VOICES OF SCOTTISH JOURNALISTS

Voices of Scottish Journalists

Recollections by 22 veteran Scottish journalists
of their life and work

IAN MACDOUGALL

THE SCOTTISH WORKING PEOPLE'S HISTORY TRUST
Scottish Charity No. SC020357
In association with
John Donald

First published in Great Britain in 2013 by
John Donald, an imprint of Birlinn Ltd

West Newington House
10 Newington Road
Edinburgh
EH9 1QS

www.birlinn.co.uk

ISBN: 978 1 906566 63 0

The publishers gratefully acknowledge the support of
The Scottish Working People's History Trust
towards the publication of this book

British Library Cataloguing-in-Publication Data
A catalogue record for this book is available on request from the British Library

Typeset by FMG using Atomik ePublisher from Easypress
Printed and bound in Britain by
Bell & Bain Ltd, Glasgow

Contents

List of Illustrations

Foreword by Neal Ascherson

Rescuing the memories of working people is not just a blow struck against 'the condescension of posterity'. It's foundational for any national history; on these highly detailed and personal individual recollections can be built the account of an age which is at once objectively truthful and subjectively revealing. In this sense, Scotland and Scottish modern history owe a debt which can never be fully assessed to the volume after volume of recorded memories put together by the painstaking, devoted and sensitive work of Ian MacDougall and the Scottish Working People's History Trust.

This latest book is particularly eloquent – and often entertaining. This is because it is concerned with a group of working people who have often been upwardly mobile, sometimes dizzily so, and whose job has been to record the experiences of others – the raw material of history. It is the trade of journalism.

Journalists are good at telling stories about other people, and dissecting other professions. They are much less inclined to examine themselves, either individually or as a trade. They record without mercy the rewards and careers of politicians, lawyers or bankers. But they have been, in general, curiously erratic and feckless about looking after their own material interests. A notorious few, in London as a rule, enjoy enormous salaries for a few precarious years. Many more end up on the scrapheap, fired on a proprietor's whim to exist on pensions which would scarcely feed a cat.

And yet when journalists do talk about their lives, they are talking history. This is because (for the last century) becoming and remaining a journalist was a journey – an upwards escalator from the crowded, plebian lower floors to the penthouse suite. Up there, the high heid yins saunter, sip their drinks and exchange confidences about who the next Labour group leader on the council should be, and why that problem with the Ministry of Defence contract needs kept under wraps. And on the edge of the carpet, listening hard and trying not to be conspicuous in his new suit, is a lad who left school at 14, whose mother did office cleaning or sold a cow to get him a shorthand and typing course. He listens and scribbles (will the news editor give him a row for only getting 100 words down a minute?). And yet he feels – always will feel – a sense of superiority. 'I am the witness. My story will tell ordinary folk the truth about how these chancers are misgoverning them.'

This wonderful book – interviews by Ian MacDougall with 22 journalists who recall their careers – is a unique contribution to Scotland's history. It's about the recent past. These journalists were born in the early twentieth century and they worked in the age of hammering typewriters, dirty glue-pots and stuffy phone booths in the corner of the office. Many of them, including many I knew myself, are sadly no longer alive. But their testimony reveals a swathe of Scottish social history as no other profession's memories could. This is because almost all of them made that steep escalator journey, from single-enders or farm kitchens to the press benches of the High Court or to the hotel lounges where Cabinet ministers and showbiz celebs answer questions you didn't ask. These journalists never forget where they came from. Outwardly respectful, they retain a deep, humorous scepticism about fame and power. And experience with a seismic industry, in which a distant proprietor can close down a fine and widely-read newspaper at a moment's notice, makes them aware of the precariousness of their own fame and power.

Some of these long interviews have the vividness and insight of novels. There's Ethel Simpson's account of growing up on a poor tenant farm in the north-east, or Bob Brown's memories of Shettleston in the late 1930s. Liz Taylor has dictated what's almost a movie script about her wild, war-damaged father rushing his family from butchers' shops in Dundee to a hotel in Earlston and riding to hounds with the Buccleuch Hunt. George Hume, the wittiest of men, recounts his years on the *Fifeshire Advertiser* (the editor bought a book of editorials and printed them one by one), covering 'little awful Highland shows', then moving to a Glasgow paper where there were no knives in the canteen in case the van boys fought with them. Like several other contributors, he remembers the droll solemnity of *The Scotsman* before Eric Mackay's reforms: if the Lord Provost had been machine-gunned in Princes Street, George suggests, *The Scotsman* headline would have been 'Untoward Event in the Capital'. (R.W. Munro records the dreadful moment when a new chief sub – 'a fairly rough type'– actually told a *Scotsman* reporter to cut his story.)

Nothing in the book is more interesting than how these men and women came into the profession. Almost none of them did a formal training course. Almost all of them remember a good English teacher at school, and library books brought home by hard-working fathers. But it was often mothers and aunts, rather than fathers, who used their contacts to get sons and daughters newspaper jobs and paid – for 'secretarial' training. 'Knowing someone' was crucial. And yet, in that staid and restrictive old Scotland, it was the wish for self-expression and adventure, rather than security, which drew young people to journalism. When he joined the Edinburgh *Evening News*, Gordon Dean was told: 'Walk in here, Mr Dean, and you walk into the Bank of England – a safe job!' But within a few years the sedate Scottish press was pitched into turmoil by takeovers and closures, as Roy Thomson moved into Scotland and London-based dailies competed vainly to loosen the grip of the *Daily Record*.

The proprietors competed, but the journalists co-operated. It wasn't just that they shared stories, as they still do – that huddle outside the Sheriff Court: 'Did ye get that bit down? Ach, you can have that quote, more your rag's sort of thing.' It was the unwritten commandment to 'bring on the juniors', to train the young on the job, to rescue a baffled kid on some rival paper by giving her the line or the name she'd missed. Back then, the bosses didn't like graduates or women. But by the end of the century, they had surrendered to both. Young women, especially, seized the chances opened by wartime. Ethel Simpson, in her touching memories of the Aberdeen *Press & Journal*, remembers how protectively the male staff treated her: she was to leave a courtroom at once if anything 'nasty' came up. In the Glasgow blitz, Max McAuslane recalls Elma Waters telephoning from beside an unexploded bomb in Great Western Road: '"It's a yellow bomb and has a red stripe round it." It was as if she was going to a wedding reception! "Get away from there!"'

Politics were usually kept private. Labour journalists often worked for Tory papers, and vice versa. Yet in many of these accounts you can trace a recurrent trajectory: early indifference is affected by witnessing the Depression of the 1930s, leading often towards Labour or sometimes Communist commitment which in turn, in the post-1945 decades, may veer towards left-leaning assertion of Scotland's need for political identity and ultimately towards the SNP.

Scotland's newspapers are in a bad way now. Circulations continue to fall; too many papers are owned by firms outwith Scotland whose local managements are craven and obsessed with the bottom line. Newspapers which can still somehow produce reporting and features of extraordinary brilliance are starved of investment. But the structure which made Scottish newspapers so strong – the 'German' pattern of city-based regional dailies with world news on the front page, quite unlike the domination by the London 'nationals' south of the Border – is eroding away fast.

It's wrong to be too nostalgic. Naturally, the older generation who speak in this book have little good to say about changes. The computer screen keeps reporters in the office; managements are too much in charge; the local papers no longer carry the careful reporting of functions and councils, edition by edition, that once ensured city evening papers such loyal readerships. News is increasingly about either the struttings of top people or the crimes of the lower depths; the mass of ordinary 'respectable' working people in between, and their interests and activities, are ignored. Several journalists in this book conclude that 'there's not the fun in the profession that there was'.

I think that's too hasty. A look not only at the papers but at the Scottish blogosphere suggests that the land is still producing men and women who take naturally to new forms of journalism, though more perhaps to argue for their opinions than to report. The old Scottish press remembered in these interviews was steady and responsible – but often deeply unadventurous, and even repressive.

Tom McGowran sums up: 'All this was before the age of cynicism.' Reporters then 'felt they were in a sense lords of creation'. Perhaps they are less romantic about their status today. But George Hume shows what the job will always carry: '. . . the richness of it. You meet mass murderers, High Court judges, comic singers, fading actresses, [and] the wonderful rich pattern of loonies that keeps the country going – I mean, wonderful.' That richness, sane and loony, is still there waiting for those who dare to report Scotland.

Introduction

These personal, spoken, edited recollections by 22 men and women veteran Scottish journalists cover a wide range of people, events, institutions, and places during the 20th century, not only north of the Border but also elsewhere in Britain and some, especially during the Second World War, overseas too.

The recollections, recorded during 1996–9 by the Scottish Working People's History Trust, a charitable body formed in 1991–2, are thus not only about newspapers and their staffs, proprietors, readers, contents, production, distribution, views, influence, problems, successes and failures, but also will inform or remind the reader about many other aspects and issues of the past century. Max McAuslane, earliest of the 22 veterans to begin, in 1929 aged 17, working as a journalist, recalls, for example, his reporting the events surrounding the landing by parachute near Eaglesham, Renfrewshire, in May 1941 of Hitler's deputy leader of the Nazi Party, Rudolf Hess. Tom McGowran, captured like tens of thousands of other British and Allied servicemen at the fall of Singapore in 1942, recounts how he succeeded in surviving the barbarous ill-treatment endured by so many of those prisoners of war forced by their Japanese captors to build the notorious Siam–Burma railway and the bridge over the River Kwai. Liz Taylor, married and with four children, lived and worked in India for ten years, and 'interviewed Krishna Menon, followed the Pope, reported air crashes and gold smugglers'. Thus, in recalling their daily work for morning, evening, Sunday, or weekly newspapers or other journals, these 22 veterans also present kaleidoscopic views of other aspects of their own experiences – their childhood and their families, schooling, housing, and sporting, recreational, political, or other activities – as well as of the experiences of many other people. As George Hume, the youngest of the 22 and, more or less simultaneously with Lorna Blackie, the last of them to enter journalism (in 1956), in his case as a junior reporter on the weekly *Fifeshire Advertiser* at Kirkcaldy, puts it in his inimitable way: 'Surely the charm of journalism is the richness of it? You meet mass murderers, High Court judges, comic singers, fading actresses, [and] the wonderful rich pattern of loonies that keeps the country going.' Readers interested in people and events during the past century, and how these 22 veteran journalists contributed to the reporting of those that came their way, will, it is hoped, find in the pages below an abundance to explore.

The veterans appear in the chronological order in which they began working on newspapers. The first three of them were born shortly before the 1914–18 war, the next four during that war, the following ten during the 1920s, and the last five in the 1930s – the youngest of them, George Hume, only a few weeks before the outbreak of the 1939–45 war. Two of the 22, Hector McSporran and Jack Sutherland, though they spent respectively all or most of their working lives on newspapers north of the border, were not actually born in Scotland. Hector McSporran, son of Scots parents from Kintyre, was born in Canada but came in 1919, when he was six years old, to live permanently in Scotland. Jack Sutherland, his father a Highland Scot and his mother from Northumberland, grew up in the latter county and began working on newspapers in Berwick-upon-Tweed when he was 16 in 1943; but after a further five years on papers at Clacton and Darlington, he came in 1952 to the *Scottish Daily Mail* in Edinburgh, and, apart from a brief period working on that paper in Manchester, he worked in Edinburgh until he retired in 1992.

Of the 22, four are women. There would have been five had not one, who began work on a Scottish evening paper in the 1930s, agreed to be interviewed and recorded but then exercised her right to change her mind, and declined to take part in the project. But why otherwise are there so few women among the 22 veterans? As Liz Taylor recalls below, she herself in 1950, aged 19, left Galashiels Academy, well-equipped educationally with her Higher Leaving Certificate in English, history, French, physics, chemistry, and art, plus Lower Latin and maths; and having been, moreover, editor of the school magazine, she 'went round all the local newspapers asking for a job. I even went to the *Daily Express* in Glasgow, and they said: "It's not a job for a woman." Nobody would give me a job.' Four years later, as an MA Honours graduate of Aberdeen University, having been assistant woman editor of the University student newspaper, and still keen to become a journalist, Liz Taylor at last found a job with the Edinburgh *Evening Dispatch* – but only, it seems, because her father, who owned two bars and a restaurant, had the editor of the *Dispatch* as one of his customers and put in a successful word with him on Liz's behalf. Similarly, in 1950 Lorna Blackie, newly graduated from Glasgow University with Honours in English language and literature, and having worked as a student on the University newspaper there, suffered a sharp setback when she applied to Kemsley Newspapers for an application form for a trainee post, but received a reply that 'they never took women trainees'. It was only in 1956, when she was 28, the oldest entrant by some five years among these 22 journalists, and apparently through her father's influence with its then editor, that she was able at last to begin work as a reporter on the *Scottish Daily Express*. She went on to become what an experienced male colleague later described as one of the best reporters he had ever worked with. No doubt in the earlier and mid-20th century, numbers of boys and youths (for example, Ron Thompson, below, in the case of the Dundee *Courier*) also tried unsuccessfully to be taken on even as newspaper office or copy boys, let alone junior reporters. But for girls and young women, it could prove in that era particularly difficult to find such employment. It was only in the second half of the century that more, even many more, women journalists began to appear on the full-time staffs of newspapers in Scotland.

If on their entry to journalism three of the four women among these 22 veterans were university graduates, none of the 18 men was. James Gunn Henderson was the only one of them on leaving school to apply to enter university – St Andrews, in his case. He was accepted, but did not go, because he had always felt he owed it to his mother that he should 'get a job and work'. Half a dozen others among the 18 men left school with, it seems, sufficient Highers passes to have been able to apply to enter university, had they wished to do so. But in that era many fewer young people than nowadays followed that path. Of the other dozen men veterans, most – for example, Ernie McIntyre, Tom McGowran, Bob Scott, George MacDougall, Gordon Dean, Ron Thompson, and John Cairns – had left school at age 14, 15 or 16. So also did one of the four women veteran journalists, Ethel Simpson. Ron Thompson, indeed, when he left school 'without any certificates', was not quite 14.

Liz Taylor and Lorna Blackie were thus highly qualified academically before they became journalists. So also was the fourth woman among these 22 veterans, Nancy Mackenzie. She, too, was a graduate, in 1941 from Edinburgh University, with an Ordinary degree in French and German. Her entry, too, into journalism, like that of Liz Taylor and Lorna Blackie, was delayed for several years, until 1948. But most of the delay in Nancy Mackenzie's case was due to her volunteering for war service, 1942–6, in the Women's Royal Naval Service.

So how important was a record of academic success at school, college, or university for young entrants to journalism in Scotland during the decades of the mid and later 20th century which these 22 veterans recall?

When Ron Thompson, not yet 14, left school in 1943 and applied for a job with the Dundee *Courier*, he was told his lack of qualifications prevented him from being considered. Instead he found work as a clerk in the jute industry for seven years, before at last he was able to begin working on newspapers. Decades later, Ron ended his working life as a highly respected newspaper and Grampian TV reporter, and author of several books. Bill Rae, who had not enjoyed his five years at the prestigious Boroughmuir Senior Secondary School in Edinburgh – 'I was never so glad to get away from anywhere in my life' – nonetheless left, aged 17, in 1945 with Higher English and Geography and Lower French, German, and maths. Before the Highers exams he had been interviewed by the chief reporter of the Edinburgh *Evening News*, who 'told me if I passed my Higher English (they didn't seem to bother about anything else) they would take me on as a copy boy. And that's what happened.' It appears, however, to have helped Bill's entry into the *Evening News* that his grandfather and his mother were already employed by that paper, even if not in its editorial department.

Possession of a university degree was not considered by some of these veterans to be a necessary or, by one or two, even perhaps a desirable qualification for entry into, or success in, journalism. Jack Sutherland, who had himself left school at 16, and who years later became night editor of the *Scottish Daily Mail*, recalls below that among the sub-editors on that paper quite a few had no previous experience as reporters. 'We got an awful lot of graduate entries in the late 1940s and up to the middle 1950s, oh, an awful lot. I looked with disdain on the graduates that appeared in the office. I think their approach was just young arrogance mainly. They were probably trying to improve our writings.' Lorna Blackie, graduate of Glasgow University, who had found in the earlier 1950s that 'For women it was almost impossible then' to get into journalism, found also that having 'a degree was no help at all'.

Skills that certainly were desirable in that era for the young entrant to possess, or without delay to acquire, were the ability to write shorthand (the higher the speed the better, always assuming the shorthand could be easily read back by its writer) and to type. In those days before the spread of handheld tape recorders, most of these 22 veterans had good, and some had excellent, shorthand speeds either by the time they became full-time journalists or soon afterward. A speed of around 120 words per minute was regarded as a desirable minimum; Hector McSporran could write shorthand at between 150 and 180 words per minute, Bob Brown, Bob Scott, and Ron Thompson at 160, Gordon Dean and George Hume at 140, and most of the others at between 100 and 120. Colin Dakers and Liz Taylor appear to have felt diffident about their shorthand; James Gunn Henderson decided his was not speedy enough to enable him to report the trial in Glasgow in 1958 which resulted in the conviction of the notorious murderer Peter Manuel.

Full-time training for journalists under the sponsorship of the National Joint Council for the Training of Journalists was not begun until 1964. However, before – even long before – then, there were available some correspondence or distance learning courses, and at least one external degree course, in journalism. But generally whatever introduction or even elementary training young entrants received was on the job, with, if they were fortunate, a mentor or tutor – either a senior office or copy boy, or a junior or experienced reporter. Ethel Simpson, for instance, beginning aged 17 as a junior reporter on the Aberdeen *Press & Journal* in 1944, was shown the ropes by another junior with some experience who was about to be called up for his wartime service in the armed forces. On the other hand, David M. Smith, beginning likewise as a junior reporter in 1930 on the bi-weekly *Perthshire Constitutional*, seems to have been thrown in at the deep end, without much or any preliminary guidance or training. The first reporting task he undertook for the paper resulted in his receiving a thunderous reprimand from his news editor and, a short time later, an ominous warning that, 'Unless you pull your socks up and improve, you'll be out in a fortnight.' Liz Taylor, given a fortnight's trial by the editor of the *Evening Dispatch*, who had already reduced to tears her sacked girl predecessor, convinced herself that by the end of the fortnight the editor had decided to sack her, too. At the eleventh hour, however, Liz was saved by an unexpected piece of luck. Uniquely among the 22 veterans, George Hume was formally apprenticed for four years as a junior reporter at the *Fifeshire Advertiser* in Kirkcaldy. He recalls that in 1960 he was the 16th in Scotland to pass the National Joint Training Council examinations, his newspaper having put through eight of the 16.

Some of the 22 veterans began as office or copy boys, fetching to the office copy (handwritten reports) from meetings, courts, or other events being covered by the reporters, or ('the worst job of the lot') filling up gluepots, as Bill Rae did at the Edinburgh *Evening News*, or, as he, Gordon Dean, George MacDougall, and most other office boys did, dealing with the reporters' daily orders for cigarettes and similar menial tasks. Other young entrants among the 22, such as Max McAuslane in 1929 on the weekly *Clydebank Press*, Ethel Simpson in 1944 on the Aberdeen *Press & Journal* and *Evening Express*, and Christopher Reekie in 1953 on the *Southern Reporter* at Selkirk, began a step higher on the ladder as junior reporters. Christopher Reekie's experience as a junior was not untypical on a local weekly paper: 'I just did about everything.' In his search for news stories, he visited every week the local ministers at their manses, went to the Sheriff Court and to caged bird shows, sometimes down to the town's textile mills, and to meetings of all kinds of local government bodies. R.J. (Bob) Brown appears to have been unique among these boys and youths in beginning, aged 17, in the winter of 1941–2 on the *Ayr Advertiser* not as an office or copy boy or junior reporter but as a reporter, a surprising fact he attributes to wartime conditions – shortage of staff and newspapers much reduced in size.

Hours of work for editorial staff on local weekly and evening papers could be long: from 8 or 9am to 5 or 6pm and then, even after a break for a meal, out covering evening meetings two or three times a week, plus sport on Saturday afternoons. On the weekly *Berwick Journal*, where Jack Sutherland began work aged 16 in 1943, he recalls that 'You were probably working 45 to 50 hours a week, that was the norm.' On daily morning papers, hours of work that included some late shifts could also for reporters be somewhat unsocial, as Gordon Dean, for example, found in his later years on the *Daily Record*. For those papers' sub-editors and other editorial production staff, working as they did into the early hours of the mornings, the hours were chronically unsocial. Many examples of these conditions are recalled in the pages below.

Wages or salaries of those staff reporters who acted also as local correspondents or stringers for other newspapers or journals were thus normally supplemented by linage – payment by the latter being per line published. But juniors sometimes had a struggle, as, for instance, Max McAuslane, Jack Sutherland and George MacDougall say they did, to receive a fair share, or indeed any share, of linage. Wages in that era might also sometimes be supplemented by somewhat inflated claims for, or generous management grants of, expenses. Ernie McIntyre describes, for instance, an apparently spurious claim for Wellington boots by a colleague in the Edinburgh office of the *Daily Herald*, for covering the Border floods in 1948. And Bob Brown recalls the *Daily Mirror*'s Scotland correspondent telling him that for years he had banked his salary and lived off his expenses. Thus a junior reporter submitting his or her first claim for expenses not seldom found himself or herself, as for example Liz Taylor did, firmly instructed to increase markedly the sum claimed, so that any less scrupulously exact claims made by more senior colleagues would not be exposed. A life member of the National Union of Journalists, writing in March 1974 in the *Journalist*, organ of the Union, asserted that: 'In half a century's experience I never met a journalist whose expenses claims would stand up to close scrutiny – my own included.'

*　　　　*　　　　*

During their working lives these 22 veteran Scottish journalists worked full-time on the staff of one or more out of a combined total of some 45 newspapers or journals. Hector McSporran and George MacDougall each worked successively on nine separate papers, Gordon Dean and Christopher Reekie on eight, Ernie McIntyre and Ron Thompson on seven, Max McAuslane, Jack Sutherland and George Hume on six, David M. Smith, Colin Dakers, and Bob Brown on five, Bob Scott on four, Tom McGowran, James Gunn Henderson and Lorna Blackie on three, R.W. (Billy) Munro and Ethel Simpson on two, and Bill Rae, Nancy Mackenzie (both Edinburgh *Evening News*), John Cairns (*Alloa Journal*), and Liz Taylor (Edinburgh *Evening Dispatch*) on only one. Ron Thompson and George Hume also worked respectively for many or some years full-time as TV reporters, and George Hume for BBC Radio Scotland also. David M. Smith, Hector McSporran, John Cairns, Liz Taylor, Lorna Blackie, and George Hume worked in addition for varying periods as freelances. Quite a few of the 22 worked also at one time or another as non-staff local correspondents (or stringers) for papers or journals other than those which employed them full-time. Bill Rae and Gordon Dean became later in their careers members of a small full-time team who ran their own news agency.

Those newspapers or journals on which one or more of the 22 worked at one period or another as full-time staff included, in the Highlands and north of Scotland, the *Highland News* at Inverness, the *Campbeltown Courier* and, also at Campbeltown, the *Argyllshire Leader*, the *Northern Times* at Golspie, and the *John o'Groat Journal* at Wick. In the north-east, the Aberdeen *Press & Journal* and *Evening Express*. In Dundee, the *Courier*, *Evening Telegraph*, and *People's Journal*. In Fife, the *Fife Herald* at Cupar, and the *Fifeshire Advertiser* at Kirkcaldy. Elsewhere in central Scotland, the *Perthshire Constitutional, Kirriemuir Free Press, Stirling Journal, Falkirk Herald, Alloa Journal*. In the west of Scotland (other than Glasgow), the *Clydebank Press, Renfrew Press*, and *Ayr Advertiser*. In the Borders, the *Southern Reporter* at Selkirk, *Kelso Chronicle & Mail, Berwickshire Advertiser, Berwick Advertiser, Berwickshire News, Berwick Journal, Dumfries & Galloway Standard*. In Edinburgh, *The Scotsman, Evening Dispatch, Evening News, Scottish Daily Mail*, and the *Leith Gazette*. In Glasgow, the principal centre of journalism and newspaper production in Scotland, the *Glasgow Herald* (retitled in 1992 *The Herald*), *The Bulletin, Evening Times, Sunday Standard, Daily Record, Evening News, Sunday Mail, Scottish Daily Express, Evening Citizen*. In addition, several of the 22 worked full-time at one period or another in the Edinburgh, or Dundee, or Aberdeen, or Inverness branch office of one or more of these newspapers: *Glasgow Herald, The Bulletin, Evening Times, Daily Record,* Glasgow *Evening News, Sunday Mail, Scottish Daily Express,* Glasgow *Evening Citizen, Sunday Express.* Ernie McIntyre worked full-time for several years as Edinburgh correspondent of the *Daily Herald,* Bob Brown, based in Glasgow, worked as Scotland correspondent successively for *The Times* and the *Guardian.* Six of the 22 veterans worked full-time for varying periods on newspapers in England: David M. Smith and Jack Sutherland on two or more of the four Berwick-upon-Tweed papers, and Jack Sutherland also on the *East Essex Weekly Gazette* and the *Northern Echo* at Darlington; Ernie McIntyre on the *Birkenhead News, Liverpool Daily Post,* and *Liverpool Echo*; George MacDougall in London on the *Daily Worker, Challenge, Scope,* and the *Daily Express*; Gordon Dean on the *North Shields News*; and Christopher Reekie on the *Newcastle Journal,* Newcastle *Evening Chronicle, Sunday Sun,* and *Sunderland Echo.*

Moreover, freelances among the 22, such as David M. Smith and John Cairns, contributed in their regular work to some or many of the newspapers above. George MacDougall during his full-time employment with the *Daily Worker* contributed regularly also to three newspapers in East Germany and Poland. Liz Taylor in or from India contributed to the *Daily Herald,* a newspaper at Bombay and another in Cyprus, as well as to the BBC Radio programme *Woman's Hour,* and, once returned permanently to Britain, she contributed to several papers or journals, such as *The Scotsman* and *Country Life.* Tom McGowran, while in the wartime army at Singapore, wrote a weekly column in the *Straits Times.* Bob Brown also contributed to various papers or journals while employed full-time elsewhere: the magazine of the Glasgow Citizens Theatre, for example, as well as *The Economist* and, while he was in the army during the war, the Royal Pay Corps journal. Bob Scott did some part-time journalistic work for the *Dalkeith Advertiser,* Jack Sutherland for the *Edinburgh Advertiser* and the Forestry Commission staff newspaper. Ernie McIntyre also edited the Edinburgh Labour paper *Clarion.* James Gunn Henderson, Ron Thompson, Lorna Blackie, and George Hume also contributed to one or more of other papers or magazines such as the *Weekly Scotsman, Sunday Post, Sunday Standard,* and, in George Hume's case, to some in Germany and the United States, as well as to BBC Radio and TV.

Thus these 22 veterans accumulated, individually and collectively, a mass of experience in journalism, experience which they present in the pages below. It must be emphasised, however, that these recollections do not, nor do they make any claim to, constitute a comprehensive and systematic study either of newspapers and journalism in Scotland or of the biographies of the 22 veterans themselves.

As has been indicated, an attempt was made in recording these recollections to achieve so far as possible some balance among the newspapers or journals on which they had worked: north, south, east, west, daily mornings and evenings, Sundays, Scottish nationals such as the *Glasgow Herald*, *The Scotsman*, *Daily Record*, *The Bulletin*, and the strongly Scottish editions of such UK national dailies as the *Daily Express* and *Daily Mail*, published respectively in Glasgow and Edinburgh; the Scottish regional papers Aberdeen *Press & Journal* and Dundee *Courier*; UK national papers such as *The Times*, the *Guardian*, *Daily Herald*, and *Daily Worker*; and local weekly or bi-weekly papers such as the *John o'Groat Journal*, *Highland News*, *Perthshire Constitutional*, *Campbeltown Courier*, *Ayr Advertiser*, *Fife Herald*, *Dumfries & Galloway Standard*, and *Southern Reporter*.

An attempt was also made to include among the 22 the various categories of newspaper journalists: from those who had been office or copy boys, then junior, senior, or chief reporters, feature writers, specialists such as industrial or local government correspondents, columnists, leader writers, sub-editors, to senior production staff such as copy tasters, chief sub-editors, night editors, and on to assistant and deputy editors, editors and editors-in-chief, but also one or two freelances, as John Cairns was more or less from the outset of his journalistic career, and as David M. Smith became after 20 years or so of his. It is regretted that lack of space made it impracticable to include also, as originally hoped, two or three sets of recollections by press photographers.

Among the myriad of issues, events, persons, places, and institutions that the recollections of these 22 veteran journalists cover, or at the least touch upon, are: newspaper proprietors and the degree of their interference in editorial matters; fires, accidents, and disasters; industrial disputes; trade unionism (mainly, the National Union of Journalists and the Institute of Journalists) and non-unionism or anti-unionism (not least at the D.C. Thomson press of Dundee for decades after the 1926 General Strike); crimes and offences, courts and trials; relations between press and police; local government; public relations work; journalists' ethics; chequebook journalism; interviewing; newspaper circulations, mergers and takeovers; family members who fought in the 1914–18 war; the 1939–45 war (during which nine of the 22 veterans served in the armed forces); peacetime National Service (which four of the 22 experienced); growing up in Glasgow, Wick, Perth, Aberdeenshire, Edinburgh, Galashiels, Broughty Ferry, Shotts, Stirling, Dundee, Campbeltown, Earlston, Northumberland, Arbroath, Selkirk; children's wartime evacuation; schoolboy employments; schooling, and further and higher education; housing conditions; poverty; churchgoing; competition, sometimes fierce, between newspapers;

co-operation between reporters from different papers; freelancing; linage; sport; occupational hazards; 'characters' on newspaper staffs; redundancy, retirement and pensions; wages, hours and working conditions; the annexation of Rockall; parliamentary and other elections; the General Assembly of the Church of Scotland; royal visits; humorous anecdotes; political views or activities of journalists.

On that last subject, a majority, it seems 14, of the 22 veterans themselves appear not to have held any strong political views, or taken part in political activities, or joined any political party. 'I don't think,' says Max McAuslane, 'many journalists do get drawn into political activity: it's maybe the nature of their job, you don't want to identify too much . . .' Of the minority of eight who do indicate or imply their political views, and in several cases their activities, Ernie McIntyre recalls that his views developed when before the 1939–45 war he saw the terrible poverty at Birkenhead, where he worked on the *Birkenhead News*; and he joined the Labour Party when in 1947 he came to Edinburgh to work on the *Daily Herald*, whose political views were congenial to him. 'I always took the view,' he says, 'that if you were writing for a Tory paper, well, you didn't have to hold a view, but . . . if you were a competent journalist you could write a story to suit their purpose – which you often had to do in papers like the *Daily Mail*. I don't think it was an embarrassment when I worked for other papers. I think you were a journalist first, and your politics were your own. Many a good left-winger worked for the *Daily Express* and the *Daily Mail*, and many a good Tory for the *Daily Herald*, but they were good writers . . .' Tom McGowran, Bob Brown, George MacDougall and Jack Sutherland each also describes his political views and, in the case of the first three, specific involvement, at one time or another, in or with political parties while working as journalists. Colin Dakers, R.W. (Billy) Munro, and Lorna Blackie (who was evidently invited by both the SNP and the Conservatives to stand in elections) at least mention explicitly or implicitly their political views or inclinations.

None of these recollections has ever, so far as is known, been published before. In editing the recollections for publication, an attempt has been made throughout to preserve the actual spoken words of the 22 veteran journalists, subject to some necessary transpositions and deletions of repetitious and some other matter (much of it, during the recording of the interviews, concerned with checking details). One reviewer of the preceding Trust volume *Through the Mill*, which presented the recollections of 33 veteran Penicuik, Midlothian, paper mill workers, referred (mistakenly, I hope) to my methodology as being to present 'volumes of virtually unedited personal recollections'. In fact, the editing of the Penicuik workers' recollections had reduced by about half the number of words in the verbatim transcripts of those 33 veterans. In the case of the 22 journalists, their verbatim transcripts before editing ran to some 740,000 words altogether, the edited versions below to some 267,000.

As always with oral history of this kind, the question arises of how accurate and reliable are these recollections, dependent as they are on the memory of the recorded interviewees rather than on documentary sources such as diaries, minutes, annual reports, etc. Where the recollections are those of the veteran as eyewitness, presenting his or her own direct personal experience, then they are likely to be at their most reliable, although of course no more infallible than any other single historical source. Of such eyewitness testimonies there are innumerable examples in the pages below. Moreover, between at least some of these testimonies comparisons can be made, since one or more of the veterans worked on the same newspaper at or around the same period. Relevant documentary sources, such as histories, biographies, and back numbers of newspapers and journals, as well as numbers of the persons referred to *en passant* by the 22 veterans, have been consulted to check dates and other details. The notes near the end of this volume are intended to help confirm, complement or elaborate, or to contradict and correct, these spoken recollections wherever that has seemed necessary. The reader may conclude, in assessing the accuracy and reliability of these recollections, that there are some similarities with a court case in which witnesses successively provide their testimonies (even if, in the pages below, not under oath or affirmation). The fullness, detail and reliability of recollection vary, not only within any individual witness's or interviewee's testimony, but also between the accounts of any two or more. No one, whether an interviewee, as each of these 22 veteran journalists is here, recalling events and persons from years or decades earlier, or a writer of contemporaneous minutes, diaries, letters, or other documentary sources, has a monopoly of truth. Successive witnesses of the same event may recall certain aspects but be forgetful or oblivious of others. Differing interpretations of the same event or of the character or motivation of a person are the stuff of history, whether based on documentary or oral history. Some hearsay is also presented by some of these 22 veteran journalists as they recall what their parents or grandparents or others told them about events or persons before they were born, or at least at which they were not themselves present: it is hoped further research in contemporary newspapers and other sources may yet establish whether such hearsay is accurate and reliable.

This is the seventh volume of oral recollections resulting from the work of the Scottish Working People's History Trust in interviewing occupational groups of veteran working people throughout Scotland and recording their memories of their working lives, and of their housing, educational, recreational, and other experiences. Founded in 1991–2 as a charitable body, the Trust began interviewing and recording such recollections in 1996. Its first volume, *Oh! Ye Had Tae Be Careful,* published in 2000, presented the recollections of 11 veteran workers at the former gunpowder mill and bomb factory at Roslin, Midlothian, in production for 150 years till its closure in 1954. There followed *Bondagers* (2001), recollections by eight veteran women former farm workers in south-east Scotland; *Voices of Leith Dockers* (2001), recollections by seven veteran dockers employed at those docks at one period or another between 1928 and 1989; *Onion Johnnies* (2002) the recollections of nine Bretons (including one woman 'Onion Jenny'), who had all at one time or another between the 1920s and 1970s sold in Scotland from their bicycles, or on foot, or from their vans, onions transported from their homeland around the port of Roscoff in Brittany; *Lewis in the Passing* (2007), the work of Calum Ferguson of Stornoway, an acclaimed Gaelic-speaking author, and radio, television and film producer, presented the recollections, several of them in Gaelic and English, of 20 Lewis veteran crofters, seamen, women herring gutters, hotel workers, domestic servants, and other islanders; and *Through the Mill* (2009), the recollections of 33 men and women veteran Penicuik paper mill workers, covering almost the entire 20th century. In addition, the Trust, in a collaborative project, edited for publication by the Scottish History Society in 2003 a volume of documentary source materials: *Mid and East Lothian Miners' Association Minutes, 1894–1918,* the first such volume of any Scottish trade union's minutes ever to be published in edited form so extensively. The Trust during the past 15 or so years has also secured or facilitated the deposit in public repositories in Scotland of considerable numbers of documentary sources and some artefacts, such as old banners, concerning working people and their trade union, Co-operative Society, political, Friendly Society, and other organisations. The next volume of oral recollections the Trust hopes to publish will be those, covering virtually the entire 20th century, of two dozen miners from the various former coalfields in Scotland. Other recorded recollections presently awaiting transcription and/or editing are those by Leith seamen, Peeblesshire textile mill workers, Borders farm workers, Leith shipyard and women workers, public librarians, railway workers, Co-operative Society workers, and farm workers other than in the Borders. Interviewing and recording of building workers, Glasgow secondary school teachers, and lighthousemen are also presently proceeding.

* * *

The Trust wishes to express its warmest thanks to the 22 veterans who generously gave so much of their time to enable their recollections to be recorded and now at last published. The gathering and preparation for publication of such occupational sets of recollections is slow, time-consuming work. Because the Trust tries to find, if possible, a representative score or so of the oldest surviving workers in a given occupation, provided they have good clear memories of their working lives, sadly it is often the case that by the time the volume containing their memories is published, or even by the time the verbatim transcriptions and their edited versions are ready to submit to them for their approval of the latter, they themselves have passed away. This, very sadly, has been the case with 17 of these 22 veteran journalists: Max McAuslane, David M. Smith, Ernie McIntyre, Hector McSporran, Colin Dakers, R.W. (Billy) Munro, Tom McGowran, R.J. (Bob) Brown, Bob Scott, Jack Sutherland, Nancy Mackenzie, James Gunn Henderson, Ron Thompson, John Cairns, Liz Taylor, Lorna Blackie, and George Hume. It is greatly regretted that the Trust's thanks to them are therefore posthumous.

Never well-funded for carrying out its aims and activities, the Trust is deeply grateful to all those persons, charitable bodies, and other organisations that responded so generously to its appeal for funding to secure the publication of this volume of veteran journalists' recollections: F.P.M. Johnston, Kathleen Dalyell, Dr Gordon Prestoungrange, Laurie Flynn, Ivor Guild, Professor Karl Miller, Professor Alexander McCall Smith, Iain Anderson, The W.M. Mann Foundation, The Binks Trust, Unite the Union (Scottish Region), Transport Salaried Staffs Association, University and College Union Scotland, Dr Norman and Mrs Trish Godman, Gordon Dalyell, The Nancie Massey Charitable Trust, Educational Institute of Scotland, UNISON Scotland, and Grahame Smith, General Secretary, STUC, for its appeal to all its affiliated organisations on behalf of the Trust.

To a large number of other persons and institutions are also due the thanks of the Trust. They include Dr Neal Ascherson, for his Foreword to this volume; the Heritage Lottery Fund, which in 2003–5 provided a grant that enabled the Trust to employ for the first time a professional typist who transcribed the audio tapes of the veteran journalists' recollections; Jackie Grant (the professional typist); and, for providing information (or further information) and/or photographs or other practical help, Dr Jean Munro, Andy Brown, Roy Scott, Alex Hogg, George MacDougall, Ethel Simpson, Bill Rae, Gordon Dean, Mrs Christine Mackay Henderson, Christopher Reekie, Liz Taylor, Mrs Audrey Lucas,

Rudolf Steiner School, Edinburgh, Hamish Coghill, Eric Rutherford, Rev Alison Swindells, the late Mrs Jean Simpson, Phil Watson, Gordon Dalyell, Professor Emeritus W. Hamish Fraser, Ian D. McGowan, Lorne Boswell, John Weir, Rev. Rolf Billes, Euan Robertson, David Scrimgeour, Albert (Bert) Morris, Kenneth Roy, Leslie Gunn (Wick High School), the late Jean Smith, Mrs Dinah Stevenson, Andrew Hood, Frances Horsburgh, Sheila MacNamara, Mamie Magnusson, Sally Magnusson, Calum Ferguson, Stewart Boyd, Norrie Bryce, Agnes Watt, Andrew Fyall, Walter Gunn, Ian Nimmo, David Scott (formerly of *The Scotsman*), Professor Emeritus John Foster, Professors Christopher A. Whatley and Jim Tomlinson (Dundee University), Brian Rafferty, Peter Esson, Bruce Cannon, Bill Oliver, Bob Atack, David Fletcher, Noel Donaldson (Wick), Mrs Marjorie Crawford, Stan Hunter, Denis Straughan, Frank Beattie, James Frame, Ken Smart, Ian B. Smith (Berwick), Bill Sinclair, Brian McGuire, Ross Anderson, Jim Seaton, James Grassie, George Broadlie, Bill Gilchrist, Douglas Hill, Craigie Veitch, Willis Pickard, Bob Ross, Findlay McQuarrie, Harry Diamond, Mrs Margaret Sutherland, Tony Langmark, and the following librarians, archivists, officials or representatives: Craig Nelson, *The Scotsman*, Campbell Thomson, *Daily Record*, Miriam Yamin and Hannah Jenkinson, *The Guardian*, Steve Baker and Tim Dale, News International Newspapers Ltd, Peter Aldrich, *Daily Express*, Irene K. Duncan, D.C. Thomson & Co. Ltd, David Moffett, *Daily Mail*, Duncan Smith, *Press & Journal*, Alison Cameron, editor, *Northern Times*, the editor, *John o' Groat Journal*, Sarah Bond, Johnston Press plc, Susan Windram and Edith Scott, Tweeddale Press, *Falkirk Herald*, Graeme Scott, editor, *Fife Herald*, Alan Woodison, editor, *Kilmarnock Standard*, Janice Gillies, *Berwick Advertiser*, Jim Raeburn, Scottish Newspaper Society, Norman Bartlett, President, Chartered Institute of Journalists, Dr Patricia Allerston, National Galleries of Scotland, David Catto, Aberdeenshire Library and Information Service, Sheila Campbell and Audrey Brown, Kirkcaldy Central Library, Enda Ryan, The Mitchell Library, Glasgow, Christine McGilly and Rosemary O'Hare, Culture & Sport, & Business @ The Mitchell, Glasgow, Janice Goldie, Dumfries & Galloway Libraries, Louisa Costelloe, Aberdeen Central Library, Tom Barclay, Carnegie Library, Ayr, Jamie Gaukroger, Highland Local Studies Library, Inverness, Alasdair M. Sutherland, Local Studies, Angus Council, Catherine K. Dunlop, East Ayrshire Council, Marjorie Donald, A.K. Bell Library, Perth, Kirsty Crawford, BBC Scotland, Louise North, BBC Written Archives Centre, Reading, Julian Reid, Corpus Christie College, Oxford, Laura Maffioli-Brown, Royal Star & Garter Homes, Richmond, Surrey, David Young, Hamilton Town House Library, Sybil Cavanagh, West Lothian Local

Studies Library, Michelle Gait, King's College, Aberdeen University, Julie Hutchison, Glasgow University Library, Dr Hugh Hagan, National Archives of Scotland, Jane McTavish, Jackie Szpera, Anne Morrison, James Hogg, Karen O'Brien, and their colleagues in the Scottish and Reference Departments and Edinburgh Room, Edinburgh Public Library, Dr Maria Castrillo, Dougie Mathieson and colleagues, National Library of Scotland, Janet McBain, Scottish Screen Archive, Zilla Oddy, Hawick Heritage Hub, Angus Martin, Kintyre Antiquarian & Natural History Society, Ian C. Copland, Cupar Heritage, Sarah Mason, Saltire Society, Anna Dyer, Scotland–Russia Society, Frances Jessop, Vintage Books, Paul Smith, St Johnstone FC Ltd, Sandy Jardine, Rangers FC Ltd, Society of Motor Manufacturers & Traders Ltd, London, Amy Rolph, World Rugby Museum, Twickenham. The Scottish Working People's History Trust and I are especially grateful to John Donald, an imprint of Birlinn Ltd, and to Neville Moir and Mairi Sutherland personally for publishing this work, and to David Fletcher of the Scottish Working People's History Trust for his major contribution to bringing that about. In my absence through ill health, Roger Smith skilfully constructed the index. Terry Blundell has expertly and selflessly guided me through the mysteries of the computer. Without the constant practical help, encouragement, and tolerance of my wife Sandra, the work would have taken even longer to complete.

Ian MacDougall,
Edinburgh

Max McAuslane

My mother was Ayrshire. I think she had a journalistic connection. Her uncle was called Johnston and I believe he was in the *Glasgow Herald*.[1] I never met him. I think that's probably why I went in for journalism, because when you're a young man people push you this way and that way. They say, 'Oh, you'll be a lawyer, you'll be . . .' I was quite interested in English at the school, and my mother said, 'Why don't you think of journalism?' 'Why?' I said. 'Well,' she said, 'I had an uncle who was a journalist.'

I was born in Apsley Street, Partick, Glasgow, on 20 May 1912. My father was a postman, born and bred in Glasgow. I knew none of my grandparents. But my grandfather McAuslane worked in the shipyards. He and my grandmother McAuslane were dead before I was born. My other grandfather was on the railway but he was killed in a railway accident when he was quite young. My grandmother remarried but I never met her second husband. In fact, I knew very little about my grandparents at all, I mean, we didn't discuss them. Today people do discuss these things, and people are living longer so they know their grandparents. But it was very different when I was a youngster.

I had three brothers above me and a younger sister, Jeanie. Alex, my oldest brother, was born in 1899 in Parnie Street in the centre of Glasgow. Then my parents and he moved to Partick, but I can't think now of the name of the street. Then they moved round the corner to No. 37 Apsley Street, then, before I was born, to No. 45, and then round the corner again to Glenavon Terrace. Alex was in the Scottish Rifles in the First World War and was wounded. My father, a Liberal, wasn't too keen on the war or on anything military, even the Boys' Brigade: he wouldn't let my brothers join the Boys' Brigade.[2] Alex became a chartered accountant and spent most of his life abroad in Burma with the Burmah Oil Company. Tom, my second brother, was a commercial traveller for a bit. But he was very interested in the church – they all were – and eventually he was a Church of Scotland minister in Fife and Aberdeen and finished up at Huntly, and was 90 when he died. Jim, my third brother, worked in the Prudential Insurance Company and then joined the civil service, the Department of Health. He died in his sixties of cancer. My sister Jeanie arrived in 1920, and when my mother died in 1929 Jeanie, aged nine, went to live with my brother Tom, the minister, in Cowdenbeath. So Alex was about 21 years older than Jeanie and about 13 years older than me.

At 45 Apsley Street, where I was born and lived until I was about 12, it was a tenement and we were on the top flat. There was one bedroom, a kitchen, sitting room, a parlour and a bathroom. There was a bedroom – a 'hole in the wall' bed in the kitchen – where my parents slept. My three brothers and I slept in the other bedroom, and my sister Jeanie, a baby at the time, slept with my parents. The lighting was electricity, and there was a bath and a flush toilet. Then about 1924, when I'd be 12, we moved round the corner to Glenavon Terrace. It was a bigger house, the ground floor of a tenement, a main door and upstairs downstairs, so there was more room there. It had a dining room, a sitting room and two bedrooms up the stairs, and down the stairs – a basement really – a bedroom, bathroom, kitchen, and a sort of lumber room. It was an older tenement, so the lighting was gas; and there was a bath and a flush toilet. Then when I was 17 in 1929, just after my mother died, we moved up to Kelvindale – it's called Kelvinside, but really it was Kelvindale – in the west end of Glasgow, to a new house, one of the first built by MacTaggart & Mickel, and set up on a hill.

As soon as I was five in 1917 I went to Hyndland School. I used to walk to school, it'd be a good couple of miles. Hyndland was an all-through school and I went there from primary through to my Highers. You paid fees there, five shillings [25p] a quarter in the primary, then 15 shillings [75p] in the secondary department. But eventually it became free. My sister Jeanie started at Hyndland primary, too, until our mother died, then, as I've said, she went to live with my minister brother Tom in Cowdenbeath and they sent Jeanie to Dollar Academy as a boarder. So she finished her education there. My brothers had gone to our local primary, Thornwood School, but later to Hyndland. Hyndland was a very modern school built, I think, in 1910, and it had a very good reputation. I can't recall the primary very much. I was happy enough at school, I wasn't mad on it. It was a very strict regime, even in the primary. The headmistress was very strict, so were all the others. In my third year in primary Miss Nicol was the first teacher to make some impression on me. She was very friendly with all the class and a very good teacher. I had a great regard for her. I remember one door which had the number 50 on it: that was the number of children in the room. Certainly the numbers got less as you went up the school, but 30 would be the average, I would think. When I was older I took Greek of all things, and there were only about four boys in the class; and in Latin there wasn't an awful lot of people. But in the other subjects of course there was quite a big group. I sat and passed the Qualifying exam when I was 11 or 12 and proceeded into the secondary department.

I was good at English, and that and French was my favourite subject. We didn't do physics or chemistry but what they called Lower Science – botany and geology and that sort of thing. I don't think I did that too well. But I'll tell you why I took Greek. My mother wanted me to go on into the church. So the Greek you had to take for that. My oldest brother Alex, the accountant, thought the law would be a good thing for me to try for, so I took Latin as well. So I remained at Hyndland School until I was 17 in 1929, and passed my Highers in English, French, Maths, Latin, Greek, I think, and Lower Science.

As a boy I was a keen reader. I joined Partick public library in Dumbarton Road. I liked reading anything at all, any book that was on the go at the time. I used to read a lot of R.M. Ballantyne's books – *Martin Rattler, Coral Island*.[3] I got the classical books, Scott and Stevenson, as school work. *The Fair Maid of Perth* was the only Scott book that really tickled my fancy; the other ones, I just couldn't take them. I was very keen on Dickens. I remember at ten years of age reading *Oliver Twist*. I was a keen reader and read quite widely, and I was quite encouraged by my parents to read. An interesting thing I remember about my parents was them sitting on either side of the fire in the kitchen and they divided the Glasgow *Evening Citizen* between them.[4] They would have a piece of the paper each and had a conversation about the paper: 'I see so-and-so's done this and . . .' This was the conversation. They were quite interested in local government. They used to talk about the Lord Provost and the councillors and what was going on – very local: Glasgow, that was their interest. My father, a Liberal, was interested in politics too. He had a cousin, Walter Smith, though I called him Uncle, who stood for Parliament as a Liberal for Camlachie, a terrible constituency in the east end of Glasgow – not a hope![5] Compared to us Walter Smith's family were quite wealthy, they all went to a good school and had a good education. Then Walter Smith went as a missionary to Africa or somewhere, came back, joined the Church of Scotland and got the job of going round all the churches preaching and getting people interested in the freewill offering scheme. Then he went into journalism. Of all things he went into the local weekly *Govan Press*. When I eventually joined the *Govan Press* one of the old printers there remembered Walter Smith and said, 'He used to go to cover the launches of ships on a bicycle, dressed in a morning coat!' Eventually he joined the BBC and was a sort of public relations officer for the BBC in London. Maybe Walter Smith unwittingly developed my own interest in newspapers.

Well, latterly at Hyndland School, once I got the idea of the church and entering the ministry out of my system, I seemed to home in on journalism. I had a very good English master called MacDougall, a big fat chap, and he got interested in me. Once I wrote a story for him as an essay, and he said, 'Did you write this yourself?' 'Yes,' I said. 'Are you sure you wrote it yourself?' 'Oh, yes.' 'Well,' he says, 'that's very good. I thought it was too good for you to have written it.' Then while I was still at school I read the newspapers avidly. My parents always got the *Evening Citizen* and the *Daily Record*. So I decided to write for the papers, and I wrote a piece for the *Daily Record* while I was still at school. It didn't appear in the *Record*. But I got a cheque for 30 shillings [£1.50] from the *Sunday Mail*, the *Record*'s sister paper. Now we didn't take Sunday papers: father didn't believe in Sunday papers. But he got hold of the postman who delivered letters to the *Daily Record* and asked him if he could get a copy of the *Sunday Mail* for us.[6] So I was quite proud of myself when I saw the article, though there was no name, no byline, on it. So I began to dabble in things and that was really the start of it. And in my final year at school I got an old typewriter from an old joiner in the housing scheme where we lived and who knew I was interested in journalism. And I bashed away on that old typewriter and taught myself to type.

So I left school with my Highers when I was 17 in 1929, and began to send from June to August to every Glasgow newspaper these typed letters asking for a job. I went through *Willings Press Guide*.[7] I got nice replies from them, but nobody offered me a job – except Cossar, who owned the weekly *Govan Press*. He sent for me and gave me a job. Cossar owned half a dozen local papers: the *Govan Press*, the *Southern Press*, *Clydebank Press*, and *Renfrew Press*, and at one time the Maryhill, the Partick, and a Pollokshaws paper as well. Anyway, when I joined him he had the first four papers and I joined the *Clydebank Press* as a junior reporter only.[8]

I had no experience and no idea what to expect when I began at the *Clydebank Press* in September 1929. It was all very weird and wonderful to me. I went around with a young English reporter from Manchester named Clayton who was 21 and who was my mentor. Clayton was very good, a very enthusiastic young chap, and took me under his wing. His uncle was chief sub-editor of the Manchester *Evening Chronicle*, and Clayton's father worked, I think, in Singer's at Clydebank.[9] His uncle had obviously taken an interest in Clayton and shown him a few tricks of the reporter's trade. But Clayton died about a year after I began on the *Clydebank Press*. We were both at the opening of a new church in Knightswood in Glasgow. We were out in the open and he got soaking wet and a bad cold, pneumonia set in, and the next thing Clayton was dead. It was a terrible shock to me.

But before Clayton died he had given me a few tips about reporting, and I took over from him. My job really was to work outside Clydebank: Duntocher, Bowling, Old Kilpatrick, Yoker, Knightswood – that was my beat. Each day you went to a different place. The paper at that time was an old-fashioned one of course that had in it various districts. Yoker would have a column, Bowling would have a column, and so on. And you had to sort those columns. No use coming back to the office with nothing, you had to produce something, which was quite an incentive. It wasn't an easy job for a young person like me without experience. I had a bit of shorthand, not much, and I had to learn fast. My father wrote shorthand and he used to teach me before I'd even left school. And when I was in the Greek class at school but eventually decided the church wasn't for me and I wasn't really going to have any use for Greek, I used to sit in the class and do shorthand. After I left school I went maybe a couple of nights a week to night school at the High School in Glasgow for shorthand.

When I first began at the *Clydebank Press* my wages were 25 shillings [£1.25] a week. Looking back on it now, it was really quite a good wage then for a lad of 17. The hours of work were not too bad really to start with. You were in at nine in the morning till six – it really depended when you got finished. You didn't get away before six, but if you were kept on, you know, you were kept on. As a junior reporter I did evening jobs, meetings and that sort of thing, maybe one or two evenings a week. It wasn't a standard evening shift, just if a job came up you were there. And by that time I think I'd given up evening classes for shorthand. At the start I wasn't trusted to cover a meeting for I hadn't much shorthand, so I had to get some facility in shorthand before I was sent to cover meetings. There were just four of us on the reporting staff of the *Clydebank Press*: the chief reporter and his deputy, Clayton, and myself. The office was a little one, and there was a front office where they sold the newspaper. The *Clydebank Press* wasn't printed there but in Govan, where all the other papers were printed. The flatbed Cossar press was invented by the brother of the owner of the *Govan Press*. Every Friday I used to go with the chief reporter to take the paper over to the Govan office, and you corrected proofs and made up a page. That was good experience.

On the *Clydebank Press* I didn't realise there was a thing called linage.[10] The chief reporter had the linage there for all the papers and I didn't know this. One night the chief reporter was going to play bowls and I was told to do the police calls. I dutifully did the calls and noticed there was a lot of activity at the police station. Usually it was dead quiet, but that night everybody at the police station was buzzing about and nobody was paying any attention to me. 'What's going on?' I asked. 'There's a guy been shot in a bank in Kilbowie Road,' a policeman says. 'What bank?' 'The Commercial Bank.' Kilbowie Road wasn't far and I got to the bank. A policeman was standing at the door and I says, 'I'm from the *Clydebank Press*. What's going on?' 'Oh,' he says, 'a guy walked in just after three o'clock and demanded money from the till and then shot the bank man. He's away with £600.' I knew the local police quite well by this time, asked for the detective in charge, and he told me the story. So I got back to the office again and phoned the bowling club for the chief reporter. He wasn't there; I phoned his home, he wasn't there. So I said to myself, 'What am I going to do with this?' Well, I sat down and wrote the story, left it on the chief reporter's desk, and went away home. We didn't have a phone at home: not many people did at that time. So next morning the place was crawling with newsmen – the *Daily Record, Daily Express*, all in there.[11] My chief reporter had a face like fizz: 'You were supposed to do the calls last night, and you leave a story for me?' 'That's right,' I said. 'Why did you no' phone me?' 'I phoned you and couldn't get you at the bowling or at your home.' 'Well,' he says, 'all the papers are on to me about this story.' 'Why?' as an innocent I asked. One of the reporters said to my chief, 'You shouldnae send a boy to do a man's work.' I said, 'What's the connection?' 'Well,' my chief said, 'it's no' you that's doing this story at all. You're no' a big crime reporter. You go and do your district stuff as usual.' So I was sent up to Duntocher, but I met a policeman there I knew quite well. He said the police had traced the suspected bank robber: 'There's blood on his face, he'd jumped on a bus with a wee bag about the time of the killing, jumped off the bus before it stopped and ran up the road, and the conductress had a very good view of him.' 'Who's the conductress?' I asked. 'Oh, she lives in Knightswood.' 'By gosh,' I said to myself, 'I'm going to sit on this story.' Of course most of the daily papers were still all milling around. So I said nothing about it at all. But the following night I went out to Knightswood and saw this conductress, who told me all about it. So next morning I got into the office bright and early: 'I've got a good story.' 'What is it?' 'This Clydebank bank murder.' 'Oh, nothing to do with you, by Christ!' 'Oh,' says my chief reporter, 'that's a very good story. It should be on the front page of course. And I'll cut you in on it.' So that was where the linage fiddle arrived. I certainly hadn't realised all the stories I'd been doing had meant linage for the chief reporter but not for me. Anyway, that was my first little scoop.

Well, I was about two years with the *Clydebank Press*, then at the age of 19 I was put in sole charge of the *Renfrew Press*. There was a central editor of the four papers. He was in Govan. But I ran the *Renfrew Press* entirely and I was on my tod – completely. It was really rather ridiculous, because nobody was very interested in me at all, as long as I did it! But, oh, it was a great experience. By then I knew how to put a paper together. But covering things was a terrible job: will I cover the sheriff court, will I cover this – or that? I got £2 a week for that job, and that's where I came adrift after about a year.

What happened was that I went one night to a Burns's Supper. The main speaker was the Provost of Renfrew, Colonel Somebody, factor for the Elderslie estates. Suddenly he said, 'Renfrew Town Council proposes to sell the Renfrew Flying Club to Glasgow Corporation.' They were going to make it an airport. So, och, this was great stuff and I splashed that in the *Renfrew Press*. But the Provost was a great pal of Cossar, owner of the paper – they were great freemasons – and he went to Cossar and said, 'What's this in your paper? That wasn't supposed to get out. It is a secret thing. Nobody's supposed to know this. You'll have to do something about it – contradict it.' So of course they sent for me: 'What do you mean printing this?' 'Well,' I said, 'it was a good story and nobody told me it wasn't supposed to be known. He shouldn't have said it if it was secret. And,' I said, 'you can't contradict that. The whole audience heard it. You can't say it didnae happen.' They said, 'You'll have to do something, you've got to do it.' 'I can't think of any way I can possibly do that,' I said. 'You must do it!' they said. I said, 'I can't do it this week.' 'Next week,' they said, 'is too late. You've got to put something in the paper this week.' 'You tell me what to put in, or you write it. I'm not going to,' I said. So there was a real row, and the central editor didn't back me at all and said, 'Oh, I've got nothing to do with it.' So I said, 'Stuff your job', and walked out.

The *Renfrew Press* job was too demanding, it was impossible, hopeless to do on my own, and so I walked out. But I did my last Renfrew round-up and went to Babcock & Wilcox's big tube works there where usually you got some local football news. I saw the company secretary, who said, 'Great news. We've won a terrific order worth half a million pounds' – a lot of money at that time in the early 1930s, especially as Clydeside was in trouble during the Depression. So I told him I'd left the *Renfrew Press* now, but I said, 'What about the *Glasgow Herald*?' 'Well,' he said, 'we're going to put out a hand-out to the *Herald*.' 'What about me putting it in there?' 'Well,' he said, 'I'll give you all the information you want.' So I got it into the *Glasgow Herald*, *The Scotsman*,[12] and the *Daily Record*, and I got paid for that. The great value of that was that it gave me an in: they knew my name now. I got on well with John Simpson, the chief reporter of the *Daily Record*, he was a very good chap. The chief reporter of the Glasgow *Evening News*,[13] sister paper of the *Daily Record*, said to me, 'We could do with somebody to watch the Govan court for us.' I said, 'I'll do it.' 'Right, you're on.' So I did that, and then I would also do assignments for the *Daily Record* itself. They didn't have a man to cover Govan itself. And I used to do stuff for *The Bulletin*, too,[14] and the *Glasgow Herald*. There was plenty of work being offered me. So I built up quite a good freelance business, and I really made far more money than I had made in the *Clydebank* or *Renfrew Press*. I was freelancing for maybe about two years.

I was a reporter, I'd never been a sub-editor.[15] But one day I got a call from the chief sub-editor of the *Daily Record*: 'How are you fixed for the summer?' he asked me. I says, 'I've no' anything.' 'Would you like to do holiday relief for us as a sub-editor?' 'Well,' I said, 'I must be honest with you, really I'd love to do it, but I haven't really been a sub.' He said, 'I've talked to John Simpson. He thinks you'd do all right.' So I went into the *Daily Record* subs. I worked on the Scots desk, as it was called at that time. John Lees, who was six feet three, showed me how to use type, and so on. I picked it up quite quickly, so that was great. The summer went past but I was still there – I was accepted, you see. And sometimes, if a late-night story broke in Glasgow, the chief reporter would say, 'Can I have Max to help out on this one?' So I would leave the subs' desk and jump out reporting. I was still a sub-editor on the *Record* and really I'd by then, 1934, become a staff man, though nobody had told me that!

So not long after that John Allan, the editor of the *Daily Record*, sent me as a *Record* staff reporter up to their Aberdeen office.[16] The *Daily Record* was doing very badly up the east coast from Edinburgh to Aberdeen. The *Daily Express* were pushing ahead very strongly, not so much in Glasgow, though they were there, but up the east coast. They'd been very negligent on the management side in the *Daily Record*. They'd just kidded themselves on they were doing fine: they weren't doing fine at all. So eventually they'd begun to send people on an ad hoc basis up to Aberdeen. We had a paper there, the *Press & Journal*, in the same Kemsley Newspapers group as the *Record*.[17]

When John Allan asked me to go to Aberdeen, I said, 'Well, I've never been up in Aberdeen in my life before. I don't know anything about it.

What are you going to pay me, and what's the condition of the job?' He says, 'Well, the editor in chief, David Anderson, will decide what you're going to get paid.' David Anderson was the editor in chief and general manager, a very colourful chap. He was an artist as well, had style and was very up in the clouds where I was concerned. John Allan said I should go and see Mr Anderson's secretary about an appointment with him. His secretary, a dead pompous guy, arranged an appointment for 5pm. So I went along and sat outside Mr Anderson's room. Suddenly Anderson walked out from it, wearing an artist's cape. I says, 'I'm McAuslane.' 'Yes?' 'I've an appointment with you.' Anderson just stood there, didn't take me into his room. I said, 'I'm supposed to be going to Aberdeen but I don't know what the conditions of the job are.' 'Aberdeen?' He says, 'People go there for their holidays. It's a lovely place.' And he swept by me![18] Anyway, eventually John Allan told me I was to get £6 a week, which was quite good, and my expenses would be paid of course. I was only on £5 a week as a sub-editor in Glasgow with the *Record*, though I had been doing a shift for the *Sunday Mail* which I was paid 50 shillings [£2.50] for, and also did work for the *Sunday Chronicle* in London, which had started up a Scottish edition because the *Sunday Express* had started one, and I had £2 from the *Chronicle*.[19] Allan said I should be able to continue to do my *Sunday Mail* shift in Aberdeen. So that was quite good, I was quite well paid in Aberdeen. I was to stay in the Douglas Hotel there but in due course find myself digs. I asked how long I'd be in Aberdeen and said I didn't want to spend the rest of my life there. John Allan said he didn't know but just to take it as it went, but maybe it would be for a year or two because they really wanted to establish me there.

Well, I got on fine in Aberdeen. It was a great experience, because I'd never been in a town like that, a fishing centre, granite, agriculture, the University, and all that, especially the fishing. You went on these stories that I'd never got in Glasgow. Every winter you'd a trawler disaster without fail. I went to sea myself in pursuit of trawler disasters. One of them was where the entire crew were lost fishing off Iceland. Another one was where a whole family of father, son and uncle were wiped out in a herring drifter. So that was really an education, Aberdeen was very interesting, and I enjoyed my time there. I was the sole reporter there for the *Daily Record*. The *Press & Journal* staff were quite separate, but they would help you. They tipped me off on things, which was very useful. And I also covered an area outside Aberdeen city itself: Fraserburgh, Buchan. Incidentally, the *Press & Journal* had a deal with a car hire firm in Aberdeen that provided only second-hand Rolls-Royces, one of which I used for my work. All these Rolls-Royces had belonged to quite famous people: Barbara Hutton, the Woolworth heiress, for instance, and King Carol II of Romania.[20] Then, too, I was married in 1937 when I was in Aberdeen. My wife was a Skye girl working as a nurse in the Southern General Hospital in Glasgow, and we were married in Skye. And then in 1938 the *Daily Record* recalled me to Glasgow.

*   *   *

From the early 1930s the *Scottish Daily Express*, which had begun to publish in Glasgow in 1929, was very much beginning to develop and penetrate in Scotland. At that stage there was no *Scottish Daily Mail*.[21] So until then the *Daily Record* had had pretty well a monopoly of the popular press. The *Record*'s circulation at that time was about 350,000, which was very good. But the *Express* really were very skilled, with a very big staff and all the money in the world to spend, and they had 13 editions in Scotland every night! A Paisley edition, a Greenock edition – you name it. The *Record* was very sleepy really, because it had its own way for so long. Its territory was really Glasgow and the west of Scotland. They didn't bother much about anywhere else. But, as I've said, the *Express*, very smart, decided to concentrate on Edinburgh, Dundee, Aberdeen, Inverness. They did a lot in Glasgow of course, but mainly in those areas where we in the *Record* were neglecting. We sold hardly any *Records* in places like Aberdeen. There was a *Daily Record* office then in Edinburgh, I don't think they had one in Dundee. We did eventually have two chaps there, and before there was an office I think the chap just worked from his home. But until just before I went there we'd had no staff reporter in Aberdeen or in Dumfries. The paper was very much centred in Glasgow.

The *Daily Record*'s political line was sort of independent Tory. It was a funny thing really, because it was said that if anybody was *Daily Record* the working classes were *Daily Record*. I remember one election when the front page heading in the paper was 'Vote Tory!' The miners and the dockers were the people who read the *Record*: they must have had a laugh at that heading. Anyway, the *Record* was the daily paper in Scotland with the largest circulation in the 1930s. But the *Scottish Daily Express* was creeping up on it, oh, very much so. Bogle, the *Record*'s general manager at that time, was less than honest about the circulation, which was going down. So we were really being misled about that until Clem Livingstone became editor of the *Record* about 1936–7. Even before he was editor he was the one who began to stir things up, and that was when I'd been sent to Aberdeen.[22]

When I came back to the *Record* in Glasgow I was probably the fourth reporter. John Simpson was chief reporter, Jimmy MacDowell deputy chief, and a chap Stevenson came from the *Glasgow Herald* and *The Bulletin* who took over as third man. I was probably the main working reporter. I was sent up and down the country quite a bit until the war broke out and until I was called up in 1941.

In March that year I'd been sent out to report on the Clydebank Blitz. We knew there'd been a blitz all right. But somehow you didn't realise what it was like until you went down to Clydebank. The blitz had taken place on the two nights Thursday–Friday, 13th–14th, and Friday–Saturday, 14th–15th. I went down on the Saturday for the *Sunday Mail*. I was absolutely shattered when I realized . . . People were pushing prams up the road with all their belongings. Buses were taking people along to shipping, to friends, or whatever, and then you saw these buildings absolutely flattened. I knew Clydebank well because I'd reported the area for the *Clydebank Press* for about two years from 1929. I couldn't believe what I saw. Up on the hill – they called it The Holy City: Parkhall, I think, was the official name – it was all small bungalows and they were absolutely flattened. I headed for there and discovered the Provost and the town clerk in a ruined house, just sitting there, trying to trace where people had gone. People were coming and going and saying, 'Where's so-and-so?' They had a terrible job. People had just got out and gone off, ran off into the countryside, or gone to stay with relatives or whoever. And, oh, there were mass graves. They buried them in a mass grave. Whole families were written off. I couldn't believe it. It was frightening.[23]

A woman reporter, Elma Waters, even before the war worked for us in the *Daily Record*. In my earlier years in newspapers women reporters were relatively rare, and we only had Elma in the *Record*. And of course we kept her protected, wouldn't let her out. But she was out this night and a bomb landed in Great Western Road. She said, 'I'm quite near there, I'll look at this there.' 'Well, be careful. Keep your distance if it's . . .' Eventually she was back on the phone. 'Well?' 'It's a great big hole, a huge hole, and in this hole there's this bomb. It's a yellow bomb and has a red stripe round it.' It was as if she was going to a wedding reception! 'Get away from there!' When she came back in to the office: 'How were you allowed to get so close to it?' 'I just walked up and had a look at it.' 'What if it had gone off?'

The main news story I think I ever encountered was ten days before I was called up in May 1941 to the RAF. During the war of course censorship made it very difficult to get information at all. Anyway, I was on duty on Sunday the 11th of May. John Simpson, the chief reporter, was already in and had a memo left by a *Sunday Mail* colleague which said, 'A German plane has crashed at Eaglesham but it was too late for us to do anything about it.' Well, at that time a lot of enemy planes were shot down or crashed every week in this country, so another one wasn't really a big deal. But I made the usual routine calls. There was a war room in Bothwell Street, Glasgow, at that time, so I phoned them up: 'Oh, can't say anything about that. It hasn't been cleared yet.' Well, that was understandable because they didn't want the enemy to know where their plane had crashed or whether the crew were alive or dead. So I said, 'Oh, well, I'll come back to you on that one.'

Then I got a phone call from our general manager, who lived at Eaglesham. 'I was just walking the dog this morning,' he says, 'and I heard about this plane that's crashed. The funny thing is, the pilot has asked to see the Duke of Hamilton.' John Simpson had just gone to the Press Club for his lunch, so I phoned him and says, 'John, did you know anything about this pilot asking to see the Duke of Hamilton?' 'No.' 'Well,' I said, 'apparently he has. I think we'd better have a look at this.' 'Och,' John says, 'it's just another airplane. It could be anybody.' I said, 'I don't know. Why the Duke of Hamilton?' So I phoned the Duke of Hamilton, who was commanding officer at Turnhouse aerodrome at Edinburgh. I got the duty officer: 'Oh, the Duke's not here.' 'Where is he?' 'Oh, he's away.' So I said, 'It's this aircraft that's landed at Eaglesham. The pilot apparently asked to see him.' 'I don't know anything about that. Anyway, it's gone to RAF Command now.' The duty officer knew about it obviously, but that was the brush-off there. And unfortunately that night there had been a heavy, heavy raid on London and the telephone lines between London and Scotland were down. We'd a teleprinter link, but no telephone. So I couldn't get on to London.

When John Simpson came back from his lunch I said, 'I think we should go out to Eaglesham.' 'OK.' So I went to Eaglesham with John Simpson and a photographer. Sure enough here is this Messerschmitt aircraft lying in a field and surrounded by RAF people. I didn't know much about planes, but I said to John Simpson, 'But that's not a bomber. That's a Messerschmitt. Why would you have a Messerschmitt?' We went down to the field and spoke to some of the RAF chaps. There was no senior officer there, just a sergeant. They were quite good, matey. Some of them had been inside the plane. They said it had extra fuel tanks, and you could see where they had been before they were discarded, and they said, 'Yes, how did the plane get here?' I asked what had happened to the crew. 'There's only one.' 'Where is he?' 'Oh, he's been taken away to Maryhill Barracks in Glasgow.' They said, 'A ploughman up there apparently found him.'

John Simpson was standing by himself, trying to take a picture of the plane while I was talking to the RAF men. I said to John, 'Amazing story this. Apparently this ploughman found him.' 'Oh, hell,' said John, 'we cannae stay on here. We've got to get back to the office.' He was chief reporter, he had other things to do. I said, 'Well, John, I'm staying on anyway. Send the car back for me later. The photographer and I'll go up to see the ploughman.' But the photographer says, 'I'm not going anywhere. There's a war on, you know, and plates are rationed. I've got my picture of the plane.' I said, 'But there's this ploughman.' But the photographer had no interest in him: 'You're just kidding yourself on.' So John and the photographer sat in the car and I went to see the ploughman.

A fantastic story Donald McLean, the ploughman, had to tell me. He said he and his mother and sister had seen this aircraft flying round, saw it coming down and crash-land in a field just 300 yards from his house. And he saw the parachutist coming down and found him with his ankle broken or damaged. The German spoke English very well and said, 'All right. I'm not armed.' So Donald McLean was quite brave, because he was just a wee chap, about 5 feet 2, and the pilot was over 6 feet. He helped the pilot across to his house, put him into his parlour and gave him a big comfortable seat. The first thing the pilot said was, 'I want to see the Duke of Hamilton.' 'Oh,' says the ploughman, 'I can't do that for you.' 'Well, who can? It's important I see him.' The ploughman said, 'Will you have a cup of tea?' 'I don't want tea.' So he took a drink of water, then he relaxed and chatted just about his son. He gave the ploughman his name – which later proved phoney – said he was an oberleutnant, equivalent of a squadron leader, and told him he'd been in the infantry in the First World War and then in the air force, flying over the Somme where the ploughman himself was in the infantry. Both men were 47. I asked the ploughman, 'What's a 47-year old man doing flying a Messerschmitt?' 'Oh, I don't know about that.' I said, 'He's an oberleutnant, he's 47 and that's all the rank he has reached, and he gets flying this super aeroplane from Germany to here? And he asked for the Duke of Hamilton? That doesn't make sense to me. Did he tell you what his job was?' 'No, no, just a pilot.' I really was fascinated by this business. I thought it could be the pilot had met the Duke of Hamilton, a great airman, even before the war, in civil flying clubs, and that he might be a count, a society man. But what was he doing? And then he'd said again, 'I've got to see the Duke of Hamilton – an important message for him.' Of course the wee ploughman was frankly bemused by all this and had just said, 'I can't do anything for you. I don't know the Duke of Hamilton.' He was hoping the police and the army'd come and take the guy off his hands. But he told me enough to know this pilot really was important.

29

So I went back to John Simpson and the photographer, who were still sitting in the car. I said to the photographer: 'Get the ploughman's picture.' 'Ah'm not moving. Ah'm going back to the office.' 'Get his picture!' 'No!' I said, 'Well, you'll be back out before the day's out to take that ploughman's picture.' Well, we went back to the office, I wrote everything I knew about the story. That day Clem Livingstone, the editor of the *Daily Record*, was visiting friends in Lenzie, and John Lees, the acting editor, says, 'I'm baffled with this.' I said, 'I'm going to take this entire story down to the War Office censor in Bothwell Street myself, and watch their reaction.' So the censor said, 'Oh, you can't print this.' 'What's wrong with it? The menace of German planes crashing, and this pilot asked for the Duke of Hamilton.' 'No, no.' So we were banned from printing anything on it. That made me more suspicious than ever. I went back to the office, wrote a very simple story, didn't even say the aircraft had crashed in the west of Scotland, didn't mention crew or anything, and took it back to the censor: 'Are you back again?' 'Yes.' 'You're not printing that.' I said, 'I've had many stories printed about German aircraft and you've let them in. Why not this one?' 'You're not printing this. It's a lot of nonsense anyway. There's nothing in it, nothing in it.' I said, 'I've been up seeing the aeroplane. Half of Eaglesham know about it.' The censor took it to a boss man who said, 'It's not on.' So I says, 'We'll see about this.'

So we worked on the story, went back out to Eaglesham and saw the ploughman and his family again. I didn't know where I could take it. The Duke of Hamilton was not available. But it so happened our editor, Clem Livingstone, before the war had set up a radio receiving station at Gleniffer Braes outside Paisley. And he engaged refugees from Europe who spoke various languages to listen out for foreign broadcasts. Clem thought it could be useful but I'm surprised he got away with it. So I phoned Clem at his mother-in-law's house. 'I'm coming in now,' he said, 'just wait till I come in.' He was in in no time at all: 'What's this?' He was very interested in the story, but, 'What do you mean you havenae got a picture of the ploughman?' So he phoned the photographer: 'Get out to Eaglesham and get a picture of this ploughman.' Clem says, 'Now I wonder if we can get any help from the radio receiving station?' So I phoned, but: 'No, nothing interesting, nothing that measures up to that at all, no.' I said, 'Well, could you listen out on the German waveband, especially any domestic broadcasts?' So that was it, the thing was dead, you couldn't move on it, nothing else was going. Anyway, I wrote the story up, every detail of it, all without names. It never struck me that the pilot could be a political figure.

Well, on the Monday, when I went into the office the receiving station had picked up a broadcast from Germany: mournful music in Berlin – Rudolf Hess had apparently been lost at sea out on a flight. I said, 'That's him!' I did the final version of the story, and said to Clem Livingstone, 'What are you going to do about the censorship?' He said, 'I'm not going to the censor.' 'Dangerous,' I said. 'No, we're not,' Clem says. 'We're running the story, Max. Hell mend them.' And he ran it. And, once we ran it, over the teleprinter came a signal, 'Hess has landed.' Well, the censor up here had seen our paper, we had broken the story, so they used it themselves and it came up on the teleprinter. Then they called a press conference in London about Hess. When the pressmen asked any questions, they said, 'We're just giving the broad outlines. Ask the *Daily Record* in Glasgow, they know the detail.' We'd got an exclusive story in the *Daily Record*. They held the press conference at midnight, and I sat on the phone in our office until six in the morning, answering phone calls from newspapers, news agencies and what not, all over the world, and we gave them the stuff. Oh, it was a tremendous story.

After the war, I spoke to the Duke of Hamilton. You would meet him at things, and I knew him quite well. We were at Edinburgh airport one day, both going to London, and I said to the Duke: 'What about Hess? Tell me about it.' 'No, Max, I can't,' he says. 'My son, Lord James Douglas-Hamilton, he's doing a biography of Hess. I'm giving all my stuff to him, so I'm not telling you. But,' he said, 'I'll tell you this. I was asked to go to Lisbon to meet somebody who would be Hess or Hess's brother, who was a middleman in this. I was the undercover. I'd have to go on my own and if anything happened they didn't know me. I wanted the consul or the ambassador in Lisbon to cover or look after me but they wouldn't do that. So I wasn't prepared to do it.' Before Lord James published his book he told me, 'My father was absolutely in the clear. There was no question of him being an agent or anything else. But he was asked to be, and there was communication between our Special Branch and the anti-Hitler group in Germany. They were in touch with him and they were arranging this meeting.' Germany, in order to attack Russia, wanted Britain out of the war. So they arranged with this anti-Hitler professor chap to contact the Duke of Hamilton, who was a friend of his, that he would arrange for somebody to meet him in Lisbon. Hess himself was to go. But of course that wasn't on because the Duke of Hamilton wouldn't wear it. There were people in this country of course who didn't dislike Hitler at all and thought him preferable to Stalin. But I don't think the Duke of Hamilton was that at all.

I never myself saw Hess, he was already off the scene at Eaglesham. But Willie Ross, later Secretary of State for Scotland, met him then. At a lunch we had in Edinburgh when I was chairman of the Scottish Newspaper Proprietors, I was sitting beside Willie Ross. He said to me, 'You were involved in the Hess story? I met Hess. I was a sergeant at Maryhill Barracks in Glasgow when he was brought in there.' I said, 'I could have done with you that night to give us some information.'

A lot of people would know their own bit of the story, for example, the Home Guard and the police, who took Hess in. McLean the ploughman was sitting in his house with Hess when the farmer came in, saw Hess, and alerted the Home Guard and the police. They, and the army Signals, who had a unit there, all turned up. It must have been rather comical. I did a thing for the BBC, was out at the scene of Hess's landing, and a woman at a nearby house says, 'I remember it vividly. I couldn't help laughing. There was a sort of farm road leading down to the main road, the police cars were down there, and Hess was walking from the house down to them. They were all walking down as if it was a parade. Hess was the tallest and most military looking of them all.'[24]

*   *   *

I'd already received my call-up papers and, as I've said, I was in the RAF ten days after the Hess landing. Incidentally, after I was into the RAF I got a letter from my wife saying: 'You've got a letter from your office with a cheque for £6 as payment for the linage for the Hess story.' By Jove – six quid! It was nothing at all, I was taken to the cleaners. Anyway, in the RAF I was a very short time at Wittering, a fighter station in Northampton, then at Duxford fighter station in Cambridgeshire, and then I went to Egypt, at Daba. Alexandria was the nearest town to Daba, and El Alamein was close by in the desert. Daba was on the west side – the German side – of El Alamein but I was out of it before the Germans occupied it. I was in radar. My job eventually was to control fighter aircraft and beam them on to enemy aircraft. You got signals from your radar stations, got a fix on where the enemy aircraft was, and vectored your aircraft on to it. It was an interesting job, I liked it, and eventually I became a sergeant. We weren't in the battle front at El Alamein, but it was a very hot spot where we were. If the enemy could knock out your radar it was very useful to them, so they tended to go for the radar, but it was very well protected. Then when the Eighth Army pushed ahead we followed them up right through North Africa to Tripoli. From there we went to Toulon in the south of France.[25] There'd been a bit of fighting there but that was over by the time we landed. I came home from there and was demobbed after the end of the war in 1945.

I think the war changed my views politically. I wasn't a bit surprised when Labour got in with a landslide in the 1945 election, because the troops were all very left-wing.[26] What struck me during the war was the tremendous waste, people doing things that weren't necessary, and conniving and fiddling things. For example, we had a commanding officer who went away to Tunis and flew back himself a big aircraft that cost £80 just to take off. He wasn't operational, just being self-important. That was just a trifle compared to some other things that were happening. Then on the way to Egypt we went to South Africa and I was a bit shattered at the apartheid there.[27]

I wasn't involved in any journalistic activities in the RAF, except on the troopship to Egypt. To keep the troops amused, they said, 'Can we not produce some magazine we can read, no matter what ship you're on?' So I was recruited to that, sort of designed the thing and wrote a couple of pieces for it. What annoyed me about the war were the lost years. I was 29 when I was called up and 33 when I came back: I felt them a terrible waste of years. I didn't consider taking up some other occupation at the end of the war, and just wanted to get back to newspapers. And by that time I had a daughter. So the thing was to settle down and just get on with the job.

I went back to the *Daily Record* as a senior reporter, just what I'd been before. It was an interesting life, I enjoyed it, and it was a good paper to work for. The paper was doing well. But I felt I might have been moved up earlier on. They did away with the appointment of chief reporter. John Simpson, the chief reporter, at that time'd be in his 60s. Then in 1954–5 Alastair Dunnett, who'd become editor of the *Daily Record* in 1946, asked me to take over as news editor.[28] I said, 'Well, you'll have to clear it with John Simpson.' So they made John a sort of general reporter at large and features writer for the three sister papers, the *Record*, the Glasgow *Evening News*, and the *Sunday Mail*. Of course John wasn't daft. The *Record* was, I think, the only paper he'd worked for and he'd probably been there 40 years or so. 'Oh,' he says, 'I've suspected this for some time, because I've been sort of pushed aside a bit.'

I found there was quite a contrast between being a senior reporter and being the news editor. You'd to get yourself off this habit of going out on a story: news editor was a desk job where you worked ahead, planning the news. The *Daily Mirror* took over the *Daily Record* and its sister papers in Glasgow from Kemsley Newspapers in 1955,[29] and I remember one Sunday sitting at the news desk when there were great problems with a story. I said to the reporter doing it, 'I don't understand why you can't break this story. I've a good mind to go out on it myself.' Sitting beside me was Hugh Cudlipp, boss of the *Mirror*, and suddenly his fist hit the desk beside me. 'Max,' he said, 'never say that! You know you're not going out. You've got to sit here at the desk.'[30] But I built up a first-class team, they were excellent chaps, in Glasgow and in the branch offices in Edinburgh, Aberdeen, etc. You didn't really have to tell them anything.

Well, it took a little time to get the message across in Edinburgh and other branch offices because they were just that much removed. They'd had a certain way, and you didn't want to stir things up too much. Tom Nicholson, for instance, the chief reporter in Edinburgh, had been in the job so long and he'd got a way of life going for him that he didn't like to change. I remember, for example, going across once to Edinburgh to visit them there, and Tom said, 'We'll go to the Press Club. I always go there to play my father at draughts.' His father was a nice old chap. Let him play draughts in the evening, but as a newspaperman you don't say, 'Wednesday's the day I play the old man come hell or high water.' Tom was a very handsome, striking man, and a good speaker, a good chap. But he had this fixed . . . When Bulganin and Khrushchev visited Edinburgh I sent some reporters through to Edinburgh to help Tom. They'd been there all day with the whole story, it was a good story. All they had at night was a dinner and Tom came on and was proceeding to give me a long-winded story. But I said, 'Tom, I don't . . . What's the menu? What did they get to eat and drink? That's what I'm interested in. That's all I want. I've had all the stuff all day. You should know that.'[31]

Then in 1957 I was asked to come over to *The Scotsman* in Edinburgh as news editor. Roy Thomson had bought *The Scotsman* and its sister paper the Edinburgh *Evening Dispatch* in 1953, and Alastair Dunnett had become editor of *The Scotsman* early in 1956.[32] *The Scotsman* was a good paper, but it was still pretty stodgy – they still had adverts on the front page – and it obviously had to change. It was definitely in a rut and seemed to have been left behind by the rest of the press. My brief as news editor was to sort of get things going, a different approach to the news and the kind of story that makes front page news, generally giving the news an uplift, developing the pictorial content, and preparing for news on the front page.

I got on well with Alastair Dunnett, who of course had been editor of the *Daily Record* for ten years from 1946. He was a very good chap, a very tough guy, but very straight and enthusiastic. He couldn't stand people who weren't enthusiastic and would do anything for an easy life. I remember a chap, a sub-editor, at the *Daily Record*, who used to have a book in his desk drawer so we wouldn't see him. He'd just got old and tired on the job. Well, Alastair Dunnett had been watching him and told him to smarten his act up. Eventually, Alastair said to him, 'Jimmy, the navy are offering a fortnight's trip on a ship. Would you like to take it up?' When Jimmy came back from the trip his job was taken! He had virtually nothing to do.

There were some very bright people working on *The Scotsman*. Some of them had very, very good education at university. I remember the Principal telling me that Jim Vassie, who did economics for the paper, was the brightest economics student he'd ever seen coming out of Edinburgh University. Another chap on *The Scotsman*, Arthur J. Arthur, a graduate of Glasgow University, was terribly bright.[33] Among the reporters you'd people who had special knowledge of things. But they weren't being used, exploited. The six leader writers did two leaders a week each if they were lucky. So when Alastair Dunnett became editor he took his leader writers out for a drink and explained things. One of them said, 'I won't have a drink, Mr Dunnett, I'm writing a leader tonight.' Alastair said, 'These chaps are terribly bright but they're wasted. Why don't we use them as feature writers?' So he did, and they became very good. I sent Arthur J. Arthur down with a reporter to the press conference when the nuclear power station at Calder Hall was opened. I got a letter afterward from the Nuclear Energy Authority: 'We've never been so embarrassed as by questions from your Mr Arthur. We'd to stop and check up.' He knew more about nuclear energy than they did![34]

And then *The Scotsman* used to have an arrangement of exchanging newspapers and information with the Russian paper *Izvestia*.[35] The chief leader writer spoke Russian fluently. He would go through these papers and pass them to colleagues that specialised in Italian or French, and pass economics stuff to Jim Vassie and so on. So they built up a terrific knowledge. Arthur J. Arthur went later to the BBC, and another chap who did European affairs for *The Scotsman* joined the Foreign Office. Oh, they were a tremendous crowd on *The Scotsman*, oh, gosh, an entirely different world from my earlier experience on the *Daily Record*.

But then also there was the funny sort of snobbishness on *The Scotsman*, there were those and such as those on the paper. There were the older reporters who just ambled along. They would phone up the office in the morning and ask, 'What am I doing today?' 'Well, I see you're marked for a presbytery meeting.' 'Oh, fine. I'll have a round of golf before then.' They went to the meeting and wandered off again! It was ridiculous. I said, 'This is daft, this needs sorting out.' Some did certain jobs. One did shipping, he had no special training, I suppose. Some others had some other special thing. And that's all they would do. They wouldn't do anything else. We had to stop all that nonsense of course. And then again the older chaps had these columns; the younger reporters were doing all the dashing about! George Philip covered the Court of Session, that was a full job, that was fine. But Philip Stalker, a terribly posh, entertaining wee chap, he was one of these 'What am I doing today?' sort of chaps. He did presbytery reports and specialised on church, religious affairs.[36] Of course some had got set in their ways. It was very difficult to change them because they weren't very good at anything else. And they were relatively elderly, in their later fifties or sixties. So you just encouraged the young chaps. First, I appointed a very good chap as deputy news editor, Stuart Brown. He'd come to *The Scotsman* from the *Daily Mail* and he'd been a reporter before he was a sub-editor. Then I wanted a third man, a night man, and I picked on a young reporter who was only 25, but a very good chap – Allen Wright. When I asked him if he'd be third man at the news desk, he said, 'You must be joking', but he took the job and was a great fellow, tremendous.[37]

I was news editor of *The Scotsman* from 1957 to 1960, then I joined its sister paper the Edinburgh *Evening Dispatch* as its editor. The *Dispatch* was in a very bad way and everybody knew it was in a bad way. Edinburgh, with Glasgow, was one of the few cities of size to run two evening papers. By then the Glasgow *Evening News* had ceased publication, though the *Evening Times* and *Evening Citizen* were still there. London was, I think, reduced to two and eventually just one; Birmingham and Manchester each had only one evening paper. So obviously you couldn't expect two papers to survive in Edinburgh, and it was obvious the paper that was going to survive was the *Evening News*.

The *News* was the best paper. It had a much bigger circulation than the *Dispatch*, and it was a tremendous advertising medium. The only time the *Dispatch* was on top was with its sports edition, the Saturday *Green*, over the *News*'s Saturday *Pink*. Although Roy Thomson didn't say it at the time, I knew it was in his mind, anybody knew. So I said, 'I'll do what I can with the *Dispatch*.' Not that Roy Thomson expected me to do wonders, and you knew you couldn't win. There wasn't time to change the paper round. You'd to take the staff you had, and they were actually quite a good staff in the *Dispatch*. But to get them motivated, to get them working the way you wanted them doing, there really wasn't time. But what Roy Thomson wanted me to do was to make life difficult for the *Evening News*, force the *News* to spend money to fight us – and eventually he would get the *Evening News*: he'd already tried every way to get it. So that was really my brief, what I had to do was just that. And in doing so of course you got the *Dispatch* staff on your side. They were very good, but I didn't push them too hard, though sometimes you felt you had to put the boot in a bit. But they always reacted well, they'd have a go.

Unfortunately, we'd had several editors of the *Dispatch*. There'd been A.D. Mackie, then Jack Miller came up from the *Daily Mirror*. Well, Jack Miller had made such a hash of the *Dispatch*, really terrible.[38] So it'd been decided to bring a *Scotsman* man in to steady the boat. But he went into reverse and turned the *Dispatch* into a sort of evening *Scotsman*, which wasn't what they wanted at all. So eventually he decided to resign and I took over as editor.

So we started by tackling the news service and making it bright – pictures, special pages, good layouts, and so on. I know that doesn't sell a paper, but it helps. At that time the daily circulation of the *Dispatch* was about 70,000; the *Evening News* was, oh, something like 140,000. There was no way you could catch the *News*! But we did give it a good shot and what we intended to do, and did do, was force them to spend money.

Our circulation was going up very slowly. But we were doing a lot of things the *News* weren't doing, not only on the editorial side, but publicity-wise, marketing, and so on. And we were exploring outside Edinburgh – special editions in Falkirk, Fife, and places like that. That was doing us some good, adding circulation, though still no hope of catching up on the *News*. But then the *News* began to spend money on publicity and various promotions. The owner of the *News*, who lived in Yorkshire – all his other papers were Yorkshire – had run buses originally, he wasn't a newspaperman basically. And of course when he had to spend money he wasn't interested in it. So Roy Thomson had him on the run. And by the end the Yorkshire man said, 'Get rid of this lot.' Roy Thomson said to him, 'I'll tell you what. I'll swap one of my Sheffield papers for your Edinburgh *Evening News*.' The *Sheffield Star* that Thomson swapped, a sort of *Dispatch* really in Sheffield, which had two evening papers, wasn't doing very well! Anyway, he did the deal, and so Roy Thomson got the *Evening News* at last in 1963.[39] They kept it a secret. They invited the manager of the *Evening News* up to *The Scotsman* and *Dispatch* office and we were told there that that was it.

In the *Evening News* I discovered the staff were so laid back. They'd had things so easy for years, and they all had their own little fiddles going – one guy, for instance, did the Press Association and the BBC on the side.[40] So of course they had to change their tune a bit. I don't blame them, I mean, the *Evening News* was so successful, great for them. They were so successful because of the *Dispatch*'s defects. Well, the *News* staff were sitting back and they were very, very lazy. Some of them were naturally bright; others were inclined to, 'Oh, what's all the fuss? Why should we do that?' When the two papers were merged, some staff left from both papers, well, mostly from the *News* naturally enough, because they had been on a winner and they'd been taken over and didn't like it. But some at the *Dispatch* we got rid of, because we couldn't carry the two staffs. What we did was we took young people, young chaps, and placed them in jobs in other places in the Thomson group – in Aberdeen or whatever, and so nobody lost their job, I don't think. But on the *News* side some left voluntarily, out of pique or whatever. One chap, George Millar, a nice bloke in his 40s, came to me very honestly and said, 'Max, I don't think I'm going to enjoy working for the new set-up.' I said, 'Well, it's a free country. What are you going to do for a living?' He said, 'I thought I'd set up a press agency.' 'Great,' I says, 'can I help you in any way?' He says, 'I don't know.' 'Well,' I said, 'I'll tell you what I'll do for starters – it's a very good thing to get into sport. We've now got into the Kemsley Group. Say I get you all the sports coverage for Edinburgh for the *Sunday Times, Sunday Graphic . . .*? And the Court of Session: if we can't on occasion cover it, you cover it.' 'Oh, that'd be terrific.' So George Millar and Bill Rae, the two of them, left us at the same time and took friends with them, and made a great success of the United News agency. Both were excellent experienced reporters.[41]

The *Dispatch* ceased publication, though we copied a lot of the *Dispatch* into the *News*, and for two or three years called the new paper the *Evening News & Dispatch*. The editor of the old *Evening News* was a chap called Cairns, a nice chap, but completely under the will of Barnetson, the boss. If Barnetson'd said 'Sneeze', Cairns sneezed, and he'd really lost any will to do anything. Frankly, the *News* had been going so well he didn't even need to bother. I was asked to become editor of the *News & Dispatch*, but I said, 'You can't change editors overnight. He must remain as editor.' So Cairns was called editor and I was given some fancy title of consultant editor or something. But actually I was running the paper from the start. It all went very well, and then eventually we just dropped the *& Dispatch* bit from its title. Cairns was getting on to retirement and he retired and I became editor and remained editor until my own retirement in 1976, though I stayed on as editor consultant, *Scotsman* Publications, until 1977 until the new editor had got settled in. I didn't interfere in any way. If he wanted any advice, I would say, 'Well, this is the way we did it, but that's that.' You can't look over the guy's shoulder, you know.[42]

We went on to front-page news as well – until then the *Evening News* had adverts on its front page. I didn't know how I was going to do that, but eventually what did it was the assassination in November 1963 of

President Kennedy. A circulation chap says, 'Put this news on the front page.' Some of the adverts of course were sort of fixtures: you couldn't just change the whole front page overnight. So I just sort of cleared a window on the front page, and put in the window: KENNEDY SHOT! And that gave me an in. From there I managed after the next day to make the window a bit bigger and eventually I took over the page, so that was it. So that was almost 100 years after the *News* had been founded in 1873 that news was put on its front page.[43] I spoke at the centenary dinner and we were well established by that time, no problem. The circulation of the *News* went up naturally when the *Dispatch* ceased and there was no competitor, then it came down: some people stayed with the *News*, some didn't. The circulation kept a fairly steady course of maybe about 145,000, and when I left it was 146,000. The challenge was no longer other papers, it was people's time. Television had come in in the 1950s, and commercial radio to some extent. There was a sort of new look at newspapers. People buy one paper: buy an evening paper, don't buy a morning paper. And this was the pattern. People didn't spend so much time reading as they used to do. So that affected circulation. Toward the end of the twentieth century the circulation of the *Evening News* was down to about 80,000, not much more than half of what it was when I became its editor. But that fall is not all to blame on the paper. It's people's attitude to newspapers.

I did quite a lot of broadcasting in the early days of television. But I realised I wasn't a television person. I don't know what it was – the voice, or something. TV is a different medium from newspapers and I realised it wasn't my scene. It wasn't the actual content, it was more projecting yourself on television: you needed to be something of an actor. The kind of person they want you don't get, unfortunately, both in the same parcel: you don't get the chap who knows and can handle news and the guy who can put it over. So eventually television went to presenters and somebody behind the scenes who produced the news for them. This is the way it happens now. But unfortunately the presenters become more important than the news man.

*   *   *

I joined the National Union of Journalists as a young reporter in my Clydebank days before the war. I became quite active in the Union, and I was chairman of the Aberdeen branch when I was up there with the *Daily Record* for three or four years until 1938. Aberdeen was a very small branch, a very haudin' doon branch.[44] Then after the war I was secretary of the Glasgow branch and then did a year as chairman. Och, it wasn't much of a union at that time, it wasn't very militant.

I was never politically involved. I didn't have much time or inclination for that. I mean, I was interested enough, detached, but I was never a member of any political party. I remember though as a youngster going to my first Scottish Nationalist meeting to report Oliver Brown, a great chap. I was fascinated by what he said.[45] But, as I say, I never joined the Nationalist Party or any other Party. I don't think many journalists do get drawn into political activity: it's maybe the nature of their job, you don't want to identify too much . . . One chap, Liam Regan, we had on the *Daily Record* and then later he was news editor of the *Sunday Mail*, was a great left-wing chap and used to be out working for the Labour Party and so on.[46]

As a boy I went to church and the Sunday School regularly. The churches we went to were very strait-laced, so they didn't have any of these badminton clubs or that kind of thing. Though my mother wanted me to go into the ministry I was never enthusiastic about that. But once I went to work on a daily newspaper you couldn't go to church because you'd work on a Sunday and you lost touch with the church. When I came to *The Scotsman* in Edinburgh in 1957 I could pick and choose my hours, and went then to church.

Well, looking back over my career in journalism I suppose the job that gave me most satisfaction was the *Daily Record*, because I was there at a creative time, especially after the war. Before the war the staff had been there a long time and they were all set in their ways a little bit. When I was news editor and got choosing my own staff I found them, and some I inherited, too, very, very good. They would bash on with stories, and knock holes in windows, as people used to say. They were self-motivated, tremendous, so that was very stimulating. When I came to *The Scotsman* I was on a fighting wicket. *The Scotsman* was not doing all that well, so that was different and you'd to work on the staff and get them going. I found my job at the *Dispatch* definitely the most frustrating. You knew you couldn't win.

Comparing newspapers now with when I first began all those years ago on the *Clydebank Press*, *Renfrew Press*, and the *Daily Record*, I don't think there's enough effort now going into newspapers journalistically. We seem to have lost the way. I was pointing out one day to the editor of the *Evening News* that if I buy an early edition of an evening paper at 11am and another one at 5pm there's hardly any difference in it at all. 'Why is it like that? Is there nothing happening in the city between 11am and 4 pm – no courts, nothing?' 'Well,' he says, 'we change the paper as little as possible. We've only one machine and you can't change it too much. The marketing people who really run the thing don't care as long as the paper is selling.' I said, 'That's wrong. There's not an incentive for anybody.' And the number of editions has declined as well. The evening paper has only declined because they've allowed it to decline. If that's everyone's philosophy, then it's going to be a very poorly-educated democracy. People aren't going to know what's happening. Even locally I notice how little I know what's happening in Edinburgh City Council. What's happening in all the committees, how many houses are built, who's getting houses? And that's happening in all fields. We're not getting detailed coverage. People are relying on television and its coverage is abysmal. The interviewing leaves a lot to be desired.

Then another thing is youngsters coming through in newspapers. I think there's more to be done for them. I don't know what they're learning. But I've got a bit distressed about what's going to happen about journalism. These schools of journalism are run by people who haven't been too successful as journalists. So they escape and become teachers. The youngsters are maybe getting quite a good basic grounding, but I don't think there's too much know-how going into it. I don't think they're getting the right kind of training. Everybody should start off on a weekly or a small daily because there you get personal attention.

I remember the first day I turned up in 1929 at the *Clydebank Press* my father had said, 'You'd better put on your good Sunday suit.' I turned up with my good suit and a bowler hat. And I remember the chief reporter, this big chap with a cigarette, looking at me, asking me if I had any shorthand, and laughing as he said to me, 'Well, son, you're no' really dressed for the job. The only folk who wear bowlers doon here work in the shipyairds.'

David M. Smith

The first job I got to do, after joining in the summer of 1930 as a junior reporter aged 16 the bi-weekly *Perthshire Constitutional*, was to report on a Perthshire Colts cricket match.[1] It was on the Saturday afternoon, and on the Monday morning I went into the office and sat down to write the report. The news editor of the *Constitutional* was Peter Winton, one of the very hard, old-fashioned types of journalists. He was almost blind, but he was still in charge and he ran the paper. He said to me, 'What are you doing?' I said, 'I'm writing the report, sir, of the match.' He says, 'Writing a report? The report should have been written yesterday. It should be lying on my desk now.' I said, 'Oh, but I've just come in.' He says, 'No, no. You'll have to learn. If you're at a job today you write the job today – it doesn't matter when you bloody well finish – and have it on my desk in the morning. I don't care when you finish – on my desk in the morning. In future get that into your head. You don't carry news over a day. News goes on all the time, and you've just got to do it.'

I was born in Perth in August 1914 – a very ominous month. I was an only child. Before her marriage my mother was a domestic servant in a farmer's house called The Makum, at Bilmakum near Cupar in Fife. She didn't return to work after her marriage: married women didn't do that then.

My father, who was born about 1890 and died in 1963, was a police sergeant in Perth. He left school at probably 12 or 13 and had started work as a farm hand, but wasn't interested in that, and after a few years he worked on the Dunalastair estate beside Loch Rannoch. He must have liked the lifestyle there, for years later he used to drive us up there from Perth once a month or so as a Sunday outing. He was a very good fiddler and was in a band there, and used to tell me how they thought nothing of walking, after a day's work, ten miles across the hill to play at a dance and then walk ten miles back again to start work on the estate in the morning. But there was no future in that job, and Rannoch was and still is a pretty desolate place. Then he worked on the railway for a very short time as a fireman before he became a policeman around the time I was born. He and some other young constables who were from the country and hadn't had great education went by private arrangement once or twice a week to the house of one of the sergeants, where a teacher came and gave them tuition in the three Rs. My father was a sergeant for ten or more years before he retired from the police about 1940.

I don't know what my grandmother Smith had done for a living before her marriage. She came from Aberfeldy, and her family were brought up, and were friendly, with the Dewars of Dewar Whisky before they started out in the whisky venture there. She died about 1928 but I remember her very well. My grandfather Smith was grieve on New Downie farm, in Angus near Monifeith, where he worked for 36 years till he retired in 1928. He would be about 83 when he died in 1942. As a boy I spent most of my holidays, summer, Easter and Christmas, with my grandparents on the farm there, while my parents went away on their own on summer holiday to Aberdeen: only once, I think, I went there with them. My grandparents lived in the farmhouse at New Downie, which had a very big living room, kitchen, a bedroom-cum-sitting room, and then up the stairs there were four rooms.

Our house in Leith Buildings, the last house in Dunkeld Road, Perth, was on the second floor of the tenement. It was ten minutes' walk from my father's police station in Tay Street – though he cycled to work. Our house was just a room and kitchen, and I slept in the room. The lighting was gas. There was only cold running water. Friday night was bath night in a big tin bath. The toilet was shared with another family. There were four houses on a landing, and there were two toilets on a lower level.

When I was five I started at Northern District primary school in Perth. History interested me most, and I liked geography and arithmetic. I didn't like English grammar, I thought it was dreadful. But I liked the primary school, got on well there, and, as far as I remember, passed the Qualifying exam. I then went on to Perth Academy, which was fee-paying. I walked back and forth to the school, a quarter of an hour's walk, and went home at dinnertime. At the Academy I enjoyed history, but also English – because I liked the English teacher, Mr Kerr, who also took history. English at the Academy was more interesting than at the primary, because we had literature. I wasn't a keen reader at all as a boy. I got comics – the *Rover* and the *Wizard*.[2] But I didn't join the public library till after I left school. As a boy my chief interest was football. I played wing half for the primary school team, but it was rugby at the Academy, and a disappointment that they didn't offer football there. So I was conscripted into playing full back in rugby at the Academy, though I quite enjoyed it. But unofficially we also played football on the North Inch, which was the Academy's playground. The Academy, for boys and girls, was a big school. I suppose you were given a good basic education there. But for some reason I wasn't really much interested in it. It may well have been because I was really more interested in football and cricket. Anyway I stayed at the Academy till I was about 14½ or 15.

What happened then was that as I was quite good at cricket the sports master decided I should join the Perthshire County Colts – but that involved being equipped with whites, etc. My father wasn't impressed with the concentration on sport and the lack of educational knowledge. So he immediately took me away from the Academy and I went for a year to Ross Commercial Training College in the centre of Perth, to do shorthand, typing and English literature – I think they assumed you already had the grammar. The courses were excellent and I would be doing about 120 words a minute in shorthand when I left, and I could type fluently.

As a boy I had no ambitions, none, till I was about 14. My mother thought, God only knows why, I should become a minister! I think she thought it was a very respectable job. My father thought I should be a banker, and while I was at the commercial college and starting to look for jobs I actually had an interview for the bank. It must have been when I was about 14, I think, I had said to my father: 'I want to be a newspaper reporter. That's what I want to be.' I don't know how that idea came about. I'd never met a reporter, there was nobody in our family on a newspaper. We did get the Dundee *Courier* regularly at home, and my mother got the *People's Friend*, which I read devoutly, to the annoyance of my father, who did not approve of that paper.[3] I don't know what it was made me want to become a reporter, but that was one of the reasons I was keen to learn shorthand quickly. Anyway I had made up my mind even before I had left Perth Academy that I wanted to become a newspaper reporter.

When my father arranged an interview with this banker friend who was prepared to give me a job, I said: 'I don't want the job. I can't imagine sitting behind a desk counting money.' My father was not very pleased. But as a police sergeant he was in touch with the press, and he must have mentioned my keenness to the two local newspaper offices, the *Perthshire Constitutional* and the *Perthshire Advertiser*.[4] The Ross Commercial Training College was next door to the *Constitutional* office. Well, I was told there was a vacancy there, I went to see them, and they said they would start me.

I started, not as office boy, but as a junior reporter. The job then had several ramifications. Well, the *Constitutional* was a bi-weekly of eight to twelve pages, and for one thing the brown paper wrappers, the stuff for the post, had to be made up every morning. It was a lot of work, and we had to get into the office at half-past six in the morning to do these wrappers. It was a task for the junior reporter, but office staff did the wrappers as well. Then some mornings you had to get up and go out with the van to deliver the papers in Perth, though not outside the town. So the driver drove and you jumped out at the newsagents' shops. And sometimes on publication nights, if they were short-staffed, they would say to the other junior reporter and myself, 'Oh, you might just wait on and feed some of these . . .' So we helped with that, and then got the papers out and folded them, and that sort of thing. So you were maybe there till, well, half-past eleven or midnight doing that sort of caper. It was a long day, but you had to help, there was no choice: that was part of our job as junior reporters.

In the two mornings each week you were on those duties you were up at half-past five, and had to be in the office at half-past six. The two early mornings and the two late nights per week didn't always coincide. It just depended often on what you were doing. But there wasn't much choice about doing the wrappers and that sort of thing: you had to be in to do that. It was really the sort of work you would associate with a circulation department, but the junior reporters did it.

The *Perthshire Constitutional* was privately owned by the Hunter family. The paper was founded about 1830. Thomas Hunter, the proprietor in my time there, concentrated on local government. He was more interested in that than in newspapers, although he remained editor–proprietor. He ultimately became Lord Provost of Perth and contributed more to Perth as Lord Provost than probably anyone. Later he became the MP for Perth and was knighted. His son Harris Hunter was very keen on the Territorial Army, and became a colonel in the 51st Highland Division but was captured at St Valery in 1940 and spent six years in a prisoner of war camp. That pretty well finished the *Constitutional*, because by the time he came home at the end of the war and tried to pick up the threads it was too late.[5] So the paper closed down then. By then the rival Perth weekly paper, the *Perthshire Advertiser*, which had been founded after the *Constitutional*, had virtually captured the castle. The *Advertiser* was part of the Munro Press, itself part of the Outram Press which had the *Glasgow Herald, Glasgow Evening Times*, and *The Bulletin*.[6]

But when I began on the *Constitutional* as a junior reporter in 1930, Sir Thomas Hunter was still very much flourishing as editor and proprietor, a leading figure, an outstanding figure, in the town and county of Perth. If he had concentrated his energies on the paper it would probably still be flourishing. But instead he concentrated on local government. Politically, the *Constitutional* was Conservative (the *Advertiser* was Independent). But then, with the development of the National Liberals, the *Constitutional* became National Liberal so that Sir Thomas could become the local MP. When Sir Francis Norie-Miller, founder and head of the General Accident Insurance Company based in Perth, gave up as local MP, Tommy Hunter got the job. There was a very close association between General Accident and the *Constitutional*, which did all the GA's printing for it: that was good business.[7]

*   *   *

When I started as a junior reporter in 1930 my wages were 7s 6d (37½ p) a week. The hours were very elastic always but, oh, they were long days, there's no doubt about that. As a junior reporter you didn't do much evening reporting then, so you finished normally about five-ish. When the paper went to press we could probably clear off then. That was it. It was haphazard. There was very little definition on hours. You had time off in the evenings, and I was still interested in sport outside of the job itself. In fact, I'd been at the *Constitutional* three months when Mr Winton, the news editor, called me in to his office and said, 'Look, I'm just going to tell you straight. Unless you pull your socks up and improve, you'll be out in a fortnight. You can get your head down and decide if you're goin' to be a journalist or not.' I think it was the case with myself then that being young and newly begun at work you're not taking it very seriously. You really had to produce the goods or Mr Winton was down on your top. He was a very hard taskmaster.

Mr Winton had himself been a very good reporter. He had been with the *Constitutional* a long, long time. He and Tommy Hunter, the proprietor, had been reporters together, I think. But by then Mr Winton couldn't do any reporting because his eyesight was so bad. He overcame it wonderfully, but his eyesight was really very, very bad. But thanks to him I had a very good training, because I had to do everything. When you covered the Sheriff Court, for instance, as a young reporter, you went there, took your notes, came back to the office, and you had to read your note over to Mr Winton quickly. He summarised it and re-dictated it to you, I took his dictation down in shorthand and just read it straight from my note then to wherever it was going – to the Glasgow, Edinburgh, or Aberdeen papers, wherever it was going. Football was another example. St Johnstone, the Perth team, were in the First Division then, and football was done for the evening papers. There weren't sufficient phones at Muirton Park, St Johnstone's ground, for everyone. So what happened was:

Mr Winton sat in his office at the *Constitutional*, a runner cycled the mile and a half from Muirton Park to the office with the copy. My future wife, who worked in the office on the clerical side, used to go in to the office on a Saturday afternoon, read the copy over to Mr Winton as it arrived, and he either subbed it or shortened or lengthened it as he wanted, and then she'd phone it to the evening papers. Maybe it was a sign, too, that Sir Thomas Hunter was a bit paternalistic, in that other proprietors or managers might not have kept on somebody with Mr Winton's serious disability. Of course, however expert Mr Winton was, those arrangements involved some complications and some delay which could have been avoided if the *Constitutional* had got a normal sighted person.

Of the other editorial staff, Eddie Balfour was a mature, experienced reporter. Eddie would be about 25 or 28 then, a very nice fella and a very beautiful shorthand writer. He wasn't keen on too much work really, he liked to take time over things![8] Harris Hunter, son of Sir Thomas and in his thirties then, also did reporting – some news and all the sport. But he gradually concentrated more on the commercial side of the business. Then there was another lad, Andrew Boyd, who started as a junior reporter the same time as me. I suppose it would be unusual for a bi-weekly local paper to have two junior reporters, but it was just the way it worked out. Andrew had gone to Queen Victoria School in Dunblane.[9] His brother was a printer with the *Constitutional*. Then of course there was Sir Thomas Hunter as the editor. There were no women on the editorial side. Then on the printing, advertising and circulation side there was a foreman printer, three or four compositors and one or two juniors, two advertising agents and some office workers. The *Constitutional* did commercial printing, too, and that was quite an important part of the business. One of the jobs also of the junior reporters was proofreading. The foreman printer did the proofreading and you read with him. He was a well-educated man of good experience and with good English. So that was the best training you could get. Mind you, proofreading was boring work, but the training was excellent. I was doing that after only a few weeks at the *Constitutional*.

After a while as junior reporter the only regular job I had to do was Perth police court. It was every morning at half-past nine. At one time Colin Dakers, who was younger than me, was one who went with me to the police court; he was on the Dundee *Courier* in Perth then. But the *Courier* always had a senior reporter who went to the police court. The *Perthshire Advertiser* generally had a junior like myself there. But we were very much dependent on the senior reporter, who kept us right. Andrew Boyd, my fellow junior at the *Constitutional*, had other work and hardly ever did the police court. I enjoyed reporting the police court: it certainly broadened your knowledge of life – lots of characters, drunks, minor offenders in Perth, some coming up regularly.

The inter-war depression more or less coincided with my years on the *Constitutional*. I remember the unions then were becoming stronger, there was a much more aggressive attitude amongst union officials in Perth. The railway unions were the main ones in Perth, which was a big railway junction, with both the LNER and LMS. I don't remember his name now but I used to interview the local secretary of the National Union of Railwaymen and, you know, there was more aggression and they weren't interested in conciliation really.[10]

Our own union, the National Union of Journalists, came into being about 1935 in Perth. There hadn't been anything before that.[11] By that time we had begun to realise our wages were not just as good as they should be. Of course our wages were supplemented by linage, because the custom in local papers then was for the editor or the proprietor to hold correspondence for the national papers. But of course the actual work was done by the reporters. As time passed I did a lot of linage work. Harris Hunter had *The Scotsman*'s correspondence for Perth, and that included also the Edinburgh *Evening Dispatch*; he also had the Aberdeen *Press & Journal*, and I think we held the Glasgow *Evening Citizen* and Glasgow *Evening News* as well. The *Glasgow Herald* and Glasgow *Evening Times* were handled by the Dundee *Courier* office in Perth. Someone else did the *Daily Express* correspondence, I don't remember who it was, but later on I did that. The *Daily Record* had their own staff reporter in Perth. A chap who was a printer held the correspondence for the *Daily Mail*: they didn't take very much then, only sport. But the primary one was *The Scotsman*, and once I had developed a bit I did practically all the reporting work in Perth for it: I did all the sheep, bull, and horse sales in Perth, which were very big as Perth was a very important agricultural centre. For the bull sales we would run at least a full column in *The Scotsman*.

So the linage for those national or evening papers was a lot of work for us local weekly paper reporters. We were paid. Well, that was the point. Because one or two of us discovered that we were all getting a very poor share of the payment. What we had thought reasonable proved to be not reasonable. We were doing the work but, on the *Constitutional*, Harris Hunter was taking the greater part of the fee paid. The same applied at the Dundee *Courier* Perth office, where a very fine reporter named Jimmy Littlejohn held the agencies and was taking the greater share while the boys were having to do the work: he was paying them, but a very small proportion only. So someone must have got in touch with some of the lads in the city, and the result was that two chaps came up to Perth from the *Stirling Observer* to see us about starting a union.[12] We were all very interested on the *Constitutional* and the *Perthshire Advertiser*, and so was John Dawson, the *Daily Record* staff reporter – but not, of course, the staff in the Perth office of the Dundee *Courier*, because D.C. Thomson, the proprietors, were strictly non-union, indeed anti-union. Well, I should say their Perth reporters were interested, but for that reason they couldn't do anything.[13]

The *Constitutional* refused, I think, to deal with the union or refused to make any move at all. But by that time Sir Thomas Hunter, the editor–proprietor, had become MP for Perth. So they said, 'Well, we don't want to hold threats. But if you don't take action and agree to this we'll have to raise the matter in the Commons.' So the result was we joined the National Union of Journalists then in 1935. But for the first couple of years we were members of the Stirling branch of the Union. The first Perth branch was formed in 1937. There never had been a Perth branch before then. I became its first treasurer. But I was treasurer for only a month before I left Perth. Eddie Balfour, formerly of the *Constitutional*, was branch secretary. There were four of us from the *Constitutional* who were branch members. Mr Winton, the news editor, had died in 1933–4; but Andrew Boyd and I, and Bill Wylie and Jimmy Jeffers, two other reporters who had joined us by then, were all branch members.

Eddie Balfour had left the *Constitutional* before Mr Winton died. So I took over as news editor in 1933–4, when I was between 20 and 21 years old, and I remodelled the paper then. It was difficult to do it because Sir Thomas was still the boss and he wasn't so keen on radical changes. But for one thing I introduced a page of pictures. The *Constitutional* had occasionally bought in photographs, but I said we should have our own. Sir Thomas said, 'Well, how are you going to do it?' I said, 'I'll learn the camera and take the pictures myself.' So I did the pictures as well. Before then I hadn't been at all interested in photography and knew nothing about it. But Bob Watson, chief photographer of the *Perthshire Advertiser*, helped me out. Bob was a very good photographer, we became very friendly, and we used to do all the social functions in Perth together in the evening. We took all the dance pictures, all the staff pictures. There were plenty of firms in Perth, there was always stuff on, and Bob and I were well entertained when we went round the dances. So after I became news editor the *Constitutional* had a regular full page of pictures – not many landscapes, I never went in for them, but faces. I really believed that faces were what we required to sell the paper. You had to have faces or people doing things. They would then buy the paper to see themselves or their family and so on. So circulation went up as a result. But I don't know if Sir Thomas Hunter was pleased or even interested. He came into the office every week to write his leading article as editor, and sometimes that was the only time you saw him. His son Harris was in control but he was concentrating more then on the commercial side of the business. So I had a relatively free hand, and it was a tremendous experience for me.

It was very generous on Bob Watson's part to help me as he did with the photography, because there was very much enmity between our two papers, at one time it was cut-throat. The *Advertiser*'s circulation was substantially bigger than the *Constitutional*'s. It had overtaken the *Constitutional* completely. I really don't know the *Constitutional*'s circulation when I joined it – it was a closely guarded figure – but I would think it was about 4,000. The *Perthshire Advertiser* always came out with their circulation figures and they were always very substantial. Of course by that time the *Advertiser* had been taken over by Munro Press and was very substantially backed.

Another thing I did as news editor was I persuaded John Keir Cross, a well-known figure on the BBC, to write me one or two articles. John was a great friend of mine, a very nice fella, and he and I had been at school together. He was a very good writer, very broad-minded in his attitudes. He introduced sex into his articles for the *Constitutional*. And I can remember Sir Tommy Hunter coming in nearly purple in the face, with red rings all round the sentences in John Keir Cross's article: 'What do you think my bloody paper is?!' In fact, it was mild stuff I had read and passed. But this was going too far, so John Keir Cross was dropped. I had to curtail that aspect of local journalism![14]

Then the old papers always had stereotyped introductions to everything. They never changed the style of anything. I changed the style and tried to make the *Constitutional* more readable, with bigger types, and setting out the paper more. I also got all the local organisations persuaded to send me a weekly column, and I had a minister who wrote me something controversial every week – quite good stuff. When I brought out the first edition after changing the paper like this, one or two of the senior reporters in Perth on the *Advertiser* and the *Courier* said, 'Oh, the *Constitutional* is more like a magazine than a newspaper now.' I said, 'It may be but the news is there as well.' Well, a lot of newspapers now are more like magazines than newspapers. That's partly the result of television – but there was no television in those days and radio was still relatively young. So those were the sorts of changes I introduced on the *Constitutional*. I would have changed the front page, too, with its solid columns of advertising; but Sir Thomas and Harris Hunter wouldn't let me change that.

As for wages, we got annual increases. When after seven years, the last three as news editor–chief reporter, I finished working at the *Constitutional* in 1937 I must have been getting about £2 or £2 5s [£2.25] a week. It wasn't an enormous sum, but, I mean, it was a local family newspaper and they were not paying the top wages ever. And that wage was excluding what I could make on linage, which might be £1 or £1.50 a week. By that time we had a better share of that, though the linage was always less than the weekly wage.

On the *Constitutional* you had a fortnight's paid holiday. You didn't normally get public holidays – not Christmas Day nor New Year's Day, normally you were working then, there was always something on. My future wife and I had seaside summer holidays from about 1936, Bridlington first, then North Wales. We were on holiday in Belfast in 1938 when we got engaged. When we came back from holiday we were generally completely broke, we didn't have a penny! It wasn't a big wage really on weekly papers then. But I did manage to earn £100 for one job, which was very considerable. The Scottish Typographical Association held its annual conference in Perth, and its local secretary, with whom I was very friendly, got the job for me as shorthand writer to produce their book. Mind, it was a fortnight of slavery. You had to produce every night a summary of that day's proceedings which had to be printed and ready in the morning for the members at the conference. And then at the end of the conference I had to complete all my transcription within a week, a very heavy load of work. To do it, I took a week off work from the *Constitutional*.[15]

*   *   *

By 1937, after seven years on the *Constitutional*, I wanted to go south. I had been applying for other jobs. For the previous year I had haunted Glasgow, Edinburgh, Dundee, for jobs. I wanted to go, too, to Manchester, Nottingham, Yorkshire, Devon – anywhere in England, though I never applied for anything in London. I wanted to get on to national newspapers. I felt I had had enough of local papers. I had written applications all over the country. But jobs were tight. I had haunted the *Courier* office in Dundee, because it's a very good firm the Dundee *Courier*. So in 1937 I came to Berwick to work for the Tweeddale Press on the *Berwick Advertiser*. And the week after I got the job in Berwick I got a letter from the *Courier* offering me a job in Dundee!

When I came to Berwick as chief reporter to the *Berwick Advertiser*, the Tweeddale Press, the owners, limited me to 18 months. A limited contract like that was not normal at that time but, well, it suited me because I really wanted to go further south. I wasn't interested in staying on in Berwick-on-Tweed then. But the 18 months' contract was the Tweeddale Press's idea. Printers had a seven years' apprenticeship in the printing trade, and at the end of seven years they were finished because they were due to go on to a very much higher rate of wages. Major Smail, owner of the Tweeddale Press, operated his journalists in the same way: 'If you stay for 18 months you'll earn so much and that's the maximum I'm going to pay a journalist.'[16] You weren't compelled to go then. If you were fortunate you might be kept on. But so far as normal things were concerned it was an 18 months' contract. So for me Berwick was a staging post.

What I came primarily to Berwick to learn was the court and local government work. I could have a foot in both camps in Berwick, because the *Advertiser* was covering both sides of the Border. Court work in Scotland is entirely different from court work in England, as was local government. So Berwick was an ideal place for me to learn these things.

At that time the Tweeddale Press had only three papers: the *Berwickshire Advertiser*, which we on the *Berwick Advertiser* also worked for, and the *Kelso Chronicle*, for which I and the other *Advertiser* reporters had little or nothing to do. The *Berwick Advertiser* and the *Berwickshire Advertiser* were both published in Berwick, the *Kelso Chronicle* in Kelso. The *Berwick Advertiser* circulated in Berwick itself and in Northumberland; the *Berwickshire Advertiser* in Berwick and in Berwickshire in Scotland. The rivals to the three Tweeddale Press papers were the *Berwick Journal* and the *Berwickshire News*, both published in Berwick.[17]

When I began as chief reporter of the *Berwick Advertiser* in 1937 my salary was £2 15s [£2.75] a week. That was an increase on the *Perthshire Constitutional*. The chief reporter of the *Advertiser* held the linage, but I think it was only for one paper, the *Newcastle Journal*.[18] But when I came to Berwick I knew I could supplement my wage by some other linage, because I had also worked for the Glasgow evening papers. Glasgow holidaymakers came to Berwick in those days – Spittal was a major holiday resort – and there was always something happening with them. So I generally made in the summer a wee bit of linage out of the Glasgows. Berwick was also a good agricultural area, and as I had always done work in Perth for the *Scottish Farmer* the first linage work I did in Berwick was for it. They used to send me a postal order for about five bob [25p] a month![19]

*   *   *

As I've said, I first met my wife when we both worked in the *Perthshire Constitutional* office. We got engaged in 1938 and we were married in Perth on 1 September 1939. So I was born in the month the First World War broke out, and got married two days before Britain entered the Second World War. Of course we didn't know the war was going to break out two days later. We got a rented house over in Tweedmouth, on the south bank of the Tweed. So of course when the war started, well, it was obvious I would be called up in due course. What would my wife do – join the Forces or go back home to Perth? She said, 'No. We've got a home here. We'll just stay here.' We'd gone about together for so many years, she'd been to so many reporting jobs with me, she'd done as much typing and phoning for me – so she was well equipped to do anything. Major Smail, proprietor of the Tweeddale Press, said to her, 'Well, if you'd like to, what about taking over Dave's job while he's away at the war?' So she took over my job at the *Advertiser* when I was called up in May 1940, and she continued with it until I was demobbed in 1946. It was a very unusual arrangement. The editor of the *Advertiser* when I went there in 1937 was a woman, Miss Mary Gray. She was, I think, the first woman editor. When I came she viewed me with a lot of suspicion, because before my time she had had one or two men reporters whom she didn't think were any good. But I went with her to my first council meeting, I took a complete shorthand note, went back to the office, typed it up, and she got it in the morning. She was impressed and changed her attitude altogether.[20]

Women reporters were rare in those days. There were none on the *Perthshire Constitutional* or *Advertiser*, or the Dundee *Courier* in Perth. I didn't have any qualms when I had learned it was a woman editor on the *Berwick Advertiser*. There I, as chief reporter, was the only experienced reporter. We had two junior reporters, Douglas Blackhall and Stuart Brown. That was the editorial staff, four of us. Then on the printing and commercial side, it was much the same at the *Advertiser* as on the *Perthshire Constitutional*. They had four linotype machines, and about the same number of printers. But they also produced the *Berwickshire Advertiser*, which came out on a Monday, the *Berwick Advertiser* on a Thursday.

I'd never had any army connection at all when I was called up in May 1940, at the time of the evacuation from Dunkirk. When they asked which regiment you preferred to join, being from Perth I naturally said the Black Watch.[21] So I was called up to the Royal Signals, and as we arrived for training at Darlington barracks, the Dunkirk people were coming back. We were all paraded in our civvies, and the first thing they said was: 'Is there a shorthand writer and typist amongst you?' I put up my hand. I was the only one. They said, 'Right. Fall out. Straight into the orderly room and start work.' This was even before I got a uniform.

So in the orderly room, where all the administration was done, it was shorthand and typing I was doing. The adjutant was in charge, and he dictated letters to me. The work in the office was in a dreadful state. They'd been Territorials who were in there, and with all due deference to Territorials they had very little knowledge of administration. It was a bit of a shambles. Not that I had much knowledge of administration either, but I was able to do a certain amount.

I'd been there about a fortnight when the sergeant major called me out the office and sent me with a squad to peel a big pile of potatoes. The adjutant came round like a raging lion, collared the sergeant major, and says: 'Smith goes back to the bloody office and he stays in the bloody office. He doesn't waste his time peeling potatoes!'

We were at Darlington only about six weeks. As it was not far from Berwick I sometimes got home at weekends. Then we moved into Hildebrand Barracks in Harrogate, where this Signals training battalion for NCOs was set up. I was there for three and a half years. I became a lance-corporal, a corporal, then a lance-sergeant. At the end of that three and a half years I was sent to Catterick and I was left in limbo there for about a month, doing no work, just attached to the School of Signals. I didn't know what was happening. Then one morning the sergeant major called me: 'Your old colonel's arrived, Lewis Barclay. He wants to see you.' I'd got on very well with him. He was a very keen cricketer and I played cricket all the time in Harrogate with him when I was in the orderly room there. 'Well,' Colonel Barclay said, 'the War Office are setting up a special team. There's only five in the team: myself, a captain, a sergeant major, a sergeant, and a lance-sergeant. We have to go round checking all the training in this country then go abroad and check training there and rewrite the manuals for the future.' So I became the lance-sergeant in the team. I didn't travel with them in Britain, I stayed at the base in Catterick looking after the office, and only went away with them twice – once to Lincoln and somewhere else. But later we went to Italy, from Italy to Palestine, up to Syria, then all over India, to Ceylon, then all over Australia, to New Guinea, to the Solomon Islands, and to another group of islands down there. That was my first time abroad, I'd never flown in an aeroplane before, and we flew 35,000 miles around the world. It was an amazing experience that lasted almost 18 months. When we'd been in Italy and in New Guinea the fighting was still going on. Of all the places we went to, Australia made the greatest impression on me. We were in Perth, Adelaide, Melbourne, Sydney, Cairns, Townsville – the lot. I think if I'd not been married I'd never have come back home from Australia. Oh, my army experience broadened my mind completely.

We must have been in Australia when the war finished and the colonel said, 'Right, you're due for demobilisation. We're going on to America for another tour of up to six months. Or you can be sent home now to be demobbed. What do you want to do?' I said, 'Listen, I've had six and a half years. I've had enough. I want to go back home.' And the other sergeant – he was in insurance in civilian life – said the same.

So I arrived back in Berwick in 1946, where my wife had been doing my job as chief reporter on the *Advertiser* throughout the war – indeed she was the only reporter as all the others were in the Forces. She and Miss Gray produced the *Advertiser*. Though when I'd been on leave I worked there, and so did Douglas Blackhall when he was on leave. Stuart Brown of course was a prisoner of war. He'd stupidly joined the Territorial Army on 1 September 1939, the day I got married, though I told him not to, and he left a note on Miss Gray's desk: 'Gone to join the army'. He was captured at St Valéry in 1940, and was next seen in the *Advertiser* office at the end of the war. So when I came back in 1946 my wife worked on for a few months and then just packed up. She didn't mind being displaced as chief reporter by her husband, and she might have welcomed it! Douglas Blackhall and, as I say, Stuart Brown came back as well. We just restarted and carried on more or less where we'd left off.

Miss Gray retired in 1948 and I became editor then. I'd be 34 then. I suppose in some ways it was quite young to be editor of a weekly paper. But I'd had massive experience in journalism by then. Earlier that same year, when Major Smail, proprietor of the Tweeddale Press and himself a bachelor, died, his half-cousin, Colonel J.I.M. Smail, a New Zealander, became the proprietor. Colonel Smail had got leave during the war from the New Zealand army in Italy and decided he would come to Berwick to see his relative Major Smail, who was a generation older. The Smails had owned the *Berwick Advertiser* for six generations. So at the end of the war Major Smail, who had had two nephews in Darlington who were always assumed likely to succeed to the business but who were both killed in the war, wrote to Colonel Smail and suggested he come and stay with him at Berwick and come into the business. That's what happened, and Colonel Smail became the proprietor. But he had no experience, none at all, in newspapers. Miss Gray, the editor, and he never gelled. So very shortly after his arrival as proprietor Miss Gray retired.[22]

So as the new editor I was very much in charge of the paper, indeed I only took on the editorship on condition that I was in charge. I was very much opposed always to proprietorial interference in newspapers. I believed that journalists should run the papers and not the proprietors. Mind, I've been proved quite wrong in that respect and my wife has explained to me often that I was wrong. But that was my view. Colonel Smail was a young man when he came to Berwick after the war and I had been very friendly with him. We were on very good terms. Originally he didn't attempt to interfere on the paper. But later on, once he got a knowledge of the business, we didn't see eye to eye.

As time went on he naturally took over more of the management of the paper. He was very active, very progressive in his ideas, no doubt about that. He sometimes didn't like the way I handled the paper. Relations between us were very easy at first but they became more difficult. And of course by that time, as we were still doing correspondence for other papers, I had acquired quite a number and had set up a fair agency. I was prepared to send stuff under the signature 'Smith, Berwick' to papers anywhere. It became a very well-known name, because I simply sent stuff out of anything that was happening to papers in all the main cities – Glasgow, Edinburgh, London, Manchester, Newcastle, anywhere, and regardless of whether we were their official correspondents or not. I created what I believed should have been done before, a pool where all those who took part in it were all paid accordingly. All the *Advertiser* reporters, Douglas Blackhall, Stuart Brown and Tommy Leach, a junior, all participated in the pool. Some weeks they actually got more money from the pool than from their *Advertiser* wage, because we had such a big coverage, and it was properly run and distributed. I just dictated it, but the others were quite happy with my dictation and it was a fair system, unlike the one I had suffered under at the *Perthshire Constitutional*. So it all worked very well.

I remained editor of the *Berwick Advertiser* from 1948 until 1951, when in the last few months relations with Colonel Smail became less easy. But for that I might well have remained in the job. I liked the job, I was quite happy in it. I also remodelled the *Advertiser*. It was the front-page news to begin with, and photographs. They didn't have a photographer, so I did the same as I'd done in Perth. Even while Miss Gray was still there as editor I had got a camera and did photographs. I started the photography then. I could do both press photography and journalism. That was very unusual in those days. It caused a little trouble with the union, because some of the strong union members objected to that. I had gone back into the National Union of Journalists as soon as I came back from the war. Ultimately there was an East Northumberland branch formed that took in down near Newcastle, and Blyth, Morpeth and Alnwick, all round that area. In the *Advertiser* we all joined that and went to the branch meetings once a month in Morpeth or Alnwick. Stuart Brown was the only one with a car and he drove us down. Later, about 1947–8, I formed the Berwick branch and became its first chairman and was chairman for quite a few years. The *Berwick Journal* people joined the union, so we had about eight or ten members in the branch. Anyway after I became editor of the *Advertiser* I established about 1949–50 the photography department and we then employed a photographer. One of the first was Denis Straughan, who later worked for *The Scotsman*.[23]

Well, Colonel Smail as proprietor and I as editor disagreed over proprietorial interference in handling copy for the *Advertiser*. He also objected to the correspondence business, to us editorial staff working for other papers. He said I was being disloyal to the Tweeddale Press while I was working for those other papers. That was the thing that annoyed me intensely. I said, 'Right. You can take a month's notice. I'll be finished in a month.' What I was really annoyed about was that when I came to the *Advertiser* first before the war its circulation was not very good and was dwindling. I think it was down to about 2,500 copies. I think it rose during the war. When I left in 1951 it was up to over 7,000. So that was the thing that really finished me, when Colonel Smail said I was disloyal to his firm. But another thing I had done when I came first to the *Advertiser* was to start a children's column. I used to be very bored then on a Sunday night in Berwick. I was in digs, my friends were all away home in Newcastle or elsewhere, I was on my own. I had done a children's column in the *Perthshire Constitutional*. But Major Smail, then the proprietor, was very hidebound and very much opposed to it in the *Berwick Advertiser*, just because I think he didn't trust the people he'd previously employed. But I persuaded him it'd be a good thing to start it. It was just children's news. And I persuaded Tweeddale Press to get certificates and badges for the kids. The badge said 'Uncle Bob's Child, *Advertiser* Children's Nook', and the certificate said they were members of the '*Advertiser*'s Children's Notes'. They had to come to the office to collect their badges and certificates. Major Smail then thought it was a wonderful thing, because a lot of people thought he was 'Uncle Bob'. One or two girls used to come religiously every Saturday morning to see 'Uncle Bob'. But he always had to be out. He couldn't be there.

My wife carried all this on during the war and it built up enormously. The children collected stuff for the troops, stuff for the small naval vessels that used to come into Berwick, and loads of vegetables, salvage, everything. It did tremendously well. There were several hundreds in the club then. Membership extended through the *Advertiser* circulation area on both sides of the Border. Then there were small competitions they ran, with prizes, and they collected and exchanged stamps, and everything like that. I said to the Tweeddale Press then, 'You realise these are the readers of the next 20 years?' But long after I left the *Advertiser* they stopped the children's column: unless you got someone interested, an enthusiast, to run it, it was no use. But it built the circulation. There's no question of that.

*   *   *

When I resigned from the *Berwick Advertiser* in 1951 I immediately set up as a freelance. It was an idea I'd had for some time, since things were not going well in my relations with Colonel Smail. I hadn't been looking round for other possibilities or other jobs, and I really had no other job to go to when I gave my notice in at the *Advertiser*. But I had a lot of journalistic experience and I'd made a lot of contacts, particularly in the *Newcastle Journal*. The chief news editor there was Arthur Wilson, I got to know him fairly well with sending him stuff, and he had said to me, 'If you ever decide to set up on your own, we'll back you.' They had three papers in Newcastle: the *Journal*, the *Evening Chronicle*, and the *Sunday Sun*. They were all part of Kemsley Newspapers at that time.[24]

So I finished at the *Advertiser* on the Friday and started my own freelance business on the Monday – plunged in immediately. My wife entirely supported me. By that time we had our son Ian, aged three. I had a friend who was a plumber up the main street near the arch in Berwick, and he said, 'I have an old room up there. If you like you can have that to start in.' It was rent free and excellent. I put a phone in and made a small darkroom. I was intent on doing both the words and pictures. The pictures were important: the market for them was very much better in those pre-television days.

I was on my own. Well, my wife did quite a bit of the phoning and taking messages at home. Most of the work when I began was general news, sport was secondary. I was supplying all my old contacts in Edinburgh, Aberdeen, Newcastle, Glasgow, Manchester and the BBC in Newcastle. But I didn't hold all the papers then. The *Berwick Journal* held quite a few – the *Sunday Post* for one, and quite a few others.[25] Well, that was really fair game for me because I was now an open freelance. So I cut in at every opportunity, which was pretty unscrupulous but it was the only way to do it. So I acquired the lot. For the *Berwick Journal* and others it was an extra, for me it was my livelihood. That's how I looked at it: 'All right, if I'm prepared to start as a freelance, pay my own expenses and everything like that, I'm quite justified in moving into any market I want to.' Once or twice they tried to have me expelled from the union because I was doing the double job of journalism and photographs. But the threat wasn't carried out.

Denis Straughan left the *Berwick Advertiser* and came to me as photographer, and that helped me to concentrate on the written work. Then I had another chap, Dennis Hay, who left the *Advertiser* and came to me. From 1951 there was fairly continuous growth in the work. But I only stayed in the plumber's old room for about a year, because the roof was leaking and when there was rain you had to run over with a bucket to catch it! So I got out of there and got offices in the middle of the town in Hydehill, where the Universal Building Society were converting their premises. I was quite friendly with the chap there. He said, 'Look, there's two rooms up there. You can get them at a reasonable rent.' So I was there for about three years. Then in the early 1950s I got a much bigger place, a former solicitor's office, in Ravensdowne, again in the centre of Berwick. The solicitor's office itself was very nice, but the rest of the place was pretty dilapidated. Altogether it had two rooms on the ground floor, two up the stairs and a darkroom, and a cellar where I used to have a darkroom as well. It was ideal for the purpose. It was then, too, that I started a retail shop business because when I did the photography I started doing weddings as a purely commercial photographer. I had done a bit of that in Perth, too. And I started photographing children as well. At one time we had two photographers. After Denis Straughan and Dennis Hay went away I got a very nice chap, Stuart Rennie, a press photographer from Falkirk, who had done a lot of sport work there. Then for a long time I had Eddie Sanderson, who ultimately went to America and became one of its leading photographers – did all Joan Crawford's stuff.[26] Actually Eddie went from me direct to the *Daily Mirror* and he never looked back. Crawford Tait worked for me as well and then went on to the Edinburgh *Evening News*. Stuart Gilbert trained with me as a journalist and later became editor of a paper in Birmingham. Stuart Brown, who worked with me on the *Berwick Advertiser*, went on to become news editor of *The Scotsman*; and Douglas Blackhall, another junior reporter from my *Berwick Advertiser* days, later became editor of the Shields paper. So young fellows like those who trained with me at the *Advertiser* or later in my freelance business went on to greater things. Douglas Aikman, who went on to the *Daily Mail* in London, was another.

As I say, I employed usually one photographer but occasionally two. On the reporting side I had a reporter based in Alnwick: the first one was Bert James from Perth, who later became editor of the *Mearns Leader*.[27] The reporter at Alnwick just worked from his digs. And in Berwick I generally had a junior reporter, in the late 1960s it was my son Ian, who came into the business then. And my wife was always giving practical help in the background.

But after a time the press photography side of the business dwindled a lot. The start of the decline was in the later '50s. When I started I could be sure I would have half a dozen pictures a week in *The Bulletin* in Glasgow, and the *People's Journal* [28] was also a very lucrative market for which you could do stories and pictures. Sometimes I used to have maybe a couple of page spreads on something. But these died. *The Bulletin* ceased publication in 1960. It was the result of the coming of television. We also lost around that time the *Daily Herald*, the *News Chronicle*, and the Edinburgh *Evening Dispatch*.[29] These were all markets that just disappeared. And then later on in the '60s or '70s another factor was the railways. We used to have contract parcels where you could send pictures by rail and there was no charge to you. If we got anything decent it would maybe go to half a dozen places. But that stopped. By the 1990s if you wanted to send a parcel it cost about £30 to send it from Berwick to Newcastle. Well, no newspaper was going to pay for that. By the late 1990s it had to be something exceptional if they even wanted a picture. So the market for that disappeared. So the last press photographer I employed would be about the early 1980s. But for about 20 years after I set up the business in 1951 the press photographic side was very good.

So when the pictures side had pretty well died by about 1980 the business had become one rather of words. By that time, too, the *Newcastle Journal* had decided to put one of their staff reporters into Alnwick. So soon after that I no longer employed a junior based there. That finished our interest on the Northumberland side and we became concentrated exclusively in the office in Berwick. There was then myself, my son Ian, and for seven years my younger son David who, however, left in the middle 1990s to go into teaching. Newspapers are progressively not looking at parochial news now. It's a different attitude. Andrew Neil said in *The Scotsman* he wasn't interested in the small-time news, only in the big national or international news. I spoke soon afterward to three old readers of *The Scotsman* who'd had the paper for 50 years, and they were all cancelling their orders. *The Herald*'s a far better paper than *The Scotsman*, and it's still using small-time news.[30]

In the last 20 or 25 years of the twentieth century I don't think being a freelance newspaper reporter-cum-photographer has become difficult in the cities, because there's been so many staff men sacked who have then started as freelances. And the papers are still needing the news, therefore they're quite happy to take it from the freelance. So the freelance market there is better than it has ever been. But for freelances on the outskirts it's more difficult. We still do a lot on Border Television, for instance, and on Radio Tweed.[31] And the lucrative return from television is much greater than it ever was from the newspapers! What we've lost on the swings we've gained on the roundabouts. So far as we're concerned it's balanced out. My son Ian, who now does most of the work, and I are still working away. And I employ a girl full-time in commercial photography, and she does press work as well if necessary. So there are not many fewer of us than at the height of the business's expansion.

Incidentally, not long after I left the *Berwick Advertiser* and was free-lancing I took over the editorship of the *Berwick Journal* as well. Alex Steven, the proprietor and editor of the *Journal*, died. There were three sons in the business but none of them were interested in the journalistic side. They were very hard pushed for an editor. I suggested Stuart Brown and Douglas Blackhall, but they didn't fancy the job. So the *Journal* finally came to me and asked, 'Will you take over the editorship and carry on running your own business?' I said I would take on the editorship for 18 months or two years at the most, and during that time train their second-eldest son to become editor. So I took the job over and quite enjoyed it. Their office was on the main street, and I worked between there and my own office. Of course the *Journal* was in direct rivalry with Colonel Smail's *Berwick Advertiser* and *Berwickshire Advertiser*. I relished that! The *Journal* also had the *Berwickshire News*, which was very strong. The *News* was selling 6,000 copies, the *Berwickshire Advertiser* only about 700 copies. We were also rapidly catching up on the *Berwick Advertiser*'s circulation. The *Journal* and *News* had a big gift shop, Border Series Gift Shop. I said, 'Look, we've got all this stuff here. Why don't we give a weekly prize, just reasonable gifts, in a small competition?' And it went well of course. Our circulation just kept coming up. But then there was a tremendous family fall-out among the Stevens – and they sold out virtually overnight to Colonel Smail. I was ill at home with jaundice and was running the paper from my house. The proofs were being brought over to me there to check and pass them. Someone came in last thing at night and said, 'Here, you know what's happened? They've sold out to Colonel Smail.' So the last issue of the *Journal* came out. Smail, in fairness to him, took over all the staff. But I insisted there was a two-line entry put on the front page: 'Mr D.M. Smith, editor of the *Journal*, resigned last night.' I didn't want to work with Colonel Smail again. I believe he had made it a condition of the deal that I must not be told anything about it, because he would have a good idea that I could do something about it if I had known. In fairness to Colonel Smail, we got on all right personally, and I was always invited after I became freelance to any event or function the *Advertiser* put on. But professionally over the years we had big arguments, big fall-outs, really serious. The day he took over the *Berwick Journal* he saw me in the street and gave me a V-sign. But Colonel Smail built a big business, a much better business than I would ever have imagined. He really did well. I was editor of the *Berwick Advertiser* when he took over the *Southern Reporter* and the *Kelso Mail*. The *Southern* was the biggest of all, a real prize.[32]

Well, looking back over my 70 years in journalism, I think newspapers have improved in their appearance and generally in their content as well. But I don't think in the nationals and the local papers there's the same standard of accuracy there used to be. Shorthand, I think, has deteriorated but it's not just that. I detect a deterioration in the general attitude. I haven't any regrets that I became a freelance rather than remained a staff newspaper journalist. I've always preferred just to work. Freelancing did involve seven days and seven nights a week. There's obviously much less financial security in it than for the staff reporter. On the other hand, staff reporters' jobs have become less secure than they used to be. As a freelance it's up to yourself entirely. No good going into freelancing if you're not prepared to work. Freelancing is becoming crowded. It seems everyone who loses his staff job thinks, 'Oh, I'll have a go at freelancing.' Well, the cake isn't as big as it used to be, and there are more people trying to slice it. But I've no regrets about becoming a journalist. To young people thinking about entering journalism, if they like variety in life, and wide interests without actual participation, I would think it's an ideal job. But you have to sacrifice a certain amount. I used to play a lot of golf, but when I started freelancing I said, 'Well, it's either the golf or the freelancing.' So the golf had to go.

Ernie McIntyre

I came actually from an engineering family and when I left Riverside School in Stirling at the age of 15 I'd hoped to become a marine engineer. My one ambition was to go to sea as an engineer. But unfortunately that was 1931, in the height of the Depression, and no one was taking on apprentices. I tried one or two places in Stirling, Alloa, and places like that – but nothing doing, they just didn't want to look at an apprenticeship. Well, I'd heard through an aunt of mine who knew the advertising man in the *Stirling Journal* that there might be a vacancy there for a junior reporter. I applied for it and got it.[1]

I was born on 18 June 1916 at Causewayhead, Stirling. Causewayhead at that time wasn't within the Stirling burgh boundaries; it's within them now. Mine was a very pleasant childhood because we lived at the foot of Abbey Craig, where the Wallace Monument stands, and you always had the close proximity to Stirling, which is a fair- sized town – so it was sort of town and country.[2] I spent a lot of my boyhood on a farm, helping out and watching. I did the milk and milk round and things like that. I had a very happy childhood.

My mother was from Oban and my father was from Loch Awe side, and they had settled in Stirling. Both were Gaelic speakers. Quite a number of Gaelic speakers could only speak it, but my father could also read and write Gaelic. Unfortunately my folks used the language to communicate between each other, instead of teaching it to us kids, so we never learned Gaelic. I was fourth in the family: I had two elder brothers, one elder sister, too, and a younger sister.

My father had served his time in the North British Locomotive works in Glasgow, and he did some time working as an engineer on the pleasure boats on Loch Etive, near Oban. He came to Stirling to work with the Grampian Engineering Company and worked there for several years. Latterly he was head engineer for the Abbey Craig Laundry in Causewayhead, Stirling. He was never a seagoing engineer but I think he'd have liked to have been one. But even during the

Depression my father was always in work, which made a difference.

I remember the crowds of unemployed congregating at Causewayhead Corner, nothing else to do. We played pitch and toss on Abbey Craig and pontoon on a Sunday then. I was there, too, just a laddie. The policeman would come and chase us. Why he bothered to chase us, I don't know. We weren't doing any harm, only playing in pennies and shillings.[3]

We went to Bridge of Allan school. It was a primary and secondary in those days, I think. There was a village school at Causewayhead where we lived, but my mother didn't like the headmaster too much. He had been in the First World War and I think he had suffered a bit of shell shock or something, and he could be a bit rough with the kids sometimes.

We took the bus mainly to Bridge of Allan school – about a mile and a half to two miles from Causewayhead. They were the old Tilling Stevens buses – petrol electric buses. They had a dynamo which was driven by a petrol engine and the electricity drove the bus. One of my earliest recollections was going to school in the 1926 General Strike, with the buses boarded up. The Stirling–Aberdeen and Oban railway line passed very close to Causewayhead and during the Strike there was a lot of picketing at Cornton Junction there on the railways. But the buses still ran: they were very much non-union, and I remember wire netting round their windows, and things like that.

Later on, when it came to going to secondary school, Riverside was built as a new secondary in Stirling on the Causewayhead side. The headmaster at Bridge of Allan school had become headmaster at Riverside, so we joined him there. At the secondary school my interest was in science. I can't say English was my best subject, but we'd a very good English master. He was a fellow called Smart, who taught me all the Shakespeare I ever knew. You got so much to learn every night, and if you didn't know it the following morning you were liable to get the belt. But as a result you learnt Mark Antony's speech and all these things.

I wouldn't say I was a keen reader at school. School was school and that was it. I did fairly well there and I was always up among the sort of leaders. I never had any great problems with exams or anything like that. At Riverside School I took a sort of commercial course and learned shorthand and typing. I think I was put into the commercial course because of my sort of scholastic rating. We got English, science, history, geography, French, maths, and shorthand and typing. I was pretty good at maths. It was a three-year course, a very comprehensive course. I just can't remember the typing speed but I came out of school with about 120 words a minute shorthand. The shorthand speed was the important one. Shorthand of course was a question just of memory – memory and practice. So that equipped me for a job on the local newspaper, the *Stirling Journal*.

So that was my first job when I left school. I didn't want to continue at school, perhaps unwisely. I was fairly desperate to start earning money. You see, my mother had four other kids and I felt it was time I should be earning some money. My parents didn't put any pressure on me to leave or to stay at school, they left the decision to me.

So I started with the *Stirling Journal* at the beginning of September 1931. I was 15. The money was ten shillings [50 pence] a week. Some people in England had to pay indentures to become a journalist. The *Journal* paid me ten shillings a week but the annual increments were only five shillings a week. Anyway I took the job.

I started right in at the deep end. One of my early jobs was going along to Stirling Burgh Court. I remember a policeman in the Burgh Court questioning my age, because you weren't supposed to be in the courtroom under the age of 16 and I was only 15 at the time.

A weekly paper like the *Stirling Journal* was a very good training because you were thrown in at the deep end. And Stirling was the county town. You had all the sort of local organisations – town councils, county councils, Burgh and Sheriff Courts, and occasionally a High Court sat there on circuit. There wasn't very much hard news in Stirling. But the Scottish National Party were rising there in Stirling itself. When I started work I had just missed Wendy Wood climbing the ramparts of Stirling Castle and substituting the Scottish Standard for the official flag. I think that was about 1930. And the Wallace sword was stolen, too, from the Wallace Monument about 1934–5. I think the sword was stolen twice, once after I left the *Journal*. Nationalists were suspected on both occasions. And of course there was always the annual Bannockburn Day. One of the main speakers I recall there was R.B. Cunninghame Graham, an old Labour man. I heard him speak at Bannockburn Day, a very impressive guy, very tall and big white hair. He lived in Gartmore, which was actually in Perthshire but next door to West Stirlingshire. He was a great adventurer in South America, and one of his saddles had been gifted to the Smith Institute, the local museum in Stirling.[4]

When I began on the *Journal* in 1931 there were three weekly papers in Stirling. The *Stirling Observer* was owned by James Munro, the *Stirling Sentinel* by David Pearson,[5] and the *Journal* by Andrew Learmonth. I don't think these three papers had any politics as such. I mean, I think any of them would have been Tory. Both Stirling parliamentary constituencies – West Stirlingshire particularly – was sort of see-saw. Tom Johnston was the MP in West Stirlingshire against Guy D. Fanshawe and I think they both had a spell of the seat.[6] A lot of people voted for Tom Johnston because of the man, not so much his politics. I used to travel West Stirlingshire with him, when electioneering meant seven (days), four or five meetings a night, and you would travel around West Stirlingshire – maybe three in a night: Kippen, Buchlyvie, Balfron – saying the same thing. You'd to try and get something different for the paper. And then of course Tom Johnston would switch to the east side of the constituency, which took in places like Fallin and Plean – miners, you see, and more left-wing. And sometimes Johnston got a rougher ride in the left-wing areas of the constituency than in the others. You know, at these meetings you always got the rebel who wanted to ask questions, and I would say it was Labour Party members, working-class people, not uncritical of the Labour Party. I don't think they were critical of Johnston personally – well, there was one guy that was a bit critical of him personally but I just forget what the criticism was for.

When I started on the *Stirling Journal* in 1931 there was the editor and three reporters. The *Stirling Observer*, I think, had an editor and four reporters, and the *Sentinel* an editor and two reporters. The first editor I worked with on the *Journal* was a guy called Scott. Unfortunately, he was very sort of colourful in his English: he liked the big flamboyant words. I remember one intro I wrote about a British Legion dinner in the Royal Hotel, Bridge of Allan: 'The ballroom of the Hotel was a paradisical dugout last night.' Scott thought paradisical was a wonderful word, I think it was terrible! Unfortunately, later on he had a bit of a nervous breakdown.

On the *Journal* it was really a five-and-a-half-day week. But you were doing football and sport on a Saturday afternoon, too, so it was a six-day week. The football and sport weren't paid. You didn't volunteer, you worked. Then, though there was no photographer on the *Journal*, there was a camera in the office. I stupidly decided to take some pictures for the paper with it. So I was doubling the job – reporting and taking pictures. It meant being late at night at dances and things like that. There was a lot of society functions in Stirling. The society people were very reluctant to meet your request for a photograph until one of their leaders agreed, then they all followed like sheep. But sometimes you had to wait until they'd had a good drink round about midnight. You were getting home late most nights – and no overtime or anything like that.

I must have joined the National Union of Journalists very quickly after I got the job on the *Journal*. Doubling the job with a camera was against union rules, but I didn't know that and they never said anything about it. It was the Forth Valley branch of the union, the members were mainly in Falkirk and Stirling, with one or two perhaps from Alloa. You had journalists in Falkirk and Grangemouth – the *Falkirk Herald* and the *Falkirk Mail*, and the Grangemouth paper was an offshoot of the *Falkirk Herald*.[7] The union branch had maybe 30 or 40 members, but it wasn't a very active branch. All the *Stirling Journal* reporters were in the union. The Forth Valley branch was about 100 per cent, but it wasn't 100 per cent strength. It was more a social organisation than a militant trade union organisation, it wasn't effective as a trade union at all.

I didn't even develop the photographs I took. A local photographer developed the negatives and the prints had to be sent to Glasgow for the photographic plate. One night Scott, the editor, had me round at his flat with the camera. It was then he was taking a nervous breakdown. He had me take a picture of a hole in the wall through which he alleged his next-door neighbours were trying to gas him. When Scott ended up in hospital he was succeeded as editor by Alex Budge, the chief reporter, who eventually became a sub-editor on the *Glasgow Herald*. But the *Journal* didn't employ another reporter to replace Alex Budge. Later on, Jimmy MacIntosh became the editor of the *Journal*, then Jimmy became a sub-editor on *The Bulletin* in Glasgow.[8]

So on the *Stirling Journal* you worked long hours and you got no recompense for them. They weren't paying union rates or anything like it, and the trade union in Stirling didn't help me in the least. You started work between nine and ten in the morning and you'd finish about six o'clock at night. Although if you were on the Sheriff Court, say, you could have an hour in the local pool room on the way back to the *Journal* office. So I became a fairly competent snooker player. That was all part of the game. I mean, as journalists you didn't have as tight a rein on you as did some other workers, you had a wee bit of freedom. On the other hand, as I say, you might go home at six o'clock at night but have to go back out again to report a dinner. The press were invited to most of the annual dinners of the local organisations that took up a whole evening, in winter time two or three evenings a week.

On Saturday afternoons you covered mainly junior football. St Ninian's Thistle were a fairly good junior team. King's Park, the predecessors of Stirling Albion, were the senior team and occasionally I'd cover them. I remember once getting to Hampden Park in Glasgow with King's Park for a semi-final or something: it must have been very unusual for them because they were always a Second Division team.[9]

The *Stirling Journal* was published every Thursday, the *Sentinel* on a Tuesday, and the *Observer*, which had the largest circulation of the three, was bi-weekly and came out on Tuesdays and Thursdays. I think the *Journal* was quite a good paper, but it was very difficult to acquire new readers. I mean, most of the readers were interested in the births, marriages, and deaths, or the adverts. We were more, I think, the Stirling county paper, because people got the *Observer* and the *Sentinel* in the town itself. I think the *Journal's* circulation was only 2,000 or 3,000. I think it was more or less static all the seven years I was there. There was never any sort of panic about falling or rising circulation. I always thought local paper readers were a very solid readership, accustomed to one paper they got week after week, and it's very difficult to make them change their mind. The three Stirling papers all had accompanying printing shops – jobbing printing – and I think the newspaper was a sort of sideline for them.

Stirling was a very staid town, really almost devoid of characters. But one character I remember was an old woman named Jane Brannigan or Smith who, I think, by the time I left the *Journal* in 1938, had had 88 appearances at the Burgh Court for drunk and incapable. Once when she came up to the court the magistrate said to her, 'Well, what will you have: fined £2 or ten days in prison?' She says, 'Oh, my mind's made up, your honour. I'll bide a week wi' you.' I think it was that she got food, shelter and clothing in jail.

I used to travel for a weekly column of local news for the *Journal* round the nearby mining villages of Fallin and Plean. We had quite a good Miners' Welfare Institute in Stirling, and there was one in Plean. I got on very well with the miners, they were always very hospitable and always seemed to have a pot of tea on the hob. But then you also got your first taste of mining accidents there. I remember one at Fallin: about six miners were killed when the cage went to the hollows, as they called the big wheels, and one went right down to the sump at the bottom. That's when also I found out that you never know whether you're intruding into private grief until you knock on the door, because people regard death very differently. Some welcome you as a reporter into the house, some don't want to see you. If they didn't want to see you, you just went away. But you could never tell until you knocked on the door.

So as part of the routine of gathering news you had weekly visits. I did my weekly rounds by bus, Alexander's buses. Fallin and Plean would take maybe half a day. You recorded things like bowling matches, so the visit'd be perhaps to the secretary of the bowling club. And of course the weekly papers also had a lot of people in these villages who acted as local correspondents. My wife's father, for instance, a watchmaker and jeweller who was also the postmaster in Kippen, 10 miles from Stirling, wrote quite a lot of the local Kippen news for the local paper – unpaid, but it was nice to see your name in the paper. Well, you always like to see what you've written appear in print. I think even the journalists liked it. In those days, maybe nowadays, too, the weeklies, unlike the dailies and the Sundays, wouldn't have the money to spend on a whole lot of local correspondents like my father-in-law.

Most of the time in the *Journal* office we were busy writing up. We had Stirling town council – we didn't attend town council committees in these days, just the full council, and Stirling county council, and other bodies like Rotary clubs. One paper did it as an official arrangement for the three to save on money. As I've said, in wintertime there'd be possibly three or four dinners in the evenings each week, and in my camera days there were a lot of dances, sales of work, and local competitions. Once I went with my camera to a Voluntary Aid Detachment competition, where society ladies did their part as auxiliary nurses.[10] That was in the old days when you operated the flash with magnesium in an open tray. You could hear the touch paper going *zzzttthhh*, then it stopped and I thought, 'It's gone out.' So I looked down – and it went up in my eyes! One of the ladies present was Lady Elizabeth Younger, aunt of George Younger, later Secretary of State for Scotland, and I always remember her comment: 'What's the first aid for burns?'[11]

Stirling wasn't a very political town, a bit Conservative–Liberal, you know. My own political views were developed later on in Birkenhead. But, oh, in Stirling you were so busy you had no time for anything, except the odd game of snooker. Most of our free time was in the morning, as I say, on the way back from the courts, for instance. No one in the office knew or really cared very much how long you were in the courts as long as you got them covered. An important trial'd be all day. But if it was pleading diets and things like that you might have only a few in Stirling. The sheriff was Dean-Leslie, who had the reputation of not being very kind to miners and people like that. If you were a miner you were liable to get a heavier fine than if you were the local lawyer or something like that.[12]

As a local newspaper reporter you weren't looking for stories to highlight poverty in the 1930s. Poverty existed, although any miner's home I went to at that time didn't give you the impression of great poverty. There were the occasional evictions. They built a new housing estate in Stirling called the Raploch. It was a deprived area, they'd no sort of amenities. The authorities just built houses and nothing else. There was a lot of poverty in there and one or two of the local criminals came from the Raploch area, but you never really got into the guts of it. I don't think the Stirling papers even carried leaders in those days which gave any opinion. The *Journal* once or twice carried a leader but they were very apolitical. I think they thought of themselves just as newspapers reporting events as they happened – women's bowling, the county cricket match, the town council.

The army in Stirling kept itself very much apart. We didn't have a great deal of contact with the army. They were the Argyll and Sutherland Highlanders and they were very much a family on their own, as all these Scottish regiments were. They had their own officers' and sergeants' mess, their own entertainment, and they just didn't seem to want to know. We were never invited to anything, except that the army officers had an annual garden party where again, as photographers, we had to wait till the leader decided to have his picture taken, otherwise they were all turning their heads away.[13] I remember on one occasion the chief guest was the Maharajah the Gaekwar of Baroda, whose wealth was not beyond the dreams of avarice but out of sight of the dreams of avarice. He drew up in a Rolls-Royce, which parked on the Castle esplanade, didnae even drive into the Castle. The Maharajah and his aide-de-camp, just dressed in normal lounge suits, strolled towards the Castle gates. No one was there to meet him. The attendant at the gate wanted to charge him the usual 6d admission fee. But the great man of wealth didn't have 6d in his possession! Then I think he made himself known and was duly admitted.[14] So there wasn't much contact between the army and the people of Stirling. There was no sort of recruiting drives, they seemed to get all the recruits they wanted. And no court martials: we never heard of them.

I had seven years' experience on the *Stirling Journal*. I think it was a valuable experience because you became a competent reporter. You could provide an accurate story of anything that happened, you know, good shorthand writer and all that sort of thing. It was all about verbatim reporting. The town council was more or less verbatim. The *Journal* was a big full-size paper and plenty of pages to fill. Bridge of Allan and Dunblane had their own councils. You covered these. In Bridge of Allan a new faction got into the council to stir things up because a great arrears in rates had built up. The council was split into two factions, those who wanted things cleared up and those who wanted the status quo. It was a great test of shorthand that, because you had more or less to do a verbatim report. Two speakers might be speaking at the same time. You had to get one down and then the other! After maybe an hour and a half of that you came out really fatigued.

Your shorthand speed was increasing all the time with the passage of the years. You were verbatim or next to verbatim all the time, and with the weekly paper you'd got to be really accurate. I remember being put on the carpet and given a tremendous dressing-down for spelling Libby's with two ls. On another occasion I referred to the English master at Stirling

High using the word 'teached' – and that almost got me the sack! Well, the English master wrote in, but of course the editor would have passed my copy with 'teached' in it! Nowadays when you see where the papers get away with that sort of thing! By the time I left the *Journal* I think I had about 140 words a minute shorthand, which was quite adequate for most things. Shorthand never gave me a great deal of trouble, I'd had an excellent foundation at school, and even yet I take all my notes in shorthand. After the Second World War an awful lot of reporters didn't have shorthand at all. How they got on, I don't know.

I left the *Stirling Journal* in 1938 after about seven years. I left because of money. As I've said, they weren't paying union rates or anything like it. I think it was five shillings a year extra you got, so that'd be perhaps 35 shillings [£1.75] or £2 a week or something like that I was getting by 1938. It was miserable. The compositors and printers on the paper were in their own union. Whether they got union wages or not I don't know, but the editorial staff certainly didn't get union rates. There were still difficult times in the early 1930s. I decided very early on, 'I want to get out of it,' but it was difficult to get out. I wrote all round the country looking for jobs. I had a big pile of letters thanking me for my application but they'd no vacancies. I was ready to move anywhere.

I eventually got a job on the *Birkenhead News*.[15] I'd written to the *Liverpool Daily Post* and the *Post* had passed on my letter to the *Birkenhead News*, which was a bi-weekly.[16] The *News* paid union rates, which I think at the age of 24 was £4 7s 6d [£4.37½]. I was about 22, so I think I got about £3 17s 6d [£3.87½]. It was a livable wage, as my digs in Birkenhead were 30 shillings [£1.50] a week. I was sorry to leave Stirling as I'd a lot of friends there, and of course in the newspaper game you do make a lot of friends and acquaintances. I was sorry to leave them, but I felt I was getting nowhere at an increase of five shillings a week each year. It was really the financial aspect that made me move.

As a bi-weekly the *Birkenhead News* was published on Wednesday and Saturday. There was one other weekly competitor, the *Birkenhead Advertiser*.[17] We had by far the largest circulation. The *Birkenhead News* had editions for Wallasey and Heswall, both in the Wirral. I think the *Birkenhead News* Saturday edition was up around 20,000, and of course they had those local editions, too. The *News* was quite a good successful paper, and quite good journalists on it, too. The editorial staff of the *News* would be about eight or nine reporters. The proprietor, Wrayford Wilmer, a nice chap, called himself the editor but he was just a sort of figurehead. He was a decent guy who wanted to give you trade union wages and that sort of stuff – and did. Birkenhead was a good news area so it was a good training. And we got extra money doing linage for the *Liverpool Daily Post* just across the Mersey. For me it was an altogether bigger world than Stirling had been, an exciting sort of job to be in, and especially at that time.

Most of the big stories at Birkenhead came from the Cammell Laird shipyards. Just because no one else had asked before, I was the first reporter to be on the deck of a big ship launched at Cammell Laird's – the second *Mauretania*. She was a 30,000 tonner, I think. I had suggested we write to Cammell Laird and ask them if we could get on deck, and Cammell Laird said, 'Yes, sure, come in. There's only a few people on deck in any case.' It was a wonderful experience, I was standing right on the forepeak. You see this great mass just starting to move and then . . . Of course the Mersey had very spectacular launches because, unlike the Clyde, it was a wide river or estuary and there was no drag chains on the ships. They just pulled the chocks away and let her go and she ended up in the middle of the river.[18]

I did the same with the *Prince of Wales* battleship, later sunk near Singapore by the Japanese on the same day as HMS *Repulse*.[19] I think the launch of the submarine *Thetis* was the first launch I was at. Then a year later, in the worst peacetime submarine disaster, the *Thetis* went down during her trials in Liverpool Bay. It went down on a Friday morning in June 1939, and our deadline for publication was a Friday night. The stern of the *Thetis* came up again, but no one thought of putting a rope round her stern. They thought, 'Oh, well, the stern's up so the bow'll come up.' But the stern sank again. I think three of the crew escaped but 99 died. It was a very impressive funeral service at sea. I was aboard a minesweeper and the relatives of the dead men were on board a minesweeper ahead of us. All the way out this yeoman of signals on our ship was semaphoring to the ship ahead. A little man from the *Daily Herald*, I forget his name now, as we were nearing the spot where the *Thetis* went down said to the yeoman of signals, 'What is that ship ahead signalling?' With a disdainful look down on him, the yeoman said, 'I haven't the faintest idea.' The press of course weren't too popular with the navy then either. I mean, it was only when they started to want recruits that the armed services and their public relations officers became less of a closed world.[20]

As I say, it was a good news area, Birkenhead, because we had Port Sunlight, Lever Brothers' model village. There neighbours weren't allowed to talk over the garden fence or to hang out their washing – all sorts of restrictive stuff. But Lever put a marvellous art gallery down in the middle of the village, and they had a nice dance hall – plenty of entertainment for them. They were really nice people down there in Birkenhead area and very helpful.[21]

One of my recollections of those days is going to a meeting and being told that the basic wage of a top railway engine driver was then 50 shillings [£2.50] per week. These were the guys that were driving the *Flying Scotsman* and engines like that with 300 passengers behind them. But they all had to work overtime to get anything like a decent wage. And there was tremendous poverty in Birkenhead. It still hadn't really recovered from the Depression. There were very big docks in Birkenhead, and the dockers had to go to the docks every morning whether they had a job or not, in the hope that, you know, someone loves you. My friend in Birkenhead had a pub in the dock area and the dockers used to come into the pub a lot about 11 o'clock in the morning. They hadn't been able to get a job that day. I always remember one or two of them used to drink two pints at a time. I was behind the bar one day and a docker came in – it was the first time I experienced this – and he asked, 'Two pints.' I looked round for his friend, in vain. The first pint went over in one gulp, the second was for chatting over and might take 15 or 20 minutes. But they were great guys these dockers, I mean, they'd a tremendous sense of humour. I don't know what it is about Birkenhead and Liverpool but, something like Glasgow, it's got its own sort of sense of humour.

As for the pay, as I've said, I think I started with £3 17s 6d [£3.87½] and later I got £4 7s 6d [£4.37½]. That was a fairly good wage then. It was supplemented of course, because if you were doing some local authority meetings in Birkenhead you could always sell it in linage to the *Liverpool Post* and the *Liverpool Echo*.[22] The linage wasn't much more than a penny a line. But I also did a Saturday afternoon job on the football results with the *Echo*. The *Echo* had a wonderful circulation as one of the main papers in the north of England. I think it was about 250,000 in these days before the war. The *Post*, a morning paper, and the *Echo*, an evening, operated on the one staff. The *Post* didn't have a great deal of circulation but it sort of regarded itself as the quality newspaper. You could pump stuff into the *Echo*, the evening paper, until twenty past or half past four in the afternoon. And of course the daily paper boys sitting in the Liverpool Press Club just milked the last edition of the *Echo*. You never saw those boys out on stories! The *Echo* had the same make-up every day: column one with a banner headline right across the back page, and then every other story single column. And of course you could just shovel it in!

On the *Birkenhead News* we were or became members of the Liverpool branch of the National Union of Journalists: there wasn't a separate Birkenhead branch. The Liverpool branch was fairly big, because they had the *Post* and *Echo* and *Liverpool Evening Express*.[23] I wasn't active in the union then but I was a good attender at the branch meetings because it gave us the chance to get across the water to see some of the boys in the Liverpool Press Club, where all the branch meetings were held.

It was also in Birkenhead where you came face to face with a lot of poverty. There was a lot of poverty cases in the courts. You got to realise how people were really living then. You know, women were coming up to court, claiming their husband hadn't paid up, and husbands coming up to say how they couldn't pay and all that sort of stuff. And then if they didn't pay up I think they were jailed. So I think this had some sort of effect on my own political awareness. You saw how the other half had to live sometimes, and that something should be done about it. So I think my main political views were developed in Birkenhead.

From Birkenhead, too, I remember people going to the Spanish Civil War. Most of my friends were in the Territorials. I didn't myself join the Territorials because it meant giving up holidays. But when the Second War broke out in 1939 I tried for both the navy and the army. What attracted me to the navy was, I suppose, I'd always wanted to go to sea. The navy offered me a job as a stoker but I didn't want to go in the stoke-hole! I tried to get into the army to join some of my friends there who had been Territorials in the Royal Army Service Corps. The same day the navy offered me a job as a stoker the army took me into the RASC, but by then my friends had gone overseas. I must have volunteered in November 1939. But you just couldn't walk in and be taken. They hadn't got places to put all the men in. So you volunteered and then you waited for your call-up. So it was December 1939 I joined up. And of course I wasn't long in the army till someone spotted I could do shorthand. The RASC were short of people with shorthand and typing.

I did my training, however, at Warrington with a Lancashire infantry regiment. That was a bad winter, 1939–40. I remember lying on the barrack square in deep snow. On my first day in the army, in fact, in a Nissen hut, I went to bed with all my clothes on – even my soft hat. There was no heating, and of course you didn't know how to make up a camp bed. I think the floor of the hut was concrete. But they taught us how to make an army bed like an envelope.

Then they wanted me for work at the War Office. I was sent to this holding unit in London which supplied people for all sorts of different jobs all over the world. Then the War Office said they didn't want me because I was A1 in health. So they started sending me off to be clerk to the officer commanding troops on troop-ships. The first ship I was sent to in March 1940 was the liner *Empress of Britain* at King George IV Dock, Glasgow.[24] We thought we must be going to the Middle East or somewhere like that. And then this regiment of Scots Guards arrived on the quayside, all as brown as berries and some had RAF wings on their battledress. They came on board: 'Where have you been?' They said, 'We've been down at Chamonix in the French Alps practising skiing.' So there was only one place we could be going on the *Empress of Britain* and that was Finland: the papers were full of Finns and Russians dying in the snow. Unfortunately, Finland signed peace before we sailed from King George IV Dock.[25] So I went back to London. But a few weeks later I was up again in Glasgow, this time to join HMS *Victoria*. We were going to Norway – Narvik. But Norway was subjugated by the Germans before we got away.[26]

Norway was where one of my two elder brothers was lost. I think he'd have liked to have been a marine engineer but unfortunately he'd joined the navy and he was lost on the cruiser HMS *Glorious*, off Narvik in June 1940.[27] My other elder brother, who'd worked in the post office, had volunteered for the Royal Engineers, postal section. He was lost also in 1940 coming back from Dunkirk when the ship he was on was sunk. After losing two brothers I never volunteered again.

From the Glasgow docks I was sent back to this holding company in London, then to an RASC headquarters near Ashford in Kent. We were all quietly settled in this nice peaceful country mansion, then one day after Dunkirk we were told a new general was arriving: General Sir Bernard Montgomery. One of the first things he did was to order every officer in XII Corps, which we in the RASC supplied, to meet him in a cinema at Folkestone. They all crowded into this cinema, and he says, 'You've got ten minutes to cough. After that I don't want any more to cough.' The officers came back and told us everyone at our headquarters must be out at six o'clock in the morning doing PT. I suppose that's the way you win wars.[28]

Then they sent me to an army administration course at Aldershot. In my spare time, just for the sake of reading something, I used to read all the manuals that the army's full of: *King's Regulations*, the *Manual of Military Law*, and all that, infantry, artillery, every service, they've all got their manuals. I'd been reading these just for interest; I went to Aldershot and I came out top! I didn't even do any swotting. So the War Office, which rejected me before, had me back then, about 1941–2. So I was there till the end of the war. I got fairly good promotion. The troop-ship job had been for a corporal. I missed sergeant: the job with RASC headquarters in Kent was staff sergeant. This holding company supplied odd bodies for embassies and military attachés and that, and there was some very rapid promotion. I recall one fellow who went from private to staff sergeant major. I went to the War Office as a staff sergeant and finished as staff sergeant major.

I could have stayed on as a Regular in the army at the end of the war as a lieutenant quartermaster but I'd had enough of the 'yes, sir, no, sir'. I'd no regrets, though I lost financially. As a staff sergeant major I think I was paid about £10 and a small allowance of 3s a day for living in London. I could save, and I certainly lost money going back to newspapers.

I went back to the *Birkenhead News*. I was demobbed 1st of January 1946 at Olympia. You were allowed to keep your overcoat, and you got a striped suit and a hat. I certainly had no use for this greatcoat, and I went down to the Salvation Army to hand it in. The woman at the door there gave me the bum's rush. She says she didn't want it, and it was not right coming there trying to sell my coat! I think the money then on the *News* was over £5 a week. I was only there a few months when I joined the *Liverpool Daily Post* and *Echo*.

The *Post* and *Echo* had quite a big staff. The head office might have had 60, 70 journalists; of course it was two papers. We had our own annual dinner and all that stuff, and there was a good sense of sort of comrade-ship. But then, again after a few months, I heard the *Daily Herald* were opening up and wanted a man in Edinburgh. We used to get double wages on the *Post* and *Echo* at Christmas, which was very good. I must have handed in my notice, however, just before Christmas, because when I opened up my wage packet there was no double wages! I went to see Spencer, the general manager, and I said, 'Look, I haven't had my double wages at Christmas.' He said, 'Oh, you're under notice.' I said, 'No, I'm not under notice,' I says, 'you're under notice!' He said, 'You've just been using the *Daily Post* as a stepping stone to better things.' And I possibly said, 'Well, do you blame me for that?' Anyway I went and reported this to the chapel there and then. The *Post* and *Echo* had a very good active chapel, with regular meetings. It was the first time I'd seen the union really working. The chapel immediately held an emergency meeting, the first I'd ever been at. By that same evening Spencer had to give me my double Christmas wages. So that's when I really started to take an interest in the union.

As I say, I must have handed in my notice at the *Post* and *Echo* just before Christmas 1946. I came to Edinburgh on New Year's Day, 1947. By then the *Scottish Daily Mail* had opened up in Edinburgh. The *Scottish Daily Express* were well established and of course the *Daily Record*. The *Daily Herald* had six or seven people in Glasgow. Pat Dollan, former Lord Provost of Glasgow, called himself Scottish editor,[29]although I worked directly with the *Daily Herald* in Manchester, where the editor was Frank Machin, well known in trade union circles. They already had one man in Edinburgh, David Moir, and decided to double the staff and make it two.

David Moir, a Labour councillor in Edinburgh, had been an auxiliary fireman during the war and drove a fire engine. He was coming back from a fire one day when a member of the royal family's car had broken down. David Moir must have had some sort of news sense and tipped off the *Daily Herald*. So the *Daily Herald* got an exclusive on this and he was taken on the staff. He had no journalistic background experience whatever, a kind of wartime recruit. Well, a lot of people were recruited like that in wartime.

But the *Daily Herald* was a great paper, the first to reach a circulation of two million copies. Lord Southwood, who wasn't a left-winger, was quite prepared to put up the money and run the *Daily Herald* as long as it made money. Lord Southwood's Odhams Press owned 51 per cent of the *Herald*, the Trades Union Congress had 49 per cent. So in effect the *Daily Herald* was only a name: every light bulb, every pen, pencil, notebook, was supplied to the *Herald* by Odhams Press, and Odhams Press made sure the paper never made too much money for the TUC.[30]

But they were quite lavish in the way of staff and salary. When I came to Edinburgh in 1947 my basic salary was £11 a week – about £3 more than the top reporters' salaries in Edinburgh. And they were very generous in expenses, they didn't quibble. David Moir put in his expenses one day for decorating the office on VJ Day! We had an upstairs office in Cockburn Street and 18 months or more after I arrived they were shifting to a downstairs office there. Next door there was a waterproof shop. The week before the flitting, Moir had put in his expenses – £4 or something – for buying Wellingtons to cover the Border floods. The manager, Mr Moody, wrote back: 'I note the purchase of Wellingtons to cover Border floods.' He says, 'Please ensure that they're added to the office inventory.' So a few weeks later Mr Moody came up to supervise the shift from the office upstairs. He and Moir decided to repair to the George Hotel, an expensive one, for lunch. Before they went to lunch he said to Moir, 'Oh, by the way, Moir, I thought you had some Wellington boots here?' And Dave says, 'Oh, yeah, I must have left them upstairs.' So he dashed next door to the waterproof shop and said, 'For God's sake, give me a pair of Wellington boots,' took them back into the new office, and slung them on the counter. So they went to the George for lunch and they're talking things over, and Mr Moody said to Moir, 'By the way, Moir,' he said, 'these boots,' he said, 'the Wellington boots: did you find them useful?' 'Oh, very useful, Mr Moody. We've had a lot of floods in the Borders and they're really indispensable.' Mr Moody asked, 'Are they comfortable, Moir?' 'Oh, yes,' he says, 'very comfortable.' 'I thought,' said Mr Moody, 'they'd be more comfortable if you took the string off them.'

The Wellington boots had little eyelets at the top where you could tie them together with a bit string. Then I was only a few months at the *Daily Herald* when I had a perforated duodenum. It happened at the Edinburgh Press Club, and I was whipped round to the Royal Infirmary, which was very close at hand. David Moir handed in his expenses that week: 'So much to nurses looking after Mr McIntyre.' And he got away with it.

Well, I was two or three years in the Edinburgh office with David Moir till he got sacked. We were co-equal: I was told when I went to Edinburgh, 'Your boss is Manchester.' The first thing David said to me was, 'Oh, let me see your expenses before you send it to Manchester.' I said, 'No. You don't see my expenses. They go direct to Manchester.' So we were on the same footing. The Labour government put out some housing figures, where they were doing very well – a record number of completions in new houses. This came out at five o'clock in a press handout from St Andrew's House, but Moir went to the Press Club and forgot about it. Next day the figures were splashed in all the papers, even in the *Daily Express*, but the *Daily Herald* didn't have a line about it. Of course, Arthur Woodburn, the Labour Secretary of State for Scotland, was kicking up a fuss about this.[31] There was an inquest at the *Herald* in Manchester, and Moir happened to be on duty when Manchester phoned: 'What happened to this story?' Moir said, 'Oh, I don't know. Ernie McIntyre was on last night.' Of course, Manchester came on to me: 'Editor wants a memo on this.' I told them, 'I wasn't on duty last night. It was Moir.' That's the sort of character he was. David borrowed money from everyone. He was an inveterate borrower and then he would go and buy you a drink with the money. The *Daily Herald* were very good to him. He got himself heavily in debt once, it got to the ears of the *Herald*, and they cleared off his debts. Money was his sort of power and the way he bought popularity. But eventually the police took him up to the Burgh Court for fraud, and that was the straw that broke the camel's back. David Moir never got a job in journalism again. He went after that to an advertising agency and later died.[32]

As I've said, there must have been about six or seven in the *Daily Herald* Glasgow office, including Pat Dollan, his son Jimmy, and Ishbel McInnes.[33] There was always a man did politics, another industry, and a third agriculture. And we had a staff reporter in Aberdeen and in Dundee. We didn't have one in Inverness. From Edinburgh we did the Borders.

Pat Dollan called himself Scottish editor, but he'd nothing to do with me at all, he didn't exercise any control over me. There were a lot of good points about Pat, but he was very jealous of his territory: you mustn't muscle in on his territory. Our boundary was Harthill, midway between

Edinburgh and Glasgow. Pat had of course been the wartime Lord Provost of Glasgow. He got closely involved in the development of Prestwick airport and then the miners – coal was big news immediately after the war, not only nationalisation of the mines, but also because coal was in short supply because it was short of manpower. There was a big fight for Prestwick Airport, and that was the first thing Pat showed me when I went to his office was his cuttings, about three feet thick, on the airport. Pat had a photographic memory and could dictate half a column on coal without even looking at a reference book. He'd originally been a miner himself and had written regularly in his earlier days for *Forward*. Ishbel McInnes was down as a staff reporter but she was really Pat's secretary. Pat dictated everything to her. I got on with Pat, he was quite a nice guy. When I ended up in Edinburgh Royal Infirmary in May 1947 with a duodenal ulcer Pat came in to see me the next day. He was no longer Lord Provost by then but he'd been knighted, and all the people in the ward got quite a kick out of having Sir Pat there.

The *Daily Herald* didn't have a great circulation in Scotland. I couldn't give you any exact figure. But it laboured under the handicap that it had only one edition for the whole of Scotland, where its main rivals, the *Daily Express* and the *Daily Record*, could editionise the stories. The *Herald* never did publish in Scotland, and of course we went to press in Manchester at nine o'clock at night, which was quite early. The Scottish edition had to get away on time from Manchester because it preceded the north-east of England edition, which was the *Daily Herald*'s best-selling edition, in the Northumberland mining area and places like that. It was the bible for people in these areas. So in Scotland you missed any big story that happened after nine o'clock at night, which was a handicap. In later years the *Daily Mail* and the *Daily Express* were finding that, too, when they ceased publishing in Scotland. They looked silly the next day.

Our readership fell into two categories: people like trade union secretaries and organisers, who felt they had to buy it, and the genuine Labour Party members who wanted to buy it. I mean, you'd quite often go into a trade union office and you'd see the *Daily Express* open on the desk and the *Daily Herald* still in the in-tray. And of course they had these difficulties about finance, I mean, where the money came from. So the paper used to spend unlimited money on pictures, used to hire taxis to take us down to Berwick-on-Tweed or Scremerston if there was a ship ran aground there. I remember a ship ran aground at Scremerston. We used to hire Page's taxis in Edinburgh, and for long-distance runs Page had a vintage Rolls-Royce. And that's what the *Daily Herald* man arrived in – the *Daily Express* came in Austin Tens and cars like that! But the

Herald was a very good paper to work for. A lot of people thought you had to be a member of the Labour Party to work on it. But no one on the *Daily Herald* ever asked about your politics: you were there as a journalist.

I joined the Labour Party myself after I came to Edinburgh. I hadn't been in a political party before that. But as it happened I hadn't actually paid my sub to the Party. Dougie Henderson, who used to live beside me out at The Inch, was standing as a Scottish National Party candidate for Edinburgh council. He needed people to second his nomination and he comes round to my house one night. 'Och,' I said, 'I don't agree with your politics, but I agree with your right to stand.' So of course my name appeared up at the City Chambers as one of Dougie's seconders or proposers.[34] And Magnus Williamson, a Labour councillor and journalist, who was a colleague of mine on the *Daily Herald*, spotted this. Oh, Magnus wanted me expelled from the Labour Party and from the editorship of *The Clarion*, the local labour movement monthly paper! The editorial board of *The Clarion* told Magnus where to get off. In any case I hadn't at that stage paid my sub to the Labour Party so I couldn't be expelled. Magnus Williamson was one that took notes of everything – every phone call you made, he took notes. Magnus made his money through employing a lot of little boys, you know, sending in the results of football matches, and he'd give them half a crown. And then Harold Wilson gave Magnus the OBE for his services to journalism![35]

In my time at the *Daily Herald* we had the big Border floods in 1948. I covered the floods. We were down at Ayton in Berwickshire in a hotel, and of course there was a big build-up of flooding behind the railway there. If that embankment had gone, the flood would have gone right down the valley to Eyemouth and wiped out Eyemouth. And of course that's what we were waiting for down there. Then at midnight there was a report that a sea mine was floating at the same time towards Eyemouth harbour! So this was Eyemouth threatened from both sides.

The first Secretary of State for Scotland I remember when I came to the *Daily Herald* in Edinburgh was wee Joe Westwood. The first meeting I remember I went to where he was speaking was of farmers in the North British Hotel. The government were encouraging farmers to increase their output. Joe got a bit of heckling during his speech, but at the end of the meeting he was more or less given a rousing reception for his plea for a 10 per cent increase in output. Of course the *Daily Express* heading next morning was 'Farmers jeer Joe Westwood', or words to that effect; the *Daily Herald*'s, 'Farmers agree to . . .' To a certain extent both reports were true. But, I mean, you begin to wonder if there's such a thing as objective reporting.[36]

Old Hannen Swaffer, probably the best known of the *Daily Herald* journalists, told me that on the night of the 1945 election results, Lord Beaverbrook was in the big *Daily Express* newsroom in Fleet Street, and every Labour win that came through almost the whole of the sub-editors' table stood up and cheered![37] I ran across Hannen several times, a great guy he was. He used to come up from London for the Edinburgh Festival.[38] An outstanding man in every way, in some ways he was very humble and in some ways extrovert – not arrogant, extrovert. He was very deaf; I was more or less his eyes and ears when he came to Edinburgh. I said, 'Why don't you get a hearing aid?' 'Oh,' he says, 'it makes you too damned conspicuous.' And there he was with his big black hat and the front of his tie covered in cigarette ash. But he was a great journalist. There were some very good guys in the *Daily Herald*, but they never lasted as long as Swaffer. He was a bit of an institution. Out on a royal story in London one day he walked into the newsroom and said to Percy Cudlipp, the editor, 'He's failing, Percy.' Cudlipp says, 'Who's failing?' Hannen says, 'King George.' 'How's that?' Hannen said, 'He didn't recognise me today.'[39] Another fantastic story he told me was how Harry Lauder invited him up to Scotland to see the salmon mating in the pools and the deer roaming the hills. They were up in the Highlands, and Hannen said, 'We were approaching this little cottage with a woman standing at the door. She sees these two figures coming towards her, her eyes light up, she starts to walk towards us, she puts out her hand, and she says, 'How are you, Hannen?'[40]

Well, I was with the *Daily Herald* ten years, from 1947 to about 1957. Then because of a clash of personalities with Maurice Linden I went to the *Scottish Daily Mail*. I think Linden may have been on the staff of the *Daily Mirror*, but they made him Scottish editor of the *Daily Herald* and put me under him. And, och, I was never done having a row with him. He had me at Glamis Castle at midnight one night to find out why the Queen wasn't going there, and that sort of stuff. *Time* magazine[41] came out with an advert for Rolex watches, and it was of a man cut off from the nose upwards with a medal round his neck and wearing a Rolex wristwatch. Linden was convinced the man was the Duke of Edinburgh and he shouldn't be doing it. The Duke happened to be in Edinburgh and I'd to get a quote from the Duke that the man was him or wasn't him. I eventually got the quote from the Duke's equerry that it couldn't be the Duke because he never wore a wristwatch, he wore a fob watch. When I told Linden that, he said, 'OK, do a story on that.' So I'd to do a story on that: it never appeared.[42]

I think the quality of the *Daily Herald* was declining as the years went by. It was working against the collar all the time. Some of the old loyalists were leaving it for other papers. The *Daily Express*, give it its due, was a very popular paper. The *Daily Herald*'s main rivals were, well, the *Express* and the *Daily Mail*. We didn't worry about the *Glasgow Herald* and *The Scotsman*. They very seldom had anything we didn't have. But we were quite often beaten by the *Express* and the *Mail* because they had more staff and they also had this tip-off system. If you phoned the *Express* or the *Mail* you got paid so much in return. This became well known among the public. But no one thought of phoning the *Daily Herald*. And then we had the fundamental problem that we didn't publish in Scotland. And of course at that time, from the middle 1950s onwards, there was also the sort of growth of cheque-book journalism, and it came into a real force. But I found after I joined the *Scottish Daily Mail* that a lot of people objected to being bought. Anyway, later on the *Daily Herald* became *The Sun*.[43]

The *Scottish Daily Mail* was a good paper. It was a boozy paper – I mean, the staff. Of course, the big majority of journalists in these days were heavy boozers. I think it was because they seemed to have more time on their hands. I remember when the *Daily Record*'s Edinburgh office was in Bank Street, at the top of the Mound, most of the forenoons were spent in either the Rendezvous Bar or Hardie's Bar. There might be three or four *Record* men, there'd be odd bods like myself, and there might be about eight or nine journalists in that bar all morning. They went back to their office in the afternoon, got the first edition of the Edinburgh *Evening News* to see what was doing, and if there was anything worth milking they could milk it. And even in these days the *Evening Dispatch* and *Evening News*, the *News* particularly, had a very good news service right up to their last edition. You'd get things like morning court cases that you don't get today. And then of course all the handouts and that came out, and I think the public relations officers took a lot of the initiative out of journalists. You couldn't get past the front door in St Andrew's House. Willie Ballantyne, in charge of public relations there, took their press office down at the front door and you only had to walk about six yards into it and you stopped there, you couldn't get anywhere else.[44]

After I joined the *Scottish Daily Mail* about 1957 I found, as I say, a lot of people objected to being bought by cheque-book journalism. You could get stories by cultivating them without paying them anything, and even though they'd been paid by other papers. One famous story illustrated that: Andrew Condron, a West Lothian soldier who stayed behind in China after the Korean War in 1950–3. I think 11 or 12 Yanks plus Condron stayed behind and didn't want to come home. Of course, this was a big thing, especially in America, GIs preferring Communist China to America.[45] I used to go to see Andrew Condron's old father Pat at Bathgate and we'd have a drink together. He said to me he'd been bought up by the *Daily Express*, and he got money from the *Daily Record*, too. All Pat wanted from me was his airfare to London if Andrew came into London. 'No problem,' I said, 'I'll be going down with you.' 'Aye,' he says, 'when I meet Andrew you'll be there.' So one night when I was sleeping about three o'clock in the morning, the *Daily Mail* phoned me and said, 'Andrew Condron has just left Moscow for Copenhagen.' So I got out to Bathgate about four or five in the morning, knocked up old Pat, and says, 'Right, your son's coming home. We're off.' John Blackwood, editor of the *Scottish Daily Mail*, came on the phone and said, 'Get this man over the border quick. The *Express* is taking out an injunction to prevent you taking him over the border.'[46] I said, 'If they take out an injunction against me, they've got to expose all their cheque-book journalism.' But, oh, no, I'd to get over the border. Pat Condron was quite happy to come with me by road to London. Of course, we didn't know the *Express* had sent a plane to Copenhagen to pick up Andrew Condron there, and of course they could come in anywhere, even at John o' Groats! Dick Russell was on the story for the *Express* from Glasgow, Hugh Farmer of *The People*[47] and Alex Murray from the *Daily Record*, both also from Glasgow, and they were all down at Heathrow. Hugh Farmer phoned up the *Express* newsdesk in Fleet Street and, speaking in a Glasgow accent, he says, 'Is Dick Russell there?' 'No, he's at such-and-such hotel in Southend.' So I had old Pat Condron, and Hugh Farmer and Alex Murray knew where the *Express* were. We did a deal and went down to Southend about five o'clock in the morning. The *Express* men there had been boozing till three o'clock celebrating, and were all in their beds. We were sitting in this wee lounge at the hotel when Andrew Condron comes down the stair with a baby in his arms. It was the first meeting of Andrew and Pat for so many years. Andrew had been bought up by the *Express* for £600. We paid nothing. So we got all the story, second-hand of course, but we still got the story. The *Express* headline next day was: 'The Big Reunion, and Only the *Express* Were There'. The guy in charge of the *Express* – I forget his name now, but he'd been a colleague of mine in the *Daily Herald*'s Glasgow office – didn't look at me and wouldn't speak to me.[48] Of course a lot of them on the *Express* were sort of brainwashed into the idea that they were working for the best paper in the world. I think they got a higher rate of pay, they were quite well paid. And the *Express* spent an awful lot of money on staff – they were grossly overstaffed. In Edinburgh, I know for sure, they covered everything, down to maybe Women's Guild meetings and things like that, in the hope there was a story there. I remember one *Express* man telling me it was quite an event for them to get a story in the paper because they were reporting stuff there was no room for in the paper. When I joined the *Scottish Daily Mail* it wasn't unusual for you to go out on a story and find there were four or five *Express* men against you. One of them confessed to me on one occasion that his job that particular day was to look after me, I mean, 'Just keep your eye on what the *Daily Mail* man's doing' – and that was all his job was.

I was with the *Scottish Daily Mail* till it folded, ceased publication, in December 1968. See, there again it was in a sort of similar position to the *Daily Herald*. All the expense of all newsgathering and general running of the paper was charged to the *Scottish Daily Mail*. But a lot of these stories went to the English *Daily Mail*, and for them the Scottish paper got no financial credit. So the burden grew just too heavy. And I think they made a mistake coming to publish in Edinburgh instead of in Glasgow. I mean, even people in Edinburgh didn't know the *Mail* was a Scottish paper, because there was no sort of visible presence. In Glasgow the *Express* had a big glass office in the centre of the city. The *Mail* had a wee shop in Princes Street for a short time: it was not an impressive building. Tanfield, where the *Scottish Daily Mail* had its editorial and other offices and was published, was tucked away down at Canonmills. You could pass Tanfield and you didn't know there was a newspaper there.

But we were very fortunate in the *Mail* because we had quite a good chapel there, too. And we had quite a good name as journalists throughout Britain. When the paper folded in December 1968 there was about 110 people had to be found editorial jobs. I was father of the chapel and George Strathie was clerk,[49] and we had 150 jobs on the board – vacancies; and I think there was only two or three that never got a job when the *Mail* folded. It may have been the state of the market at that time, but, you know, there were people writing to us from all over England and Scotland offering us jobs. Not all the *Mail* staff got jobs in Scotland, a lot of them had to go to England. Of course, some went to England to run the *Mail's* Scottish edition there. I myself finished after 11 years with the *Scottish Daily Mail* on Friday night and started with the *Glasgow Herald* on Monday.

I was with the *Glasgow Herald* 13 years, from December 1968 to 1981. I started off in its Glasgow office. But a vacancy quickly arose in Edinburgh and I came back through, which I was quite pleased about. The *Glasgow Herald* is a better paper now, but then it was very pedestrian. I remember asking for some cuttings on the Bay City Rollers, who were never out of the papers in these days.[50] The *Glasgow Herald* had, I think, only one cutting on them. That was the sort of paper it was then. They didn't want anything flimsy. Old George Cabarrack, who had the spaghetti shop in Brougham Place, Edinburgh, came out one day with tartan spaghetti. He'd got spaghetti dyed, some with onion skins, some with carrot skins, and he was serving up this tartan spaghetti. I thought it'd make a nice wee story. But it was pooh-poohed in the *Herald* office. I said, 'Well, I'm going to do it in any case.' So I took a photographer with me and had a picture of George at his tartan spaghetti: it made the front page. Well, of course, two or three people from the *Scottish Daily Mail* went like me to the *Glasgow Herald*, and I think it sort of brought about a change in it.

In the late 1950s, near the end of my *Daily Herald* days, I had gone on the National Executive of the National Union of Journalists. My experience with the *Liverpool Daily Post* showed me what the union could do, and I was very grateful to them, because I wasn't an old member of the *Post* staff but my colleagues there stood behind me a hundred per cent. After I came in 1947 to Edinburgh and the *Daily Herald*, which was a closed shop and your colleagues expected you to play a part in the union, I was the branch treasurer for a long time. Magnus Williamson got on to the National Executive of the union, though I could have got on to it before him because of who I knew in Edinburgh. Then Magnus gave up the union, and he was gonna be succeeded on the National Executive by John Scott, a commercial photographer who wasn't really a newspaperman at all. I said to myself, 'Well, this is not the guy to represent Edinburgh.' So that's when I went on the National Executive, and I was on it all through my *Scottish Daily Mail* days and when I was on the *Glasgow Herald*.

Two big men I ran across were Roy Thomson and Robert Maxwell. Roy Thomson came to Edinburgh and got *The Scotsman*. It's reckoned he got it for nothing because he got all that property surrounding *The Scotsman*, and when he sold off the property he was left with the paper for nothing. But he also was in for Scottish Television. There was never a man more confident of getting the STV franchise than him, because at that time he was the only person who knew how to run a television station. Hugh Fraser and one or two others were after it, but they didn't know anything about television.[51] Anyway I met Thomson one day when I was on the National Executive of the union and on a deputation to Thomson from the Printing and Kindred Trades Federation, of which our union were members.[52] *The Scotsman* was very badly organised, the editorial department at least and in some other departments as well. We all sat round the table with Roy Thomson and he told us no trade unionist was going to tell him how to run his business. If any of his men had a complaint, or wanted to say something, his door was always open, and they could come and talk to him individually. The secretary of the P&KTF – I think his name was Fletcher – explained to Thomson, 'Well, that's not the way trade unions work in this country, and,' he says, 'we could just stop your paper tomorrow.' At that time stereotypers in *The Scotsman* were 100 per cent union and the stereotypers were always a very well-organised union.[53] Thomson says, 'Oh, well, in that case we'll talk.' It was after that *The Scotsman* formed their first editorial chapel, and I sat in on a meeting. *The Scotsman* eventually became 99½ per cent. But even so, there were some that weren't very good trade unionists in the chapel. We had obtained a five-day week, but Albert Mackie, editor then of the Edinburgh *Evening Dispatch*, a stablemate of *The Scotsman*, decided he was going on to a five-and-a-half-day week. Jim Bradley, general secretary of the National Union of Journalists, said, 'Oh, they can't take unilateral action like this, and if they do,' he says, 'we'll pull out *The Scotsman* as well within the same building.'[54] I was on the National Executive of the union, and there was two guys from *The Scotsman* came down to my office and said, 'If you talk about *The Scotsman* going on strike, we'll resign from the NUJ.' Well, to them it was an honour to work with *The Scotsman*, you know; never mind about the money, it was an honour to work there.

Then there was Robert Maxwell. I remember at one National Executive meeting I was put up to speak against some of the conditions of work on the *Scottish Daily News*, the paper that followed the *Scottish Daily Express* when it ceased publication in Glasgow. Of course, I was getting all the abuse in the world for speaking against the *Scottish Daily News*.[55] But it was Robert Maxwell was running it then. I had first met Maxwell when he bought a medical publishers' up in Edinburgh. I remember doing the story at the time and finding him thoroughly objectionable, domineering and arrogant. A most objectionable character then he was![56]

I was a member of the Labour Party but I wasn't very active. Well, you didn't have time to be active. And I didn't get on very well with some people in the Party in Edinburgh. There was some I admired a lot. But then there were some others. You know, James Miller of the Progressive Party, a more uncontroversial Lord Provost you could not meet – I never knew him to make a controversial statement during his three years of office. But James Miller, a big city builder, used to hire so-called opponents in the city council, give them jobs and things like that. Well, guys like that I didn't want to know. I wouldn't say they were corrupt but, I mean, they could be bought and their price was cheap. I remember one Labour councillor, he was a baillie, he used to give me a lot of stories and I got on very well with him. He was one of James Miller's frequent critics in the council, you know, about Miller buying up this bit of land and that bit of land. He eventually retired and I says to him one day, 'What are you doing now?' He says, 'Oh, I'm working for Jimmy Miller.'[57]

Two men I admired were both named Moffat. Jack Moffat was chairman of St Cuthbert's Co-operative Association and was on the board of *The Clarion*, of which I was editor. He was responsible for setting up the Co-op supermarket in Leven Street. He had great opposition to it. The Co-op didn't want a place like that. Jack Moffat was a fairly good guy and he's got at least two memorial seats in Princes Street Gardens.[58] Abe Moffat, a very strong, powerful, dominating sort of character, who could manipulate the press very, very well, was another character I admired. In the late 1940s, early 1950s, coal was news. Abe, as president of the Scottish miners, had a press conference every fortnight after his Scottish Executive meeting and he'd come out with very controversial stuff which was splashed in the Edinburgh *Evening Dispatch* and every other paper the following day. Abe knew very well that if it didn't go with the National Executive of the National Union of Mineworkers in London he'd be overturned, but by that time he had his headlines. And of course he did well in the Knockshinnoch Castle colliery disaster inquiry, where he stood against the QCs. Abe was a sort of genuine character.[59]

Well, looking back, I think the job I enjoyed most was the *Daily Herald*. The political stuff gave me most satisfaction. My own political views were congenial. I always took the view that if you were writing for a Tory paper, well, you didn't have to hold a view but you could write a story. If you were a competent journalist you could write a story to suit their purpose – which you often had to do in papers like the *Daily Mail*. Whereas in the *Daily Herald* you were always writing a story that you yourself believed in. I don't think it was an embarrassment when I worked for other papers. I think you're a journalist first, and your politics were your own. Many a good left-winger worked for the *Daily Express* and the *Daily Mail*, and many a good Tory for the *Daily Herald*, but they were good writers – well, I wouldn't say they were members of the Tory Party, but they were Conservative-inclined. The *Daily Herald* paid good money and it employed good writers. I didn't myself feel a conflict of principle working for non-Labour papers. I felt I was a reporter first and foremost.

Hector McSporran

I got into the upper grade of the secondary at Campbeltown Grammar School, where you had to take two languages. I took Latin and French. Our woman teacher in Latin was a very soft mark and we took advantage of it. I never did any homework. She was off ill, and the principal teacher of Latin came in. None of us knew anything about what we were supposed to know about. He belted the first six, I was next in line. But the bell went to change class, so I was saved by the bell! Well, four of those boys he had belted made up their minds they were leaving Latin, and I decided to leave with the four. I went into commercial subjects instead. And that was why I became a journalist – because I'd typing and shorthand.

I was born in Toronto, Canada, on 12 January 1913. My father had a farm there. My earliest memories are really sketchy. Apart from chasing the ducks with a rake, I can remember going to get the cows in. They'd all bells round their neck: I don't think there were any fences and the cattle wandered about, but you knew where they were because of the bells. Ours was a wooden house and I was blamed for trying once to set it on fire. I had built something behind the house and set fire to it, fortunately my mother was there at the time and spotted it right away, otherwise the house might have gone up in flames! Another memory is as a wee boy skating – I could skate even at that age, about five or six. In Canada you didn't start school until you were six. I came over to live in Scotland in 1919.

My father belonged to Kintyre. He was born in 1870 and died in 1923. He started off as a farm worker. The farm he worked on he married the farmer's daughter – they eloped, in fact – and after two or three years they went to Canada. He started off in hydroelectric works in Canada until he became established, and then he had a farm.

My mother also belonged to Kintyre. Before she married I think she was a domestic worker. Her father, my grandfather, Hector Thomson, whom I'm named after, was quite a substantial man and had the shop, the post office, and the local inn in the village of Glenbarr on the west coast of Kintyre, and he owned a farm. It was his farm my father worked on when he ran away with my mother and they got married. My mother died in Canada in the big 'flu after World War One. She died in either 1918 or 1919. By that time there were four of us children: I had two older sisters who were born in this country, and a younger brother, who was only about a year old when my mother died.

So my father took us back to this country in 1919, in March, I think, and settled in Campbeltown. He worked just as a labourer with his uncle, who was a farmer and cattle dealer. Then he became the foreman or grieve on one of his uncle's farms ten miles out of Campbeltown. I remember he used to drive in in a wee horse and buggy and spend the weekend with us in Campbeltown. He went away again the Sunday night. So we only saw him at weekends. He died in 1923. So I was orphaned at the age of 10.

My grandfather McSporran was dead long before I was growing up. All I know about him was he was a crofter and a drainer. I don't think the croft made enough money so he worked also as a drainer. After working all day on draining somewhere in Kintyre he was going home by taking a shortcut over a hill, it was a very windy night, and he was blown off the hill to his death.

In Campbeltown we lived on the top flat in a big four-storey tenement in Barrochan Place. It was built in 1908 on the site of old army barracks by my father's uncle, who was a farmer and a builder. My aunt, a dressmaker, had the top flat: on one side the residence, on the other side the dressmaking. At one time she had occupied about 30 girls, but when the ready-mades came in she had to dispose of so many of her workers. When we came there in 1919 I suppose at the most she would employ about six girls. It was still quite a big business even at that, with six working full-time. But long before she died about 1935, there were only four working there. One of my sisters took over the business then and, although she was losing money, kept one of the girls there until the girl retired, because she'd been there from the very start about 50 years earlier as a wee girl from school.

My sisters were Mary and Helen. Mary was five years older than me, and Helen two years; my brother Duncan was five years younger than me. Mary's first job was looking after the child of our English master in Campbeltown Grammar School. She did that for years, and then went into domestic service with a family McFadyen in Campbeltown, whose daughter was a great friend of Vivien Leigh, the actress, who used to go to Campbeltown on holiday, and my sister looked after her.[1] My sister

Helen from leaving school took over my aunt's dressmaking business. And until a few years ago she still did a bit of dressmaking. When my brother Duncan left school he started off as a stonemason and became the foreman quite early. I remember being in a bus once and we were passing some new houses that had been built. There was a couple of men behind me on the bus and one of them said, 'I wonder whit like these houses are?' The other man says, 'They'll be good houses. McSporran built them.'

I started school in 1919 in the primary department of Campbeltown Grammar School. I liked the school and got on well there. I sat the Qualifying exam and got into the upper grade of the secondary department. One thing I didn't like about the secondary was algebra. I was very good at mental arithmetic and geometry, and always good at arithmetic. In some of the exams right up until the third year I was getting 90s in geometry but only about 25 in algebra. And I was good in English. I was always good at writing an essay in English and sometimes the teacher would read my essay out to the class to show how it should be done. I got the prize in English, and I think it was third prize I got in French in the third year. But, as I've already said, Latin was another matter! Incidentally, one of the two boys among the six belted by the Latin principal teacher who didn't leave Latin was Willie MacVicar. Willie was the minister's son, and he was frightened his old man would have chased him if he'd left Latin.

As a laddie I was very keen on football, that was my principal interest. I joined the Boys' Brigade when I was about 11 or 12, then I was asked to join the Scouts. The Scouts had a football team and they wanted me to play in it. I was a good player, though I say it myself. But I didn't stay long in the Scouts. The Scout master got into bother or something and the Scouts disintegrated. Then I started climbing the hills. There were a few of us used to go away on a Sunday especially, but even in the evenings, away up the hills round about Campbeltown. Some nights we'd just walk down the promenade and, well, past the promenade right down by the shore at Campbeltown Loch – a two-mile walk there and back. I was quite keen on walking but I preferred hill-walking.

As a laddie, too, I was a regular attender at Sunday school, and when I was probably about 18 I joined the Church of Scotland and at one time I was a Sunday school teacher. Not that I did any teaching, I hadn't a class as such. I was a sort of supernumerary or supervisor as a teacher and used to do the collection and go round to see everyone had a teacher. The only time I ever taught a class was when a teacher was missing. But at that time I played football quite a lot and I'd quite a good reputation as an outside left. And if it was boys I was teaching in the Sunday school, they knew about me and were far more interested in talking about the game I'd played in than the divinity or theology lesson I was supposed to teach them.

In football I started off in a churches and Sunday school league which had about ten teams in it, and I played in the church team. I also played for Campbeltown United. We had a mid-Argyll league: three teams in Campbeltown, a team in Tarbert, one in Lochgilphead. There was one in Oban, Oban Combi; it was never part of our league, but we used to play friendlies with them. We played in the Junior League and one year went to the fifth round of the Scottish Junior Cup, but were beaten by Tranent, who won the Cup that year.[2] I was right-footed but I could kick with my left foot as well as I could with my right, and that was why I was always put at outside left. Later on I played inside left and was far more effective. One of the frequent visitors on holiday to Campbeltown was Campbell Caskie, father of Jimmy Caskie who played for St Johnstone, Rangers, and Everton. I used to play with Jimmy and his brother Alex out on the local green.[3] But through Campbell Caskie they brought to Campbeltown the Glasgow schools champions – I think it was Possilpark School – to play a Campbeltown select team, and I was chosen for the select team.

I was 17 and in my fourth year when I left Campbeltown Grammar School. Why I left school was I had a big operation – perforated stomach – and I missed a complete term and part of another. They wanted to push me ahead but I reckoned I could never have made up for the year I'd missed. I was a bit older than the others in my class, having not started until I was six. I left before I could sit my Highers.

I hadn't really got any ambitions. All I wanted was a job. I wanted to work, I was keen to work – at anything. Anyway I got a job with my father's uncle who had an ironmonger's business. Even when I was at school I used to go in there and do odd jobs, such as delivering messages, especially carrying cans of paraffin for lighting. A wifie would come in and order paraffin and the can was a bit heavy for her to carry, so I used to carry it and get paid for that. I did all sorts of jobs in the shop. I worked there for about 18 months after leaving the school.

I became a reporter by accident really. My great uncle the ironmonger was a great churchman and was session clerk of the United Free Church. He was very friendly with the minister there, Rev. Bruce Blackwood, and with my minister, Rev. Tom MacPherson. They always came about the business in the shop. I think it was my great-uncle asked them if they'd heard of any prospects of a job for me. Blackwood says, 'There's a job going at the *Argyllshire Leader*.' Blackwood was very friendly with Alex

Ramsay, who had opened the *Leader* in Campbeltown against the long-established paper, the *Campbeltown Courier*.[4] Alex Ramsay was an excellent journalist who'd worked out in China, in Peking, and came back, started the *Leader*, and was looking for somebody to start off in the paper. Well, Rev. Blackwood recommended me and I started there. That's how it began. I hadn't had any ambition till then to become a reporter. So I was about 18½ or 19 when I started in 1931–2 on the *Leader*.[5]

Alex Ramsay was the editor and the owner. There was just the two of us editorial workers. But there were three compositors, and then they had a Monotype. But Alex Ramsay eventually lost the Monotype because he couldn't afford to keep up the payments on it. And we hand-set the paper. I helped to do that, and I was the fastest hand-setter of them all.[6] But my main job was reporting. It was excellent experience, though it proved to be brief.

The *Leader* was never doing well. Its circulation at the most was probably about 1,000 copies. The opposition was the long-established *Campbeltown Courier*. Its circulation would be about 3,500. Alex Ramsay was a great newspaperman and a very nice man personally. But he was a daily newspaper man, not a country weekly newspaper man. The mistake he made was he went left-wing and people stopped buying his paper. He was really a socialist, and a pretty left-wing socialist, though I don't think he was a member of any political party. The *Courier* was very much associated with the Conservative Party, and the *Leader* was to sort of counteract the *Courier*.[7]

Well, I wasn't long with the *Leader*, about 18 month, when I was invited to take over at the *Courier*. Alex Ramsay took me up to his solicitor Archie Stewart, who was also my solicitor, for advice. I remember Archie Stewart saying to Alex Ramsay, 'Can you guarantee Hector's future in the *Leader*?' Ramsay was honest enough to say, 'No.' So Archie Stewart says to me, 'Hector, take the *Courier* job.' And I did. The *Leader* foundered about a year afterwards. I don't know what happened to Alex Ramsay then. But I'll tell you, he was very good to me when I took over the *Courier* first, with very little experience to bring out the paper. If I was in trouble at all, he always told me to go and seek his advice, and I did, and he helped me.

At the *Courier* I was just described as reporter, but I was actually the acting editor, because I did everything. What had happened was that Angus MacVicar, who was really a novelist, had run the *Courier*. Then he decided he was going to give up working as a journalist and devote his time to writing books, and I was invited to take over from him as acting editor.[8] Angus MacVicar had himself actually been standing in for the editor of the *Courier*, Alex McLeod. McLeod, who belonged to

Campbeltown, had been right through the First War in, I think, the Argyll and Sutherland Highlanders. He sometimes spoke about his experiences in the war, and I would imagine they had led him into alcoholism. He must always have worked for the *Courier* and he had inherited it when the man, named Wilson, who owned it before him died unmarried and with no family and willed the *Courier* and the business – a big newsagent's shop and a big jobbing printing business, because it was the only printers in Campbeltown – to Alex McLeod. Well, there was another printer, Alex Keith, in a very small way who just maybe did business cards, funeral notices, and things like that. Anyway Alex McLeod was bequeathed the *Courier*, did very well for a while, but then went on to drink and went off the rails. He would come into the office and maybe work for three weeks, and was excellent when he was working. Then he would disappear for three weeks on the bottle. But Alex McLeod was a natural country weekly paper editor, and so the opposite of Alex Ramsay of the *Leader*.

When I started on the *Courier* about 1933 as reporter-cum-acting editor, Pat McKay was the office boy or junior reporter. Later on he went to a paper in Ayr or somewhere. Alex McLeod came in and out, but he died after I'd been there four or five years. Broom, the new editor they appointed, came from the *Daily Record*. He was an alcoholic, too. I don't think they knew that when they appointed him. I got on with Broom but of course I was left to do all the work: the editorial staff was Broom and me. He was usually there in the office. But he had a half bottle in his pocket all the time and was drinking all the time. The only time he absented himself was once when he went to do the county council meeting at Oban or Dunoon. He was missing for a few days. I asked Archie McNair, the local Provost, if Broom had attended the meeting and if he was sober. 'Well,' he says, 'to my surprise he was very abstemious the time he was at the meeting.' Anyway he reappeared the day before the *Courier*'s publication and wrote up his copy in double- quick time and I got it into the paper. Broom was a competent journalist.

I don't know why to this day, but in 1938 I left the *Campbeltown Courier* and went to the *Kirriemuir Free Press* in Angus.[9] I've regretted it ever since. I saw this advertisement for a reporter, replied to it, and was accepted. I remember interviewing Anna Neagle and her husband Herbert Wilcox at Kirriemuir when they came to see Barrie's birthplace. But I boobed, being a young innocent from the country, when I asked her if she'd ever played Peter Pan, she says, 'Yes, three times.'[10] But I was never happy in Kirriemuir. The paper, whose circulation might have been 4,000, was owned by a man, a ploughman, who, I was told, had won the Irish Sweep and bought the *Kirriemuir Free Press*. His son was the editor and his younger son the photographer. The younger son wasn't too bad, but the older son was useless, hopeless, hadn't a clue. There were just the three of us and I was supposed to do everything. On my afternoon off I was expected to go to the cattle market to get the cattle prices for the paper. On my Saturday afternoon off, when I had arranged to play outside left for Kirriemuir Thistle, a Junior team, and was supposed to go and play with them in Dundee and all sorts of places, I was expected by the *Free Press* never to leave Kirriemuir. I stuck the job for three months then packed it in.

I was very friendly with Ian Stewart, son of Archie, in Campbeltown, where the Stewarts had stayed just below us in the tenement in Barrochan Street. Ian was a reporter for a while with the *Daily Express*, he had a law degree, gave up the *Express*, went back to Campeltown and became sheriff clerk and town clerk. Ian recommended me to Donald Brown, news editor of the *Express*. Donald Brown said, 'Hector, I can give you a job here tomorrow. But you'd have to start at the minimum wage' – which at that time was £5 7s 6d (£5.37½) a week. 'But,' he said, 'I'll tell you what to do. Go up to Fort William. The freelance there has left and joined the *Daily Record*.' So I went to Fort William and stuck that for about 18 months until just after the war started. I remember the evacuees from Glasgow arriving at Fort William. The papers, some of them only four or eight pages, were full of war news and nothing else: the market had dried up. So I'd to give that up and I went back to Campbeltown. I did a wee bit of freelance work there. But then Donald Henderson, the editor of the *Campbeltown Courier*, who had gone there from the *Express*, was called up and I was invited to become editor of the *Courier*.

I know I made a good job of being editor of the *Campbeltown Courier*, because the boss, the big white chief, Charles Mactaggart – a lawyer, one of these arrogant tyrant sort of buggers, known as Lord God Almighty in Campbeltown – stopped in the middle of the street and called me over to congratulate me on my first issue. He said, 'It's the best *Courier* I've seen for many's a year.'[11] But I was lucky because I had always the suspicion I'd be called in as editor of the *Courier* and I was preparing in my own mind what I was gonnae do. By then I had tried twice to get into the Forces but had failed the medical both for the army and the RAF because of two stomach operations I had had for ulcer trouble. I think it was in the army medical, when I went before them stripped naked, the chairman says, 'Have you not a letter from your doctor?' I says, 'If I have, it'll be in my jacket pocket.' He says, 'Go and get it.' When I gave it to him he says, 'Good God, laddie, if you'd shown us this to begin with there'd have been no need for a medical!' So it was a hopeless quest – grade four or something.

Alex McLeod's brother-in-law had become the proprietor of the *Courier*, but he had no money, and Charles Mactaggart, who was the secretary of the board, subsidised the paper till McLeod got established. I got on very well with Mactaggart for years, and he was very appreciative of what I did on the *Courier*. But eventually during the war his sister was charged with hoarding coal. Everyone in Campbeltown knew about it, and they were at me: 'I bet you don't publish this in the *Courier*.' But when Mactaggart's sister appeared in court I was determined her name was going to be in the paper. Mactaggart got to hear of this and he called a board meeting: 'By decision of the board, you cannot publish this case.' Well, just by chance that same day there was an advert for a reporter in the *Glasgow Herald* in Glasgow. I applied for it without telling Mactaggart. Meantime, another case arrived in Campbeltown court and Ian Stewart, by then the procurator fiscal, said in court: 'I hope that, unlike other cases, this case will be reported in the *Courier*.' Well, I did a wrong thing for a journalist. I changed Ian's words to: 'I hope the editor of the *Courier* will publish this case – unlike other cases where he was prohibited from . . .' Mactaggart came down on me like a ton of bricks. I told him, 'It's you to blame. Everyone in the town knows about your sister. And what they're saying is she was hoarding ten ton of coal, not ten hundredweight, and it'd have been far better to have published the case.' Though at that point I didn't know whether I was getting the *Glasgow Herald* job or not, I was determined to resign, so I says to Mactaggart, 'You can accept my resignation right now.' A few days later I got a letter from the *Glasgow Herald* inviting me up for an interview.

There I met Tom Chalmers, the news editor, and Jimmy Ross, the chief reporter, and they took me down to J.M. Reid, editor of the *Bulletin*, a sister paper but completely different from the *Herald*. Two days later I got a letter from Sir William Robieson, editor of the *Glasgow Herald*. He said he was impressed by the reports he had got from these others, offered me the job at so much a week – double what I was getting at the *Courier*, and said if I proved satisfactory the wage would be increased considerably within a year.[12] Well, I didn't go off then to the *Glasgow Herald*, because at the *Campbeltown Courier* they'd a hell of a job getting an editor. Charles Mactaggart there must have had some connection with Willie Adair, the agricultural editor of the *Glasgow Herald*. And without them even consulting me, the next I knew Tom Chalmers came to me and says, 'Hector, the *Courier* wants you to wait for three months because they've a job getting a replacement for you. It's up to you, Hector. But if you want to go back, your job at the *Herald* will still be here for you.' So I went back to the *Courier* on condition

I wouldn't be there for more than three months. They paid me, but I was a wee bit disappointed with what they gave me: £25. I had saved that paper. When I was editor I became managing editor, because I'd to look after the shop, the bills, and everything. The woman there who did the accounts was three years behind with them, and when people got the accounts I was the one who got all their bloody complaints! Eventually Mactaggart employed an accountant, but I had to go in with the accountant at nights and price the accounts. And I got £25 for all that. However, I was glad to get away!

Getting a job at the beginning of 1944 as a reporter on the *Glasgow Herald* was really my entry into big-time journalism. The staff was maybe reduced a bit by the war but they'd quite a few reporters, some helluva good reporters, mostly older chaps. There was Tom Chalmers, Jimmy Ross, Jimmy Chalmers and Bob Taylor, who were all over military age, and there was a fella Stewart, and Macdonald, two Milnes, and Bob Russell, who later went to the *Express*. Bob Russell's wife Meg, who worked under several names, was a good all-round woman reporter. Then maybe just after the war we'd another girl reporter. Her father was a big butcher in Motherwell. She was a beautiful girl, she should have been a bloody film star or a mannequin. She was very good when she was there. But she didn't last long. Och, this night she went out on a story, went on the bash, didn't turn in her story, and that was it.

Between the three papers – *Herald*, *Bulletin*, and Glasgow *Evening Times* – there'd be about 20 reporters. So it was a much bigger outfit than I'd worked with up to then. It was a challenge to me. I'd to prove myself against these people. One thing in my favour was I was a hell of a good shorthand writer. At one time I had taken a test for a job advertised in Geneva, where the minimum shorthand was 180 words a minute. I made 180, but I didn't apply for that job because I knew I could never have maintained that speed over a period of time. I suppose I could do my 150 all the time. The one man I could never take in shorthand, even at my best, was Donald Dewar. Oh, God, he was hopeless. But I took Churchill several times. He was a measured speaker, but he could be very difficult to take because he had this ball in his mouth, and it was a word he would say but you could never get the meaning of it.[13] I remember on the *Glasgow Herald* John Ritchie, who was a hell of a good shorthand writer, and I were taken down to the editor's room as the best two shorthand writers in the office, to try and beat the Press Association on the budget – and we did that. At that time shorthand was absolutely indispensable for a reporter. They tell me they don't need it now. Well, I'd a reputation that I could go on to the phone without sitting down first preparing my story – just dictate it straight over the phone. I think it's got to do with confidence in being able to do it and never getting flurried.

In the *Glasgow Herald* during the war years, partly because of the shortage of staff and for economic reasons as well, we worked for all three papers – the *Bulletin* and Glasgow *Evening Times* as well. If you went out in the morning on a story you were doing it for the *Evening Times*. When you came back into the office and you'd done the *Times*, you'd rewrite the story for the *Herald* and the *Bulletin*. It was quite a load of work. They were smaller papers then of course. I remember I was sent through to Dundee for the *Herald* to report the annual conference of the British Association for the Advancement of Science: oh, the most awkward bloody job you can ever do. You've got to take a pick, there's so many things going on at the conference. It was all Greek to me: I'd no scientific background. The one boy that helped me in that was Ben Allison, who worked for the *Express* for years, a great fellow and a first-class reporter.[14] I was very friendly with Ben and had met him first in Fort William, where he ran the Ben Nevis Race: well, he went up so far and back down, but he made a story out of it.

I remember during the war interviewing Joe Louis, the boxer, for the *Herald*. I couldn't understand what he was saying. I thought he was talking about horse pills. He was on a tour cheering up the American boys away from home in horse pills. Then it dawned on me – hospitals.[15] But, och, I met so many people when I worked for the *Herald*. One was Hector McNeil, the MP for Greenock, who'd been a journalist himself and later became Secretary of State for Scotland. I'll be quite honest, McNeil was a bastard. Once in George Square in Glasgow he was in the chair, and we pressmen were all around. I was at a corner below his chair and asked him a question. He says, 'Don't you ask me questions at a time like this.' I fell out with him from then on. He was self-important and pompous.[16] Then I knew Pat Dollan, the Scottish editor of the *Daily Herald*, a good man, but a man out for himself, an opportunist. I knew his son Jimmy, too, a nice fellow, who also worked for the *Daily Herald*; but I knew Pat's nephew, also called Jimmy, better than his son.

Well, I was with the *Glasgow Herald* from 1944 to 1949–50, certainly five years. It was a great experience on what was a very prestigious paper. You had to be absolutely accurate then. I read the *Herald* now and I still think it's a hell of a good paper, but there's an awful lot of mistakes in it. What's wrong is they used to have readers to pick up the mistakes. There's no readers now. Another thing, Glasgow was the centre of journalism in Scotland, you had all these papers, a lot of professional colleagues – rivals as reporters during working hours but generally friendly.

But one thing I realised not only when I was in Glasgow but after I left it and went elsewhere: there was some hell of a poor reporters in the big papers in Glasgow. Well, Donald Henderson of the *Express*, who went to the *Campbeltown Courier*, to me he hadn't a bloody clue. His *Courier* was mostly stories lifted out of the nationals. Tommy Sharp, who was with the *Daily Record*, who was in the same digs as me one time in Glasgow, could talk but he couldn't write! I think the reasons to begin with were a lack of education. They never stayed long enough at school to take their Highers. On the other hand, some of the poorest reporters were graduates. They hadn't the nose for the job, they'd no news sense. It's all right writing beautiful English, but you've got to recognise a story when you see it, you've got to know there's a story there. It's not just a question of shorthand speed either: if you have 250 words a minute it doesn't mean you're going to be a good reporter. A good reporter needed a combination of qualities: perseverance, a sense of curiosity, inquisitiveness . . . This is what's lacking now.

What led me to leave the *Herald* was I was married in 1946 and couldn't get a house in Glasgow. I had one of a family and another on the road, and I was in sub-lets the whole time I was in Glasgow. Well, I was down in Ayr covering the Tarbolton air crash by a KLM plane.[17] Jimmy Parker, who was down there for the *Evening Times*, picked up a paper, saw this job advertised in Dumfries, house available, and says, 'Hector, this is what you're looking for.' I applied for it and got it – again without an interview!

I'd never been to Dumfries. But, oh, it was a lovely town to live in. But the work on the *Dumfries & Galloway Standard*, a bi-weekly, was bloody awful.[18] Oh, I missed the *Glasgow Herald*, and after I'd been in Dumfries a couple of years I regretted going. The *Standard* was unusual – a bi-weekly paper, a paper on the Wednesday and a paper on the Saturday. The Saturday edition had a circulation of about 30,000, the Wednesday one maybe 15,000 to 17,000. I went there as a reporter, and what bugged me was that between me and Davie Dunbar, the other boy there and one of the best shorthand writers I ever met, the two of us had to fill two pages in both papers. There was another reporter who did other things but couldn't report council meetings, courts, or things like that. And I stuck it out for years, far too many years – eight years, I suppose, I was there.

I stuck it out because of housing and family rather than journalistic reasons. My wife loved it down there in Dumfries, we had three boys eventually at school, and we made friends. Dumfries was a most friendly town, a lovely place to live, with bonny countryside all round. I enjoyed living there, it was the working I didn't enjoy. But I tholed that because of the family. When I was offered a job in South Shields on a Newcastle paper I accepted it – but I couldn't afford to go. When I put my resignation in at Dumfries I just got a big increase to keep me there – so I couldn't afford to go!

On the *Dumfries and Galloway Standard* there was an editor who was fully paid but did nothing except write the leading article. Then there was Willie Muir, sub-editor, a first-class newspaperman, two reporters, and two freelance photographers – one of the photographers became a staff man eventually, because pictures were becoming more and more important then. We did eventually, long before I left, have a woman reporter, Vivien Lauder. Women were fairly rare then on the editorial side. The *Standard* also had a big jobbing printing business and a shop, and I think the girls in the shop would also be maybe what they would call the office boy, doing the sort of nitty-gritty stuff.

When I went to Dumfries I had to travel around a lot. It was a huge area and it had poor public transport. So the first thing they wanted to know was did I drive. When I said, 'No' – 'Well, you'd better start.' They paid for me to learn and they put me through. I used to go as far as Stranraer and Langholm for a story, and once across the Border in Carlisle there was a big celebration and I was through for that. Twice I had to do holiday features about the Isle of Man, so I flew from Cumberland to the Isle of Man, and they took us round the TT track there – by car of course! I was never involved in reporting runaway marriage couples in the 1950s at Gretna Green.

And I used to report Burns Suppers. The speaker at one of them – a very well-known lawyer from Glasgow, who was a teetotaller, when he was about to propose the toast and the president said to him, 'I'm sorry I can't offer you a decent drink to propose the toast,' – says, 'What's wrong with water?'!

When I went to Fort William just before the war I had joined the union – the National Union of Journalists. I used to send my contribution to Willie Hannigan at the *Daily Record* in Glasgow. But he either died or disappeared, because when I sent my contribution I got it back, so I let my membership lapse. I joined the union again when I went on the *Glasgow Herald* in 1944 – they insisted. I think if you were a member of the Institute of Journalists that was OK, but you had to be in one or the other.[19] But most of them in the *Herald* were NUJ anyway. I kept going wi' that, but when I went down to Dumfries in 1949–50 I let it lapse again, but not for very long, because I got interested again in the union and revived union interest in Dumfries. I formed a sub-branch there. I was encouraged to do that by the new editor, Williamson, who was a bit of a head case. He was in the Salvation Army and used to go out with his uniform on, sing, and wave the flag and all that.[20] But he was very keen on unions, encouraged me, and I became the first secretary of the branch or sub-branch there. I'm a life member now of the union. If I could have had my contributions collected regularly I'd have been a union man since about 1938.

*   *   *

Well, but for family reasons I might have moved on sooner from Dumfries. Then after eight years there, I fell out with the man who came up from London to become editor of the *Standard*. I had worked with him at the *Glasgow Herald* and he'd made his reputation on me. He was very friendly with Niall Macpherson, National Liberal MP for the area. Our bosses on the *Standard* at that time were National Liberals, and they went to Niall Macpherson and asked for his recommendation for an editor.[21] I couldn't get on in the office with this editor, though we got on well enough socially. And the one thing that bugged me more than anything else was when he was writing the leading article. We'd all our stuff through, maybe by seven o'clock in the evening, but at nine o'clock he hadn't started writing his leading article. It was not only me and the other reporters he was keeping hanging on, it was the boys down in the machine room, too. Later on he died, drank himself to death, I think, through brandy.

Anyway, eventually I saw a job for a reporter advertised in the Aberdeen *Press & Journal*. I applied for the job and got a reply back within a day from Peter Craighead, the news editor, offering me the job. I'd never worked in Aberdeen before, except for an odd day now and again when the *Glasgow Herald* used to send me up. The Aberdeen job was for Aberdeen Journals – that was the *Press & Journal* and the *Evening Express*. There had been the *Weekly Journal*, too, but by that time it had maybe folded. Peter Craighead was news editor of the two papers and knew me. We had met at Edinburgh on what was the famous coffins trial, where in the crematorium at Aberdeen they had been throwing kids' bodies in with adults' and flogging the coffins. George MacDonald senior (his son George retired in the 1990s from the *Glasgow Herald*) and I were sent through from the *Herald* to cover the trial and Peter Craighead and George Ley Smith were doing it for the *Press & Journal*.[22] George MacDonald and I did the *Evening Times* in relays, then George did the *Herald* and I did the *Bulletin*. Well, a *Daily Herald* man came up to me after the first day and wanted to share my *Bulletin* story with the *Daily Herald*. He says, 'I'll rejig it a wee bit just to show . . .' I says, 'Fair enough, it's all the same to me.' He says, 'Because you've had the best story of them all.' He rejigged my story and used it in the *Daily Herald* and I never even got a dram from him! Och, not that I was worrying, but afterwards I thought he might have showed some appreciation.

Well, when I left Dumfries for Aberdeen, I think it was early in 1959, I thought my wife was reasonably happy about moving – until the day we left, when she wasn't very happy. We'd made such good friends in Dumfries and it was a big step to go from one corner of the country to the opposite corner. As I've said, we had three children by then. Duncan, the oldest boy, who was 12, got into Aberdeen Grammar School, which I think had just stopped being fee-paying. The middle boy went to Aberdeen Academy at Schoolhill, and the youngest one went to the local school in Broomhill Road.

The day I arrived at Aberdeen Journals it was freezing hard. Two reporters were out on the hills looking for lost climbers. Another reporter was out on the North Sea for some reason, and there was a fourth on some dangerous job. I said to myself, 'What the hell have I let myself in for here?' I felt like running away! I took the 'flu within the first week I was there and was off for three or four days. But I settled in very quickly as a reporter for both the *Press & Journal* and the *Evening Express*: one week *P&J*, one week *Evening Express*. My first week was at the *P&J*. How they worked it was you worked from two o'clock one week Monday to Friday. And then you were off at the weekend, went on at eight or nine the following morning, had a day off during the week, and then you worked the weekend. So you worked every second weekend, and there was a day off each week to make up for that. I got used to it very quickly, and of course I had been accustomed to that to some extent at the *Glasgow Herald* and *Evening Times*. It was nothing new to me, and I quite enjoyed it. The only time I felt unsocial hours was if you were out on a story, especially sent up to Peterhead, as I was on one occasion, and worked right through the night because there was a boat reported missing. Of course missing boats are big news up in the north-east. Then it was found, but missing again, found again, missing again. I was writing a story about a boat that was missing and the next thing I knew the bloody boat was moored up in Peterhead harbour. I'd to rejig my story and I phoned the office in Aberdeen and the editor, Jimmy Grant, came on. I says, 'Well, Jimmy, you've enough there for the first edition and I'll rejig the story for later.' He says, 'No, Hector. Rejig the story now.' And I'd to rejig the story when he was still on the bloody phone![23]

When I went to Aberdeen first there were certainly 20 reporters on the *P&J* and *Evening Express* – quite a big office. There were four women in the newsroom, and at least two, three or four in women's features. That was quite a lot of women for those days, and it would certainly be unusual in any paper except maybe the national papers. More women journalists were coming in by then and I think had started coming in during the war when men were scarce. Ethel Simpson was in Aberdeen Journals from the start of that. And the Journals when I first began there had, I suppose, half a dozen photographers: another sign pictures were becoming more important.

Jimmy Grant, the editor of the *P&J*, was in a class of his own. Such a gentle benign man away from the office – but in the office he would bite your head off! The least wee mistake, oh – then the next day or minute he was as if nothing had happened. But, oh, he was a gem of a man and such an excellent editor for the *P&J*. He wasn't the editor when I arrived. Ken Peters was editor but he became managing editor, and Jimmy Grant succeeded him.[24] Aberdeen Journals were owned by Kemsley when I went there, but two or three years later the papers were taken over by Lord Thomson. It was all right under Thomson, but later on ownership changed again and the *Daily Mail* own it now. It's a completely different paper since they took it over. That's maybe not their fault. I think it's the fault of that big strike they had.[25]

Around the time I went to Aberdeen the circulation of the *P&J* would be about 110,000. It went up to 115,000 at one time under Jimmy Grant. The *Evening Express* was between 80,000 and 90,000. I think they're both less now. The great strength of the *P&J* was that it was respected by its readers, and it spread over such a wide area and had special editions for each of these areas. The *P&J* became part of family life. The *Evening Express*'s great thing was that people in the city of Aberdeen expected to have the *Express* in their home every evening, it was their sort of local paper. There was a great deal of loyalty. I don't think Grampian Television, which came in the early 1960s, had the effect people thought it would have.[26] I know nothing at all about the advertising revenue of the Aberdeen papers, and Grampian might have had an effect on that. Apart from that, I suppose the coming of Grampian made us on the Aberdeen Journals more alert: we knew we had competition. We hadn't had much up till then. The *Glasgow Herald* and *The Scotsman* didn't circulate very widely in the north-east, though the *Daily Record* did and it was the main rival of the *P&J*. The *Daily Record* had an office in Aberdeen, with two reporters and a photographer. So did the *Daily Express* at one time, and the *Daily Mail* also at one time had a reporter in Aberdeen. But there was no real competition from other papers with the *P&J*: you see, it did wee stories that the nationals would never touch. Naturally, local people were interested in local stories.

Though I was working as a general reporter in Aberdeen, after a time I was offered jobs as a sub-editor. But I wanted out of the office – I could never sit in an office eight hours a day. And I was never very ambitious, though I wouldn't have said no if they'd made me chief reporter. So I carried on doing stories for the *P&J* one week and for the *Evening Express* the other week until, about 1967, Aberdeen Journals moved out from Broad Street in the centre of Aberdeen to the city outskirts at Mastrick. After that the staffs of the two papers were separated. I went to the *Evening Express*. The deputy editor of the *Evening Express* suggested I should become its local government correspondent. I said, 'No, I'll go as a general reporter. I don't want to go as local government correspondent.' At that time my three sons had flown the nest, and if I went to the *Evening Express* it meant I finished work at four or five o'clock and would be home with my wife at night instead of her sitting alone if I went to the *P&J*. So I did go to the *Evening Express* as a general reporter. One of the stories I covered was the famous Garvie trial. It was the story of the year.[27]

But I found myself more and more getting local government work to do, because I was more experienced in it than anybody else in the office. Eventually Bob Smith, the editor, says, 'Hector, you're doing all the local government, so you might as well be officially recognised as Municipal Correspondent.' 'And how's that gonna affect me?' 'Oh,' he says, 'you'll get an increase.' I got about £200 a year extra. I should have taken that to begin with, but I'd been working maybe for three years without it. But I didn't mind that. The one thing I liked about it was it took me out of the office, and I was more or less my own boss. I was in the Town House all day or, when local government was changed in 1974–5, I was always out at Woodhill House, headquarters of Grampian Regional Council, or in the centre of the town at St Nicholas House, HQ of Aberdeen City Council. I was very seldom in the office.

Every councillor in the city knew me by my Christian name. If they wanted their story, they would come to me. It was different in Grampian Regional Council. I knew Sandy Mutch, the convener, on Christian-name terms, and a lot of other people there.[28] But in the Region they came from Elgin, Kintore, all over. I knew them well enough, but not on Christian name terms. They were more distant than the city councillors, put it that way.

So I was the municipal correspondent of the *Evening Express* for seven years. That was the first time I'd really specialised, until then I'd always been a general reporter. Maybe it was a sign of getting old! I think it was that I liked general reporting but, after all those years, I felt I could do with a change. But then I could have done with a change when I was local government! I'll put it this way, I was glad when the time came, when I was 65 in 1978, for me to retire.

Well, I was a journalist for nearly half a century. The only regret I ever had was leaving the *Glasgow Herald* to go to Dumfries, because if I'd stayed with the *Herald* all my life I'd have had a far better pension from the *Herald* than the pension I have now. They had the best pension scheme in Scotland at that time. But I was five years with the *Herald* and ten years with the *Dumfries and Galloway Standard*, which to begin with anyway had no pension scheme. I just got peanuts back from them.

If I had my life to live again, if I opted for not being in journalism, I'd probably have wanted to go into law. But I knew from the beginning, having left school before going through my Highers, that I could never go into law anyway. I never thought of that at the time, to be quite honest. I always wanted to work, and I'd have taken any job to work.

As a reporter I met an awful lot of people. I remember once in Ayr, when I was reporting the KLM plane-crash story at Tarbolton, we stayed in the same hotel as John Cameron, the KC for KLM. We used to have a drink with him at night. I didn't meet him again until years later when he was judging a case in Dumfries and I met him in the street. He lifted his hat to me.[29] And I've shaken hands with the Queen when she invited those of us who were regular reporters at the General Assembly of the Church of Scotland in Edinburgh to a cocktail party at the Palace of Holyroodhouse. We were all introduced individually to the Queen, Prince Philip, and Princess Anne, and they shook hands with all of us. You couldn't meet a more genuine person than the Queen, and so friendly. I happened to mention to her that Lord Reith needed a pacemaker because of the pressure of his work, and the Queen says, 'Do you know, I often think I could do with a pacemaker myself.'[30]

Colin Dakers

When I went to Arbroath High School, rather than leave at age 15 I decided
– and my mother fortunately backed me – that the career I wanted was
journalism. You can't just come out of school and into journalism right
away. So I hung on for an extra year where I honed both my English
and my foreign languages, including German, and I started after school
hours helping out as a sort of runabout boy in the local *Arbroath Herald*
newspaper office.[1] And from there I went to D.C. Thomson in Dundee,
really the cradle of journalism in Scotland, where I got excellent training.

I was born in 1915. My grandfather Dakers was a tailor. My father
was born in Edinburgh, so was my mother, but he was employed in a
local tailor's shop in Arbroath. When things became recessional he did
his own work, worked up a clientele of the local well-to-do, made suits
for them, and became a master tailor in Arbroath, where I stayed most
of my young life.

Away back, my family originated in the Low Countries at the time
the Huguenots in France were being persecuted. Among the Huguenots
were a large number of weavers and they decided they would leave.
Most of them settled in Angus, where there are still today two places
with Low Countries' names – Brechin and Friockheim. Friockheim was
what you might call the home of the weavers. In Brechin, on the end
of a building, there is a plaque with an 1860 date and the two spellings,
Dacre and Dakers. That suggests to me there was, if not a French, at least
a Flemish connection of some kind. So my forebears stayed in Angus, in
and around Arbroath.

I don't know a great deal about my mother's family, except that her
father was in the engineering business. I never had any contact with my
maternal grandparents. They lived in Edinburgh and they didn't really
come on to my scene at all.

I was the second youngest in a family of six – I had three brothers and
two sisters: David, then William, Lindsay, Jean, myself, and Margaret. My
eldest brother Dave was very, very interested in folk music and was well

known in the area for his ability at concerts to sing traditional Scottish songs. My sister Jean was interested in poetry and could recite very many old Scots poems. My brother Lindsay, who died about the age of 23, his interest was ballroom dancing. Both Dave and my other older brother Bill were in the Territorials and were among the first to be called during the Second War. Dave went to the merchant navy, and Bill became a physical education instructor to the paratroops. Both survived the war. Incidentally, my father was in the Royal Flying Corps in the First World War. I think he was a conscript, but I'm not certain: with a family, I don't think he would volunteer. He had an unfortunate experience. With his tailoring skills his job in the RFC was repairing aircraft wings. He was on the wing of an aircraft repairing it on a plateau on a hillside when the bloody plane was blown off the hillside with him on the wing. He dropped off, got a leg injury, and that got him out early from the war.

My earliest memories are of growing up in Arbroath. I was unusual in my schooling because I went to primary school like everybody else and then went to what was called an intermediary secondary, which was Keptie. Now the unusual thing was that I was the first pupil to be transferred from Keptie Intermediary to Arbroath High School, a rather superior type of school. I think the main reason was because right from the beginning I was very good at French and English, and I think my headmaster recommended I switch courses from what was virtually a junior secondary school where I would have ended up doing joinery or something like that.

At school I was particularly interested in English, French and German; at mathematics I was useless! I did physics, but didn't stay long with physics. As I've said, the career I wanted was journalism.

What sparked off my ambition to become a journalist was simply that I was an avid reader of newspapers. It came no higher than that. I decided the main source of information for any young advancing man was the newspapers and, like my father, I read newspapers voraciously. I haunted the local library because I was an avid reader. That was always the case. My family took the Dundee daily *Courier & Advertiser* and the local weekly *Arbroath Herald*. I think my mother got *The People's Friend*, which I didn't read, and occasionally the *Weekly News*.[2] The corollary to that is that I quickly learned there was no way I'd ever become a reporter unless I had the skills of shorthand and typing. I took this problem to my mum, who'd a big family to bring up and couldn't really afford lessons in shorthand and typing which had to be taken privately, although I got a little of those subjects at Keptie Intermediary School but not at Arbroath High. So my mother said, 'Right, you're the last of the boys', because two of my older brothers were already in work as engineers and the third was a clerk in an engineering firm. So she sacrificed quite a bit to pay for my getting shorthand and typing, and of course I applied myself and got them. In shorthand I got up to around 40 to 50 words a minute – a pass mark was between 40 and 60; typing of course improved with practice. But my shorthand was never my strongest suit, and I couldn't do really high speeds until much, much later in my career.

All this study and learning knocked into my leisure time. So about the only thing I had leisure time for was walking. I had an old paternal grandfather who at that time must have been in his seventies, and he used to say, 'Come on, Colin, we're going for a wee walk.' He'd take me by the hand, and his wee walks were about 15 miles into the country. The one small skill he passed to me was he always said, 'Now don't just look, Colin – listen.' And he taught me how to listen to birds. So I got to know every bird there is and to imitate them, because grandfather showed me how to whistle. So my interests outside my work have been mainly in nature, art and the theatre.

Well, by the time I left school, I'd had some little experience working with the *Arbroath Herald*. Anyway I stayed on for three years and was actually 17 when I left school in 1932. That was quite an advanced age for most working class boys of that time. That was due almost entirely to my mother, who decided that since there was income coming from most of the family except me, she would give me a better chance than they had had. There was a tradition of them handing over their pay at the end of the week and getting their pocket money – and that was it. You had to live with whatever my mother decided you could have, because she was the treasurer of the family.

I wasn't unemployed for any time after I left school. I applied for a job to the *Courier* in Dundee. They said they would keep me in mind, and very shortly after that they called me in. They gave me an interview which involved a general knowledge and a sports test. Fortunately I knew quite a lot about both because, as I say, I was a voracious reader, reading the papers from back to front, not just the news pages but the sports as well. The good thing about D.C. Thomson was you were expected to cover everything – sport, general reporting, specialist reporting, feature writing, what have you. I got top marks in the general knowledge. They took me on right away.

I didn't play sport a great deal myself. I remember one of my first assignments with D.C. Thomson. When you come into the office, there's a book – a diary – which details what your duties are for the day. And when I looked at my spot for that day it was the Scottish Women's Open Golf

Championship at Gleneagles. I went to the chief reporter and I says, 'I think you've made a mistake. You've got me down for the Women's Golf Championship.' I said, 'I don't know the first thing about golf.' And he says, 'What an excellent qualification!' So I was dropped in at the deep end. But I found, not for the first or last time, that if you've got helpful colleagues – that's the secret. And I had Gair Henderson of the *Glasgow Herald*. He was most helpful to me.[3] What astonished me when I went to cover this Women's Championship was that I was the only one out on the course, you know, questioning the players, 'What did you do at that hole and this?' The other reporters were sitting in the clubhouse having a drink, but at the end of the day they produced far better reports than me!

At that time it was a dual thing, because D.C. Thomson had the *Courier* and the *Evening Telegraph & Post*.[4] And you used to do a week on one paper and then move over to the other one. So you got sort of two disciplines: the very urgent discipline of the evening paper, because your deadline was much tighter on an evening paper than on a daily; and then you'd do a week on the daily paper. That was very unusual but that was the way they worked.

When I began at D.C. Thomson I wasn't the only junior reporter there, there was one or two others. And then there were several quite experienced reporters. I would say they had at that time about 20 to 25 reporters altogether. And they had no sex barriers. Women were allowed to work there, too, although there weren't very many good women reporters around at that time. On the two Dundee papers the proportion then would be about 70 per cent men to 30 per cent women.

I can't remember what my salary was when I first began in 1932. But D.C. Thomson paid you well because they wanted good staff. Anyway I wasn't actually greatly concerned about the cash element because I was interested in the career as such. And I must say that if I was giving any young lad a recommendation it would be to go to a paper like the *Courier* or the Aberdeen *Press & Journal* or even a local paper, and get your training right – what you can and can't do in journalism. Because if you make a mistake in journalism it's fatal, you're up shit creek. It's there in black and white. So I felt I had a very good training in the *Courier & Advertiser* and *Evening Telegraph*. In fact, it was a passport to other jobs. If a rival firm knew you'd been trained with D.C. Thomson, you were on a good thing.

But at D.C. Thomson I found there was one aspect I couldn't live with. The 1926 General Strike had taken place just six years before I joined the firm, and it had gone non-union then. I'd lived through the General Strike, but I was only 11 then and I didn't have any memories of it in Arbroath. I didn't know till after I'd joined D.C. Thomson actually that they had a non-union policy. I wasn't strong pro-union or anything like that. But I felt very strongly that the denial of your freedom to be a member of a trade union was something I didn't like, particularly as I grew a bit older and got two or three years' experience. I gradually came to the view that my future, wherever it was, didn't lie with D.C. Thomson for that reason. In the office there were people like me of the same view. One whose name I can't remember now – Harry . . . but he ultimately became diplomatic or political correspondent of the *Daily Telegraph* – at any rate Harry, like so many of the staff and like me, went to the Second War and came back with really strong views about this non-union situation. Journalists were scarce and Harry was told, 'Right. You'll get your old job back at an enhanced salary, but you must not join the union.' And Harry walked out. Now it was his example that impressed itself on my mind. I said, 'Well, here's a very experienced journalist who was formerly chief reporter, and he doesn't like it either.' And after that I decided I was going to get out.[5]

There was no one else who left D.C. Thomson for the same reason, not that I can recall. In fact, some of them stayed for the reverse reason, because they agreed with the policy of non-unionism. But I had the issue impressed on my mind very strongly on the other side of the coin, because before the war when I was a young lad, maybe about 1935–6, there was a big strike amongst the jute workers and I was sent to cover it. I was to cover this particular mill that was out on strike, and it was only then that I discovered that the militancy of the unions could be a very ugly thing as well. When I arrived on the scene I just stood around and began asking questions about what the strike was all about. And of course a group of about 30 or 40 workers on a picket line twigged that I was a reporter with D.C. Thomson, the hated non-union shop, and they actually attacked me physically. I ended up beside a lamp post. I was really fearing, not for my life, but being injured, because they were very, very violent. 'What the f— are you doing here?! Get the hell out of here!' sort of thing. I said, 'I'm only doing my job, the same as you.' So they had me up against this lamp post, punching and hitting me, and I put my arms behind me and locked them on to the lamp post. And I don't know what would have happened. The police didn't appear. It was a woman, oddly enough, one of the workers, stood in front of me and said, 'Leave him alone. He's only doing his job.' And because of her stance I got free. But it was a frightening experience. Despite that, I decided quite early in my career that the unions were a good thing for working people, and that there were people like that who let their minds overrule their hearts.[6]

It quickly became clear to me because of my personal experiences that D.C. Thomson were very reluctant to give wage rises and they were minimal really when you did get them, and you got them on merit only. I was lucky in that respect. I got my wage rises on merit only. But I gradually came to the view that the only way to break this grip they had was to get out of it, or to join the union and get the hell. There wasn't any attempt by Harry or anybody else to form a branch or chapel of the National Union of Journalists inside D.C. Thomson's. But the first thing Harry did later on when he left the firm was to join the union. There was a lot of talk about a clandestine organisation of journalists. But, I mean, the great thing to me about unions is that they are a united thing. The bosses don't understand individual conscience approaches. The only thing the bosses understand and fear is joint approaches, when you all get together and say, 'Here, we're not having this.' There was nothing at all like a united front like that in D.C. Thomson.

We were all working at different rates, as we were paid on merit to some extent. It wasn't entirely a bad scheme actually. But it meant that a lot of people got a raw deal. In fact, very often it was personal dislike – another case of divide and rule. If they didn't like somebody's face, they would make life difficult for them. And I think that's what appalled them about Harry. He wasn't the chief reporter when I joined – that was a guy called Gordon Beattie – but Harry became the chief reporter later. He was a brilliant reporter and, as I say, later on became political or diplomatic correspondent at the *Daily Telegraph*.

*   *   *

Well, when the war came in 1939 I volunteered within a matter of weeks for the Royal Army Ordnance Corps. I thought it would be easy – and it wasn't! As I've said, my two brothers were in the Territorial Army before the war, but not me. I wasn't militarily minded. In fact, I was probably one of the worst soldiers the war ever spawned! The companionship you get in the Forces is about its only good aspect, because stick a rifle in my hand, as they did, and I am away on another planet. I couldn't kill a fellow human being ever and, thank God, I never had to. That was my main reason for joining the Ordnance Corps! It wasn't really a fighting unit. What I didn't realise of course is that all service units are expected to fight if necessary. I never had to. I don't know what would ha' happened if they'd stuck me on the front line and said, 'Shoot a couple of Germans, Colin.' I don't think I could have done it. All my life I've been opposed to devaluing human life. I never considered registering as a conscientious objector, definitely not. I didn't feel as strongly as that. My feeling was that Nazi Germany really had to be defeated. I hated everything the Nazis stood for. I mean, I knew what was happening to the Jews. And that, to me, is one of the most appalling things about this country of ours: they didn't want to know. The politicians of that time were either absolutely thick or they just didn't care. I felt strongly about that. I knew what was going on and I couldn't believe that this country was allowing it to happen without making minimal protest. It's perhaps from that time stems my utter contempt for most politicians. I think politicians are the pits, they really are. I never myself joined a political party. I veered towards Liberalism, but there's a lot of the policies of Liberals, Labour, Tory, I don't like.

Well, I went first for training in the RAOC to Monkton Farley, outside Bath. Monkton Farley is a curious place most people don't know about. It's a hill riddled with caves, ideal for storing ammunition – very dangerous, but ideal. Now we used to work twelve-hour shifts, humping this stuff. An order would come in for ammunition, we'd have to handle it irrespective of time and energy, and we weren't very well fed. I had three guys from Birmingham who were particular buddies of mine, and I said to them one day: 'You know, if this was a union, we'd be on strike because we're working under the most appalling conditions.' They looked at me and said, 'You're bloody right, Colin. Let's have a strike!' This was unheard of. In fact, it amounted to mutiny. So what we said was, 'We're staying down here until we get proper shifts and proper food.' They sent a lieutenant colonel from Headquarters, Army Ordnance Corps, down to us and he gave us a right bollocking about how we were letting down our fellow soldiers at the front. And we said, 'Well, our fellow soldiers at the front are properly fed at least and we're not.' The outcome of it was they improved our food and our shifts. So don't say that rebellion doesn't pay! That no doubt strengthened my trade union inclinations which had already been growing in D.C. Thomson.

Well, that's what the army is all about – co-operation amongst other ranks, because most of the officers, not all of them, don't give a monkey's fart for you or your fellow workers. You're just units, numbers. I got a very strong feeling at that time that if I ever got back to civvy street, which I did, I would join a union.

In the Ordnance Corps I got to the dizzy heights of corporal. I never got any further, for the very simple reason that I couldn't stand a regime in which you were expected to shout and bawl at people. In fact, at this depot somebody decided that the Ordnance Corps weren't sufficiently trained in warfare, that they would have to be retrained in rifle drill and what have you. I was useless at anything to do with that aspect. I was good at the job I was doing, but not at that. So this guy come down, he was a major, got all the NCOs together, which included me, and lined us up on the road through the base. Now the road passed under an overhead pulley scheme which took the ammunition down to the rail depot. We had to get a squad and march them up, about turn, quick march, left, right, left, right, all this crap. When it came my turn I was as nervous as anything because I was no good at it and I knew that. So I lined up my squad. When you give them the about-turn you have to catch them on the right foot. Well, I kept hanging off and hanging off, until to my eternal dismay they were right under this rather noisy overhead thing. Then I shouted, 'About turn!' They didn't hear me and of course just kept on marching. So I had the humiliation of running after them and shouting, 'For Christ's sake, about turn!'

Then after Monkton Farley I was posted first of all back to Scotland on an ammunition dump in Perthshire, then I was posted to the Middle East. It was about the beginning of 1942, for on my way out I heard about the disaster of the *Prince of Wales* being sunk in the Far East. That appalled us. When we heard that we thought, God, the war's over.[7]

The troopship we were on was the *Oriana*. I was the only guy on this ship that could do shorthand and typing, so they got to know that and I got a lot of work in the office. Now in the course of the trip to the Middle East, a young officer volunteered to give a talk to the officers aboard on Germany's Nazism. He had fluent German because he'd lived in Germany from his student days, so he knew what he was talking about. I wasn't present at the talk, but apparently some of the old blimps there were absolutely appalled because the young officer thought Hitler was a good thing for Germany. How an intelligent guy stands up in front of officers and even thinks that, never mind says it, in the midst of a war! So they nailed him for sedition and court-martialled him. The problem with the court martial was that there was nobody who could take notes except me! So I was called into this very interesting court martial in which this young officer was defended, would you believe, by Quintin Hogg, at that time a young lieutenant but later Lord Hailsham.[8] Quintin Hogg didn't get him off, but what he got him was that a report would be prepared and sent to his unit in the Middle East and they would then decide what the punishment, if any, would be. It gave me a fascinating insight on the way the army mind works, because there was this poor bugger who'd stood up and given them what I've no doubt was an interesting lecture, and the next thing he knew he was nailed for sedition. He hadn't been a member of Mosley's Blackshirts or anything like that. I mean, I took a note of his evidence and the guy to me was just an innocent caught unwarily in a trap.[9]

I was in the Middle East two years, based in Alexandria. I was on running ammunition overland twice a week by lorry convoys to the Mersa Matruh–Tobruk area from Alexandria. It was a horrible bloody assignment, because the Stukas quickly twigged that that's what we were doing, and used to attack us quite frequently.[10] They bombed us repeatedly and I lost quite a few of my fellow soldiers whom I'd been with since I joined. I mean, I came up against this dreadful horror I have of seeing dead people, because guys were getting blown up. All the protection you had was to drive into the side of the road or dive under the lorry, and of course the lorry was loaded with ammunition – not the best place to dive! Well, the army gradually broke up the convoys because they were a sitting duck, and they used to send instead maybe two lorries spaced out. So I was lucky to survive that experience. I lost a lot of my mates. As I said, I joined the Ordnance Corps for an easy life, but I didn't have it!

We were overworked because, you know, we weren't accustomed to the kind of temperatures you got there. When you hump ammunition you have to hump it out of lorries, or you've to hump it 15 cases high. We even handled some 9.2 inch navy shells, great big bloody things about four feet long, that you could only roll into position. It was very heavy physical work. I've never worked so hard in my life as I did in the army.

Then, round about 1944, before D-Day, I was invalided out. I got sunstroke and was invalided to South Africa, then I was posted back to this country and discharged. I needn't tell you I was absolutely delighted. So before the end of the war I was a reporter again, on the loose in an area when there weren't a lot of reporters around. D.C. Thomson were very glad to see me back, because they knew I was a fairly experienced reporter and they were short of bodies at that time. But I only came back temporarily to Dundee because they put me in charge of the Perth branch. I loved it in Perth. I thought it was a nice wee city, and I enjoyed my reportorial career there for the *Courier* and the *Evening Telegraph*.

But what was really a turning point for me was an accident in Kinross of all places. One of the things you had to do was call the police and the fire station in Perth to ask if there was anything going on. I was actually in the fire station when a call came through saying, 'There's been a bad accident near Kinross in which a lorry and a car are involved and there's some deaths.' I had no means of transport at that time. It was late at night. So I went to the firemaster and said, 'Look, the only way I can report this is for you to take me up there.' 'Right,' he says, 'put a helmet and a jacket on.' So I was temporarily a fireman, and we got up to the scene of this accident.

It was horrible. A bloke in a car had picked up some guy hitch-hiking and he'd run slap bang on a bend into a lorry. The petrol from the car had spread over both vehicles and the whole thing had gone up in flames. Now lying at the side of the road were four blackened bodies: three from the car, and the driver of the lorry. Although I've seen a lot of bad accidents, I'm not immune from emotions caused by accidents. I decided then and there I was going to change, not my career but my area of work. And I gradually after that came round to the idea of going over to the production side of the newspaper.

So after this Kinross thing I was no longer interested in reporting, and I said to the bosses, 'I want to get out of this.' And they were very good, I must say. They said, 'Right, Colin. You know all about news and you know all the legal pitfalls and things to avoid, and you're good at spelling and correcting errors and that kind of thing.' So they said, 'How about sub-editing?' I said, 'Right, you're on.' The chief sub-editor at that time was John Cameron. He took me under his wing and told me all the ins and outs of typography. I mean, it was a whole new ball game because you had to know about how to measure a story in the space, how to lay out a page, how to give a story prominence or not give it prominence – all this kind of thing. It was a great experience on the other side of the coin altogether in journalism. I'd had no experience of that, none at all, up to then. To me, the sub-editor had been the enemy, the guy that cut your story! So I joined the enemy and took to that like a duck to water, I really enjoyed it. One change on becoming a sub-editor was I was on constant late shift or night shift. But I didn't find that irksome – though later on my wife did! I quite liked night work because it gave you the best of the day in the summer. But my wife had to bring up our family more or less without me, except during the day.

So I was back with D.C. Thomson for a time after I left the army in 1944. But I'd become kind of discontented with the union situation. There was still this business of wages being held down and journalists being exploited by a company which were very good in training but hopeless at public relations with their staff. And I was thinking of getting married. So I decided to leave D.C. Thomson. I was married about then, my wife was a teacher in Arbroath, we got a house in Edinburgh, and we moved. I was disillusioned with D.C. Thomson. They'd done a lot for me, but their whole outlook on inter-union co-operation was . . . They were beginning to change their mind but they weren't changing it rapidly enough for me.

I moved on to the *Evening Dispatch* in Edinburgh in 1945, and that was a whole new ball game. I loved the *Evening Dispatch*. I was just a sub-editor. Don Elliot at that time was the chief sub-editor there, and he was pro-union. It was a union office, thanks largely to Don Elliot, who was a member of the National Executive Committee of the National Union of Journalists. He encouraged all his journalists to become union members. So when I went to the *Dispatch* the staff were mainly in the union. I joined the National Union of Journalists there then.[11] Of course, the *Dispatch* and *The Scotsman* were stablemates. But they had separate staffs – they had nothing to do with each other. Mind you, a lot of *The Scotsman* guys didn't like trade unionism. They didn't want to join a union. There was snobbery about joining a union, you see. So some of *The Scotsman* staff were in the union, a lot of them weren't.

Well, I didn't stay long at the *Dispatch*, because I joined the *Scottish Daily Mail* as a sub-editor when they opened up in Scotland in 1946 with an office in Edinburgh. The *Scottish Daily Mail* was a sort of first venture of a British national newspaper to print in Scotland.[12] That was a new step for journalism in Scotland, and I was delighted to be in on it. Well, during the next 22 years from being a sub-editor I was appointed deputy chief sub-editor, then chief sub-editor, and after that night editor in overall charge of night production of the *Scottish Daily Mail*, and finally assistant editor. There was a staff based in Edinburgh of round about 40 to 50 journalists – reporters and sub-editors.

Most people don't realise that sub-editing's not just a case of marking up copy and correcting errors. Copy pours in from all sides. You're overwhelmed with it and you've got to have guys you can depend on to assess it. So as the years passed and I became chief sub-editor, George MacDougall and Jack Sutherland, as deputy chief sub-editors, and we had to decide what to do with this vast amount. So what I did was: 'Right. You're in charge of the inside of the paper. I'll do the front page and page 2.' And that's about the way it worked. I had an excellent staff and they worked hard. I had two very, very good deputies in George MacDougall and Jack Sutherland, who were very good at their job.

The two main agencies for copy were Reuters, a worldwide organisation of newsgathering – and since those days they've expanded considerably into the electronic era as well;[13] and the Press Association. In addition, you had all your own *Daily Mail* staff in Scotland as well as down in England. So my role as chief sub-editor was to look at the copy and decide what you want for the main pages – page one and two. Page two was normally a foreign news page. Then you decide on your display. What you do is, you get a sheet of paper lined into columns, and you draw a plan and put down on that plan which story goes where. And you get the sub-editors to knock it into shape. You tell them what length the story's got to be. They've got to cut it and rewrite it and fit it into that particular space. So you have to map out the whole paper. The detail is divided between the night editor, the chief sub-editor, who's in charge of the inside of the paper, and his deputy. If you make a mistake – and we all make mistakes – you take the can back.

I'll give you a human interest story which is a reflection on my profession. I had a brilliant, very fast-working sub-editor who had a drink problem. So much so that he used to go to the toilet and hide his bottle in the cistern. And he was a problem to me for a long, long time. I'm the last person to sack anybody and I couldn't bring myself to sack him because he was such a hell of an able journalist and a nice guy. But it came to the point where one night he lost the splash, which is the main story on page one. He'd put it in the wastepaper basket, unwittingly. So I went to the editor and I says, 'We're going to have to sack this guy because you can't depend on him.' And the editor says, 'Right. You sack him.' And I got the job of sacking him. And the guy was shattered. But the funny thing was that the day after I sacked him, his wife come on the phone and asked for me. 'You're the man that sacked my husband?' I said, 'Yes.' She says, 'It's the best thing you ever did.' She says, 'The shock has made him a different man.' What happened to him after that, I don't know. But it was a salutary lesson.

Well, over that period of almost 25 years I was on the *Scottish Daily Mail* there was an excellent reporting staff led by the late Frank Walker, who was the news editor, and there were various others. We had experienced journalists like Charlie McCorry and Ernie McIntyre. In fact, I interviewed Ernie McIntyre for the job. He was a very canny, quiet-spoken but able reporter. You could give Ernie anything, even if it involved the biggest bore of the year – the General Assembly of the Church of Scotland![14]

We occasionally got men up from London who were made editors of the *Scottish Daily Mail*. There was Frank Stefani, but I forget the other one. They were good at their job. But they didn't know anything about Scotland. They thought all you had to do was shovel London stuff into the paper. That was a bad period. But then we got John Blackwood, who was formerly on the *Glasgow Herald*, and he was excellent. He just sat back and let you get on with it. He was the editor in the latter years.[15]

Any journalist who lived through that era'll tell you that all journalists had a great respect for the *Scottish Daily Mail*. I can't remember what the circulation of the *Mail* was, but it was less than the *Daily Express* and it was always less than the *Daily Record*. The *Record* is an example of a paper that is sneered at because it's a tabloid. Actually, I think it's an excellent paper. It has a bigger circulation than all the other locally printed papers in Scotland put together. That either says something for its quality, or it says something for John Public. He wants a paper that he can sit down at the breakfast table and read in half an hour. The *Record* has always done well in Scotland, but, oh, the *Daily Express* was always in the lead.

And then in the 1960s *The Sun* came along. And, you see, there's been an inclination under the Murdochs and the Maxwells of appealing to the lowest common denominator – what I call the morons – of this country. They don't want to read something in depth like *The Scotsman* or *The Independent*.[16] They just want a paper that's easily read and touches lightly upon the politics, even ignores the City, and that's it. We tried on the *Scottish Daily Mail* to raise the tone a bit, but didn't succeed. There weren't enough readers interested.

That was a fatal error, to publish the *Scottish Daily Mail* in Edinburgh. I mean, the Edinburgh–Glasgow rivalry has always existed. Whether we like it or not, the biggest population centre is in the west coast. And if you have a population that buys a certain paper and gets into the habit of buying it, they'll keep on buying it, they won't change. It's very difficult to get somebody to change from one newspaper to another, especially if it's a paper they like and whose views they like. I don't know why the decision was taken to publish the *Scottish Daily Mail* in Edinburgh rather than Glasgow. The London management made the decision. They never explained it. They just thought that here was a big population area that didn't have a locally printed paper: let's have a go. And it took off, the *Mail* really did well to begin with.

But what that new step engendered was one of the most debased episodes in newspaper journalism, namely, the rivalry between the *Mail* and the *Daily Express*. Because journalists from 1946 onwards were called upon to do things that normally they wouldn't have done. There was an intense circulation war. The thing about the circulation war is that they'll do anything, including bribery, to get the story that they want. And journalists were asked to engage in this, as I call it, bribery and corruption aspect of journalism, paying people to tell their stories, paying to collect pictures, and paying them more than the other paper'd pay. I'm glad that aspect has kind of died down, although it'll come back, as sure as I'm sitting here.

You see, one of the big changes I've seen in my time is the advent of [some newspaper proprietors] such as that swine [Robert] Maxwell who stole our pension money. These guys have no principles at all, certainly no journalistic principles, and they're not interested in journalists who have principles. So they have debased the coinage of journalism more than any other person I can think of.

This brings me to another aspect of our society that I cannot understand, and that is apathy. People see what's going on, and they know what's going on – and I'm not just talking about journalists, I'm talking about the public in general – but they don't do anything about it. Why is that? Why do people see the evil things that are happening in this country, its decline into a greedy society, and they don't do anything about it? They cannae even turn up to the polls on a municipal or general election to register their protest. Then they wonder how it happens. The only thing that explains it is, 'Sod you, Jack, I'm all right.' And this is an attitude that has permeated our society in my time. It never used to be like that.

Well, the end of the *Scottish Daily Mail* in December 1968 was interesting in a sense, because annually I organised a dinner dance for the staff and their wives, and it was a great event. We were foregathered for this event and a phone call came through to me from *The Scotsman*, saying, 'We hear that your paper's folding.' I says, 'Well, if you've heard about it I haven't.' And that was how we first learned. Next day I got on to London: 'What's this?' 'Yes, we've decided to close you up. Circulation's not big enough.' I can't remember what the circulation at that time actually was. But it was stable. What it was not doing was catching up with the *Scottish Daily Express*. Of course, after our demise the *Express* and the *Daily Record* grabbed as much of our circulation – and then set off on the same battle, and ultimately the *Record* was winning hands down. Then the *Scottish Daily Express* went the same way as the *Scottish Daily Mail* had gone. But, oh, it was a terrible shock when the *Mail* ceased publication in Edinburgh. There had been rumours from time to time, which nobody believed, because it was a thriving paper and it was a good paper.

The majority of the sub-editors and reporters in the *Mail* got jobs fairly quickly. When I left the *Mail* in December 1968 I went as deputy chief sub to the *Daily Record*. I was offered deputy chief sub on the *Glasgow Herald*, too. But when I had my interview at the *Herald* I got the impression the guys there were dead in the water: I wasn't impressed by any of their interviewers. And – the clinching factor – the *Record* offered me more money. I travelled to Glasgow by train in the winter and by car in the summer: my wife, son and daughter had refused to move to Glasgow! I was deputy chief sub on the *Record* for about four or five years, then I became copy taster. All the copy – Scottish, national and foreign news – comes in through the copy taster and he has to decide what's going in the bucket and what's passed on to the night editor. Copy taster is a very responsible job, really an exercise of journalistic judgement, with about the same seniority as deputy chief sub. Then after about ten years with the *Record* I retired. But they phoned me and said would I like to do reporting in their Edinburgh office. And I enjoyed doing that for a further ten years. But I was getting so bloody old. One night a call came into the office: 'There's been a murder at Sighthill.' So I got a taxi and off I went to Sighthill. When I got there – and I got there before the police – there was a guy lying in the gutter with a knife in his heart, bleeding to death. That Sighthill experience was a bit like my Kinross experience all those years earlier. When I came home late I explained to my wife what had happened. 'Och,' she said, 'you're getting too old for this life. Give it up. Forget the money. Let's just enjoy life.' By then I was 75. So that's what we did.

R.W. (Billy) Munro

I think it was through this aunt of mine who was secretary of the Queen's Club in Frederick Street, Edinburgh, of which one of the owners of *The Scotsman* was a member, that they got me an interview with the editor, Dr, later Sir, George Waters.[1] I can't remember exactly but I must have shown some interest in writing and reading which made my family think that, well, now is there something in that? My family took *The Scotsman* as a daily paper, and I think perhaps this aunt may have said, 'Well, I think I can probably get you an interview.' These things were very much less formal, I would say, in those days. I mean, there was no training – except that when I met the editor he said, 'Well, the only thing you would have to do, you would have to learn typing and shorthand up to a certain speed,' and that was the only qualification required. And he having, I suppose, judged in some way that I'd perhaps fit in, I must have shown some interest in current affairs. So it was in 1933 that I joined the paper.

I was born on 3 February 1914, just before the First War, in the parish of Kiltearn in Ross and Cromarty, north of Inverness and near Evanton. My father was a farmer there at Newton of Novar. But I left there when I was about two or three years old and we lived in Perth till I was about 10. My father was in the Territorial Army, and when the 1914–18 war came he couldn't go overseas because he was very deaf. So he worked in the army record office in Perth. After the war, when the smallholding system was becoming really important in the land fit for heroes to live in – three acres and a cow, and some of the chaps in the army had been promised land when they came back from the war – my father became one of the earliest commissioners under the Board of Agriculture smallholding scheme. He went all round the Highlands particularly. He moved the family then from Perth to Edinburgh, where he was based, and we lived in Polwarth Terrace. Then about 1925 he bought the farm of Hillend, near Lothianburn, at the north-eastern end of the Pentland Hills. But he had to give up the farm in the early 1930s when his Aberdeen Angus herd got foot and mouth disease; after that he was doing secretarial jobs of one kind or another.

My grandfather Munro had been a Free Church minister in the parish of Alness, next to Kiltearn. My mother's father had been a factor on the island of Bressay in Shetland, before he became a factor on the estate near Evanton of Munro-Ferguson, Lord Novar, who was a great forestry enthusiast.[2] So my grandfather knew a lot about forestry as well as general agriculture.

My mother was born in 1882 and married in 1905. She was one of five sisters, all the others of whom were in the professions. The eldest one was secretary, and virtually the founder I think, of the Queen's Club in Edinburgh; another was a doctor and finished her life as a medical missionary in Africa; and there was one in the civil service who was one of the earliest ladies to become an inspector of factories and wrote an official report, which I think is quite a classic, on the truck system in Shetland.[3] They were all unmarried except my mother. Before her marriage she worked for a bit in her father's office at Novar, so she had some secretarial training in that way.

We were five of a family: I had two brothers and two sisters. I was the second youngest, the eldest was a sister, and my younger sister Peggy and I were twins. The five of us were born between 1905 and 1914.

I started at school in Edinburgh. My older sister and my two brothers were at school in Perth, but not me or my twin sister. My first schooling was at home by my mother, who was a very intelligent person. She got some system whereby if you could prove that your children were being educated at home you were excused compulsory education. And I remember learning my alphabet from something like a pack of cards of letters. She taught us to read, and write presumably, at home. So I didn't go to school until we came to Edinburgh after the war. I began at Cranley School in Colinton Road, not far away from our home in Polwarth Terrace. Then I went to Edinburgh Academy.[4] We used to travel there every morning from Hillend Farm by bus. One of the bus conductors, a big red-faced burly chap, used to have us all organised. There was no sitting for us while there were adults on board: 'Up you get.' He sort of ran the show for us. It was great fun.

At Edinburgh Academy I started in the prep and then into the gytes – the first class in the upper school. I think they gave us a pretty good general education. Quite a lot of the masters were English, but it had a very good reputation for its Scottish content as well. There were two or three real very Scots schoolmasters, a chap called Taylor that we called Jas T., because he signed Jas Taylor; and another one, 'Boab' McEwan, was very, very Scots.[5] I remember being interested in geography particularly. And there was one master who spotted that I was interested in writing and he encouraged that. Essays were normally a plague but I enjoyed them. There was one I wrote for one of these English masters, and he wrote at the bottom of it: 'I like your vigour but I loathe your sentiments entirely.' I forget whether there was something particularly Scottish about what I'd written. A school friend and I started writing detective stories, but I didn't write for local papers at all, and I don't think I wrote articles for the school magazine. I just got pleasure from writing, and I've realised since I have a pleasure in words, the use of words and the construction of sentences.

I was a great reader, and started collecting books at the age of about 10 or 11. I still have one or two from 1925. R.M. Ballantyne was my great hero. He wrote about 80 books and I had every one of them. I picked them up in second-hand bookshops. In George IV Bridge there were about half a dozen bookshops when I was a boy, and coming back from school I would zigzag across the street and look in the threepenny trays outside the bookshops. If you went in and asked for a book, they would charge you a big fee for it. But if you kept your eye on the trays outside you could build up a library, and that's how I did it.

Travel was another interest I had, and later on I took to biography, too. History didn't interest me a lot at first, but on my father's side there was an aunt who lived in Bridge of Allan. She was widow of a Provost of Grangemouth who had been a bit of a shipowner. She was always very kind to us, asked us to stay, and took us round all the castles, and I enjoyed that. I mean, Stirling Castle and the window where the king chucked Douglas out, and this kind of thing, the Bruce statue, the Wallace Monument.[6] And so I think I got hooked on the historical business fairly young, largely through this, when I was still at school.

I think I was one of the problem children: I didn't have any particular ambitions. I sat Highers at school but I can't remember what they were. When I left school in 1932 I would be 18, but I don't think I had any clues really about what I wanted to do. I helped my father in an office that he ran for a bit after he had that bad luck with his farm at Hillend. Although it was a mixed farm with stock and crops, he was particularly interested in stock. We used to have rows of first- and second-class winning tickets from the Highland Show up in the byre. But when foot and mouth disease got into the Aberdeen Angus herd, which was his pride and joy, it was a great sorrow to him that he had to give up the farm. So, as I've said, he was doing secretarial jobs of one kind or another, and I gave him a help with that.

*   *   *

Well, you could say it was undue influence perhaps that I was actually interviewed for a job by the editor of *The Scotsman* himself. I mean, there may have been a vacancy. And he may well have said to Lady Harriet Findlay, the proprietor's mother, quite a personality in Edinburgh at the time, 'If you hear of any likely person, I'll be prepared to meet them' – something like that.[7] I wouldn't say it was an influence on the editor's decision, but it might be at least the open door. But I didn't get a job on *The Scotsman* straight away. The editor said, 'Come back to me', or come back to the office, or probably to the chief reporter, James Herries.[8] At any rate I then took a year at Nelson's College in North Charlotte Street and trained in typewriting and shorthand. I may have bashed a typewriter before then in my father's office, but I hadn't tackled shorthand. By the time I left Nelson's I think I was doing 100 words a minute in shorthand. I reckoned I'd got up to the mark that they expected at *The Scotsman*. [9]

So I joined *The Scotsman* in 1933 and was on the editorial staff to 1959, and again from 1963 to 1969. I had not much idea about newspapers and journalism to start with. You learnt as you went along, and for any important occasions you were always out with a senior. The first day I was on the paper I was sent along to see somebody – it may have been James Mollison – about Amy Johnson flying to the Cape. It was some world flight business or something. I didn't know anything about it but I was quite capable of putting down what the chap told me.[10] Something more important I went to early on was when J.M. Barrie was made Chancellor of Edinburgh University. I went along with David Terris, later chief reporter, who became a very good friend of mine and taught me a lot of journalism, to see how it was done. David had cut his finger that morning and couldn't write shorthand. So there was me, just joined the paper, taking shorthand notes of the speech by Sir James Barrie. One of the things he quoted was, 'The wreck of the rough world shall be my fortune or your fortune'. But nobody in the hall – where the acoustics are exceedingly bad – knew whether he said 'wreck' or 'ruck'. But one of these wise guys at the press table said, 'Oh, that's from, not Shakespeare, but from some famous writer. Check it up when you get back to the office.' But I found when I went back to the office that Pope, I think it was, had misquoted it, and the misquotation was just as common as the other version. Still nobody knows what Barrie said! That same day, though somebody else was reporting it, I went to the Assembly Hall and listened to George Bernard Shaw talking about plays. Barrie and Shaw in one day! Shaw was up in the Moderator's chair in the Assembly Hall. He was interrupted towards the end of his speech when somebody went up and whispered to him. We could hear over the microphones, 'Oh,' said Shaw, 'well, they can cut me off if they want.' This was the BBC saying to Shaw, 'You're going over your time'! Oh, Bernard Shaw was a good speaker. Mind you, of the two Barrie was the more sensitive man – a complete contrast. And Barrie probably only said about 20 sentences; Bernard Shaw kept us at it for probably an hour![11]

At first I found reporting quite strenuous and the responsibility worried me. For instance, I used to go every month to the meeting in George IV Bridge of Midlothian county council. Well, I had no real knowledge of what local government was. There were special reporters doing Edinburgh town council regularly and they got to know the members and so on. But I remember feeling my lack of background at the Midlothian meetings. However, at the monthly budget meeting there was always an official came and sat at the press table and helped us, which was very thoughtful.

My shorthand was adequate for all purposes. I don't think my speed went up beyond 100 words a minute. It was very rarely that you had to take a verbatim of anybody. The like of Bernard Shaw and Barrie got verbatim reports, but otherwise you had to summarise. So if you could take down a few sentences this was all that was required. My speed was adequate for most people in public life. It was the Compton Mackenzies who would speak about 300 words a minute and leave you gasping.[12] If speakers complained of being misrepresented it was their own fault. I mean, a man in public affairs, an MP or somebody, got to know that he had to discipline himself to speak slowly both so that his hearers could absorb it and that the reporters could get it down.

There were no hand-outs in those days. A Cabinet minister would come to Edinburgh and speak in the Usher Hall and there was no hand-out to the press of his speech. I remember, for instance, Stanley Baldwin, Neville Chamberlain, Anthony Eden, and so on, if they were speaking *The Scotsman* sent I think it was six reporters.[13] The chief reporter was at the head of the table with a watch, and we each took what we called a take – about three minutes, which was all you could manage at the speed an ordinary politician or lecturer would be speaking at. The *Glasgow Herald* had their team there as well, and the politician or other speaker knew his words were being taken down by these chaps. So while the others were doing their take, you wrote up your three minutes. The result was, apart from the last take, going back to the office the whole speech was ready to hand into the printers, and they set it. You wrote your take in shorthand, then you wrote it up in longhand while the others did their takes, and then you were ready to do the next stint in shorthand. It was a very efficient system. I remember later on, after the war, an important speech by Churchill in Perth. There were a lot of pressmen there and we were assured there would be a copy of the speech for us on the table half an hour beforehand. Then General Smuts died.[14] One of us went along to the Station Hotel to see Churchill. Oh, Mr Churchill was busy writing a little personal tribute to his old friend Jan Christian Smuts and the promised speech wouldn't be ready beforehand as expected. It would be on the desk when we came to the meeting hall. When we got to the meeting hall there was no copy of the speech. I was there with Bob Urquhart, agricultural reporter of *The Scotsman*, who had come for his own interest to hear Churchill.[15] The Edinburgh *Evening Dispatch* man was there, so the three of us made a verbatim team and we took the whole of Churchill's speech down. Churchill spoke beautiful English, and he paused, but the sweat was pouring off us by the end of the evening, and we hadn't got it written up. We had to write it up in the car going back to the office – then we found they already had the speech in the office! Anyway, with a hand-out you always had to check it against what was actually said at the meeting. There was a lot of those kinds of illustrations, I can tell you.

When I joined *The Scotsman* in 1933 there must have been about a dozen reporters. The chief reporter was James Herries, who was a bright chap. He was an art critic, and I remember I used to take the shorthand notes of his articles. He didn't use a typewriter but wrote everything out in longhand or dictated it. You can be very wordy if you're dictating unless you're very accustomed to it, and he used to ramble on rather. But James Herries was a very helpful, friendly chap, a delightful character of many gifts and with an uncanny instinct for being in the right place at the right time – which he sometimes attributed to guidance from the spiritual world: he was in fact a spiritualist. We used to have to go down to the spiritualist society in Albany Street once a week to get a note of what the speaker there had been saying. Herries was the hero of one of the most remarkable bits of newspaper influence on public affairs that I know of. It was in 1930, a few years before I went to *The Scotsman*. There was a great controversy going on about the design for the new government buildings, now St Andrew's House, to be built on the site at Calton. There was a great secrecy in the Office of Works. The fear was we were going to be landed with some ghastly building designed in London. Word got round there was a model of the building in the City Chambers that was going to be discussed by a committee. Photographers were not allowed at committee meetings in the City Chambers. So Herries went up there himself, saw the model, started trying to sketch it but realised he wasn't able to do it. He tried around other newspapermen but none of them felt competent either to draw this model. So he had a hunch he should go back to the office – a hunch he attributed to a spiritualist influence. He thought he would get in touch with some of his architect friends in Edinburgh and ask if they could sketch the model, but it was holiday time and they were all out of Edinburgh. As Herries was walking down the High Street he saw a chap sitting in an old knockabout car sketching the Tron Church. So Herries tapped him on the shoulder and said, 'Would you like a job?' So the chap went with him up to the City Chambers and drew the model and *The Scotsman* published the sketch over half a page the following day.[16] The plan was killed stone dead from that moment. The town clerk was very angry: 'Oh, you're not allowed to draw.' Herries said, 'I know there is a ban on cameras, but there is no ban on drawing.' And they got away with it. Well, that was the influence a daily paper had, and it was the influence that one person by a little bit of initiative and know-how was able to get round the problem. It was a coup. But that illustrates a little bit of the independence then of the individual reporter: here was the man on the spot, not the man at the desk back at the office, deciding what's going to be done. That was the change in my time that I saw in newspapers when in the 1960s I went back to *The Scotsman*.

Among the reporters the oldest one that I remember was David MacKail, the agricultural correspondent. He was constantly smoking a pipe, never had a match, and was always borrowing matches. They all regarded him as an old fogey, but I realised later on that here was a man who had been in *The Scotsman* for possibly 20 years before any of us, and he remembered things. He knew precedents, and if you had the right attitude you could go and say to him, 'Has this ever happened before?' That can be very useful – but it's getting less and less so: I mean, precedents are not regarded with the importance they had in the 1930s.

Another old experienced reporter I recall when I was starting off was George Philip, an awful nice man and a great expert on the Court of Session. Another nice friendly reporter, considerably older than me, was Pip Stalker (I always called him Philip), born in Dundee: jam, jute and journalism, you know. Philip came from the Dundee *Courier* or the *Dundee Advertiser*.[17] One of Philip's jobs was to go along to report a series of lectures being given by the Outlook Tower man, Patrick Geddes, and there was an old usher chap or janitor there. And this janitor said to Philip, 'I see you're going along to this Professor Geddes's lectures every time.' 'Oh,' Philip said, 'I'm just from the Dundee *Courier*, you see.' 'Oh,' said the janitor, 'I'm glad, because there's aye something queer about those that gang wi' Geddes.'[18] But the character round whom all the stories accumulated was Charles Graves, a most distinguished man, who was several times mistaken for the chief proprietor of *The Scotsman*. Charles Graves was a great theatre man, did splendid crits and knew a lot about the theatre, so he always did the main theatre on a Monday evening. One time Frank Moran, the golf man, who was out most of the summer, was on late duty, which meant he was in charge of reporting in the reporters' room for the evening and up to three o'clock in the morning: any emergency, and Frank was responsible.[19] Well, Charles Graves rang up the office about ten minutes before the theatre went in and said, 'Look here, Moran, I'm afraid I shan't be able to cover the King's tonight.' Frank said, 'Graves, you can't do this. I can't get anybody else to go to the King's at ten minutes' notice. It isn't fair. What's the trouble?' 'Oh,' said Graves, 'as a matter of fact, my house is on fire!' And indeed it was. He was once sent down to the Waverley Market in Edinburgh to a circus, and he wrote it up as a sort of dramatic performance. He came back to the office, handed in his copy, and just as he was going out the door said, 'Oh, by the way, when you're going round to the Infirmary,' – we had to go round what we called the calls: the police station, Royal Infirmary, fire brigade, and so on – 'if there's any admission of somebody mauled by a lion, it's perfectly true.' Graves then shut the door and went away! He took the view he was the dramatic critic, he was writing about the circus as a performance, and news was not his affair.[20] But Charles Graves was the only real writer, I would say, in those days on *The Scotsman*, the only chap with a real feel for words. Graves wrote the obituary column. I can't imagine anybody on the staff being able to write as he did, for example, about General Sir Ian Hamilton, who, Graves wrote, had walked with giants, had marched with Roberts from Kabul to Kandahar, and had understudied the Olympic Kitchener.[21] Graves wrote a book of poetry, James Herries, the chief reporter, wrote a book titled *Storm Island* and another, *I Came, I Saw*, and Philip Stalker wrote *The Elephant, The Tiger and the Gentle Kingdom*.

Speaking of obituaries reminds me of the morgue in the office – a series of box files of envelopes with material for obituary purposes mainly, a huge thing that expanded along a whole shelf. When I joined *The Scotsman* in 1933 I was interested in people and people's careers, and one day was looking through the morgue when James Herries happened to come along just as I'd happened on an envelope with details of Ernest Shackleton, the Antarctic explorer.[22] I drew Herries' attention to the fact there hadn't been a proper obituary of Shackleton, and I said to him that the morgue didn't seem to be very carefully looked after. Herries said it was nobody's job at the moment and would I like to take it over? So I was put in charge of it, and that meant cutting out bits from the paper and other sources if I could get them, about people who were likely to be mentioned in *The Scotsman*. I found the work absolutely fascinating. My own historical interests were growing as, later on, *The Scotsman*'s were going down, I would say. But I remember years later an obituary Philip Stalker was doing, and he was having difficulty finding the age of some member of the nobility who had died. He was looking up Debrett, so I said, 'Look up *Burke's Peerage*, it has the exact dates.' 'Oh,' Philip said, 'I never knew that.' And he'd been 20 or 30 years on the paper. An outcome was:

> 'Some things I cannot understand as yet
> and one of them is why the great Debrett
> in dealing with the uncle of a peer
> gives him as born in such and such a year,
> whereas the careful Burke is moved to state
> the year, the month, the all-important date,
> whereby the noble nephews of the nation
> may nicely time each calm congratulation.'

That appeared in *The Scotsman*'s 'Log', which Wilfred Taylor of course did – and that I think was one of the disasters. The Log was started during the war and it was Sir George Waters's idea. At that time so much of newspapers was the same material – dispatches from war events. That was the moment Sir George chose to say, 'Well, now it's time *The Scotsman* started a gossip column.' We were all encouraged to contribute to it – I think we got 7s 6d [37½ pence] for each paragraph we contributed. Then more and more Wilfred Taylor took it over and we were not encouraged to contribute to it. It gradually became Wilfred's column, and he gossiped on and on about his days in St Andrews and so on, and it was rather tedious really at times.[23]

There were women reporters on *The Scotsman* in pre-war days. Elsie Adam was one. She was a lively person, sort of elderly, I suppose a spinster. The only joke I ever remember Sir George Waters producing was when they decided to change the name of a column either from or to 'Women to Date'. He said in his rather sort of gruff way, 'Something essentially dull, Miss Adam, I think.' When I went there she was very inexperienced, but very much doing her own thing. She was liable to be put on any sort of meetings and jobs, as we called them. But she wrote her own column. Well, it was a weekly column I think she did. So the day before that she would probably not have any kind of diary engagement at all. She probably could say to the chief reporter, 'Look here,

I'm doing something or other today,' or, 'I've got my column.' I don't think she was unusual in Edinburgh newspaper circles as being a woman reporter when I first began.[24] There was another woman on *The Scotsman*, and there were two or three assistants who came in: two sisters called Watt, one the editor's secretary, the other I think helped Elsie Adam out. I think James Herries' daughter Connie was on the staff for a bit, too. I also think Lynne Gladstone-Millar was there for a time.

As well as the reporters and chief reporter there was a news editor on *The Scotsman* – Neil Fraser, when I went there, and he didn't decide what were the main news items. Neil was an immensely knowledgeable person – you could go to him and ask him about something, and though he wasn't all that much senior in years, he had a sort of encyclopedic memory and very considerable intelligence and forcefulness. He had very much the editor's eye and ear. He'd just got into the right job. I've often wondered what Neil Fraser actually did.[25]

The editor, Sir George Waters, was very much an indoor man, you had to go to the editorial sanctum to meet him, and it was quite an occasion if you had to go and see the editor. As a young fellow just starting I really didn't come much in contact with him. The only time I had strong words with him was once when – because we used to get invitations to all sorts of public dinners and so on and they were nearly always addressed to the editor but it wasn't expected he would actually go – he did go and I found him wandering around looking at the table plan and he wasn't on it. I'd got his ticket. It's the only time I remember him being rather brusque with me. But we got it sorted out. He very, very rarely went to public events, I rarely saw him at these, and he never spoke. Sir George Waters had a very good knowledge of public affairs and some very firm views. I remember hearing him as an elder getting shouted down in the General Assembly of the Church of Scotland on the matter of Scottish Home Rule, which he was very strongly in favour of, and he carried *The Scotsman* along with him on that subject. Earlier he had got a letter from the moderator of the Church of Scotland, thanking *The Scotsman* for the support it had given to the union in 1929 of the Church and the United Free Church. So he was a sort of *éminence grise* in the background. After Sir George the editor was Murray Watson, a different character, a much more forceful man than Sir George, but less cultured, I would say, less respected in the way that Sir George was. But later on, in the 1950s, when Roy Thomson became proprietor of *The Scotsman*, I don't think Murray Watson could really get on with him.[26]

Then when I joined the paper there would be 20 or more sub-editors. They were dealing with foreign correspondents and home affairs, and there were different desks. The chief sub-editor, a chap called Dixon, was an important person. He was a fairly rough type in some ways: a chief sub had to be fairly ruthless. The staff reporters had a lot of independence then: we wrote our own headings, and within limits decided how long the story was to be. But I remember one of my colleagues went to Dixon, and Dixon said, 'Oh, we're very full tonight. If you cut it by about half, I think.' If our own headings were changed you could go and argue with somebody – not at the time: everything had to be done at the moment, but the following morning you could go and say, 'Look here, that heading of mine, you made a mess of it and the heading didn't say what the story said,' or something like that.

Then at that time I think there were about three or four photographers on *The Scotsman*. Nowadays I find it rather deplorable watching the rat races of photographers sticking cameras in people's faces. It looks awful, but on the other hand they've got to be there. If a reporter misses something he can make up. But if a photographer hasn't got anything in the box, he's had it.

*   *   *

One of the things I enjoyed on *The Scotsman* were general elections. We were all scattered round the country, and each given two or three constituencies to write a sort of review of prospects about. I always reckoned I would see every candidate or go to his meeting or, if I couldn't do either, go to his office and speak to his agent. One of the questions I always used to ask candidates and agents was, 'What do you think is your biggest problem or your best asset?' So I remember going to the Tory agent in Banff, for which Sir Edmund Findlay, chief proprietor of *The Scotsman*, was MP. The agent, a solicitor, looked at me rather sad-faced and said, 'Do you really want to know?' So I said, 'Yes, I wouldn't ask you if I didn't.' The agent said, 'It's the reputation of the sitting member that is our biggest liability, because he doesn't attend.' I think he meant Sir Edmund didn't attend the House of Commons or the constituency meetings, but the House particularly. I couldn't obviously report it in just these words in *The Scotsman*.[27]

But elections were great fun. My first experience of reporting them was in the 1935 general election. I remember trailing over a tattie field to pursue John Colville, later governor of Bombay, who was a farmer as well as an MP.[28] I wouldn't say I wouldn't still walk over a tattie field to meet a Cabinet minister, but then you felt, as James Herries put it, 'in the front seat in the stalls': you weren't on the stage but you were very near it. There you were, sitting perhaps in a little schoolroom, perhaps away out in the country, with the audience sitting at the school desks, and the Cabinet minister having to come and, even if there were only a dozen people, to speak to them and answer questions. I remember James Stuart in Moray and Nairn who, when somebody at a meeting in Banff shouted 'Speak up!', said, 'Oh, I didn't realise anybody was listening.'[29] *The Scotsman* itself was very definitely Tory. But we were left very much to ourselves. You knew that Findlay, the chief proprietor, was a Tory MP, and you knew the paper's attitude to certain things. But I don't remember ever being ordered to give a good show to so-and-so because he's in a difficult constituency, or anything like that.

In those days you were expected to wear a suit and a collar and tie always of course. I would say a dark suit generally, because you didn't quite know what you were going to be landed with until you went in in the morning. There was a diary that was kept marked up by the chief reporter as to who was allocated to the different jobs. You might know the night before, and if there was anything really important you would know the day before so that you could do a little bit of reading up or whatever. Incidentally, the photographers were a bit more informal in their dress than the reporters.

As for working hours, this is one of the problems of journalism. These unsocial hours, as we call them, are pretty damaging to one's social life. *The Scotsman* was not strict about our appearing, say, at 9 or 10 o'clock in the morning. On Mondays, the people who were doing theatres were not expected to be in in the morning at all. The courts began at 10am, and the court man had to be in. I did some court reporting but very little. George Philip and one assistant normally did the lot at the Court of Session and the High Court. For the Sheriff Court I think we depended largely on our sister paper, the *Evening Dispatch* – unless there was a big case on, then the whole lot would be in on it. Fortunately I just missed the Kosmo Club sex scandal.[30] But people would wander into the office about 11 o'clock in the morning, and very often I'd got an hour's work done on some of my own hobby interests before I went into the office. But if you started about 11 o'clock in the morning you'd be working till six or seven in the evening. You were quite likely doing a 7.30pm meeting. And of course there was definitely a risk that you'd spend the interval in the pub. There were a lot of pubs round about Cockburn Street. So there's no doubt this was a menace, and at first, well, I fell for it a bit. I know I took too much in those days. Because of the irregularity of hours and when you're doing nothing and filling in time between one thing and another, that was a common problem for journalists before the war. There was a particular pub where *The Scotsman* reporters gathered. There was one that we used to haunt in Cockburn Street, almost directly across from *The Scotsman* steps, but I've forgotten what it was called. And there was one with a cellar where they were supposed to have signed the Act of Union in 1707. And George Philip was terribly particular. Once the pubs started giving short measure, George would say, 'We'll have to move.' And then the late duty was from 6pm to 3am, and that, once you got experience, was in charge of the reporters' room. There were people out doing jobs, attending meetings or whatever. And if there was an emergency of any kind you had to go out. But normally, well, you were more or less chief reporter and in contact with the sub-editors.

I wasn't invited to join a union when I went to *The Scotsman*. But I remember as if it were yesterday Fred Johnston, who was on the reporting staff of *The Scotsman* and who was at the desk opposite me where we shared a common swivel light, got me into the National Union of Journalists.[31] I think otherwise I'd probably have drifted by preference into the Institute of Journalists. I think, too, it was soon after I went to *The Scotsman* that Fred roped me in. Actually a lot of the time I found it most uncongenial. Don Elliot, a splendid journalist on the *Evening Dispatch*, was the important man in the union. In fact, he would have been president if the office hadn't indicated it wouldn't do – or at least he wasn't allowed to be off as much as he would have needed to be. But I think of Don more as a politician than a union man. To me he was very left-wing and very aggressively so. I wasn't particularly happy in the union. It was a sort of hostile atmosphere. I think the people who supported it and were particularly keen on it were to me hostile to the management, whatever they did more or less. Because of my family background, my father being a farmer, it was the only experience I ever had really of trade unionism. Besides Fred Johnston and myself there were other *Scotsman* reporters in the union. I'm sure though there would be quite a few Institute men among the reporters, too. Then there were some neither in the Institute nor the National Union – the likes of Charles Graves, I should think, couldn't care less. There was certainly no ban of any kind in *The Scotsman* on the union, and nobody ever asked me whether I was or wasn't a member.

And then before the war I was an active supporter for a few years of Scottish nationalism. I think my interest in political issues, which happened to be a nationalist point of view, probably informed and helped my journalism. And as my political views were a bit of a side issue it didn't interfere with my journalism. I mean, one could hold these views without upsetting anyone. I was always made welcome in Labour and Liberal offices, partly I suppose because I was polite to them and, well, they knew that my paper had Tory leanings. I don't think I ever did really find any conflict between my personal political views, which favoured nationalism, and the official views of *The Scotsman*, which were Conservative.

*   *   *

When the war came in 1939 and I, one of the babies on the staff, was aged 25, that was one of the times when I was summoned, on my own, to the editorial sanctum. I remember Sir George Waters saying, 'I don't really want to lose any of my staff.' It was a reserved occupation up to a point, but beyond that point whether he had to drop the proportion I don't know. 'But,' he said, 'I'm afraid I can't really claim that you are all necessary' – and so more or less indicated that *The Scotsman* would not stand in the way when I was called up. Well, I had been in the Officers' Training Corps at Edinburgh Academy and I had a Certificate A, which was more or less reckoned to be a stepping stone to a commission. And I suppose out of a sense of duty, and to some extent because my father was in the Territorials and I think would dearly have loved to have been a soldier if he hadn't been deaf, I put in for interview for a commission. I got an army note back saying to report to the High School Yards in Edinburgh at 8am on whatever date it was. I thought that was a darned funny time to be holding a meeting, but I went along. The place was closed up and there was nobody there at all. So I went back at 8pm and of course the interviewing board were all sitting there in a row. The late A.H.C. Hope (Little Arthur we called him), whose son later became Lord President of the Court of Session, was chairman of the board.[32] When I handed in my notice of calling and pointed out it said 8am, Little Arthur said: 'And were you there then?' I said, 'Yes, sir, I was, but you weren't.' Well, I didn't say it quite as cheekily as that. 'Oh,' he said, 'I don't think we need to ask you any more questions. You're through.' But then I went for a medical, my eyesight was bad and it was classed C3, so that ruled out my getting a commission.

I had to wait then till I was called up in the Royal Army Service Corps and did a little stint in that, during which I became a lance-corporal. I did six weeks' square-bashing first at Ossett in Yorkshire, where we were in an old rag store. It hadn't been very well brushed out. I'm subject to asthma and this got me with the old rag store. If I had gone to the Medical Officer at one point I'd have been back to *The Scotsman* in a brace of shakes. So there was another medical examination eventually, and this one included an oculist. He said, 'You'll be thinking of going for a commission?' 'Oh,' I said, 'I'm ruled out on eyesight.' He took up a piece of paper. 'H'm, C3,' he said, then scored it out and wrote: A1. He knew a doctor in Edinburgh that I knew as well – this is the sort of old boy network I suppose you'd call it. Anyway he'd done a much more careful examination than the first one had been, and he presumably thought that with glasses I could be brought up to a proper standard. What you did with glasses inside a gas mask I never quite knew! So that was that, and I then did a darg at the Officer Cadet Training Unit at Dunbar, where a wild sergeant major gave us hell. I got commissioned in the Seaforth Highlanders, my father's regiment, which he was very pleased about.[33]

I did about four months then with the Seaforths up in Aberdeenshire, including a bit of sort of coast defence stuff. And then they thought the Indian army was going to revolute and all the Indian officers were going to resign. So they took two officers from every battalion in the Highland Division, which I was with, and shipped us off to India on a magnificent Cape liner with a splendid Cape library where I learned a lot about South Africa. We nearly saw Halifax and Brazil on the way round the Cape of Good Hope to India. We had three days in Durban, and in a house up in the brae above Durban I heard Churchill announcing the fall of Singapore.[34]

So we landed in Bombay, and they said, 'Well, what are you doing here?' After a day or so footering around they brought a list and said, 'Now what would you like on this? We've got some boats on the Irrawaddy.' When they heard I'd been in newspapers I got pushed to the public relations. There was an Edinburgh geology professor's son named Jehu who was head of it. He'd been a lieutenant one day and was now a major general in charge of public relations. I was I think three years in India, in Rawalpindi first, then I had some months of press censorship in Bombay and Delhi. So I had a very interesting time in the north-west army. Unfortunately, most of the funny things were happening in the north-east. I was attached to the Indian army. They tried to transfer us to the Indian army. But I thought, well, having got into the Seaforths I'll stick to my coat. In New Delhi Wavell was the GOC first, then Auchinleck. One can say rather grandly that I was on Wavell's staff there, but . . .! Then I was posted to Italy, where I celebrated both VE and VJ Day, and then I was for a bit in the Middle East.[35]

My three years in India cured me of my Scottish nationalism. I saw what a disastrous effect nationalist theory could have. I found myself on the opposite side there. The generations that have grown up since the British empire disappeared have, I think, a very false impression of what the empire was. I mean, I think I've got quite a lot of time for it. My eldest brother was in the Indian Civil Service for 16 years and acted as a magistrate and administrator, but came out at the time India became independent. Of course there were a lot of openings and jobs which, there's no doubt, were very useful from the point of view of the people in this little island. My own brother, well, he'd have been a sheep farmer if he hadn't gone to India, and in fact he went to sheep after the India thing blew up. On the other hand, I think they did a great deal of good in India, too. And the Partition in 1947, particularly the rushing of it by Mountbatten by a whole year, led to disastrous results on the boundary between India and Pakistan.[36] The people who represented the move for independence in India were, to my way of thinking, the worst of them – the resentful ones, the envious ones, perhaps. I know everything wasn't perfect at all in India before independence. But I think that, with the divisions particularly between Muslim and Hindu, and the line that Jinnah took which created Pakistan,[37] they were very much better off under us really. I think probably inevitably independence would have come. But I don't think it would have come in such a divisive shape as it did in the end. I think definitely the British Empire had been a worthwhile institution. We did a lot of good both in India and in Africa and in a good many other places. But my experience in India didn't lead me to join the Conservative Party in Britain, which had traditionally been the great upholder of Empire.

Well, I was in Italy, just outside Rome, for maybe a year or so, as captain and adjutant of a unit where the previous commanding officer and his chief assistant were under open arrest for having, with the best of motives, flogged petrol to the poor Italians in the south of Italy. The chief assistant was actually a photographer and he was marrying, in a Catholic wedding, an Italian woman. The chap who was to be best man was shifted and I, a black Presbyterian member of the Church of Scotland, had to be the best man at this Catholic wedding in Rome! Then in the Middle East, by which time I was a major, I was in Cairo all the time. But I did manage to get a weekend up to Luxor and saw the Valley of the Tombs of the Kings. I had started when I was only eight to keep newspaper cuttings when they found Tutankhamen's tomb in 1922. All my travels during the war were very interesting and satisfying. When I was demobbed from Cairo in 1946 I came back to *The Scotsman*.

I was quite happy to get back and didn't really have any difficulties in settling down. Some people had a worse time. There was one chap, a reporter I think, in the *Evening Dispatch* who had come back as a lieutenant colonel and I think he was very fed up because he had got back to the ranks. Obviously I was not aiming for the editor's job or anything like that. I didn't have any ambitions of that sort and was content to be a reporter, though eventually I did become an editor, but my ambitions didn't grow in that way. The way up was through being a sub-editor. But the sub-editors were indoors men only. A chap with the ambition to be an editor would normally go through this process and graduate to sub-editing. I never fancied sub-editing at all. It was dealing with other people's stuff, and I never fancied it – and very awkward hours of course. I liked meeting people and seeing what happened and writing about what I saw and heard. And then for my part, I don't think I would ever have fancied the kind of rough and tumble journalism really, and I may have sort of fallen down on that because soon after I came back I was technically chief reporter. I took over from David Terris, though I forget now when.[38] But by that time the job of chief reporter had really disappeared because the news desk ruled the roost and reporters were just sent out and told what questions to ask, and that sort of thing. After the war the situation had changed. However, I did some liaison with St Andrew's House and went up every day to the press office there and sat in on most of the early Labour government press conferences. Joe Westwood was the Secretary of State for Scotland, then Arthur Woodburn. Arthur Woodburn wasn't too bad but Joe Westwood was really hopeless. I remember he was giving a speech at the opening of Tulliallan Police College. He had the script there, obviously hadn't had time to look at it, and was just reading it by rote and lost his place completely. He said he had had many years of experience of the police, 'but never once in their hands'. I think Joe Westwood was the father virtually of the new town of Glenrothes. A namesake of mine, Captain D.J. Munro, used to write regular letters to *The Scotsman* and said, 'Call the town after its father, Westwood Burn.' Of course Tom Johnston was a great asset in many ways and I saw a lot of him in connection with the Hydro Board. So after I came back from the war in 1946 I remained as a general reporter with *The Scotsman*, doing much the same kind of work as I'd done before. I never specialised, though specialisation was beginning to come in then, people were drifting into it; but I preferred general reporting and managed to keep out of it until 1959. Well, though I had no hesitation at the time when I came back from the war and didn't consider trying any other occupation, I think I should have actually. I think it was a mistake to have gone back to *The Scotsman*.

By 1959 Roy Thomson had taken over *The Scotsman* and Alastair Dunnett, who had previously been with the *Daily Record*, was editor. Things by then had changed so much that I obviously was not fitting in. There were times when I was overruled by the people in the desks in the office. The freedom we had, the influence we had on what our own first-hand knowledge produced, had disappeared. I remember somebody at the desk said to Bob Urquhart, the agricultural editor, a very experienced chap, very much senior to the man at the desk who said to him: 'Well, ask the chairman of the . . .' – the National Farmers' Union or whatever it was – 'what his views on this are.' Bob said, 'There's no point in asking that man. It's perfectly obvious what his views would be.' 'Oh,' the chap at the desk said, 'of course if you won't ask the question I'll have to get somebody who will.' So I think the new regime at *The Scotsman* might have – I wouldn't say would have – given me the push. At any rate Alastair Dunnett, when he spoke to me about moving from *The Scotsman* to the *Highland News*, which Roy Thomson had also taken over, sort of indicated there wasn't much future for me in *The Scotsman* – a conclusion I was by then reaching myself, though I hadn't taken it to the point of applying for jobs outside *The Scotsman*.

So in 1959 I went from *The Scotsman* in Edinburgh to become editor-in-chief of the Highland News Group in Inverness. When Thomson took over the Highland News Group, rather surprisingly, and to their credit, they seemed to think somebody with a knowledge of the Highlands would be an advantage there. Well, to me, it was an interesting world there because Inverness did not know an editor. The *Highland News*, founded about 1890, was definitely the infant. It had started really as a radical paper. The rival *Inverness Courier*, founded in 1817, the same year as *The Scotsman*, was the one that was always called 'The Paper': you know, 'Let's have something in The Paper.' Yet during the Battle of the Braes in 1882 the *Courier*, pro-landlord, was burnt solemnly in a cave in Skye every day.[39] But the editor of the *Courier*, Evan Barron, an old boy who'd been an infant at the time of the Battle of the Braes, lived in Nairn and never came to Inverness. He always discussed his leader with Jim MacKay, his chief reporter, on the telephone, and fixed it up in that way. But I don't think Evan Barron was ever in Inverness in my time. He was very much his own man. His leaders were marvellous. Evelyn Barron, his daughter, was never called editor, but she was in charge. I remember when I was editor of the *Highland News* I was once in the *Courier* office looking at one of their old files, I think for my historical things. I was up at the top of a ladder in their outside office. Miss Barron came in and looked up: 'Surprised to find you here, Mr Munro.' 'Oh,' I said, 'I always get a very nice welcome here, thank you, Miss Barron.' And I did. I got on very well with them all. But to me, to be an editor meant something, and I think to one or two other people it meant something, too. So I was the only editor in Inverness. Evan Barron completely ignored me. I'd met him once or twice before: his brother and my father knew each other. Once a year the Barron Trophy was presented to the journalist in

Inverness who had done most for the profession during the year. And in the last week I was in Inverness with the *Highland News*, as my replacement or disappearance had been announced, the committee, apparently with Barron's permission, agreed to the trophy being given to me. And Barron asked me and Jean, my wife, out to lunch – the first time that he had paid the slightest attention to me. Once I was on the way out he was prepared to acknowledge my existence![40]

So the *Highland News*, even in 1959 when I became its editor, was still the new boy. I never found anybody particularly critical of it and didn't find myself embarrassed by that view. But there's no doubt which paper was what they all regarded as 'The Paper'. It was an interesting process being editor, seeing you had to fill your front page every day with something, whether it was the vegetable show or a disaster. So it was a bit different from *The Scotsman*. One of the things that I never quite could find acceptable at the *News* was that there were very few letters to the editor: a guide to what people think of as their own paper. And the *News* was definitely thin, very thin, compared to the *Courier*.

We published the *Highland News* the day before the *Inverness Courier*, which was deliberately provocative. The *Courier* came out two days a week. The *News* tied up with the *Football Times*, which was a Saturday paper. I've never taken the slightest interest in sport, so the *Football Times* was a dead loss to me, I'm afraid. Then Thomson's Highland News Group, of which I was editor-in-chief, also had papers in Dingwall, Forres and Thurso. The Thurso paper was quite interesting to me, and we used to go up to Caithness now and again. But these amalgamations were an unsatisfactory arrangement.[41]

I got on well in Inverness, enjoyed the place, and knew a lot of people up there. I think we were making something of the *Highland News*, too. Working on this weekly paper I got to know the nuts and bolts of newspaper production that I did not need to know working on a daily paper like *The Scotsman*. On a daily paper you don't need to know how it's done, how it's produced, at all. I liked to go round *The Scotsman* and I had friends in all the departments, so I got to know myself and saw the paper printed. But as a reporter you didn't need to know at all. On the other hand, when I went to Inverness, the very first night I had to pass the paper for printing. The type was set up for each page on a big solid desk table and there was no way of getting a page proof. You got galley proofs as the different stories were set up. But when I went there you never saw a proof of the whole page. My predecessor as editor I wasn't allowed to meet (he was out before his successor was allowed in, this was Roy Thomson's idea). So I was confronted that first night with having to read type upside down and back to front. I remember I pointed to a heading in the middle, 'Ice Siege in Badenoch', where there was then a very heavy eight inches of frost. So I pointed to the word 'siege' to the chief compositor and asked, 'Is that spelt rightly?' I can spell pretty well usually but 'siege' and 'seize' is one of my problems. So they all stood back and waited for my editorial decision! I knew there was a book-shelf in the office, which I'd taken over only that morning, so I hurried through to look for a dictionary. There was no dictionary. There were three volumes of an encyclopedia but they didn't go as far as 'S'. But there was a Bible, and having been well brought up I looked up Jericho and found out how to spell siege.

My understanding when I went to Inverness was that I was to be the editor of a new daily paper. But there was some confusion because when Thomson bought some of the Kemsley newspapers I don't think they realised they had in the bag as well the Aberdeen *Press & Journal*, with which a daily paper in Inverness would be competing. So the daily paper in Inverness never emerged. That made the Inverness job even – well, I wouldn't say necessarily more attractive, but at least more important.

After three years and some months with the *Highland News*, I came back again in 1963 to *The Scotsman* in Edinburgh. They gave me a presentation in Inverness which I still have – a briefcase. I remember hearing this manager, my colleague, in a separate room the door of which had been left ajar, making some remark about, 'Of course, we're not making it obvious that he's been asked to go!' So moving from Inverness was certainly not only my choice. There was a general manager sent in whom I did not get on with. He overruled me on one occasion and deleted a whole lot of material from one issue of the paper against my wishes, and I made that quite plain. So I think he probably recommended my removal back to Edinburgh.

Oh, hire and fire was a Thomson operation. This general manager was the successor to Sandy MacRae, Provost of Dingwall. Sandy had been general manager of the *Highland News* because he was proprietor of the Dingwall paper which the *News* had taken over. We got on quite well together, and he was a good local provost. Sandy, however, got a notice one day that his appointment as general manager of the *News* was at an end, that he would not come in the following day, and that arrangements would be made for his desk to be cleared. So Sandy came to me almost in tears and showed me the letter. I said, 'You can't accept that. You're the Provost of Dingwall and people will think you've had your hand in the till.' He was very grateful to me, though I was his junior strictly speaking. But I said, 'This treatment may be all very well in London or in Toronto, but it will not do in Inverness.' That kind of treatment in a small town would have looked exceedingly bad. So Sandy objected, and they relaxed the thing in some way and gave him three days, or some proper notice anyway.[42] But I think this was the kind of way the Thomson organisation worked. I remember Roy Thomson, when they took over *The Scotsman*, going round insisting on meeting all the telephone clerks, which was a good line: 'I'm Roy Thomson. Meet my son Kenneth.' Then one day a notice appeared above the desk diary: 'Editors will write on one side of the paper only. They will type in double spacing.'

Back at *The Scotsman* I carried on working as a general reporter. There was a good deal more of contact with St Andrew's House, daily calls there, and a good deal of national news handling. Another job I contributed to then was *The Glorious Privilege*, the history of *The Scotsman*. Magnus Magnusson was the nominal writer, but in fact it was half a dozen of us: Robert Warren, who edited *The Weekend Scotsman*, was a leader writer, and wrote some of the crosswords; Philip Stalker and David Terris did the modern stuff; Matthew Moulton took a stint; and I took the earliest period because I was interested in historical things by then. Magnus Magnusson wasn't in it at all at first. It was when Roy Thomson took over *The Scotsman* he'd said it was time to have a history of the paper, and this group of us, less Magnusson, divided the work between us, with encouragement from Murray Watson, then the editor. But then for some reason it fell on evil times and was never produced. It just lay in type-script, and then somebody – I don't know who – reactivated it and said, 'Look here, this must be produced.' Magnusson, a very able chap, with whom I kept up a friendship, was given our copy and he improved it a lot. He brought a unity into it and gave quite a lot of his own distinctive ability to it. But fortunately we, the ones who had written the thing, got wind of this, and I remember getting my contribution back, and quietly and without comment, restoring some of the things that Magnusson had slaughtered![43]

So that from my return to *The Scotsman* in 1963 I was at first at least more my own master – except that if there was a big news story this blinking desk'd send somebody else supposedly to help. It was getting less and less attractive a job. I was getting more and more things taken out of my hands, and I suppose they were quite glad to see the end of me. Well, honestly I was glad to see the end of them, too. By that time I'd been with *The Scotsman* for 36 years, apart from war service. I wasn't entirely sorry to give it up and take some sort of early retirement. Unfortunately, the financial arrangements probably weren't as good as they might have been. I did get the best advice I could within the firm from the company secretary, who was an old colleague and I'm sure gave me the best advice he possibly could.

I didn't actually put in my notice until I'd fixed up with the Edinburgh educational publishers W. & A.K. Johnston to work on editing a completely new edition of their *Gazetteer of Scotland*. With a fairly wide knowledge of Scotland, I knew my sources and could turn up where to find all the new industrial centres or water and hydroelectric schemes, and all the rest of it. I was working on contract to Johnston, or Johnston & Bacon as they became, as a freelance. There was another thing I fixed up with Johnston's: *Kinsmen and Clansmen*, about clan history. My wife Jean and I collaborated on some books, and a history of Tain took us quite a while.[44] I enjoyed this kind of work, and, as I've said, the historical side had been interesting me more and more at the time when *The Scotsman* was less and less interesting really. Whether I was ever entirely fitted for newspaper work I'm not quite sure, except that it did give me an outlet for my writing interest and my interest in public affairs. But I don't know that I'm really a newshound in a way and certainly in the conditions as they are now. I'm thankful to be able to dissociate myself from it quite honestly – which is a sad thing in a way to say about one's own profession. But it's not one to be proud of now, I'm afraid. So I have no regret at all about having given up *The Scotsman* in order to concentrate on more creative writing.

Tom McGowran

I wanted to be a journalist, from quite an early age. My mother encouraged me in this really. I think it was the encouragement I got when I wrote essays. They seemed to think that they were good. And if you get encouragement like that, then you tend to want to go along that path.

I was born on 2 May 1918 at 5 Annfield, Newhaven, then a wee fishing village on the Forth, just outside Edinburgh. My father, born in Leith about 1893, was an apprentice engineer with Henry Robb, the shipbuilders there. During the First World War he was an engineer aboard oil tankers, which I imagine must have been a pretty hairy experience. Then towards the end of the war he went ashore at Tampico, on the Gulf of Mexico, to take charge of a department in the oil refinery there operated by British interests. It was known as Agila Mexicana, Mexican Eagle. I think Royal Dutch Shell also had an interest in it. The refinery was expropriated by the Mexicans about 1932, and it was rather amusing to find six months later the Americans were operating the factory! So my father retired from that job about 1932 and came back to this country. He bought himself a small engineering shop and used to tinker about in that, but he had a very generous pension by which he was sufficiently well provided for. He often told me that if you want to make real money – this was true of his generation at least – you had to go abroad to work.

My mother was born and brought up in Newhaven. From the age of 11 she was a seamstress, because her mother had been widowed with four children when she was only in her thirties and had to bring up all four. So the minute my mother was of age she was put out as a seamstress. They used to work something like 16 hours a day at their sewing machines. The result was that my mother could make a sewing machine do anything. She did some most elaborate and beautiful tapestries and all sorts of things on a sewing machine. She could make it talk.

The Newhaven people would have abhorred the thought of marrying a Leither. There was a very strict code there. The economic reason behind it was that the Newhaven womenfolk took a very active part in the life of the fishing community and had to have the skills necessary. If a Newhaven man married a Leith girl, it was reckoned that she would be useless. So there was no intermarriage, or very little – oh, it was *infra* dig. – though they were two adjoining communities with only a bridge between them. I think you'll find that is true of all the fishing communities round the coast, right up as far as Peterhead and beyond. They were very closed communities. There must have been a hell of a lot of interbreeding. But my mother did break away in that she married a Leither. She was the daughter of a fisherman. There was a long line of fishermen in her family. That's really what put me on much later to writing a book about it. I went to one of these summer school courses on tracing your ancestors and ended up writing a book about fishermen of the Forth.[1]

My grandfather McGowran was an engineer with Bruce Peebles in Edinburgh.[2] My granny – my mother's mother – worked as a fishwife. She bought a house in Prince Regent Street, Leith, but she would leave her house in her best togs, go down to Newhaven to work, change there into her fishwives' clothes, and never let the Leith folk know.

I was the oldest of three brothers. My brother David, 18 months younger than me, became a doctor; my brother Al was nine years younger than me.

When my parents got married they had their own house in Annfield, Newhaven. In Newhaven in those days it wasn't uncommon for people to have their own houses, not rented but actually own them. I have no recollection of Annfield as a child. I was three when I left there to join my father at Tampico in Mexico and I was at Tampico till I was about 11 in 1929. I came back then to attend secondary school. Up to that point I hadn't been at school: my mother taught me at home, and I did a great deal of reading. *The Water Babies* was my favourite book, but I also recall reading *Don Quixote* and Nathaniel Hawthorne's *Tanglewood Tales*. I don't recall *Don Quixote* as hard going and I still remember the story quite well.[3] So my mother provided tuition herself in English, helped me with grammar, syntax, spelling, and encouraged me to read and write. Spanish of course we picked up because we were living with native people – servants, and that sort of thing. We had our own sizeable house provided by the oil company, with servants. It was natural for white colonials then to have servants all over the empire. That's what was the difficulty when you came back home: you found you couldnae afford the servants you'd had out there. But the maths and science side of my early education was a difficulty, as my mother wasn't able to teach me them. So I had no grounding in them, nothing at all. And my father was always very busy, led a busy life, and left it to my mother. After I came back to Scotland in 1929 I remember the headmaster coming in on one occasion with the results for the maths exams. 'Now, boys, guess who's first in maths?' And some idiot shouted: 'Tom McGowran!' The headmaster said, 'No, no. We're starting at the top, not the bottom!' Many years later, when I did the management course at Heriot Watt College in Edinburgh, we had one year of statistics and there was a hell of a lot of Higher Maths in that and that just about drove me up the wall. But I actually came out then second in the exam. I tended not to look at things as conventionally as some other people because of my unconventional background. But I don't think that educationally I ever found a disadvantage in having spent my boyhood in Mexico.

I certainly found in Mexico an early interest in creative writing, and my mother encouraged that. When I returned home in 1929 and went to Daniel Stewart's College in Edinburgh they put me in a class based on a general examination they'd given me. On the basis of my writing, I shot over two other classes the following year. So writing seemed to come easily. History and geography followed naturally, I picked them up. But beyond writing I didn't seem to have any academic qualifications, and one subject I really found difficult was maths. I could never understand the importance of maths. It was so obvious to the teachers that they didn't think it needed explanation of course.

But I fitted in fairly quickly at Daniel Stewart's. Where I did feel completely different was that in America at that time kids wore long trousers. Now I turned up on the first morning at Stewart's in long trousers. That was a definite clanger. It took a while to live that one down! You could wear long trousers when you were more senior, but not in the first year. I quite enjoyed my time at Stewart's. I was keen on sports, took part in rugby – the third XV, and swimming was a great thing, and I used to take prizes for diving when I was in the Scouts, and followed that up later by doing a lot of scuba diving.

As a boy at school I wanted to be a journalist. There was nobody in the family who'd gone into journalism. I left Daniel Stewart's when I was 15¾. And my father apprenticed me at Bruce Peebles where his father had been, because he wanted me to be an engineer. That was quite a traumatic change for me. The alternatives didn't present themselves. The engineering was there. There was no suggestion that there might be an opening for journalism. I accepted my father's decision. I liked working with my hands. I wouldn't say I actually shuddered at the whole experience at Bruce Peebles. Well, it didn't last long: about three months. The ambition was still there to write, so when I saw the opportunity arise through an advert in the press I took it. My life has been a succession of violent changes, so that I've got into the habit of taking them as they come!

The advert was for a copy boy in the Edinburgh *Evening Dispatch*, I applied and got an interview, and started there on my 16th birthday in May 1934. It would be David Glenn, the chief reporter, and Robert Leishman, his assistant, who was on the *Dispatch* for many, many years, who interviewed me.[4]

My first pay as a copy boy was 10 shillings [50p] a week. The hours were 7.30am till 4.30pm, because the *Dispatch* was an evening paper so you tended to finish early. I worked all day Saturday, too. We would normally have had a Saturday afternoon off, but of course that was a busy time with the sport. Sports stuff just used to flood in and you'd be glued to a telephone on a Saturday afternoon taking down results from all your correspondents. What we did in advance was to cut the names out and paste them on to a piece of paper so all we had to do was fill in Arniston Rangers 0, Somebody Else 1. You would either take down in shorthand the reports that came in and take them along to one of the other chaps who was doing the typing, or you'd take it down yourself straight on to the typewriter.

I had no shorthand when I started in the *Dispatch*, so I went to the Royal High School evening classes to learn it. But I invented a method which I haven't heard of anybody else using, of learning to picture an outline alongside its word, simply writing down the shorthand word on top of the printed word. And we'd go down the column just writing it all out, and it tended to form an association. Anyway I learned shorthand fairly rapidly – but not very well! I would say my speed at the very top was 120 words a minute. Typing never presented the least difficulty, and even now I keep up my touch typing all the time.

As a copy boy you were really a bit of a message boy. You'd be sent up to the Sheriff Court to bring back the copy for the first edition. Or it might be at the General Assembly you'd sit behind the *Dispatch* reporter and bring his copy down to the office. As the trial or meeting or whatever was progressing, the reporter'd be writing his report simultaneously. I always thought this was quite a skill because there was a good deal of condensation required and he'd no opportunity of backtracking and saying, 'Well, I could have done that better.' So that was the copy boy's principal job, and going down to the press room, collecting copies and taking them round all the desks in the office. The *Dispatch* in those days ran I'd say maybe five or six editions each day. The first edition came out in the morning. Of course the race results were the important thing, so I think the last edition came out about teatime.

I think there would be about five of us copy boys on the *Dispatch*. You gradually worked up. After a couple of years you'd move on to the next stage – the tubes. The tubes were these pneumatic tubes you'd sometimes see in department stores for sending change round the place, but in the *Dispatch* they conveyed the copy. Robert Leishman's job as assistant chief reporter was to sub-edit the staff reporters' copy. It didn't go through the sub-editors, who dealt with the agency copy coming in and that sort of thing. There were about half a dozen sub-editors. Don Elliot and Archie Meldrum were the two principals on the editorial subs' table, and there were three other subs there. The sports department had three sub-editors – Lawson, Cairns and Robson. The tube boy took the copy from them, or got the copy down the tube from the Creed room upstairs.[5] And I invented what to me seemed simplicity itself but was regarded as a great leap forward. I put an aluminium strip along the edge of the counter so that as tube boy I could tear the paper instead of folding or cutting it, and there was great rejoicing about it! It was much quicker.

After the tubes you went on to the phones. Well, when the phone rang you'd put the earphones on and get your typewriter. The *Dispatch* had correspondents all over, and it might be Innes, Cupar, from Cupar in Fife: 'This is Innes, Cupar. Today's stories for you.' You'd sit there and simply type them up. And that's what you were doing for a good part of the day. You weren't entirely employed on that, because you had periods between phone calls, but you weren't sent out to collect copy: the copy boy was the lowest rung in the kind of hierarchy or grading of boys.

All this was before the age of cynicism. The reporters did enjoy their work and they felt they were in a sense the lords of creation. It was a prestigious job in those days, as you see from the films made around that time: the reporter was usually the hero. It's very much a different picture nowadays. But then it was a prestigious job, and there was generally a sort of constructive friendly atmosphere that I as a young lad found encouraging. And the reporters helped you a great deal, took an interest in you, and encouraged you.

When I began in the *Dispatch* in 1934 there'd be about 10 reporters. I've mentioned David Glenn, the chief reporter, and his assistant Robert Leishman. I remember Bill Garden, whose son Neville was later a music correspondent. Then there was Bill Aitken and Robin Stark, Stokie Johnston, Bill Johnston, and Pat Garrow. And, it might be by 1935, there were a couple of women reporters. One was Lorna Rhind, a regular reporter, though she might have concentrated on women's interests.[6] The other woman was a rather ladylike person, a bit aloof. I can't remember her name at all. She was a very attractive woman but kept herself a bit separate from the rest of the reporters.

The editor of the *Dispatch* when I was there was called MacLachlan, a delightful old boy with flowing white locks and a huge bow tie, an absolute gentleman. I remember one reporter saying, 'Who's going to tell the old boy that his leg's being pulled?' Because there was a series of letters in the paper all about blue tits. I won't go into details but this thing got more and more outrageous. Everyone must have known except old MacLachlan, who did the choosing of the letters. Somebody finally must have told him because the series ceased like that![7] I, of course, had no sooner started as a copy boy aged 16 than, uninvited, I was writing leaders for the paper. MacLachlan was very understanding about it. He'd take a little bit out maybe and insert it as a leader. He was the leader writer, but he didn't want to discourage me. He'd call me into his office and say, 'Now look, you should put it this way.' But I gradually got the picture: it wasnae my job to write leaders for the *Evening Dispatch*! I should have got my arse kicked, but he was quite encouraging. It must have been unique in journalism for a copy boy to be contributing to the leaders. From my point of view as a trainee journalist, however, it was a marvellous experience.

Between the *Dispatch* and the Edinburgh *Evening News* there was keen competition. The *Dispatch* was the middle-class paper – rugby and all that sort of thing. The *Evening News* had the big grip on Edinburgh, it was the paper that really got down to the folk, with a much bigger circulation and more advertising, too. On the *Dispatch*, I think there was a kind of snobbery about it: we quite liked being the paper of the middle classes, even if we had to give up circulation for it! But between the *Dispatch* and *Evening News* reporters there was a good deal of camaraderie. They didn't really try to scoop each other. They might be at a Trades Council meeting[8] and there'd be an agreement, they'd say, 'Well, what about it, chaps? Will we put our pencils down now, or . . .?' One wouldn't stay behind and see if he could get a scoop on the others. If one did that it would build up. So I don't recollect any cut-throat competition among the reporters themselves. Post-war it was a different story, but not then. We were all in our little niches and we were content to stay there.

As a boy you'd have to hang on on the phones until there was a vacancy, then you'd go into the editorial team as a junior reporter. That's what happened to me. About the end of 1938 I went not into the *Dispatch* but *The Scotsman*, its sister paper that shared the same building, as a junior reporter. I had no regrets about leaving the *Dispatch* after four and a half years; on the contrary, moving to *The Scotsman*, a more prestigious paper than the *Dispatch*, was promotion!

But *The Scotsman* proved to be a very limiting job, a fairly menial one, a sort of rubbish job really. There might be a political meeting which nobody wanted to go to and you'd go along and do a paragraph of about an inch on it. If I went to the theatre to do a review it was a play nobody else wanted to do. And then as a junior reporter you were still answering phones, and the reporters gave you stuff. I didn't find it very satisfying work. By then I had a very strong ambition eventually to get to Fleet Street. You were expected in those days to go out from your training paper in like Edinburgh or Glasgow and get experience in weeklies. You'd do a stint there and then, if you were lucky enough, get into some big paper in Fleet Street. Many people did this. It was very much my inclination to move from *The Scotsman* to a weekly paper because of the width of experience you got. So *The Scotsman* job wasn't any great shakes. Of course, it led on if you were prepared to wait. Well, I was impatient. So when I saw a job advertised for a junior reporter on the *Falkirk Herald*, a paper I never even knew existed, I applied for it and got it. It wasn't that I had to get this job in the *Falkirk Herald*, it was simply that it presented itself, looked a better job than the one I was doing on *The Scotsman*, and I moved on. What may have helped in getting me the job at the *Herald* was the fact that Fred Johnston, the owner, himself had been at Daniel Stewart's College.[9]

Junior reporter meant a lot more on the *Falkirk Herald* than in *The Scotsman*, because at Falkirk there wasn't a large staff when I joined it in June 1939. Well, it was a big staff for a local paper: there was an editor, a chief reporter, a senior reporter, a less senior reporter, and myself. We'd no photographers. We bought in a local commercial photographer, who used to have one of these ruddy great magnesium flashes which persisted until after the war. The editor was W.C. Murray, who seemed to be ancient to me as a young lad. His father had been editor before him, though there wasn't any general hereditary element in the editorial department.[10]

The sorts of jobs I did as junior reporter at the *Falkirk Herald* were the Police Court of course daily, and interminable meetings at night about which you had to turn out virtually a verbatim report. The meetings might be of the council, or political meetings. I know that reporters now, especially on a weekly paper, don't like evening assignments. But in those days you would attend anything that was on. The hours were long, but then it was relaxed. You might start at 9.30 or 10 in the morning, and in time for the Police Court. Then you might go on to the Sheriff Court, though the senior man would probably be doing that. Then it might be a meeting, which would be held during the day, of the county council in Stirling, though there again it would tend to be a more senior reporter who went there. You might go and interview some local worthy or other, or somebody about an accident. That was the type of work we were doing

– unimportant in a sense, but quite wide in range. That period is all a bit vague now in my mind because it only lasted a very short time, from June till the beginning of October 1939, when I volunteered for the army.

My pay was £2 10s [£2.50] a week. My father said that was far too little to live on. But actually I managed quite comfortably on it, and even managed to buy a gramophone record every week. As I recall, classical records then were not all that cheap at about 5 shillings [25p] each. But I know that Woolworth's, which had a shop in Falkirk, were selling popular records for as little as 3d [1¼ pence]! I was in digs in Falkirk. My mother was unhappy about that: she'd have preferred me to live at home. In those days they didn't expect you to leave home practically until you got married. But by this time I was 21, and also it was much too expensive and time-consuming to travel home. I suppose every youngster wants to try to see if they can fly the nest, although I wouldn't say that was the principal reason in my case. So in Falkirk I had digs where I had quite a comfortable room to myself, and only about 50 or 60 yards away from the office. I went home more or less every weekend.

I joined the National Union of Journalists in Falkirk more or less as soon as I went there. I think in the *Falkirk Herald* you were required to join. It wasn't a closed shop, in the sense you could be in the Institute of Journalists if you would. The other fellows in the *Herald* were all members of the NUJ. It was just one of those things that was expected. It didn't carry any political significance. I mean they wouldn't let you in if you weren't a bona fide journalist, so it was a badge of office. Personally I had no qualms at all about it. I tended to be a bit pro-unions, though I hadn't joined a union in either *The Scotsman* or the *Evening Dispatch*.

In Falkirk at that time there was a lot of poverty, a lot of unemployment, and a lot of street gangs. There was one street gang which threatened on one occasion to beat us up because we'd reported one of their members in the Police Court. They were just a gang of toughs, not sectarians. I didn't particularly like Falkirk. Well, if you come from the capital city, Falkirk seemed just a wee bit downmarket! And of course I didn't know enough folk to realise that it was quite a couthie place. Eventually I did discover this – but that was long afterwards. I think I felt a bit lonely or homesick to start with. I found it was a fairly closed community. But then you were so busy that you didn't get a lot of time for self-indulgence, as you were out reporting most evenings. And of course you had a privileged position as a member of the press. But I was hardly there long enough to put down any roots.

*　　　　*　　　　*

I clearly remember the outbreak of the Second World War. I was home that weekend. Almost immediately there was the raid on the Forth Bridge, the sirens went and we thought, 'Oh, my God, we've just been watching H.G. Wells's film *The Shape of Things to Come*, where they bombed the hell out of cities the minute the war broke out.'[11] And we thought that's what was going to happen. We had made no preparation for air raid shelters. We didn't have one at home: we jolly well had one not long after that!

I had been concerned for some time before 1939 about the general political situation and the approach of war. I was pretty left-wing. At the time of the Spanish Civil War I was greatly exercised to volunteer. I was connected with most of those – I knew George Drever, for instance – who did volunteer in Edinburgh.[12] That's not a side I generally talk much about. It's no great secret of course, but . . . But I was interested in the issues of the Spanish War from the beginning. It was fairly obvious to me and to the circles I was in at that time that this was no less than a prelude to something much more serious, as indeed it proved to be. I was already interested from an early age in politics sufficiently to associate with political activists. I think you could say I was on the fringes. I didn't actually become a member. I was Scottish correspondent for the *Daily Worker* for a bit: they didn't pay! But I did actually volunteer for the International Brigade.[13] At that time of course, when I was working for the *Evening Dispatch*, I was quite a valuable addition to those who wanted to get information into the press. I could put stories into the *Dispatch*, stories from Spain concerning local people. And I did that, and the *Dispatch* welcomed that because there were some very good stories actually. There was an admiral's son – he was about 18 at the time, but I can't remember the name – who'd gone missing and then he suddenly showed up again. I wrote the story up.[14] Another story I particularly recollect was a cruise ship with German tourists aboard landing at Leith. And I think a Young Communist League man had chalked up on the side of the ship, *Mit Hitler Nieder*. Of course I'd been tipped that this was going to happen. So I got the story and the photograph, and the *Dispatch* was delighted![15] The *Dispatch* was further to the right than the *Evening News* was. But you knew what the score was on the *Dispatch* and you had to try to work round it, and those were news stories.

Anyhow – I think it was 1937 or 1938, I was still with the *Dispatch* anyway – I volunteered for the International Brigade. They had an office in the High Street in Edinburgh: it was the Communist Party or the Young Communist League, one or the other. They handled the volunteers, and it was arranged that I would join a party for Spain. I said I wanted to go, and a chap called Park, who was an absolute crackpot, said he would arrange it.[16] So I duly wrote to my parents telling them I was pushing off – and they wrote to the *Dispatch*. I think I must have caused my parents quite a lot of distress in that period, but it was unintentional. I think they were highly unchuffed about my political views. They were Liberals, and any association with the Communist Party in those days was, oh, quite drastic. But I didn't do it to upset my parents, but because I felt that was the correct route to take. The rise of fascism and Nazism, and the struggle in Spain, was a great catalyst for people of my generation. It was much more a case of black and white in those days than it is now. Anyway, then I showed up with my toothbrush and spare shirt on the Friday night. Park said, 'You're no' goin'.' I said, 'Why not?' And he says, 'Oh, we've had word from London you're not to go. You're too young.' I must have been 18 or 19 at the time. So that was it. But thinking about it afterwards, I realised that what must have been the deciding factor was that I was in a position – I was a plant, in other words – much more useful to them where I was in the *Evening Dispatch* than I would have been as cannon fodder over in Spain. But I always regretted that I didn't have a bash at it. I was quite disappointed when I was turned down, because I was keen to go. But I'll tell you what did happen as a result of that. When, 30 years after the Spanish War, I first applied in the 1960s for a visa to go to the United States there was a long hiatus and I was called into the consulate in Edinburgh and asked to explain all this. So they reluctantly gave me a visa. But this is what it was all about. And every year for about 20 years when I went to the States I had to go through the same. Finally, I said to them: 'Look, this is a piece of bloody nonsense. You know you're going to give me a visa anyway. Why not just draw a line under it and say that's it?' And they said, 'Well, yes. We're quite prepared to do that, provided you write us a series of articles saying what a wonderful place the States is.' I think the States is a wonderful place, and if I felt like writing an article and saying that, I would do it. But I'm not going to be . . .! I never even got to Spain during the Civil War, but they knew about it.

So when the Second World War came along I volunteered in October 1939. My concern about the rise of fascism in Europe may have been an element in it, but possibly also was the desire for adventure and movement. I was enjoying the job in Falkirk, doing what I wanted to do. The trouble is I keep volunteering for things and wishing afterwards I hadnae. It was the army I volunteered for. I went to the Assembly Rooms in George Street, Edinburgh. In retrospect I should have volunteered for the navy, because that's where my interest has always been. It was just one of those accidents. I must have got in the wrong queue, not necessarily that I felt I was in the wrong queue. I just got put in the army, and that was it. Then I got posted to Hillsea Barracks in Portsmouth. I got put in the Royal Army Ordnance Corps because I could type, I think, and immediately I got shoved in the company office with a friend, Denis Carter of Leeds, I still keep in touch with. We joined on the same day, were in the company office together, got posted to the Far East together, went through prison camp together, and came out together. Well, being in the company office with the skills required for office work, they had in mind to send me to York. But they were making up a draft for somewhere they didn't say where it was, and Denis volunteered me for the draft so we could go together. The company officer said to me, 'Well, we've got you down for York, or you can go on this draft.' I said, 'Oh, is it Egypt?' And he said, 'No, I can't say.' In fact it was Singapore. We sailed in December 1939 and arrived in January 1940 into Singapore. We had two marvellous years before the shooting started.

In Singapore city I was put in stores to start with, keeping records. Then gradually I was put in charge of a department, motor transport, to keep a census of all the unit's holdings of motor transport. Then I was given a job as secretary to Colonel Linnie, later a general in the War Office. But at that time he was a colonel on line of communication, and our job was really dashing up and down Malaya checking that the ordnance stores were in a position for use in the event of an attack. I remember arriving on a beautiful sunny morning in Penang on the overnight train from Kuala Lumpur, and stepping off the train to get the news that the Japs had started the war.[17] I saw this plane being shot down out of the sky, and I was standing there cheering, unaware that it was one of ours that was being shot down. We had nothing but rubbish – old Buffaloes with a top speed of about 120 mph.[18] The Jap Zeros were of course as good as our Spitfires. And on that same day at Penang I said to Colonel Linnie, 'I've just heard on the radio that the *Prince of Wales* and the *Repulse* have been sunk.' 'Oh, you can't. That can't possibly be true.' And we rushed off, and sure enough he said, 'Oh, my God, that's the end.' The two battleships had shot off north without any air cover and they were lost for the loss of three Japanese planes. It was really the end of the capital ship era. Only the aircraft carrier counted after that.[19]

By that time I was a sergeant, and was based at army headquarters in Fort Canning, on a hill in Singapore itself. Round about 1937 the British wrote Singapore off. It had been built as an enormous naval base with all the big guns pointing out to sea. So to defend Singapore would require something like ten capital ships – an enormous fleet. And it was realised that if we had commitments elsewhere we simply couldn't defend it. They hadn't anticipated that the Japs would come overland to Singapore through Malaya. Well, that is the popular mythology, that the big guns were all pointing out to sea. I think some of them could have been swung round to cover parts of Johore.[20] But all we had was armour-piercing ammunition, which would have been useless against the invading Jap troops. I wasn't aware of that at the time. I was doing a weekly column for the *Straits Times*, mainly about fitba' matches, social events and that sort of thing, which the army authorities had approved and which the commanding officer had asked me to take on. The work was quite welcome, because it brought me in four quid a week, which was a lot of money. I was able to run a car on that, which most of the other squaddies couldnae do! And I remember writing an article for the *Straits Times* in October 1941, saying that the Japs had their hands full in China and any thought they could take on the entire Far East was absurd: the war started at the beginning of December 1941.[21]

The British civilians in Singapore really didn't want us. They didn't fraternise with us much. I remember being a member of a gramophone society, and that was about the only contact I had with the civilian side. They used to come to it, or we went to them – I forget whose gramophone society it was. But generally speaking there was no great contact between us. It was the old colonial attitude. I know about that because it was exactly the same when I was in Mexico. Once the British get abroad, they get snooty ideas. I don't know how that attitude applied to the officer ranks. I know the officers were . . . well, Raffles Hotel, for instance, wouldn't allow NCOs or other ranks to use it. It was a very stratified society in Singapore. It was exemplified by the Governor. Up to the point of the surrender to the Japanese he was still insisting on everyone dressing for dinner and having the menu printed.[22] That attitude of mind persisted throughout. He saw his duty as continuing to produce as much rubber and tin as he could for the war effort, and anything else was an irrelevance. He wouldn't allow air raid precautions to be taken in Singapore because he said that would alarm the natives. The result was when the first waves of Jap bombers came over they caught us completely unprepared and many lives were lost. It was a shocking experience. The Japs just wiped us out and they did it in ten weeks. Some of our units fought very well. Most of them didn't because they were raw kids. An entire Division, the 18th, arrived about a fortnight before the end and walked straight out of school into prison camp. Many of them didn't survive, of course.

Although based at Malaya Command headquarters at Fort Canning in Singapore, I was up and down the line quite a bit. I felt towards the end that I wasn't going to get out of Singapore. Fort Canning HQ was where all the thinking was done – what thinking there was. I remember seeing two of our major generals standing in front of a map. The Japs had just broken through one of the lines drawn on the map, and I remember one general saying to the other, 'What the hell are we going to do now?' I thought, Jesus, if they don't know! Towards the end, when we were forced right off the mainland, I thought perhaps we might be able to hold the island of Singapore. But within days of course it became obvious that we couldn't, especially as the water supply for the island came from the mainland, and the Japs had quickly cut that off. Even when we were back on the island and they were digging trenches everywhere for the final stand, the secretary of the golf club refused to allow anyone to dig trenches on the golf course.

Well, we retreated and retreated and retreated. I'd been deputed to run various people down to the docks to get away from the island – a bit messy that. There'd been a storming of ships and that. But we won't go into that. I remember giving this officer a message for my mother. Well, 52 ships left Singapore and only four got through. The other 48 went to the bottom. Some of these ships were full of nurses, and as they waded ashore they were machine-gunned in the surf.[23]

Finally, I was in our office which overlooked the central quadrangle at Fort Canning. That morning I had thought, 'Well, it's getting towards the end now. Either we escape, which is highly unlikely, or we get bumped off, which is much more likely, or we get taken prisoner.' And looking out on this central quadrangle, I saw the General Officer Commanding, Percival, come out, preceded by one of his staff with a Union Jack.[24] Somebody else was carrying a huge white flag. Some of our chaps, Regular soldiers, were absolutely in tears at this great disaster of the British Empire, the laying down of our arms. Churchill said it was the worst thing that had ever happened. But he must have known that it was going to happen. It was very obvious with the troops we had. Our troops were green. The Japs were the seasoned Imperial Guard from China, unstoppable, marvellous fighters. They came down mainly on bicycles with a bag of rice and a rifle, infiltrated the lines and started their own war somewhere far behind. Panic stations – we'd all withdraw, form a new line, only to find they'd curved round on the outside and come in behind us. There was a complete inevitability about it.

I ended up in Changi. Changi was a civilian prison, but also a village, and also a district – and we were there. The Japs put a fence round the place and left us alone for weeks and weeks. It must have been an overwhelming surprise to them that they'd got so many prisoners – something like 60,000.[25] They didn't know what to do with them. Food supplies were fairly good to start with, because we'd left them mountains of food, most of it appropriated for their own use. Gradually that petered out, and we were on to rice. Our main diet was rice and a sort of vegetable soup made with cabbage leaves and this sort of thing, three times a day. Maybe twice a week you'd find a wee bit meat in it. It obviously wasn't enough to sustain life and a lot of people started dying of malnutrition and disease. Then the Japs started using us on working parties, clearing up the town, unloading ships in the docks.

After maybe four or five months the Japs said: 'You must sign a certificate that you will not attempt to escape.' Our commanding officer said, 'This is nonsense. The Hague Convention says it is a soldier's duty to attempt to escape.' The Japs said: 'We're not signatories of the Hague Convention. You will sign this certificate or be shot.' All the top brass had been taken away by this time to Taiwan. The officer in charge was only a major, but he gave the order to sign anything: 'We're signing under duress and you're not committed.' So we elected not to be shot and we all signed. But we didn't all sign our own name. The number of Greta Garbos that got in there was quite astonishing![26]

The Japs then marched us off first to Roberts Barracks at Sellarang, which was the Gordons' Barracks, built to accommodate about 1,500 men. There were about 15,000 of us there, with one water tap. We were there for four days without food, or only with what food we were able to carry in, and no hygiene at all. We dug trenches and shat into them, and we buried people on the barrack square. It must have given any sergeant major there an absolute headache to see the beautiful square dug up like that. Then we were marched back the five or six miles to our camp at Changi. What a relief it was to get back into these very humble tumble-down shacks that had been part of Changi village.

Then the Japs gave us all sorts of marvellous promises: 'You're going to a holiday camp. Take all your possessions with you. You'll thoroughly enjoy it.' And the parties of prisoners started going up to Siam, now Thailand, to build the Siam–Burma railway. To get there we were four days in cattle trucks, 30-odd of us to a small truck, which meant there wasn't room to lie down. So night and day for four days we tried lying down by shifts, with very little food, the heat overpowering. We'd have what they called a benjo stop, where you got out, shat on the ground, and then got back into the truck. We arrived at Bampong, which was really the beginning of the railway which was to link Bangkok with Moulmein in Burma, a distance of about 280 miles through virgin jungle. At the beginning of the century the ground had been surveyed by the Germans, who reckoned it was impossible to build a connecting railway there – unless there was an expendable labour force, as there was then for the building of the Panama Canal, because you had all these tropical diseases. Well, the Japs had an expendable labour force, they didn't want them, and that was the only thing they could think of doing with them. So we prisoners of war began to build the railway.

You'll have seen these films where the Chinese fill a basket with earth and then carry it up and empty it to build a dam. Well, that's the way we built up the embankment for the railway. We'd sow it with grass and then along would come people who would lay chips on top, and behind them would come some of our chaps laying the rails. We built a light single line railway that way, right through the jungle, building bridges as we went. First, we had to build a bridge over the River Kwai, and I was on that. The later film about the bridge was very much romanticised. But then who'd have watched it if it hadn't been?[27] No, life was very grubby and minimal: not enough food, overwork, dying. You'd wake up in the morning and find the bloke next to you had died either of overwork and malnutrition or of malaria, beri-beri, dysentery. Dysentery was the worst. Dysentery was dreadful. Typhus, cholera, jungle sores – ulcers – that ate your leg off. Our method of coping with jungle sores was to stand in the stream and let the fish nibble away at the dead flesh until your leg started bleeding, then it would start healing. But it wouldn't heal unless you got rid of the dead flesh. Maggots wrapped in a banana leaf and bandaged on to the leg was another method. But usually people who got bad sores like that got their leg amputated without anaesthetic by our own surgeons, who had tremendous work to do.

The Jap engineers in charge of the building of the railway were an elite. They took very little to do with us. But below them were a sprinkling of Japanese sergeants, and below them again were Koreans – and the Koreans were really the most brutal. The Koreans were certainly wearing Japanese uniforms, but recently somebody told me that they were actually not in the army. In fact, at the end the Japs were going to kill all us prisoners, and they were going to kill all the Korean guards, too.[28]

I was on the prisoners' wireless at various times. It may have been my journalist's instinct for news. I'd been on the wireless in Changi under a chap called Hugh, and also I operated the wireless intermittently at various points and had supplied batteries off the lorries. I took a small, not a major, part. I think it was an act of bloody stupidity, looking back on it. The Japs chopped your heid off if you were caught. But one didn't think too much about the consequences. Yet in the back of my mind I knew that that's what would happen, and it did happen in one camp. I'd actually brought a piece of equipment. We were operating a set in

Changi and it was broken up into bits and I was given a bit to take up. I got as far as Camp Kanburi [Kanchanaburi] with it. We arrived at the camp and – kit inspection. Standing there with this bit in my kitbag: 'Jesus Christ, how am I going to deal with this one?', I opened the kitbag for inspection, managed to get the bit out and slipped it down between my legs and covered it over with mud: 'Yeah, OK.' I managed to recover it and take it back to Lance Thew, who said, 'What the hell have you been doing with this?!' Thew rebuilt the set and had it in a Huntley & Palmer tin, with the top half filled with peanuts. But he was a careless bugger. The Kempetai, the Jap secret police, walked round, picked up the biscuit tin, threw it down – and there was the wireless set. Well, three of them got beaten to death. Thew was taken up. One of the group was Eric Lomax, the Railway Man.[29] Fortunately, I wasn't in the camp at the time or I might very well have been involved, because my job was usually to take the news down in shorthand from the wireless. Subsequently I was involved in a wireless set towards the end of the war, so we knew the atomic bomb had been dropped.

The Kempetai weren't part of the Jap organisation within the camp. They were apart, but did a raid on you from time to time. My job was to dish out petrol to the ration lorries in a small camp in the jungle when suddenly the Kempetai descended on us. I had been given a sparking plug, which was very valuable, to flog to the natives. Very fortunately for me a lorry came in needing diesel or petrol and I was able to go back to the hut. I couldn't think what to do with this sparking plug. However, there was a half drunk mug of tea – well, a bean can with a handle soldered on to it that was used as a mug. So I popped the sparking plug into the bean can and the Kempetai never noticed it. But it was touch and go on that one.

There was another occasion when, as I've said, I had to try to get the batteries off the lorries. The Japs realised we must be getting power from somewhere off a vehicle. So they said, 'You must form a guard at night to make sure the batteries are not taken.' Well, of course we kept turning a blind eye to the batteries disappearing. But one night I was on guard about two o'clock in the morning. Suddenly this tall Jap officer, absolutely naked, came rushing down on me, with his sword naked too, and screaming at the top of his voice. They went mad, you know, just flipped completely, screaming and shouting. I'd been sitting there reading. Fortunately, I heard him coming, stood up, bowed, and said, '*Skokosan*: Officer, sir.' If I hadnae spotted him, my heid would have been on the flair. Anyhow I stood there with bowed head, expecting at any minute that the sword would come down on my neck. They had complete life and death control over us, they could do what they liked with us – and often did. He stormed and raged and hacked away at this bush beside me until there was nothing of it left. Then suddenly he switched off like that and walked away. And I thought, 'What the hell was all that about?' Then I realised he had felt I should not have been reading but walking about, looking to see that the batteries were not taken off. Fortunately, I had twigged: I had spotted him through the side of my eye, jumped up, saluted, and bowed to him – and that had saved my life. Added to which I'd had a sort of teasing relationship with him in the past, because I could speak a certain amount of Japanese and used to ask him, 'What are you goin' to do after you've lost the war?', this sort of thing. He had a sense of humour. You couldn't have got away with that with one of the less educated ones. They'd have beaten you to death. The Japanese officers treated their own men much the same as they treated us: it was very brutal.

During our captivity we got no mail from home, none whatever. We once got a delivery of postcards. But it must have been at the end of the war, because it told me that my father had died of a heart attack in October 1944 at the age of 51, unaware that I was alive and that my brother David was a prisoner of war in Germany, and when my youngest brother Al had just joined the Royal Scots and was posted to Palestine. We were allowed, I think three times, to fill in blanks on a postcard: 'I am well. I am working for money. Give my regards to Winnie and the kids' – you know, that sort of thing. We did receive some money. We got 10 cents, which was enough to buy some tobacco or a boiled egg. You got that once every ten days. I was up for the tobacco.

While we were building the railway we had some contacts with the native population, the Chinese in particular. They helped us quite considerably. Some of our own Intelligence Corps, themselves prisoners, in fact had a circuit going, which passed news between camps. And we did what we could. You know, we'd co-ordinate all the wireless bulletins, and it was a result of that that the set was discovered in Kanburi:[30] some idiot had been seen removing from a sack of rice a message that was discovered to be a news bulletin.

Being a prisoner was depressing, particularly in the early part when the Japanese were evidently winning the war and pushing on towards India. Well, some of the prisoners – the kids who had no realisation – thought there would be an immediate push to get us out. I said at the time that it'd take two or three years before we'd be free again. Well, when three years had passed and nothing had happened, I began to despair. It was a long time. Towards the end I was getting very suicidal almost. But there weren't high suicide rates among the prisoners: you didn't need to commit suicide, you just needed to lose spirit in the end and you'd go down very rapidly. And of course in the end we were down to nothing in clothes, you know, mainly G-strings. But some of us managed to hang on to something. I got an old kitbag and made a pair of shorts out of that which lasted me right through.

The spreading of news was a key factor in keeping up morale, especially when things began to happen in our favour. But rumour was a tremendous thing. Alex Young of Bearsden had a little pocket diary, now in the Mitchell Library in Glasgow, and in microscopic writing he kept a day to day record of events right through. Alex kept it in a pocket inside his shorts. Once he got back after the war it took him 20 years to type his diary up using a magnifying glass. He tells some of the early rumours. And the funny thing was that these rumours all – well, not all but some of them – came true: but they were only about three or four years ahead of the time![31]

Well, our liberation at the end of the war came as a bit of an anticlimax. The order had gone out, and I have a copy of it, to camp commandants that in the event of an Allied invasion, as they expected, the Japs were to eliminate the prisoners of war, just get rid of them, and 'do this in any way you find practical, but leave no trace.' The order specified different ways: you could machine-gun them, bury them alive, march them to death, or . . . In Borneo the Japs practically wiped out the entire prisoner of war population on a death march which started off with 2,500 of whom only six survived – because the six took off into the jungle. The Japs'd simply wiped them out by keeping them marching until they all died.[32] But in our case the Japs'd got us down to dig these enormous trenches round the camps, about 12 or 14 feet deep. They put us in these trenches with their machine guns on us, and they'd do this practice once a week. That went on for several weeks towards the end of the war. We knew what was happening of course. So at that point we didn't expect to survive really. And we knew from the various rumours that the Korean guards were going to be bumped off, too. Well, this was in August 1945, the invasion of Malaya and Burma had actually started. The ships were all at sea, the invasion date was the 18th. But the atom bombs were dropped on the 6th and 9th, and on the 14th the Emperor of Japan capitulated.[33] So that day or the next the camp commandant was called to Bangkok, came back, and immediately started to relax. Now the rumours started flying round. Then he called us all on parade in the evening and told us that the war was over. He didnae say who'd won. Then the Japs simply disappeared into the jungle. But there had been a machine-gun battalion in the jungle near our camp, ready to come in and shoot the lot of us.

That was the way they were going to eliminate our particular camp. It was a close-called thing, touch and go, three or four days in it.

In that particular camp there were maybe about a couple of thousand of us prisoners. But overall some 25,000 went in, and about one in three didn't come out – that was British.[34] But overall they'd taken about 60,000 to 80,000 prisoners, including Indians and Australians. Well, that's what happened there. The Japs simply disappeared. I remember that night walking about, none of us wanted to sleep. Finally, I lay down in the open air just on the ground, scared to go back into the hut in case the whole thing vanished in a dream. Next day the Thais came in and told us it was all over. They had us down to their village and celebrated and what not. Then about six weeks later the planes, mainly American, started coming over, dropping us books and parcels. They broke us in gradually with food over the six weeks before they pulled us out. Some of them over-ate, in fact one or two Australians died as a result of just gorging themselves on bully beef and things like that. And then we went by barge to Bangkok and flew out to Rangoon. Oh, it was marvellous in Rangoon, to see white sheets – something we'd forgotten, curtains at the window, and women. Then home by ship. And that was it.

I'd been three and a half years in captivity. When I'd joined the army in 1939 I was 9½ stones. I was down to six stones when the war ended. Some prisoners were down to three stones. Of course, they died: you couldn't survive at that weight. But the will was the thing. If you believed that we would win and that it was only a question of time, then you hung on. But a lot of them couldn't relate to what was happening to them. They'd been in school, Good Lord, they'd lived sheltered lives. That 18th Division that'd come out to Singapore were just young laddies.

Well, when I came back home I had about a couple of months off, then I started back in the *Falkirk Herald* and I was with them until I retired in 1980. Those years as a prisoner of war simply disappeared down a black hole. I was more or less 21 again, I didn't feel any older. And I got married at the age of 28 after I'd been home about 18 months. My wife, who's about eight years younger than me, was old Fred Johnston's secretary and I hadn't really met her till I came back from the war. I can't recall I found it difficult settling down again, I think it was quite smooth. I had a lot of nightmares of course, as practically everybody did. The recurring nightmare was that the whole experience of being freed was a dream, and that in fact we were back in prison camp. It was a recurring nightmare not every night but for many years. Some people's minds have been turned. But my members – 650 of them – in the Far East Prisoners of War Association are probably the more adaptable ones.

But there are a lot of ex-prisoners who never joined, have been unable to speak about their experiences, and have become social recluses and suffer all sorts of ailments as a result. Our group in the Association is more or less self-contained in Scotland but we're part of a federation for the whole of Britain.[35]

I went back to the *Falkirk Herald* as a fully-fledged reporter. I'd done a great deal of writing and journalism in the army. There was no change at all in the editorial department, it was as though the war had never happened. It was still the same verbatim reporting. But they hadnae got the newsprint, because of rationing; that was the only limiting factor. I think the circulation was below 20,000 before the war, when I came back it would be in the lower 20s; when I left it was about 40,000: the reason for that was we took over the upper ward of Lanarkshire from the *Hamilton Advertiser*.[36] The only rival to the *Herald* was the *Falkirk Mail*, a bitter rivalry, although a phantom rivalry, because the *Mail* was of no consequence really, with a very much smaller circulation. Old Tom Mackie was the proprietor and editor of the *Mail*, and when he died we were asked if we would buy it. I was all in favour, just as an act of grace. But the rivalry and bitterness was so built in that Fred Johnston wouldn't touch it, and the *Mail* just fizzled out. Politically, I suppose you could say the *Falkirk Herald* was Liberal, but it never had any strong political persuasions. Falkirk wasn't that greatly political, it was a working-class area – mining, light engineering, foundries, above all the Carron Iron Works of course.[37] As a reporter in Falkirk I used to do the annual review of the iron founding industry and it was a big thing. We'd turn out a 64-page tabloid once a year. There isn't a foundry left now as far as I know, it's all gone. There was a lot of skill and real craftsmanship in it, too. Anyway our leader writer in those days was actually John Terris, a reporter on *The Scotsman*. We paid him so much, and honestly it was the most awful tosh. I used to sometimes nip through to Edinburgh and ask him if he could jazz it up a bit.

I wasn't long back in Falkirk, about a year maybe, when the Grangemouth office of the paper became vacant. As I lived above the Grangemouth office and it suited my personality really to be working on my own, I asked for the job. The editor said, 'Not bloody likely. We need you here in Falkirk.' But I kept persisting and finally I was allowed to go and work in Grangemouth. There you were a one-man newspaper, the Grangemouth correspondent of the *Falkirk Herald*. There was a rival *Grangemouth Advertiser*, which I subsequently bought for the *Herald*. You were really your own boss. You were given three or four columns to fill, but usually I filled a page because it was a wonderfully good news source.

At that time Grangemouth was beginning to boom, and of course there was the docks, ICI, and a community of about 20,000 people. So it was really a gift and you could make your own hours and work all day and night if you felt like it.

I remained in Grangemouth for about five years till October 1952. The manager in Falkirk died, and a short time later one particular issue of the *Falkirk Herald* contained no Falkirk news at all – it was all Grangemouth. It was just fortuitous – not only was there my contribution but the county council had been dealing with Grangemouth. So I got a phone call: 'Want to see you.' And old Fred said to me: 'I want to make you assistant manager.' I said, 'Oh, heavens, I don't know anything about manage-ment. And who's the manager?' He said, 'There isn't one. You've got to start at the bottom.' So I said, 'Well, I'm not very sure about that.' Old Fred looked quite upset. I think he expected me to say, 'Oh, thanks.' I said, 'Will you give me a couple of days to think?' He went a bit sour at that, he wasn't pleased at all. However, a couple of days later I said I'd be delighted to do it.

Well, that was rough. I found it very uncomfortable to start with. We had a staff of about 60, and about 59 of them reckoned they should have had the manager's job. So the first year or two was a wee bit sticky. After a few months I decided I needed to equip myself with some of the paper skills that were needed. So I went to the Heriot Watt Management School in Edinburgh. I was spending about 20 hours a week studying on that for five years. It was evening classes for the first three years, 6.30pm till 9.30pm. Then you got an intermediate diploma in management. The second part was a two-year course in the full diploma, which was day release for a couple of days, and the rest was evenings. By the time I'd travelled backwards and forwards between Falkirk and Edinburgh I reckoned I'd been to the moon and back about half a dozen times. I can't believe how good my wife was about it, and that was at the time we were having all our weans – four of our own, and we adopted a grandson, who became a photographer with the *Herald*. I got the College prize in the end through sheer bloody persistence: 30-odd had started the course, only five of us survived to the end.

As for giving up journalism and reporting, well, you got fascinated by the business of trying to make a better profit than last year, and building the firm up. The Johnston family business had started in 1767 when Patrick Mair established himself as a printer in Falkirk. His daughter married a young printer named Johnston in the 1790s, and that's when the Johnston connection came in. About 1845 a Glasgow crowd started a paper in Falkirk that lasted a year and then the Johnstons took it over. My boss was Fred Johnston the second, the present chairman of Johnston's is Fred the third, and he has a son and a grandson, so the family succession's assured!

Och, I don't know, I enjoyed the management side of newspapers. It was a challenge. However much you enjoy a job there's always the chance you can grow a bit stale maybe if you stay too long. And that's what happened in Grangemouth. I was five years there, and a perfect job. But at the end you get fed up eating rich cake.

R.J. (Bob) Brown

I remember my grandpa Brown, the ironmoulder man, telling me when I was young (I was quite lucky – I had grandparents who talked to me) that when he was a young man in Shettleston, Glasgow, he and some of his peer group pooled their meagre resources and three days a week bought the *Glasgow Herald*. And on summer nights particularly (I'm never sure where they did it on dreich winter nights) they would sit by the Burn Brig down near Carntyne Station and read stories out of the *Glasgow Herald* – foreign affairs, parliamentary affairs. They took turns to read out the stories, then discuss the political, economic and social implications of these stories. When as a schoolboy I began to think of journalism perhaps this was subconsciously the beginnings of it.

I was born in Shettleston in 1924, February 27. Shettleston at that time was an industrial suburb of Glasgow. But my own people, who had been in these parishes and neighbouring parishes for generations, never really thought of themselves as Glaswegians in the way I did, because they had been absorbed in the big city boundary extension of 1912. It took in Partick, Govan, the Shaws and elsewhere, and they knew a different Shettleston. I was a city boy but Shettleston was still close to being rural. You crossed the main Glasgow–Hamilton railway line and you were in open country, with working farms and all the rest of it. So I knew about street games in Glesga and about plunderin' nests in country places. I had this dual background which in fact was very useful.

We lived in better than average circumstances, in a little place called West Bank Terrace behind the main street. It didnae have a great outlook: you looked into the Cleansing Department! But it was a row of terraced houses with a pend in the back and overshadowed by the main street tenements. It was a nice place to grow up. The houses in West Bank Terrace were ground-floor and upper-floor. We were in a ground-floor house, with another family above us. I lived there till I was about 12. The accommodation was quite small. There was a scullery at the back, what we called the kitchen – today it would be the living room or lounge, then a long lobby to the front door, one bedroom, a bathroom, the parlour through in the front, and an indoor flush toilet: so basically two rooms and a kitchen, but very good compared to many others. It was gaslit. There was a range in the kitchen, where my mother did the cooking when I was a wee laddie. I remember the toasted cheese being done with the bread held in front of the open fire; later we got a gas cooker.

Washing facilities were limited, and my father when he came home grubby from a day's work would wash himself at the kitchen sink. But we had a bath. I took a bath only once a week, which was fairly standard working-class behaviour. For folk in the tenements wi' nae bathroom, the Shettleston public baths built about 1930 were a great boon: for a couple of coppers you just went for a bath there. When at a later stage I jined the Boys' Brigade (which my father was a bit dubious about: he regarded it as a military organisation) for the fitba', whiles on a very dirty wet Saturday afternoon on Shettleston Hill, if you could run to a penny or tuppence I've seen us sprint down wi' our clothes under our oxters 150 yards to Shettleston baths and have a bath. It was heaven – unlimited hot water, whereas at home your mother'd get angry if ye ran the hot water away.

All the ground-floor houses at West Bank Terrace had a very small garden at the front, where the path from the door to the pavement was barely six yards. The back was common ground – a drying green, with several communal wash houses dotted along the length of the terrace. There were either four or six families to each wash house. In fact my mother didn't use the wash house all that much. Her own mother as far back as I remember was crippled with rheumatoid arthritis, so my mother went once a week to do her mother's washing elsewhere in Shettleston and tended to take her own major washing with her and do it all together. She took the washing in a case. In those days if you took it in an old pram or basket on wheels you were going to the steamie. Mother wisnae in the social league, I suppose, that went to the steamie, so she wasnae in the business of drawing the washing through the streets.

But I don't recall any problems with the wash houses at West Bank Terrace. The days were allocated of course, and if you drew a wet Monday . . . I remember the family Mackay diagonally up the stair from us – an outside stone stair that went up on a dog leg and had a little landing that covered the two upstairs houses. The Mackays were from Buchan, Mr Mackay was in the Glesga polis, and Mrs Mackay, a big broad Buchan peasant, was a lovely woman in many ways. I remember as a kid watching Mrs Mackay at the weekly wash, a big event. She had a leathery waterproof apron, a big bratty that came right down her shoulders. It was a formidable sight. It was like a platoon of guardsmen going into the attack in some foreign field.

My understanding was that at an earlier stage West Bank Terrace had been quite a select semi-professional row of residences, but it had come down and it was full of working-class families by my time. There's the respectable working class who in the main don't drink, and there are the feckless ones who drink and fecht. When you put it this way it sounds very patronising, but we all know it's true. There were no problems in West Bank Terrace. And it was beside Shettleston Co-operative Public Hall, which was a great venue for all sorts of events in the place at that time.

My father, born in 1890, was a Clydeside engine fitter, a skilled craftsman. He had served his time with Sir William Arrol in Bridgeton.[1] Unfortunately, when he finished his apprenticeship there the state of world trade meant he couldnae be kept on. So he worked in the shipyards for a good many years. In the First World War he engined submarines. He was a near-casualty then of the K37 submarine disaster in the Gare Loch. He was scheduled to be on her final trial trip, but had a row with the gaffer because he refused to go up the forward end of the sub, where the red leaders had been in and the place was stinking with new red lead paint. The gaffer gave him his jotters on the spot. Otherwise he would have been in the part where the casualties were when the K37 did her dive in Gare Loch.[2] My father saw the problems of shipbuilding coming, and he came out of the yards after the war and switched to work with Stewart & Lloyds in Tollcross tubeworks.[3] Later on my father told me that he had a good Depression in the 1930s, by which time he was a maintenance engineer, because on average he was brought in one week in three throughout those years to maintain and service largely idle machinery. And, as he and my mother pointed out, this made a very considerable difference to the capacity of our family to survive hard times. I remember the Depression, though not so clearly as my older brother Jimmy, but I have quite clear recollections of its effects. My father stayed on at Stewarts & Lloyds tubeworks until he retired.

My parents were Shettleston. Of course Shettleston at that time was relatively small. It wisnae as populous a place as Bridgeton. It was the outer industrial suburb. There was a kind of hiatus between Parkhead and Shettleston of open space. Shettleston was basically a mixed pit, weaving and engineering village. When I was a kid my father pointed out that the Railway Tavern in the main street – a pub, but originally a dwelling-house – had a brick lean-to on it where, he said, a forebear of ours was the last handloom weaver to work in Shettleston and that was where the loom had been. And Shettleston was a very mixed community. I remember there were fancy names in Shettleston: my father and mother used to talk about a mutual friend called Landy Manson. He was christened Orlando. Now there you are: I'll bet there werenae Orlandos in Morningside.

My mother was born in a tenement at Shettleston Cross, within 100 yards of our house in West Bank Terrace. She was less than a year older than my father. My brother Jimmy was six years older than I was, and there were just the two of us.

My grandpa Brown was, as already mentioned, an ironmoulder. His brother Bob was an engineer who worked most of his life with John Brown, shipbuilders, at Clydebank.[4] Bob got the workmen's train right through from Shettleston to Clydebank, and he worked constant night shift most of his life. So there was a craft tradition on the Brown side of the family for two generations ahead of mine. Grandpa Brown, in fact, with a brother, latterly set up in a small business they worked themselves as ironmoulders. He had bought a house in Easdale Drive, and my understanding was it was collateral against the setting up of the iron-founding business with his brother. After grandpa died and my granny Brown was still alive, we moved about 1936 when I was 12 from West Bank Terrace to my grand-parents' house in 49 Easdale Drive. It was a small semi-detached cottage with a small front garden and a fair-sized back garden. Easdale Drive had been renamed: it had earlier been Hamilton Drive – and this harks back to what I was saying about the absorption in 1912 of Shettleston into Glasgow. There was duplication of street names in Shettleston with established names in the city. As for granny Brown, she came when young from Chryston to live in Shettleston, about six or seven miles from it. She worked in Bridgeton cotton mills until she married, and walked four miles back and forth every day from Shettleston to Brigton [Bridgeton].

My other grandmother, who, I think, even as a young woman had the beginnings of rheumatoid arthritis, was of that generation of young women who never went out to work but stayed at home and helped run the house. She was 83 or 85 when she died while I was in the army in wartime. Grandpa Jackson, my maternal grandfather, who also lived into his eighties, had gone to work as a kid at Shettleston Ropework. When I was wee he would whiles pick me up on his knee, and in his Calvinist work ethic way, would tell me to stick in at my books and get on, because he was a gaffer when he was 10 years old. Later on I discovered he had in fact been a gaffer at 10. Apparently at the ropeworks there was a squad of wee laddies – I'm no' sure whether it included lassies – whose job was to tease down the yarn before the rope-spinning began. He was presumably an eident laddie at his job and was put in charge of the squad of wee laddies. But grandpa Jackson must have been quite a remarkable man, because in this same Easdale Drive where my other grandpa bought the house at No. 49, grandpa Jackson had a double cottage built in 1902 – at No. 46. Now he was a working man – his death certificate says he was a foreman yarn spinner, retired. But in 1902 he borrowed money, commissioned an architect in Shettleston (there *was* an architect in Shettleston), designated the quarries from which the stone was to come, and when the house was built and was valued at about £700, he sold off the other half, and presumably that cleared part of his debt. I came on all these documents years later when my mother's only sister, who never married because her fiancé had come back from the trenches in the First World War then died in the great influenza epidemic, and who had had the life rent of the house herself, died in 1979. I then disposed of the house. I put all the documents into Glasgow City Archives at the Mitchell Library, because perhaps there werenae terribly many records of the building of small town houses in working-class areas.

Of my great-grandparents I'm not sure, but I know there were miners and other artisans in the family. In fact, it would be maybe a great-great-uncle who came in from the pit one Saturday, washed and cleaned himself up, came out wi' a Gladstone bag, and said to his mother, 'Well, that's me off.' And she says, 'Where are ye off to?' And he says, 'Australia.' And naebody ever heard o' him again! I kept hoping there'd be a notice in the paper: 'Would the descendants of X . . .?', and that I would be able to retire at an early age.

*   *   *

I would start Wellshot primary school in Tollcross at age five. I was a guid scholar, had no problem with my lessons, and scored very highly in the old Qualifying exam. I was also very handy at drawing. In fact myself and a lassie called Elsie Bonnar were slightly embarrassed in our last year at the primary school, because we were both talented with the drawing pad and the headmaster insisted we were transferred to the art room of the old advanced division school, which was for the less academically endowed between the end of primary and the leaving age at 14. It was perhaps an enlightened move by the heidie in encouraging our artistic talents. But it was poor psychology, because we paid a heavy price, being greeted with some derision by these bigger laddies who thought we were wee sooks and teacher's pets. But there was one memorable occasion at Wellshot primary when I would be about 10. It was the last night of the Easter holidays when the school went on fire. We were due back the next day but half the school was destroyed. It was a great affair, because we were all standing there on the firemen's hoses to prevent the water getting through, the firemen were shoutin' at us, and the polis were chasin' us. We reported to the school next morning and were sent home for a week because the school was in a terrible mess. Until the summer holidays, the school was segregated: half of us went in one week from 9am till 1pm to the bit that was certified safe, the other half went in from 1pm till 5pm. By the time we went back after the summer holidays the school was rebuilt. But it was a great year that. I think schools should go on fire every year at Easter!

But I was a keen scholar in the sense that, apart from my grandpa Jackson's knee which I've referred to, my dad qualified as a working-class intellectual. When I was just a bairn I was used to my dad coming in from Shettleston Public Library, a new and extensive district library, wi' his books under his oxter. So I grew naturally used to books. There were a few books in our house actually, mostly reference books of various kinds, very little fiction because fiction was a great luxury to spend your money on: working-class families couldnae afford to acquire libraries. But the library books marched in and out, and I, as did my brother, grew readily into this custom. My father took me along to the library and joined me when I was seven, eight or nine. There was a big junior section there, and the reading room was also a great boon as I grew up. Because money to buy newspapers was limited, I early learned the habit of reading the newspapers there, both the broadsheets and the others, and it was a good catholic (in the non-sectarian sense) selection. I used even to read the *Cork Examiner* there from time to time, and *Forward* and the *Daily Worker*.[5] I was probably at secondary school before I began to really read the newspapers seriously.

When I was beginning to form notions of what I might do after school my father in no way shaped me towards journalism – except that when I began to talk about it I suppose there was a kind of respectability in that his own younger brother Sandy had been a not undistinguished journalist in his day, cut off at his prime when I was barely 10 years old, and thus had no role in shaping my own career in newspapers. But Uncle Sandy as a boy had completed the three-year secondary course at what was then the new Eastbank Academy, which I later attended myself. Then to complete his Highers he transferred to Hamilton Academy for the last two years: you could go to Hamilton in a few minutes by train quite easily from Shettleston on the old LNER line. Sandy became a journalist on the *Falkirk Herald* or the *Falkirk Mail*, and, with a commendation from his editor, left there quite early to join the D.C. Thomson press. That was before the 1926 General Strike, which produced the infamous D.C. Thomson attitude to trade unionism which my generation of journalists, or people like myself who had a strong political view, detested greatly. As a matter of principle I have never in my life worked for D.C. Thomson newspapers. But before 1926, when Uncle Sandy joined Thomson's, there was no virulent anti-trade unionism there. Indeed, Jimmy Aitken, one of the revered figures of the National Union of Journalists in Scotland, and municipal correspondent of the Glasgow *Evening News* when I knew him, had formed with one or two others the first Dundee branch of the union in 1909.[6] Anyway Uncle Sandy had been a D.C. Thomson journalist in Dundee, then went to London where he was their literary man, but returned to Dundee. Unlike my father he was always fairly frail, and he died in the mid-1930s. Then my mother, for whom I had, as most of us do for our mothers, great affection and respect, had lived through the First World War and the Depression, and for her two boys she wanted above all security. My brother Jimmy, more conformist than I was, was academically OK. He completed the full secondary course, too, sat the Civil Service examination and the Glasgow Corporation competitive entrance exam, and took a job in the City Assessor's office. My mother was very keen that, when I came to that stage, I did something of the same sort. But by that time I was intent on going into newspapers. At first she took a fair bit of convincing that this was not a dangerous and hazardous occupation to follow.

Anyway after passing the Qualy I went to Eastbank Academy in Shettleston. The Academy had been founded by the old Shettleston School Board, though by the time I joined it it was called Eastbank Senior Secondary School. There were three secondary schools under the Glasgow Corporation Education Department in the east end at that time. The two others were John Street Secondary in Bridgeton, which served that inner-city area, and Whitehill Secondary, which served the posher end of Dennistoun and wider parts. Eastbank Academy or Senior Secondary was at the Edinburgh end of the main street in Shettleston in a little cul-de-sac called Academy Street. It was a solid two-storey sandstone building, very old-fashioned by today's standards, with few of the facilities that modern schools have. It had a big intake because it served a wide area: Shettleston, Tollcross, parts of Carntyne (one of the early Corporation housing schemes between the wars), and in towards Parkhead. Even though, as my father said, he had a good Depression, it still entailed some sacrifice to keep youngsters at school, although by the time I went to secondary we had free books. My father and mother were very keen that my brother, who had started work in 1935, and I completed the full secondary course. There weren't all that many who stayed on to the fifth year. But many of my peer group at school were from families where the father was not an artisan: Elsie Hogg, for instance, a smashing-looking lassie whom we all fancied, her father was the manager of the Broadway Cinema, and there were quite a number at school with that kind of white-collar, semi-professional background. My pal Robin Stevenson, his father was a Libby commercial traveller – with a car![7] He was the only guy I knew whose father had a car. Quite a number of the Academy pupils lived in the Sandyhills housing scheme. Like Mosspark, it was not a slum clearance scheme but one of the better quality Corporation developments between the wars. Neil Carmichael, MP, later Lord Carmichael, whom I'm still friendly with and whose father had been election agent for Jimmy Maxton and succeeded him as MP for Bridgeton when Maxton died in 1946, and Cliff Hanley, whose first novel was *Dancing in the Street*, both came from Sandyhills. Cliff Hanley was a year ahead of me at school, Neil Carmichael a couple of years ahead. I remember Cliff Hanley saying years later to me, 'You know, Bob, we thought we were somebody going to Eastbank.' And so we did: they used to shout at us, 'Eastbank toffs!' Everything's relative, I suppose.[8]

Eastbank Academy was a co-educational school of course, as they all were. I started in 1C, a class of the clever mixed group; 1A was the clever laddies, 1B the clever girls. Then you went down to 1F. It was a big first-year intake, but by the time the fifth year came along there were about 23 or 24 of us sat our Highers then. There was no sixth year *per se*: you only went back for a sixth year, which was a repeat fifth year, if you failed to get your Highers and needed them for access to university or something. You had to get a group of Highers – it was all or nothing. There was a bit of a vogue at that time among the boys to go to Jordanhill Training College to become physical education teachers, and you needed your Highers. I remember quite a number of them repeating the fifth year because they'd failed maybe in one subject. English was my best subject, I was an indifferent linguist, and I struggled with maths. At the end of the first year at the Academy you had to start making a selection of subjects. I could have taken a Higher history nae bother, but I was an ardent reader of history anyway, so I thought I'd do geography, which opened horizons on the contemporary. But I also took Higher commercial, an odd choice for a laddie: it was mostly lassies took that. I took commercial because by that time my mind was moving to newspapers. I wasnae committed even in my own mind, and because I was still very good in the art room, I swithered whether art might not be a good thing to do. But by the time I was moving into the second year at school, I'd be about 13, I was thinking newspapers might not be a bad idea. By that time I was dipping into the newspapers in the public library reading room, so the one thing fed into the other. The more I saw the papers, the more I thought of journalism, and the converse.

The commercial course, if you were going to be a newspaper reporter, taught you shorthand and typing. Nowadays we're all journalists, but when I was going into newspapers 'reporter' was the word. I began to feel that being a reporter and conveying essential information wasnae a bad aspiration to hold. That was the real reason I took the commercial course, which only two or three laddies took; and only four of us, two boys and two girls, eventually took the Higher commercial exam. The war had broken out in September 1939 when I was entering my fourth year, and I remember sitting one of the Higher commercial papers the morning after one of the nights of the Clydebank Blitz in March 1941, when I was in an Anderson shelter a' nicht wi' these planes coming over. So when I left school to go into journalism I had Higher English, Geography and Commercial, Lower French and Maths, I was typing at upwards of 50 words a minute and had a shorthand speed of 160 words a minute, which was very fast.

*   *   *

When I left school at 17½ in 1941 the tentative notion of the first year had solidified: I just wanted to be a newspaper reporter. The call-up to the Forces was on then for age 18½. Going to the university had been a possibility, but in my own case there were the costs, and the further complication that the only university degree courses exempt from the call-up were the hard ones like medicine. Otherwise you were called up anyway when you were 18½. So for me university was never really a runner. As I say, I just wanted to be a newspaper reporter.

But I couldn't get a job. There weren't many weekly papers in and about Glasgow city area. There was the *Eastern Standard*, which circulated from Bridgeton out. That would have been handy because it was the nearest one, just in Broad Street, Brigton. But I couldn't get a job there. Then there was the *Airdrie & Coatbridge Advertiser* just up the road: the tram ran to Airdrie through Shettleston. But there was no vacancy. I tried the *Motherwell Times*. I tried all round: papers like the *Rutherglen Reformer*.[9] I extended my applications beyond Glasgow and the immediate Lanarkshire area – Paisley and Clydebank, tried them all. But there was nothing. And extending it to papers further afield created problems of travelling or alternatively going to live there. My parents weren't keen on that, and there was the concern I wouldnae get paid enough. I was conscious then of all this, that I was now of work age but I still wasnae working. I couldnae get a job at what I wanted to do. So I looked at the adverts in the *Glasgow Herald* and got a job in a lawyer's office in Glasgow.

It was a small two-partnership firm called Blair & Marshall, whose offices were at 58 Bath Street. I went in by train or sometimes tram. Mr Blair was an irascible man with whom I early fell out, Mr Marshall was a gentleman, who was also an assessor in the Burgh Courts. There were six divisional courts in Glasgow, following the police divisions. And Mr Marshall, as legal assessor, every week sat on the bench with the lay magistrate, to avoid the good bailie sending the accused to the penal colonies for nicking a bar o' chocolate oot o' R.S. McColl's. That happened, or nearly happened, from time to time, and the legal assessor had to lean forward and say, 'You cannae dae that.' Ironically, I, who desperately wanted to be a newspaper reporter, went as part of my duties every morning with Mr Marshall, successively to the Eastern Court, to the Marine, to Govan, to Maryhill. I sat beneath the bench, and when the charge sheets were signed by the magistrate they were passed down to me and I filled in what the verdict was. In a city which still had three evening newspapers the Burgh Court, even in wartime with short, small papers, was not ignored. Every morning I sat and watched three reporters from the three evening papers smiling and laughing and looking pityingly at me, knowing fine that I wanted to be a reporter, too. And here I was sitting filling in charge sheets while they were writin' stories for their papers. It was very hard to take – oh, frustrating! I could have killed each of them and taken their jobs immediately. Mr Marshall and I got on fine. Coming from the courts, he would sometimes take me for a coffee on the way back to 58 Bath Street. He knew that I wanted to go into newspapers, and he took a cautious legalistic view, like my mother in a different way, that maybe this wasnae the best career option for me. He said, 'You know, you could go to Glasgow University and take a law degree. That might be better.' He at least understood my aspirations.

Mr Blair, on the other hand, was not a nice man. He and I had a number of rows. In the office there was a smashing lassie from Motherwell called Miss Craig – I never knew her first name. Quite a young girl, she'd be in her late twenties then. She knew I wanted to be a newspaper reporter, and she counselled me to be patient. She was a good interventionist with Mr Blair, as I suspect maybe Mr Marshall was, too. Anyway, I was in Blair & Marshall for several months, did what office boys do, took their mail to Hope Street post office, got the stamps. I was paid 15 shillings [75p] a week.

Then one morning in November or December 1941 an advert appeared in the *Glasgow Herald*: 'Reporter Wanted' by a west of Scotland weekly, which turned out to be the *Ayr Advertiser*. I wrote, was summoned to Ayr, had an interview, and got the job. It was as a reporter; in more expansive times it probably would have been junior reporter, but there was then such a shortage. In wartime they were tiny newspapers. The *Ayr Advertiser* at that time, I think, had an eight-page paper most weeks, maybe twelve on an odd occasion. But the staff shortage was very acute, and really there was no differentiation because reporters were so hard to come by. They were all in the Forces, except the old ones. Years later George Goodfellow, the editor of the *Advertiser*, told me he had been hoping he would get a reply to the ad from somebody maybe discharged or whatever from the Forces, a more experienced, senior man, who could take some of the burden, because George himself was not only editing the paper but having to go out reporting.[10]

When I went there I was the second reporter on the staff. Henry Hay, an Ayr boy, about a couple of years older than me, was the established reporter. Henry had had rheumatic fever as a kid and was unfit for the Forces. He was desperately keen to join the RAF, and even in the time I was at Ayr made further efforts to get in, but was always rejected on medical grounds. He later went to work for the Kemsley *Evening News* in Glasgow, worked latterly, I think, for STV, but died young. So Henry was the senior of us two reporters on the *Ayr Advertiser*, but was not totally experienced himself at that time. So George – we didn't call him George except behind his back, he was Mr Goodfellow – did the big meetings: Ayr town council and often Ayr county council, because really neither Henry nor I were particularly up to it. I'd just begun and was only learning the business. I was a very good shorthand writer, far better than Henry or even George Goodfellow. But I really didnae understand very much about how local government worked.

It was too far to travel daily from Shettleston, so I got digs in Ayr. I was subsidised, yet again, by my parents, who had said I was to take the job. George Goodfellow had said to me at the interview the salary would be one guinea [£1.05] a week. I was never cheeky, but never blate, and I said to him that it wasn't a great deal of money, but I was very anxious to get the job. 'However, I would have to be in digs, Mr Goodfellow.' That was going to cause financial problems. 'Well,' he said, 'if it would help, I'll increase it. I'll give you 22s 6d [£1.12½].' The structure of newspaper wages in those days was such that if you got more than the union minimum you were known as a 'merit man' – you got a merit award that lifted you above the minimum rate. So sometimes I brag (particularly to my wife, who was also a reporter), 'Of course, I was a merit man from the start.' This was a cachet very few reporters could claim. It had nothing to do with my ability; it was a humane editor who gave me 7½p extra to ease my financial problems! I can't remember how much I was given weekly by my parents to help pay my way, but, as you can imagine, I lived very frugally in Ayr.

I paid my own digs, which were in Queen's Terrace, a row of larger houses, all terraced, different shapes and sizes, down near the seafront. The digs were run by a woman bombed out in London, whose son was at Ayr Academy. I got this room at a very cheap rate in the winter months – about 15 shillings [75p]. That left me with nothing. Well, that was the digs until I was called up. But the great advantage of course of reporting was that quite often, even in wartime, the jobs you did sometimes included a cup of tea and this and that. Our household at home was largely teetotal, like many Scots households. There had been a drink problem in a previous generation and my mother was very strongly anti-drink. So that I didnae drink in those days. I didnae drink until I went to the sojers. I've never been a heavy drinker at any time, so I had no problems with pubs and funding boozing. And even then, of course, there was a limited amount of linage to be made at the *Ayr Advertiser* which supplemented the income – och, if it was five or six bob [25 or 30p] a week that would be the maximum.

The *Advertiser*, founded in 1803, was originally printed by the same printer, Wilson, who printed the Kilmarnock edition of Burns.[11] I've really worked for most of the world's ancient newspapers. But at the *Advertiser* it was the first time I'd come across newspaper files that had accounts of the battle of Waterloo. The Dunlop family (who I'm sure would not have approved George Goodfellow paying me an extra 7½p a week) were the owners of the *Advertiser*. They were what we called in Scotland minor gentry. They lived in some style out at Doonside at Alloway. George Goodfellow, the editor, had a tied cottage, a rented house, on the Doonside estate. Colonel Charles Dunlop, a minor landowner, had been a regular soldier. Occasionally we saw him, but he was a very shadowy figure: I wouldnae ken him if he chapped my door. Later on he became Sir Charles. His great claim to local fame was that he was the boss man of the Western Meeting – the Ayr Racecourse, then, as now, the prestige meeting in Scotland. And the *Advertiser* had a very lucrative jobbing printing contract: they did the race-cards for all the Scottish race meetings, including Musselburgh, Perth, Bogside, Hamilton, and Ayr itself.[12] In fact, the apprentices and indeed some of the linotype men and compositors did a lucrative extra paid shift. When Musselburgh and Hamilton were racing they were allowed off at the end of the week, once the paper was away, and they sold race-cards at the venues and pocketed a bit of extra cash. So the *Ayr Advertiser* gave me a very considerable insight into the mysteries of the print trade, which was quite fascinating. And I learned almost the first week I was there that I couldnae touch a bit of type as the form was lying on the stone. I was given a hell of a row – and that was a lesson you only were taught once. But I had good relations with the five lino men in the *Advertiser*.

There had been two Ayr papers that merged, presumably for economic reasons, in the early 1930s: the *Ayr Observer*, which was the town paper, loosely called, and the *Advertiser*, which was the country paper.[13] The *Advertiser* had a heavy agricultural interest and circulated heavily in the south of the county: Girvan, Maybole, all the towns, and the rural villages – Kirkmichael, Straiton, Dailly, Colmonell, Ballantrae, and goodness knows where. The *Observer* printing works, still functioning as a jobbing shop, was in the hinterland of Burns Statue Square. The *Advertiser* was heavily geared to the paper itself, but it still did printing jobbing work. When I walked into that office you could smell the ink, and it was romantic. Oh, I had arrived.

It was nine or ten months before I was called up. By the time I was leaving the *Advertiser* I was doing Prestwick town council, Maybole town council, the presbytery of Ayr, a big and powerful one, and, och, all the organisations. The hours I worked depended to some extent on the job you were going to. Newspapers at that time was largely a diary job: the events of your community and the ordered way the community went about its business dictated how the newspaper went about its business. Reporters were indeed reporters: they reported. The diary was the bedrock of the office. Certainly, if something happened that wasnae a diary marking, you of course broke off and attended to it as if it was. Figuratively, if a ship at that time being repaired fell aff the stocks at Ayr shipyard and 14 folk were killed, then you stopped going to Ayr toon cooncil and went doon tae the shipyard and did the story. But the day's work really pivoted on the reporters' diary, which George Goodfellow, as editor, marked. If the letters GG appeared against Ayr county council, George Goodfellow was going to that council. If it was a new minister being inducted at the Sandgate Kirk or whatever, and a reporter was going to the induction, it would be HH or BB (by that time, I was Bob, although I was aye Robert at home). So most days started surprisingly leisurely, in that you'd maybe get in the back of 9am. The first diary marking of the day was almost exclusively the Burgh Court at 10am at the Town Hall, and the Sheriff Court was at 10.30am down at the County Buildings. So that very often, if short-staffed, whoever was doing the Burgh Court would also go on to the Sheriff Court. But you phoned in advance to find out what was on the agenda at each, and so you balanced it.

Speaking of phones, when I went to work on the *Ayr Advertiser* I had never used a phone in my life. I had certainly done the Glesca keelie thing. I knew fine that if you went to the red Post Office phone box on the street corner and stuck a bit of newspaper up the Button B return money call, and somebody used the phone, didnae get through, wanted their money back and banged Button B but nae money came, they would walk away and lose it. Then you could nip in to the box and get tuppence. I knew that. But nane of our family friends or acquaintances were on the phone. People didnae communicate by telephone. So at the *Advertiser* I, a wee bit like the stoat and the rabbit, had to learn how to use this instrument in the corner of the reporters' room.

As a newspaper reporter, the *Ayr Advertiser* was an invaluable introduction for me. I was no different from other kids wi' a bit of writing ability. I loved discovering adjectives, and purple prose was a joy and a delight to me in my formative days. But there wis nae space for purple prose in wartime, or even post-war, journalism. And I learned a thing at Ayr that I've retained to this day: if I'm asked for 600 words I'll give you 600 words. If it really should be 1,800 words but they have to put it into 600, I'll distil down to 600. It taught me the virtue of tight, economical writing. Brevity is more than the soul of wit, it also is a great aid to lucidity. One of the things that irritates me about contemporary journalism is the long convoluted umpteenth paragraph piled on paragraph that tells you damn all at the end of the day. I shall be eternally grateful that, in that professional sense, my time couldnae have been a better time.

I tried to join the union before I was called up, but there were nae National Union of Journalist members in Ayr. George Goodfellow and old Jimmy Moffat, chief reporter on the *Ayrshire Post*,[14] great buddies the two of them, were both members of the Institute of Journalists. Now I didnae know much about it, except I knew that the Institute wasnae a trade union. I got a name in Glasgow of a union man, and I wrote. But wartime . . . Anyway I tried, but couldnae find a way then to join the union – but I joined it immediately after I was demobbed after the war. I'm now a life member of my union. I'm a trade unionist by conviction, not convenience. Well, when I came to Ayr I had all this. I had a severe culture shock – although I didnae use the phrase at that time. I was a stranger, not only physically: Ayr was very predominantly a middle-class town.

I didnae have a full year at the *Ayr Advertiser* before I was called up. But, oh, it was an invaluable experience. In retrospect, it didnae mean very much in terms of my acquisition of any newspaper skills. I was feeling my way. The jobs I was given were limited, for obvious reasons. George Goodfellow hadnae a lot of time to train ye: he was hard pushed just to get his paper out. But George was kind enough afterwards to say that I was a quick learner, and he had total confidence that I produced accurate, well-written reports.

*   *   *

I was called up in October 1942. I actually asked to go to the navy. There was no family connection to the navy, except that my father had worked in shipyards and had engined ships. But I didnae get to the navy, I was ca'ed up to the sojers. I went to Richmond in Yorkshire, the Green Howards' depot, for a basic six weeks' infantry training.[15] This was presumably one of the lessons of Dunkirk, when clerks and drivers and cooks didnae know how to handle a rifle. You also got aptitude tests, to decide whether you were brigadier material or cook material. After Richmond, I went to the East Yorks regiment and was posted to Fulford Barracks, York. Playing football there I scraped my legs very badly on an ash pitch, and had a very severe dermatitis condition which stayed with me on and off for a good many years even after the army. I was eventually taken off a medical grading by the army and given a preventative grading, because it was ruled this dermatitis would flare up if I went overseas. So I was posted to the Royal Army Pay Corps and did the rest of my wartime service in that. It was a much more genteel and sedentary kind of soldier to be than a rude, rough infantryman: with hindsight, I was not ungrateful for the intervention of fate. I was never posted overseas. I got terribly fed up with the Pay Corps at one stage and made a serious effort to get back to the infantry, but did not succeed.

Ironically, given my basic political attitude, I was posted to Officers' Accounts in Manchester, where all the commissioned ranks' accounts were held centrally. So I became very familiar with allowances paid at second lieutenant, major, and brigadier rates. But in terms of newspapers, I really held great power at the end of my army career, because after VE and VJ Days the colonel of that Pay Corps unit, which was housed in Pownall's Mill, a huge old cotton mill, was appointed editor of the revived Pay Corps journal. Colonel Dunhill had no idea how you edited a magazine, and put up a notice asking if there were any spare journalists kicking aboot. Bold as brass, I marched in and, despite my mere ten months' experience at the *Ayr Advertiser*, said I was the world's greatest journalist. Before I knew where I was, I was Col. Dunhill's right-hand man. The Pay Corps magazine, printed on the most beautiful art paper stored since pre-1939, came out periodically. It had a captive circulation because a' these guys in this huge old mill several storeys high and seeming to run about as far as Sauchiehall Street, had their demob group numbers ahead of mine, so they were hardly allowed to be demobbed without first forking up a year's subscription to the magazine. So I had a splendid year being Col. Dunhill's editor, chief sub and news editor, and producing the magazine, with the help of the printers. The job enabled me to commandeer a truck and go to the likes of Preston and York and address groups of second lieutenants on the need to provide material for the magazine. And we had a world exclusive. When General Montgomery was brought back from North Africa to take a leading part in preparations for D-Day, there was a Monty lookalike who walked about North Africa and Sicily to fox the German High Command. Now this lookalike, it turned out, had been a Pay Corps officer – and we got the first news of that into the Pay Corps journal. It wasnae really my exclusive, but I basked in the reflected glory.[16] Col. Dunhill wanted me to sign on as a Regular so that I could keep producing the Pay Corps journal for him. Having had more than enough of H.M.'s Forces by that time, I declined the invitation. I was demobbed about March or April 1947, took my full two months' statutory leave, and went to Ireland and various other places. My formative period in newspapers really began post-army service.

*   *   *

I was anxious to get back, and did two years with the *Ayr Advertiser* after my demob. Even after the war, newsprint remained rationed, but less severely so. I can't recall now what our weekly ration on the *Advertiser* was. I think it was an annual allocation with flexibility to decide when you went up. For instance, the week of the Ayr Cattle Show, second in importance in Scottish agriculture only to the Highland Show, was one of the first shows in the year. We always had an extra newsprint allocation then.

The *Ayrshire Post*, the rival paper, came out on a Friday, a day after the *Advertiser*. If we had a good exclusive we could never scoop the *Post*, because they would lift it. Young fellow as I was, you had imbibed all the romantic prose about newspapers, and the thing you most dearly wanted was a world-shattering scoop. When you couldnae get one frae the *Ayrshire Post* you whiles became crabbit.

The *Ayrshire Post* had two retired lady schoolteachers who came in on the Wednesday and Thursday and read the proofs. This was a luxury that the more penny-pinching management of the good Colonel Dunlop didnae run to: the reporters had to read their own proofs. It was a very time-consuming chore you could have done without. But again it taught me a lot I wouldnae have been taught if I hadnae had to read my ain proofs. And sometimes on a Tuesday morning – Wednesday was press day – we would come in bang on 9am and do 50 minutes of proofreading before nipping down to the courts. Equally on a Tuesday, you would come off the typewriter in the office, och, half past seven or eight o'clock at night, and there'd be a mountain of proofs waiting to be read, with the lino men screaming at ye for proof corrections. So you learned to proofread fast and fluently. The casualness and complacency of modern print under the new technology, where any damned error seems to slip through – I can understand it: it's perhaps not too easy to correct mistakes in printing now as it was in the older method. Nonetheless, there's now a casualness about word usage and everything else that would never have been tolerated in my day. The apostrophe is a case in point. I think now we'd just be as well to abolish the apostrophe because nobody, except old fogies like me, understands how apostrophes work!

The circulation of the *Ayr Advertiser* at that time was about 14,000–15,000. The *Post* was a bit higher – about 20,000, their circulation area was the more populous part of the county. The *Post* went into Troon; we didn't sell at all in Troon. The *Post* to some extent tried to sell in Cumnock, although that was *Cumnock Chronicle* territory.[17] We didn't really try Cumnock very much, although we circulated heavily up the Doon Valley – Patna, Dalmellington, etc. We circulated in Prestwick, Ayr burgh, and the south.

The *Ayrshire Post* didn't devote as much space as we did to agricultural affairs. We reported not only Ayrshire agriculture but national agriculture – although there was no way the *Advertiser* would ever send a reporter to the Highland Show. George Goodfellow was the same kind of old-style journalist as I suppose I've become in my day, in that every morning he would go through the London *Times* and *Daily Telegraph* largely on the social gazette type pages, because the Ayrshire landed gentry was very deeply established and very closely identified with the kind of stuff in *The Times* and *Telegraph*.[18] It was not uncommon for you to go into the office of a morning and find, say, a cutting from *The Times* pasted on a bit of copy paper stuck on your typewriter, saying, 'Go and see', or 'Phone about this', and it would be something that had happened to one of the Ayrshire connected gentry that required a paragraph.

I remember when Lord Malahide died in Dublin, George Goodfellow, who, immersed in south Ayrshire lore as he was, knew there was a connection, sent me round to Boswell Park in Ayr, to talk to these two very old ladies, direct descendants of James Boswell. The Boswell town house there was from the days of James and his father, the famous Scots-spoken High Court judge, who wasnae quite Braxfield but had things in common.[19] It wasnae a muckle house, but a fair-sized town house with Doric pillars and just a narrow garden off the pavement. I rang the bell. Of course in those days you simply announced yourself as 'I'm from the *Advertiser*'. I had my wee cutting from *The Times* with me, and said to the old lady who answered the door that the old guy had died in Dublin. I was never invited in, but the sister I got shouted over her shoulder and the other one came toddling through, och, in a dim light: they were obviously living in genteel poverty. And the first one said to her, 'This young man from the *Advertiser* has come to tell us that . . . (and she used the Christian name) has died. Isn't that nice of him? And he's brought this cutting to let us see it. Do you want it back, young man?' I said, 'Well, yes, please, if you don't mind.' But before I could say again what I was there for, I was in the most polite way shuffled off this doorstep. It was almost enough to make me abandon my chosen career. I fear I was not a very good reporter that night. I was young!

The *Ayr Advertiser* was very Conservative, the *Ayrshire Post* was Liberal. The *Post*, incidentally, was edited by my father's cousin, J. Ferguson Macnair. A Shettleston man originally, he'd been a *Glasgow Herald* parliamentary correspondent, had had enough of Fleet Street, had come back to Scotland to be editor of the *Post*. He was slightly snooty, and when I tentatively introduced myself as the son of his cousin, he kind of looked down his nose at me. It made no impact on him at all. Thereafter he was just Mr Macnair. He hadn't been an influence in my decision to go into journalism, because I didn't know of him until I went to work in Ayr.[20] Anyway the fact the *Advertiser* was strongly Tory caused me some problems post-war. South Ayrshire had a long Labour history. In the 1930s, Jimmy Brown, about whom there was a touch of the Ramsay MacDonald, was the miners' MP. Then Sanny Sloan, from my wife's village of Coylton, came in. Sanny never forgot that his brothers' names were on the Coylton war memorial and he was pacifist. When Sanny died, Emrys Hughes, who had married Keir Hardie's daughter Nan, got the Labour nomination. The Tory agent and organiser in Ayr Burgh, the seat held by the strongly Tory Sir Thomas Moore, was a rather nice lady called Miss Laidlaw.[21] She didnae raise my left wing high at all. She was just a nice woman who came into the *Advertiser* office with her wee bits and pieces about the Party, and was perfectly civil and polite. Miss Heron, however, the Party's South Ayrshire agent, was one of these Tory women I would have had no hesitation in stringing up on a lamp post – an arrogant, objectionable, bigoted upper-class woman in a tweed suit, and wi' a bonnet wi' a feather in it. She came in and issued orders until one day she and I fell oot and I bloody near got the sack over it. As I'd got older my political ideas had developed and become more radical – but I'll come back later to that.

Ayr was a good news centre in its own right. It was the county town where the county council etc. met, it had a coalfield, it had a thriving wee port, the dairy industry, and the farming industry was big. And by the time I returned from the army in 1947 Prestwick was an international airport and made Ayr a very big news centre. Prestwick had been pioneered in wartime, now suddenly there were five major carriers flying through Prestwick. So we had this huge traffic through the fog-free airport, and it was full of human interest stories – old grannies flying oot to Detroit to see their sons that had emigrated in the 1920s, and what not. The dailies sent staff men down to Ayr. *The Scotsman*, the *Express*, and the *Daily Mail*, newly arrived in Tanfield, Edinburgh, each had one, the *Daily Record* had two, and the evening papers were also represented. Now a great many of these staff men hardly moved outside the airport, because apart from the human interest it was the period when the Labour government was grappling with the problem of airport development in the UK, and Prestwick had a very vigorous political lobby pressing for recognition of its unique status. Lindgren, Ministry of Aviation parliamentary secretary, was never out of Prestwick, it seemed, having meetings with the local lobbies.[22] All that meant that folk like me, working in the *Ayr Advertiser*, made an awful lot of money in linage. I had the *Daily Herald* and *Daily Mail* linage, and *The Scotsman* paid me a retainer of £1 per week plus linage. My future wife Margaret, who had got my job on the *Advertiser* when I went to the army, had the Kemsley linage and she made a lot of money, too.

So that not only had I had almost a year's apprenticeship before the army, I had been properly learning this business of journalism for two and a bit years after my demob. But I wanted to move on in journalism, I wanted to work in daily journalism, and I wanted to come back home to Glasgow. I had hoped to join the *Daily Herald*. Jimmy Dollan, news editor in its Glasgow office, was waiting on a vacancy to offer the job to me. But it was a small office and vacancies werenae all that frequent. In the interval, Willie Kyle, staff man in Ayr of the *Glasgow Herald*, said to me, 'How would you like to work for the *Glasgow Herald*, Bob?' I said, 'Oh, aye, I wouldnae be averse.' In those days the *Glasgow Herald* didnae put ads in the paper when it wanted a reporter: you had your shoulder touched. To flash back for a moment, too, to the day I'd left Ayr to go to the army, Henry Hay, the other reporter then on the *Advertiser*, came up to Ayr station, saw me on the train, and gave me a bit of advice from his vastly enhanced 18 months' more experience than mine, and said, 'Bob, when you come back from the war, if you survive, you should work for a paper like the *The Observer*. It's more your style.'[23] So, I mean, I was interested in the *Glasgow Herald*. Anyway, in due course Willie Kyle said to me, 'You've to go up to Glasgow and see Tom Chalmers, the news editor. Unless you make an awful botch of it, there's a job for you.' So I went and saw Tom Chalmers in his wee doocot. Tom Chalmers, whom I was ultimately to succeed as news editor, wore a very distinctive white eye patch, and it must have been a clean one every morning. It was always immaculate, never any sign of soiling on it. He was supposed to have had his eye shot out on the Western Front in the First World War by a German machine gun. Tom's good eye blinked cheerily like a railway signalin' lamp whiles. At the interview he talked about what I'd been doing in Ayr. He knew George Goodfellow, who was the *Glasgow Herald*'s non-staff racing correspondent in Ayr and who wrote under the byline of 'Black and Gold': in those days you didnae have many personal bylines. So George must have given me a good reference, and I got the job. The only small hitch was the money. When Tom (TC we called him, but always Mr Chalmers to his face) said to me, 'Well, that only leaves the starting salary, Robert. It'll be £9 a week.' I said, 'Oh, yes.' He said, 'Is there something wrong?' And I said, 'Well, I had hoped for a wee bit more, Mr Chalmers.' 'Oh?' he said. 'That's the rate.' Very diffidently I said, 'Well, you know, Mr Chalmers, Ayr's outside the city. It's just about the best news centre in Scotland. I make an awful lot of money in my linage.' He says, 'Oh ? How much do you make?' I said, 'Well, I'm earning twice £9 a week between my *Advertiser* staff pay and my linage.' And he said, 'Oh, as much as that? You surprise me.' I thought, 'Oh, aye, he's beginning to take notice.' 'Well,' he said, 'young man, you'll have to make up your mind. You can stay with the fleshpots of your linage in Ayr. Or you can embark on a career in daily journalism with one of the UK's most noted newspapers. It's your choice.' So I surrendered and took the plunge as a reporter with the *Glasgow Herald* at £9 a week.

There were about 14 or 15 reporters in the newsroom at 65 Buchanan Street, Glasgow, at that time. I was the most recent arrival, but within a short time there were two or three other new arrivals. There was a fair amount of movement out of the *Glasgow Herald* because they did in fact pay lower than average rates. You could get more elsewhere. Some of the guys who had maybe got married and had young families went to the *Express*, where the money was better. George Harvey came down to the *Herald* about a month after me from the *Press & Journal* in Aberdeen – we sat for five years on opposite sides of one of the *Herald*'s huge mahogany desks you could have played a fitba' match on, they were about the size of Hampden Park – and George and I did the Citizens Theatre *Prompter* magazine for several years for, I think it was £10 an issue we got: we split it.[24] And the *Glasgow Herald* held linage, but, och, it was buttons, and the expenses were poor. People on the *Express* and the *Mail* made a lot of money out of their expenses.

Among the 14 or 15 reporters there was just one woman. She was English and had come up from the south with her husband, an air controller at Prestwick airport. Molly Plowright was very fluttery, very English, a nice enough woman, but nobody took Molly seriously. She later became the film correspondent. But, very unusual in those days, there was a woman sub-editor, Nan . . . – her surname's gone. Of Outram's two other papers, the *Evening Times* had a good woman reporter when I first went there called Sally Russell. Then she became women's editor and ceased to be a reporter. The *Bulletin* acquired a woman reporter eventually from the Borders; later on she wrote for *The Scotsman* on racing and what not. But there werenae many women then on newspapers. Margaret, my wife, had left Ayr Academy before completing her secondary course, became office girl in a glazier's office, then, when I was called up, got my job on the *Ayr Advertiser*. There had been one woman reporter in the *Ayr Advertiser* previously; then post-war there was a lassie, Christine McCracken, taken on in the *Advertiser*. So then there were two women reporters on the *Advertiser* when there weren't all that many women reporters as such, though there were a few women specialist writers, and women's page. I think it was pre-war the National Union of Journalists had made a very enlightened deal with the employers that there was no differential in pay rates between men and women.

At Outram's, the staffs had been merged in wartime, to combat manpower called up to the Forces. I gather you could find yourself working for the *Bulletin* one week and the *Herald* the next. That lasted until the war finished, then the papers reformed into their separate staffs. One legacy though was that Tom Chalmers, who had been news editor of the joint wartime staffs, retained the news editorship of all three newspapers, including the *Evening Times*, although each had its own chief reporter and staff functioning independently. Tom Chalmers as news editor had a largely administrative job. He didnae really have a lot to do day-to-day organising news, which was done independently at each paper's desk. There was a rough co-operation worked out.

When I was in the *Glasgow Herald* from 1949 to 1954, if you did a story and got a byline on it you felt you had really done a most meritorious story. The byline wasnae your own name, it was 'By a staff reporter'.

And, by Jove, if you finished up in the paper one morning with 'By a staff reporter', you had hit the big time that day. It was an achievement.

The 1950 general election came soon after I got the job in the *Glasgow Herald*. Of course we were all on duty that night into the wee sma' hours to do the election. And I forget now which constituency it was, but one of the marginal English constituencies: how it went the election'd go. Well, Labour won it. And I remember in the reporters' room saying instinctively, 'Oh, we've held it!' Jimmy Harrison, the deputy chief reporter and a terrible Tory, says to me: 'What did you say?! Are you a Labour man?' And I said, 'Aye, well, yes, aye.' 'Oh,' he says, 'you'd better not let that be known about here.' In a sense he was right. I wouldnae have been sacked, but it was non-U, like whistling in church.

Well, in my schooldays at Eastbank Academy I was active in the school debating society. It wasnae particularly political, more kind of highfalutin moral issues. A teacher at Eastbank for whom I had great affection at the time and retrospectively was Mr MacCormick, whom we knew as Monty, younger brother of King John MacCormick of Nationalist fame. Monty taught us history. But he also clearly was touched by the same tinge as his more famous brother. Whiles he would say, 'Of course there's another way of looking at this.' To that extent he certainly encouraged me toward what has been a constant political preoccupation of my adult life: the Scottish dimension in politics. It would be to malign Monty's professionalism to say he subverted my view of history, but he set my curiosity running.[25] It would be wrong to claim my family background was highly political in the way some families were. But we discussed world events. I remember the first thing that profoundly moved me was the Spanish Civil War. When the fall of Bilbao was reported it was almost like a death in the house.[26] My father was never a member of a political party, although he was very active in the Amalgamated Engineering Union. He was also a friend of old Willie Cuthbert, a famous ILPer in Shettleston and nationally in the Maxton–Wheatley era, and a nice old man. So I was fortunate in that we discussed things in the house. And so when I went to work in Ayr on the *Ayr Advertiser* it was a profound cultural shock. I moved from, if not a highly politicised family, a highly politicised environment in the east end of Glasgow, which of course was Independent Labour Party territory – Bridgeton, Camlachie, Shettleston. John Wheatley had lived in Shettleston, in a big hoose up the Sandyhills golf course. My father had told me about the riot at Wheatley's house, organised by militant Catholics. Willie Regan – father of Liam Regan, a later friend and colleague of mine who worked for Kemsley newspapers and then freelanced – had been one of the group of four Catholics who really broke the hierarchy over the matter of Catholics being permitted to be socialists. Liam himself was anti-church to his dying day, on the grounds of the shabby treatment the Catholic church devoted to his father.[27] Shettleston was ILP territory and we just voted ILP automatically. I've seen me in my late schoolboy teens whiles walk from the house on a Sunday night from Shettleston through Tollcross to London Road, the famous Auchenshoogle tram terminus, where you got the tram to Dalmuir, get a penny fare to Brigton Cross and go into the Olympia Cinema, where Jimmy Maxton had a Sunday night once a month that, I think, promised us the millennium was coming. *Socialism in Our Time* was the ILP slogan at the time.[28] I profoundly believed, after hearing Jimmy on a Sunday night, that by Monday morning it would all have happened, and by Tuesday morning I was bitterly regretful that it hadnae. But I never joined a political party. In Ayr after the war there was only one overtly political journalist and that was Allan Hewitson, a Labour councillor. Allan, an ex-*Ayrshire Post* man, was working for Kemsley newspapers: the *Daily Record*, Glasgow *Evening News*, and *Sunday Mail*. Naturally Allan and I very swiftly became very good friends. Older than me, he had been in the navy most of the war. In some ways a kind of feckless man, Allan was a good reporter and a good guy. He died relatively young, in his late fifties.[29] Then when I came in 1949 to the *Glasgow Herald* I wouldn't say it was a very overtly political bunch of reporters I worked with. Equally I didn't make a lot of political noises in the newsroom – apart from my spontaneous reaction in the general election of 1950! Again I was still very much learning this trade. I mean, there was a lot of pretension, which didnae really rub off on me, about it being a profession. And then I had been in Manchester in the army in the previous 1945 election. There was a shortage of barrack accommodation and we were in civvy digs, with a civilian accommodation allowance. So I got my civilian clothing brought down. It was the first election campaign I took part in. I was furious at the time, because although I was by then 21 I wasnae on the register and couldnae vote. But I was oot in the Rushholme division of Manchester and knocked on doors for Lester Hutchinson, a very left-wing MP. I sometimes look back, smile wryly, and say, 'God, I've no' half been a supporter of lost causes a' ma days!' Because Lester Hutchinson, a man after my own heart who believed in socialism in our time, too, as I did then, had the distinction later of being expelled from the Attlee-led Labour Party for left-wing deviationism. So, I mean, I was politically interested.[30]

But I also had this belief that news was important. Although I worked in Ayr for a Tory-inclined paper, then I joined the *Glasgow Herald*, which was theoretically independent but in reality was a Conservative paper, I took the view that, though I was politically interested, to be a good newspaperman I had to have no Party affiliation. So I didn't join a Party until 1964, by which time I was working for *The Guardian*. I joined the Labour Party in 1964 because I came home after the first '64 election, when the Wilson administration was first elected, very angry and despondent that after 13 wasted years (the great slogan of the time) Labour had squeaked in by such a narrow margin that obviously another election was goin' tae be needed. I was so angry that my wife said to me, 'Well, maybe you should go and join the Labour Party and do something about it.' And, by God, I did – in a fury. I hadnae really meant to join the Labour Party, because I still strongly believed there should be no Party affiliation, that as a reporter I had to maintain a strict neutrality. It didn't mean I didn't have private sympathies. But it was only in '64 I harnessed my political conviction to Party membership.[31]

*   *   *

I was about five to six years, from 1949 to 1954, with the *Glasgow Herald*. Towards the end of 1954 I moved to the London *Times* as their first ever Scottish staff man. By that time I was a very experienced *Glasgow Herald* reporter. I think I had quite a good reputation, but very localised. You could be marked in the *Herald* diary to go to the annual general meeting of the North Glasgow Washing Green Society. Now that was big stuff: you got a fat paragraph if you were lucky. So these jobs . . . And in that era when the Scottish staff correspondent was a highly prized job. You did the best of the day's stories every day of the week. Well, I watched two Scottish staff men, Bill Coulter o' the *News Chronicle* and Frank Gillespie o' the *Daily Telegraph*, and I thought, 'I could do that job a damn sight better than them.'[32] Neither of them were bad reporters, but they were both a wee bit lazy. I didnae want to go to London. I didnae like London as a city, it was too big. I wouldnae have minded going to London for five years in the Commons Lobby. But I felt even then that if I went there, 'I'll come hame efter five years,' because of my political attitudes. I felt drawn both as a newspaperman and because of my private inclinations to seeing how far we could improve things, because these were my people. I wasnae chauvinist, but Scotland is where I live. I've wore Scotland like a comfy old jaicket. I was at hame here, I felt relaxed. As I say, if I could have gone to London for five years and come home, I would have done it. But I also realised that if I did, the odds against me breaking off would have been difficult. And even that early there was much about Westminster that irritated me. All the needless mumbo-jumbo would have driven me daft. So I didnae really want to go south.

Well, I wrote to Ernie Cockburn, a Scot and an ex-Outram man away before my time, who was news editor in Manchester of the *Guardian*. I'd never met him but I knew of him. On the *Glasgow Herald* we provided the *Manchester Guardian*, as it was still called in those days, with some stories, and the *Herald* contributed, as I understand it, about a third of the *Guardian*'s foreign costs for a service to itself. I suggested to Ernie Cockburn that as the *Daily Telegraph*, the *News Chronicle*, and the *Daily Herald* all had a Scottish staff man, it was high time the *Manchester Guardian* put a staff man in Scotland. I thought I wrote him a very convincing piece, and I got a very courteous reply from Ernie Cockburn that there were good reasons why his paper didn't have a staff man in Scotland, but would I be interested in coming to Manchester? I wrote back and said I would be interested, but I would really like to work in Scotland for one of the UK papers. Within a few months I got another courteous note from him saying that *The Times* was thinking of appointing a staff man in Scotland. So I got in touch with *The Times*, and was told later that R.M. Dobson, its Home News Editor, said when my letter came in, 'I think this is our man.'[33] So I was summoned down to London immediately – I had to go at such short notice that I couldnae get a day off and went 'sick' – had the interview and got the job. Most of my changes of job have been virtual touches on the shoulder. I'm vain enough to think that that's because I was a good reporter and a valuable acquisition. But *The Times* job, no. That was how I came to be *The Times* Scottish staff man.

The Times at that time appointed three staff men outside London for the first time ever. They put a man in Birmingham, a man in Manchester, and a man in Scotland, who happily was me. Of all the newspapers I've worked for, I think it was probably my most productive and enjoyable job. They were good to work for. And, oh, I was given enormous freedom: I think that was what made it so attractive. And it was also of course the mighty *Times*, The Thunderer. Sir William Haley hadn't then long been appointed editor. I think Haley's enormous achievement was that, without ruining or changing the format of the paper, the way for a while it wavered later under Rupert Murdoch, he modernised the paper thoroughly and retained all its essential qualities. Haley was a moderniser with a great sense of historic consequences.[34]

When I joined *The Times* at the end of 1954 there were occasions when, if something happened and I missed it, a day late I would file just a short story for the record, the guts of it, an inch or an inch and a half. So Haley didn't betray the paper's traditions, but he modernised it. Anyway, I went down for what I called a week's indoctrination to old Printing House Square. I discovered then that the paper was subdivided totally and operated on two distinct legs: home and foreign news. That was apart from all the specialties. Of course, I was home news.

One of the troika of deputy editors was also the foreign editor, and he was, I think, a second-generation removed Scot, of Caithness extraction, who rejoiced in the name Iverach McDonald. And he was your romantic Scot *par excellence*. He had a dewy, misty, Landseer-stag-in-the-mountain view of Scotland, which caused me considerable problems at times as a staff writer, when I had to gently disengage from Iverach's notion of how a particular story should maybe be done. For although he was foreign editor, Iverach had this great attachment to the Scottish correspondent, and what he was about. It led to the joke in Printing House Square that Bob Brown really wasnae in the home news at all, but should be in Iverach McDonald's foreign correspondent list.[35]

My only instruction when I joined *The Times* was that I was to write for the late London edition, which was the last edition. If a story was of interest in the final edition, then it was intrinsically a good story, and I wasnae to waste my time chasing my tail on stories that were of no consequence. In reality, most stories I wrote were of course for the first edition, the one that came to Scotland. Incidentally, at that time *The Times* and the *Daily Worker* jointly chartered a plane that flew up from London to Renfrew airport with their respective first editions, for distribution onwards from Glasgow. It still meant you couldnae get a *Times* in, say, Inverness before about 1pm, or in Wick or Thurso before about 4pm, and in Stornoway it was 9.30pm when the boat came in with the paper.

The Times was also a very satisfying paper for a reporter to work on in that there was good sub-editing: you didnae get any butchery. Even if you lost a third of a story between the first edition and the last, it was intelligibly put together. Equally, as I've said, I had total freedom. I got the odd directive. When something interested them, R.M. Dobson (Dobbie, as we called him, a smashing guy), home news editor, would phone me and say, 'We think you should maybe do a piece about X. Were you thinking of doing it?' And I would sometimes say, 'Well, no. But if you want it . . .' Because I got few directives it wasnae worth arguing over 400 miles of phone: I had a good relationship with Dobson. He was a kindly man, a good news editor, he gave me my head, and he trusted me. And so did they all.

I would make occasional visits to Printing House Square for specific purposes. I always went down for a working week in the first week of the New Year. This was a double convenience: there wasnae a lot of news in Scotland just after the New Year. *The Times* profoundly believed that all Scots were paralytic drunk post-New Year for about four days and that they wouldnae get a line out of me anyway – a theory that I never discouraged. Margaret, my wife, used to come down to London with me. So I went down for a week and would work while I was there. But it was largely a grand tour: I went to see all the folk whose specialty I served from time to time. John Hennessy, the sports editor, always wanted to see me because I did a bit of sport, the Scottish Cup Final, for example. And when the grand curling match was revived for the first time after the war, and played on Loch Leven – I wasnae a curler, you didnae have many curlers in the east end of Glesca – I did this (though I say it myself) splendid piece for the sports page, nearly a column of 1,400 words or so. That was one of these peculiarly Scottish stories that was romantic in many ways: I discovered that there was a lot of kind of Masonic ritual in curling that I'd never realised. Roy Hodson, *The Times* staff man in Manchester, used to say to me, 'Oh, God, Bob, I wish I was working out of Scotland. You've such a variety of different stories up there.' And I had a good reputation for being able to do that kind of stuff as well as the hard stuff. In fact, when I left *The Times* in 1960, Frank Roberts, the deputy news editor, told me, 'You know, you're leaving as the highest-paid reporter on the staff.' And, I mean, at that time I think I was only on £1,400 a year or something.[36]

I had left the *Glasgow Herald* in 1954 for the immense financial advantage of a fiver a week. In 1954 a fiver was a lot of money, and I went from roughly £900 a year. Of course *The Times* was careful wi' its money. It didnae lash out money. But I got a rise with great regularity, some of them on Haley's direct intervention. Bob Dobson, the news editor, however, raised a test case on behalf of Birmingham. Jeff Preece, the staff man there, about 1956–7 submitted to the management a case for providing him, and progressively Roy Hodson in Manchester and me in Glasgow, with company cars. He showed the benefit this would represent for these men doing their job over scattered territories. This was carefully evaluated by Francis Mathew, the general manager.[37] A note finally came back which Dobbie circulated to the three of us: it had been decided that this was an unnecessary innovation and that the job could be perfectly well done utilising public transport and hiring a taxi when occasion demanded it. I mean, I covered general elections using public transport. I've gone from Aberdeen to Inverness along that railway line you don't really use if you can avoid it. Willie Lyle from Macduff in Banffshire, who worked with me on the *Glasgow Herald* and went to the *News Chronicle* and the *Daily Mail* later, used to tell the story of the two Macduff men that got on the train at Macduff to go to Aberdeen on a winter's night. As they got off and one of them hauled his bag off the rack he says to the other yin, 'Well, that's the worst of the journey over.' And the other yin says, 'Och, where are you going?' And he says, 'China!' So when I think back about covering the likes of a three-week general election campaign in that period of terrible political quietude, when there were not highly political stories coming out of Scotland, sometimes you had a job getting constituencies where onything was likely to happen in terms of result . . . But the other thing was, I had complete freedom. That's probably the crucial point. They trusted my judgement, and I provided a wide variety of well-written stories.

When I was appointed *The Times* staff man in Scotland, Sir William Robieson, editor of the *Glasgow Herald*, on the grounds that the Outram Board took the perfectly legitimate view that if *The Times* put a staff man into Scotland this represented competition and they didn't see why they should help, refused me accommodation in the *Herald* office where I could do my work. So for a year I worked out of Kemsley House in Glasgow (where the *Daily Record*, Glasgow *Evening News*, and *Sunday Mail* were published). But I was struggling in Kemsley House because I had an awful job getting background there that I needed for referencing. It really was an impediment that there wasnae any kind of House library that I needed for my work. But when Sir William Robieson retired as editor of the *Glasgow Herald* and was succeeded by James Holburn, who had been a London *Times* foreign correspondent in Berlin during the Nazi period before 1939, I was allowed to work out of the *Herald* office at 65 Buchanan Street.[38] I had a desk there by convenience, which gave me access to the *Herald* library, which was the best Scottish newspaper library by far. *The Scotsman* had a good library, but the *Glasgow Herald* maintained an index: you could find things quickly. Incidentally, my desk in Kemsley House was in their Features room, which housed all sorts of weird folk – including the doo man, The Gangrel, and wee Elky Clark. Wee Elky, who had the sight of only one eye, and I became great friends. Now Kemsley House was full of very narrow corridors. And one day when I was hashing out to go somewhere and wee Elky was pursuing his amiable amble, the pace he traditionally went at, I met him right in the corner of one of these narrow corridors and almost bowled him over. For all Elky's normally slow movements and slow diction, before I could say, 'Oh!', his hands were instinctively up and he was ready for the noble art of self-defence. He could have had me stretched out cold. He got as big a fright as I did at meeting him, but, by God, was he ready and I wasnae! He could have laid me low! That wouldnae have done relations between *The Times* and Kemsley Newspapers much good![39]

When I wrote a story for *The Times* out of Glasgow or Edinburgh I was bylined and datelined. I was 'From our own correspondent, Glasgow,

September 10th . . . Edinburgh, April 6th.' But if I wrote a story from Penicuik or Ayr or Portree, I became 'From our special correspondent, Portree, January 10th.' The 'own' and the 'special' denoted a staff man. If the byline was 'From our correspondent, Glasgow, September 6th', then it was the stringer (a non-staff reporter). And these lines were deeply cherished at that time in *The Times* newspaper. In fact, I got an early rebuke from Dobbie – Bob Dobson, the news editor, with whom I had good cordial relations the whole time I worked for the paper. There was a sudden flash flood in the Laigh of Moray. The river Spey rose in its wrath and poured watter a' o'er the Laigh o' Moray and it was a very serious flooding story. It just happened, as the best floods happen, in the bat of an eyelid. Well, I used to call London in the morning and I would call them again before the late-afternoon editorial conference to confirm or change what I was doing for the schedule, the basis of discussion at the conference as to the contents of the next day's paper. So I had said to Dobbie in the afternoon that this story was breaking in Moray and that I would do it. Of course I did it by telephone from Glasgow: phoned the polis, phoned the shirra [sheriff], things any reporter would dae, and I finished up with a good enough story. But I put on it 'From our special correspondent' (internally we abbreviated that to FOSC, or FOOC if I was doing it from Glasgow or Edinburgh). At breakfast time next morning the phone rang in my house; it was Bob Dobson phoning from his own home in Ealing. He said, 'Robert, were you in this place Fochabers yesterday to do this story?' 'No, no, Mr Dobson,' I said, 'I did it by phone from Glasgow.' He said, 'You didn't?!' I said, 'Yes, I did.' I thought I'd made some terrible faux pas. 'You didn't file a story from Glasgow as FOSC, Fochabers?' 'Yes,' I said. 'Oh, Good God,' he says, 'you mustn't ever do that again. That's dreadful. You weren't in Fochabers?' 'No,' I said. 'Oh,' he says, 'that's terrible. I'll need to tell the editor this. We've had a story in the paper supposedly from Fochabers and you weren't even there!' 'Well,' I said, 'Mr Dobson, I can see if something happens in Denver, Colorado, or in Vladivostock, nobody expects our staff man in New York or Washington to get to Denver, or from Moscow to Vladivostock. I can see it's acceptable to the reader that the staff man in Moscow is filing a story about something that's happened 2,000 miles away. It's a bit ludicrous daein' a story about Speyside floods in the Laigh of Moray from Glasgow when, you know, we're a small place.' I said, 'When you live and work in a wee small place, you know it's a wee small place. So I never gave it a . . .' 'Well,' he said, 'I can understand now why you did it. But you mustn't ever again do anything like that. That is not allowed.' He was nice, but he left me in no doubt that I had really blotted my copybook.

This was before the era, even in the popular press, of very much in the way of personal bylines. In some ways I think that the personal byline has been the ruination of much good reporting, because it gave too many young fellows a false notion of their own importance. They couldnae see the wood for the trees whiles, they were getting so intoxicated with their personal byline.

Another point about *The Times* policy on bylines: when I was based for a time at first as their Scottish staff man in Kemsley House, Glasgow, I got on fine with Donald Bruce, then news editor on the *Daily Record*, a kind of taciturn, moody, ex-Jap POW, as many ex-Japanese prisoners were. Donald was passing me one day at my desk, looked over my shoulder and saw a bit of paper I had with just 'FOOC, Glasgow' on it, and said, 'What's FOOC?' Of course the *Daily Record* didnae have things like 'From our own correspondent'. I explained. 'Oh,' he says, 'That's nice. I would like to be an FOOC.' Thereafter, if there was some reception or something on and I walked in and Donald was there and got his eye on me, he scandalised the whole gathering and almost embarrassed me by shouting, 'Hi, FOOC, how are you getting on?'

Some time after the Laigh o' Moray story, Britain made its last great imperial expansion by annexing Rockall. We didnae realise at the time it was all to do with mineral resources and what not. But the Admiralty made this announcement in London about 11 o'clock one morning. My phone rang almost immediately. It was Mr Dobson, the home news editor, who said: 'There's a statement here from the Admiralty which I shall read to you.' It was a very terse statement saying HMS *Whatever* had landed a party on Rockall at 14.20 hours on such and such a date, a Union flag had been run up, a plaque stuck on the rock, and Rockall was now part of the British Empire. Dobbie says to me, 'We're still not terribly clear why we've annexed Rockall. We'll try and do something at this end. I'll put Basil Gingell, our naval correspondent, on to it.' Basil was a very old world *Times* man. Then Dobbie says to me: 'Can you get to Rockall?' 'No,' I said, 'there's no way I can get to Rockall. I know very little about Rockall, Mr Dobson, except, as we say in Scotland, it's a muckle lump o' rock sticking out the Atlantic. Even if we were prepared to charter a helicopter (which were then just beginning to come into use),' I said, 'we couldnae land on Rockall. And there's nothing there but gannets and seaspray.' 'Well,' he said, 'what's the nearest part that you can get to Rockall?' By this time of course I had the business at Fochabers and the Laigh o' Moray behind me, remember, so I said warily: 'Well, I could go to the Outer Isles and look kind of south from maybe about Barra, or I could go to Ardnamurchan, the nearest point on the mainland.' 'Well,' he said, 'go to Ardnamurchan.' 'Mr Dobson,' I said, 'I cannae get to Ardnamurchan. Francis Mathew wouldnae give us a car, remember. I would have to take a train to Oban or Fort William and sprachle my way away west. And,' I said, 'there's nae phones except call boxes on the way. How could I get anything to write aboot, unless you want fiction – and I take it we're no' writing fiction.' He seldom got shirty, but this time he got quite ratty. But at the finish, with enormous reluctance, he let me stay in Glasgow, though he said, 'Right, I won't alert Gingell. You'll just do it with the Admiralty yourself.' That, I took it, was a punishment. But you'll find in the files of *The Times* that I recorded the annexation of Rockall, the last addition to the British Empire, and we didnae really get much very much oot the Admiralty. I was into the *Encyclopedia Britannica*, meteorological records and everything else I could remotely think of, because naebody really knew anything about Rockall. It was sea area Rockall, sea area Malin – and that was as much as anybody knew. So, I mean, I was Scottish correspondent, but I was a kind of foreign correspondent.[40]

The year after Rockall came the Suez crisis of 1956. When Suez occurred, *The Times* in the first spasm of the crisis backed what the British government had done, and it offended me deeply. Suez really split Britain in two. I was astonished at the time by colleagues of mine who were much more conservatively inclined but how many of whom were outraged by what we did in cahoots with the others in Suez. Suez upset me so much that it was almost the only time in my newspaper life when I seriously considered resigning because I could not take the line of the paper that employed me. But by the grace of God, or whatever deity intervened, after a few days *The Times* came to its senses, found it difficult to retract completely, but greatly modified its line by adopting a much more sensible and cautious one. I felt the crisis for me personally was over and I could carry on working for this paper which I enjoyed working for, which gave me great freedom, and, in hindsight, gave me the happiest newspaper years of my life.[41]

*   *   *

After six years on *The Times* I was induced in 1960 to go back to the *Glasgow Herald*. Again it was the touch on the shoulder. As I've said, I was working out of the *Herald* office in Buchanan Street again for most of my period with *The Times*, and that gave me access to these facilities that were imperative. When Tom Chalmers, who had been the *Herald* group news editor, died shortly before he was due to retire, Reggie Biles, the deputy editor, came through after Tom had been decently buried and said the editor, James Holburn, wondered if I would be interested in rejoining the *Herald* as successor to Tom Chalmers as news editor. I went through to see Holburn, who said he had read my Scottish copy for *The Times* with interest and approval and thought I had done some very distinguished work. I said, 'Well, I'm not uninterested in becoming news editor of the *Herald*, but I'm not anxious to leave *The Times*. It's a very congenial berth and it has realised all my expectations. If it's a question of taking over the group news editorship of three newspapers, then we can forget it. I am not interested. It's an impossible job. It's an administrative job, and if I'm going to be news editor then I want to be a news editor. I want to control and direct the editorial services. I'd be willing to discuss the news editorship of the *Glasgow Herald* if that was acceptable to you.' 'Well,' Holburn said, 'I was rather hoping you might say that, because I don't think the group news editorship at present works particularly well.' But it took another few days, because the *Herald* were not good payers and their first financial offer was substantially below what I was getting from *The Times*. So after several days of fencing I agreed to go as news editor of the *Glasgow Herald*, with a remit to develop, expand, and modernise the paper's news coverage. And I went for £1,800 a year, which made me paid much higher than the chief sub-editor and various other senior editorial functionaries. The chief sub-editor got wind of what I was being paid and just about went through the roof. But I went for that.

Well, it was a bad move which I regret, because Outrams was moving. The *Herald* was floundering badly and moving into that period which led to the struggle for control between Fraser and Roy Thomson. Fraser was invited in, and he as the company doctor syndrome, sorted it out. So within a few months of my taking over as news editor of the *Herald* the *Bulletin* was closed down. There was a period then of intense cost-cutting. Latterly I joked that if I wanted to send a reporter in the tram to Dalmuir there was a board meeting; and if I wanted to send a photographer with the reporter there was an extraordinary general meeting of shareholders before I was authorised to spend the money on the tram fare. It was a most frustrating period. Of course, I didn't get the freedom I'd been promised to develop the news services, although I did have some successes. Charlie McCorry by this time was back in the *Herald*'s Edinburgh branch office, and I used Charlie to break a lot of the stuffiness in the *Herald*'s features material. I got Charlie to do two splendid pieces about pigeon racing in Scotland, the secretary of which was a guy in Baillieston – I lived in Garrowhill at the time. We did this two-day piece on the Scots doo men and used a jargon that *Glasgow Herald* West End readers werenae familiar with. It was a great breakthrough. Charlie and I ran over the bones of it together. I had benefited greatly from being given a free hand, and as news editor I had a very light rein on my writers: they got a free hand, too. I also had a piece done on Jeannie Robertson when she was little known: I had a great admiration for Jeannie's range and what not.[42] Now that was something the *Glasgow Herald* didnae have. So in a sense I would lay a modest claim to bringing the *Glasgow Herald* into some of a recognisably different world from its traditional narrow, West End mercantile concept of things. But I didnae have the freedom that I had hoped for. I never had a budget. Budgets were unheard of in the *Glasgow Herald* in those days. Och, it was a frustrating period. The paper was in the control of Gordon Allan, an accountant. Everything was a cash-book entry to him. James Holburn, the editor, who was also a good newspaperman, although with a very different outlook from me on affairs, latterly had very little to do with Gordon Allan, who exercised an iron discipline in the paper's daily affairs. Holburn used to send me down to the next floor to negotiate with Gordon Allan until one day I came up absolutely bilin'. I said to Holburn: 'Don't send me down there again because one of these bloody days you're goin' tae have tae explain to your board of directors why your news editor threw Gordon Allan right oot the windae into the well of the building.' Allan was a wee nyaff of a man who had total control and you couldnae budge him. So, as I say, it was a very frustrating period, and afterwards I bitterly regretted going back to the *Glasgow Herald*.

I left the *Herald* in 1964, just before the Fraser/Thomson battle was joined, because I decided there was no future for me on the paper. So I put it about on the grapevine in newspapers that I was not averse to being offered a new job. My old friend John Cole, who later became the BBC's political correspondent and whom I had known when he was still on the *Belfast Telegraph* as its Stormont man and I used to go over there and do the Ulster elections for the *Glasgow Herald*, had joined the *Manchester Guardian* and used to come up to Glasgow. John and I became very friendly and have remained good friends. He was an industrial man for years. Anyway John phoned me. It was just at the time the *Manchester Guardian* was in transition from Manchester to London and was dropping *Manchester* from its title. Alastair Hetherington was its editor, ex-*Glasgow Herald* leader writer of course, son of Sir Hector, principal and vice chancellor for so long at Glasgow University. Hetherington was editing the paper for about two days a week in Manchester and about three days in London, and, och, it was a daft arrangement. It couldnae work. Well, when John Cole phoned me he said, 'Bob, I hear you're wanting a move. Well, we're at last putting a staff man into Scotland.' John said

Ernie Cockburn, to whom I'd written on this subject some years before, was away but, he said, 'I'm authorised to offer you the job of Scottish correspondent. Are you interested?' 'Oh, God, aye,' I said, 'I'm interested.' It was like getting my old job on *The Times* back again. Of course, by that time *The Times* was as admirably served by their new Scottish staff man, Hugh Cochrane, as I hope I had served them. Hugh, in fact, was my nominee to succeed me there. When I was leaving *The Times* Dobbie, its home news editor, had asked me to draw up a small list of potential successors, put the name of the man I recommended in an envelope and seal it – and I wrote 'Hugh Cochrane'. Dobbie came up to Glasgow and did the interviews himself and Hugh was given the job and proved a highly successful *Times* Scottish staff man. Hugh and I were the best of friends and good comrades until his death, and I was privileged to write an obituary of him in *The Scotsman*.[43]

So in leaving the *Glasgow Herald* I was lucky. I went down to London and saw Hetherington, who said, 'I cannae pay you very much because we're in a difficult transition. What are you getting on the *Herald*?' 'Well,' I said, 'I'm getting £1,800.' 'All right,' he says, 'I can manage £1,900. How about that?' Little did he know I would have come for £1,600! So that was fine.

I've been very lucky in my editors. George Goodfellow on the *Ayr Advertiser* was very old fashioned, a very up-and-down conformist, but a very good editor and taught me a lot. On the other hand, I didnae think a lot of Sir William Robieson on the *Glasgow Herald*. I didnae think he was a particularly good newspaperman. He had a dead hand in the *Glasgow Herald* as I knew it, though there were a lot of good newspapermen in the *Herald* that you learned from. Then, well, Haley of *The Times*: it was just a good newspaper.

In my new job as Scottish correspondent of the *Guardian*, the manner in which the day-to-day work was conducted was very similar to *The Times*. As time went on though it became with the *Guardian* more structured, and I had greater control from the *Guardian* than I'd had from *The Times*, who had been extremely good and had virtually let me do as I decided ought to be done, with occasional exceptions when there was something of special interest they'd asked me to do. The *Guardian* was, with hindsight, disappointing. On getting the offer from them I was very pleased and very keen, because in a sense it gave me my *Times* job back again with the freedom, or so it had seemed, to cover all that was worth covering in Scotland for another quality newspaper and, for the first time, one that came somewhere closer to my own private slant on the way the world should be organised. That was possibly more important to me than to many journalists – not all: people like John Hossack and Philip Stein were the same, but we were the exceptions rather than the rule. Most of the lads were extremely good reporters, but were often politically neutral or with no great strong belief in anything pertaining to that.[44]

So, with hindsight, in fact I was joining the *Guardian* at rather a bad time in the paper's history, because they were in the midst of the transition from being the *Manchester Guardian* to being the *Guardian*. It had been C.P. Scott's *Manchester Guardian* and here they were launching into a terrible commercial adventure to try and establish themselves as a London Fleet Street national newspaper.[45] *Manchester* was dropped from the title. This was a very brave exercise and a very dodgy one. In emotional, readership, and financial terms they were so conscious of the strength of their north of England roots. Almost all the paper's circulation was there.

When I joined the paper Hetherington, as I've said, was commuting back and forth, editing the paper about three days a week from Manchester and two days a week, or three days the next week, from London. That was part of the problem of not wishing to appear to a readership who were not (any more than the Scots) enamoured of London as a concept, to surrender their roots. And there was great anxiety in the north of England about the paper taking off for Fleet Street. So the *Guardian* management – a Trust even in those days – was very concerned to retain the north of England thing generally and not alienate a very loyal readership. Of course, the readership was not confined to the north of England: many Liberal and liberal-minded people elsewhere read the *Guardian*. When I joined the paper the foreign side, if my memory serves me right, was retained in Manchester. There was a substantial office left in Manchester, but the main thrust was moving south. The internal tensions were there. The north – the old Manchester office, the Dean Street and Cross Street office – wanted to retain their identity. This was where the paper had been run from and they were reluctant to see power pass.

With Harry Whewell, the news editor, I got on well. Harry was determined, as was the north office generally, that their old supremacy remain intact, and that their schedule was as busy, big, and important as London's, where of course parliament and all the rest were. So Harry was very anxious to maintain the daily schedule. They had a daily contact editorial conference – a telephone hook-up. By today's standards it was very primitive. People like John Cole, the industrial correspondent, operated from London, as did Peter Jenkins and all the well-known names of that period who worked on the *Guardian*.[46] So that if I wanted to go off for a day or two to do something special in Scotland (which *The Times* had been very happy to let me do, because I could arrange the stringers, the non-staff correspondents, to cover for me), Harry was very reluctant to see me go off his schedule. He wanted a good story out of Scotland every damn day. So sometimes things were very difficult. From my own point of view this was a wee bit frustrating. If there was a good story out of the Scottish Office or the Scottish TUC[47] or there was this or that – all the things that were run-of-the-mill, day-to-day, important news – it nonetheless meant I was cut off from a good bit of the kind of background features work that I'd done for *The Times*. That wasn't completely so, because, for example, when Tam Dalyell, a new youngish MP, got a severe rap on the knuckles over allegedly leaking a Porton Down chemical warfare secret, the *Guardian* asked me to do a profile of Tam, which was great.[48] But these kind of features tend to stick in one's memory with the *Guardian*, whereas I forget, without reference, much of what I did likewise for *The Times*. Harry Whewell was very reluctant to have you take off into the great blue out yonder and disappear for three days. I could see Harry's point of view. But it was a bit irksome.

Harry was, I think, of Welsh extraction, although Manchester-born and bred. He'd never worked in Scotland and hadn't any idea of distances north of the Border or the problems of travelling there. London often accuses the Scots, when they get introspective, of parochialism. In my experience there's nobody more parochial than Londoners. But sometimes folk from other parts of England can be equally parochial. It can be a very irritating feature of working with English people.

Unlike *The Times*, where there had been only three staff men outside of London, the *Guardian* had quite a network of them. I was in Scotland, I think there were, for instance, two in Newcastle and two in Leeds – the junior one of whom incidentally was the very embryonic Mr Bernard Ingham who privately was in his early Labour Party days. I never cared much for Bernard Ingham. I met him once or twice in London when we were summoned there.[49] Alastair Hetherington, as editor of the *Guardian*, was a great believer in working lunches where we discussed how the paper should move forward. It was a democratic paper, the *Guardian*, much more so than most I worked for.

You really got a chance to make suggestions about the paper's policies. For example, J.F. Kennedy of course had won the American presidential election in 1960 and there was all the ballyhoo about the first 100 days of the Kennedy administration. So when Harold Wilson and Labour won the 1964 election here, the *Guardian* was especially obsessed with the first 100 days, and we – quite a lot of the paper's correspondents strewn around the UK – were all summoned to London for a big working lunch confab on the subject. I was regarded as the ultimate expert on regionalism because of Scotland's peculiar situation even then, without devolved parliament but with devolved Scottish Office, bodies like the Scottish Council,[50] plus the Kirk, education, and all the distinctions Scotland had both historically and administratively. The working lunch conference then decided – and it was the kind of tactical error that even good editors like Hetherington can make – that for a fortnight we would run the leader page article on the first 100 days of the Wilson administration from different angles – och, the usual. I was to come in early on about day three, if my memory serves me right, with how it was working in the regions, viz., Scotland. Privately, of course, I never accepted that Scotland was a region. I had a very strict private agenda of my own which wanted more devolved autonomy for Scotland, but that was neither here nor there. But all this was a feature of the *Guardian* and a characteristic of Hetherington's editorship. It was also said at the time that if you werenae in the Labour Party you didnae get on in the *Guardian*. Well, as a matter of fact, as I've already said, I only joined the Labour Party in 1964 out of frustration at the failure of Labour, after 13 years of the Tories, to get in with more than a narrow majority.

The routine on the *Guardian* from places like Scotland was that you would have a morning call to say what you were likely to be doing and see if there was anything that they specifically were wanting done. They would call you back in between if need be of course from wherever your operating base was; and then you would have a call in the afternoon to say what it was and to give some indication of the strength of the story, etc. It was all done by telephone in those days – nae faxes: they hadnae been invented, thank God in some ways, although fax would have been very useful in other ways. So that, without realising it, Harry Whewell leaned on you quite heavily. On the other hand, Harry was also very relaxed, as for instance when the Michael Colliery in East Fife went on fire in 1967. It was a Saturday, and I think it was a maintenance shift that were down the pit. I heard it on the radio that evening. Hugh Cochrane, who had taken over from me as *The Times*'s Scottish staff correspondent, and I, as *Guardian* correspondent, worked together quite amicably in situations like that because our interests and our responsibilities in the type of story were broadly the same, and we each went after our own material on the job. But in a case like the Michael Colliery fire Hugh and I pooled basic information (as had happened between me and Phil Stein and Bill Myle of the *News Chronicle* when I had been *The Times* correspondent), so that we could compete with the big battalions from the Scots papers, who could put four, five, six reporters in on a big story. Hugh phoned me that Saturday night and said, 'I'm going up to the Michael in the morning. Are you going?' So we went up in Hugh's car to East Wemyss.

I phoned Harry Whewell at the office about 2pm and he said, 'I thought you were never coming on. I thought you would have phoned me a wee bit earlier.' I said, 'How the hell did you know I was in Fife anyway?' 'Och,' he says, 'I knew you'd be in Fife. I just never bothered phoning you at your house. But I was beginning to get a wee bit jumpy in case you hadnae gone.'[51] So that illustrates the easy, relaxed manner in which we operated. I don't want to give the impression that for me working for the *Guardian* was a frustrating and disappointing period. Guys who worked as I did had great freedom of movement compared to a staff man in head office or in Manchester. Nonetheless, if you landed a job in Scotland for *The Times*, *Guardian*, or *Daily Telegraph* – and these were highly prized jobs of course, at that time – you had to have considerable versatility, capacity to work independently, not to get worried by events, and ability to cope. It took, I suppose, a special kind of temperament, as well as experience. You had basically to be a good reporter.

Harry Whewell just wanted stories all the time. Another example was when the Sabbath was broken on Skye by Calmac and British Rail with the running of the first Sunday ferry. I had a story in the *Guardian* on Saturday morning and I went up with Hugh Cochrane to Skye on the Sunday. We cadged a lift on a launch run by British Rail out of Kyle of Lochalsh early that morning to Kyleakin, and we were on the jetty when the first ferry came in there. Next morning Allan Campbell Maclean, a good left-winger, chairman of the Labour Party, a splendid novelist of teenage children's books, phoned me and gave me hell for my *Guardian* story. 'It clearly leant in favour of these bloody Wee Frees,' he said, 'and I'm very disappointed in you. I thought you were far too pro the Wee Frees.' 'But, Allan,' I said, 'when I saw these big Inverness constabulary guys belting into these fellas who were laid down on the quay to prevent the cars coming up, and hauling them off and thumpin' them with batons,' I said, 'my instinctive distrust of the polis overcame my anti-Wee Free prejudice!' But it didn't satisfy Mr Maclean, who I don't think ever forgave me for showing a slight bias in my report, which I tried never to have.[52]

When I left the *Glasgow Herald* to join the *Guardian* in 1964 I was able to negotiate with James Holburn, editor of the *Herald*, that I could retain my previous corner in its newsroom. So my base really for virtually 20 years and three successive papers was the *Glasgow Herald*, apart from that one year in Kemsley House, Hope Street. And the *Guardian*, unlike *The Times*, had no style differential concerning 'our correspondent': I was just 'From our Scottish correspondent'. While I was there the *Guardian* introduced personal bylines. I was one of a small group of us who were awarded these from the start, although bylines never bothered me. I think they're a waste of time. Some of the deterioration in the standards of journalism, of reporting over a good many years, is because too many young reporters are awarded personal bylines far too soon and go on an ego trip from which they never recover. That's my personal view, an old man's verdict, which is probably not very sustainable in fierce debate. But there you are. And then I used to say of certain people that in their youth they'd seen too many Jimmy Cagney Hollywood films containing newspapermen. Some reporters in the *Daily Mail* office in Glasgow, before it began publishing in 1946 in Edinburgh, were particularly prone to that.[53]

I think the circulation in Scotland of the *Guardian* was then, in the mid–later 1960s, about 10,000 – if it was 15,000 that would be an absolute outside figure. As I've already said, there was also the progressive readership who took the *Guardian* because by that time, too, the *Daily Herald* was losing its old cachet and was becoming just another newspaper. In fact, in 1964 it ceased to be the *Daily Herald* and became *The Sun*; and the *News Chronicle* had gone as well. So it was really down to the *Guardian* and on Sundays the *Observer*. I bought the *Observer* all my life until, och, it went off in the '80s, I think, and because I was getting irritated I stopped taking it.

Before then, I would have loved to have worked for the *Observer*, but they were not in the market for staff men. Robert Kemp, the Scots playwright, who for many years wrote a small piece every week in the edition of the *Observer* that came up to Scotland, suggested to me and then to the *Observer* when he bowed out that I might take over the box. It was really quite a small piece he wrote every Sunday, but it was a discerning piece.[54] Had I done it, which I didn't, I would have done it perhaps not in the same way but I hope it would have been as worthwhile to read. But that was the nearest I came to working for the *Observer*. The economics of a staff man for a once-a-week paper was not on. In those days it was a much more conservative (small 'c') newspaper world, in the sense that the most recent decade or more of lavish spending was unheard of in almost any newspaper, apart from maybe in the *Daily Express*, who spent money like drunken sailors. Indeed, the quality broadsheets, daily or Sunday, in those days operated in a uniformly cheese-paring way. You didnae make money out of your expenses. There was a fella called David Craig, an ex-*Glasgow Herald* sub-editor, went to be the *Daily Mirror* staff man in Scotland – I'm talking about the 1950s now. David died young of cancer. But he told me, when there was a bunch of us on some job, that he banked his *Mirror* salary and lived on his expenses for years. Now that was unheard of in quality broadsheets, whether they were British or Scottish, like the

Glasgow Herald and *The Scotsman*. *The Scotsman* were always particularly cheese-paring, the *Glasgow Herald* were very extravagant compared to *The Scotsman*, and the *Glasgow Herald* wasnae in the same league as even the *Daily Record*. As Scotland staff correspondent for the *Guardian* and earlier *The Times*, I always operated on the principle that I was conscientious, worked hard, and not infrequently worked, och, a twelve-hour day – not necessarily even on a big story. It was just that in reporting there's a lot of hinging aboot, no matter how you do it. If it was a busy day and there were four or five stories that merited your attention, you tried to do them all – and sometimes you did, sometimes you'd to farm them out to your local correspondent, your non-staff stringer like Bert Morris in Edinburgh, a staff man on *The Scotsman*, or in Glasgow Hughie Davidson, a freelance (there werenae many freelances in Scotland in those days).[55] Then, when you got the damn thing written, you could have an hour or an hour and a half on the phone, telephoning to Manchester or London. Many a night I trailed home at eight o'clock. I never started early unless there was a job that merited me being physically present first thing in the morning: I was a slow starter because I was a late finisher. For instance, when in September 1959 Auchengeich pit went on fire I was with *The Times*. The story broke just after breakfast time and you were out there until, och, after midnight.[56] On other stories out of my Glasgow base and away in the Highlands or the Borders you could be away for three days and you just worked. So I tried to award myself a relaxed day or even a day off, because otherwise you just never got time off. And then I was a youngish fellow with a wife and family. Looking back on it, I really don't think I took a very honest share of helping my wife Margaret to raise three bairns. Even years earlier on the *Ayr Advertiser* you worked long hours: at the end of the week, once the paper was away, when it was quieter, you still had all sorts of routine things that had to be done for the next week's paper. But sometimes if David Johnston, my counterpart on the *Ayrshire Post*, and I went down to the Sheriff Court in the county buildings in the Low Green and there was nothing much on there and it was a fine summer's morning, we would nip oot the side door, away across the Low Green and we would have 18 holes on the smashing wee pitch-and-putt course down in Blackburn area, nip back up into Gilchrist the baker in Boswell Park, have a cup of coffee and a cream bun – and say we'd been stuck in the Court and there wisnae a line in it. I never had a qualm of conscience about that because, by Jove, they got their pound of flesh out of ye at other times. And particularly guys like me were appointed as reporters and staff men because in the main we were reliable, conscientious, and experienced. You knew when to let your sails down and when to keep them taut.

When you were working single-handed as a staff correspondent you negotiated your main or annual holiday, and by and large took your days off when it was quiet. In fairness, too, neither *The Times* nor the *Guardian* were difficult. You did tend to be off a wee bit of the weekend, because there was no paper on a Sunday. But if there was a major story on the Saturday you were working that day and usually writing on the Sunday. On the *Guardian*, with the tremendous internal pressure to preserve its identity in those difficult times of transition, Harry Whewell, the news editor, used to really aye want a story for Monday's paper. So I worked many a weekend then when in fact there wisnae very much doing in the way of immediate hard news. I've seen me leave my house on a Sunday morning, maybe 11-ish, to go in to my desk in Buchanan Street to try and put something in Harry's schedule for Monday's paper without a damned clue in my head what I was goin' to do. In those days the Sunday papers didnae carry a lot of hard news: it was mostly background features and what not. So that you werenae getting much of a lead from them. Nowadays one of my criticisms of contemporary newspapers is that you seem able to write about anything whether there's any great relevance or no'. But in those days if you didnae have something to tell in a new story then you didnae do it: the paper didnae carry flam. Readers wanted to know that President Kennedy had been shot deid, but no' that President Clinton maybe, just maybe, had sex in a room in the White Hoose wi' a lassie. Then and now are two totally different eras.[57]

If I had a day off and, alerted by me, my stringers – the network of non-staff correspondents up and down the country, all experienced, qualified professional reporters such as Bert Morris and Hugh Davidson – contributed something to *The Guardian*, the paper had to pay them. Though it was a time of cheese-paring, there was obviously a ready recognition that one man couldnae work seven days a week, 24 hours a day. And there was a budget, in which I wasnae involved, so I never knew what budgets were in the *Guardian* or *The Times*. But in fairness, neither paper ever cribbed much. In Aberdeen, for instance, our *Guardian* stringers were the *Press & Journal* reporters. The newsroom there ran what in those days we called a linage pool. They exported stories to other papers, and if they sent a story to the *Guardian*, *The Times*, the *Daily Telegraph*, the *Mirror* or whatever, they got paid. In offices like the *Press & Journal* the money was pooled. Sometimes a news editor took a bigger whack of it than he should ha' done, but in good offices it was a straight share. If you had a busy month exporting a lot of stories, you didnae get extra payment, because you would get the benefit the next month when you hadnae done so many. If I was on a day or a couple of days off, I would know what was likely to be happening. Obviously you couldn't legislate for a pit disaster or a lifeboat drowning. But on programmed stories, say, an issue before Aberdeen or Inverness town council that was controversial and I was goin' tae be off, I would sometimes phone the local stringer and say, 'I've put it on the schedule and I want at least half a column.' So in a sense I was a kind of mini news editor within Scotland as part of my role as Scottish correspondent: I administered as well as wrote. Of clerical or secretarial assistance I had none – unheard of. You really were a one-man band. For these jobs I did, you really needed the right temperament and to be able to cope. When Hugh Cochrane, who had succeeded me in *The Times*, left it to join the BBC, the third staff man for *The Times* in Scotland was Dick Sharpe, a Rutherglen boy, a first-class reporter who had been on the *Glasgow Herald* as their industrial correspondent. Dick died relatively young some years ago. I wouldn't want even remotely to imply that Dick Sharpe was an incompetent. He stayed with *The Times* for only two years then came back to the *Glasgow Herald*. As I say, Dick was a first-class reporter: fast, accurate, trustworthy, reliable, and with plenty of flair. My impression, although Dick would never say, was that he found himself temperamentally unsuited to the onus of working on a one-man basis. I think maybe Dick didnae sleep as well at night as he might have done, whereas I could sleep like a babe and so could Hugh Cochrane. So Dick, I think, was not equipped to cope with the stress of the job, and he had the wit to get out before it did him harm – and, let me repeat, Dick was a first-class reporter.[58]

When you went on annual holiday, well, at the time our kids were small we rented a house on Bute every summer for a very elastic month. Margaret, my wife, would take the kids down and I would try to get three weeks' holiday, to compensate for what I've mentioned as all those periods when I was missing from home on reporting jobs. Whether it was three weeks or a fortnight I was off, I've seen me come back to the desk I had at the *Glasgow Herald* office in Buchanan Street to find three big tall wickerwork baskets full of mail, put there for me while I was away by Margaret Cairns, who was my secretary when I was news editor of the *Herald*.[59] You couldnae just tip it all into the wastepaper bin because you didnae know what was in that mail. You had to slit open every damned envelope. So I always prayed my first day back was a quiet day, so I could say to London or Manchester, 'Look, I've got a pile of mail higher than Everest.' If in fact it was a busy day I would stay on at night to slit these damned envelopes, 95 per cent of which you could dump because it was history by then. So as sole correspondent covering the whole of Scotland you had to have all these other skills, too, to deploy.

Perhaps that was why Hugh Cochrane and I were such good friends as well as friendly rivals: we could co-operate and we could haul off. Hugh only needed to say, 'I'm doing something special, Bob,' and I just laid off and never asked, and he did likewise with me. Phil Stein, hardworking correspondent in Scotland of the *Daily Worker* (which later became the *Morning Star*),[60] was also able to cope with all these things. In some ways the pressure on Phil was a lot less than on Hugh Cochrane and me, in other ways it was a lot heavier. Phil's role was to do mainly with political and industrial stories: there was much of what happened that Phil could just ignore – it didnae enter into the *Worker*'s scheme of things, royal tours being one! The *Guardian* was much less monarchist than *The Times*, but for *The Times* I had to do a number of stories about the royals that I could well have done without, and it reinforced my innate republicanism enormously. Though I've never actually seen it, my understanding was that when George V died, the *Worker* had a paragraph at the bottom of a column on page three of what then was only a four-page paper, saying: 'George Windsor died yesterday aged 76.'[61] Phil was under enormous pressure because he was writing for a paper that had a raft of people in the trade unions who were acutely concerned that that kind of industrial–political story was well covered. So Phil had limited financial resources at his disposal (in those days the paper's staff man paid part of his salary anyway to the Communist Party), he had no great network of experienced, qualified journalists as correspondents such as the conventional orthodox papers had, and he had this readership who bought the *Worker* for political reasons, and read it with a political eye, and he had the members of the Party who were very censorious of what he wrote. Of a random couple of illustrations of Phil's position one was when the big Bonus Joe dispute at Rolls-Royce, Hillington, East Kilbride, and Hamilton was on in 1956 or 1957. It was a bitter strike over a guy who wouldnae go slow wi' his workmates and worked away at the machine as though his life depended on it, so the boys put on an overtime and output ban and walked oot and it took seven weeks to repair the dispute, famous in its day.[62] The day they went back to work was a filthy day of rain in Govan, and the big Hillington meeting was in old Govan town hall, with the polis pretty obnoxious to us all. Phil Stein was arrested, quite wrongly. It should have been *The Times* correspondent – me – that was arrested. We didnae get into the meeting, we were huddled outside, it was raining heavens hard, and these two polis kept moving us. As we were moved for about the fourth time from one doorway to another I said to Phil, 'If that bloody polis moves me again, so help me, I'll clatter him.' Five minutes later they came along and moved us. Phil was standing nearest them and said, 'Oh, for God's sake, constable, have a heart. You know who we are.' The polis put his hand on Philip's shoulder and said, 'Move on now.' Phil knocked his hand away and three seconds later he was in the police box. Once we got the result of the workers' meeting, we all of us press men went to Govan police station. Phil was just then coming up frae the cells, facing five charges, including police assault. But when I phoned the *Daily Worker* to tell them what had happened, they were more concerned whether I would dae the story for them than whether Phil was goin' tae get sent to the penal colonies! Then the last day, a Friday, of a Scottish TUC annual congress in the late 1950s, was also the first day of our National Union of Journalists' Annual Delegate Meeting at Weymouth or somewhere. Phil Stein was Glasgow branch delegate to the NUJ meeting and asked me would I cover the last day of the STUC for him for the Saturday's *Daily Worker*. But that day at the STUC a motion was approved demanding some increase in Old Age Pensions, and the sum was much higher than Labour, who were then in Opposition, had been asking for. Well, I hadnae checked the figures, and when I was on the phone to the *Worker* in London I said it was sixpence or something mair than Labour were asking for. So when Phil came back from our NUJ conference he phoned to thank me. I said, 'Everything OK?' 'No' really,' he said, 'I had Abe Moffat on this morning.' Abe Moffat was president of the National Union of Mineworkers in Scotland and of course was a lifelong Communist. Abe and I got on well, but Abe didnae know that I, no' Phil, had done the story from the STUC. He just assumed it was Philip's story, because it was, like *The Times*, 'From our Scottish corre-spondent', nae personal byline. And Phil said to me, 'Aye, I'd Abe on. He's no' at all pleased.' 'Why? What was up?' I said. 'Oh, Bob,' said Phil, 'that figure you gave for the Labour Party, it wasnae quite right. It was about thruppence oot. And,' he says, and I quote, 'Abe rebuked Philip for including in his story a grave error of historical fact', end quote. Now I got many a roasting in my years on newspapers from irate readers who thought that I'd maligned them in a story. But it's the only time I've ever been upbraided for perpetrating a grave error of historical fact. But Phil Stein had to live daily on the *Worker* with that kind of thing – a very graphic illustration of pressures on Stein that werenae on guys like me. Well, I was quite grateful to Philip for taking the blame. On my book-shelf there's a copy of Page Arnot's beautifully bound – not the cheap one, the posh one – history of the Scottish miners,[63] and on the flyleaf in Abe Moffat's hand is: 'To my good friend Bob Brown, Journalist'. I got that from him when I left *The Times*, and I know Abe regarded me with some favour because I reported accurately, even when the mineworkers and the Communist Party were deeply involved. I was quite touched that a hard political man like Abe gave the posh volume to a guy from the capitalist press, because *The Times* was the capitalist press. I said to Phil Stein, 'Thank God you didnae tell him about the grave error of historical fact!'

*   *   *

It was 1964 when I went to the *Guardian* and it was 1969 when I left. As I've said, I'd arrived at the *Guardian* at a very bad time, because internally the paper had this constant concern with its roots in the north of England while it was basically being produced in London. Another senior reporter on the *Guardian* in Manchester with whom I became very friendly as well as professionally attuned was Joe Minogue, a Salford man. Joe had a not dissimilar background to myself. Under Harry Whewell as news editor Joe became a kind of regional news editor: he handled all us guys out doing jobs daily in the sticks, as it were. It was really Joe, a very pro-*Guardian* man, too, who played a big part in my departing from the paper. At that time, in the late 1960s, Joe was very despondent. And of course he had more access to what was being talked about in the office than I had, stuck away up in Scotland. Joe was very pessimistic that the *Guardian* was goin' tae survive, and he was very insistent I should look around and see where I could go. 'One of these days,' he said, 'the axe is goin' to fall on us all, and guys like you are goin' to be in the first batch.' Joe was not an alarmist and I took what he was saying very seriously, and he said, 'If there's anything comes up, Bob, I would strongly urge you to make a move.'[64] When I did leave the *Guardian* my friend John Cole also acknowledged it had been a difficult period to work for the paper, particularly for people like me, away on the periphery. But in fairness it wasnae just that. I wasnae buckling at the knees, but as I've said before, by the time you were doing your twentieth Labour Party conference, eighteenth Tory Party conference, and nineteenth Scottish TUC, you were beginning to say, 'God, have I written about this so often . . .' When you choose, as I did, to live and work in Scotland, you're able to say, with great affection and humility, 'Scotland's no' a parochial wee place, but it is a wee place.' And when you're doing stories like this time and time again, you begin to . . . That comes with any job. It's job fatigue, to make it sound grand. So it wasnae so much that I was responding to Joe Minogue's warning to get out before something dire happened, that I began to look around and wonder what I could do. I didnae know what I wanted to do, to tell you the truth – except I didnae want to leave journalism, which was still kind to me. I had an enormous range of people I'd got to know, some well, in all kinds of different trades. David Murison, for instance, of the *Scottish National Dictionary*: I thought wee Davie was one of the great Scots of history.[65] Journalism is an enormously privileged job. I never had any regrets about doing it, you know, recording and reporting a nation's life. Particularly, I was very fortunate to work for these two quality papers, *The Times* and the *Guardian*, as well as for *The Economist* when I came to do that,[66] because it was all tied up with the constitutional shape of the United Kingdom, and my profound belief that Scotland didn't get as much time at Westminster and in the corridors of London power as it should, and that it required good reporting by good reporters from Scotland to put Scotland's needs, ambitions, hopes, and actualities of day to day living, in a perspective that would have some impact on these buggers in the corridors of power, particularly those reading *The Times* newspaper. This is why I feel my *Times* years were perhaps my best and my most important, because undoubtedly, writing for *The Times*, there was attention paid. I could cite now references, attentions paid, to things by people in power in London, who took decisions that were partly influenced, I think, by accounts *The Times* carried, because *The Times* at that time was a very powerful and profound influence. I was extremely conscious of all this and felt very privileged to have had the luck to do that. So, coming back to my leaving the *Guardian*: I was not keen on public relations, which was then in its infancy in Scotland, although it had been kind of established in London for a wee while. I took a severe view of public relations, which I still do. It's a propaganda machine, a load of codswallop: you present selective information. I was about non-selective information, about reporting the facts as far as one could establish and discern them. Well, Professor Ken Alexander at Strathclyde University was a good contact and friend of mine, one of the guys that, working as I was doing on newspapers, you turned to. I think it was probably Ken who said to me he'd heard I was getting a wee bit jumpy and did I know Strathclyde University was looking for a press officer? It wasnae public relations as such, it was to be the press officer. Sam Curran, Principal of the University, wanted the world to know that Glasgow had two internationally renowned universities, and he also wanted a kind of half-decent University gazette.[67] If it had been straight public relations I would never have gone to Strathclyde. But also I was reinforced in taking on the job by a phone call I made to Alastair Burnet, editor of *The Economist*, for which I'd written pieces until I'd gone to the *Guardian*.[68] 'Alastair,' I said, 'as far as I know you never had anybody in Scotland do anything for *The Economist* after I quit when I went to the *Guardian*. If I was available would you be interested?' 'Oh,' he said, 'yes,

I would reinstate you immediately as Scottish correspondent and pay you a retainer again.' So in a sense that clinched the Strathclyde job as far as I was concerned, because I knew that no matter how diligent I was at Strathclyde I wasnae goin' tae be working five days a week at full steam the way I'd been used to working. And indeed that proved so, because producing this University gazette was a doddle. And although we were making professorial appointments and setting up new departments in the University, all of which were the subject of press material, it was easy work compared to what I had been doing. At the same time I worked regularly for *The Economist*, certainly a piece every fortnight – but never during my working hours at the University. Incidentally, Alastair Burnet had said to me that if I wished to join *The Economist* staff he'd be happy to appoint me full-time. He knew I did not want to come to London, and he said, 'If you take on everything north of the Trent I'll base you in Glasgow.' It was a very tempting offer and I wrestled with it, och, for several days. Then I thought, 'Do I really want this? This is the kind of thing I was glad to be done with.'

After I went to Strathclyde I also formed an unofficial liaison with Chris Baur, later editor of *The Scotsman* but then its industrial correspondent. With the rise of the Scottish National Party, Alastair Dunnett, then editor of the paper, told Baur he wanted him to begin doing Scottish politics, in which Chris's background was a bit sketchy and hazy.[69] So he and I did a private deal, that he would be kind of my eyes and ears at political stuff and would brief me on what had happened, and I would keep him right and give him, I suppose, tutorials about political history in Scotland. So it worked very well, I was quite well briefed for writing pieces for *The Economist*.

During my years at Strathclyde University there were big political developments in Scotland in which I became involved. As I've said, I had joined a political party – the Labour Party – for the first time in 1964. My friend and fellow journalist Hamish MacKinven and I served incognito as the press advisers to the Party's Scottish Executive until I left the Labour Party in 1975–6 over the then Labour government's failure to introduce a proper white paper on devolution with powers for Scotland.[70] And that was when Jim Sillars, Labour MP since 1970 for South Ayrshire, Alex Neil, research officer for the Labour Party Scottish Executive, and I set up the Scottish Labour Party.[71] Well, as I mentioned earlier, Monty MacCormick, my history teacher at Eastbank Academy and brother of King John MacCormick of Scottish Nationalist fame, had encouraged me then to think about the Scottish dimension in politics, which became a constant political preoccupation of my adult life. As I've said, from my early years I was not only politically interested in socialism in our time, but also culturally interested in the Scottish dimension. I remember when I would be about 16 or 17 I picked a book off the shelf in Shettleston public library: *A Scots Quair*, by Lewis Grassic Gibbon. I had never heard of Gibbon but was utterly fascinated by his book.[72] At that time I was friendly wi' Willie Smith, Chris Grieve's [Hugh MacDiarmid] election agent in Kelvingrove in the 1945 election, when Grieve was SNP candidate.[73] Because I was intensely interested in the whole relationship of the Scots and Scotland within the United Kingdom and again as part of the wider international socialist movement, I went once or twice around those years to a meeting in 59 Elmbank Street, Glasgow, then SNP national headquarters, where they had a kind of headquarters branch. But I really was repelled, because they were kilted folk and romantics, and I could see no relevance. They didnae even have, as I recall it, a lot of interest in the Scottish dimension that I had an interest in. It was all kind of slightly heedrum-hodrum. But I was aware we Scots were a small five-million unit of an imperial parliament that didnae seem to me to be as concerned about our welfare as it should have been. And this view was reinforced when I went to work for the *Glasgow Herald* and then the London *Times*. It seemed to me that so often in a parliament where so little time was devoted to Scottish affairs we were concocting solutions to economic and social problems in Scotland that were not necessarily the best solutions. My work progressively reinforced my view that the failure to have any real control over so many areas of activity affecting the people was a serious flaw and ought to be put right: Scotland just wasnae well run. When Churchill won the 1951 election we then had that terrible long period of inept Scottish Secretaries, folk like James Stuart. I mean, the English are always talking about how you couldnae run a whelk stall. I wouldnae have let Jimmy Stuart near the Women's Rural Institute in Elgin or wherever. I exempt from this criticism Jack Maclay, but then his roots were Liberal, he was a Liberal Unionist, a nice guy, and didnae raise my hackles the way a lot of Tories did. By Tory standards, Maclay was an excellent Secretary of State for Scotland.[74] Good organisations like the old Scottish Council (Development and Industry) in the 1950s were almost the only vehicle we had for any kind of self-generating economic and social progress. I have a lot of respect for people like Steven Bilsland, Lord Bilsland, and others, because set against the period they were operating in they put in a lot of effort to try and give Scotland a modern economy.[75] But the old Scottish Council whiles hit the problem of Westminster and English indifference, not contempt; but in more recent years it's been rightly said Scotland is the last colony, because that typifies much of the unintentionally offensive attitude, particularly of the south of England. I make a great distinction between the Midlands and North of England, and the metropolitan south which really at times is hard to take and might make you into a raving loony Nationalist. Londonisation is a very insidious thing that operates against places like the north-east of England, Yorkshire and Lancashire as well as Scotland. The difference between those areas and Scotland is that we have these clear historic differentials that make us that bit different from our counterparts in Wearside and Tyneside.

When I had got my call-up papers in 1942 I came home from Ayr for a few days before I went off to Richmond, Yorkshire, about a week before the battle of Alamein. At that time Churchill addressed a big meeting in the Usher Hall, Edinburgh, that was well reported next day. Sir Harry Lauder was at the Usher Hall and sang 'Keep Right On to the End of the Road' – all very patriotic, except that Churchill didnae say a bloody word about what we were all fechtin' aboot. I was very angry because by that time I had very strong views about what we should do with the world, and my war aims were quite different from Mr Churchill's. So I wrote an article and bunged it off to *Forward*. Emrys Hughes, the editor, sent it back almost immediately: he wasnae using it. So I was then very indignant with Emrys as well as with Churchill. There was only one other paper at that time I knew you could send anything like that, and that was the *Scots Independent*, which I saw in the reading room of the public library. So I sent it off to the *Scots Independent* about a day before I set off for the army, and they used it in the *Independent* with a two deck headline: 'Soft Soap and Stale Ginger at Usher Hall. National Comedians of Scotland and England on the Same Bill'.[76] Years later when I was working for the London *Times* I was talking with David Murison, who dropped a remark that politically he was a Scottish Nationalist and had had a spell as editor of the *Scots Independent*. It turned out my piece about the Usher Hall had landed then on Murison's desk and he'd put these headings on it and printed it. That had been the period in the SNP when the MacCormick faction, the Willie Power faction and Douglas Young faction were clashing. David Murison said his publication of my article had provoked an internal row, and had been the straw that finally broke the camel's back: the moderates had broken off and formed the Scottish Convention. So, in a sense I feel that at 18 here I was playing a major part in bursting up the SNP![77]

All this relates to my part as one of the founders in January 1976 of the Scottish Labour Party. When Jim Sillars, as Labour candidate, won the South Ayrshire by-election after the death in 1969 of Emrys Hughes, he vigorously attacked the SNP. In 1967 Winnie Ewing had won Hamilton for the SNP in a by-election, and the SNP were at the start of that run that led up to their successes in the two 1974 general elections.[78] After the 1970 election, when Sillars was re-elected, I began to notice he was making strange noises at Westminster for a guy who had behaved as the Hammer o' the Nats. I then discovered that when Sillars had got to Westminster he was appalled at the indifference shown to Scottish affairs. As he said, he couldnae get an argument oot o' half of them, and he began to make these noises that ultimately led to the formation of the Scottish Labour Party. But we did then form a group which became loosely known as the Watchdog Committee. There were four Scots Labour MPs: Sillars, Alex Eadie, John Robertson, and Harry Ewing, and myself and Jimmy Frame, the Edinburgh *Evening News* industrial correspondent, with Chris Baur of *The Scotsman* also sitting in quite often. I don't remember Neal Ascherson, who also was working for *The Scotsman*, taking part but he was hovering in the background.[79] Labour was edging up to devolution and we monitored it. Hamish MacKinven and I largely produced the 1974 Labour general election sheet that went everywhere in Scotland and in it we had the controversial centre page spread, headed 'A Powerhouse for Scotland' about the Bill that was coming. Harry Ewing, the junior devolution minister in 1974 under Ted Short, really misled us.[80] He assured us that most of what we wanted was going to be in the Bill. But when the Bill was published on the Friday morning it was such a bloody damp squib that we were all furious. I went down on the Saturday morning to Sillars's house. Alex Neil was there. They were determined to break away from the Labour Party. I was the cautionary one and reminded them they were respectively a Labour MP with a safe seat and a Labour Party official. 'I'm the genuine amateur in all this,' I said. 'I've nothing to lose. I can be the most eccentric politician that I care to be.' But to their credit they were very principled. And I naturally said, 'Well, if that's what you want to do, then of course I'll go along with you.' So Sillars and Alex Neil both gave up a lot. For me, it was the kind of culmination, the fusion of my newspaper work and my political belief kind of came together at that point. To get the Scottish Labour Party off the ground I became its chairman. But I never believed the Scottish Labour Party would make it. We did better in some ways than I expected, and I said at the time we would be a footnote to the history of the times. I think in any future evaluation we should be more than a footnote. I think that what we did then was significant in the evolution of the Labour Party towards a stronger role on Scottish devolution.

After the first meeting of the SLP, the academic registrar of Strathclyde University came to me and said, 'Bob, I'm a wee bit concerned. I think we could maybe have questions at the University Court. Is it essential that you do this?' 'No,' I said, 'it's not essential. Indeed it's an unusual role for me. Normally I'm your essential backroom man. I'm doing this,' I said, 'simply while the SLP gets off the ground.' He said, 'Well, I'm not asking you to stop doing it, but that would be a good idea from the University's point of view.' 'I'm not terribly anxious to have a public role,' I said. 'So if you give me just enough time to find somebody else to do it . . .' And that's what happened: within, I think, two months we got Don Robertson from Fife to do it.[81] I remained very active but I was no longer a public spokesman for the SLP. I mean, Sillars and I wrote his 1979 election newspaper in about two hours one night in Annbank, and it was a cracker although I say it myself. We were canvassing in New Cumnock and I bumped into George Foulkes, the Labour candidate, and gave him a copy myself. It was a highly professional publication – far better than what the Labour Party had. George went six shades of green.[82] Well, I have been a member of no political party since the Scottish Labour Party went down in 1979–80. I remain a very firm believer in political objectives, but I have never rejoined. Jim Sillars and Alex Neil both joined the SNP. I have worked for the SNP but never joined it. In the SNP's post-'79 group era I did an enormous amount of work writing pamphlets, and I produced virtually single-handed the Govan by-election newspaper – a cracker, though I say it myself.[83] I don't care much for some of the people who are members of the SNP, and I just find that some of the continuing romanticism of the SNP jars a wee bit.

*   *   *

Well, the job at Strathclyde University was quite a happy job, and I was nine years there – longer than I had been in any job before. I didn't write for *The Economist* during all that time, because they began to reorganise. Andrew Neil (a ferociously capable journalist but about whom I had reservations from the first day I met him as a young fella) joined the paper and Alastair Burnet made him a kind of regions correspondent, which obviously included Scotland. So to some extent I had to bow out at that stage and later terminated my contributions altogether. Another aspect of my Strathclyde job was the terrible row Judith Hart, Labour MP for Lanark, gave me. Judith was very conscious of my status when I was a reporter and said I was a stupid idiot throwing myself away in going to Strathclyde.[84] In some ways, maybe she was right, in that it was a much lower-key job, although a very important job for Strathclyde University. When I joined the University I said at home to Margaret, my wife, 'I don't care if I never see another hotel bedroom in my life.' But after about a year I was beginning to say, 'I wonder what lies on the far side of Blythswood Square?' Because for the first time in my life I went to work in the morning wi' a pretty reasonable idea of where I was going and what I was doing, and that I would come hame at half past five at night. It had never happened to me before. It was a luxury for a while – and then it became a wee bit irksome. So I have mixed feelings on Strathclyde. I was quite happy there and met a lot of good academic people like Professor Edgar Lythe, a great guy, a nice man and an interesting man.[85] I had gone to Strathclyde in 1969 as one of the highest-paid people in Scotland in newspapers. But I discovered in the later 1970s there were now quite youngish reporters getting mair money than I was. It was then I went to be a public relations man.

I went to the South of Scotland Electricity Board simply for the money, because they were offering what seemed to me an obscene amount of money. I went purely to increase my pension right. There had been no transferable pensions in journalism, and I was a wee bit concerned. So for the first and only time in my life I moved to the SSEB purely for money. It was a success in money terms, and a disaster in every other sense. I was a good reporter but I was a bloody awful PR man because I didnae believe a word of what I was saying. It was a shame my working life should end in that way. I retired from choice early – and gladly – from that job at the age of 60. I hated every minute of the South of Scotland Electricity Board.

Well, a general-duties reporter is a jack of all trades and a master o' none. In many ways perhaps that was the great stimulus and enjoyment of the job.

Bob Scott

I'd always wanted to be a journalist. Oh, from the age of about 10 I knew I wanted to be a reporter. But there were no openings at the time I was enquiring around, so I had to work as an office boy in the British Legion.

I was born in November 1925, in Morrison Street, Edinburgh. My father was a grocer. He was in the Royal Artillery in the First World War, but was too old to go in the Second War, apart from which he had ulcer trouble. My mother was a housewife. My brother, eight years younger than me, became a cost accountant.

At the age of five I went to school first of all at Torphichen Street School. I don't mean to be snobbish, but Torphichen Street was down by Rutland Square, was in a nice area, and it wasn't a very big school. I liked it, it was fine. But I was only there a few months when the school closed for some reason, and I was sent to Tollcross School, which I didn't like very much. It was a big school, a big playground, and it was too rough – a bit frightening for a wee lad. I was pretty unhappy at Tollcross School until I went to Darroch Junior Secondary. Sean Connery went there, too, he was in a class about two years below me, so I didn't know him.[1]

Well, at Tollcross primary school we didn't do much in the way of writing essays. But there was an essay competition there by the Royal Society for the Prevention of Accidents. I went in for that, won it, and went to the Usher Hall to get my prize. I went in for it the next year and won it again! But it wasn't that essay competition that aroused my interest in language and in writing: I'd always been interested. As a youngster I was a very keen reader, a regular reader of mainly story papers like the *Skipper*, the *Hotspur*, the *Wizard*, and the *Adventure*. And they had other boys' papers as well – *Champion*, and *Triumph*. Nowadays I look at the kids' stuff and it's all comics, how can they learn like that? I would sit up in bed at night with a torch even, if necessary, reading. I read *Biggles*, and the *Magnet* and the *Gem*, Billy Bunter.[2] But I could never settle to reading a long story: I've got loads of books upstairs here now, they're all short stories! Well, not so much in my boyhood days, but later on, when I was starting out to work, I was keen to get as much experience as possible. So I went and did jobs because I wanted to get the experience. So I didn't have time to do anything else but read a quick short story – and that was it. But I kept the reading up all the time.

At Tollcross primary I sat the Qualy. I just got through to Darroch Junior Secondary, which I wanted, by the way, because at Boroughmuir Senior Secondary, the other school, I wouldn't have got shorthand until my third year. I wanted a commercial course where I'd get shorthand right through, because, as I've said, from the age of 10 I knew I wanted to be a reporter.

I got that ambition first of all from films, another thing as a boy I used to like. In those days before the 1939–45 war the cinema was your only entertainment. Well, the radio had just been coming in, and I can remember sitting with the earphones. My mother had a pair, my father had a pair, and I had one single. That was our radio. I saw the films and loved the films, newspaper films. I think they were more true to the fact in those days than in some respects nowadays. So that fired me with enthusiasm. I can remember particularly the *Five Star Final*, with Edward G. Robinson, a newspaper editor who wanted to change broadsheets into tabloids: a revolutionary thing. So that was a big influence on me.[3]

The cinema I went to mainly was my favourite, my local fleapit, the Coliseum in Fountainbridge. Poole's Synod Hall was one I went to quite a lot, and the Blue Halls, later called the Beverley, in Lauriston, and if I felt a bit affluent I would go to the Rutland, later called the Gaumont, in Torphichen Street. As a laddie I went twice a week anyway to the cinema, not Saturday – I was usually playing with my pals on a Saturday, or reading. But weekdays I used to get sandwiches in my schoolbag, off to school, and then when school finished, just into the Coliseum.

I liked Darroch Junior Secondary much, much better than Tollcross primary. In the commercial course there was shorthand, typing eventually – not at first, but I wasn't as much concerned about that because ma dad got me a second-hand typewriter and I could bash around on that at home. Having got the rudiments of shorthand I'd then to get the speed up. That was why I wanted it right away, instead of waiting at Boroughmuir for three years. Then there was bookkeeping, which was not much good to me, and the usual, maths, English – well, English was very essential. The English was stimulating at Darroch.

But I was a rebel at school. I wouldn't do my homework at all. I reckoned if I went to school five days a week, morning and afternoon, that was enough. So I don't know how many times I got the belt for not having done my homework. I don't think I told my parents about it!

The English teacher knew I was a conscientious objector to homework. So the first thing when it came to his class, 'Come out. Let me see your homework.' 'Haven't done it.' 'Right.' But that man was fair, because there was one day when we had been asked to do an essay. He was handing out all the books and mine was never coming. I thought, 'Oh, that's me for it this time. I must be the worst of the lot.' When he'd one left, he said: 'This book was the one that was absolutely 100 per cent perfect, even to the last semi-colon.' And he brought me out to the front of the class and praised me up to the eyes. The next day I got back of course . . .! He very probably was terribly anxious I should develop my writing skills further by doing the homework. But I never looked on it that way, because you never do when you're 12 or so. Anyway it was just usually one of the belt I got, a token, I think, but every day that we got homework – sometimes you just didn't get homework at all. Well, when I came to leave school at 14 in 1940 I was the only one that English teacher spoke to about trying to get a job. He tried to help me find a job. But he couldn't get one for journalism: he didn't have the contacts. I had no regrets about leaving school. I was glad to shake the dust of school off my feet, because I knew what I wanted to do. It was not then like it is now. It's worth their while for kids to stay on now, especially when the chances are not so very great as they used to be.

*   *   *

I was 13 when the war broke out. I remember hearing Chamberlain's broadcast and the air raid that followed it. My mother wanted us to go down to the air raid shelter. I said, 'I'm not going down there.'[4] The idea of a wee shelter stopping a bomb . . . If you were going to get it, you were going to get it. The shelter was intended just to protect people from splinters and shrapnel. The same when there was an air raid at night, I was sleeping, my mother was getting me up, and I said, 'I'm not gettin' up, I'm not goin' to the shelter,' and I'd turn round and go to sleep again. By that time we'd moved from Morrison Street to Upper Grove Place, nearby, and to a bigger house there.

As I've said, when I left school and wanted to be a journalist there were no openings. I looked to see if there were any jobs marked in newspapers. But there weren't. So I just answered an advert for this other job, got it, and so I had to work as an office boy in the British Legion office for Scotland at St Andrew Square. Well, it was a job, not what I wanted. It was just marking time and earning a bit money, and with the intention of remaining there only until a vacancy arose in a newspaper. And

I knew once I as the office boy got beyond a certain age they'd have to pay me more, so they'd get rid of me and get another one in. It seemed a good idea, too, that I might get help there as time passed, because the British Legion obviously had connections with the press. Well, I worked as office boy at the British Legion for three years. But eventually my boss there knew somebody in the Edinburgh *Evening Dispatch*, phoned him and asked if I could get an interview. So I went up to the *Dispatch* and started I think it was the next day!

In those days on newspapers you had to have good shorthand. Well, when I left Darroch Secondary School I had about 150 words a minute. Oh, I loved Pitman's shorthand, being able to take things down in squiggly lines and to read it back. That was the greatest pleasure, reading it back. After I left school I used to go to Boroughmuir night school just purely to get my shorthand speed up away beyond 150. I was in a class of young ladies, except on occasions a man stationed in the army somewhere round about Edinburgh used to come, and he was aiming for 200 words a minute. When you were aiming for a speed you always went higher – for 140 you went for 160, so this army man went for 220. The poor teacher could hardly speak at 200 words a minute, so he had to say to her, 'Just forget it.' I think I eventually reached about 160. I used to take 180, but I found 180 was just a wee bit beyond me, and at that speed if you get stuck for a couple of seconds, that's you lost about ten words. I never timed my typing, but I was fairly fast. Well, shorthand was a very necessary and desirable tool of the trade, so was typing, but not now.

So when I was 17 I was started in the telephone room of the *Evening Dispatch* in Market Street. When I left the British Legion I was getting £1 a week, when I joined the *Dispatch* my salary shot up 50 per cent to £1.50! There were two other lads the same age as me and we were known as shorthand telephonists. A middle-aged woman named Jean, who'd been there many years, was in charge of the department. The *Dispatch* had bags of telephones in this telephone room, and reporters who were out on jobs, or local correspondents, phoned in their stories. It was a very wide range of stories: meetings, accidents, sport, court work, things like that. At lunchtime it was bedlam, because that's when most of them phoned in. In a way that had to do with the editions of the paper. But it was also because the correspondents, especially Innes, correspondent from Cupar, Fife, had about a dozen court cases every day and wanted to get them off his hands and get a bite to eat before he went back to cover the court again. In short, things happen in the morning and the reporters report at the end of the meeting or the proceedings. So you'd be left with almost a book of shorthand notes which you had then to transcribe and type up and get them sent through to the sub-editors. So you had to have very good shorthand or you were out. Then there were further meetings, etc., in the afternoon. So I got something to eat myself at lunchtime – with difficulty at times.

Our day started about 8 o'clock in the morning. The *Evening News* had the big small ads and required a long time to get their paper out. The *Dispatch* could get out early and did so. We came out with full race-cards and tips and everything for the punter. But that meant we'd to get a very early edition out. Everything had to be finished by about 9am so that we could print the first edition and be out with it on the street by about 11am. The other editions followed on: we'd about seven editions during the course of the day, roughly an hour between each edition.

Well, I did that for about ten months and then I was taken on to the reporting staff. At that time, during the war, there'd be a dozen to 14 reporters in the *Dispatch*. There was David Glenn, chief reporter, who did no reporting but sat at his desk the whole day. He organised the diary. But the real boss of the place was Robert Leishman, the deputy chief reporter. He was the municipal reporter for years and years, knew all the town councillors intimately, and he also did court work. He took me under his wing, taught me just about everything, and I always had great admiration and respect for him. I don't really know if he acted as a kind of tutor to young lads coming into the *Dispatch* reporting staff, because I was the only one there then. I don't know if he'd done that before or later, I just know he did that with me. So the organisation of the diary and the allocation of the jobs reporters were to cover was done sort of jointly between David Glenn and Bobby Leishman. Above them there was a news editor, chief sub-editor, deputy editor, and the editor. T.B. MacLachlan was the first editor I remember. After that was a man Smith,[5] and after him it was Albert Mackie, and after him in the early 1950s Jack Miller, who came up from London.

You were working long hours in the *Dispatch*. You went in at eight in the morning and the shift lasted normally until five in the evening. After the last edition, about 4.45pm, that was it. But if you were working on a story, you had to keep on that story. Even though you were gathering facts for the next day's paper, you had to stay. And also of course there were evening meetings to cover. So you might find yourself working till 5pm, going home for your tea, and then out to a meeting. That happened quite often. That was part of the normal day, no paid overtime for it, no time off in lieu. You just did it and that was it. And that persisted after the war. But I wanted to do that, because I was so keen to get the experience that I did jobs I didn't have to do and I didn't mind that. But you had to take your turn of certain jobs. Maybe once a week for a recognised job, two or three times more if you wanted to try doing more.

So we had to go in the morning about 8am, and we did rewrites from *The Scotsman*, our stablemate daily paper, or we wrote up stories from handouts sent in by public relations officers, and so on. That got rid of the first-edition stuff. Then I had to go round the calls, that was the ambulance, fire brigade, police, the Royal Infirmary for accidents to coal miners. I didn't go to the Castle to check for notices of court martials; they usually sent things in automatically. Then after that to the Burgh Court and report the cases that came up before the magistrates. The *Dispatch* used to send a copy boy up to the court, so you had your copy written and ready for him. A lot of people tell me they can remember being my copy boy: Neville Garden was one of them for a while. Anyway, after the Burgh Court we'd go to the Sheriff Court, and after that we'd to go back to the office in case there was more work for us to do before the lunch break. It was a heavy routine of work. You never got time to worry or feel bored, especially with six or seven editions within an hour of each other. You were working against the clock all the time. It was quite strenuous, especially if you found yourself in a big case up at the Sheriff Court that was going on two or three days. Then you'd to write a different introduction for every edition. So you'd be writing seven different intros, each one bringing the case up to date, as well as adding to the story you'd been sending in. It was a slog, but, by gosh, you couldn't get any better training.

When I was at the Sheriff Court I was called in one day to the chief reporter's office, and they said they were getting an experienced man in to do the court. They added that it was no reflection on my work, but they felt I was just a bit young to be doing responsible court cases. I'd be just nineteen. But they said, 'Carry on going to the Sheriff Court and see how it's done', sort of thing. So the first day this experienced guy sent a wrong sentence down. He came from somewhere in England and with a reputation for being experienced. So I had to tell him he'd sent the wrong sentence down to the office. Before very long that guy was out and I was back on the Sheriff Court again.

I loved court work. I liked doing a big case where I could send the different stories through. I found court work more interesting and stimulating than general reporting. I mean, I've done everything in my time. There was a case in Glasgow years ago about a policeman who had a mistress, wanted to get rid of her, so he knocked her down then drove the car over her. Our office in Glasgow phoned through to Edinburgh and said, 'We can't cover it, we've got too many other things on. You'll need to send somebody.' So I was sent through to Glasgow every day to cover the court case. In those days there was the Glasgow *Evening News*, *Evening Citizen*, and *Evening Times*. Each one of these papers had three reporters covering the court case. One took about ten minutes' notes then went to phone it over to his office. The second one, then the third one, did the same. Then the first one was back again and it started all over. I was there for the *Dispatch* all on my own! I had to send a story for every edition. That was a slog.[6] Sir John Cameron was defence counsel in that case. I got on very well with him. I managed to get a sandwich after phoning my story and was just making my way back to the court when Sir John came along, looked at me and said, 'Ah, one of the ghouls of the press, eh?'

Another famous case, the coffins case, Bobby Leishman and I were at was during the war. Two workers at the crematorium in Aberdeen took bodies from coffins, put them in another coffin, and used the coffins to make coffee tables. There was such an outcry in Aberdeen that the authorities didn't think the men would get a fair trial there, so they were brought down to the High Court in Edinburgh, and found guilty. But once a case was finished that was us, and the next one was the one that mattered to me.

At one time the police in Edinburgh issued special crime reporter cards to the press. Not everybody got them. It was supposedly to accredited journalists and to help you do your job. If, say, there was a murder case you showed your card and got through the police lines when other reporters were held back. So I was a crime reporter for a while with the *Dispatch*. Actually, I didn't do much in the way of crime reporting. It was mostly court reporting and crime feature-writing. There was one murder case, though it didn't really get a big sensational show, where I had to chase through back gardens with a photographer to try and get pictures for the story. But these were very few and far between. It was mostly court reporting and routine stuff. At the time I was a crime reporter though, I used to write feature articles for the *Dispatch* on various aspects of crime, one of which was safe-blowing. And I was asked to go up to the police office, was brought before one of the high officials there, and he tried to tell me I was putting ideas into the heads of criminals. So I had to tell him, 'That's a load of rubbish.' I was writing about things anybody could know. Shortly after that, my chief, Bobby Leishman, got a letter from Edinburgh University, wanting to know if they could get permission to use the series of articles as a basis for a thesis. So he was chuffed about that, and I was quite pleased myself.

Just to show you how forgetful I was in these times, I got a pass to go and do this feature article about Saughton Prison. I was shown round the prison and spoke to various people, one of them this nice, mild-mannered guy. The man who was showing me round says to me, 'You no' remember him?' I said, 'No.' He says, 'That's the Polish watchmaker from Peebles who emptied a gun into his wife.' I said, 'Oh, God.'

Speaking of the war, reminds me that I had worked at the *Dispatch* for about six to nine months and was 17¾ when I got my call-up to the Forces. The choice I got was the navy or a Bevin Boy. So I said, 'Oh, to pot with the Bevin Boy. I'll plump for the navy.'[7] So I went along to get my medical. After so long they said, 'Get your clothes on and go away home.' I said, 'What's wrong?' 'Oh, just get your clothes and go home.' And they handed me a card which I think was C3. I'd had no inkling and had felt perfectly well. But they wouldn't tell me what was wrong and said, 'Go and see your own doctor.' I never went. I was too scared to go! So I don't know to this day what the trouble was. Anyway, my chief reporter, short of manpower, just about fell on my neck, he was so glad I wasn't being taken away from the *Dispatch* to the Forces. On the other hand, I was in the Home Guard, and what you see about it in *Dad's Army* is absolutely true, every bit of it.

During the war years we had short newspapers of course, they cut down the size of the paper and I think we were down then to eight pages from maybe, oh, twice as many before the war. But you learned how to abbreviate a story, not have too much verbiage in it. That was another thing you got a good training in. One of the most distasteful jobs I ever had to do, though it was normal *Dispatch* policy, was to go along to homes where a son, father, or brother had been killed, and ask if we could have a picture so we could print that. You weren't expected to ask for any comments, but to ask for details of them for a biographical sketch. That was one job I hated. It was the only job in journalism that I utterly detested, the only job. Then when the war was finishing they wanted to do special editions and they got the reporters doing various things. My job was to go through all the files, day by day, and put on a map how far the Germans had got into Russia before they were halted and driven back.

The *Dispatch* circulated in Fife, East Lothian, the Borders, and out to the west – Falkirk and Stirlingshire. It didn't circulate in north Fife – the Dundee papers would do that, and west of Falkirk the Glasgow papers. There was a great rivalry between the *Dispatch* and the Edinburgh *Evening News*, but there was also a great camaraderie! I liked it because we all got on very well together, and there was no sense of personal rivalry or, still less, animosity between *Dispatch* and *News* reporters. So though there was tight competition you could do that without damaging relationships. I mean, everybody knew if you got a story by yourself that was your thing, you didn't have to be dirty about it. In my day I used to go up to the police office at the High Street, walk into the Deputy Chief Constable's office, I'd be asked to sit down and maybe get a cup of coffee, and they would hand me a sheet with all the incidents in it, with all the details. And they'd say, 'If you're wanting anything . . .' And I would say, 'Yeah, I'd like that one.' 'That's all right.' Then 'How about that one?', and they'd say, 'Could you leave that one for a couple of days? We're still making some enquiries.' I'd say, 'Yes, that's fine.' I mean, as a newspaperman I was always looking for a scoop and, without boasting, I got many scoops. But I pride myself that I never did anything nasty to get them. In my early days on the *Dispatch* the national papers didn't have the men to cover the stories. It was only after the war and things began to settle that the national papers decided they'd spread their wings a bit, and their guys starting coming in much more.

When I began on the *Dispatch* in 1943, or later just after the war, well, apart from the *Evening News*, I remember the *Daily Express* had Gilbert Cole and I think one other man in an office in India Buildings in Victoria Street. Ernie McIntyre of the *Daily Herald* was another. There was the *Sunday Post*, though I can't remember where their office was, it was maybe in India Buildings, too. Then there was the *News Chronicle*, I think in Victoria Street, just before you got to the Grassmarket. The *Daily Record* were in Bank Street before they went to Frederick Street. I didn't have much contact with *Daily Record* reporters.[8] There were very few national paper reporters at all in my early days at the *Dispatch*. I think the *Daily Mail* had a reporter somewhere in the centre of the town before the *Scottish Daily Mail* began publishing at Tanfield in 1946.

Another aspect in those early years I was at the *Dispatch* was that I joined the National Union of Journalists as soon as I was a reporter. In the *Dispatch* the chief sub was a very strong union man – not a troublemaker. But every time somebody young came in he would grab them and tell them all the benefits they could get from being a member of the union. So it was through him I became a member of the NUJ. I went to chapel meetings, but I was never active in the union. Once because they were stuck for somebody to attend officially in Glasgow from the Edinburgh branch I was nominated, so I went, took notes, came back and passed it on, and that was it. I regarded myself always as a loyal member of the union and I hold a life member's card now.

*   *   *

I was always a football fan. I grew up in a Heart of Midlothian family. My father, uncles and cousins were all Hearts fans, and I used to go to the football every week. So at the *Dispatch* I'd asked if I could write features on one or two sports things. So I did articles on Helen Elliot, a Scottish table-tennis champion, and various other personalities.[9] Then I thought I'd like to do some sports reporting. So the *Dispatch* started me off doing Edinburgh University and Edinburgh City matches! From there I got to doing the bigger games on Saturday afternoons, while I was still continuing with general and court reporting during the week. Then in the early 1950s Alex Young, the *Dispatch* football writer, left to go to the *Scottish Daily Mail*. So I got his job. I had to change my whole style completely. It was quite a big change, because I had to do a page every day, and then I had virtually to fill a sports edition on Saturday nights. It meant I had two feature pages, front-page news, a match report, and bits of snippets! So it was a slog, oh, it was a slog. But again I enjoyed it. I did that myself, I didn't have an assistant. So I did that for about three or four years.

Then in 1955 I got a phone call from Bruce Swaddell of the *Scottish Daily Express* in Glasgow, asking me if I would go through and see him. I was going through to report a football match at Hampden Park, so he said he would see me then. When we did a match in Hampden Park for the *Dispatch*, Albert Mackie, the editor at that time, used to come too. He would write his report of the match in verse and I wrote mine of course in prose, and we used to send pictures. We took a wire machine through with us, and it was all – verse, prose, and pictures – wired. When I saw Bruce Swaddell and he asked, 'How do you get your copy?', I told him and he was astonished. The upshot was Bruce Swaddell asked me if I'd like to join the *Express*, and I was offered a lot more money than I was getting with the *Dispatch*. I told him I'd like to think it over because I was first and foremost a football reporter. I could write feature articles on other sports, but I didn't know enough about them or the people in them to put myself forward as an expert. So I either phoned or wrote back saying, 'I'm sorry. Thanks for your offer, but I don't feel I can take it up.' He phoned me and told me, 'I can assure you that you'll not be asked to do many, if any, of these other things, and if you are, you'd be able to handle it all right. And by the way we'll add another couple of quid on to your starting offer.' So what could I do? I had got married in 1949, had a son, and my wife was just on the point of presenting me with another child. So that was it. I was sorry about leaving the *Dispatch*, because those had been my formative years in journalism and I'd learned an awful lot there. It was the fact I was given the chance to learn a lot for which I was always very grateful. You were doing work which in effect the national papers were doing. But on the *Dispatch* you were doing it for a limited public, a more localised readership, for your own people, as it were. I realised that I had to leave the *Dispatch* if I was going to develop my talents and make more of my career. You could go so far with the *Dispatch* and that was it.

So I went in 1955 to the *Daily Express*, based in its Edinburgh office which was in Bank Street, at the top of the Mound. When I'd got married in 1949 I was earning £7.50 a week at the *Dispatch*, when I went to the *Express* it went up considerably above that but I can't remember now what it was. Supposing I was getting £12 a week by the time I left the *Dispatch*, then the *Express* offered me £14 and then upped it to £16. Oh, that was a huge salary that! It was above the standard NUJ rate. The *Express* tended to pay higher rates and, apart from NUJ-negotiated rises, they had a merit scheme and if they thought you were worth it you got extra money. There was no quibble about that in those days. You didn't have to apply for the merit money, it came through as a bonus, an accolade!

The *Express* office in Glasgow was in Albion Street. They had a batch of sports reporters in Glasgow of course. The staff over there was fantastic. They had a man to cover Aberdeen, Ronnie Main, for Dundee John Mann, and for Dumfries John Enos. I covered Edinburgh and the southern half of Fife. In the Edinburgh office Gilbert Cole was the chief reporter, Ray Mackenzie deputy chief reporter, and there'd be about a dozen reporters. I was the only sports writer there. I didn't cover general news stories unless it was a news sports story – a sports story with news connotations.

I spent my day and my week going out to Tynecastle and Easter Road, and less often across to Fife to Kirkcaldy for Raith Rovers, to Methil for East Fife, and to Cowdenbeath and Dunfermline for the teams there. You'd keep in touch by phone. And then of course you had to keep your ear open for stories. A lot depended on tips. One of the greatest scoops I ever had was when I was down at Dunbar, covering the Scottish football team, who were going to play an international. So when our photographer and me were on our way home we were approached by two Hearts players who were members of the team pool and who asked us for a lift back to Edinburgh. On the way one of them said, 'Are you interested in a story?' I said, 'I'm always interested in a story.' 'Well, Hearts are going to Australia for a tour. But what's even more interesting is that we're going round the world to do it – going out one way and coming back the other way.' So I got the whole story without having to approach anybody else. And it came out the next day, because Bruce Swaddell, my sports editor at that time, was a great guy and if you did a story he took it. He never phoned me back, just took the story, and got somebody to draw a map of this world trip. That was the big heading: 'Around the World in 87 Days'. Next day all hell broke loose. The *Mail* and the *Daily Record* and the other papers were all on to the Hearts, saying, 'Why didn't we get this?' Tommy Walker, Hearts' manager, had said: 'I don't know how he got it, because he wasn't supposed to get it.' You kept quiet or you'd get the other players into trouble.[10]

More or less at the time I moved to the *Express*, cheque-book journalism was coming in. Later on the *Express*, the *Mail* and the *Daily Record* were throwing money around like nobody's business. Not long after I started on the *Express* I remember being sent out to do a story about a Rangers player in Glasgow. There was some row with his club, I asked him about it and he gave me it without any question of any payment. On the other hand, I would go to another Rangers player for a story and he would say, 'Well, what are you going to pay?' And I'd say, 'Well, I'm not going to pay you anything, but I'll get in touch with my sports editor and see what he says.' And the player says, 'Well, you see, I need to know what size it's goin' tae be, because if it's only a wee story, a certain amount, and if it's bigger it's more, and . . .' I says, 'Oh, well, I'll speak to them.' We paid. I didn't like the development of cheque-book journalism. I didn't see why you should have to pay for a story. But you had to grow accustomed to it, and I came to accept it. They used to tell you, 'You can get a team picture but it'll cost you so much a head.' Personally, I would have told them to go and get stuffed. But I couldn't do that. I had to refer it upwards and the decision nearly always was to pay.

About a year or so after I'd gone to the *Express* I sent a story through to Glasgow about an injury to a player. And the same day I got on to a news story connected with sport: I think it was that the Hearts directors wouldn't attend their yearly get-together, because it was being held on a Sunday. So I got two stories and thought to myself, 'That's not a bad day's work.' The next day I looked at page one and there was my news story, not with my byline on it but just '*Express* staff reporter'. I thought, 'That's bad that.' So I turned to the back page and there's my other story, with an eight column headline, but 'By Tommy Muirhead'. Tommy Muirhead was an old Rangers player. When his career finished he went to the *Express*.[11] So I was blazing angry. Mind you, I wouldn't have done it in my later years, but young as I was then I was hotheaded enough to risk it. So I wrote to Glasgow to say I was aghast and, 'If that's the sort of thing . . . I'd be as well not working for the *Express*.' Well, I got a phone call from Bruce Swaddell, the sports editor: he was coming through to see me. I thought, 'I'm for the high jump now.' He took me for lunch and said, 'As far as the front page is concerned, I can't do anything about that. When it's a news story, I've got to hand it over to the news desk. What they do with it is their business, nothing to do with me. So I can't help you. I'll take the blame for the other one,' he says, 'because Tommy Muirhead,' who was supposed to be the top sports writer at that time, 'had nothing. So we had to give him a story and yours was the best story that was in.' So Bruce Swaddell said, 'I'll take the blame for that. By the way, will you accept a £2 rise?' So my vanity paid off at that! Well, that happened quite often in the *Express*, but it didn't happen too much to me after that. It did happen again once or twice but over nothing that mattered very much, so I never bothered about that.

Oh, I've loved it, I've loved every minute of it. Well, at times I cursed it. An example was that I used to be very well up with Hearts players. You had to be if you were to run a column like that. Two of them were involved in a transfer, and the manager arranging it told me about it, so I got the first beat on the story. And he told me, 'It's not goin' to happen till two or three days yet.' At that time I was working morning, afternoon and night for the *Express*. So I said to them, 'I'm on day off tomorrow.' They said, 'Oh, you can't go on a day off tomorrow. This story's for you.' I said, 'Nothing'll happen tomorrow. I've got the transfer story sewn up.' 'No,' they said, 'you'll have to work tomorrow.' I said, 'Well, I'm not working tomorrow. I'm just about flat out on my feet. I've got to have some time off.' 'Well,' they said, 'if something happens you'll have to be reported to the editor.' I said, 'Well, go and report me then.' So that had me cursing.

For a spell latterly, as I say, I was working a seven-day week, morning, afternoon and night. I got half a day off, if I was lucky, on a Friday. Well, it caught up with me about 1963–4. I had to go to the doctor and he sent me to a specialist who said I had been grossly overworked. I had to get drugged, a very powerful sedative. I got this liquid drug and a couple of minutes afterwards that'd be me out. I woke up to get some lunch. My poor wife had an awful job. Drugged again until tea time, took some tea, then drugged till the next morning at breakfast. That went on for a solid week. The specialist at the Royal Infirmary said, 'If you want my advice, you'll change your job. If you don't,' he said, 'I'm sorry, pal, I'm no' goin' tae be responsible for the consequences.' So I was ready to pack it in at the *Express*, but they gave me a desk job. That's how I went on to administration. So for the rest of my time with the *Express* I ceased to be based in the Edinburgh office and I was travelling daily by train between Edinburgh and Glasgow doing an admin job.

I had to keep a diary of the big sports events that were coming up and assign various people to the jobs, and tell them what to do, where to go. I was a kind of news editor in sport. For the first time in my life I had to go into editorial conferences. That was a bit of an experience. But I wasn't being harassed any longer in the way I'd been before. When my shift finished, that was it. I started work about 9am and got home about 7pm, if that. It was a long day. To get a train, I was up at home in Edinburgh by quarter to seven in the morning at the latest, then I just walked from Queen Street station in Glasgow to 195 Albion Street, it wasn't very far. It was regular and I didn't have any hassle: nobody coming, nobody phoning me up at two o'clock in the morning and saying, 'The *Mail* have got a story that you haven't got.' That had been the case when I was a sports writer, when I wasn't getting my sleep. In a way I had regrets about giving up sports writing, because I liked the writing very much. But after I got the desk job I still used to go sometimes to a match at the weekend to get wee snippets. We had a 'Behind the Score' feature, I think it was called, so I used to write pieces for that. That kept my hand in and gave me a certain amount of satisfaction. My wife welcomed the change, it had been a difficult life for her, her sleep was interrupted too. As I say, I used to work Monday, Tuesday, Wednesday, Thursday, Saturday and Sunday, and very often it was morning, afternoon and night. Friday was supposed to be my day off. But I'd had to go in to the office on Friday to do stories. If I was lucky I got Friday afternoon off. Then Saturday it was a match and I could be away down at Stranraer or up at Aberdeen. And of course my family were growing up and I hardly ever saw them. So my wife liked the change and I enjoyed it, too, except for the fact I wasn't writing as much. I always liked the writing. It was a psychological shock to me to have to give it up. Admin's a different thing altogether. But there was a certain amount of pleasure to be got from admin, too, because if you suggested a thing be done and it paid off, you found yourself getting a mention from the editor, and, you know, that vanity again – job satisfaction.

I'd maybe better not say things about relations with colleagues in the Glasgow office. Well, you had people who resented . . . If I'd been much older they might have accepted it. But here's a guy they knew as a sports writer coming on as sports news editor and telling them what they've got to do, you know. So they resented it to a certain extent, and I could understand their position. I'm not myself an aggressive person, far from it. Then another thing, because I was working in Glasgow but living in Edinburgh, they gave me Saturday and Sunday off. I didn't have to do a match unless I wanted. But the ones who who were on Sunday objected I had Sunday off: 'He should take his turn on Sunday', and so on. I had to say, 'Right, I'll take a day off during the week and go in on Sunday.' So that and a combination of other things just got on top of me and I got thoroughly disgusted and fed up.

Then as for characters, we had a drunk. I'd be sitting at my desk in the morning when I'd get a phone call from him: 'Been on a binge.' 'Where are you?' I said. 'Don't know.' 'Well,' I said, 'leave the phone and go out wherever you are and see.' He was in some hotel and had no recollection of getting there. Several times, not me specially, but other people had to cover up for him or he would have been out, finished. For a number of journalists over-heavy drinking was an occupational hazard. It may be because of the stress – there was terrific competition between the papers. You could get ten exclusives, but if you missed the eleventh one the management were down on you like a ton of bricks. I remember once in the football close season – I never even got a rest from it then, I had to provide stuff every day – I was at Saughton enclosure in Edinburgh one Saturday afternoon watching a schoolboy game when I heard two men behind me say, 'See that left winger? Great isn't he?' And the other one says, 'Yeah, he's going to Hearts.' And of course my ears picked up. 'But,' he says, 'there's goin' tae be trouble, because Hearts have approached him illegally.' So I checked up, that was right, and I got the story exclusively. I was then delegated to get something every day on it, and did so until the top *Daily Record* reporter at that time, who was very friendly with one of the Hearts' directors, had gone to him and said, 'Look, you've got to give me something. The *Express* have been getting away with this story all the time.' So the director said, 'Right, ok, we're getting fined because o' him,' and he came out with the story. I was called up by my editor, who came from London. And my sports editor said to him, 'Look, Bob Scott broke the story in the first place, and he's carried an exclusive on it every day since until now.' 'Ah, but he didn't get the last one did he?' At that stage I decided, och, well, what the hell? You could never win with somebody like that.

The terrific competition was mainly between the *Express* and the *Daily Record*, and the *Scottish Daily Mail* to a lesser extent. That was partly because the *Mail* was published in Edinburgh, the other two in Glasgow. They always thought the *Mail* did badly because it did publish in Edinburgh, not Glasgow. The *Express* used to have the biggest circulation – about 600,000 in Scotland. But the unions started demanding more and more money. They should have stopped and listened. The Glasgow office was grossly overstaffed. The result was they had unofficial strikes. Papers very often went away without the first edition, the Aberdeen and the Glasgow streets edition. And people just got fed up and stopped buying the *Express*. So what happened was the *Mail* went down, but the *Daily Record* went up and passed us. The *Express*, riding the crest of the wave, threw it in.

I don't think television was an important factor. If you stand in a shop and watch the sales of papers, you'll find that while the price of the papers goes up people don't stop buying them. They maybe stop buying one, but get another one in place of it. The corny old joke of course is you can't wrap a fish supper up in a television set. You can see something on television and then once it's away that's it. On paper you've got it there and if you don't read it when you've got something else to do you can come back to it and read it when you've got time. And there's far more detail and news content in a newspaper than on TV. Obviously television may have something to do with falling paper sales, but I don't think it's all.

*   *   *

Well, I started with the *Express* in Edinburgh in 1955 and did about eight years of sports reporting there, then I went through to Glasgow to do that admin job. I was 25 years altogether with the *Express*, most of it in Glasgow in admin. Then what happened was all that trouble and in March 1974 they just closed the Glasgow office. They decided they were going to print in Manchester. So a lot of the subs working in Glasgow were offered jobs in Manchester. If they did not want to take them they just got redundancy money. A number of officials were kept on. It was a skeleton staff in Glasgow. I was kept on and so was my sports editor, Bruce Swaddell. Bruce went down to Manchester, supervising the subs there. But I was kept on in Scotland, more or less the one contact sports man there. They appointed an editor in Scotland directly responsible to Manchester and London. I didn't get on with him at all. When Bruce Swaddell died I was sent down from time to time to Manchester, to attend meetings and discuss what we would do, and so on. Then when the *Daily News*, run by former *Express* staff, started up they were allowed the use of the *Express* offices in Albion Street that we were also occupying. There was a lot of rancour and bitterness: the *Daily News* people saw us working there for the *Express* and thought it all wrong that we shouldn't be joining them. But if you've got families you can't just be gallant, take the Errol Flynn attitude, and say, 'Gung ho!'[12]

Then the edict came from London, I suppose, that they were going to cut back in Scotland again, and in Manchester, too. I talked it over with my wife. I said, 'If you say no I won't do it, but if you think I should . . .' God bless her, she said, 'You do what you want and that'll be all right.'

So I turned to the union and said, 'I want to go.' The editorial tried to say who would go. The union said, 'No. We'll say who wants to go.' So the others let me put my name on top of the list. They knew I was so disgusted. Very few had as long service with the *Express* as I had – 25 years. And lo and behold they told me I could have a pension. They said, 'It won't be as much as it would if you'd stayed on till the end, but you can have it and it won't affect your redundancy money. So I took a pension, it's index linked and has been increased just about every year since, and came out. That'd be about 1980.

I meant to do nothing for a little while and then see if I could do a wee bit freelancing. But six months after, I got a phone call from some of my old colleagues inviting me to a lunch in Glasgow. I found out then they were starting up the *Sunday Standard* and my name had been put forward to try and get sport off the ground. They gave me a completely free hand to buy anything I wanted – files, books, just to get it started. After it was off the ground they asked me if I'd like to carry on on a sort of freelance basis, doing admin, the same sort of job I was doing in the *Express*. They were a great staff. And the *Standard* office was beside the *Herald* and the *Evening Times* in the old *Express* Albion Street office. So that was me until after nearly three years the *Sunday Standard* closed. I got a settlement from the *Standard* which surprised me, but they were so appreciative.[13]

But even before it closed I was working again. My son Roy, who was deputy editor of the *Dalkeith Advertiser* at the Scottish County Press, asked me if I'd like to take over the running of one of the Press's other papers, the *Leith Gazette*. Later they had to close the *Leith Gazette* because that wasn't doing very well, but they started up five freesheets.[14] So I was there for five years and quite enjoyed it because again I had a free hand. They let me work less than a full week and paid me accordingly. It wasn't much, but what was more important to me was that I was keeping my hand in. Then I fell ill and had to have an operation. I was 62. So I just packed the job in. I'm not a rich man, but I don't have to worry about where the next meal's comin' from.

Well, I had nearly half a century in journalism. I don't regret one minute of it. I'm grateful that I managed to realise my ambition, and I achieved a certain amount. My father was always very proud of me and I used to take him to football matches. One day he was in Glasgow and they had a huge hoarding up with pictures of top football writers, and I was in one of them. He thought this was great – a son up on a building in Glasgow. Not many Edinburgh people have that distinction in Glasgow! But I didn't do probably as much as I would have liked to have done – maybe be a foreign correspondent or something like that, in English-speaking places – I didn't have any foreign languages. I would have liked to try my hand at that when I was much younger, but with two children, you know . . . I used to shudder when they sent me abroad to a football match, because when you left this country you weren't a sports man or a features man, you were an *Express* reporter. I used to keep my fingers crossed that nothing was goin' to happen that would keep me away from home for weeks or maybe months! I was very much a home man. I didn't want to live in Glasgow, I didn't like Glasgow. And then the children were at school and they had their friends, and to take the children away it disrupts them and their teaching. So I decided just to travel back and forward between Edinburgh and Glasgow.

Oh, it's a different world now in newspapers. After I retired my son Roy was having a tough time with people off at the *Dalkeith Advertiser*, and I went in there to do some sub-editing for him. All I could see were computers in front of me. 'Oh,' I said, 'I couldn't do this, I'm too old to start this.' So I just did ordinary subbing, put headings on. But even when I was in the *Sunday Standard* it was beginning to get like that. The old linotype had finished. They don't phone in stuff now, they just do it on their tape. When I was helping my son on the *Dalkeith Advertiser* he had all the stories on his computer. It's away above my head. I mean, I was used to the old writing of a story – writing it if you were in court, or typing it if you were in the office, or phoning it in if you were outside the office. Now it's a completely different technique that I find bewildering. As for shorthand, I think it's always a good thing for anybody to have, not just for reporters, but a lot of bosses in business like to be able to take a note in shorthand so they don't miss anything.

I was never politically inclined and wasn't all that interested in politics. I don't think I would have bothered being a political correspondent anyway – too boring from my point of view. I used to like the sort of things that were different every day – a crime story, the Sheriff Court . . . I used to dislike the General Assembly of the Church of Scotland, because they would start on a subject and before you know where you are you're bogged down in addendums and you're trying to find a story. The first General Assembly I did was for the *Evening Dispatch* when I was 18. There were three gentlemen from *The Scotsman* covering the General Assembly, they'd done it for donkey's years. Adding up their ages, it'd probably come to nearly 200 years. And there's me, 18 years old, and, oh, dear me. I got in a hopeless tangle, which was sorted out eventually. The next day I looked at the diary and I was marked again for the General Assembly! This is something for which I'll be eternally grateful to Smith, the editor. Well, after that mess I'd made the previous day I got a front-page banner headline story out of the Assembly, because after one day I was beginning to get used to it. Dropped in at the deep end? The double depth end! Youngsters had to be dropped in at the deep end. I was fortunate in that I used to volunteer for things, go to meetings and various things which gave me a grounding in different aspects of the work. One of my heroes then was Doon Campbell, who later became a war correspondent and lost an arm doing his job. He was a top reporter. So I said, 'Can I come wi' you?' 'Of course, come on.' So I used to go out with him and he would give me tips all the time.[15]

Jack Sutherland

Not a bit of journalistic legacy was passed on to me in my family. As a boy I had no particular ambitions. I hadn't thought of anything at all. I just got interested in newspapers after one of my pals left school the year before me, joined the local paper, and got me to write one or two pieces for it, sports reports mainly.

I was born in Rothbury, a small village in Northumberland, about 12 miles from Morpeth, on 14 May 1927. My father was a village policeman in Rothbury and met my mother there. He came from Helmsdale in Sutherland, one of 15 children. He'd been in the Gordon Highlanders in the First World War, came back, and worked on farms with his father.[1] He got fed up with that, came down to Northumberland about 1923–4, and joined the police force. After a few years at Rothbury he was transferred to Guide Post, a mining village nearer Morpeth. From there he was promoted sergeant to Blyth, and then about 1938 moved up to Berwick-on-Tweed.

My mother was born and brought up in Rothbury, a member of quite a large family of four sisters and three brothers. So she stayed at home and helped her mother. Her mother, my grandmother, came from a wealthy farming family in Northumberland, and had defied their wishes and married my grandfather, a widower. He'd had a family up Arbroath way and he'd come down to work in Rothbury on the LNER railway as a guard. Two of his sons also worked on the railway.

My grandfather Sutherland was a ploughman, and most of his sons were ploughmen with him. They went round all the farms up north in Scotland. Oh, he moved all over the Highlands, there was quite a lot of movement and different houses. It was a hard, hard job, and he was a hard man. I remember him, he was still alive as I was growing up and he used to visit us. He never told me about his working conditions as a ploughman. He was stone deaf. He was kicked on the head by a horse when he was eight years old and he'd been stone deaf ever since. He used to have this big ear trumpet, though I'm sure he could hardly hear. He was a fine man, a fine-built man. He used to get us up at six o'clock every morning, make us porridge, and he would read the Bible to us for about ten minutes. Before every meal the big Bible came out, and you couldn't eat until you'd had the good word. He was a keen churchgoer – Church of Scotland. He died when he was 86 in 1942–3. My grandmother Sutherland had an Orkney connection, though I'm not sure what it was. There was talk about her mother had gone to America or Canada in or after the Clearances, had come back, and my grandmother was supposed to have born on a boat coming back.[2] She was a very hardy Highlander and outlived my grandfather by a couple of years. She had failing eyesight, but she never protested, never murmured anything at all about it. Then one holiday we were up seeing her and she put her hand out to get the kettle on the fire, but missed the kettle and put her hand right into the cinders. We realised then she was blind. She hadn't told anyone. What a hard life for her, bringing up 15 children, and moving from farm to farm and, och, terrible housing conditions. In the 1960s I used to get a cottage up at Nigg Bay for a holiday with the family, merely because grandfather and grandmother had had their last cottage just about seven miles away from there. I walked to it once and it was a ruin, just collapsed. But the whole cottage was just basically one room, no bigger than this room, with a sort of boarded piece where there was another bed, and a huge old range.

I'm the middle one in our family. My older sister Phyllis was born at Rothbury; my younger sister Barbara at Morpeth.

I was about three and a half when we left Rothbury and moved to Guide Post, though we went back for holidays every year to Rothbury. So I started school at Guide Post. I enjoyed my primary school days and particularly enjoyed painting and writing. Then we moved to Blyth and I sat my Eleven Plus there, but then we moved to Berwick, where I was at the primary school about a term, during which I learnt I'd passed the exam and could be admitted to Berwick Grammar School. When I went to the Grammar School it was purely boys, but we had only a year there and then we were transferred and amalgamated with the girls' school at the top end of the town.

Initially I enjoyed the secondary school, but not the last couple of years. We had a family problem: my father went to prison. He had some kind of an affair with a local woman, in fact one of my teachers at the primary school. Before he went to prison he'd left the police force with more or less a mental breakdown after about 25 years' service. He and my mother had become tenants of an hotel, it had nine bedrooms and was a very good business.

It was very upsetting. The publicity had a bad effect on the family. But it didn't break up my parents' marriage. When my father came out of prison he came back home. He never indicated his mental breakdown was an effect of his experiences in the war, though he was wounded twice. So my days at the Grammar School were overshadowed by these family problems. In fact, when my father went to prison I didn't go to school for about six or nine months, because I felt ashamed and my mother needed help at the hotel. So I just more or less played hookey. I just couldn't face it. It was wartime and the school didn't press; I suppose they realised the circumstances, the small-town atmosphere. I think with my mother's persuasion, eventually I went back to school. I sat and got my School Leaving Certificate. As I've said, I didn't have any particular ambitions, I just got interested in newspapers after my pal John Shaw asked me to write one or two pieces for the *Berwick Journal* and *Berwickshire News*. And then it was that John said, 'Look. There's a job going. See if you can get it.' So as soon as I left school at 16 in the summer of 1943 I started working for the *Berwick Journal* and *Berwickshire News*.

By the time I began I had a wee bit of experience in reporting wee jobs, Saturday afternoon sport and so on, while I was still at school. That was for free, I wasn't paid. It was just for the experience. It was a non-union shop anyway. But I'd been in the office and I knew most of the staff. I had had neither shorthand nor typing at school. I was able to type: I had my father's typewriter at home. So when I began full-time on the paper I went to night class twice a week to learn shorthand. I had two years' reporting experience then before I went off to do National Service.

I started off on a pay of £1 5s [£1.25] a week at the *Berwick Journal* as a sort of office gofer. I used to do all the wrappers for the postal orders papers, to go down into England and out all over the world really. I used to have to wrap all those up. There must have been about 400 or 500 of them every Thursday morning. There was no self-adhesive stuff then and, oh, messy, messy glue.

The reporting I did was all general – just local fairs, and an awful lot of going to visit families of people who'd been killed in the war. For instance, there was an awful lot of Arnhem victims from Berwick and north Northumberland.[3] I remember a whole page of thumbnail sketches of these local lads, and going from house to house collecting these pictures, and speaking to grieving families. And there was an awful lot of prisoners of war as well from Dunkirk and Singapore, a lot of Northumberland Fusiliers were caught there as well. Ian Johnston, the brother of one of my best pals, was taken prisoner at Singapore, and when news started to filter through that so-and-so was there, there was no word of Ian. It transpired, oh, about six months after the war that he in fact had died on the infamous Burma–Siam railway.[4] Another case was where we got word this local airman had been killed off Hong Kong. The editor, Alex Steven, asked me to go to Tweedmouth, see the airman's father, and collect a picture and get a wee bit history about his son. Duly my report came out the following Thursday: 'Local Air Force Hero Killed Off Hong Kong.' About two weeks later a court of enquiry report came through. In fact, the airman had taken the plane up and deliberately crashed it into the sea, committed suicide. That was one of the worst moments of my life, that I'd written all about this war hero and then in fact he'd gone over the top. So reporting those things was a harrowing experience. I was only 16, 17, 18. That was one reason why eventually I gave up reporting and moved inside to sub-editing.

But the sort of jobs I reported on included attending funerals. Well, it was local personalities. You'd go to the cemetery gates and no matter what the weather was you'd just have to stand there and ask everybody arriving, 'Your name, please? Your name, please?' Some of them had the gumption to come and say, 'I'm so-and-so. I'm representing such and such an organisation.' Then after the coffin had been lowered into the grave and everybody had dispersed, you would take a copy of all the inscriptions on the cards on the wreaths and flowers. And woe betide you if you missed somebody out.

It was so easy to make a mistake, not least on a local paper like the *Journal* and the *News*. And all the people in the locality are ready to pounce. Oh, the number of councillors that would come in to the office and say, 'I've been misquoted', when they hadn't. But they always used us as an excuse because somebody else had criticised them for saying that. Even at the age of 16, 17, I was sent out to cover town council meetings because there was only the chief reporter and myself and a part-time woman. My pal John, he'd volunteered to join the army when he'd just turned 17. He joined the Horse Guards. From the point of view of getting experience, in some ways it was grand being thrown in at the deep end – and without any training. The chief reporter did guide you along the right lines. He wasn't himself a particularly good reporter. I didn't realise that at the time, but as I grew older and wiser I realised that he wasn't. And of course my shorthand speed took a year or two to build up.

When I began in the *Journal*, on the editorial staff of the paper there was Alex Steven, the editor, Alan Pass, the chief reporter, my friend John Shaw – we'd started in the Grammar School together – and this woman Ellie Stewart, whose husband was in the Forces. She did part-time, about two, three days a week. It was maybe unusual that two young lads of the same age, John and myself, should be there. But, well, again it was wartime and there was a shortage of qualified staff really. One reporter who'd gone away to the war and was a captain was killed. That was the first time I ever saw a man in tears – Alex Steven, the editor, when he got the news that this reporter had been killed in action in North Africa. Gloom descended on the office that week. There was another reporter, Arthur Wood, away in the navy. He didn't come back to Berwick after the war, I think he sought his fortunes in the south straight away and later he became a respected agricultural journalist on the *Daily Telegraph* in London.

Well, I was 18 in May 1945, just as the war ended. I was called up to the navy. But I'd done only six weeks when I was kicked out because I had severe attacks of asthma. Again I think it was a lot of the nervousness from the strain and troubles with my father. I ended up with asthma, was discharged from the navy on medical grounds, and came back to the *Journal*. I came out from the navy with all my quota of clothing ration coupons, and the full demob outfit, after just six weeks!

I'd always played a lot of football. There were a lot of servicemen coming back in 1945. I joined the British Legion directly I came out of the navy, the committee persuaded me to join the committee and said, 'What can we do for some of these young fellows?' The idea of a football team was mentioned, so I said, 'I'll organise the football team.' I played goalkeeper myself. They were mainly charity games. Then I was always a keen reader, I mainly went for biographies and autobiographies. When I was a youngster at Blyth I was about four years in the Church of England choir, but then interest waned. Then I was in the Scouts and the Air Training Corps.[5] When I was called up I went into the navy because there were no vacancies in the Air Force at that stage.

Well, the hours at the *Journal* were nine o'clock in the morning till whatever it was at night. If there was a night job on, you might get away at four o'clock instead of five. But you never recouped the hours that you spent at night. You worked just the afternoon on Saturdays at football matches, not in the morning. Occasionally you worked on Sundays – you got church services and so forth. You were probably working 45 to 50 hours a week, that was the norm. There was never any difficulty in me getting the two evenings a week to attend my shorthand classes. But the other three evenings you might well be out reporting. Certainly you were out at least one night a week. Quite often it could be two or three, especially in the autumn when they seemed to have an awful lot of local associations' annual meetings. And you were back and forward to these.

And one major day in early 1947 we had the Goswick train disaster. Goswick was a place about seven miles south of Berwick. I was having my lunch in my folks' hotel bar when the editor's son arrived. 'Jack,' he said, 'dad wants us to go out to Goswick. There's been a train crash.' We didn't know how bad it was. We got out there and it was carnage. It was an Edinburgh to London train. There must have been about ten carriages absolutely splintered. There were eventually 27 people died. The locomotive had jumped the tracks. They've never known to this day whether it was a cow or some other obstacle on the line.[6] Everybody got in on it, including the rival reporters. My job was to glean as much information from them, collate the facts, phone Alex Steven, the editor, who would then send it away: he had a lot of freelance links. A friend who worked in the local accountant's tipped me off two or three months later – he shouldn't have done this – that Alex Steven, for that one day's work that we did, had got £90, which was a hell of a lot of money then. My pay was then about £2.5.0. a week. But he'd called Lincoln Shaw and myself into the office and gave us £1 each for our efforts that day. That was one of the things that made me vow: 'I'm not staying here.'

The paper's politics were, oh, very much independent. Alex Steven was very much a Tory, but non-party. A local paper like the *Journal* would almost have to be independent, because you can't align yourself like that. Berwick was a traditional Unionist seat until Sir William Beveridge was persuaded by the Liberals to stand, because he'd just produced his Report, and he won the seat in a by-election in 1944: Captain Grey, the MP, a Tory, had been killed in action.[7]

The *Journal* was a non-union office. As a policeman, my father hadn't been in a union. But at an early stage I had notions about trade unionism, because Bob Clemenson, one of the permanent lodgers at my mother's hotel, was an ex-policeman who was also an out-and-out Communist. He'd come out of the police force as a sergeant and he'd applied and applied for the chief constableship of various places, which was unheard of for a sergeant! Bob Clemenson was quite a brilliant man. He was staying at the hotel because he got a wartime appointment as the local weights and measures inspector. But he gained quite a reputation amongst policemen that he was going to challenge the accepted order of things – all the ex-army colonels and what have you who were becoming chief constables. He was going to apply because he had the experience on the ground. Bob Clemenson brainwashed me from an early stage! He had quite an influence on my political thinking, very much so. And, with my father going to prison, he was a great help to my mother, and was more or less a second father for a long stage. I couldn't say what Bob's background was before he'd joined the police, and whether he was a member of the Communist Party – that I don't know. Eventually, when Bob retired, he went back to his home in Bedlington. But he was a very, very strong Communist, very strong in his opinions, oh, a great character. He encouraged me to think in trade unionist terms and certainly in socialist terms. I became a socialist myself, very much so, when I was with the *Berwick Journal*.

I didn't at that stage join a political party. But I did try and persuade Alan Pass, the chief reporter, that we should join the union together. The *Berwickshire Advertiser*, the rival weekly, was a union shop, and obviously they were getting more money than we were. But Alan again wouldn't challenge the accepted order. He had a nice little number and he wasn't going to spoil it. I didn't attempt myself to join the union, I didn't think it was worth it just going it alone. That was one reason why Lincoln Shaw left and then I left.

Lincoln Shaw was one of the lads who came back from the Air Force to the *Journal*. But, as I say, it was a non-union shop and the pay was terrible. So Lincoln just stayed about three months and then went down to Essex. He'd been there about three months and I got a phone call from him at the end of November 1947 to say, 'There's a job here on this local weekly series in Essex.' So I applied, got the job, and started there as a reporter in December 1947. The paper was the *East Essex Gazette* series, based in Clacton, and run by Arnold B. Quick, who was a very, very good Essex county cricketer.[8] Lincoln Shaw worked in the Clacton office, I worked in the Harwich office. It was good safe reporting on various local events, especially sport, which I always enjoyed. That was a damn good two and a half years there. It was a union shop. I joined the union – the National Union of Journalists – there.

But my mother wasn't too well. So I decided to get closer to home and applied for a job on the *Northern Echo*, a daily paper published in Darlington, as a branch reporter, in charge of a branch office. I got a letter back from the editor to say the position had been filled, but would I like to try sub-editing? So I wrote back and said yes. From about £7 a week in the *Essex* weekly series I was going up to £11 something at the *Northern Echo*. It was good money at the time. I didn't even know at that stage what a sub-editor did – you didn't have subs really on weekly papers at all. But I just arrived there, got digs, and began to learn all over again, a new aspect of newspapers. I realised very early on, I think basically because of the all-round experience I'd had on local weeklies, that 'I'm going to be good at this.'

You found that quite a lot of the subs hadn't had any outside journalistic experience at all. They came from university, or from school as copy boys, or something like that, and they were given a vacancy on the subs' table without having done any journalism at all. There was one woman there – she'd been there 45, 50 years, the daughter of a local bigwig. I think he had a lot of shares in the Westminster Press,[9] and she had a job on the subs' desk. She was unmarried, she was the bearded lady. She had hair, surplus hair, and she couldn't get a man. She was a very, very nice woman actually.

So I had about two and a half years on the *Northern Echo*. I became active there in the union. I was treasurer of the Darlington branch and delegate to the Annual Delegate Meeting. There was a group of four of us at the *Echo*, close pals, all subs, and one, Jim Moffatt from Paisley, left to join the *Scottish Daily Mail*. He'd only been there a couple of months and he says, 'Phone me. There's a vacancy.' So I applied and was asked to come up for an interview. That was in 1952, when Andy Ferguson was the first editor of the *Mail*, and I was offered a sub's job at £13 – about £1 more than I was getting at the *Northern Echo*. I went back, gave my notice in, and Reggie Gray offered me another five shillings a week to stay. So I said, 'No thanks.' He tried to persuade me: 'All these daily papers up there, they've got a short lifespan. You're just better staying here.' But I said, 'No, I'm going up.' When I got there, there was another job going, so I phoned another of the four at Darlington and he came up to join us. About three months later there was a job going on the features desk, so I phoned the fourth pal. So the four of us all migrated from the *Northern Echo* to the *Scottish Daily Mail* within about seven months. Only Jim Moffatt of the four of us had worked in Scotland before. But of course I'd worked on the *Berwickshire News* and had a Scottish involvement there. And as a schoolboy I'd been in Edinburgh: it was only an hour and a quarter up the railway line. But the other two were English and had never been to Scotland in their lives. But they all did very well on newspapers, they all did very well.

So I wanted to move on from the *Northern Echo*. In fact, my aim had earlier been to do two years in three or four papers and then make my way to London. But on my visits to London I never liked the place, I'd never have liked to live there. When I was in Essex, I used to go down to London every six weeks for a weekend with Lincoln Shaw. His parents lived in Hounslow, but Lincoln and I stayed in a hotel in Bloomsbury – I'm sure the proprietor thought we were a couple of homosexuals! – go dancing, meet a friend in the police force, and always go to the Sunday afternoon concerts at the Albert Hall, up in the gods for five shillings. We both liked music. Lincoln's parents were both very good musicians and used to get jobs with the London Symphony Orchestra and so forth. But London itself never appealed to me. On the other hand, I'd fallen in love with Edinburgh when I'd come there with the school choir when I was about 10 or 11 and sang in the Usher Hall. So when I came to Edinburgh in 1952 to work on the *Mail*, I thought, 'This is my city!'

By then the *Scottish Daily Mail* had been published in Edinburgh for six years. When I joined it it had 72 editorial staff in Scotland, and I think about 59 of them were at Tanfield in Edinburgh. There were about six or seven, including a full-time sports reporter, in Glasgow; there was one reporter in Inverness, one in Aberdeen, one at Prestwick covering the south-west, and Jimmy Henderson in Dundee.

The principal competitor of the *Scottish Daily Mail* was the *Scottish Daily Express*, which was published in Glasgow. When before 1946 the *Daily Mail* board had discussed opening up in Scotland, one of the directors who had east-coast connections appears to have stepped in and said, 'Look, the east coast is going to be the gateway to Europe after the war. And Edinburgh and the Forth area is going to be a massive conurbation, a lot of industry, etc., because we've got closer links with Europe.' And he persuaded the board to open in Edinburgh instead of Glasgow, which was a grave, grave mistake. Everybody on the staff felt that. In fact, one editor put a bulletin on the notice board, saying: 'All this defeatist attitude that we shouldn't be printing in Edinburgh has to stop. We are here. We've got to make the best of it. That's it.' I don't think there was ever any serious consideration by management of transferring publication to Glasgow. But all the rivals were in the west. That was where the population was. I think in Glasgow it was a million, whereas Edinburgh was much less than half that.[10]

Publication of the *Mail* in Edinburgh didn't, however, make things more difficult from the point of view of production or distribution of the paper. Our edition times were fairly similar to the *Daily Express*'s. Our first edition was off at 9.25pm, for the Highlands and certain parts of the Borders. These papers went by train; if they missed the train they obviously had to go by van. The very odd times we missed the edition time and were running very tight timewise, then we had to take the vans. I remember one time there was a late football match involving Aberdeen. We had to hold back the presses, we missed the train, and therefore the papers had to go by van. There were 35,000 papers in this van already north of Perth when Aberdeen office phoned to say we had the wrong score for the match! Colin Dakers took the decision: 'Stop this bloody van and bring the papers back!' We had to get the police to stop the van, send it back, do a reprint with the correct score – and off again to Aberdeen. That was a costly night for the *Mail*, a costly night. The outcome would have been even more disastrous if the wrong score had been given, the sales of the *Mail* would have plummeted. They were bad enough. We had to fight to get circulation. In 1952 the circulation was about 105,000 in Scotland. The *Express* was a lot more than that, and the *Daily Record* also much more. The *Record* at that time had the highest circulation. But we didn't really look to the *Record* as a competitor, it was mainly the *Express*. The *Record* was directed to a lower readership, that was mainly working class, whereas the *Mail* was aiming at middle class as well as working class – to the prospective Tory voter, and you didn't find many of those in the working class!

Well, I started in the *Mail* as an ordinary sub-editor. Then I became splash sub,[11] did a couple of months' copy tasting, was appointed deputy chief sub to Colin Dakers, and then I was appointed chief sub when I was 29 in 1956. I was chief sub at the time of the Suez Crisis then, and the Hungarian uprising.[12] Colin was my mentor there, guided me along, and was very good. He was a bit of a scatterbrain but he knew the job.

There were about 14 sub-editors on the *Mail*. We'd have the copy taster, the night editor, the chief sub, deputy chief sub, and 10 others. Then there would be three or four on the features desk. So you're getting on for 20 subs. Quite a few of the subs hadn't worked as reporters. We got an awful lot of graduate entries in the late 1940s and up to the middle 1950s, oh, an awful lot. I looked with disdain – and I can only speak for myself – on the graduates that appeared in the office. I think their approach was just young arrogance mainly. They were probably trying to improve our writings. But at the same time we did try to guide them to our way of thinking. And I think we won the battle – the workers won. They eventually came round to our way of thinking. We merged. In fact, the *Mail* was a bloody good team, it really was, of sub-editors and reporters.

The reporters I recall from the 1950s and '60s were Ian Ramsay, Len Lord, Hugh Moran. I think Hugh joined the *Mail* after me. Five or six years I think he was there, then he went to the BBC as industrial correspondent, and then went outside journalism altogether to some development body, and then he suddenly disappeared from the scene, though I think he got a job on the *Express* for a short spell.[13]

The *Mail* had possibly the best features team, mainly people from London who occasionally came up to Scotland and wrote from a Scottish perspective. But in Edinburgh we had features writers like Charlie McCorry, and Ernie McIntyre used to do some features. Charlie was a very experienced man. I recall one night when we'd only about half an hour to go to the edition time, and it was discovered there was a big gap where there should have been an article about angling. Charlie suddenly appeared in the office from the pub across the road. I was night editor then, and I appealed to Charlie: 'For God's sake give us 250 words.' Charlie sat down, rattled something off, and it was very readable. Within about 20 minutes I had those 250 words. Then sport, mainly football, was well covered, too, we had some very capable men in sport: Alex Young, Alex Cameron, who eventually went to the *Daily Record*, Peter Donald did the rugby and cricket, and John Fairgrieve was an absolutely first-class writer who did an all-embracing column as well. Then there was John Rafferty, a splendid writer who'd been a schoolteacher and we gave him his first chance in journalism before he went to *The Scotsman*. He was covering a Welsh–Scottish football match the night of the Aberfan disaster, and he gave a brilliant report of it. He died relatively young. So sport was a strong feature of the *Mail*.[14]

I was with the *Mail* for 16 years, and on the whole during those years its circulation was edging up. Its top circulation was 122,000, or something like that, in, I think, 1959–61. I don't think it ever went below 100,000 in the time I was there. But the *Daily Express*'s circulation was going up and they were outranking us day after day really. I think then there was a gradual growth in overall reading, that more and more people were buying more and more papers. The *Daily Herald* disappeared or was transformed into *The Sun* about 1964, *The Bulletin* had disappeared a bit earlier, and we'd absorbed the *News Chronicle* in the middle 1950s. And despite the fact they said television would kill off a lot of the papers, I think there was a gradual increase.

The number of editions of the *Scottish Daily Mail* remained much the same. In the second edition, about 11.30pm, we covered mainly Ayrshire and Dumfries. There was a slip edition about midnight for Fife, I think we had two pages for Fife.[15] Then the third edition, a main edition, I think about 1am, was Glasgow, the Clydeside area. And then the last edition was 2am for Edinburgh and part of the Borders within reach. I think we did try as an experiment a Falkirk–Stirling edition, mainly a slip, for a spell, but I don't think it lasted very long. The trains dictated to a large extent when we printed the editions. The bulk, at least three-quarters, of the circulation of the *Mail* was in Edinburgh. We were still fighting the *Press & Journal*, published in Aberdeen, and the Dundee *Courier*. We had the occasional circulation drive, mainly based on Inverness or Aberdeen. But it was a struggle. You got readers for a fortnight, three weeks, then they just tailed off again. So we never really got any long-term advantage in those areas. The first edition going up north – Aberdeen and the islands – I think we printed about 32,000–33,000 copies. Of course, some of the early editions also came into Edinburgh: you could buy the *Mail* at 10pm at the Caledonian Station, the General Post Office, and one or two other places in the city centre. I think just over 40,000 copies were run off for Glasgow area. The rest was really Edinburgh and the Fife slip edition, which didn't sell a lot. The Dundee *Courier* came down into

Fife and they had a full-time reporting staff there; we just relied on local correspondents.

Of particular stories I remember us covering in the *Scottish Daily Mail* in the 1950s and '60s, Jimmy Goldsmith's elopement with the girl Patino was the biggest human interest story. It ran and ran. I was personally quite delighted with our coverage of the Kennedy assassination in 1963. We had a printing time half an hour earlier than the *Mail* in London; for their first edition they produced only five pages, we produced 13. Ours was then, I think, a 24- or 28-page paper. George MacDougall was the chief sub that night and I was night editor. We got the word about six o'clock that Kennedy had been shot. The editor had gone off early, the deputy editor, John Calder, came through and said about 6.30pm he was going, and left George and myself to produce the works. We really outgunned London on this. Eventually we had to toe the line with London's coverage, adapt the pages to suit them. By their second edition they had 12 or 13 pages as well. Everything just went by the board. Such a story, it was the major story of, och, the decade, the century.[16]

We were given quite a lot of freedom by London. London had a very good provincial desk which was the link between their back bench and our back bench in Edinburgh.[17] And we were on the phone with them six, eight, ten times a night, back and forward. Dan Davis was the provincial editor, and he advised us early on what London were splashing on, whether it was a dictum that we had to follow or not. But it was very rarely they interfered.

Andrew Ferguson, a Scot, was the first editor of the *Scottish Daily Mail*, from 1946 to 1954–5. Then Stefani, who had Border connections – Kelso – arrived. He had his own typographical ideas and he completely changed the look of the Scottish *Mail* as compared with the English *Mail*. His idea was a mess, terrible. London didn't like it and he was pushed aside, sacked, after about 18 months. After that I think he subbed on the *Daily Telegraph* in London. Stefani was followed by Bill Matthewman, who was English. He was a damn good man. But he got involved in the awful Lord Clyde judgement. Matthewman was the man who printed the picture of a murderer being caught in Derby. Bill Matthewman decided to print this picture, against the judgement of others in the office. And of course because of the question of identity involved, he was charged with contempt of court. He was fined £10,000 and the paper was fined £15,000 – a lot of money in those days. I was at the famous judgement by Lord Clyde that newspapermen must not interview witnesses in murders, and so forth. We were completely gagged, and that went on for years. Shortly after, Matthewman was transferred to London. The Scottish establishment would frown on any man who'd transgressed continuing as editor of a national newspaper. But Bill Matthewman became managing editor of the *Mail*, which really meant looking after expenses, the bills, and so forth. But he bounced back. Mike Randall became the London editor, saw the potential in Bill and appointed him his deputy for a spell. Then Randall was pushed out after a major overhaul of the *Mail* office, and Bill lost his position, too. After Matthewman, Donald Todhunter became editor of the *Scottish Daily Mail*. He was an out-and-out Englishman, white cuffs, always immaculately dressed. I remember being in his flat once and he showed me his shoes in his huge wardrobe: he must have had about 80 pairs of shoes. I remember there was some big story in Orkney. We had a big map of Scotland on the newsroom wall. Orkney and Shetland were transplanted and inset in the North Sea. Todhunter didn't know! And he asked, 'Can we get a man up there quickly?' 'It'll take a couple of days to get a man settled and organised up there.' Todhunter says, 'But look, it's only . . . Can you get a boat from Arbroath?'[18] Well, Todhunter went down to London as assistant editor or something, and he was succeeded by John Blackwood, the last editor of the *Scottish Daily Mail*. John was a Scot, Paisley born and bred, a very polished, very capable man. Again, he had never had any reporting background. He'd been a copy boy and then a sub on the old *Bulletin*. He knew how to handle people, which is more than I ever did. I was considered a hard, hard man. I didn't feel myself to be so, I was firm and fair. But I remember at the funeral of Pat Ford, a sub on the *Mail*, I was sitting beside Pat's brother at the funeral tea, and mentioned I'd worked alongside Pat. His brother said, 'Oh, you're the hard man, you're the hard man.'[19]

*   *   *

In 1963, when I was night editor in Edinburgh, there was a staff crisis in Manchester and I was transferred there as chief sub. Manchester had a far bigger circulation – which meant a lot more money. I agreed to go down for two months until they got the staff crisis resolved. Well, things dragged on and I was there two and a half years. I wasn't married then, still single. I got married down there. So I went down to London to see Mike Randall, the editor, and I said, 'Look, as soon as there's a vacancy in Edinburgh I want to go back.' Mike Randall says, 'You stay on here at Manchester and you're in the running for the editorship in Edinburgh eventually.' Things dragged on and on in Manchester so I went down to London a second time to speak to Mike Randall. I finally got my wish and came back to Edinburgh as night editor, but retaining my Manchester salary. But he warned me then – this was in 1965, 'Look, the *Scottish Daily Mail*'s time is limited.'

Oh, off and on down the years there was the odd rumour about the paper closing. Well, I was back in Edinburgh only two and a half years when the *Scottish Daily Mail* closed altogether in December 1968. My wife and I had been to the theatre and went to the Press Club for a drink. There I was greeted by Ian Calcott of the *Daily Record* with the news that, 'Have you heard the *Mail*'s folding?' I said, 'Ach, away. I've heard this all before.' Then the club steward said, 'There's been a couple of phone calls for you from your office. Will you phone them?' I got John Blackwood on the phone there and he said, 'Can't discuss it on the phone. Come down at once.' I got a taxi, it dropped me off at Tanfield, my wife carried on home in the taxi. I was given the sad news: the paper was closing in a few days. Bill Matthewman, the previous editor, was also there, overseeing the close-down, and John Blackwood and he called me in and said, 'Look, we're closing here but we want you to go down and be the Scottish editor at Manchester. All the papers are going to be produced from Manchester.' So I flew down the next day to see the Manchester editor, who was the infamous Larry Lamb, a hard, hard man, who went on to become the editor of the *Daily Mirror* and then of *The Sun* – Murdoch's boy, then he went to Australia. He told me point-blank right at the start: 'This is my office. No one's going to tell me who to appoint. I will appoint my own Scottish editor. It may be you. But it's going to be my decision and nobody else's.' I said, 'I can see now we're not going to get on at all. I just want nothing more to do with it.' I realised I was being used as a tool in a power struggle between the London, Edinburgh, and Manchester offices. So I went back to Edinburgh and said, 'I'm not having anything to do with it. I'll take my handshake and that's it.' Of course I'd worked in Manchester already and didn't care for it. Larry the Lamb reinforced my decision.[20]

So I took my golden handshake from the *Scottish Daily Mail*. But before the paper folded I collapsed – stomach problems – and had a major stomach operation. It was partly the strain, but I'd had ulcer problems for a few years and had had treatment. But this time the surgeon said it had to be cut out, so it duly was. I was back home recuperating on the last night of the *Scottish Daily Mail*. I was pretty weak, so Margaret, my wife, drove me down to Marshall's bar, the local hostelry of the *Mail* staff, at Canonmills, to see some of the old faces for half an hour. The place was absolutely mobbed. Of course Marshall's bar died a death the next day: it lost all its customers. Well, I'd completely missed out on the last four or five weeks since we were first told the paper had died, so I'd missed the awful atmosphere of the office.

Before I went into hospital I'd phoned Max McAuslane, the editor of the Edinburgh *Evening News*, and asked him for a job there, and I duly got word there was a sub's job available. Obviously it was a big reduction in salary. But I didn't want to leave Edinburgh. I'd been married four years by then and had two sons. Fortunately, my wife was working as well then. Her mother was staying with us, so Margaret, who had a big nursing and social work background, was working as an attendant at the Thistle Foundation in Edinburgh, a very good job.[21] And with the golden handshake I was able to pay off my mortgage, so that reduced the overheads.

When I went up to the *Evening News*, I had an interview with the personnel man, Mr Byers, and *The Scotsman* deputy editor, Eric Mackay. Mackay tried to persuade me to join *The Scotsman*.[22] I said, 'No. I have worked nights over 20 years. It's about time I had nights off.' I wished afterwards I'd gone to *The Scotsman*. But I got a job as sub-editor with the *News*. It was difficult to go from being night editor at the *Mail*, but I coped. I knew that if I didn't like it, I'd also had the chance to join the *Glasgow Herald* in Glasgow. They'd offered me an executive job while I was in hospital. But . . . I love Edinburgh. Well, it was good for the ego that I'd been offered four jobs – in Manchester, Glasgow, and two in Edinburgh. And I know myself I was a damn good production journalist, I was highly rated in various papers. That's not boasting, that's straight fact.

The main difference I found in starting on the *Evening News* was – getting up in the morning! And I found it difficult to adjust to parochial journalism rather than national journalism. About three years after joining I became deputy chief sub there. I was told by Max McAuslane I would never be chief sub, it would always go to a younger person. I was just over 40 then. After Max left and was succeeded as editor by Ian Nimmo he appointed me leader writer.[23] I hadn't done that kind of work before, but I enjoyed the challenge. But I was a good writer, and there was always a conference with the editor in the morning on what the subject would be. He would give a rough idea of the line he wanted taken and I would just do my leader. Ian Nimmo never discarded a leader from me. I did the leader for about three or four years. I was also in charge of planning all the overnight pages, which was mainly an afternoon job, every afternoon. I did the leader in the morning, out with the first edition between, say, 11.30am and 1pm, and then went over to the overnight pages. The overnight situation became pretty intense and took longer and longer. We were producing 13, 14, 15 overnight pages. It was a big lump of the total *Evening News*. I asked eventually to give up the leader writing because of the pressure, it was too much. In fact, I went down with a near nervous breakdown and was off for about five weeks. I was good at page planning, so I enjoyed that when I did it. If the demands of overnights hadn't grown so strong I would have kept the two going, overnights and leaders. But it was too much.

As I've said, I'd become a socialist years earlier when I was with the *Berwick Journal*. After I came to Edinburgh to the *Scottish Daily Mail*, I joined the Labour Party. I'd be in my late twenties, and I hadn't been a member of any party before then. The *Mail* of course was a Tory paper but that didn't set up any tension for me, because I went there as a sub-editor and wasn't involved in editorial conferences on policy, not to begin with, but I was as I became more senior. Of course, in those days the *Scottish Daily Mail* wasn't a blatant Tory paper – by stealth, let's say. We always had to carry the London *Mail*'s leaders, but we did have an independent voice. But I wasn't politically very active during my days at the *Mail*, because of working at nights, the antisocial hours. It wasn't until I went to the *Evening News* that I had my nights to spare and it was much easier. The *News* of course was not a Labour paper and never has been. So I warned the editor, Ian Nimmo, from the start when he asked me to do the leaders, 'I'm socialist inclined. If I go overboard at times, OK, just tell me and I'll try . . .' But, as I say, he never altered one. So my *News* leaders were slightly inclined to the Left! But there were no letters of protest from irate readers! But I was never ultra-biased, never. I never fretted at all that, as a socialist, I was employed by papers like the *Mail* and the *News*. You learned to counteract your own leanings. I certainly never felt like resigning on grounds of political principle, never. I had to live with it on the *Mail* for years. I wonder how I'd manage on the *Daily Mirror*! In fact, I was offered a job on the *Mirror* when I was in Manchester. I've never been short of offers of employment.

Well, I was 59 when I took early retirement in 1986. The office made it clear they would accept anybody that applied for early retirement. By then I'd worked for 43 years on newspapers and I thought enough was enough.

At Christmas that year Margaret and I went off to Australia, and had nearly three months with friends there, and then California. I'd been back home only about a month and I got a phone call from the general manager of the *Edinburgh Advertiser* freesheet, asking me to work two days a week, really to edit the paper and collate all the stuff that came in from correspondents and what have you. I was supposed to do it for a couple of months. In fact I was there for two and a half years.[24] I was then asked to edit the Forestry Commission staff newspaper. It was six times a year, five days out of every two months. It was child's play. I thoroughly enjoyed doing that for about four or five years. It just kept me a little ahead of my basic pension and so forth. Then I got my Old Age Pension and I said, 'OK, that's it,' and I packed in in 1992.

Well, looking back over all my years in journalism, I've no regrets, except possibly that I didn't go to *The Scotsman* instead of the Edinburgh *Evening News*. It was a good life. The best years of my life were without a doubt at the *Scottish Daily Mail*. It was a good paper, a good team.

During my working life from 1943 to 1992 the main changes in newspapers were that from the middle 1950s onwards, the accountants took control of the national papers and helped to reduce the ratio of money available to the editorial side. Then of course after that, the computerisation. But I never got involved in it. I got out at the right time. I think a lot had to do with Roy Thomson, Lord Thomson of Fleet as he became, coming into the British newspapers scene. He took control of the financial side, and a large financial team tried to curb the excesses of the editorial people. That ended really the good national foreign writing and teams that were out in the capitals of Europe. I mean, the *Daily Mail* had a tremendous coverage of Europe and the Far East. Well, of course, its decline could be seen too, maybe, as a reflection of the decline of the British empire.

And then I think young entrants to journalism are not getting the basic background that we did. I gather there's some lassies moving into one local paper now straight from school. And there's no older guiding hands to help them out. They're getting rid of all the older, experienced types. One of the important elements of journalism is your contacts. These young people that are coming in have no contacts at all. Well, I was a summer lecturer with the National Council for the Training of Journalists. I think that helped a lot, just a week's intensive course helped a lot. But I think basic work on the ground is the only answer. I haven't so far met any brilliant journalists produced from the college. At the end of the day they've got to get down-to-earth experience.[25]

George MacDougall

When I was leaving primary for secondary school I wanted to be an engineer like my father. He had been an engineer officer in the merchant navy for almost 20 years by that time, had steadily been promoted, seemed to be doing a good job and was well thought of, and I, then aged 11, thought, well, I could get into that kind of life. It was a nebulous feeling, because there was no way I could ever have become an engineer. My mind didn't work that way. Well, I signed myself out of secondary school at the age of 14 in January 1943, because by that time I'd become convinced I wanted a job having something to do with books or newspapers.

I was born in Edinburgh on 26 March 1928. My father had begun as an engineering apprentice with Ramage & Ferguson Ltd, shipbuilders in Leith, but was called up to the Royal Scots in 1917,[1] returned after the war to complete his apprenticeship, then, like so many others, found himself unemployed, and reluctantly decided to go to sea as a junior engineer. He was with the Ben Line first,[2] then from about 1930 with the New Zealand Shipping Co. He sailed to the Far East, China, Japan, New Zealand, Australia, and then during the war, by the beginning of which he was a chief engineer, he was on the North Atlantic convoys and the Mediterranean run. He was awarded the OBE in 1942 for saving his ship from sinking after it was torpedoed, and later he won the oak leaves after his ship was attacked at Gibraltar by a midget submarine. After the war he returned to regular voyages on a passenger liner, and latterly a cargo ship, between Britain, New Zealand and Australia until he retired in 1959.

My father was the youngest of three brothers and a sister. His eldest brother Alex, who, like so many others, had joined the Royal Scots Dandy 9th Territorial Battalion before the war in order to get a paid holiday, was killed aged 21 at the second Battle of Ypres in May 1915;[3] his other brother, Fred, lost a leg in action as an artilleryman and probably as a result died, barely aged 30, in 1924; his sister Mary Ann, for many years manageress of a prestigious women's clothing shop in Edinburgh, died in her early fifties. My grandmother MacDougall, who belonged to Thurso, died in 1926. My father's family were, I suppose, typical of so many other families in Scotland who suffered similar losses during and just after the 1914–18 War. Father, always away at sea, missed all their funerals; in his brother Alex's case there was no funeral as his body, no doubt blown to bits as were thousands of others in the Ypres salient, was never found.

My grandfather Peter MacDougall, born in 1867, was a coachman, then chauffeur, and gardener. The third of four sons of a Black Isle crofter at Fortrose, he had come to Edinburgh about 1890 in search of work. He died in 1948. An old photograph of his father showed my great-grandfather, Alexander MacDougall, who died in 1912, to have been a huge man with a big white beard. Surviving family papers testify that the MacDougalls were small crofters on the top of the Hill of Fortrose from the middle of the nineteenth century. But they must originally have come there, perhaps as victims of clearances, from MacDougall clan country in Argyll.

My mother, Mary Laurenson, born in Leith in 1898, second oldest of three sisters and a younger brother, worked as an ironer in various laundries in Edinburgh from almost the time she left school at the age of 14 until she married my father in 1927. She didn't have a regular paid job thereafter ever again. Her father, who died relatively young, was a joiner in Edinburgh and Leith. His father, my great-grandfather Laurenson, apparently was a Shetland fisherman who settled in Newhaven about the 1860s and worked as a fisherman from there. Until her death in 1941, my granny Laurenson lived as a widow in the Canongate area, including for a time in Robertson's Close and Queensberry House.

But there were no people whatsoever that I know of in the extended MacDougall–Laurenson families who were ever in journalism. I was the first.

My earliest memories are of growing up in Edinburgh. I was the eldest of three brothers, one two years and the other almost six years younger than me. When my mother had me in 1928 she was living in a room in Clarence Street, Stockbridge. But about a year after I was born the family got allocated a council house in the new scheme at Stenhouse, on the west side of the city. The house, at 56 Stenhouse Place East, was part of a four-in-a-block, two-storey type. We were up the stair. It was a small two-bedroomed house, with its own little bathroom and scullery. I would think we were the first tenants of the house. We remained in that house about four years, and then we moved further along the Place East to No. 49. There, upstairs again, we had our own door at the side of the four in the block, and a bit of back green. The house also had slightly bigger rooms, so it was a wee bit better than the smaller house at No. 56. By that time I had two brothers, David and then Ian.

I can't remember for sure, but we were probably just into No. 49 when I started school at Stenhouse Primary in the summer of 1933. The school was just five minutes' walk up the road from the Place East. I can't remember much of my early schooling. I think I was, well, OK, probably just above average. The headmaster was Mr William Cowe, a very large man with a huge face, who frightened me as a small child, but in fact he was apparently quite a gentle fellow. I can't really remember a lot of my teachers, except two in the later stages, Miss Robertson and Miss White. I was usually all right at spelling and arithmetic, although my teachers criticised my handwriting, which apparently wasn't very good. I was good at reading, and one of my earliest memories is joining the public library, children's section, at nearby Balgreen when I was seven or eight. I enjoyed picking out books and used to go once or twice a week to the library. I was a very keen reader and of course always enjoyed the children's comics. I think we used to get comics for very young children, then we started reading *Radio Fun* and *Film Fun*,[4] which dealt with comedians of the day, including Laurel and Hardy and Charlie Chaplin. Then we went on to the boys' adventure story magazines like *Adventure*, *Skipper*, *Hotspur*, *Wizard* and *Rover*. I was allowed to buy the *Wizard* and the *Hotspur*, but I had to trade them with other boys in order to get the *Rover*, *Adventure* and *Skipper*. Trading was the usual practice. By the time I was 10 or 11 there was a boy along the road who used to get the *Magnet*, which specialised in stories about public schools. Of course we knew nothing about public schools, except they seemed to have in these books a very high kind of boy. So we enjoyed reading about their adventures in the tuck shop – boys like Billy Bunter, Harry Wharton, Bob Cherry, who were from backgrounds far removed from those of us in the housing scheme, but which seemed to have a bit of an edge about them, much more exciting than our lives.[5]

I can't remember being gripped by any particular desire at the primary school to write stories or star with my essays. I didn't sit the Qualifying exam because in September 1939, at the beginning of my last year at Stenhouse School, of course the Second World War broke out. I, having read all these comic books, was in a state of panic about what was going to happen in the war. I thought we were all going to get bombed to bits by the German air force, as soon as the war started. I therefore wanted to be evacuated straight away, although my mother (father, as usual, was away at sea) said it wasn't necessary. In fact, I had the great idea, because of my father's contacts there, that maybe I could be evacuated to New Zealand, which I thought was far safer than anywhere else. But that was pooh-poohed by my mother. Eventually I said, 'Well, I'm going to be evacuated anyway,' and persuaded her. So by the time my mother managed to get me registered the first lot of evacuees had gone. I was in the second lot, which went early in October.

It was an organised school evacuation. Quite a few of us all went together in the train from Edinburgh to Aberdeen, changed trains there and on to the local train which took us to Keith in Banffshire. There were some evacuees from my own class at Stenhouse; I can't remember all the names but remember one boy called Quinn who came with me. When we arrived at Keith there seemed to be a lot of coming and going about who was going where. Obviously all the girls went quite quickly. But I remember that I and several other lads about my age had to hang about. Finally, they must have been persuading people, I think, to take us. This very large bossy woman, who was obviously in charge, eventually took me to a house in Fife Keith, over the water from the main part of Keith. There a lady called Mrs Simpson, who had one boy of her own aged about three or four, was perusaded to take me into her home. I don't think she welcomed me, shall we say, with open arms.

The house in Fife Keith was rather primitive. I was used to a reasonably good corporation house which had all mod cons. There in Mrs Simpson's house they still had gas lamps rather than electricity, and in the attic bedroom I shared with her small boy there were oil lamps. At night she lit them and then she came up and put them out.

I think I was treated fairly by Mr and Mrs Simpson, but of course they had their ways. He worked in a grocer's shop and probably didn't get very high wages. They got to a certain extent money for my lodging. I don't know what it was, but it wouldn't be very much.[6] I remember two incidents. One was where I was helping myself to butter and got a sharp reprimand: 'Don't you realise that that butter cost 1s 5d [7p] a pound?', which made me draw my horns in. On the other occasion, well, I was all right with fish if it was fried haddock and chips or fried cod and chips, but I had a Finnan haddie with all its bones put in front of me. I hated it, couldn't eat it, and got a row.[7]

At first at Keith I was quite excited because it was a new place. I went to the local school, the primary section of Keith Grammar School. I met new boys at the school, and girls, and they seemed to have a good sort of social life among themselves. I made friends with a couple of boys, one of whom was a farmer's son, and we used to run about the woods in the vicinity of Keith, playing all the games 11-year-old boys play. But eventually I fell out with the boys, and I felt I was getting picked on as an incomer with a different accent. They had very much the Banffshire accent and talked about queans and loons – being called a loon I thought was being called daft.[8] But I got used to that and soon picked up all the nuances of the local dialect. I don't think my own accent changed: I was at Keith too short a time.

Then there was another boy named Steven Laird who lived across the courtyard in this pend where I was with Mr and Mrs Simpson. Steven's father was a bit more well-to-do, in fact I think he ran a garage. Well, it turned out Mr and Mrs Laird and Steven were friends of relatives of my father who lived in Macduff, next to Banff. I had hardly been in a motor car before then, so I remember vividly Mr and Mrs Laird were going to visit relatives in Banff and offered to take me to see my relatives in Macduff. It must have been in November or early December 1939, so that was a great adventure. At Macduff I was made very welcome by my father's relatives – cousins, I think. They were an older woman, two younger women, and a man. I had a lovely meal there and enjoyed my Sunday afternoon. Mr Laird picked me up in his car again and took me with his family back to Keith.

But I remember feeling very homesick at Keith and, especially after I fell out with some of my friends, I really wanted by December to get back home again. My mother came up for the day to Keith with my two young brothers just before Christmas with Christmas presents. We all had a meal with Mr and Mrs Simpson. After my visitors went away I felt really homesick. So I began writing, agitating, to my mother. 'Please allow me to come home,' I used to write. 'I'll do all your messages for you, run all your errands, if you'll only let me come back home.' So eventually she sent me £1, and I waved this £1 note in front of Mrs Simspon saying, 'I'm going to buy my rail ticket home, Mrs Simpson!' I think she was quite glad to get rid of me. So she went down with me to Keith Station, we bought my ticket to Edinburgh, she got me packed and saw me off on the train to Aberdeen, where I changed to the Edinburgh train. I always remember coming out of Waverley Station to get on the tram back home feeling, 'Oh, isn't this marvellous!'

Once home I thought, 'That was daft going away from Edinburgh. I'm not going to do anything daft like that again.' We didn't have any serious bombing in Edinburgh, although there were a few bombs dropped, some people were killed and some houses demolished.[9] But by about 1941 I got personally fed up going down to the air raid shelter in the back garden and I told my mother, 'No, I'm just goin' tae stay in my bed.' And that's what I did, I just stayed in my bed during any night-time air raid alerts. My evacuation in Keith left me quite interested in what was going on up in the north-east. Many years later I revisited Keith, stayed there in a rented flat for a fortnight, and went all over my old hunting grounds in Banffshire. It was quite pleasant to go back there. But I really wasn't evacuated there long enough for the experience to leave any significant effects on me. I think the teaching skills in Keith Grammar School primary section, where I was in the top class, were quite high, despite all the disruptions with the war. What also impressed me at the time was that it was a school at which quite a range of social classes were all in together; Stenhouse Primary was more kids of working-class people. For instance, the father of one of the girls in my class in Keith was then Provost of the town, a sort of middle-class family living in a big house which quite impressed me when I passed it going to and from the school.

*   *   *

As a lad I was, as I've said, a keen reader. There were also a number of places around where we lived in Edinburgh where we could play. We used to have very imaginative games, based on traditional things like playing cowboys and Indians and soldiers. We were quite near Corstorphine Woods and liked to go to Corstorphine Hill, which resembled many of the sort of Western scenic landscapes we saw in the Hollywood movies. Then, too, I joined the Life Boys, and later on the Scouts, and then during the war the Army Cadets.[10] In May 1939, just before the war broke out, our family had moved about half a mile away to Chesser, another corporation housing scheme, a little bit more upmarket, near the cattle market. Chesser combined rented council houses with some which people had already bought from the council. Our new council house, upstairs in a four in a block that was stone-built, was also bigger than at Stenhouse, with four bedrooms, a bigger living room and kitchen. Two of the bedrooms were up an internal stair, and there were also several large walk-in cupboards. So we were really moving upmarket. By that time my father had been promoted to chief engineer and was obviously getting a better income, so my parents were able to expend more on housing rent and other things. I was a bit upset at leaving Stenhouse, where I had quite a number of chums in the same street. Because we were going slightly up the social scale I felt we were going among snobs at Chesser. A lot of the boys and girls there went to fee-paying schools like George Heriot's, George Watson's, Daniel Stewart's, Mary Erskine's. But in fact I soon found there was a very wide range of kids from all classes in Chesser. So we made new friends quite quickly there again. I also kept in touch with one particular friend, Peter Cameron, I'd had at Stenhouse. Peter's family also moved away from Stenhouse about 1939, to a succession of addresses, but eventually they ended up in Morningside. So every weekend I used to go on my bike – which I got for my 12th birthday in March 1940 – to see Peter at Maxwell Street in Morningside, and we'd roam the Blackford Hills and the Braids together. I liked to get out and about. From the time I had the bike I used to go cycling with several lads, away into the countryside of West and East Lothian, etc. I couldn't do that before I got the bike. I mean, if you visited your granny in the Canongate area, or went to the beach at Portobello, that was the furthest you'd gone.

Boyhood was a very happy time. And then my pals and I, and certainly my brother Dave, used to go every Saturday afternoon to the cinema. If we could persuade my mother, she would occasionally take us to the cinema in the middle of the week at night. Saturday we went with the boys to the local cinemas like the New Tivoli in Gorgie Road, and later from about 1938 to Poole's Roxy, a magnificent new cinema also in Gorgie Road but nearer where we lived.

As I've said, I missed taking the Qualifying exam at Stenhouse and never took it at Keith either, and when I started back at Stenhouse for the last months of my primary schooling the teachers agreed, on the basis of my previous performance in the class, that I should get the Qualifying certificate without sitting the exam. Just as the war began in September 1939, Edinburgh Corporation had built a new secondary school, Saughton Junior Secondary, for the Stenhouse, Sighthill and other local areas. Boys and girls could go to Saughton Junior Secondary for a three-year course based really on practical things. Boys could do, for instance, technical work like woodwork, metalwork, technical drawing, etc., and the girls could be trained in domestic work like cooking, laundry, sewing, all that kind of thing. Well, after I came back from Keith my mother said to me that she and my father (who, again, was away at sea, this time on a cargo ship, from just before the outbreak of the war until about the middle of 1940) would like me to go to George Heriot's, one of the leading fee-paying schools in Edinburgh. I immediately objected that Heriot's boys were a lot of snobs and I didn't want to be associated with them, whereas my friends would all be going to Saughton, and anyway I wanted to be an engineer like my father and therefore the technical course at Saughton was a good idea. I was a very insistent child. With father away at sea all the time my mother had to control us, but I was often able to shout her down. So I wore her down and I was allowed to go to Saughton Junior Secondary. This proved a very bad mistake on my part, because the boy who came bottom of the class for all practical subjects – woodwork, metalwork, technical drawing, etc. – was me, whereas I was usually among the top three in English, history, geography, maths, and similar subjects. I don't remember any discussion at all about my going to Tynecastle or

Boroughmuir, both of which were senior secondary corporation schools and reasonably near Chesser. You see, I had my mind fixed on Saughton. It was the brand new local secondary, cheek by jowl with Stenhouse Primary, just ten minutes' walk from our house in Chesser. And – an important thing – quite a few of my friends were going to Saughton: although when I arrived at Saughton in March 1940 I found that some of my friends had actually gone to Boroughmuir or George Heriot's!

So at Saughton I was duff at woodwork, metalwork, technical drawing, and also science and art. Mr Brown, the woodwork teacher, a very peppery man, with a big moustache and a loud voice, once threw a block of wood at me because I'd made a mess of it in the woodwork class. He would say, 'Help ma boab, you're an awfy laddie!' But very surprisingly, the science teacher, who was our register teacher, in the first week suddenly pointed to me and said, 'MacDougall, I'm going to make you the class captain.' So I was in charge. I had to make sure the register was always provided and generally be responsible for the discipline of the class but really for answering for the class – which shocked me, because a lot of the boys in my class, some of whom I'd never met before, were a lot bigger and certainly tougher than I was. To think I might be challenging these boys at any time sent waves of fear through me!

But I liked Saughton School. There were some excellent teachers there, particularly, as far as I was concerned, in English, maths, history, and geography. Dr James Kinghorn, my English teacher, was a brilliant chap, interested us a lot in reading, and later on when I left school I joined his amateur drama class at the School's Former Pupils' Club and was very much influenced by him. Mr Corbett, an excellent teacher as well, taught us geography and I later became very friendly with him as well in the FP Club, which he helped to run. My history teacher, whose name I've forgotten, had a metal plate in his head as he'd been shot in the First World War. He, too, was a very good teacher and in fact while he was my teacher I was top of the class in history and won a school prize – a book – at the end of my second year. I also had two excellent maths teachers, Mr Houston and Dr George Reith. After the war Dr Reith became Director of Education for Edinburgh.[11]

After two months at Saughton my ambition to become an engineer like my father disappeared. As I've said, it was a nebulous feeling and it became clear I could never have become an engineer. There was another course I could have taken at Saughton, and I often wished I'd gone into – the commercial course, where you got shorthand, typing, and French, and where the girls were in the same class as the boys, whereas in the technical classes there were only boys.

By the time I was 14 in March 1942 I'd become interested in newspapers, and of course the war was on and I was reading newspapers about the war. Before the war, my mother used to read the *Daily Express*, which was delivered to us daily. In 1940 I became a newspaper delivery boy myself at the local newsagent. I think that also inspired me to read newspapers, because I remember reading on the front pages in late summer 1940 about a ship, with evacuees on their way to America, being sunk in the Atlantic and many of these youngsters being drowned, and saying to myself, 'Oh, thank God I didn't go on a ship to America.'[12] My mother also got the Edinburgh *Evening News*, which I used to read assiduously to get the war news. For a while she got the *Daily Herald* because it had been offering free books or a set of encyclopaedias if you bought it for so long; but eventually she reverted to the *Daily Express*. Anyway I got fed up after about three months from July 1940 of delivering newspapers. It was a six-day-a-week job, for which I got 3s 6d [17½p]. But it was an early start: I had to be at the paper shop about 7am, so I'd to get up about 6.30. So I gave it up. But then I did a dafter thing. By winter 1940 I wanted to make more pocket money, so I decided to work as a milk delivery boy for the local dairy at the foot of Chesser Avenue. It was a six-day-a-week job, too, with pay 2s 6d [12½p]. You had to be there at 6am, you got a nice free half pint of milk to drink, and then you delivered the milk, a lot of it in cans. So on an icy winter morning you'd be going up some dark staircases with two big cold cans in your hands. It was hard work. I lasted there only two or three months and gave that up as well. Some of my pay for these two jobs I gave to my mother, but I think I got most of it as my pocket money, so she didn't have to give me any more money. I would go to the cinema and get my own sweets with my money.

In June 1942 the number of boys in my class at school dwindled because a lot of them left school at 14 after two years to start apprenticeships. When I went back to school in August after the holidays we had a new young history teacher, Miss MacGregor, not long out of Edinburgh University, and she also was an excellent teacher and again I did very well in history. She was obviously a left-wing person, and got me interested also in politics. Later on I discovered she had been a member of a very left-wing club inside the University. In 1945, the year of the post-war general election, Miss MacGregor appeared as election agent for Mrs Kitty Wintringham, Commonwealth Party candidate in North Midlothian. Her husband, Tom Wintringham, a former commander of the British Battalion in the International Brigades in the Spanish Civil War, and one of the founders of the Home Guard, had fought a by-election in North Midlothian in 1943 for the Party, and had finished a good second. He had died, however, in 1944.[13] Anyway Miss MacGregor got me interested in politics, and when I was still at school I went to a Commonwealth Party meeting at Tollcross. Just before I left school in January 1943 I had gone to another meeting, called The Coming Revolution and organised by the Independent Labour Party, and sat beside Miss MacGregor and her friends. The meeting starred a man called Sergeant Pitcairn or Pitman or Pit-something, who'd just been thrown out of the army in North Africa because, according to the authorities, he'd been spreading Communist or revolutionary ideas among the troops.[14] So at the age of 14 I became imbued with left-wing ideas, partly through the influence of Miss MacGregor but also through reading books in the library; and of course in the war the Red Army in the winter of 1942 was beginning to smash the Germans at Stalingrad, and that had a big effect on us all.[15]

Well, officially I could have gone on at Saughton Junior Secondary School until June 1943. But, as I've said, I signed myself out at the age of 14 in January that year, because by that time I'd become convinced I wanted to have a job having something to do with books or newspapers. I saw a job advertised in the Edinburgh *Evening News* for a junior librarian at Edinburgh University Students' Union library, and told my mother, 'I'm going to apply for that job.' She didn't want me to do it. What she wanted me to do was finish the year at Saughton and perhaps then, if I passed my leaving certificate exams, go on to do another year or two at a senior secondary school. But I was adamant: I wanted to become a librarian. So I applied for the job at the Union library and I got it.

The job was really for an office boy. There was only one librarian at the Union library, an old man, Mr McCutcheon, well, I thought of him as an old man, he must have been in his sixties then. He had obviously been quite a heavy drinker, because he had this very large red nose. He had a very gruff but friendly enough manner, was kindly, and was good at instructing me what I should do. Every morning I had to go to the newspaper shelves and put all the latest newspapers on to the hangers, sort of brass strips, and the students would read them. I also had to go into the library and get books for students who asked for them. Every week there were new books coming in and I would help to index them and put them into their appropriate places. The library had novels as well as all the various textbooks necessary for the students, and Mr McCutcheon would read the novels first and would often say to me, 'That's no' a bad novel. You could have a wee read of that yourself.' I became quite friendly with some of the students. There was one student there in his last year of studying agriculture or some kind of agricultural science who eventually became a farmer and who was also very good both at playing the piano and at having a drink. When he'd had a few drinks he'd go down to the Union bar, sit at the piano, and play all kinds of classical and jazz music. I used to stand at the door and listen to him, because he was very good. He would come occasionally and chat with me, and I always remember he gave me some advice: 'If you're going to kid anybody, kid somebody else but never kid yourself. Always tell yourself the truth.' Later on in life I tried to follow his advice.

They weren't good working hours in the Union library: they were broken. I had to be there at 8am to do my newspapers job and indexing of the books. Mr McCutcheon would roll in about 9am. I would work from 8 till 12 then go to the little staff room off the main cafeteria, where all staff, doormen and others, working in the Union could eat lunch. I got a free lunch, as well as pay of £1 1s [£1.05] a week. The lunch was usually pretty awful; the rissoles were dreadful. In term time, when we'd finished lunch I went home and had to come back again about 5pm and was in the library until about 9pm. So it was an eight-hour day but it was broken, and I didn't like that at all. In the summer holidays the Union was open, because a number of students living in Edinburgh used its facilities; but the library was open only between 9am and 5pm. So then I would work a straight day. Another thing I didn't like was I had to work sometimes on a Saturday. Depending on the shifts, I sometimes did a four-hour shift on a Saturday. But in the summer of 1943 youth employment hours became very strictly limited for all those under age 16. So – this was my first effort as a trade union representative! – I went up to the secretary of the Students' Union and pointed out that my present hours were in contravention of the Act and would have to be cut. There was a great outcry and shouting about this, but eventually they realised they had to do it. So that was much better as far as I was concerned. But by late summer 1943 I was fed up with the job. I saw it was going nowhere. And by that time I'd decided I'd like to become a journalist.

I was still very much someone who hung about the public library, and I'd begun to read the history of *The Times* and *Daily Mail* and also biographies of famous nineteenth-century journalists, people who'd been in Fleet Street and other areas of the country, and all their exciting adventures, and I became thrilled by this and decided 'I want to be a newspaper reporter'. I also decided I would offer the Saughton FP club a wall newspaper once a month. I typed this newspaper, called the *FP News*, laboriously on my typewriter, but did it in columns and headlines. A number of friends helped me produce the *FP News*: Dennis Nunnerley, Jimmy Dickson, and Alfie Thomson. That was good experience. So I began to look around for a job on newspapers. I approached Dr Kinghorn at Saughton school, with whom

I was still in contact through the FP drama club. He knew somebody in Orkney who was associated with *The Orcadian*.[16] So I wrote to *The Orcadian* asking if they could take me on as a junior trainee reporter, but I never even got a reply of course! Why would they take somebody who'd left school at 14, had no experience, and had never lived in Orkney? It was just daft. But eventually I decided to leave the Union library job, and, without having another job to go to, I left at the end of September 1943 before the new session started, because I didn't want to go back to those shifts again.

Well, an advert then appeared in the Edinburgh *Evening News* for an office boy for the *Glasgow Herald* and Glasgow *Evening Times* office in Edinburgh. So I applied for that, writing a very pompous circumlocutory letter in which I said I would like to follow the honourable profession of journalist, etc., etc., and would they please consider me as the office boy. Apparently this letter caused great hilarity in the *Glasgow Herald* office. But the manager got in touch with me, I went for an interview, and I got the job.

The office was in South St Andrew Street, off the east end of Princes Street, and very conveniently for the journalists in the office it lay between two public houses, The Grand and the Bodega. I started there in October 1943 at only £1 a week. So I took a wage cut to become an office boy in a newspaper, but found it a much more exciting job than the Union library. In the office there was a manager in charge of its commercial activities, his second-in-command, who was a woman, and there was a sort of general factotum whose first name was Cameron (I've forgotten his surname), and there was also a part-time chap called Packie who also sold newspapers up the street at St Andrew Square. Now in the morning Cameron and Packie would be in the office. I appeared at 8am, and one of my first jobs was to deliver on foot free copies of the *Glasgow Herald* to the City Chambers, the Bank of Scotland headquarters, and various other places all around Princes Street, the Mound, the High Street, etc. Then I'd be engaged in doing all kinds of messenger duties. They included going to the local tobacconist to see if I could get cigarettes for various people known to the tobacconist, because cigarettes weren't rationed but they were in very short supply. So you really had to know the tobacconist to get whatever you got per day. I would do various jobs delivering all kinds of things to various places, and picking up material from various places, including adverts for the papers. Then by mid-morning Cameron and I would be down at the Waverley Station getting the first edition of the Glasgow *Evening Times* off the train from Glasgow and delivering the papers to the various street vendors in the area, one being a man called Laing, who sold the paper at the top of the Waverley Steps, another called Whitey, who sold papers at the Wellington Monument, and then there was Packie. Once or twice a day I had to go down to the Waverley Station with maybe photographs to put on the train to Glasgow where they would be picked up by the *Glasgow Herald* or *The Bulletin*, the daily picture newspaper also then published by George Outram's. So it was a busy, eventful job, from 8am until about 5pm, with an hour off for lunch, and a five-day week.

It was really an office boy and messenger job, but of course being totally keen to become a journalist I was picking up tips from the editorial staff about their work. As it was the middle of the war, all the young men who'd worked on the newspaper had obviously been called up to the armed forces. So most of the full-timers in the office were older men, two of whom had been recalled from retirement, one of them Mr Winchester, a very peppery man in his late sixties. Tom Begbie, in charge of sport for George Outram's, was a very blustery, red-faced, hard-drinking, hard-smoking man who recruited me to do little jobs on a Saturday, picking up the scores of cricket clubs in the summer and football clubs in the winter in order to make up his linage. I got very annoyed at Mr Begbie. I thought he was a mean old basket who paid me very small sums of money for picking up the sports scores, and I also resented his sending me over all the time to the tobacconist's for fags for him. Mr Begbie would pop out quite often during the day to the Bodega or the Grand pub, come back smelling of whisky, get very pompous with the drink, and tell me he was a former officer in His Britannic Majesty's army: apparently he had served in the First World War.

Bruce Sim, who did the agriculture, was a very pleasant man. Later on I discovered he was a leading light in, I think, the Baptist church in Dublin Street. A very nice man, Mr Sim often got terribly uptight because other people would swear in front of him. Then there was another old man whose name I've forgotten but who was also quite pleasant. There was one lady reporter aged about 40, with glasses and a very severe manner – in fact, I would say she was pretty ferocious-looking. She bustled about doing the sort of women's stuff. Actually I couldn't complain about her at all, she was quite pleasant to me. A man whom I really liked and who turned up in the office about 1944 was Harold Turner, showbiz correspondent of the *Sunday Mail*, which of course was owned by Kemsleys at that time, but under a wartime arrangement the *Sunday Mail* and its stablemate the *Daily Record* both had their material provided to Glasgow by the *Glasgow Herald* staff in Edinburgh. They also provided stuff to the Aberdeen *Press & Journal*, which was also then owned by Kemsley. So our reporters made quite a bit of extra money by sending blacks, carbon copies, of their stories to these various outposts. But the most significant person for me in our office staff was the chief reporter, David Douglas. He was in his late thirties but had been exempted from military service because of his eyesight. A very, very nice man and a very, very good reporter, you could see him working away and you knew he was a very skilled person who also got on very well with the rest of his staff as well as being very nice to me. So I really admired Mr Douglas from the very beginning.[17]

In fact, it was Mr Douglas who got me made the junior trainee reporter. I was 16 and had been in the office for approximately nine months when I began to really work on Mr Douglas. I began to say to him, 'Is there any chance of becoming a junior reporter?' And he said, 'Well, I think you'd be much better off to get a job on the Edinburgh *Evening News*.' He took me over to the *Evening News* office and introduced me to the chief reporter there, a very nice man, but he had no job for me at the time. Then David Douglas took me down to what I thought was the bowels of the earth in *The Scotsman*, where people sat around at their individual desks with very shaded green lamps overlooking the desks. I was introduced there to Wilfred Taylor, one of *The Scotsman*'s leading columnists, a very effusive sort of man. He spoke grandly to Mr Douglas but of course was not interested in me. The chief reporter of *The Scotsman* was also very pleasant but said there was no opening at all for junior reporters at that time. So Mr Douglas approached our Glasgow office and said, 'We've got a very keen young chap here. I think he might be trained all right and we should allow him to become the junior reporter.' So I became junior reporter in the Edinburgh office in August 1944.

Of course the big drawback was I didn't have any shorthand or typing experience. So, even before then, I had signed myself into night classes at Boroughmuir Senior Secondary School to learn shorthand and typing: I always remember on the evening of D-Day I was at a class at Boroughmuir. Unfortunately, the teacher wasn't very good. So I didn't pick up short-hand at all at that time. However, I developed my own way of writing a kind of shorthand and managed to do my little reporting jobs. In fact, because of the shortage of manpower, I was doing jobs that normally a junior reporter wouldn't do. At the age of 16 I was reporting the Sheriff Court, where people came up for crimes in the middle range, and I would even on occasion go to the High Court and report there a more serious crime. I also reported meetings of the town council and its committees, as well as going to various functions in the city and reporting all the kind of odd things: a very wide range of activities. At that time Willie Raitt, a *Daily Record* reporter, was assigned to our Edinburgh office. Willie was very knowledgeable in that he knew lots and lots of people.[18] I remember Willie taking me to the police head office in the High Street and introducing me to the Chief Constable, Mr Morren, a very military-looking chap with a grey moustache, and the Chief Constable solemnly getting up out of his seat and shaking this 16-year-old pimply youth's hand as the new representative of the Fourth Estate, with Willie saying, 'Yes, George'll be all right,' and all this stuff.[19] Then Willie took me around, meeting inspectors and detective sergeants, lawyers, prosecutors, and defence counsel. Willie knew everybody: it was entertaining as well as instructive to go around with him. Willie did a lot of gossip-column stuff as well as straight reporting. Actually, he wasn't a very good writer but he had the sources and could get information and stories that other reporters who were better at writing the stuff couldn't get. Willie was a very friendly, kind man. I remember he had some free tickets for a Jack Radcliffe show at the old Theatre Royal at the foot of Leith Street.[20] He had one ticket spare and asked me if I'd like to go with him. So Willie and his wife and his daughter Caroline, who eventually became an opera singer, and I went to the Theatre Royal show and I was always very grateful to Willie for that ticket. As a junior reporter I was eventually given tickets by David Douglas to go to the Royal Lyceum Theatre, where the Wilson Barrett company were in repertory, and do crits on plays. Occasionally I was sent also to cover variety shows at the Empire Theatre. Once I was sent to the King's Theatre to do a crit for the *Daily Record* on a visiting D'Oyly Carte performance of *The Mikado*. I'd never seen a Gilbert and Sullivan operetta before, was totally mystified, didn't like it at all, wrote a scathing report about it which went to the *Record*, and they phoned back and said, 'We can't publish this!' So somebody else had to write a much more approving report out of their own mind but based on my notes. At that time I was still in the Saughton School FP drama club, and one of the highlights of my very limited amateur experience was in 1945 when various amateur drama clubs were asked to supply extras for the James Bridie play *The Anatomist*, about the body-snatchers Burke and Hare. Alastair Sim starred as the doctor who paid for the bodies, and I was one of the 'mob' who tried to burn his house down.[21]

So I was doing in the *Glasgow Herald* the job I wanted to do, and really getting far more experience than a junior reporter of my age in peacetime would have got. My lack of shorthand speed was a bit of a worry, but it never hampered me. I always got the story, and if I wasn't sure of some of the facts, well, the reporters on the papers at that time in Edinburgh were a friendly lot, and you would all sit together and check, 'Is this what happened?', and then go for a coffee to the Co-op cafe in Melbourne

Place after the court or council meeting (sometimes you'd even get a cup of coffee at the council). So you always got the stuff. Though there was competition between the papers, because of this wartime staff shortage in reporting there was also co-operation.

From the court I would also phone stories straight to the Glasgow *Evening Times*, if it was a story the Glasgow paper would want to publish. It was quite a pressure working for the evening paper, and you also did a story where necessary for *The Bulletin* and the *Glasgow Herald* – sometimes three versions of the same story. As things progressed, by 1945 I began to get annoyed that, because I was the junior reporter, other reporters in our Edinburgh office would take a black of my stories and send them to the *Daily Record* and *Press & Journal* and they would get the linage: I wasn't allowed to have any linage. On my own initiative I joined the National Union of Journalists in December 1944, soon after I'd become a junior reporter. Of course, a lot of the people on the *Glasgow Herald* weren't in the NUJ. They were members of the Institute of Journalists, a much more, well, employers'-orientated and 'professional' organisation, whereas the NUJ looked after its members' wages and conditions. So eventually I protested to David Douglas about the linage business and said, 'In future I, as a member of the union, refuse to allow other members of the staff to milk my copy without me being paid for it.' Mr Douglas got in touch with Glasgow, and Glasgow declared: 'In no way is this young man [I was only 17] going to get linage. But in future reporters are not allowed to touch his copy.' Of course, they still did so!

From 1944 until I was called up to the army in 1946 I never visited Glasgow head office. Head office probably affected more senior people, but it didn't affect me really. I just got on with the job and enjoyed it. Then, at the beginning of 1945, I found a new ally in the Edinburgh office: Charlie McCorry, who became a good friend of mine. Charlie had been in the Royal Artillery, but a flying bomb had exploded near where he was stationed at Woolwich. He was quite badly traumatised, and eventually given his discharge from the army. He'd gone back to his job as a reporter in the Edinburgh *Evening News*, but only stayed there a month or so and was wooed by the *Glasgow Herald*. I found Charlie, who was 10 years older than me, a very, very good instructor indeed. He used to take me around on various jobs, give me little tips and introduce me to people, and he was a very helpful, friendly man.

After the war ended quite a few reporters who'd been in the Forces came back to the office. The big change was that William Gardner, who had been the chief reporter till he'd joined the army early in the war and became an officer, came back. Of course, he became the chief reporter and David Douglas stepped down and became his deputy. Although William Gardner was a perfectly professional person he wasn't as good as David Douglas. David Douglas eventually left the paper to become an information officer with the Scottish Office. I wasn't very happy under William Gardner's leadership. He was far too distant and austere for me, not helpful like David Douglas had been. So the last two or three months before I was called up in April 1946 weren't as happy for me in the office as the previous years had been.

As a junior I was never left as a late reporter. I think there was only one reporter on duty till about 10 at night. I was either on the 9am to 5pm or 10am to 6pm shift, though occasionally of course I then had to go to the theatre to cover a show. Once, however, just after the war, when I was only 17 and I think it was probably holidays time, I remember working until 10pm. Anyway I got a phone call in the evening from the London office of the *Daily Mirror* (we stood in in Edinburgh for the *Daily Mirror* as well) saying a trawler had sunk off the north-east coast of Scotland, the survivors were being landed in Fraserburgh or Peterhead, and could I go up there and interview them as they came off? I said, 'Are you joking? Do you realise the distance between Edinburgh and there?' The London chap says, 'Well, couldn't you just take a taxi, old boy?' At which I laughed and explained Peterhead was about 180 miles away. So he lost interest and I think they went to the Press Association after that.

*   *   *

When I was called up in April 1946 I had to report to Redford Barracks, Edinburgh. I was then put on a six-week basic training course at the nearby Dreghorn Barracks, which was quite tough. Afterward, because of my experience as a reporter, they decided I would make a good army clerk, and I was immediately posted to the Royal Army Service Corps training camp at Cirencester in Gloucestershire for a 17-week shorthand and typing course. 'Oh,' I thought, 'that's good', because I'd never really mastered shorthand and I was a two-finger typist as well. I had bought my own cheap second-hand typewriter in 1943 when I was 15 and taught myself to type. At Cirencester I had an excellent corporal shorthand and typing teacher who in no time at all had me doing 100 words a minute in shorthand. As a result, in October 1946 I got a posting as a clerk to the War Office in London, became a lance-corporal in March 1947 and a corporal three months later. The top people in each squad who passed at certain levels got the best postings: if you got 100 words a minute you went either to the War Office or somewhere like Washington, as one guy did, to join the British military staff there, or to army headquarters in York, Edinburgh, or in various other parts of this country. I was posted to a War Office unit called ST6C, just off Trafalgar Square, in an office in a former hotel there. We were in charge of supplies, mostly of bread, for various army units. Every month you had to check the amount of bread being baked in army bakeries all over the country. A brigadier was in charge of the whole of the ST6 operation and he would occasionally call me in to his office and dictate letters to me. A major in charge of our Section C would dictate to me as well. I didn't get an awful lot of shorthand dictation, but I did a lot of typing, kept up my speed in both, and was quite happy later on going back to newspaper reporting with that speed. Once you were taught Pitman's shorthand and grasped its essentials it remained with you basically for life. Everybody who does shorthand develops their own little tricks as they go, and I never had any problem.

At the War Office civvy digs were provided for you. I shared a room with four or five other soldiers in a big house near Swiss Cottage run by a Mrs Brown. It was cramped, there were about a dozen soldiers billeted in the house. Mrs Brown gave us a good breakfast. But she was a pretty untidy sort of woman. There were several sergeants there and they did all right. The rest of us lower ranks didn't do so well. In February 1947, after I'd had my first leave from the War Office, I came back to Mrs Brown's to find the same dirty sheets and pillow slip on the bed that I'd left. I made a mild protest to Mrs Brown, and she immediately told me to pack my bags and get out. But she gave me a week's notice, during which I wheedled my way back into her affections and she said, 'Och, you can stay if you want.' By then, however, David Nutt, a friend of mine in the same unit in the War Office as me, had got me a place in his digs at Stockwell in South London.

I was in the army for altogether two years and three months, about 20 months of it in London. The experience had a big effect on me. David Nutt, who was a year or more older than me, had quite an influence on me because he was very much into classical music and took me along to the Winter Proms at the Albert Hall. That gave me a real interest in classical music. Though he was demobbed before me we still went along to Albert Hall concerts. David also developed in me a much more concentrated interest in politics. On the Left himself, he used to buy the *Daily Worker*, which I'd never seen before. So he'd give me it to read after he did, and this had a big influence on me politically. I began to think in terms of Communism, and from the library would take out books by Marx, Lenin, Harry Pollitt, and various other people like John Strachey, then a Labour government minister but who before the war had written a lot of left-wing books very close to Communist ideology.[22] So I decided that the idea of socialism throughout the world was a good one and I was going to support it. I became a convinced Communist. I used to go up Charing Cross Road, where there was a number of left-wing bookshops like Collet's, and buy Communist literature. I'd also buy my own copy of the *Daily Worker*. I became so enthusiastic about all this that, among various left-wing soldiers I knew either through the digs or the War Office NAAFI[23] in Halkin Street, Mayfair, I organised whip-rounds to send to the *Daily Worker* fighting fund. Of course, the authorities didn't know this was going on inside the War Office or they'd have had a fit!

About once every six months you had to do duty as a night clerk in the main War Office. There'd be an officer in charge at the telephone to deal with any calls coming in from all over the world affecting the British army, and he'd have a clerk or two to do various odd jobs for him. I remember once being night duty clerk when the officer had gone out for a drink. I looked at the memos on his desk, and there was one from the British command in Palestine. The United Nations had decided there'd be a state of Israel, and there was this message from British army HQ in the Middle East to say they were doing all they could to remove all army equipment out of the reach of the Israelis, and where it was possible to allow certain goods to get into the hands of the Arabs they should do so. Well, Emanuel Shinwell had just then been made Minister of War, he was Jewish – and here was the army command making sure the Jews didn't get any British army equipment![24]

I didn't join the Communist Party while I was in the army, because serving soldiers weren't permitted to be members of political parties. However, in the *Daily Worker* I saw an advert that the Young Communist League of Islington met once a month in a school there.[25] So I took the bus one night, went to the school, introduced myself, said I was keen to join the YCL after I'd be demobbed, and could I attend a meeting? They said, 'Certainly.' So I used to go to the Islington YCL meetings, and I also remember going to the Albert Hall in March 1948 to a rally organised by the Communist Party at which Harry Pollitt and Willie Gallacher, MP, were the main speakers, celebrating the centenary of the *Communist Manifesto*. The Hall was absolutely packed, a very great meeting that of course enthused me enormously.[26]

David Nutt and I used to read the *Daily Worker* in the War Office. The sergeant major in charge knew that. He himself read the *News Chronicle*, and he would tut-tut-tut at us, but he never did anything about it. He was a crossword fanatic so he would consult David and me about various clues to the *News Chronicle* crosswords. I also read the *News Chronicle*, thought it the best of the popular papers and was quite inspired by it. A Liberal newspaper at the time, it was quite left-wingish in its way.

Well, I felt my army service was a waste of time in some ways. But I thought being rigorously trained in shorthand and typing was an asset. And I quite enjoyed my time at the War Office. I had civvy digs, had almost every weekend free, could wear civvy dress at the office, and could enjoy all the delights of London – a much bigger range of cinemas, including the Everyman in Hampstead and the Academy in Oxford Street, both of which showed a lot of foreign films, and also I went to the theatre and classical music concerts. Then, too, I had a friend from Edinburgh in London – Dennis Nunnerley, a left-winger, whom I'd known before I was called up, and who'd been posted to the Royal Signals in London. He and I would meet two or three times a week at night, go to the War Office NAAFI, have a meal, and then walk for miles through the streets of London, discussing political and cultural questions. We often ended up at the Salvation Army canteen at Victoria, which sold very, very good bread pudding at about tuppence a slice and which helped sustain us.

I got demobbed from the army in July 1948 at the age of 20. We got some demob money, and I had a fortnight's holiday, then I went along to the *Glasgow Herald* office in Edinburgh. The office said, 'Well, you've got a month's money, why not have a month's holiday?' 'No, no,' I said, 'I want to come back.' So I went back to work at the beginning of August and more or less resumed where I'd left off in 1946. Again I went around at first with Charlie McCorry, who of course was well established on the *Glasgow Herald* by then, just to familiarise myself with what had been going on. But I soon began again to do stories – the usual reporting round of courts, committees, etc., and reviews, plays, variety shows.

When I came back from the army the chief, then still Bill Gardner, said to me: 'Now Sir William Robieson', who was then editor, 'always meets members of staff who've been demobbed. So here's a first-class return rail ticket to Glasgow. You've to go and see Sir William tomorrow.' So when I was ushered into his presence in his office in Buchanan Street, Sir William shook my hand, sat down, and said, 'Well, MacDougall, you're out of the army now. How do you feel?' 'Oh,' I said, 'I'm very glad to be back, sir.' 'Well,' he said, 'National Union of Journalists: at the moment anyone aged 20 gets £4 7s 6d [£4.37½] a week. But we always pay above the odds at the *Glasgow Herald*. So you will get £4 10s [£4.50] a week.' So there you are: I had half a crown [12½p] over the union minimum – doing all right. It was quite a good pay for someone aged 20.

I did shift work. If I was on the *Evening Times* duty, I'd be there by 9am. If I wasn't, I'd be in by 10, or else I'd be starting, say, about 1pm on to about 9pm, or I sometimes did the late shift, say, 5pm till midnight and later if necessary. Usually you were on a particular shift for a week, so you did a late shift about once every four weeks. You had also sometimes to work on a Saturday – you didn't necessarily have to come into the office, but you'd have to be in touch all the time in case a story broke, then you'd have to cover it.

My old bugbear Mr Begbie was still there as sports man, and he immediately got me again doing little jobs for him on Saturdays. He asked me to be the telephone clerk at a rugby match for D.R. Gent, then a well-known rugby reporter, who was covering a Scotland v. England international at Murrayfield.[27] I went along there and phoned Mr Gent's stuff to the *Sunday Times* as he dictated it to me. But no money came through afterward, so I went to Begbie and said, 'Look, you've been paid for this for your part, but I haven't been paid a penny yet. You must have had the money. So,' I said, 'in future I'm not doing any work for you at all.' Begbie huffed and puffed about that but didn't make an issue of it. So I got out of the sport altogether, which pleased me because I was never interested in sport.

*   *   *

As soon as I was demobbed in July 1948 I joined the Young Communist League branch in Edinburgh. Of course, I kept that a secret from my employers, I wasn't going to tell them. The YCL branch met every week in the Communist Party rooms in Buccleuch Street. The only person outside the YCL who knew about me joining was Charlie McCorry. Charlie had meantime married Evelyn Glen, who had been a member of the Communist Party since before the war and who became a very good friend of mine. So Charlie was sympathetic to me, but he said, 'For God's sake, keep it quiet. Don't tell anybody at all.' Of course, the *Glasgow Herald* was a Conservative newspaper; but apart from that, I don't think any newspaper employer would be very keen about reporting staff being members of the Communist Party.

There was just the one YCL branch covering Edinburgh and Leith. It had about 40 to 50 members altogether, with usually about 15 or 16 at the meeting. Their ages ranged from about 16 to 30. By the time they were in their late twenties, most people had, if they still were interested, gone off to join the Communist Party or were already members of the Communist Party. You could be a member of both the Communist Party and the YCL within the latter's age limits. After about three months' membership in the YCL, when I'd shown I was an active member doing all sorts of things, had a bit of a gift of the gab because I'd been studying all kinds of political tracts and learned books, and understood Marxist dialectics, I was elected chairman of the branch. I didn't do any public speaking, only internally. I was then approached by Murdoch Taylor, secretary of the Communist Party in Edinburgh, who said, 'You're now chairman of the YCL branch. Don't you think you ought to join the Communist Party as well?'[28] And of course I was delighted to join in October 1948. There were then probably four or five Party branches in Edinburgh, plus the YCL branch. There was a Central Edinburgh branch (their branch rooms were the Buccleuch Street ones where the YCL also met), Stockbridge, West Edinburgh, and one for East Edinburgh which I think also covered Leith. At that time I would say the Communist Party had about 400 or 500 members in Edinburgh, of whom at the most 100 would turn up at the aggregate or general meetings held from time to time. I think there were members of the Midlothian, East and West Lothian areas who all came into the Edinburgh area. There was at least one girl who was a member of the YCL whose father was a member of the Party, and they lived in Prestonpans in East Lothian.

I didn't feel any conflict between working for a Conservative newspaper and being a member of the YCL and the Communist Party. I was only involved in straight reporting, and in those days newspapers were a lot more objective, particularly broadsheets like the *Glasgow Herald* and *The Scotsman*. Your reporter went out and reported what he heard, saw, or was told. He tried to get a balance, one side and another side. You were taught to do that. Therefore I felt no conflict in that sense, except of course you felt if you were tackling a story for, say, a left-wing newspaper, you would tackle it sometimes from a different angle than from the right-wing. But I never felt there was a conflict.

In late 1948 I got in touch with the *Daily Worker*, told them I was a full-time reporter for the *Glasgow Herald*, a member of the YCL and the Communist Party, and that if they wanted me occasionally to send them a story in the Edinburgh area that might be of interest to them, I'd be quite happy to do that. They had of course a full-time reporter in Scotland – Harry McShane, but he was based in Glasgow.[29] So Fred Pateman, news editor of the *Daily Worker*, said, 'Come down and have a chat. We'll pay your fare.' So I went down to London on a weekend off in, I think, January 1949, and Fred Pateman told me the kind of stories he'd be interested in. So about once a week I would phone them a story, or I'd phone an item to Walter Holmes, who ran the 'Worker's Notebook', a sort of gossipy left-wing column in the *Worker*.[30] Or they would phone me up at home and say, 'What about this? Any chance of a wee story about that from our angle?' And I'd do that for them. I didn't get paid for any of this of course, it was all voluntary. I was a totally dedicated Communist, and this was wonderful to be able to help the workers' newspaper. They said, 'Of course, you know, as usual, we're in financial trouble. But if you have any particular expenses let us know.' And I said, 'Oh, not to worry. I'll just put them on my *Glasgow Herald* expenses,' because by that time I was allowed expenses by the *Herald*. So I carried on right through 1949 working for the *Glasgow Herald*, the *Evening Times*, and *The Bulletin*.

But in 1949 William Rust, the editor of the *Daily Worker*, died, and J.R., or Johnny, Campbell, an old-time Communist Party leader, was appointed in his place.[31] Fred Pateman got in touch with me about August or September 1949 and said, 'Look, there's a vacancy coming up on the *Daily Worker*, not as a reporter but as a sub-editor. Would you be interested?' Well, I had no experience of sub-editing, a pretty different job from reporting. On the other hand, I'd be working for the *Daily Worker* and I'd be in London. So I said, 'Yes, I'd be interested in it.' So I went down to London, saw Johnny Campbell and Allen Hutt, the chief sub-editor, and they decided to give me the job.[32] I gave in my notice to the *Glasgow Herald*, where there was great surprise and even consternation to learn their junior reporter was a Communist! In those days you were a junior more or less till you were 24, but you didn't really get to the top wage until you were 28, the age of the top minimum. So I handed in my month's notice and left Edinburgh in late October 1949 to join the staff of the *Daily Worker*. I had regrets about leaving Edinburgh, not so much about the *Glasgow Herald*. But colleagues in the office were all very nice, had a whip-round for me, and gave me £8 10s [£8.50], quite a considerable sum as it was quite a small staff, and my weekly pay at that time was about £5.

Incidentally, by the time I left, William Gardner, the office chief reporter, wasn't very happy and had gone off to become a sub-editor with *The Scotsman*. The new chief reporter in our *Glasgow Herald* office was Harry Boyne, who'd been I think at the Dundee *Courier*. Harry Boyne was a very, very astute man, a very good reporter, and he persuaded David Douglas to come back to the *Herald* from the Scottish Office as his deputy chief reporter. Harry Boyne subsequently became political reporter for the *Glasgow Herald* in London, and David Douglas was then made chief reporter again in Edinburgh. Harry Boyne later became Sir Harry Boyne, chief political editor of the *Daily Telegraph*. He was a disciplinarian, but he was very fair, and if you did a good job Harry Boyne backed you up. He was always very nice and kind to me. So by the time I left the *Herald* in 1949 there were about eight reporters in the Edinburgh office, including George Watt, a specialised court reporter who'd been appointed about 1947 while I was in the army,[33] and there was also Lorna Rhind, in charge of women's features, and at that time the only woman journalist in our office.

*　　　　　*　　　　　*

The *Daily Worker* office in London was in Farringdon Road. I had been in there a couple of times before. Allen Hutt was the chief sub-editor. I'd no sub-editing experience, but within a month or two I felt very confident under Allen's tutelage. He had a reputation of being short-tempered and brusque, and if he didn't like someone he could bear down on them. But he and I struck it off very quickly. He was a great teacher and was a tremendous influence on me. He was a terrific typographer, and an historian as well. He himself had been taught by the man who, quite famous at the time, had been *The Times* typographer. Allen had also worked for the *Daily Herald* and *Reynolds News*,[34] but he'd been chief sub-editor at the *Daily Worker* for some years when I went there.

My work there was straightforward sub-editing. The sub-editor's job is to process the reports which come in from the newspaper's reporters – staff reporters, correspondents local and foreign – and from news agencies like the Press Association, Reuters, which deals with all foreign news, the Associated Press in America,[35] and various other foreign press bodies. Processing reports means cutting them down to the size required. A newspaper's space is finite, and each story is approached on its merit. You might have a story of a disaster where people are injured, trapped, or killed, where there's a great amount of police, ambulance, fire brigade activity – a very big story indeed. You would want to give that a lot of space, with pictures. The sub-editor would gather all this material coming in from staff reporters, local correspondents, and so on, check the accuracy, make sure it's all reasonably balanced where balance is required, particularly in court cases, weld it into one story or a main and a supporting story, trim it to fit into the space required on the page for it, and write the headlines which would cover it. That is basically what the sub-editor does. He would have access immediately to all kinds of standard works of reference – dictionaries, Post Office telephone directories, encyclopedias, annual books of facts about government, churches, foreign institutions, etc., in order to check anything inside the story. So care is taken within the limits of time available to make sure your facts are as accurate as you can make them. That's very important, because a good newspaper wants its readers to understand that what they are reading is based on fact. A newspaper where a hurried job is done without any adequate care simply gets a bad reputation for publishing stories which are not accurate. You've got to be particularly careful in court stories, or other stories to do with individuals, that you don't libel or defame anyone, because people could take legal action against the paper.

As I became more skilled at sub-editing, I got bigger stories to sub. I remember on one or two days in January 1950 sub-editing the rather lengthy reports from the Old Bailey of the Timothy Evans case, where the main prosecution witness was John Christie. Christie had been a special constable during the war, but he had a criminal record. He swore that Evans had done this and done that. Timothy Evans was found guilty, sentenced to death, and hanged. Several years later they discovered Christie was in fact a mass murderer who'd killed Evans's baby daughter and his wife, and several other women, including his own wife, and hidden their bodies away in cupboards. So I remember sub-editing the reports of Evans's trial and saying at the time, 'I don't believe this man Christie.'[36]

The sub-editors under Allen Hutt on the *Daily Worker* when I began there numbered about eight. Reg Weston was Allen's deputy. When Allen was off, Reg, an awfully nice guy and very helpful to me, was in charge. Reg was a very capable chap, good on make-up, too. He must have been then in his late thirties, had been a YCL member in the early 1930s, and a member for a long time as well of the Communist Party. He was very well read and a mine of information about the Communist Party and about newspapers. Reg also had an excellent professional effect on me. There were two women sub-editors, Alison Macleod[37] and Ruth Hingston. Ruth Hingston, who was Jewish, had been a child refugee from Germany before the war.[38] Then there was Eric Scott and Len Robbin. Len Robbin was an awfully nice guy who'd dropped as a paratrooper at Arnhem and been very badly wounded. In fact, poor Len died in the early 1950s from his wounds. Ben Francis, an old-time member of the Communist Party, who had at one time been industrial correspondent of the paper, acted as copy taster. The copy taster's job is to read all the copy as it comes in. Whether the copy (or report) comes in from the paper's own reporters or correspondents, from the Press Association or other agencies, it all comes to the copy taster and he reads through it and decides where it should go. Normally of course in the *Daily Worker*, which was a small operation, it all went to Allen Hutt as chief sub-editor to decide what to do with it. If the copy taster thought the copy wasn't worth anything, he just put it on the spike – the equivalent almost of the waste-paper basket.

As for reporters, the *Daily Worker* had specialists, for instance, a political correspondent, who worked mainly in the House of Commons. George

Sinfield, the industrial correspondent at that time, had very good contacts with the Trades Union Congress.[39] Malcolm MacEwen, an old-timer on the *Worker*, was the diplomatic correspondent.[40] Then you had Sheila Lynd, women's editor. Fred Pateman had become production editor, so the news editor was an old seaman, Frank Gullet. Under Frank you had five or six general reporters, as well as the specialists, based in the office.

The office itself in Farringdon Road was new, opened in 1948. Before that they'd been in much more cramped surroundings in the East End of London. But due to the efforts of Bill Rust in raising a lot of money from various places, maybe even from Russia, they managed to erect this new office, have new printing presses, and produce a broadsheet for the first time: before that the *Daily Worker* had been tabloid size.

More than most papers, the *Worker* had to depend on unpaid enthusiasts, members of the Communist Party, sending copy in by phone or post, though the paper did have a full-time reporter in Glasgow – Harry McShane, as well as one in Manchester and, I think, in Leeds. But that was about all.

There was a difference between some members of the editorial staff on the *Daily Worker* and those of other newspapers like the *Daily Mirror* or *Daily Express*: some of the *Worker* staff were not professionally trained journalists. Frank Gullet, for example, as I've said, had been a seaman when he was young, had been a Communist for a long time, had done, I think, various jobs in Fleet Street, and, it must have been during the war, became a reporter on the *Worker*, stayed there and became news editor. Frank, a bit like Willie Raitt of the *Daily Record* in Edinburgh, was not very good at stringing words together, but he was a very good operator on the news desk. Then there was Rose Smith, an older lady and old-time Communist Party member – Rose must have been well into her fifties when I went to the *Worker* – who had been put on to the paper as a reporter because she'd been a stalwart in the Party, an organiser in Yorkshire in the early 1930s, and showed some kind of facility with words.[41] The editor, J.R. Campbell, had been a journalist in the sense that he'd been editor of the old *Workers' Weekly* in the 1920s, but he'd never been professionally trained.[42]

Then the deputy editor of the *Daily Worker* was John Gollan, who like me came from Edinburgh, and who eventually became general secretary of the Communist Party, but was not a professionally trained journalist.[43] The editor and deputy editor were always political appointments, not journalists. I know this rankled with Allen Hutt. I think Allen's ambition was to become editor of the *Daily Worker*. Although he'd been a member almost since the beginning of the Communist Party in 1920, had proved his worth time and again, and in later years became known as an old Stalinist, I think he was very hurt that he'd never been trusted with the actual editorship of the paper. I think the hierarchy of the Party had decided many years before that the editorship of the paper was a political job to be done by a political person – somebody who'd been a political worker for the Party, had achieved Central Committee and Executive Committee status, and therefore was one of the inner circle. Allen Hutt never achieved that status, though for a while he was a member of the Central Committee, or National Committee as they called it later. But he was never a political worker in the field for a particular area as the others had been. J.R. Campbell of course had been the British representative in the Communist International in Moscow for quite a few years.[44] So they always wanted somebody in charge of the *Daily Worker* who was one of the top political people. They never trusted a journalist as such, not in our time.

So there was always a bit of tension among *Daily Worker* editorial staff between the professional journalists and the non-professionals. And there was always suspicion, I think, within Communist Party headquarters about the *Daily Worker*. I remember that in 1952, by which time I was working as assistant editor of the YCL paper *Challenge*,[45] there was a row inside the *Daily Worker* office between on the one hand Reg Weston, the deputy chief sub, and Freddy Deards, a very good sports reporter and later sports editor, and on the other hand Allen Hutt, over the fact that Allen Hutt was being allowed extra money. You see, the *Daily Worker* had a strict system of payment: you got Party wages. When I joined the *Worker* in 1949 as a single man I was given the minimum Party wage, then £7 a week. If you were married and had children and your wife couldn't work, you got an extra 10 bob [50p] or £1. However, it was discovered Allen Hutt was being allowed I think it was an extra £5 a week because he was such a top journalist. He could have gone to another paper and got a good job, so to keep him they paid him extra money. When this was discovered, Freddy Deards and Reg Weston protested, said they were also people who could get other better-paid jobs, and claimed they, like Allen Hutt, were entitled to extra money. There was a big row. But it was decided they could not get extra money. Both of them therefore complained to the National Union of Journalists. This was a terrible sin against the Communist Party, to complain to your union about conditions inside the Party. As a result Freddy and Reg just stamped out of the *Worker*. As a further result, the Communist Party headquarters became quite suspicious about what was going on at the *Worker*. It was then they decided that I, as a loyal Young Communist League leader – by that time I was

Left. David M. Smith. Courtesy of Ian B. Smith.

Below. Ernie McIntyre (second from right), as chairman, National Union of Journalists, Edinburgh branch, presents branch member Lorna Rhind, a pioneering woman journalist, with her NUJ life membership certificate in 1976. Christopher Reekie, branch secretary, is at left, George Strathie, branch treasurer, at right. Courtesy of the late James Thomson.

Right. R.W. (Billy) Munro, a *Scotsman* journalist for some 32 years between 1933 and 1969. Courtesy of Dr Jean Munro.

Below. R.J. (Bob) Brown and Margaret, his future wife, both then reporters with the *Ayr Advertiser*, at work in the reporters' room there, c. 1948. Courtesy of Andy Brown.

Above. Six leading Scottish journalists at a news event at Inverness in the late 1950s. Left to right: Jimmy Parker and Charlie Gillies (both *Evening Times*), Dick Sharpe (*Glasgow Herald*), R.J. (Bob) Brown (*The Times*), Mike Allan (*Glasgow Herald*) and Albert Hannah (*The Bulletin*). Courtesy of Andy Brown.

Left. Bob Scott. Courtesy of Roy Scott.

Jack Sutherland. Courtesy of
Mrs Margaret Sutherland.

George MacDougall in the 1970s.
Courtesy of George MacDougall.

Ethel Simpson as a young reporter with Aberdeen Journals Ltd in 1945. Courtesy of Ethel Simpson.

Bill Rae. Courtesy of Bill Rae.

Right. Gordon Dean. Courtesy of Gordon Dean.

Below. Tom Nicholson, *Daily Record* Edinburgh office chief reporter, c. 1946 to later 1950s. Courtesy of Eric Rutherford.

Left. James Gunn Henderson in 1990. Courtesy of Alison Cameron, editor, *Northern Times.*

Below. Liz Taylor (at right of front row) as a young Edinburgh *Evening Dispatch* reporter in 1956, with colleagues Dorothy Young (at left of front row) and Pat Mullarkey (back row). The woman in the centre has not been identified. Courtesy of Liz Taylor.

Right. Lorna Blackie. Courtesy of Mrs Audrey Lucas.

Below. Whatever the occasion, c. 1950s–1960s, this must have been a rather unusual reporting assignment for (left to right) Charlie McCorry (*Glasgow Herald* and *Scottish Daily Mail*), Hugh Young (*Daily Record*) and George Hodge (*Daily Record* and *Daily Herald*). Courtesy of Eric Rutherford.

a member of the Executive Committee of the YCL – was to be drafted back from *Challenge* to the *Worker* as a steadying influence. So I went back then and became *de facto* deputy chief sub-editor to Allen Hutt. Before I went back, Betty Reid, the internal Communist Party organiser, called me into headquarters for a wee chat. She said to me, 'Look, I would like you to report back to me on things, events in the *Worker*, that you think might be worth us knowing about.' And of course I said, 'Oh, well, OK, OK.' But I said to myself, 'No way am I going to report back to her.' No way was I going to be a spy inside the *Worker*, and I never did report back to her. Anyway, these things erupted at times inside the *Worker*.

I had been at the *Worker* for just over a year, from October 1949 till the end of 1950, when I was drafted in to be assistant editor of the Young Communist League weekly newspaper *Challenge*, whose office was in the Communist Party headquarters in King Street. The editor was being transferred as an organiser to the British–Soviet Friendship Society, which was another front for the Communist Party.[46] Sid Kaufman, the deputy editor, who was a few years older than me but had no professional journalistic experience, was made editor and political person in charge. After he'd been demobbed from the army in 1947 he'd been appointed assistant editor because of his experience in the YCL. I took on the job as assistant editor gladly because it was goin' to give me more freedom. I would be making up, laying out the paper every week, deciding on the pictures, with of course Sid's approval, and also I was sent all over the country to report on youth issues. And because I was a keen YCL member, it was great to be on its weekly paper. Moreover, I'd be working during the day, not doing shifts as I had been at the *Worker* at night. So the *Challenge* job was a terrific experience. I'd be sent up to Scotland, the Manchester, Yorkshire, Bristol area, all over Kent, etc., getting the youth issues, youth complaints, youth strikes. I was also doing a lot of public speaking in London. I did one at Speaker's Corner in Hyde Park. During the earlier part of the Korean War I remember having a stand in Tottenham High Road – I was a member of Tottenham YCL – and ranting on about the Korean War and how it was an American plot, etc. People just walked past! The only time I got active hostility was in Liverpool where one weekend I was up getting stories and was asked to speak as a YCL representative at the local branch of the Communist Party. There was a lot of heckling from people who were obviously Labour Party dockers, and suddenly the crowd surged forward, this great big docker got hold of my platform, pushed it to the ground, and got me thrown off it. Once the Cold War began and the Korean War broke out they were difficult times, and the Communist Party membership, whose highest numbers had been during the Second World War, was slowly in decline. I also became film critic for *Challenge* and used to go to free film shows at various London cinemas and do up a Marxist critique of all these new Hollywood movies, etc. So I enjoyed the work.

It was a busy life. Occasionally I would go on these trips, but I'd be out of London only about once a month. And by this time I was married. When I'd first arrived in London I'd advertised in the *Daily Worker* for digs, got two or three replies, the best of which was from a single woman in her fifties who had a little flat at the edge of Tottenham in north London, next to Turnpike Lane tube station. She offered me a room in her flat. She was a very kind person and I quite enjoyed staying there. When I got married she said, 'Oh, you can bring your wife here as well.' We enjoyed it there for a year, then we decided we wanted a bigger flat and moved to share a big flat at Crystal Palace in South London with Dick Nettleton, national organiser of the Young Communist League, and his wife and their two young boys.

While I was working on *Challenge* I went as its reporter to Berlin in 1951 to cover the World Youth Festival. That was very exciting. When I arrived in France on the ferry to go by train to Belgium to join a ship going to Poland then Berlin, I and several other YCL members were turned back by the French, who'd obviously been tipped off, as we later discovered, by an undercover CIA agent in the British Youth Festival organising committee. We were then given money to buy plane tickets to Vienna, then go on to Czechoslovakia and take a tortuous route from there to Berlin. We went through Vienna to the Soviet zone, went into a Red Army post, explained we wanted to get to the railway station for Prague, and the Red Army men cheered us because we were delegates. We had a sing-song with these Red Army men: we were singing Scottish, English and American songs, they Russian songs.[47]

That same year, in the October general election I was sent up to help in the campaign by the Communist Party candidate, Bill Lauchlan, in West Fife. Willie Gallacher had lost the seat in 1950 and had stood down after that. Of course Bill only got about 5,000 votes. Nevertheless there was a lot of support in West Fife still.[48] I was asked by the YCL to see if I could recruit YCL members there, so in the course of the election campaign I recruited about eight or nine people and they set up a little branch in West Fife around the Lochore and Lochgelly area. As a result, when I got back to my job as assistant editor of *Challenge* I was elected to the National Committee and to the Executive of the YCL, a feather in my cap. I think after that they began to trust me as somebody who could be put into various things, and that was the reason why Harry

Pollitt, general secretary of the Communist Party, called me into his office in October 1952 and said, 'Look, we want you to go back to the *Daily Worker*.' Apparently a decision had been taken at the Political Committee, the top committee, that MacDougall would go back to the *Daily Worker*. Privately, I quite laughed at that, that they would worry about such a small matter at the Political Committee.

When I was on the *Daily Worker* during the 1950s, the minimum wage in Fleet Street at the time was, I think, about £14 or £15. By the time I went back to the *Worker* in October 1952 I got £8 a week. If you had children and your wife wasn't working, you got an extra 10s [50p]. Now, nobody told me that. In fact, my wife wasn't working and we had by then a young child. I didn't know about the extra 10s payment till six months later. So comrades, not me, informed Johnny Campbell about this, and Johnny Campbell got me the money. The *Daily Worker* at the time wasn't directly owned by the Communist Party but by the People's Press Printing Society, which was funded voluntarily, supposed to be, by individuals who could take out shares. If you were a shareholder you could go to the annual meeting, etc. But these shares meant nothing: you didn't get any money back on your shares. It was simply a political commitment. The secretary of the PPPS, the sort of managing director of the *Daily Worker* and its various other subsidiaries, was David Ainley, a very sharp character. I believe David Ainley did know I wasn't getting the extra 10s payment and deliberately hadn't given me it. Because when it was pointed out to him I'd been getting less than others in my circumstances, he immediately gave me the rise but wouldn't give me the money backdated. Eventually Johnny Campbell said, 'Give MacDougall his money.' So I got a few pounds backdated.[49]

Of course the *Worker* was always in financial trouble from the very beginning. What we didn't know at the time was that the Soviet Union was subsidising the paper: there was Moscow gold. I don't know if that was being paid from 1930 when the *Worker* was first published. I think the subsidy wasn't continuous. There definitely was money: people did get money if they went abroad, and they brought money back. For instance, in 1953 they decided they would send me to Bucharest to cover the World Youth Festival there, which was a Communist front really. But young people from all over the world, including people who weren't Communists, did come to it. It ran for a fortnight and you had a great time – sports events, cultural events, torchlight processions, and you were able to march around shouting 'Long Live Socialism!' Youngsters, everybody, enjoyed it, and they were in a foreign country for a short time.[50] But I was asked by Barbara Niven, organiser of the *Daily Worker* fighting fund, if I would go to the headquarters of *Scantiea*, the Romanian Workers' Party newspaper, where I could get certain goods to sell at the annual *Daily Worker* Christmas fair. So I did. There it was arranged for me to pick up all kinds of small furry animals, wooden goods, etc. Of course I couldn't carry them all back myself, but I organised YCL members I knew personally who were at the Festival to take something back, if not for the central London fair, which was the biggest one, then to their own local ones. Most of the stuff got back and we made a bit of money that way. Earlier, I had gone to the Romanian Legation in London and saw the press attaché there, who took out £120 from a safe to pay for my fare from London to Bucharest on behalf of the *Worker*. So that kind of subsidy was going on. In my time on the Worker, what the Russians did was put in a big order for *Daily Workers*: several thousand copies a day went straight to the Soviet Union and to the People's Democracies in Eastern Europe, for the Communist Party organisations. That was a subsidy, too.[51]

J.R, or Johnny, Campbell was editor of the *Daily Worker* all the time I was there. Well, basically I liked him. I suppose in modern parlance you could say he was quite cool. He stood back from things. Every day, if I was acting chief sub-editor, we'd go into conference at, say, 5pm. We'd decide generally the contents of the news pages of the paper. Johnny would let everybody talk. You would think he wasn't even bothering to listen, his eyes would be all over. But he would come in on an incisive point. He was very good at putting his finger on the most important point. He would come into the newsroom, walk about, look at you, and maybe ask you something. But he wasnae the sort of ordinary newspaper editor who was one of the boys who went out for drinks. He never went out for drinks with you. He wasn't much of a drinker at all. A lot of the old Party members were temperance. Harry Pollitt enjoyed a drink, not a great drink. But Johnny Campbell, no. The only time I ever saw Johnny Campbell take a drink was on his 60th birthday. We put on a special party for him at King Street, headquarters of the Communist Party. Sid Kaufman and I were asked to write a sort of funny script and we did a sort of show. Johnny had a drink then. But normally he wasn't a drinking man. I thought he was a very fair sort of person. Being a young man myself, and having read my history, I looked upon him as a very important Communist indeed. What I didn't know at the time of course was he knew a lot of things that were going on that he didn't tell us about and which were not very good for the image of Communism. I mean, he knew what had been happening at the Stalin trials before the war, because he'd been British representative on the Communist International in Moscow at the time. In fact, Willie Campbell, Willie the Clown, his own stepson, had been arrested there and put into a camp. Johnny kept that very, very quiet and nobody knew. Even during the later troubles in 1956–7, when Communist Parties everywhere were in ferment about the revelations by Khrushchev and the subsequent events in Poland and Hungary, Johnny Campbell kept very quiet about his stepson. I felt generally that Johnny was a person who impressed you and who in his quiet way was very likeable.[52]

He was approachable, and I approached him personally in 1954. By this time my wife was pregnant with our second child. The Nettletons had moved out of our shared flat in London. A young couple who subsequently got married had moved in with us and shared the expenses, but they later got a bigger place and moved out, and I was left with the problem of having to pay £3 a week for the flat, which was quite expensive in those days, and which I couldn't afford on my wage at the *Worker*. I went to Johnny Campbell and said, 'Look, I don't know whether I can stay with the *Worker* because of this problem.' Well, he got me fixed up quite quickly with a job as London correspondent of *Neues Deutschland*, the East German Communist or Socialist Unity Party newspaper. As a result I got money from them and that helped with my expenses.[53]

Harry Pollitt, the general secretary of the Party, I did meet quite a few times when I worked for two years in the *Challenge* office in Communist Party headquarters in King Street. He was an impressive person, friendly, and could make jokes. I was just a youngster, didn't have a lot to do with him, but at various functions he'd be there and be very friendly, and would always say hello when he saw you. To a certain extent I was very friendly with James Klugmann, who was the sort of philosophical guru of the Communist Party. He was the man who devised *The British Road to Socialism*. Once we had a special YCL summer school at which I was a sort of very junior tutor for the younger people. James Klugmann came along and he and I got on very well – he worked in King Street as well – and he was always very friendly.[54] So was Sam Aaronovitch, another sort of cultural person, whom I got on well with. Peter Kerrigan, the industrial organiser, a big man, and always a very forbidding sort of person, who had been commissar of the British Battalion of the International Brigades in Spain, obviously thought I was very small fry indeed – especially as I came from Edinburgh and he was from Glasgow. He was a very difficult person, I never had much to do with him. He was a terribly humourless sort of character who carried out Party instructions to the letter. Kerrigan was the man who'd picked up a gun in Spain that went off and wounded Wilfred Macartney, the then commander of the British Battalion. I'm quite sure Kerrigan would have pressed the trigger if necessary![55]

I had a lot of contact with John Gollan, deputy editor of the *Daily Worker*, and he was always very friendly to me. He suffered terribly from ulcers and was often in pain: you would see him sucking away at tablets. I remember on one occasion I was invited to Allen Hutt's New Year party, John Gollan was there, we had a drink, and he was very friendly. Of course, he came from Edinburgh as well, and I knew his sister Helen and his young brother Duncan, both of them leading members of the YCL in Edinburgh. Duncan, a very nice guy, worked in Menzies's bookshop, was a great reader, and would always say to me, 'George, you must read this, you must read that.' He died very young from, I think, a throat tumour. Then John Gollan's wife Elsie was also always very friendly whenever she met me. She worked for the *Daily Worker*, too, though not as a journalist.

Nobody, including me, liked Peter Zinkin, the political editor. Well, they used to say he was Stalin's bastard, because he was so appallingly bad they couldn't understand why he could have been appointed political editor unless he had some terrible pull. So the story was Peter Zinkin was a son of Stalin and had been spirited over here and given these jobs! He was English and Jewish. There was one good thing Peter did for me. When Harry Boyne, formerly chief reporter in Edinburgh for the *Glasgow Herald*, became its parliamentary correspondent Peter took me to the House of Commons and we had a meal with Harry in the press cafeteria. Well, I got on all right with Peter but I never liked him, and of course when the *Daily Worker* began to erupt in 1956 Peter was always the one who took the totally Stalinist line at staff meetings.[56]

When I went back to the *Worker* in January 1953 younger reporters had been recruited, and two of them in particular became friends of mine: Llew Gardner and Leon Griffiths. Llew Gardner's father was Scots but Llew himself came from Corby, Northamptonshire, where a lot of Scots had gone in the Depression to work in the steel mills. Leon Griffiths had been in Budapest working on Hungarian radio. Llew and Leon were both very good reporters and were my age, so we were really friendly together.[57] I never felt psychologically isolated at the *Daily Worker*. The great thing about the paper was that most of the people there were very friendly and helpful to each other, and there was a sense of working in a common cause.

I became sort of de facto deputy chief sub to Allen Hutt, who during 1953 concentrated on teaching me make-up for the paper. So by autumn that year, if Allen was off I stood in for him. I was still only 25 and that would be the sort of work which on most newspapers, unless you were one of the brilliant people like Christiansen on the *Daily Express*, you wouldn't expect to be doing until maybe you were in your thirties.[58] It was a very good experience because Allen Hutt was an outstanding typographical expert. He did a standard textbook on typography after I left the *Worker* and, even though we disagreed politically, sent me a copy which I've still got.[59] Despite his politics he was widely respected far beyond the ranks of the Communist Party, and of course he was also for many years editor of *The Journalist*, the National Union of Journalists' paper, and in the 1960s president of the union.

By 1956 I was also working as London correspondent of a weekly Polish newspaper, a thoughtful paper, a sort of Communist Party equivalent to, say, the *New Statesman*.[60] I would send them an article every fortnight for which I was paid £5, and I went every month to the Polish Embassy and got my £10 directly from the press attaché there. I also acted as correspondent for the Polish daily trade union newspaper *Trud*. The top salary I ever got at the *Worker* was £8 10s [£8.50] a week – it had gone up by only £1 10s [£1.50] in seven years. I was making probably an average of about another £10 a week from these other papers. So I was beginning to feel relatively better off. As I've said, I was faced with the possibility in 1954 of having to leave the *Worker* for purely economic reasons: they couldn't afford to pay me more, and I couldn't afford to have a flat for my wife and two children. So they did step in and they got me these other jobs. I don't know, but otherwise I might have felt forced to leave the *Worker*. It did take a wee bit time to get the money due me from *Neues Deutschland*, but by 1955 I felt a lot more secure.

*   *   *

Just at the time of my return from *Challenge* to the *Worker* in January 1953 there was the famous doctors' plot in Moscow, where Stalin alleged his doctors, particularly his Jewish doctors, were trying to poison him. And there was a great campaign among the Communist Parties in the world against Zionism: in other words, they didn't like the state of Israel. The Soviet Union had originally supported the setting up of Israel, but Stalin was basically an anti-Semite, didn't like Jews. He was a man whose mental processes had obviously been corrupted and had crumbled during the years, and he'd got this sudden idea he was being poisoned. We had a big meeting of the *Daily Worker* staff in the office in January 1953 and John Gollan, the deputy editor, addressed it. I felt very uncomfortable about what John Gollan was saying about the Jews. In fact, two girls, both Jewish, who worked as secretaries in the office were in tears and rushed out of the room. They both left their jobs soon afterward. And quite a few people, including Jewish Communists, left the Party after that. It did have an effect on us.[61]

The next thing which sort of upset people was of course in 1954, when Khrushchev suddenly descended on Yugoslavia and embraced Tito. James Klugmann had published this pamphlet titled *From Trotsky to Tito*, and people had been saying Tito was really a Trotskyite. So people began then to say, 'Well, something funny's going on.' Both Llew Gardner and Leon Griffiths were sceptical about certain things that were going on. By 1955, when suddenly there seemed to be a lull in the Cold War, Britain, Russia, America, and France were all getting together at the Vienna talks, and there seemed to be a better atmosphere all round, because Khrushchev obviously wanted to get things smoothed out a bit. On the *Daily Worker* people felt a bit happier about things.[62]

But then of course in 1956 came the famous Khrushchev speech to the 20th Congress of the Soviet Communist Party. Of course, it was at first kept secret. We didn't know about it until Reuters suddenly started chuntering this speech of Khrushchev's over the teleprinter. I was on duty, in charge, at night – in those days our last edition of the *Worker* went at 10pm – and this must have been in the middle of the evening. When I started reading it, I said, 'Oh, for God's sake!' So I phoned up Johnny Campbell at his home about it, and he said, 'Ignore it. Don't put anything in just now. Leave it to me.' So of course Campbell started making enquiries. We were told that the British Communist Party, although they'd been at the 20th Congress, hadn't been given the speech. In fact, I think Pollitt had it read to him but he never told anybody about it. But later we did publish an edited version of the speech, edited by J.R. Campbell himself.[63]

From then on things began to happen in the *Daily Worker*. You had the situation in Hungary, where suddenly it was decided Lazlo Rajk hadn't been a spy and traitor after all but he'd been framed. And by this time you had a more reforming kind of government in Hungary, some of the people who not overtly, but underneath, were trying to do certain things, to have a sort of national Communist movement. Then of course events began to move swiftly – events in Poland, where there were riots in Posnan, etc., and more things happening in Hungary.[64]

In the *Daily Worker* they began to hold meetings of all the staff. They had always had members of the Communist Party on the staff meeting to discuss things. I think all the editorial people were in the Party, with one outstanding exception: our famous tipster Cayton. He was a great tipster and got a lot of winners. He was a nice jovial wee Londoner, but he was never a member of the Party. So Cayton never came to the meetings.[65]

Some junior people and the commercial staff were probably not in the Party, although they might be relatives of people who were in the Party. But certainly all editorial staff Party members had met together about once every quarter for a general political discussion, led by some senior figure. But when the events began to happen in spring and summer 1956 we held more meetings, because a lot of the staff were extremely perturbed about it. That was particularly so with Malcolm MacEwen, who was foreign editor again, Sheila Lynd, women's editor, Gabriel, the cartoonist, Phil Bolsover, the leading feature writer, Leon Griffiths and Llew Gardner: they were all extremely concerned at what was going on, and kept raising matters. Other members of the staff, more inclined to accept anything they were told by the leadership, defended what was going on. There was a mixture of ages in both groups. Malcolm MacEwen had been in the Party a long time, so he was an older member of staff, as was Gabriel. On the other hand, people like Ben Francis, who'd been in the Party since the 1920s, were more inclined to say, 'What's all the arguing about? The Soviet Union said it is all right. It's all right.' Walter Holmes, another old-timer, was very Stalinist, so was Allen Hutt himself, and Peter Zinkin and George Sinfield, also older members of staff, were very Stalinist. So was Mick Bennett, then assistant editor but formerly national organiser where he was quite incompetent and they'd therefore shunted him into the *Worker*, where he was a laughing stock because he really wasnae up to that job either. How on earth Mick became assistant editor is just laughable. Anyway, he took meetings and he was always burbling along, trying to get everybody into line. But there were some younger people also inclined to take the leadership's point of view. So there were about 10 or 11 people, including me, of all ages and experiences who were questioning things, and others of all experiences and ages who accepted things. Some of the discussions grew quite heated, with charges and counter-charges. By that time I was also father of the union chapel, so I was always worried about what was going to happen to the staff. I could see certain people were coming to a stage where they were going to leave. Eventually of course, after the Hungarian uprising, they did walk out. The *Worker* and the Communist Party lost a lot of good people, including Malcolm MacEwen, Peter Fryer, Sheila Lynd, Phil Bolsover, Leon Griffiths, Llew Gardner, and one or two others.[66]

My point in all these discussions was, 'We are being told lies. We've got to find the truth out and stand by the truth. There is a need for a Communist Party in Britain. We are the militant left. We can influence the Labour Party. Blah, blah, blah.' All these arguments I put forward. We should therefore stand together, but with the ability to criticise our leadership and to criticise the Soviet Union. Of course I was pooh-poohed for that by the Stalinists. And of course the other side, 'It's too late now for that, George. The Communist Party has been totally corrupted. It's no longer a viable proposition.'

Johnny Campbell, I think, was sympathetic to my point of view, and he was much the most sympathetic among the leadership toward the criticisms, because he knew what had been going on. And he'd obviously been fighting inside the Political Committee to do this, where he was opposed of course by R. Palme Dutt, the arch-Stalinist, by Pollitt and by people like Peter Kerrigan, who all wanted to batten down the hatches and be loyal.[67]

So by the end of 1956 the *Daily Worker* was in a shambles. It had lost a lot of the good people on the staff. They were bringing in more people who were sort of loyal to the leadership. Then there were people like myself who were torn both ways, didn't know where to go. Alison Macleod, who years later wrote her account of all this in her book *The Death of Uncle Joe*, was an example. Alison had been a sub-editor when I first joined the *Worker* in 1949, had left later on because of her children, but had come back by 1955 to do the TV crits. At the meetings, where she made a number of criticisms all the time, she was of my feeling that the staff had to stand together.

But the final blow, as far as I was concerned, came when the Soviet Union started doing hydrogen bomb tests early in 1957.[68] I protested about those at the staff meeting. I said, 'Look, we've been criticising the British and American testing, that they would cause cancers among people all over the world. Now does a Soviet test discriminate in favour of all who support the Soviet Union? Everybody else can have cancer, but not us, we're OK, we're members of the Communist Party.' But of course, 'Oh, that's not the way to look at it, blah, blah', from people like Mick Bennett. So that really wound me up. I thought, 'I can't go on like this.' In fact I was ill for a week. I had stomach trouble, obviously caused by nervous worry. For a year or more I had been under strain. So I went to Johnny Campbell as editor of the paper and I said, 'Look, I don't want to rock the boat. I can't go on like this and it's unfair to the paper that I should be like this. So I'm going to leave in six months' time.' He was quite sympathetic. Then he called me back in and he said, 'Look, you're going and you'll get a job all right. If you stay,' he said, 'I'll make you foreign editor, and you'll be able to make a lot of extra money because you'll be writing for all sorts of Communist newspapers then.' As if I was going to be lulled by the prospect of money. So I said, 'No way, I'm sorry.' Allen Hutt was quite sympathetic, too. I mean, he didn't agree with me but he was sorry I was going. He managed to get an interview for me with the editor of the *Daily Herald*, an old pal of his, as a possible sub-editor for the *Herald*. But I never got anywhere there.

And then the whole thing erupted again. There were more bomb tests, more rows. I said, 'Right, that's it.' One Friday I went home and said to my wife, 'There's no way I can go back.' So I wrote to Campbell, and to John Gollan, who by then was general secretary of the Party. I sent them my Party card and said, 'Look, my health is such, I've been worn down, I just cannot stand any more of it. So I'm leaving now.' Of course, then the Stalinists all said, 'Oh, MacDougall's been bought by the capitalist press.' I didn't have a job to go to! Then, a few days after I left, I was personally attacked by David Ainley from the platform at the AGM of the People's Press Printing Society. Alison Macleod, who had gone along as a shareholder, stood up and protested at the attack on me. Then I was pilloried over the case of Peter Fryer. Peter had been the *Daily Worker*'s parliamentary correspondent for years, and a bloody good reporter he was. Then they made the terrible mistake of sending Peter to Hungary. Of course, when Peter saw what was actually happening there during the uprising he began to file all these reports which were sympathetic to the uprising. Of course, they weren't published in the *Worker*, and of course again that made us critics on the staff angry. We said they should be published. But Peter was more or less expelled from the Party. He and his wife were living in a house which belonged to a Party member and they got thrown out on to the streets. So I said to him, 'Peter, our basement is empty. It's not very nice, but you can have it.' So he and his wife came and lived in our basement. Of course, 'MacDougall's got Peter Fryer in his house.' So I became a Trotskyite as well, you see, though I was only offering a guy whom I'd liked and had worked with for years a place to live with his wife. So that was another thing that just upset me so much I couldn't go back.

Well, I thought, 'I'm an experienced sub-editor. I'll get a job.' But I found I couldn't get a job. I tried the *Observer* and various other papers in London but couldn't get a job. I don't know if that was because of my former membership of the Communist Party and employment on the *Daily Worker*. If I'd gone to, say, the *Daily Mail* or *Daily Express* in London and said, 'Look, I've just walked out from the *Daily Worker*. Do you want the story? Any chance of a job by the way? I'm an experienced sub-editor', I might have got a job. But no way was I going to do that. I didn't want to make a fuss, though I did write to *Tribune*, and explained I'd left because of the Soviet H-bomb tests. Of course, that too was held against me by the Stalinists, that I'd actually written to *Tribune*, even if it was a left-wing weekly paper![69] I could have gone and sold my story, which was reasonably sensational. I could have brought in all sorts of facts about how the *Daily Worker* was financed, about embassies giving people money direct from their safes, etc. But I didn't want to do that. I was not going to welsh on my old comrades. I still liked them.

I was out of a job for a month after I left the *Worker* at the beginning of April 1957. I went to the National Union of Journalists and they gave me some money, and I also did get some social security money for a few weeks which tided things over. And I had some money saved. My wife and I had bought a house for £450 in Anerley in London from a man in the Communist Party who let us pay £2 a week until the price was repaid. So that was OK. It was sheer luck I then saw an advert in the *World's Press News* for a holiday relief sub-editor in Edinburgh at the *Scottish Daily Mail*.[70] I thought they probably wouldn't employ me, but I wrote, got a sympathetic reply, and they gave me the job, starting in May.

I was there for a month when the editor said, 'Would you like to stay here full-time?' So I was with the *Mail* for two years. Then I was getting worried because there were always rumours the *Scottish Daily Mail* was going to close. I thought if the *Mail* closed the only chance of staying in Edinburgh would be if I worked on the *Evening News*, the *Evening Dispatch*, or *The Scotsman*. But everybody else from the *Mail* would be after jobs there, so would it be worthwhile going back to London which at least had a tremendous pool of employment? So I began looking around, and got an interview at Granada Television as a possible newscaster, which I decided, however, was a job I couldn't do.[71] I applied for the job as chief sub-editor with a new financial weekly paper, *Scope*. The editor interviewed me in Edinburgh, said he had another chap for chief sub but I could be his deputy, and would get X amount of money – a lot more than I was getting from the *Mail*. He said I'd get a few quid on expenses as well. So I decided to go back to London – which proved a big mistake. When I left the *Mail* I was copy taster and had stood in as chief sub once or twice. If I'd stayed on, I'd have been promoted to deputy chief sub quite quickly and would have been chief sub by 1962, then, when the chief sub left to go to Manchester in 1964, I'd have become night editor. The *Mail* actually offered me more money to stay. If I'd stayed there I'd have gone higher up the hierarchy and got a bigger salary and also would have qualified for a pension under the *Mail*'s non-contributory scheme. But you had to be there ten continuous years. Well, the *Scottish Daily Mail* lasted almost another ten years after I left it in 1959.

But also when I went back to London, *Scope* lasted for only about ten weekly issues. It was under-capitalised and it collapsed. It was a good job, it was good money, the people I worked with were very good. But the people who ran it, and who had beautiful big offices in Mayfair, were just sharks.

Old friendships, however, at that point paid off. Llew Gardner, then a reporter on the *Sunday Express*, spoke for me to Bob Edwards, managing editor of the *Daily Express*, and I got right away a three months' trial as a sub-editor. So I was unemployed only for about two weeks, started on the *Daily Express* in London in December 1959, and stayed there till April 1962.

I happened then to be in Edinburgh, where I bumped into John Calder, deputy editor of the *Scottish Daily Mail*, who asked me if there was any chance of my coming back to the *Mail*. 'Well,' I said, 'I don't really like living in London.' 'We'll get you right back on to the back bench of the sub-editors' desk,' he said. So I had an interview with John Blackwood, the editor in Edinburgh, and he immediately offered me the job as deputy chief sub. So I came back to the *Mail* in April 1962 as deputy chief sub, was made chief sub-editor in 1964, and was there until publication in Edinburgh ceased on St Andrew's Day, November 30th 1968.

That was a blow, although we all knew it was going to happen some-time. The *Scottish Daily Mail* was a very happy newspaper to work for – I'm not talking about the *Daily Mail* nationally. John Blackwood, the editor, was a genial guy, and so were most of the staff. We socialised a lot, with dances and socials, and we got together. People had a good time on the *Mail*, and they enjoyed it. The money wasn't great but it was reasonable. It was a good Scottish newspaper. But unfortunately again, London decided they had other things to do: save money, kill off the Scottish edition. As I've said, ever since publication had begun in Edinburgh in 1946 there had been rumours the *Scottish Daily Mail* was not doing well and might close.

We got a month's warning it was going to close. I immediately phoned Max McAuslane, editor of the Edinburgh *Evening News*, because I was very pally with Ted Dickenson, his son-in-law, who'd worked on the *Mail* with me in the 1950s, and asked Max, 'Any chance of a job on the *Evening News*?' 'Well,' he said, 'we'll put you on the list to be interviewed for a job either on *The Scotsman* or the *News*.' So a week later I was inter-viewed by Eric Mackay, deputy editor of *The Scotsman*, Max McAuslane, and the chief personnel officer, and it was decided I'd be taken on to *The Scotsman* subs' desk. As soon as the *Mail* closed I took a week's holiday and started on *The Scotsman*. So I wasn't unemployed and we got good redundancy money from the *Mail*.

I was with *The Scotsman* for 23 years until I retired in 1991. That was the longest continuous employment I'd had on any newspaper. I started on *The Scotsman* as a senior sub-editor, but almost as soon as I got there Eric Mackay asked me, 'Were you ever fully in charge on the *Daily Mail?*' I said, 'Yes, I was. I stood in as night editor when Jack Sutherland was off, and I was in charge at night and made the decisions, the changes, etc.' Eric said, 'We want to strengthen our back bench, but I can't give you any title.' The back bench is the group of senior sub-editors – the chief sub-editor, the deputy chief, the night editor, et al. – who prepare the pages, lay them out, decide where each story's going. They run the editorial production side of the paper. I'd only been there three months when one night the chief sub was on holiday, it was the deputy chief's night off, and the number three man was ill, so I was put in charge of *The Scotsman* that night and produced the paper. So obviously they had confidence in me. Eventually I became assistant chief sub-editor, then in 1978 deputy chief. In the last three years before I retired I was made production editor, because the new technology had been introduced, they were having problems and wanted somebody down in the composing room floor who could make decisions, get things done, speed it up.

The Scotsman wasn't up to the *Scottish Daily Mail* as far as friendliness on the job was concerned. But it was generally friendly and there were a lot of good men and women there. There were cliques, there was also a bit of stuffiness at times, and as far as promotion was concerned it was always dead's men's shoes. Eric Mackay became editor in 1972 and was excellent. Even before then he, as deputy editor, really ran *The Scotsman*, because Alastair Dunnett, who was nominally editor, was also chairman and managing director of Scotsman Publications, so he had more to do with the business than the editorial side, although he came in and took conferences now and again and what not. As editor, Eric Mackay was very, very good, although he was hands-off: he liked to let people get on with the job. He went home between 7pm and 8pm at night, and unless some terrible thing happened, you just made your own decisions after that. He knew his stuff and ran *The Scotsman* as a newspaper you could trust. Eric Mackay's deputy, Arnold Kemp, who eventually became editor of the *Glasgow Herald*, was a first-class newspaperman as well, and had lots of ideas, hands-on stuff. Again, he trusted you, and let you get on with it. Ronnie Munro, my immediate boss as chief sub-editor and then production editor, was a very good technician, and an excellent man in every way.[72] And so were other leading members of staff in the sub-editors' department. I'm not so sure about the news department. I always felt there was a lack of imagination there in the control – the people in charge of the reporters. And that wasn't only my opinion. But *The Scotsman* was a good paper, you could trust what was in it. We did try to get balance and accuracy all the time. The composing room, the printers, were very, very good people, very helpful – to me anyway, whenever I worked with them.

I also continued my union activities, and from 1973 to 1977 was father of the chapel. I think I achieved in those years quite a number of things for the staff, and had to lead them out on strike only once, and that was for only one night. Lord Thomson of Fleet, the owner of *The Scotsman*, had saved the paper in the 1950s, because under the previous owners, the Findlays, investment had been run down. Thomson got a hold of things, and by a series of shrewd business moves actually got more money out of *The Scotsman* in his first couple of years than he'd paid for it. But he did put more money into it. He got Alastair Dunnett in as a very innovative editor. For instance, adverts were taken off the front page for the first time. *The Scotsman*'s policy also appealed to me because by the 1960s I had joined the Scottish National Party, and *The Scotsman* was definitely the leader among the press in Scotland for an elected Scottish devolved parliament. They put the case forward and ran stories about it all the time. James Vassie, one of the leading writers, was an expert on the economics of a Scottish devolved parliament. So I was happy to be on a paper which had these views, although it didn't share my own views about an independent Scotland. Eric Mackay was sympathetic to the idea of an independent Scotland, because his wife was a member of the Scottish National Party.

The Scotsman, however, always grudged its journalists a decent wage. We were always trying, but never quite succeeded, to get equality with the *Glasgow Herald*, which had a much better salary structure for its journalists. We envied, but obviously couldn't emulate, the kind of money that journalists in the *Daily Record* and the old *Scottish Daily Express* were getting. But we did eventually get expenses such as our telephone bills paid, and so much per week to buy newspapers and magazines which every journalist should be able to have. If we were kept working during our supper break, we got extra money, and if we worked overtime past a certain time we got paid time and a half, neither of which had ever happened before. The biggest advance the union achieved in the 1970s on *The Scotsman* was to get a four-night week for all journalists who worked at night. So the sub-editors were able to enjoy a better family and social life. In the 1960s the right of journalists to apply every seven years for a month's sabbatical leave to study something of possible use to them and to the paper, or to go abroad for a month to study a particular country, had been won. That was another big achievement. I applied only once, about 1980, to study, particularly in the National Library of Scotland, all kinds of sources of the Scottish Home Rule Movement, and what role the Labour Party had played in it. So I did that.

But things didn't remain like that in *The Scotsman*, particularly after Lord Thomson of Fleet died in 1976 and his son took over. His son more or less stayed in Canada and ran the business from New York – a multi-business, including a holiday firm, oil interests, and newspaper, radio and television interests. It was all a question of cost-cutting, and money earned by Scotsman Publications – and they made a lot of money – being funnelled back into the United States and Canada. Very little was really spent on investment, except in the 1980s they obviously had to get in new technology as everybody else was doing it.

They decided to go for a particular system, similar to all other newspapers, where the journalists did all the inputting themselves. So Thomson's were able to save themselves a large staff bill by eliminating the compositors, the foundry, and all the other technical departments no longer required. The journalists of course said, 'Right, that's OK. But we want more money to recognise our extra responsibility.' I think we wanted to start off with £2,000 more a year. The company offered us about £500 then eventually about £1,100, which was not acceptable to us. As a result they locked us out. One night when we had a meeting they sent round security men. They'd never had a security firm operating in *The Scotsman* before, it had always been people employed on a staff basis. These security guys threw us out the building one night in 1987 and we were officially locked out for two weeks until we agreed to management's terms to operate this new technology. Then the union, which had been negotiating on our behalf, held a ballot and a great majority of us decided to go on strike, so the dispute then became a strike. By that time we were quite prepared to accept £1,500 more a year. But the weakness of our situation was that instead of having the strike to accept that sum, it was now a question of trying to get our jobs back. So the management pressed their advantage. Finally, we agreed to go back to work on the basis that everybody would go back to their job, we'd get £1,200 and we'd get it backdated to the beginning, and nobody would lose any wages. Management, however, insisted there would be no more four-night week and that we'd go back on a five-night week. We got a compromise: a nine-day fortnight. Management also demanded no more union meetings inside the office. But the union refused to accept that, and eventually management agreed we could have meetings in the office as long as they didn't last too long. So we went back. But after that it was a very unhappy office. All people who had responsible jobs were approached by the editor, Chris Baur, who had succeeded Eric Mackay in 1985, and were asked to sign an agreement that they would no longer go on strike. In other words, people in charge of various departments should give up their union rights and leave the union. Some accepted that, others refused. There was a great deal of disgruntlement and people made that very plain to Chris Baur, who before he had become editor had been a respected member of staff. He was now generally agreed to have been a very poor editor. Chris realised feelings were against him and that the management had made him the fall guy. So in 1987 he resigned and left the paper.

The Scotsman then had Magnus Linklater, who was much better, as editor. He was a hands-on editor, stayed many times till late at night, demanded hard work and got it, and was a fair guy.[73] I liked Magnus, but I didn't agree with his decision to remove Andrew Hood, a very respected senior member of staff, as editor of the letters page. Neal Ascherson, a man I greatly respected and liked and who worked for *The Scotsman* for a time while I was there, said to me after he'd left the paper that he thought *The Scotsman* letters page was the best in Britain. People of all opinions, professions and interests wrote to *The Scotsman*, and you had some splendid letters. And it was Andrew Hood who had really built it up. But Andrew refused to leave his job as letters page man and eventually had to leave the paper. Of course the union fought his case, but without much success.[74] So I didn't like Magnus's attitude and actions there. But otherwise he was good to me. Eventually he was forced by management to cut staff, and he decided some of the older people be offered golden handshakes to go. At 63, I was by that time one of the oldest persons in *The Scotsman*. Magnus called me in, made an offer, but I said no, it wasn't enough as he hadn't taken into account my promoted posts. He was offering me something he might have given an ordinary sub-editor, and also it wasn't as much as, say, the most incompetent compositor had got when made redundant. So a compromise was worked out: I got more money and also went straight on to pension. So I was quite happy to go then in 1991.

*   *   *

After leaving the *Daily Worker* and the Communist Party early in April 1957 and returning to Edinburgh to work in the *Scottish Daily Mail*, I had joined the Labour Party there in Broughton ward in September that year and within a year was chairman of the ward Party. When I went back down to London in 1959 I joined the local Labour Party in Penge and did some local election work for them. I had also joined the

Campaign for Nuclear Disarmament in Edinburgh in 1958, soon after it was formed there, continued my membership in London, and went on some of the CND marches there. I was very glad to do so, have retained ever since my ideas and supported the CND.[75] I'm still totally opposed to Britain having any nuclear weapons, and want unilateral abandonment of them, as well as a worldwide moratorium against them. After returning to Edinburgh in 1962, I was active again in the Labour Party, supported in the 1964 and 1966 general elections its candidate in North Edinburgh, Alex Reid, who'd been a boyhood neighbour at Chesser.[76] But even before the 1964 election I'd become rather discomfited by the Labour Party's attitude towards devolution. As a delegate back in 1958 to a Party conference in Glasgow on the question of a devolved parliament I had been very disappointed by the resulting recommendation of a Speaker's conference on the matter. If there's any way of putting things off, a Speaker's conference must be one of the most devious. Then, when I was back in London again in 1959–62, I began to read more Scottish history and became convinced Scotland would be better to assert its independence. After 1966 I became totally disillusioned with the Labour Party, realising that nothing was going to happen under Willie Ross toward securing a Scottish parliament. So I joined the Scottish National Party in 1967, after three years when I simply hadn't renewed my membership of the Labour Party. Within six months I became chairman of Broughton branch of the SNP – so I've been chairman of Broughton branch of both Parties!

I've remained active in the SNP since 1967. I stood three times for election to Edinburgh town council – never succeeded, of course, though in 1968 I nearly beat the Tory in Broughton: he got in with less than 200 votes more than me. Then I stood for parliament in Edinburgh East in February 1974, and was in third place with 7,100 votes. I again stood there against Gavin Strang, the Labour MP, in October 1974 and came second, beating the Tory for the first time. That was the first time any SNP candidate had ever come second in a parliamentary contest in Edinburgh. We got 11,000 votes on that occasion. But Gavin still had a good 19,000 votes – 8,000 of a majority. He was a strong candidate, had been there four years, was still young, and was vigorous and respected, a very good constituency MP. Although our support surged it was never enough to beat Labour. I fought East Edinburgh again in 1979. By then of course there was a general decline of support for the SNP, so I was in third place and unfortunately lost the deposit by 150 votes.[77] In October 1974 I had begun to think I might just be elected. I was 46, would have to give up my job in *The Scotsman*, and the most I could expect would be to be at Westminster for five years.

However, I thought, 'Well, if elected I will go to Westminster, and by the next general election I'll have paid the mortgage on our house. Even if I lost the seat then I'd only be about 50 and I'm sure I'd get a job as a sub-editor again, journalism being a job that can be followed in any part of the country.' So I wasn't worried. And of course in those days the question of ageism hadn't really arrived: people aged 50 expert at their jobs could expect to continue in employment. Of course, 20 years later in those same circumstances I might have been extremely worried!

*   *   *

Well, as I've said, about the age of 15 I became very keen on newspapers and was a journalist for 47 years, apart from two years in the army. My greatest regret is I didn't listen to my mother when she said she and my father wanted me to go to George Heriot's School. If I'd acquiesced in that I think I would have had a better education, more suited to my needs and abilities, and might have gone on to university. If I'd gone on to university I think I would have done a lot better in the newspaper profession, because really, particularly in *The Scotsman*, it was the university people who got the top promotions. That wasn't so much the case in tabloids like the *Daily Record, Daily Express, Daily Mirror*, etc. I never thought I was a genius, so I don't think I would ever have become, say, a Fleet Street editor. But I think I would have done better if I had not been such a stupid little boy and refused the chance of a better education. So I regret that.

I also regret partly that I didn't go into television in the 1950s, when I might have just got that chance with Granada. There were an awful lot of possibilities there.

And, of course, looking back now I regret nine wasted years in the Communist Party, in the sense that it was politically unproductive. If I hadn't met certain people when I was in the army, I might not have become a Communist Party member. I might have joined, say, the Labour Party. I'm not saying I would have stayed in the Labour Party, because I think I was basically always too left-wing for it. Though I regret having wasted my time politically in the Communist Party, I don't regret having been on the *Daily Worker*, because on the *Worker* there were an awful lot of interesting people and an awful lot of good people who helped me in all kinds of ways and inspired me and also taught me – people like Allen Hutt, who went to his grave still an unrepentant Stalinist, but who was a charming man and who always did have a very kindly, friendly spot for me even after I left the Party and the *Worker*.

But I was very lucky. Although I had three redundancies, one of which I caused myself by walking out of the *Daily Worker* in 1957, the other two at *Scope* and the *Scottish Daily Mail*, I was only really altogether unemployed for about a month. I never made a lot of money but always earned enough to keep my family going, enjoy a social life and holidays, and be able to buy a house. That's an awful lot more than the great majority of people of this country ever got the chance to do. And the other thing I've enjoyed is that I was active in the National Union of Journalists from an early age. The union had a lot of things wrong with it, but on the other hand a lot of things going for it. So I'm glad it's still going and still helping people.

Well, of course, it's traditional for older people in whichever profession to say, 'Ah, now it's no' like it was in our day.' And to a certain extent one feels that. I would say the big difference between today and half a century ago is that generally speaking the broadsheets then made a much bigger effort to be accurate. The worst failing I find now about newspapers is their continual errors. This is one of the results of the new technology. In the old days you had the editorial people who did the writing, the sub-editing, the layouts, the general editorial management of the contents, and you had the compositors who did all the work of setting this up in type. With the compositors you had those very valuable people, the readers – professional men who read every line of a paper, including the adverts, and if they saw anything that didn't look right they questioned it and it was corrected. Nowadays it all goes in from the reporter and the sub-editor, straight into production, being typeset by the new technology process, and often the person putting it in hasn't checked things properly. Nobody else reads it till it goes in. So now you have newspapers full of the most appalling howlers and errors, which makes any old newspaper-man's teeth grind, including mine. That is the biggest difference between newspapers now and all those years ago, this terrible lack of accuracy which in past days would never have reached that level.

Ethel Simpson

I was the first girl to start raw as a junior reporter on the Aberdeen *Press & Journal*, totally rough raw. At 17 in 1944 I started right at the nitty-gritty rock bottom.

Mr James M. Chalmers, a very courtly gentlemanly man, very, very polite, was news editor. He always called me Miss Simpson. I was the rawest red apple-cheek coming in from the country, absolutely raw. They would be sort of protective, it was an instinctive thing in those days. I can remember to this day Mr Chalmers saying, 'Now, Miss Simpson, you're going to be at the police court. You must not stay and listen to anything nasty. You must leave that court.' And I had to promise him that I wouldn't stay. There were indecency cases came up. The clerk of court had a list and you knew what was coming. Well, I was brought up to do what I was told, and I wouldn't have disobeyed Mr Chalmers. I'll tell you how protective Mr Chalmers was. One day he said to me, 'Now you can't go to the police court.' I said, 'Why?' 'Because it's raining. You'll get wet.' Women reporters were a rarity. I was young, that was the other thing.[1]

I was born at Burnside, then a cottar house for Bloodymire farm near Banff, on 2 September 1926. My father, who belonged to Ythanwells, a bare, barren place near Huntly in Aberdeenshire, was one of a family of 11. He was a farm worker, and then he got the tenancy of a farm down at Keithhall, near Inverurie. We were there until 1945, when we flitted to North Affleck, Whiterashes, about seven miles from Inverurie. My father was a tenant farmer still when he died aged 60 in 1961.

It wasn't uncommon in those days for a farm worker in the north-east to end up as a tenant farmer. They can't do it now, because the cost of starting farming is horrendous. But there were a lot of small farms then. Every farm worker wanted his own place, and worked hard to get it, although it was very difficult in those years. My father had a terrible time. I can remember when there was just no money at all coming in, nothing. It was really bad. But we never starved, because of course there was always the neep and the tattie, and things like that, and hand-me-down clothes from people. Farming was in a terribly low ebb in the Depression before the Second War. It was grim. Once there were some Irish calves that were supposed to be a good bargain, so my father got a loan of £200 from my uncle Willie, who was a police sergeant in Stirling. They got these calves home, but they all died of disease. And it was years before he could repay uncle Willie. That was the sort of thing. It was a terrible heartache. And everything was horse and cart of course, and just a slog. My father didn't employ anybody. He got help during the harvest. There was neighbours or friends would come. They loved a day at the hairst, you know, stookin' and everything that went with it. We had a lot of friends came in. They never got paid. They got tea and something to eat. Then you would help your neighbours in turn, that was the thing then. But he never had an employee, a farm worker. My older brother Douglas left the school about 1937 and then he started working on the farm. When the war came in 1939 that made a big difference to agriculture, with the demand for food, and then it began to boom. After the war things really picked up and my father had a less difficult time. But it was terrible pre-war, there's no doubt about it.

When I was a child in the 1930s my memories are of poverty. As I said, we were never without food, we were never cold, and we were never sort of neglected really in the things that mattered. Then everything was passed down. Our clothes came from my uncle Willie the police sergeant's family, all the clothes and shoes and things like that were hand-me-downs. Uncle Willie had a smaller family – two girls, and he had a regular wage, he was relatively well-off compared to my father, so we had always a bag of stuff from there.

My grandfather Simpson in turn had started with nothing and then progressed. He had a croft and managed to get on a bit, and before he retired got a farm at Rothienorman, near Fyvie. He was a tenant farmer. He and granny Simpson had all those 11 children, yet every one of them did very well. A lot of them went into the police, some, like my father and one of his brothers, went into farming and worked their way up. But there was not a bad one amongst them. They were really very sound, very good-living, very hard workers. There was never any grief till one of them, a policeman, died fairly young. I can't go back in the family beyond grandfather Simpson, but I think we've always been in the north-east, or there was a granny came down from the Highlands. But they're all round about this part of the world, the north-east.

My mother, born in 1896 and three or four years older than my father, worked on a farm before her marriage – domestic work, as a kitchen deem.[2] Oh, she would have helped out in the fields, too, she helped in

and out, in and out. I think they had to help just wherever it was. They'd
to get up early in the morning. All her life she got up early, she was up at
five or six o'clock in the morning. Then when the steam threshing mill
came they had all the cooking to do for all the men. And if there were
men – the farm workers – slept in the chaumers,[3] they sort of helped
them, catered for them. Her family lived on this tiny croft – it's gone
now – at Grange, near Keith in Banffshire. But her father was a sort of
crofter–joiner, and she had to leave school when she was 12. There were
four girls and a son in her family. She wasn't the oldest, but she was the
one that it sort of fell on to get going. So she had to leave school, get a
job and get some money so that an older sister could get an education.
Even then she was still a crack speller, could count and could read, she
was absolutely literate and numerate. It shows how excellent the teachers
were in the old days. She got married quite young to my father. She was
never ill, never in hospital, although her upbringing was harsh and hard.
She never slept in anybody's bed but her own. She never had a holiday,
worked like a slave most of her days, and lived till she was 91. She got
up early right to the end. She couldnae stand lying in bed: get up, get the
work done. A story she used to tell me, which I often think about now
when I'm in ASDA and see them coming out with these mountains of
stuff, was that as a young girl she had to walk the five miles from Grange
into Keith with this basket of eggs. She traded these eggs for sugar, meal,
or whatever, walked all the way home again, and that was it. That was
what they lived on. It was a terribly hard life.

Her mother, my grandmother, died about the 1930s. I can remember
the distress at her death. I don't know what that granny had done for a
living before she was married, but I would suspect she was a housemaid,
kitchie deem. But my mother's family all hinged around Keith, Banffshire,
that sort of area.

I have two sisters and two brothers. Winifred was the eldest, then
Douglas, then me, then Alex and Sheena. Winifred's three years older
than Douglas, and Douglas three years older than me. Then there's a
gap, because one little baby after me died of meningitis. Alex's about
eight years younger than me, and Sheena's about two years younger than
Alex. So between Winifred and Sheena there's a difference of about 16
years. Winifred went to Inverurie Academy and became a nurse, so she
was in training when Sheena was born. Douglas was very good at sums,
the dominie wanted him to go in for banking. But he didn't go. He just
decided to help my father on the farm and that was his life from then
on. But there were no newspaper reporters among my family or forebears.
I was the first.

My earliest memories are of growing up at the farm in Keithhall, because I was just a baby when we left Bleedymires, as everyone called it, near Banff, and I don't remember that. Our farmhouse at Tweeddale on the Keithhall estate was quite a sound house, with two bedrooms upstairs and one downstairs. The best room was downstairs, and my mother used to keep an incubator in it. We used to breed chickens in it, and every morning we had to go down and turn the eggs. And then there was the kitchen. There was a dry toilet outside in the garden, a bit away really.

In the kitchen we had to pump the water. For baths we had a tin bath in front of the fire. I can't remember if there was a specific bath night. I think when you were dirty you went into the bath, sort of business. And, remember, we were out playing in the farm and the fields. My mother would have had a routine obviously. Monday'd be washing day, and you would have probably changed all your clothes on the Sunday before you went back to school. And religiously as soon as we came home from school you'd to get off your school clothes, which were your best clothes, and put on old clothes. And we used to go around barefoot as children, when the weather wasnae bad. In the kitchen, too, we had the old-fashioned range, you blackleaded it. It was a very basic thing. My mother did the cooking on the fire, there was no electricity in those days. It was sticks and peats that we burned nearly all the time. And a farm house, they're terrible to heat, you know, because there's draughts come everywhere. Sticks we got from the wood round about. There was a peat bog up Keithhall and they went with the horse and cart and got it. I think you had to pay something for the peat, but I think it would be very much less than a bag of coal. Maybe we had coal, maybe an odd occasion like Christmas. And my mother used to bake. She had the girdle and there was always oatcakes and scones and bannocks. Then we had the paraffin lamps.

My parents didn't sleep in the kitchen at Keithhall. There was a bedroom downstairs. The baby must have been with my parents. We four older children were up the stairs. My brother Doug was in one bed with my younger brother Alex, and my sister Winifred and me would have had the other bed. It was the two beds in one room – that was quite common then, although there was another room and I suppose in time we sort of graduated to it. There were pillow fights. But that was when we were small. Well, you went to bed and there was the hot water bottle and the caff beds,[4] and things like that. So it was warm once you were into it, it was great. But we'd no electric fires, no nothing. And yet, as I've said, I cannot remember being cold or hungry.

When we came to North Affleck in 1945 we had to pump all our water from the well at the bottom of the road. We'd to carry it up in pails to the house. And it was the dry toilet again down in the garden. This went on for a few years until we got the pipes and the water in and a flush toilet. But it was years, into the 1960s, before we got electricity, because everybody had to agree to take it and some people wouldn't! Until then we had the paraffin lamps and then the tilly lamps, then we got a generator and you made it make your own electricity. The house was basic to start with in 1945.

I went to Keithhall school about five, the usual starting age. And we had to walk – it would have been about a couple of miles – because there were no cars, just the horse and cart. In time I probably got a bike, a pass-me-down one. I had a bike, but I can't think it would be a new bike. Everything was passed down. I cannae remember ever having a little trike or something like that. There's not much to my schooling at Keithhall school. I didn't either dislike or like it. I remember I'd done something wrong, and the teacher took me out and I had to stand in front of the class, just stand there. I was very miffed about that. I got on well enough at the school, I can't remember having great problems with anything and if I had, my mother would never have gone and complained!

To get to Inverurie Academy I must have passed the Qualy, but I have no recollection of it either. My elder sister Winifred went to Inverurie Academy, but my elder brother Doug didnae. There was a uniform at the Academy, well, it was very simple: a gym slip and a blouse, it wasn't much. It cost money, but I might have got my sister Winifred's cast downs. I biked to the Academy, about a couple of miles. But you had a terrible brae coming back up to Keithhall. So I went to the Academy about 1938 and was three years there. I had some French and Latin, and science, maths, PT, history, geography, and English, and in the second year, was it, we got music or art. But I had no commercial subjects there, no typing or shorthand. There wasn't that then. Latin gave me an awful difficulty, oh, God! This teacher we had used to come round the class and if you werenae just . . . she'd give you a skite on the lug. She maybe wasn't the most inspiring of teachers. The subject I particularly enjoyed was English. That was my main interest and that's why I decided in the later stages at the Academy I wanted to be a reporter – without knowing what being a reporter was all about. I can't remember just what it was that sparked things off, I came to it in my own way. I'd seen newspapers and got some idea, it had just gradually come to me. Looking around for a job and what to do, I thought, 'Right, I'll try for this.' Miss Bonner, the English teacher, was small and she was younger and much better, a more inspiring teacher. She was forward-looking, and there was just something about her. There was no expectation I'd remain at the Academy and take my Highers there. My parents didn't encourage me one way or the other, they left it to me, and I had made up my mind to leave, as a lot of them did at 14, and get a job. So I left Inverurie Academy in I think it was probably the summer of 1941.

But to learn shorthand and typing I went then to Webster's College in Aberdeen for about six months. Now that cost my dad money. I knew you needed shorthand and typing for a reporter. By the time I left Webster's in April 1942 I could certainly do 100 words per minute in shorthand. I can't remember my typing speed, but I could do that. And after I left Webster's I went to evening classes for a year or two to try and increase my shorthand speed. I used also to listen to the radio and try to take things down from that in shorthand. So I thought if I couldn't be anything else – a reporter, I could be a shorthand typist.

As a girl, once I was sort of 14, not much before then, I went to the cinema. Well, we were quite far out in the country, we hadn't the money, we didnae go out to anything, and we were sort of guarded. By that time, getting up to 14, there were soldiers stationed in Inverurie: Poles. I had an auntie had a shop in the High Street and she'd reported back to my mother that my chum and me had been seen talking to these soldiers after school. So I got a skelp, I really did, and 'You don't do that again.' I did read a lot, oh, all the classics that are still in the house: Scott, Dickens, the whole lot. A lot of these books were second-hand or passed on, and then there used to be a second-hand bookshop in Aberdeen that sold books for maybe just a penny or tuppence, and on rare occasions when I was older I went in there and bought books. But there were always books around at home. And then you won prize books and Sunday School books, and my mother and my granny had some books. I always loved reading, and read into the late hours if I got my head in a book. As a girl I never had comics, certainly not delivered or bought. Something like that would have been passed from others in the family. There were The Broons of course, that sort of thing, and you saw that if you got the *Sunday Post*. When they could afford a paper, or it had been passed on from somebody, my father read the Aberdeen *Press & Journal*, the local paper. My parents wouldn't have been able to afford the *P&J* every day, though it'd only be a penny or tuppence; it probably would have been the wartime that had started them getting it. But mind, they still needed to know the market prices. That was the great thing about the *P&J*: my father had to know what was going in the mart, and the prices. At the start of the war in 1939 the *P&J*'s circulation was only about 25,000 apparently; after the war, I think it rose to 50,000. And then of course before the war the wireless came in as well. We had a wireless with a battery during the war certainly; I don't know if we had it before the war. I don't know how we were able to afford it. That would be when things started to pick up and we were a wee bit more prosperous. And once my elder brother Doug began to help my father they could do more and that made things easier. Then Winifred, my elder sister, was a nurse by then and off my parents' hands. Well, they had to help me a bittie, as I say, to get into Webster's College. But really life was easing a bit. The war made a big difference.

My parents were fairly regular churchgoers to the Church of Scotland. They would never miss Communion. The minister always came and visited us. And as children we had to go to Sunday school in Keithhall, just beside the school. I went for years to Sunday school and then packed it in as the church's influence began to wane. I was never in anything like the Brownies or the Guides. My parents could never have taken me to them, you see.

*   *   *

When it was coming to the end of my time at Webster's College it was probably somebody there who said, 'Well, what are you going to do? Try writing to the editor of the *Press & Journal* – which I did. Somebody must have told me how to go about it. I could have carried on at Webster's actually but I decided to write to the *Press & Journal*, got a reply right away from William Veitch, the editor-in-chief himself, and I was asked to go in for an appointment.[5] It was staggering really. But because I had said I wanted to be a reporter and Mr Veitch was in charge of editorial, presumably that's why he saw me. He said, well, there were no vacancies for reporters then, but there was a vacancy for a shorthand typist in what was called the registry department. And would I take it? So I said yes – better a foot in the door. So I started work in Aberdeen Journals in the registry department in April 1942. The registry department dealt really with advertising: people who were wanting maidservants – kitchie deems, as we called them in the office – nannies, all that sort of thing. The applications were from all the big houses, so this is why presumably they got this bit of special treatment. But by this time, with the war, that side of the advertising had just dropped dead. And because of the shortage of staff as well, Kathleen Findlay, who was in charge of the registry, she had started typing the letters for the news editor, James M. Chalmers. She also did the mail, opened all the mail that came in, and we sorted out the mail and did odd jobs like that, because of the dearth of work in the advertising side. Everybody had to muck in. After Kathleen Findlay got married and left I was then in sole charge there. I took over typing the news editor's letters, running his messages and things like that, and gradually got more and more involved in that side of the work. I used to have to go down to the railway station and pick up packets of news, and then I had to file the blocks, the pictures, and answer the phone – just all sorts of things. So that I very gradually eased into the whole reporters' life. Then in 1944, Gordon Forbes, the junior reporter, was going to be called up. So they needed a replacement for him. And it was a toss-up. There was a boy in the sub-editors who was very keen on becoming junior reporter, and there was me. But I was there, you see, I was in with the news. I couldnae hardly lose, although I was a female. There was no way they were going to toss me out. And then James M. Chalmers, the news editor, very much relied on me. I was his legs. I had to run up and down the stairs for him. So he decided I was going to be the junior reporter. It was 1944, I would be 17, but I can't remember exactly when I officially started.

As I've said, Mr Chalmers was very, very polite. He always called me Miss Simpson. Sometimes in later years, 'Ethel' would slip out, but I was always Miss Simpson. He was always Mr Chalmers to me, and two others there, Peter Craighead and George Inglis, would be Mr Craighead and Mr Inglis.[6] Even yet I speak of them as Mr. They only got matey as the years went on. Mr Chalmers watched over me like a hawk, as they all did. They were all older, you see, apart from Gordon Forbes and the sub-editors' boy. But the editorial staff were all very caring, very protective. I think that was an instinctive thing in those days. Anyway I just blended in.

So the great thing was that I was going to finally get out on a reporting job. I was to go with Gordon Forbes before he went away to the army. He would take me round and show me how the police court worked. And, as I've said, Mr Chalmers was very protective to me about any nasty cases coming up there – but then I would try and listen outside the court! Well, I had to know when the next case was due. But when I went back inside the court Jock Adams, the town sergeant, a rough character, used to say, 'That wis a right case.' He'd tell me the gory details and I presume he embellished them because he could see I was embarrassed. So it took a while and then gradually, as I got older, I got accepted as a reporter.

I think I was probably the second female reporter with the Aberdeen Journals. The first would have been Helen Fisher, who came and left during the war and then came back some years later. She trained with a freelance.[7] Before the war, though, there had been a woman writer, Eleanor Castell, a gamekeeper's daughter or something, who belonged to Turriff, and who worked on the secretarial side of the Journals. George Fraser, who did a regular article on the countryside,[8] told me the first time she ever wrote anything was when he went away to Liverpool for a spell and she asked, 'Could I try and do your article?' So she was given a chance, and then she progressed to do some women's and society stuff. But I was the first female to start as a junior reporter, totally rough raw right at the beginning, as all the lads had to do to start with. I was aware at the time I was a sort of pioneer. But that didn't mean anything really. I was just so lucky to be in there, and was so loving it. I was the only woman in the reporters' room when I joined. Later a Mrs Murray Stewart came in. It was a man's world. They had had women in the advertising and secretarial staff, but not on the reporting staff, and not starting at rock bottom as I had to do. But I so loved the job and was so delighted to be in there, it was just great. It was what I wanted.

I was learning all the time, I just had to learn by observation really. There was no training as such. It was the war, remember. The people who were there had to work very hard. They were all really superb people, superb journalists. They were masters. They knew everything. They really were walking encyclopedias, knew their subjects, their area, their history, their grammar, everything. They were really tremendous. They told you things in a fine way: they didnae bawl you out. Once I got through, William Veitch, the editor-in-chief, always took an interest in me really. But he would never let me off with anything. During the war the papers were only four pages but were superb papers actually when you look back on them, because they covered everything and got the vital stuff in, small staff though they had. You had the Text for Today, you had the London Letter, the fish prices, the tides, all the nitty-gritty – everything. One day before the war ended I was told to do the Text for Today, and William Veitch himself told me to do it out of Isaiah. So I'd to get the big Bible and riff through it and gave the text to Mr Veitch. He read it, 'Oh, that's very good.' Then he gave me a rebuke: I'd spelt Isaiah wrong! He wouldnae let me off with it, but in a nice way.

I never felt awed among these older men. But I treated them with the greatest respect, and would defer. They all came themselves from working-class backgrounds. So even though I came in raw from the country with a toilet at the bottom of the garden, they had been just as raw in their time. Many of them started as office boys at 14, 15, same as me, and were self-taught, and things like that. George Ley Smith, who became editor, was a very fluent French speaker. One was mad on Esperanto at that time. But the *Evening Express* chief sub-editor then, George Fraser, was a graduate; and there was Sandy Mitchell, who was also university-educated; and George Rowntree Harvey, who went and studied during the day and took a first-class English degree.[9] Everybody could speak the Doric, our local tongue, so that was a common bond. So it was a great atmosphere.

It wasn't a big polished office. It was a ramshackle, rambling place. In the reporters' room on a cold day there was a great big roaring fire, beautifully built up. The cleaners knew how to build it up. Everything was very simple, it wisnae elaborate and fancy, it was very basic: plain walls, and linoleum on the floor, and that sort of thing. So I was never frightened, never overawed, because there was a great feeling of security. That was the marvellous thing. There was always this regard and respect. It was natural with them. And there was no bullying. People went around whistling, and it was happy and there was always laughter and fun. And they would never swear in my presence. Even when I was older, long after the war, when I was put down for a spell by William Veitch to have training in the sub-editors', which is where the tempers rise, they wouldn't swear. If somebody said, 'Oh, damn!' – 'Oh, sorry, Ethel,' you see. There wasn't the swearing then that there is now. When the boys came back from the war they would say to me, 'Oh, get out of the room, Ethel. We're telling these dirty stories.' And, to start with, I had to leave the room. They wouldn't say anything nasty in front of me. When it was quiet they would sit and, in what became known as bull or bullshit sessions, tell their wartime stories and the tales were really great. So it was then, 'Oh, come on, Ethel, leave the room, go on, get out.' But as I got older and more streetwise I would stay and listen. But I wish I'd written them down – hilarious tales they told, and it was really super fun. But it took them a long time before they would swear in front of me. I was never one for swearing when I was that age. I didnae like it. Then latterly everything changed: the girls could swear like the men. But it was never ever excessive, mild really, in all my years.

It was a difficult world to be plunged into without experience, but nae bother. Just, 'What about this?' And, oh, they would tell you, or somebody would try and help you to write things, and no problems. Most of them had their information in their heads. You could go to the library there of course and get stuff. But they had it in their heads. But, oh, helpful – absolutely. You see, it was ingrained into them. The Aberdeen Journals were away ahead of their field. I've a lovely book here at home: *Aberdeen Journals Ltd. Points for Guidance of Editorial Staff*, and it's dated Aberdeen, 1932. It says, 'These hints are intended as a general guide for the editorial staff. The section for sub-editors is of almost equal interest to reporters and should be just as useful.' It tells you: 'General: If you lose interest in your job then you deserve to lose your job and probably will. Cultivate the team spirit. A newspaper is not composed of independent departments, each one depends on the other. Appreciate the other man's difficulties and try to help. After all your livelihood is as dependent on him as his is upon you. Don't be afraid to show initiative. Read your paper every day.' The last point is: 'Bring on the junior with advice and help. You were once a junior and the seniors helped you then. After all, the better they are, the less onerous will be your own job.' So that was instilled into them all the time. They did always help. And you could go to the bosses, ask them anything as well. They were very good.

The house style booklet was something separate, for instance: 'Headings should reflect the tone of the story as well as the facts. Avoid freak headings and dull headings. Don't go to the other extreme and be flippant.' That was advice for the sub-editors. For the reporter there was: 'Every reporter should endeavour to become a journalist. No real journalist keeps his eye on the clock, except to make sure he does not miss the edition.' It tells you 'where you should type, how you should type', and that 'The reporters have the best chance of anyone to become a man of affairs – seize the chance. Be thoroughly interested in whatever engagement you are attending, no matter how trivial it may seem. If it is worth reporting, it is worth understanding.' I like that. 'Study the general policy and tone of your paper and write accordingly', and 'Make sure of your facts. Don't jump to conclusions – they will probably be wrong.' Well, that holds true today. Then: 'A good reporter never indulges in flamboyant writing. Good descriptive writing is best achieved by the telling of the story, not by the use of fancy words. Cut out extravagant words. If you don't the sub-editor will. Don't be a mere shorthand transcriber.' Everything like that, and this was done in 1932. They were away ahead of their field in so many ways really.

It might have been the Aberdeen/Aberdeenshire upbringing, that might be in it: the desire for knowledge, to do the best, to work like stink. For most of my years with Aberdeen Journals there was such a great sense of family, there was a tremendous number of brothers and sisters, uncles and aunties there. Bertie Bird, for instance, was the night caseroom boss. He worked there for 56 years, and his brother was there for over 60 years. Then there was a famous reporter, John Sleigh. He died before I went there, but they used to say he had been there since the Ark. He'd actually covered the opening of the Tay Bridge. He went around apparently in a long black coat and a bowler hat, and he was a right character, a brilliant journalist, took an awful drink. Now his son George Sleigh, a very fine journalist, a sports writer, had joined the Broad Street staff in 1905 and was still in the office for years after I went there. There was all this continuity. Once you went to the *P&J* you stayed with it. Some of the editorial staff moved on, of course, and then some of them came back. But there was this tremendous continuity in all the departments. You'll never find it now: they stay for five minutes and leave. But then there was this loyalty, this innate loyalty to the paper. Being in the north-east of Scotland we always had that sort of independent spirit, because up here it's totally different from the Central Belt. You had the rural thing, the farming, the fishing, the granite, a totally different kind of countryside at that time. So I think that had something to do with it. But there was this pride in both papers and in the job and everything, and that was part of the whole thing. There was great integrity and honesty and decency.

There wasn't much social contact among the editorial staff after hours in the war years. After the war, once the boys came back, a lot of them of course were very unsettled. Some used to disappear to the pub at 11 o'clock in the morning for a break. But there was great licence shown them, as long as they did the job. It was difficult for them to settle down because of what they'd been through. Well, after the war the City Bar became the great popular watering-hole for journalists – and did a roaring trade! Then there was always an annual office dance run by the Twenty Club which organised sports and dances and everything, there was the Press Cricket Club and the Golf Club. They'd all these sorts of things. Everybody from all over the building mixed at them.

You were very well treated in a way. We weren't highly paid. But neither, I think, were the bosses in those days. There wouldn't have been that much differential between what William Veitch, editor-in-chief, got and what, for instance, the head of a department got, I don't think. W.V., William Veitch himself, this great editor-in-chief, he had actually started as a copy boy with the *Evening Dispatch* in Edinburgh. So he started with nothing, at the bottom, and worked his way up. He was a brilliant journalist. He became a lobby correspondent and chairman of the lobby correspondents. He was London editor. He did everything. He covered the siege of Sydney Street in London in 1911.[10] He had been through the mill himself, so he knew what it was, and wanted his papers to be good. And everybody got that thing, they wanted to get the best. But it was also this family concern: the reporters had a sense of responsibility to each other and for helping each other.

By the time I started with the *Journal*s in 1942 they had been taken over by Kemsley Newspapers. When I began as a junior reporter two years later you worked for both papers, the *P&J* and the *Evening Express*, its sister paper. At that time there would only have been about half a dozen reporters, working for both papers. We always had to take a copy of the stories we wrote for one paper and they were rewritten – by reporters – for use in the other paper. I didn't find working for the two papers a problem – just a scutter sometimes. And sometimes you would keep a good line back from your *P&J* story to make it easier to rejig your *Evening Express* story and make it look fresher. Or vice versa. But much later on, before the office moved from Broad Street to Mastrick, on the outskirts of Aberdeen, they split the staffs because the papers were getting bigger, the areas were getting bigger, and there were more editions.

Speaking of Kemsley Newspapers reminds me that in August 1945 Lord Kemsley himself and his wife came up and made a tour of all the building. We all gathered to hear him and I quite liked him. He was a Welshman, and though he was a Lord by then his father was just an ordinary worker.[11] But it struck me years later, always Kemsley Newspapers were ahead of their day. Much of their thinking was based on a saying, and I don't know where I got it, 'The journalist is the key to the survival of newspapers.' In this talk he gave us he was looking ahead to training. And I remember he said, 'I want to get you a new building.' He said he'd spent 'the whole of my life from the age of about 15 in the newspaper business. I ought to know something about it, and I do, and I know something, too, about producing newspapers in wartime. We have to have good papers,' that was what he stressed. And he also said something about paying good rates for the job. So he wanted better training, better papers, better conditions for us. He was away ahead of his time. Just after the war, in the late 1940s, they set up the Kemsley training scheme. If as reporters you wanted to spend a week in London, you weren't obliged to go, but of course you did go. A week in London, everything laid on for you. We got talks, instructions, practical sessions. Reporters, sub-editors, photographers, each got their shot. And they produced *The Kemsley Writer*, always trying to improve things, to train you, to make you better.[12] The whole emphasis was on training, improvement. They spent a lot of money on it. You never get anything like that nowadays. So really they couldn't be faulted. And then we had talks always in the office: the leader writer gave us talks, how to write, talks on law, everything like that, for the whole editorial staff. I came upon this book which I had, about contractions when you were writing or typing – about became abt, for instance. Then there were little homilies: 'Three essential qualifications for a journalist: a well-stored mind, a ready pen, and a reputation for reliability. Never strive after effect, use words that exactly express your meaning. Journalism is a rough record of history in the making and therefore it should be correct in every detail.' And 'Be accurate' – this was hammered into me. The reporters were the first line, they had to get their story right. We would spend ages checking a trivial fact, and if you had the slightest doubt about the accuracy – don't put it in, leave it out. That was the golden rule. And, oh, aye, 'A reporter must have a reputation for absolute reliability. He should be systematic in his habits, punctual in keeping appointments, careful in making enquiries, prompt in turning out copy, and scrupulously fair in comments. News is sacred, comment is free.' Oh, you would not have dreamt of breaking a confidence, you just wouldn't have done it. So I have the greatest regard, in retrospect, for Kemsley, for what he did and for what they tried to do. When the proficiency test for journalists came in – and the National Union of Journalists was involved in that – that was quite a bit later. But we were away ahead, getting all this sort of thing. Many young reporters in other papers felt they were just dropped into the middle of things, and either sank or swam. There was maybe something to be said for that, but probably more to be said for training. And at the *P&J* they always gave you time: when a new person arrived they always were put out with an experienced reporter. I went with Gordon Forbes in 1944 for a while under his thumb, he was my mentor. And you were briefed on what was wanted and what you'd to do. There was never any briefing for political purposes – angling a story to benefit one or other political party. Ken Peters, who became managing director, always said: 'Never did either Kemsley or Thomson, who followed him, interfere in the political content. The editorial was left strictly to the editor here.' What they *were* concerned with was the accounts and of course the *Press & Journal* was losing money heavily for years, but they carried it.

As I say, you progressed in the work of reporting. I spent years doing the police court before I got the Sheriff Court. Then, before the war ended, there was a lot of deaths – servicemen dying, we'd a lot of that. Sometimes I went to their homes and tried to get a photograph, sometimes the families came in with a picture. And you used to write up weddings, and a lot of other things as well. But the saddest story I did was when the war ended and the prisoners of war were getting home. This lad had been a prisoner for about five years, and his father dropped dead the night before he got home, just from the sheer excitement. That one always haunted me. But you were never idle. There was always things to do. I had stories and blocks and pictures to file in our library and answer the phones. We had to take a lot of copy over the phones from correspondents and transcribe it. Everybody just had to wade in and do it.

When I first began I think it was the court work I most enjoyed doing, because it was a total new life to me. Really it was a mixture of everything, you got some grand cracking tales there. It could be very funny and very sad. The first woman I ever saw sent to prison was a famous prostitute named Barbara. She was then a very attractive blonde girl, aged 19. She was very well known because she was always getting taken up was Barbara. So finally she got seven days in prison, and I was in tears. I thought it was terrible. What a shame, putting a woman to prison. So I was affected by the stories. There was another one, again in the prostitution line, that sort of haunted me. This woman was about 38 and she was a war widow. As you can imagine, she had no money so she'd taken to the streets. This man she'd approached had said he would give her five shillings. She says, 'Oh, no, that's far too much. I'll just take 2s 6d [12½p]'! This was related when the poor woman was in court. So that was the innocence of those days as well.

There were a lot of unusual cases, like trawlermen failing to sail with their vessel. And drunks used to break into the compasses on board, pinch the methylated spirits, and drink the meths. That was a regular one, the theft of the meths. Oh, drunkenness was a big problem. Then there was kids playing football in the street, which was an offence. And gambling – bookies' runners. It was constant. So they made sure they'd only two betting slips on them instead of 20. What a waste of police time. Playing pitch and toss was another crime.

So I had a long, long experience. Going to council meetings, I used to like that. You'd go with all the reporters and gradually you'd get into it. But a long, long haul at it. Some reporters of course want the big time all the time. But you cannae have the murders and that sort of thing every day. Our work was very humdrum really but it was vital. Then I used to go to the Highland Show. That was great as well. There was the season when the Braemar Games and things like that took place. I reported these, but I was never involved in interviewing the royal family. Oh, every time they came somewhere it was just expected that a woman reporter would go and describe the fashions and do the things like that. And at the Braemar Gathering I used to have to take down the names of all the people in the stand, the royal sort of enclosure bit. Then they got forms to fill in. But trying to decipher some names! You had them all to type up. It was very easy to make mistakes with names and titles. There were three dreadful days: the Aboyne Games was on the Wednesday, the Braemar Gathering on the Thursday, and we'd to be up at the crack of dawn, to be up to Ballater. We'd breakfast in Ballater, and then at nine o'clock on to the field. And then there was the Aboyne Ball on Friday night. So by the end of that week, oh, my God! All these names and fancy names and all the work – you were exhausted. But it was good.

Anyway the work all fell into a pattern, a cycle, like the seasons. To me it was just good to tell a simple straightforward story about fit was goin' on.

I was never involved in going out on a trawler or anything like that, because there was always a fishing expert on the *P&J*, the fishing editor. It was a specialised job that. Well, I was out if a boat grounded on the beach in the gales. One job I always said I would not have gone and done was to go down to the harbour late at night on my own on a story. I just wouldn't, I'd have been petrified. You just didn't go into the harbour area in Aberdeen. It was totally unsafe. All my instincts were against it. They wouldnae have sent me. If they had I would have been about to rebel. The great thing about Aberdeen Journals was there was equality of wages, I and the other girls got the same wages as the men, according to age. So there should have been equality in doing the work. But going down to the harbour on my own at night was one job I would have refused to do. If latterly I did have to go down there late on I would always have the driver with me.

As I've said, after I left Webster's College I went to evening classes for a year or two to increase my speed in shorthand. Once you were reporting more and more meetings and things like that you kept your speed up a bit. But you had to watch it. The typing was OK, there was no problem with typing.

After the war, once the boys came back, I joined the union. I joined the National Union of Journalists, because once they got back and started getting organised it was the union that was the big campaigner. There always had been a union. There was the National Union of Journalists and there was the Institute of Journalists. In Aberdeen Journals there were quite a few members of the Institute. There were problems dating back to the 1926 General Strike, when some of them wouldnae come out on strike and in fact there was a paper published in Aberdeen.[13] Because of that, some of them left the NUJ and went into the Institute, which was the older journalists' body, and vice versa. But there was always a touch of antagonism among a few when it came to union matters: 'Oh, he came out in the General Strike', or 'Oh, he wouldnae come out in the General Strike', you see. The main Institute members after the war were Alex Dempster, Jimmy Forbes, and his brother Gordon, Alistair Macdonald, another sports lad, and Norman Macdonald, also sports.[14] But animosity didn't show in the daily work, people didn't refuse to co-operate with each other. It was only when finally the unions began to take off, and the NUJ had a campaign to get a closed shop. Finally they did get a closed shop. They tried desperately to get the Institute boys to change, but they dug their heels in and said, 'No, we're not.' Then, far, far later on there was a move to merge the two bodies, and it was scuppered at the end by the NUJ activists. But in Aberdeen, when this merger year was on, it worked super. Everything worked in Aberdeen, but it didn't anywhere else. I always attended union meetings and did my stint as chairman of the branch for a year – nobody else would take it on!

From the two Aberdeen Journals papers, reporters, sub-editors, photographers, we'd about 30 in the branch. Then there were union members in the other papers. All the nationals had staff men in Aberdeen and they were all in it, and then there was the BBC and later Grampian, and there was the *Bon Accord*.[15] So you could have had 50 or so members in the branch. But they didn't all turn out. The core of the membership was from Aberdeen Journals, because they were the biggest and most powerful group. To start with there wasn't the striking that came into it later. Latterly, it grew nasty over the fight to get improved conditions and always more pay. The demand was for parity with journalists in Edinburgh and Glasgow, and bigger expenses. It always involved money. Och, and the cars and the condition of the typewriters. You'd get new typewriters, and they'd get bashed to death. But where the fighting and latterly the strikes took place was about money.

The strikes started before the *P&J* moved from Broad Street to Lang Stracht in Mastrick on the outskirts of Aberdeen. There was animosity between the caseroom, the other unions, and the NUJ. It wasn't the Scottish Typographical Association then, it was the National Graphical Association.[16] They were very, very powerful. If you had dared put your finger on a linotype machine they would have downed tools. When the NUJ discovered they were making more money than the journalists that was a very bitter point. And then as the wire room began to contract and they needed less staff, the wire room boys, said, 'Right, we'll work with less staff. But you throw that man's money into the ring.' So they were always making more and more money with less and less staff – fair enough. So the thing was becoming a bit unbalanced between the editorial staff and the others. It was terrible how eventually both sides would pull the plug and down tools in turn just as you were ready to go to press. It was blackmail, that's all it was.

But away back, when Jimmy Grant was editor, you could knock on his door. He would swear at you and you could swear at him, but you would end up getting what you wanted, because Jimmy was a union man. In fact, he was the one who decreed that we could have a closed shop. That was a huge step forward. Once you had control of the entry, and everybody had to be a National Union of Journalists' member, that was a big, big move. But latterly it did turn ugly. I used to hate the union meetings latterly. In fact, there was a strike the day I retired. Oh, God, I couldn't stand it, because it was the unfairness, the blackmail tactics, I did not like. And the papers weren't making the money, you see. Some were appalled when they discovered how tight things were.

I never found any conflict between the policies the *Press & Journal* was pursuing and my personal convictions, because – I'm going back years – news was sacred. You reported what people said. You had to try and be as fair and as balanced as possible. If there was comment, the comment was in the leader. So I never had any problems with it really. I can't think of anything they did, took a line that caused me any difficulty. Our case was always to get the best for the north-east of Scotland, irrespective of what.

Of course, different brands of politics came into it. When Lady Tweedsmuir, or Lady Grant of Monymusk as she was then, won the South Aberdeen seat as a Conservative in 1946 in a by-election, there was a lot of publicity given her. She was a very tall woman, with her bonnet and everything like that, and she was a lady, sort of business. Her chum was Lady Huntly, who was a director of Aberdeen Journals. So Lady Tweedsmuir probably got more publicity.[17] And I suspect William Veitch, the editor-in-chief, was a Tory. Mind you, W.V., an NUJ man, had also been national treasurer of the NUJ, did a lot to help the NUJ in his own way, and when he was retiring, he said, 'I'm sorry I couldn't give you more pay when you wanted it. I'd have liked to do it but the money wasn't there.' But what we used to do at every election, local ones especially, was every day we kept a note of candidates' meetings, either Val Moonie or me. We counted the lines, we counted where the stories were, and everybody got their fair whack of coverage. At the end everybody had had an absolutely fair balance, their share of headlines, the same amount of words. If somebody had the top of a column, the next time they would be down the column. It was totally fair. I don't think it is now. I think that's out the window because nobody would bother. But this was our system, so that nobody could turn round and say, 'You didnae give us a fair deal.'

I'd see me go to Communist meetings and think, 'God, that's good.' I would take the line that appealed to me from the news angle, the broadest thing. It didnae matter to me who was speaking. And nobody on the *P&J* said to me how I should write a story or what I should do on a story. Never ever was there any attempt to manipulate me, as a reporter, as to how I would handle a political story. Incidentally, the Communist Party in Aberdeen was a bit stronger than in some other places. There was Bob Cooney, Dave Campbell, and Jimmy Milne. There was quite a few of them. They fought a lot of elections but never won a seat, even in the most deprived areas of the city they never won a seat. So although they were prominent they didn't make any headway electorally. I think that's the Aberdonians, you know – too hard-headed.[18]

Aberdeen was divided: the North constituency was Labour, the South Conservative, except Lady Tweedsmuir lost to Donald Dewar in 1966. When he won I'd to go up to interview him for the *Evening Express*. He was staying in this house at Kincorth. He and his wife had a kiddie then, and his wife was in a lousy temper: she obviously was not happy he'd won! She was maybe tired and everything, with the kid and things like that, but it struck me then – oh, oh, oh! I always liked Donald Dewar, I thought he was a smashing bloke. But he lost the seat in 1970.[19]

Outside Aberdeen, the countryside was Conservative or Liberal, Liberal latterly. But there was a great Conservative tradition, with Robert Boothby in Eastern Aberdeen and Kincardineshire, which became Aberdeenshire East, then latterly Banff and Buchan. I had to interview Robert Boothby. I didn't like him. He was such a tall man and I felt there was a bit of the bully in him to somebody like me. He once dictated something to me in the office, and then in a panic I had made a mistake, and he wasn't amused. He was a flamboyant character. I thought there was an insincerity somewhere about Boothby. I was always a bit suspicious of him. What shook us all was his romance with Lady Dorothy Macmillan. Never ever in the years I was there was there the tiniest whisper of it in our office in Broad Street. I don't know whether our very fine political boys in London knew about it but would not have said anything. But it was total news to me and umpteen others about this romance that had been going on in London. There was not the slightest whisper.[20]

As the years went on there were more and more university graduates coming into the *Press & Journal*. At one time they were hoping to make it sort of all-graduate. Then they realised that some of the graduates were so naïve that you were better without them really. Some were first-class and went on to great things. They would have done well whatever they did. But some just weren't going to make the grade. So then they switched back again and got school leavers with good grades. That was much better, I always thought. Then they started a scheme where you had your six months' trial, and if you didnae improve yourself within six months . . . So that also helped to weed out some of the ones who just werenae going to make it. My daughter's a BBC journalist,[21] and when I hear about the boards they've got to go through and all that stuff I howl with laughter. At the *P&J* all those years ago when somebody new joined the staff, Sandy Meston, a chief sub-editor, would get their copy down, read it through, and Jimmy Grant'd say to him, 'What do you think of that one, Sandy?' 'He'll dae,' or 'She'll dae.' And that was you in. You didnae need all these elaborate tests. It was how you did your work and produced that story that told right away whether you'd got it or you hadnae. Just the bare qualifications, and if you were honest and upright then that was it.[22]

There were very few sackings at Aberdeen Journals over the years, very, very few. It wis only if there was maybe a fight and somebody punched somebody else, and there was the odd theft. But I could count on the fingers of one hand in the early years who were sacked. So there was a great leniency and a great understanding really.

I never thought myself of going to Glasgow or to Edinburgh to work, maybe to the *Herald* or *The Scotsman*. Well, once I got more experience and I'd be in my late twenties, about 1952, I wanted to go to London for a spell, just to see how parliament ticked, just have six months. But I didn't apply for any jobs in London. But what I did, I took three months' leave of absence and a chum and I motored round the Middle East. I felt I needed a change, needed to do something else, and I liked to travel. We went through France to North Africa, right along North Africa, then through to Cyprus, flew to Israel, back to Cyprus, then flew to Jordan. Our target was Bethlehem for Christmas and Baghdad for Hogmanay – and we did it. Then I used to go holidays abroad – to Russia once. And at one stage I was thinking of packing up and going to the Far East – Hong Kong, Singapore – for a job, because I had somebody who would have vouched for me out there. But then a great friend of mine committed suicide in America and everything collapsed and I just settled down again. You get itchy feet sometimes to travel.

Well, as time wore on I was put on to the news desk and I never did reporting for a long time. I didn't object to that, didn't find it irksome. First of all it started as a stand-in, 'Come on, go on it', and I'd cover at night time. So it was a very gradual introduction to it. It wasnae stressful and I liked it. It was still in reporting, working with reporters. The heart and soul to me is reporting. And, oh, I did go into sub-editing, too, after William Veitch made me go to do the women's page. I was never one for women's fashions, etc. I didnae like to do cookery stuff, because that wasnae my scene. I was a hard news person. I tried to broaden the women's page, went and interviewed cooks, and things like that. Even then I would make blunders with blooming recipes. My heart wasnae in it. So I went to W.V. and said, 'Look, can I get back to reporters? That's what I want.' But he wouldn't. He made me go down to the night subs. So I had about six months there. But again it was for my own good. You see journalism from a different angle. But it was a shame on the subs, because they had to control their language. And apparently the joy when I left the room and they could all start swearing again! But they were so helpful. The compositors would come through and say, 'That heading doesnae fit,' and the subs would always help. Then I got back to the reporters, and the day I got back up to the reporters I said, 'Right, I'm not leaving here again. They're nae pushing me anywhere else.' So that was it, I stuck with reporting. I ended up as chief reporter, from 1975 to 1986.

But in 1970 Aberdeen Journals moved from Broad Street to Lang Stracht in Mastrick, on the outskirts of the city. And that was the finish of the great camaraderie. Things changed when they went to Mastrick, no doubt about it. We were away from the pubs, for instance. You see, across the road in Broad Street there was the men-only Bond Bar and, near at hand, the City Bar. The men could hop in and out in a minute to the Bondie, and they did.[23] Come five or six o'clock, when the reporters finished their job you'd go and have a drink together. The City Bar was a great place, superb atmosphere, with police and university staff and all sorts there as well as journalists. So you'd get rid of any aggro, anything that had upset you during the day, by chatting. But when we went to Mastrick that all went because of course you were further away from everything. The whole place was different. The atmosphere went. There was this great big noisy room, we'd terrible problems with noise, nobody would settle down to it. Old colleagues in the different departments would say, 'Oh, I cannae stick it here.' And that was really the beginning of the end: from that marvellous absolutely ramshackle Broad Street, falling to bits, we went to this modern and noisy place at Mastrick, it just had no atmosphere, no nothing, bleak. To me the rot started then. Though of course some things were much better: we'd phones on the desk. In the reporters' room when I started in Broad Street we'd only three phones. Two of them were in a little cubbyhole in the corner of the room, beside the fire. So as the day wore on, with the smoking you could cut the fug. And there was one other phone with the chief reporter. After the war it really got very difficult when you needed a phone. And then at Broad Street you were coming in at the stair, meeting everybody on the stairs. You could hide away in it, disappear. And Broad Street was so central as well. You were right smack in the centre of the town. Everybody felt at Lang Stracht it was a factory, and a factory that could be easily disposed of if Aberdeen Journals were going through a bad patch. Then when new staff came in they didn't stay the same. And then gradually the departments began to be cut – the linotype – the huge caseroom, the wire room, the process, all these flourishing departments. They're not there any more.

Nothing's there, terrible, just decimated. The new technology had just taken over. Ah, dear, it's all gone, a totally changed world.

Well, I retired when I was 60 in 1986. But, oh, I loved the job at Aberdeen Journals. It was all I'd wanted to do, total satisfaction. I didn't look forward to retirement. I was reluctant to go. I had my mother still alive then and getting on in years, and I had a teenage daughter. I would have stayed on if I hadn't had all these sorts of responsibilities. I would happily have soldiered on. But I'm glad now I didn't. I missed it like hell to start with, oh, really terrible, the whole thing. I'd look at the paper and, 'God, they shouldn't . . . A mistake.' You know, that sort of thing. It took me a while to extract myself. I'd had almost 45 years, it just ended then – and to end in a blooming strike as well! But I had left, oh, thank God, I'd left before the big dispute. That would have crucified me. That destroyed friendships, everything.[24] The continuity has gone. The young new staff don't know. You can see it in the paper. They've no background to what has been. They've neglected so much of the local stories. I'm sorry for the youngsters. But most of all, the memory of the firm has gone. When I went there all these people knew everything about it, could tell you everything. Even when we went to what was called the library, a big room up a stair – everything was up a stair – and in that library there was a great big box with all the cuttings. There were all the pictures and the blocks. And then round that room, in beautifully bound green leather, were all the papers, right to the very first *Press & Journal* and *Evening Express*, row upon row of them, right there. So, often, if you couldnae find something you were checking among the cuttings, if you had an idea of the date of the story you got the bound volume of papers out on to this 'pulpit' stand, and as you turned the pages you were turning back history. So you had that there all the time. You were so conscious that this goes back a long time. And I'll tell you this: at night time, when it was dark and there's this eerie electric light there, you could almost feel the ghosts. And then latterly everything, of course, went onto microfilm. There's nae pleasure in handling microfilm compared to turning the pages of the actual paper. When the paper came up off the presses, the first papers always went to the subs and then to the reporters. And it was, och, just such a lovely smell and feel to it, ink and everything. And now, oh! The romance went out of newspapers. The soul, I think, went out of them. It's all money nowadays, total money. There's not the fun, just dreadful.

But, oh, I did enjoy my 45 years with Aberdeen Journals. I was lucky really. If it hadn't been for the war I wouldn't have got into the Journals. I'm quite certain about that. It would have been the men. Well, in time I might have got in, but then I'd have been past it. And then landing with people who said, 'Right, we'll give you a try.' I was so naïve, of course, so green, and just very gradually it all became assimilated into this sort of general love for the whole thing, the whole profession, and then pride in the profession as well. I was proud of my job as a journalist in those days, and to be a *P&J* journalist – you were welcomed everywhere. That was a great thing. It was an institution, the *P&J*, and you got your stories because you were *P&J*. I could never have worked for a paper like *The Sun*. In fact, I couldn't go into journalism now. If I got my chance again I wouldn't go into it as it is nowadays. I really wouldn't. I couldn't stand it. They don't even report, it's not straight reporting. The accuracy was so important. I really couldnae do it today, I wouldnae like it. So I'm glad I was in the right place at the right time and that I had a great job. I loved it and I'm glad I ended up as chief reporter. So I was still a reporter at the end.

Bill Rae

I can trace our family connection with the Edinburgh *Evening News* back to about 1890. At that time my maternal great-grandmother had a news-agent's shop in the Pleasance, on the south side of the city. My grand-mother herself as a young girl was sent by her mother to the *Evening News*, then at the foot of Advocate's Close, running down from the High Street to Cockburn Street, to collect copies of the newspaper for the shop. I took my grandmother in her old age up that flight of steps from Cockburn Street to the back door of the *Evening News*. She said it hadn't changed at all from when she was there as a girl – and I can believe it! The *Evening News* itself in those days didn't change very much.

Then my mother's father, John Henderson, a compositor, was always in the printing business. I think he did his apprenticeship with one of the Edinburgh firms, then worked in Orkney and elsewhere in Scotland for a while. Anyway he came back to Edinburgh, joined the *Evening News* in 1905, and eventually became head of its composing or caseroom until he retired in 1947. I remember him saying working on an evening paper was great. During the Second World War my father, an electrical fitter at Bruce Peebles, engineers, fell ill with TB and had to give up work.[1] My mother had then to go out to work and got a job in the accounts depart-ment of the *Evening News*. So when in 1945 I began work as a copy boy at the *News* we had this very unusual situation that three members of our family were all working in the same building in Market Street for the *Evening News*.

I was born in Edinburgh on 11 June 1928, an only child – after me, they broke the mould. I always think my father was a casualty to war. At Bruce Peebles, where machine tools were made for the munitions industry, he was in a reserved occupation from the start of the war in 1939. Working conditions were so bad, so arduous, that by 1942–3 my father was working seven days a week. I still remember him getting a No. 23 tramcar from near our home in Morningside Road to make the long journey to Bruce Peebles at Granton at about 7am, winter and summer.

It finally broke his health and he ended up in the City Hospital, up past Morningside, with TB. It was quite obvious he was not going to recover, and he died in 1946.

My father's parents lived in Morningside Drive but they belonged to Aberdeen. I think my grandmother was from Mannofield in the city of Aberdeen, and my grandfather Rae came from a farming family in Aberdeenshire. He was in the seed business, and when my grandparents came to Edinburgh I think it was because of his job. He worked for a firm of seedsmen at the corner of George IV Bridge and Victoria Street.

In Edinburgh, as I've said, my parents and I lived at 322 Morningside Road, in a top flat, directly across the street from the Canny Man pub. My earliest memories are of looking out of our front window down on to Morningside Road, the Canny Man, and the chip shop next door to it. Morningside Road in the 1930s was much quieter than it is now: very few people then owned a motor car. We didn't know anybody who did. Of course the tram cars ran up and down Morningside Road. But I'll give you an example of how quiet it was then. Some time before I began at school my mother and I were standing on the pavement in Morningside Road and here, shuffling up the opposite pavement, was an old man named, I think, John Kerr, who may have been the original Canny Man. He signalled to us across the street – he had some sweets. My mother said to me, 'Run across and get the sweet' – which I did. Today if you said to a toddler, 'Run across Morningside Road', there'd be little chance he'd make the other side. Another thing I remember about Morningside Road in those days before the war was that every Sunday morning the Royal Artillery came down from Church Hill, on their way to the firing ranges beyond Fairmilehead. In our kitchen at the back of the house you could hear the horses galloping down the road over the causies. I would rush through then to our front room window and look down to see the artillerymen, in peaked caps and on their horses, with the limbers and the guns, 25-pounders, I think.

I started at South Morningside Primary School at the age of five in 1933, and was there until 1940 when I went to Boroughmuir Senior Secondary, in the other direction. I was quite happy at South Morningside Primary. When the war broke out on 3 September 1939 the school was turned into an auxiliary fire station. Everybody was expecting some sort of mass bombing to start, so we had the school evacuation programme. The school was closed for a few days and we actually held our classes in people's houses. Parents were asked to make their parlour available for classes. We were dispersed thus for a few days. But everybody soon found that wasn't working very well. We then moved back to the school itself.

But there were all sorts of auxiliary fire service vans and trucks converted into emergency fire engines and all parked in the school playground. The school was also a first-aid post; there were nurses going about, stretchers piled up in the assembly hall, and that sort of thing. There's no doubt it was a very difficult time for education. Anyway I was there until at the age of 12 in 1940 I was transferred to Boroughmuir Senior Secondary.

I was never myself evacuated, though everybody at South Morningside School was told they would be evacuated if they wanted to be. I remember being opposed to becoming an evacuee. I thought, 'Aha, they're just trying to get me out of the city.' I didn't want to miss anything exciting that was gonna happen, such as mass destruction in Morningside! These must have been early reporter's instincts. I just told my parents I wasn't goin'. Those who did go from South Morningside School were evacuated to Nethy Bridge in Inverness-shire. Some terrible tales came drifting back – how dull and boring it was in Nethy Bridge. After everybody realised that the whole of Edinburgh wasn't going to be bombed flat, the children all came drifting back within weeks.

To get to Boroughmuir Senior Secondary I must have passed the Qualifying exam, but I can't remember a thing about it. I don't think it was very difficult. My main recollection of Boroughmuir was how old all the teachers were. They must have dragged quite a few of them out of retirement, some of them were quite geriatric. I was there throughout the war years until I left, just turned 17, in 1945. We had a very good English teacher, known as Daddy Walker. I think I did get a lot of benefit from Walker and the English classes. And there were at first one or two young teachers – a maths teacher in particular, a good teacher who could get your interest and make you enthusiastic – but they were called up. I can't say as much for the others. For example, it was quite obvious from the beginning that I was never going to be any kind of a scientist. The science teacher thought I was just the most stupid pupil he had come across. We had regular tests and once, when we got the marked exercise books back, this science teacher called me out to the front of the class (a humiliating experience), held up the exercise book between his thumb and forefinger, and pointed out to everyone that Rae had got 3 out of 100. I can't remember what the 3 was for – it might have been for writing my name across the top. Eventually, by the time I left, I had scraped through with two Highers (English and geography) and three Lowers (maths, French, German). I had a very interesting German teacher named Miss Iverach, a very formidable lady, with her hair drawn back very tightly in a bun, and thick glasses. She was a rather frightening figure, but her bark was probably worse than her bite. It was pointed out to you at the beginning that you did a three-year German course in 18 months, so it was pretty concentrated. But I enjoyed the German course much better than the French course. One mannerism of Miss Iverach was that, on those rare occasions when she tried to tell a joke, you always knew, because her head or her shoulders began to shake and wobble. She was very embarrassed, looked a bit guilty about telling a joke, and those were always the signs. I did not enjoy my five years at Boroughmuir. I was too timid, diffident, and frightened. I think I was frightened most of the time I was there. I was always terrified that something awful was going to happen. When I went to Boroughmuir first we had, for example, a Latin teacher for one or two years. I was never so glad to give up a subject. The teacher, Mr Whittaker, an old man, looked to me as if he'd been brought out of retirement because of the war. He was another teacher who hated to make a joke and embarrassed himself if he ever decided to say anything amusing to the class. He was a very strange man, not very tall, and he had a gammy leg. He was always known to us pupils as Old Kicker, because of his peculiar way of walking. Then there was a French teacher called Miss Levac, very tall, very thin, with long, very white hair drawn back in a bun, a long thin nose, and always wore a black dress. If you were running along one of the school corridors Miss Levac would step out silently from her room, and without saying anything just pointed her finger at you. You knew then you had to slow down to a walk. To me she was quite a sinister figure. I don't want to be too cruel about these teachers at Boroughmuir, but I think they were far too old to teach impressionable youngsters. One or two of them were really psychiatric cases, suitable cases for treatment. I still remember leaving Boroughmuir on my last day, coming out that front door and crossing the playground towards the main gates into Viewforth. I came out with a boy named James Paul, and we were slapping each other on the back and congratulating each other on having survived five years at Boroughmuir. For me Boroughmuir just proved how resilient children are, that we managed to survive five years there, because I was scared most of the time. I was never so glad to get away from anywhere in my life.

My interests as a boy growing up in Morningside were football, reading, Life Boys and Boys' Brigade. I was a supporter of Heart of Midlothian Football Club. I was never a good player myself, just played very informally, but I did enjoy playing football. I played for the Boys' Brigade 55th Company team, based at St Matthew's, now renamed Cluny, Church near Morningside railway station. I joined the Life Boys at the age of 7, and you were in the Life Boys football team until you transferred to the BBs at age 12, where you could stay till you were 17 if you wanted to.

One of my earliest recollections in the BBs early in the war was of the air raid siren going off. So we all immediately had to evacuate the BB hall and marched down past Morningside station to the Plantation, between the station and Braid Church. There were at least three public air raid shelters there, half sunk into the ground and covered over with earth. I remember sitting in the shelter most of that Friday night, singing songs while waiting for the all-clear to go. Most of those public concrete air raid shelters were very cold and very damp. They were mostly underground, dug into a long rectangular hole about six feet deep. You could always tell a public air raid shelter because there was a mound of earth over it and an emergency escape hatch at one end in case the doorway got blocked. They were all over Edinburgh. The individual shelter of course was the Anderson shelter made of steel and in your back garden. I think most people paid something for them, but if you were poor you got one for nothing. But at the start of the war particularly, you dug this hole in your back-garden. The Anderson shelters were sort of semi-sunk in the ground and covered with earth. They were very strong. I was never myself inside an Anderson shelter, just in one of the public or communal ones. Later in the war they had surface shelters made of brick and with a flat concrete roof several inches thick in our back-green in Morningside Road. These again had the reputation of being very damp and cold. I can't remember ever going down from our top flat to the surface shelter: everybody said you were more likely to catch pneumonia inside it than be killed by a bomb. These shelters certainly ruined all the back greens for the duration of the war.

Football then was a leading interest for me as a boy. But at that time life in Edinburgh was very, very different. On a Sunday about the only thing you were allowed to do, apart from going to church, was to go for a walk. As footballers, we said, 'Och, we'd rather have a game of football.' Well, because it was frowned upon to play games on a Sunday you had to do this in a rather clandestine way. About the only place we could go, fairly unobserved, was the top of Blackford Hill, which at that time, though near Morningside, was quite isolated and long before the police radio station was put there. So on a Saturday we'd agree to go and play football quietly on the top of Blackford Hill. You didn't want to be seen carrying a football on a Sunday down Morningside Road. So we put the football inside a paper bag (no plastic bags yet in these days). But we didn't refer to it as the ball. On a Saturday, if you shouted across the street, 'Are you going to Blackford Hill tomorrow?' 'Yes.' 'Right, remember and bring the kettle.' The ball was always referred to as the kettle. So that was how we managed to get a game of football on a Sunday.

I was always a keen reader, and remember joining the public library in Morningside Road on my seventh birthday, the very day I became eligible. Oh, I thought the public library was a marvellous place, great for children. As a laddie, I read all the boys' adventure stuff. Later it was very sort of general interest: I've always been a very catholic reader, just about anything – might not finish it, but I'll start it.

When I was leaving Boroughmuir Senior Secondary School aged 17 in 1945, I remember a number of discussions in the family, sort of asking diplomatically what did I want to do. I just kept saying I didn't know – and I genuinely didn't know. At that time, in our own circle of friends, there seemed to be only two alternatives. You either applied to work in St Andrew's House in Regent Road, headquarters of the civil service in Scotland, or you went into a bank or insurance company, something like that. And when these alternatives were suggested to me, I thought, 'There's no way I'm gonna spend the rest of my life working in a bank, an insurance company, or the civil service.' They just seemed the dullest jobs. I certainly had no wish either to try and get into university – I'd had enough of school. I wanted to get into the real world and get a job. But until I was about to leave school, I had no idea what I wanted to do. My grandfather, as I've said, was head of the caseroom of the Edinburgh *Evening News* in Market Street, and it was he who suggested casually: newspaper reporter. I thought, 'Aha, that sounds a bit more interesting. I might, for example, get into football matches.'

I hadn't thought at all until then of newspapers or journalism. Anyway I was interviewed by Dave Donald, chief reporter of the *Evening News*.[2] He told me if I passed my Higher English (they didn't seem to bother about anything else) they would take me on as a copy boy. And that's what happened.

Of course at that time, everybody knew you were going to be called up for National Service six weeks after your 18th birthday. It was very disruptive. The great majority of 17-year-olds were only going to be in a job for one year then they'd be called up to the Services for two to two and a half years. I didn't myself feel unsettled about that: when you're just 17 you take things as they come from day to day. But the prospect of National Service was always hanging over you.

The first year in the *Evening News* I thoroughly enjoyed. You didn't get out to go on stories right at the beginning. You were the copy boy. In the *Evening News* in Market Street at that time there were two copy boys, the senior and the junior. Andrew Henderson, who later emigrated to Australia, was the senior, and of course I started as the junior. We both sat at a desk near the door, where you were to intercept people before they got as far as the chief reporter's desk. Andrew showed me the ropes as the new boy that first day. 'Now,' he said to me very solemnly, 'I'm going to let you into a trade secret. You mustn't tell anybody.' 'Right,' I said. 'We're going out now to buy the first edition of the *Evening Dispatch*.' That was the rival evening paper in Edinburgh, and I learned we got its first edition so our chief reporter could nervously look it over and make sure it didn't have something the *Evening News* didn't have.

*　　　　　*　　　　　*

There were of course various other jobs for the copy boys to do. One was when the printing presses started up, an orange light came on in the sub-editors' room. I had then to run down and bring up about 50 copies of the *Evening News* and distribute them round the editorial room. The worst job of the lot though was filling the gluepots. The *Evening News* building in Market Street at that time was a warren. Away down in the depths of it was where the glue was kept. This only happened about twice a year, thank God, but when a reporter would say, 'Gluepots could do with filling,' the junior copy boy had to collect all these awful gluepots with solidified glue all round them. The glue wasn't something nice and manufactured like Gloy. The *Evening News* seemed to make its own glue and kept it away down in this horrible Stygian old basement. A kind of big oil drum was full of this horrible home-made glue, and you had to try and ladle it from the oil drum into a small gluepot – not easy. That job was the big drawback about being the junior copy boy. Another job – your first duty in the morning as junior – was to go round the editorial department and take the orders (everybody smoked cigarettes in these days) for a packet of 20 here and there, Capstan, Player's, Senior Service, or what have you. You took this order down the back steps to the tobacconist across in Cockburn Street. It must have been the biggest sale of the day for him. You came back to the office each day with anything up to 20 packets, the price of each of which at that time was about 1s 6d. Every reporter, as far as I could see, went through at least 20 fags a day. No wonder most of them are dead now.

Anyway as junior copy boy you were a general dogsbody. Then of course there were the Lamson tubes. The *Evening News* had two systems of communication between the editorial floor and the caseroom where the printing was done. On the shout, 'Boy!', you would take the handwritten or typewritten copy or story from the chief reporter, stick it inside this hollow tube that was cushioned at both ends, and then you opened up the access to the Lamson system, which consisted of brass tubes going up through the ceiling. You just shoved the copy in and *whoosh*, it was away and delivered in seconds into the caseroom, where it bounced into a basket. The second system of communication, a bit slower, was a moving railway. It came out of a hole in the wall. It was a long continuous wire. Every few feet there was a sort of clamp. An empty clamp would come out of the hole in the wall, come along, turn down, never stopping, and go past the chief reporter's desk He had another clamp beside his desk, and if he wanted to send up copy he just put it in this clamp and it took it away through another hole in the wall and eventually up to the caseroom. This railway always fascinated visitors, particularly children. I can't, however, remember any school visits to the *Evening News*, certainly not on a regular basis: they would have been too disruptive.

In my grandfather's time the *Evening News* still bred homing pigeons to carry messages. The small window of the pigeon loft can still be seen under the roof of the old part of the building, at the corner of Cockburn Street and Market Street. When a bird returned and landed on a board at the entrance to the loft, an electric bell rang in the caseroom and a boy was sent up to retrieve the message, usually a football result, from the pigeon's leg. When a reporter went to a football match, he was accompanied by a boy carrying a wicker basket of pigeons. Homing pigeons had to be handled gently and with respect. If the handler was careless and the pigeon was released with ruffled feathers, the upset bird was liable to fly to the nearest tree and preen itself, while the irate handler threw stones in the hope of persuading the pigeon to take off for the newspaper office.

When I look at the *Evening News* today there's really no comparison with the *News* of those former days. The only improvement, I think, in the *Evening News* today is that visually there's a lot to admire in it. Of course they've got colour now: there was no colour in those days. And they've got new technology, which is not an unmixed blessing. Anyway the *Evening News* today looks nothing like the *Evening News* I began working for in 1945. Then there was a paper shortage. I think in 1945 they were still on only four pages. Now and again it went to six pages and, very occasionally eight – wow! That was really something.

I think the content in those days was much better than it is today. In fact, the whole ethos of the *Evening News* has changed. It's a different newspaper. It's much more shallow today. In those earlier days it was more informative than now. Of course in those days the *News* still had advertisements on its front page. They started on column one, top left-hand corner with Lost and Found. Deaths, births and marriages were all, I think, on page 2, column 1. Everything was squashed together in those days because of the paper shortage. At the end of the war Britain was on its uppers and there was very little money to spend on Canadian newsprint, and advertising was much less. Another difference then was that the *News* was a broadsheet, now it's tabloid in format.

Another difference between then and now – and this applies to other newspapers as well – was there was no formal training for youngsters like me. I mean, everybody talks today about training in every kind of job for this and that. But in newspapers in those days it was all on-the-job training. It was all experience: experience was your training. They would send you out, usually in the evening, on very safe, easy, unimportant reporting jobs, just to give you experience. They would say, 'Here, there's this meeting tonight. Take your notebook and you can try out your shorthand.' Shorthand of course was virtually compulsory in these days: you had to learn shorthand, it was essential to any reporter. Tape recorders hadn't been invented, or at least we'd never seen them, never heard of them, and the first one I ever saw was about the size of my desk!

I didn't have any shorthand at all when I left school. You could go to evening classes; in my case I went to the Royal High School in Regent Road, where there was a very good shorthand teacher, Mr MacKerracher, who also came into the *Evening News* office on a Saturday afternoon to help with the football reports. Anyway, in odd moments every day in the office I used to practise my shorthand. Then my grandfather, the head of the caseroom in the *News*, said he would pay for some private tuition to bring my shorthand on. So once or twice a week after work I went to this matronly Edinburgh lady in a flowing chiffon dress who, I think, had been a shorthand teacher and who lived somewhere in the New Town. The only snag was that the window of the room where we sat – I was the only pupil – was never open. It was very warm and stuffy and, after a day's work, I found myself falling asleep, though maybe only for a few seconds, while she would drone on and on about contractions and that sort of thing. I just desperately wanted to fall asleep. However, I think I became in time a pretty good shorthand writer.

From the first Saturday I was with the *Evening News* I was plunged into helping with its sports pink edition. It was still then a very important edition (printed on pink newsprint) because there was no television. I don't know what the sales were at that time, but there was great rivalry between the pink and the *Evening Dispatch*'s Saturday afternoon sports edition, which was green. Both papers managed to print on a Saturday afternoon reports of dozens of football matches – Hearts, Hibs, Rangers, and all the rest, but also of local teams in minor leagues, such as Loanhead Mayflower, Newtongrange Star, and many others, which got two or three inches of coverage. To handle this vast volume of reports, all of which came in by telephone, the *Evening News* recruited for the afternoon shorthand writers and girls to sit at typewriters. As I've said, Mr MacKerracher, my shorthand teacher at the Royal High School, was one of those who came in on a Saturday afternoon to help with the football. In the *Evening News* in these days there was a long row of telephones inside booths with a red light above each door. The red light came on as soon as the phone started ringing and you went into the booth, and it would be Smith, Berwick, or whoever, phoning.[3] He and other match reporters had in most cases been asked to provide the names of the teams before the kick-off, then 60 words at half-time, and then the second half play and the result. You took this down in shorthand – well, in my case as a beginner, it would be mainly in longhand to begin with, or at best half shorthand and half longhand. The strange thing was, if you ever got stuck reading back a word it was always a word you'd written in longhand that you couldn't read! Immediately you had taken down the report – and I don't think they amounted to very great writing – you rushed across to one of the girls at the typewriters and read it out to her. She typed it down very fast. Then it was rushed across to the chief reporter or one of the several senior reporters who turned out to do this work on Saturday afternoons. They checked spelling, typing, and that sort of thing – then into the Lamson tube went the story and up to the caseroom. A Saturday afternoon then on an evening paper like the *News* was just like these classic movies you see of American newsrooms full of people shouting, telephones ringing, typewriters going twenty to the dozen. The only time I ever saw a scene like that on the *Evening News* was for those two and a half hours on the Saturday afternoons. If you look back now at some of these pink sports editions of the *News* you'll be amazed at the number of words they managed to get into the paper between 3pm and 5.30pm – and then distribute it all over Edinburgh. I don't think the *Evening News* could handle that sort of thing today.

Sometimes as a copy boy I was sent out with a senior reporter to phone in for him to the office his report about a Saturday afternoon football match at Tynecastle or Easter Road. I still remember the terrible feeling of excitement as I sat there, particularly at Easter Road, where you were right down at the front of the stand, just along from the directors' box. At Tynecastle the press seats were away at the back of the stand: you had a very good view, but you always felt a bit cut off. So although I was a Hearts supporter I always enjoyed being in the press box at Easter Road more than at Tynecastle. At both places the *Evening News* had its own phone. It was kept in a locked box beside your seat, and you had of course to remember to take the key with you out from the office. I still remember the noise while you were phoning. You were shouting down the phone with the crowd of 20,000 or 30,000 round about you. You couldn't hear what the copy-taker was saying at the other end of the line, and you hoped he could hear you. I still remember holding the phone hard against one ear, holding my hand over the other ear, and shouting down this phone. But these were great days, happy days.

So I enjoyed the work as soon as I started in the *Evening News*. I was only frightened that I wouldn't be able to do the work. In newspapers you are frightened half the time: frightened you're not going to get the thing you want, that something's going to go wrong. The communications are always dicey, so getting the story back to the office . . .

Although the *Evening Dispatch* always came out first, with a late morning or noon edition, the *Evening News* in these days had four editions. For some traditional reason the first *News* edition was always called the Third, which came out a bit after noon. The second edition was called the Sixth and came out about 3pm. It was the main edition. The third edition was called the Last. And then the fourth and final edition was called the Last City: it was very restricted – distributed in Princes Street and George Street, strictly the centre of the city only. They talk now about new technology, but I'm convinced newspapers then were faster to appear than they are now. If you were out on a job in the afternoon then and you had a good story, you thought, 'I can still make the Last City with that.' You could get on the phone, or get to the office, and dictate that story up to about 4pm and still get it into a page of the Last City, for which the presses would be running at 4.30 or 4.40, because they wanted to catch the folk coming out of offices in the centre of Edinburgh at 5pm. And of course there was the box (what people outside the newspaper industry call the stop press, although the presses aren't stopped at all – that's the point): after 4pm you could still get the bones of your story into the box, which was the last column right down the front page of the *News*. You typed your story in the usual way, it went up to the caseroom, they set it in type, and then instead of putting it on the page in the usual way, the type was put round the edge of a circular metal box, this circular box was taken down to the presses and, while they were still running, inserted into them at the point where the printers knew the last column on the front page was, and thus the box made contact with the paper as it was running off. Of course they had to throw away a few first copies because they were all smudged. But in that way you could actually introduce a story on to the front page while the presses were still running. And it was quite a thing to see a story in the paper in the box a mere ten minutes after you'd written it. I don't think they do anything like that now.

As a copy boy, as I've said, you weren't given impossible reporting jobs to do until the senior men were pretty sure you had gained a little experience on unimportant reporting jobs in the evenings. On the other hand, everybody had to go out to the cinema and the theatre on a Monday night and do a review, and this was my introduction to reviewing shows. You went out with a friend to the cinema on the Monday night with your press pass, and I was always aware that while my friend was sitting back enjoying the film I was already worrying about what I was going to write about it. I'd always been a cinema fan but I'd never had to put down on paper why I thought a film was good or not. So I used to sweat blood over these reviews, particularly in the early days, because I was a very diffident sort of person. I was always very much aware that it was only one man's opinion. Some people could dash off a review and express their opinion with great confidence. I could never do that. So my diffidence ruined many a cinema and theatre visit because you thought, 'Oh, God' – then you had to go back to the office that night and write your review. Then in the morning – you started about 8.30am – you'd look at what you'd written: 'Oh, no, I can do better than that.' And you'd still be sweating over this review. I really found it quite difficult to write reviews, just because in those days you never expressed any opinions at all in the stories you were writing for the *Evening News*. On occasion a senior reporter, seeing you stuck, would come over and say, 'Havin' a problem?' 'Aye.' 'What show were you at then?' 'Oh, it was Lex McLean at the Palladium.'[4] 'Right,' he would say, 'what have you got there?' And he would sit down, brrm, brrm, brrm. 'There you are.' That was experience, he had the formula. As a copy boy you didn't have the vocabulary, you didn't have the formula. My old friend George Millar, who worked for the *Evening Dispatch* before he came to the *News*, once said: 'There's a formula, you know, to writing.' Another thing George used to say: 'A good story writes itself.' That's true: if you've got a good story, you've no trouble in writing it. But if you've got something which is not really a very interesting story, you've got an awful job sometimes to get it down on paper.

So in my first year in the *Evening News* I was struggling to write these reviews, and had learned to write shorthand but only at about 80 words a minute. But mainly as a copy boy I was the messenger who picked up reams of handwritten copy from the *News* reporters at the Burgh Court, the Sheriff Court, the Court of Session and the High Court, or the City Chambers and, just before I went to do my National Service, at the General Assembly of the Church of Scotland on the Mound. In these days you ran down the steps from the *News* into Cockburn Street, turned right, went up to the back door of the City Chambers, and got the lift up to the committee rooms or council chamber. There was sitting a senior reporter like Vincent Halton, Lewis Simpson, or later on Arthur Goodey.[5] On a council day, which was once a month, you would go up there several times, and the amount of handwritten copy that these three guys could turn out was absolutely amazing. Vincent Halton and Arthur Goodey in particular were pretty good shorthand writers. They were listening to the debates, writing their shorthand and then transcribing it on the spot into longhand on copy paper. Vincent and Arthur in particular could produce a wad of handwritten copy paper. I picked it up from them and, holding on to it very firmly because it was all loose, got back to the office, and gave it to the chief reporter David Donald or maybe Dick Campbell, another senior reporter, and they would go over it and mark it up.[6] You'd get Dave Donald or Dick Campbell saying, 'Och, too much, they're writing too much.' Then Vincent Halton would come on the phone. At the back of the reporters' room there was a telephone and a pair of headphones, and as soon as the phone rang one of the reporters would say, 'That's Vincent', or somebody who was a good typist would say, 'It's Vincent on from the City Chambers.' And David or Dick would say, 'Oh, God, tell him to keep it down, keep his hand on it,' you know. But Vincent in full flow could produce a hell of a lot of very detailed reporting from the City Chambers: in the back files of the *Evening News* there are columns of it. That's a difference between the *News* then and now. Then it was very informative, detailed reporting that went on.

Another place I went as copy boy to pick up copy was the Burgh or Police Court. You would go up there, through the swing doors, and you were at the back of the court. You were very quiet – no clumping about on the linoleum – and you went down a slope beside the public benches to your right, which were like church pews. It was better, unless you were in a tearing hurry, to wait until the witness reached the end of his evidence then, during the change-over, you slipped past the clerk of court, ducked in front of the witness box, and there were the pressmen squeezed into this sort of cubbyhole at the left hand side, with above them the bailie sitting on the bench itself. Once at the press bench you had to talk in whispers if a trial was going on. You would get the copy from the *News* reporter (any instructions were whispered), and you'd creep out again. But if you were in a tearing hurry you just had to try and slip out unobtrusively during the evidence.

It was a sad place, the Burgh Court, because you found the same people coming up again and again in the dock. There was one woman in particular I remember: Isabella Nicol or Freeman. She was very tall, thin, alcoholic,

I think – well, she must have been. A sad figure, she'd been up about 500 times for being found drunk and incapable. A big policeman with a moustache stood with the big book on the other side of the courtroom and shouted out, 'Isabella Nicol or Freeman', and she would come into the dock. Everybody knew the ritual at the Burgh Court. Mr Heatly, the city prosecutor,[7] would rise to his feet and, addressing the court, always spoke in the historic present tense in dealing with the various cases, and would tell a story: '11.30 last night, a man comes out of a pub, he walks along the street, he's approached by this man, and to his surprise the accused throws this brick through a window.' That made it a wee bit more difficult for reporters trying to write it down in shorthand. Very occasionally there was an accused so dirty, scruffy, and flea-ridden that they couldn't bring him into court, and the court had to adjourn to the cells downstairs. The press were invited to go along as well, to see justice done, I suppose. Later on, when I myself was reporting the Burgh Court I went down once and just sort of stood at the cell door. The sentence was that the accused was to be taken out to a sort of centre in the Cowgate at the foot of Candlemaker Row, where they got deloused, a bath, and clothes. You heard some terribly sad stories at the Burgh Court. There was a man or a woman from the City Mission who would sit in the public benches, and the court would call upon them: 'Can you do anything here?' 'Yes, we'll take them to the City Mission and take care of them.' It was really a question of giving them some charitable help. Of course the most dramatic moment at the Burgh Court was when somebody came up there on a murder charge. They appeared just momentarily and were immediately remitted to the Sheriff Court.

*   *   *

In that first year I worked at the *Evening News* it was really a six-day week, because you were just expected to work on a Saturday afternoon to help out with the football, which was a bit of a drag because I didn't see the Hearts for a long time. I worked as a copy boy every Saturday morning from 8.30. During the week it was from then until half past five, after the Last City edition. You got a break for lunch: one copy boy went early, the other later – just made our own arrangements, as long as there was always one of us available on the desk. The wage when I began in 1945 was either 25s [£1.25] or 35s [£1.75] a week, I can't remember. Maybe it had gone up to 35s a year later, but I'm pretty sure the first wage was 25s a week.

At that time, when the war had just ended, some of the *News* reporters were still in the army or the RAF. All these senior men kept coming back in uniform into the office during my first year there in 1945–6. Vincent Halton, a tall distinguished-looking guy, and Lewis Simpson both came back in RAF officers' uniforms. Logan Robertson, too, had been in the RAF, as had, I'm pretty sure, Jock Robertson, who later became the sports editor. Donald Esson had been in the Royal Armoured Corps – Lothians and Border Horse, it might have been. Willie Ross, too, came back from the army. John Junor was the *Evening News* war correspondent during the war, and years later became news editor.[8] And of course on the editorial staff, too, there was Dave Donald, the chief reporter, an older man. He'd been in the First World War. His hand shook a bit, it was said because of his experiences in the trenches. Dick Campbell, also already mentioned, was there. His health was never very good, he wasn't strong physically and he had quite thick glasses with a sort of blue tint in them. Then there was a lady called Mrs Dand, who was doing the women's feature titled Eve's Circle. So when I started in 1945 there must have been about 10 or a dozen reporters. The photographers I can remember were Jack Fisher, who was, I think, the chief photographer at that time, George Smith, who became the chief photographer later, Stanley Warburton, Gordon Smith, Albert Jordan, and John Wilkie.

So far as sub-editors went, the *Evening News* had a very strange arrangement, I think different from other newspapers, in that reporters and the chief reporter sub-edited each other's copy. In other newspapers, reporters' copy goes direct to the sub-editors and they assess it. But at the *Evening News* there was quite a good working arrangement between the chief reporter and the chief sub-editor. They liaised, obviously. But it was up to the chief reporter to say to the chief sub, 'Good story here, just in from the Sheriff Court,' and he would give him the gist of it. 'Right,' the chief sub would say, 'make that the right hand on page so-and-so.' The chief sub would also tell him the fount or font with the number of letters in a line. The chief reporter would then sub (edit) the reporter's copy (report or story), put the heading on it, and send it all up the Lamson tube to the caseroom. So at the *News* it was unusual in that copy was being edited in the reporters' room. Well, it was really one big room that contained the reporters and the sub-editors, but there was a very large glass partition separating the two, and there was a hatch window through which the chief sub and the chief reporter could converse with each other. Another unusual thing about the *News* was that as reporters we often wrote our own headlines to our stories – not a bad thing, because you knew what the story was and what an accurate headline would be. Whereas if it got into the hands of a stranger – a sub-editor – he just might get the wrong end of the stick and make a mess of it. From the reporter's point of view it was good wider experience, too, of course. Sometimes the chief reporter would say to a reporter, 'Hey, there's a story from so-and-so just been phoned in. Have a look at it.' After you'd done that you would usually pass it back to the chief reporter. Only very senior reporters like Vincent Halton would be allowed actually to put it up the stair themselves to the caseroom without anybody else seeing it. But generally a reporter would do all the work, put it on the chief reporter's desk, and he would mutter, 'Yeah, that's fine – up the stair.'

The reporters' (and sub-editors') room was three floors up from Market Street. If you came across Waverley Bridge and went in No. 19 Market Street, well, they had a lift there. If you came racing down Advocate's Close from the courts, in the back door of the *News*, then up the steel staircase, it was only two floors up, because the office was on a very sloping site. Another unusual thing about the *Evening News* was that the caseroom was upstairs on the top floor. I don't know who designed the building, but supposing they had about 30 linotype machines, plus all the other gear they had in a caseroom, what weight do you think was on the floor above our heads in the editorial department?!

As for the sub-editors, there might have been about 10 news subs, I suppose, and about four on the sports desk when I started in the *News*. There was also the creed or wire room, in charge of George Fisher, brother of Jack Fisher, the photographer. They had about two, maybe three people in the creed room, where the teletype stuff came in from the Press Association and that sort of thing. The editor when I began was James Seager, and his secretary was also in his room.[9] Well, they're the rough figures for the reporting and other editorial staff just after the end of the war.

At that time everybody knew, as I've said, that you were going to be called up for National Service six weeks after your 18th birthday. So I was called up in July 1946. I was sent first to Dreghorn Barracks, on the edge of the Pentland Hills just outside Edinburgh, where you had basic training for six weeks. They asked you what you did in civvy street and what your qualifications were, and as soon as they learned you wrote shorthand and could type you were bound for the Royal Army Service Corps (RASC). That's where I was sent from Dreghorn, and I ended up doing clerking duties in the south of England. I was sent first to Cirencester in Gloucestershire, to some sort of huge holding camp. It was alleged the authorities didn't know half the people who were there, and if you played your cards right you could finish your service there. The only snag was you wouldn't get any pay! But these places were quite famous as centres of disorganisation. Anyway it was announced I was going from Cirencester to Colliers End, near Ware in Hertfordshire. I always thought Colliers End was a very sinister sort of name. It's not a mining place at all, but it sounded a place where some collier had committed suicide – which, if you know Colliers End, was quite probable. Anyway I was there for the rest of my 18 months or so of army service.

Our camp at Colliers End actually was a WOSB – a War Office Selection Board place, where officer cadets came to carry out various practical tests in the field, such as getting across a wide ditch with only two planks. So I was on the admin side of that and sort of running the permanent office. It was a strange sort of place. About 20 years later I went on holiday to see my uncle who lived in Hertfordshire and I revisited the camp through a gap in the barbed wire. The camp was completely deserted, with paper blowing about. I walked down from the main gate and there was the nice wooden building with a veranda where I had spent 18 months of my life in the office, filling up forms, etc. I walked up on the veranda, looked through the window, all was deserted. Then I walked round towards the living quarters in the spider huts, all linked with corridors. And there was the parade ground and the officers' mess, all also deserted. I began to feel quite spooked. 'Gosh,' I thought, 'maybe I'll go round the corner and come across myself coming the other way.' So after I'd frightened myself with that, I crawled back through the hedge and rejoined my uncle. That was a very spooky experience.

I thought that my army experience was worthwhile for the number of people you met from other parts of the country, other environments, all sorts, some very strange guys. Of course some of them you couldn't understand what they were saying. One chap in particular from round Shepton Mallet in the west country, I had the greatest difficulty making out what he was talking about. But you met all sorts, some very educated. You usually found the really intelligent, educated people didn't look like soldiers at all. I made a special friendship with a chap from Shettleston in Glasgow. I used to bring him through on leave to our flat in Morningside Road in Edinburgh, and near the end of our service I said to him, 'We'll keep in touch.' He said, 'I predict we'll both be very old men and we'll meet accidentally.' 'Rubbish,' I said, 'I'll definitely keep in touch.' Well, I haven't seen him from that day to this!

I began to get very bored towards the end of my army service. I was still there under the wartime scheme, so I had a demob number, one of the highest in the army. One of the abiding topics was your demob number and when you were going to get out. This guy would say, 'My demob number is 55. What's yours?' I would say, 'Mine's 247.' 'What?!'

he'd say, 'you'll be in here for years.' 'Yeah,' I says, 'that's what I thought.' But when after two and a half years I came out the army in October or November 1948 I got a demob suit, a couple of shirts, underwear, socks, a pair of shoes, and a hat.

Fortunately, legislation had been passed that anybody called up for National Service had to be given their job back when they came out the Forces. Now the snag was I was coming back as a young man of 20, and all I had in the way of practical experience of newspapers was as a copy boy aged 17. So you had to try and catch up an awful lot. I don't think you were very much use to your employer for quite a while. I had been brushing up my shorthand for several months before I left the army. Just before I was demobbed the army had offered me a refresher course, and I'd spent four or six weeks in a local newspaper office in Worksop, Nottinghamshire. The editor there sent me out on one or two reporting jobs.

When I came back to the *Evening News* at the end of 1948, I think that's when I started being sent up to the dizzy heights of the Burgh Court, reporting on Isabella Nicol or Freeman. The Burgh Court was over by lunchtime, so then you were sent out on something else in the afternoon, and there were evening jobs, too. You very quickly struck up friendships with the other reporters. The *Evening News* ones were a pretty good crowd. It was a happy place to work.

Well, as time passed a lot of my work for the *News* was in the law courts. After you'd been in the Burgh Court for a while they sent you up to the Sheriff Court (then where the High Court is now in the High Street), and I must have been there about two or three years or more. Then you graduated up to the old High Court, where you got the really big dramatic cases. At that time, the death sentence was still being passed in cases of murder. There was no occasion in the law courts more solemn than the passing of the death sentence. The number of murders then was much lower than it is now. If there was a murder in Edinburgh it was a sensation – automatically a page one splash. An unsolved murder was very rare. So a murder trial was invariably dramatic. Everyone knew if the accused were found guilty he would be sentenced to death and almost certainly hanged. It was possible, in extenuating circumstances, for the Secretary of State for Scotland to commute a sentence to life imprisonment, which in my recollection meant 15 years. If the accused happened to be a woman, and that did happen sometimes, it's also my recollection that everyone rather assumed she would not be hanged.

At the High Court, which was then in the main Parliament House buildings, the press reporters sat in the front row of the public section.

As reporters we were in the row immediately behind the accused, who sat between two policemen who, I remember, wore white gloves and had their truncheons drawn and laid across their knees: a broad hint, I suppose, to the accused. A number of times I found myself sitting directly behind the accused. This depended on whether you'd been shoved further along the press bench as other reporters came into the court. Reporters like myself who were there for evening papers liked to come in last and sit near the door. I didn't like to sit behind the accused. You couldn't see so well what was going on, and also I suppose subconsciously you rather wanted to distance yourself from a man who might just make a sudden move! Often I was struck by the ordinariness of the accused, who was said to have committed the most serious of all crimes. I can't remember one who looked as if he would commit a murder. More than once I thought, 'Well, but for the Grace of God . . .'

To the right of the accused, on a table inches from the press seats, lay the exhibits, or productions as the Scottish courts call them. All carefully labelled with place, names and dates, these productions were sometimes inexplicable to look upon until their significance was explained by the Advocate Depute in the course of the trial. Sometimes, however, their significance was all too obvious – a kitchen knife perhaps, with dried blood on the blade, or clothing, perhaps also bloodstained.

Any murder trial, no matter how dramatic or horrifying, could also for long spells be boring. There was no television then, and I think TV court dramas have given a misleading impression of how a trial is conducted: proving a case to the satisfaction of a judge and jury is a slow, painstaking business. Yet during a murder trial, however harrowing, there was always a moment of humour, of something absurd, when the court dissolved in laughter. It was something to do with the release of tension, I think. In a courtroom there's a very soporific atmosphere. I've served on a jury in the High Court, though not in a murder case, and my greatest fear was that I would fall asleep after lunch. I don't know what happens if a member of the jury starts snoring – contempt of court, cancel the trial and start again, or probably just a poke in the ribs from the court macer? Certainly acute embarrassment. Fortunately I never quite fell asleep as a juror, though I did manage to yawn with my mouth closed. Now at such dull times as these, a reporter could always slip out of the court for a breather, but not so a juror.

From the reporter's point of view, the unhurried pace of a trial could be a great help. I remember in particular how W.R. Milligan, QC, the Lord Advocate of the time, later Lord Milligan, would ask a witness a question and then he would repeat the witness's answer nice and slowly.[10]

This was a great help to accurate reporting: no one was in any doubt what the witness had said. Most of our reports going back to the office were a paraphrase of the evidence. But you developed the knack of recognising when the witness was going to say something of particular importance. At that point you went into quoting direct question and answer, so your shorthand became essential. I often wondered how the judge managed to take his notes, for I don't think any of them wrote shorthand. Of course he had access later to the official court shorthand writer's transcript.

The unhurried pace of a trial also enabled the evening newspaper reporter to write up his copy in longhand as the trial went along. You developed the knack of keeping one ear on what was being said in court, while reading from your notebook and transcribing on to copy paper. If the reporter beside you suddenly began writing what the witness was saying, it was a signal to switch your whole attention back to the court. I can remember also how awkward it was to use the narrow ledge at the front of the press bench to write up your longhand account of the evidence. The ledge was too narrow to support your whole forearm. Obviously it had never been designed by anybody who had written shorthand.

At prearranged times, a copy boy would appear in the court room, and a wad of copy would be passed along by colleagues to the boy. Once there was a new copy boy for, I think, the *Evening Dispatch*, and the *Dispatch* reporters at the trial were beginning to wonder where he had got to. All of a sudden the door behind the judge on the bench opened very tentatively and slightly, and this head appeared round the door. The judge couldn't see this. But the *Dispatch* reporter of course was mortified, horrified, and was trying to signal discreetly but frantically to the copy boy to withdraw himself. The copy boy, as soon as he looked, realised he'd come to the wrong door and retreated. The old High Court was a maze of corridors, and it was very confusing to find the right door to it or courts in the Court of Session. But this wee copy boy opening the wrong door became legendary.

As a murder trial approached its climax the tension increased notice-ably, particularly if the final edition of the evening papers was about to go. There were no mobile phones in those days, but you could use the direct telephone line to the office from the press room in the courts, which at that time was somewhere down in the basement. So you reached the point when the jury returned its verdict: either guilty as charged, or not proven, or not guilty, or not guilty of murder but guilty of an alternative charge – culpable homicide. The verdict could be unanimous or by a majority of the 15 jurors. If the verdict was guilty of murder as charged, then came the passing on the accused of the only sentence that was open to the judge. That was a solemn moment, which affected the judge, sometimes visibly. With the accused – or panel, as he was called in Scots law – standing, the judge pronounced the prescribed form of words which, in my recollection, included 'hanged by the neck until you are dead', and the precise date for his execution. As the judge reached the conclusion of his sentence he would lift from the bench beside him the black tricorn hat (the sort worn by gentlemen in the 18th century), which was kept for that purpose, hold it over his own wigged head, and declare: 'Which is pronounced for doom.'

I was always surprised by the speed of what happened next. The railing gate in front of the accused was snapped open, a carpeted trapdoor in the well of the court was lifted, and the accused, escorted by the two policemen, disappeared down a flight of steps to the cells below. The accused was gone in seconds. The judge then thanked the jury, rose, as did everyone in the court, his macer retrieved the mace which throughout the trial had been on the wall behind the judge, and led the judge's departure from the court.

For the reporters it was the signal to get out quickly into the stone-flagged corridor, watch out for any passing judges and macers, and dash back to the basement to the press room and its telephone. Until about 1928, I believe, representatives of the press had been allowed to attend the execution of a convicted murderer. I suppose this was the last vestige of the historic custom of public execution. It may have been to prove that the execution had indeed taken place. But in the 1920s the newspapers, or it may have been the National Union of Journalists, or both, asked to be excused and gave up this right of attendance at an execution. Thereafter the public was represented at the scaffold by two bailies of Edinburgh town council – not a duty much sought after. I have been told that both men invariably found it a harrowing experience. In earlier times, it seems the two bailies were entitled to a breakfast afterwards that was known as 'deid chuck'. But I never ran across any old reporters who had attended an execution.

One murder trial that always sticks in my mind was the Tron Square murder in Edinburgh in 1954. I was sort of in at the beginning and also in court at the end when the accused, George Robertson, was sentenced to death. I was sent down the morning after the murder to Tron Square and remember standing in front of that sort of E-shaped building. There was this bedsheet still hanging down from one of the windows halfway up the building. When the murderer went after his son the young man, terrified, had knotted together some bedsheets and slid down them out of the window. But the bedsheets didn't go all the way down the building and he had to drop quite some distance to the ground. When you looked at the paving across the front of the building you could see the imprints of the sole of the foot and toes of the young man in his own blood. It was quite horrifying. Still pursued by his father, the terrified young man had run across to the end of the building and dived through a ground floor window, followed by his father. A man and his wife sleeping in that room woke up and the young man was stabbed to death by his father in front of them. Robertson also stabbed to death his wife, who was his son's stepmother. He stabbed his daughter, too, but she survived. It was a horrifying case.[11]

One of my most terrible court experiences was the judgement by Lord Wheatley in 1963 in the Argyll divorce case.[12] Well, the judgement was being delivered from the bench in the Court of Session. The judges always raced through these judgements, because they knew it was a formality, and that their judgement was going to be photocopied and made available in the court office three or four hours later. That was no good to us in the *Evening News*. So John Junor and I went up to the court and had to take down in shorthand as best we could what Lord Wheatley was racing through, run back to our office, sit down at a typewriter, and between John Junor's shorthand and mine get a story right away into the paper. It was an unsatisfactory and quite alarming way of reporting anything important like that judgement. But you had no choice. And you often got stuck with shorthand, John Junor as well. On an evening paper you're under great pressure from the clock. If you're a morning paper, well, you could wait until you got the written judgement.

The *Evening News* in these days, as I've said, went in for very detailed reporting. It was regarded, I think, as the local newspaper of record. Every year the *News* held in the Central Halls at Tollcross a Municipal Forum. The public were invited to come along, there was a panel of town councillors, and this was your chance to speak directly to the councillors about anything you had a gripe about. Well, the Municipal Forum was held for a number of years and we usually sent along two or three reporters, but Vincent Halton was the leading reporter there. You sat there all evening, and Vincent would take copious shorthand notes about everything that was brought up. Vincent's objective was to get all that into the *Evening News*. Well, it took several weeks of Municipal Forum articles to get to the end of that one night's meeting. Vincent used to like me typing for him because I was, though not a touch typist, pretty fast. One night after the Municipal Forum, Vincent and I went back to the office and he said, 'We'd better get it typed up tonight rather than tomorrow morning. The caseroom will be expecting it first thing.' Well, with just the two of us in the reporters' room, he dictated and dictated, and I typed and typed until it got to about two o'clock in the morning. I said, 'Look, Vincent, it's really not worthwhile going home now. We might as well just carry on. The Toddle Inn'll be open at seven o'clock in the morning across the road.' Well, that's the only time I can remember I literally typed all night. The sub-editors started coming in to work about 7am and were astonished to find Vincent and myself still dictating and typing. Vincent wrote at such length that for anything up to six weeks after the actual meeting there would still be questions and answers from the Municipal Forum. It became embarrassing.

Among reporters from the various newspapers in Edinburgh there was keen competition, but there was a great camaraderie as well. It was amazing how the reporters always got together after a meeting or a court case, etc., and said, 'Did you get that bit? What was that he said after so-and-so?' And always somebody in the group would have a reliable note and pass it on to the others there. An example of this camaraderie was the way Dick Campbell, a senior reporter on the *News* and a specialist on the mining industry, helped reporters from other papers at the weekly press conference held by Abe Moffat, president of the National Union of Mineworkers, Scottish Area, at their offices at Hillside Crescent, Edinburgh. In these days of course with the national shortage of coal the many thousands of miners in Scotland were in control. The great problem at those miners' press conferences was to stop Abe Moffat speaking so quickly. As the doyen of the reporters there, Dick had a habit, when he realised they were struggling to get down these vital words by Abe Moffat about another strike or something, of intervening and slowing him down: 'Eh, sorry, Abe,' (note the first-name terms), 'but what was that?' Or, 'Is this right?' – or something like that. And Abe would be stopped in full flow, allowing the struggling reporters to catch up with their shorthand. That was one of the tricks of the trade.

A curious thing I found after I came back from army service to the *News* was that, as you got used to the work, the reporters in the office sort of hung about at the end of the working day and chatted. Sometimes the chief reporter, Dave Donald, or Lewis Simpson, one of the seniors, would say, 'Come on, come on, you crowd, you got no homes to go to?' Everybody was very friendly and there was no clock-watching. Sometimes, maybe about half past ten in the morning, the chief reporter would say, 'Have you seen so-and-so ?', and you'd say, 'No. I think he's out having a coffee.' 'Go across to Ritchie's and see if you can find him.' If Dick Campbell, Jock Robertson, Alec Young and various other folk ever went missing and they were needed, you always knew you'd find them across at Ritchie's tearoom across in Cockburn Street, having a coffee and chatting away.

A lot of the *News* reporters went for a drink at the end of the day to Baillie's Bar in Market Street or maybe the Horseshoe, a nice Victorian bar in Cockburn Street. They would stand around in there laughing, joking, and drinking till they got the tramcar home. But nobody that I can remember 'disappeared' to the pub during working hours, and I can't think of anybody who had a drink problem. The *Evening Dispatch* men hung out up the hill in Cockburn Street in the Adelphi Hotel.

In the late 1940s, if you asked in the Horseshoe Bar for a pint of light beer it was 11d [almost 5p]. If you were particularly flush with money you had the heavy beer at 1s 1d [5½p] a pint. Before I was married in 1963 I was running a car from 1958, going abroad for a fortnight's holiday every summer, smoking at least 20 cigarettes a day, and going out several nights a week to the pubs – and I still had money left over at the end of the week. You could get by on what nowadays seems obviously a very small wage. Of course on a newspaper you were always slightly above the average national wage. Well, I think we deserved it because it was a great strain. That I was smoking more than 20 fags a day suggests that. You got into the habit of smoking. You would come back to the office with maybe only half an hour to go to the next edition, you had this idea you couldn't concentrate unless you lit up a cigarette. All the way back to the office you'd be thinking what your lead sentence, your intro, was going to be. The first thing you did when you opened up your notebook and put the paper in the typewriter, was to reach for your fags. You wouldn't have been typing very long before the chief reporter said, 'Have you got the start o' that?' And then you were just passing it over in short takes.

The *Evening News* was an out-and-out Institute of Journalists branch, or chapel as it was called. I'd been working there as a copy boy only a week or so in 1945 when somebody said, 'You'll have to join the Institute.' So I did. Everybody in the *News* was in it; I don't think there was a single member of the National Union of Journalists in the *News* at that time. You quickly learned there were loggerheads between the two. The NUJ hated the Institute; the Institute took a very sort of gentlemanly attitude towards the NUJ. This went on for years and years. I remained a member of the Institute until 1963, and in fact some time before then, when the Institute had held their annual conference in Edinburgh and because of all the great work I had done in organising bus trips and that sort of thing, I was made a Fellow! The Institute was always regarded as a sort of gentlemanly organisation. Once, round about 1960, I was nominated to be part of the negotiating team for a wage rise. I remember travelling down at least once to London and all sitting round this table, and somebody saying, 'Well, when we approach the employers I think we should go for £20 a week minimum.' Somebody else said, 'Oh, no, no. Och, we'll never get that.' So at that period our minimum wage was less than £20 a week. The *Evening News* was the stronghold of the Institute in Edinburgh, but I didn't think much about trade union affairs at all. And I've never been a member of a political party or a supporter of any particular party: I reckon I'm a floating voter, but I always seem to vote for the guy who loses.

*   *   *

Well, I worked on the *Evening News*, first as a copy boy then from 1948 as a reporter, until 1963. During those years the *News* went on and on very smoothly. It was a very happy place to work and it really had a very experienced staff. Maybe it just happened by chance, but people tended to stick with the *Evening News*, they very rarely moved to another paper. It was regarded as a good paper to work for, a sensible paper. I don't know what the recruitment policy was, but they seemed to bring in very good chaps from school who fitted in. I can't remember any sort of ructions at all.

That made it all the more dramatic, all the more horrific, when on 18 November 1963 the takeover of the *News* by the *Dispatch* was announced. That morning a vague sort of rumour circulated on the editorial floor of the *Evening News* that some momentous announcement was going to be made that afternoon. Nobody knew what it was. At three o'clock that afternoon a very small piece of paper was pinned up in the reporters' room, a similar piece in the subs' room, and presumably throughout the rest of the building as well. I can't remember the exact words now, but it was one or two sentences to say that the *Evening News* had been acquired by Thomson Newspapers. It was just a thunderbolt. Nobody on the *News* could believe it.

Roy Thomson, the Canadian newspaper magnate, had of course bought over *The Scotsman* and the *Evening Dispatch* from the Findlay family in the 1950s. The *Dispatch* had always played second fiddle to the *Evening News*, which was owned by Provincial Newspapers Ltd, a subsidiary of United Newspapers, based in London. Anyway there was some sort of deal by which Roy Thomson got the *Evening News* and he gave up some newspaper in Yorkshire. On the *News* we just felt then that we were in the grip of big business. The result was a merger of the *News* and the *Evening Dispatch* – a reverse takeover, because it was the smaller, weaker, less financially successful paper, the *Dispatch*, taking over the bigger, stronger, and financially successful paper, the *News*. Now the *Dispatch* had always been a good paper with a very good staff and, as I've said, we on the *News* watched it like a hawk. But the *Dispatch* was the younger paper and was also sort of struggling; the *News* had been founded in 1873 and it had a stranglehold on press advertising in Edinburgh. The circulation figures proved that. Incidentally, long before the takeover by Thomson quite a few of us on the *News* had joined a scheme launched by its owners Provincial Newspapers and taken a few five-shilling shares in the paper. To make any money out of it, of course, you would have had to have thousands of five-bob shares. But it was nice to have a stake in the paper you were working for. I've still got my few shares.

Just before the merger or takeover in 1963, Bill Barnetson had been editor of the *News*. But he got a chance to go down south to United Newspapers (Vincent Halton accepted his invitation to go with him) and Barnetson was succeeded as editor by Bob Cairns, who had been a *News* sub-editor till then. I may be wrong, but I would assume Bill Barnetson had had some hint that something awful was going to happen to the *Evening News*. So it was Bob Cairns who was left holding the baby and had to preside over the reverse takeover. It was awful, it was quite horrible. It destroyed the whole atmosphere in the *Evening News*. The *Evening Dispatch* ceased publication that day. So all the people on the *Dispatch* who were in no doubt they'd been promised they'd be looked after in the new set-up came into the *Evening News* building in Market Street. You then had the most embarrassing situations where you had two newspaper staffs. Most people who had worked for the *Evening News* resented that staff from the 'failed' *Dispatch* were being given superior posts. It was pretty clear the *Dispatch* staff were the victors; the *News* staff felt they were the losers. It was a rotten atmosphere. Then there was talk immediately about redundancies: obviously the one newspaper could not carry two staffs. And this was in the days before voluntary redundancies. Nowadays it's more or less standard practice that if something like that happens, the first thing a management will do is call for volunteers to take early retirement or redundancy with compensation. But that was not the situation in 1963, certainly not at 18 Market Street. Redundancy pay then was based on your years of service, two weeks for each year or something. But compared with the handsome pay-offs you read about now, it was going to be very tough then for people, particularly if they were married with families. I had got married shortly before. I think I could take things with a bit more equanimity than perhaps otherwise, as it was just my wife and me, and she was working then at a publisher's in Edinburgh. Anyway all this situation went on for several weeks. The atmosphere was still pretty horrible.

Then George Millar, who had joined the *News* from the *Dispatch* quite some time before the takeover, came up with this idea that some of us *News* folk could get together and start an independent news agency. At that period there was a great deal of linage (payment for reports sent to other newspapers, such as the *Guardian, The Times,* the Dundee *Courier*) available at the *Evening News,* because it was the number-one newspaper in Edinburgh. George Millar himself was a correspondent for several other newspapers. 'Well,' he said, 'I think we could make a go of this news agency idea. Anything's better than working for this lot.' So George and I resigned from the *News,* we teamed up with Gordon Smith and Gordon Dean, who'd been made redundant, and the four of us created on the first of January 1964 this news agency, United News Service.[13]

The Service couldn't really have started unless it had made a fundamental guaranteed contract with the BBC. Jimmy Kemp, who always wore waistcoats with his jackets, was the man in charge of BBC Scotland news at that time, and he was looking for somebody to provide him every day with a news service from Edinburgh for the BBC in Glasgow. So this annual contract underpinned at the beginning the whole finances of United News Service. It also underpinned a lot of other casual work that was gradually built up. George Millar was correspondent for the *Daily Telegraph,* for instance, which took a lot of stuff from Edinburgh. Our first office was in Shandwick Place, at the West End, then we moved to Fleshmarket Close, off the High Street.

Because of the experience of the four founding partners, United News Service became recognised quickly as a very good training ground for journalists. Two very good examples were Ian Burrell and Chrisma Mackay, both of whom became our specialists in reporting the law courts.

But it was very hard going. I clearly remember Lewis Simpson pursing his lips doubtfully when we told him we were adding *four* freelances to Edinburgh. In time we found that those of us who were married with children were indeed under pressure, because no matter how much news UNS churned out and sold to newspapers, the rate of payment by newspapers was seldom generous. News editors were glad to take anything we offered them. But payment was really regulated by the newspaper accountants, who were taking over the world. Gordon Dean, who had a family, was the first to return to a staff job: it was all very amicable.

Freelance work of the sort we were doing is a terrible slog, in particular where there is no formal contract: the only written contract we had was with the BBC in Glasgow. We were working virtually seven days a week. On Saturdays Gordon Smith was covering rugby matches, and I reported football matches for the *Sunday Telegraph*. About noon I would get into the office Mini, drive furiously to Fife (Stark's Park, Kirkcaldy), or Dundee (Dens Park or Tannadice), or, worse still, all the way to Aberdeen (Pittodrie). There were no mobile phones in those days: a loyal friend, Joe McTernan, would accompany me to phone the copy from a local newsagent's shop or, in the case of Perth, a public kiosk near the football stadium. In the latter case there might be a member of the public making a phone call, and one hopped about making agitated signals, because the London-based *Sunday Telegraph* demanded the report at the final whistle. Then we drove back to Edinburgh, sometimes in the dark. On the Sunday one might be on call, usually praying there would not be a murder, a big fire, or some other weekend calamity. I remember quite a few times talking a London news desk out of some vague assignment they wanted followed up. But I retained a permanent dislike of ever working again for Thomson Newspapers.

I remained with the United News Service until 1975. Then I was approached by Lorna Rhind, publicity officer for Edinburgh Corporation as it then was, but about to become Edinburgh District Council at local government reorganization. Lorna was to be the head of a new department of public relations and tourism in the new council and she was looking for a press officer.

I had known the old town council very well as an *Evening News* reporter. But working for Edinburgh District Council was completely different. About a year after I started, Lorna Rhind retired after she had a bad fall in the office, and Andrew Fyall, who had been a foreign correspondent on the London *Daily Express* for years, was her successor.[14] When I retired at 65 in 1993 I had been in the City Chambers for 18 years.

Apart from my two years in the army, I always think of my working life as two-thirds journalism, one-third local government. The journalism years were exciting and the happiest. Local government in Edinburgh proved to be politically lively, particularly after Labour gained control of the council in the 1980s. But that is another story!

Nancy Mackenzie

My entry into journalism was pure chance. I had been in the Women's Royal Naval Service during the war and came back afterwards about September–October 1946, not knowing what I was going to do. I'd taken a secretarial course between graduating and waiting to be called up, so I applied around various jobs and was going down to Newcastle to be trained as a secretary in one of the big detergent firms, either Procter & Gamble or Lever Brothers, something like that. And then somewhere about November 1946 Bill Coghill, who was the assistant editor of the Edinburgh *Evening News* and who knew my father through church, said they were looking for someone to come and join the *News* staff.[1] They were just building it up after the war, and would I consider that? I went to see Jimmy Seager, the editor, and it was arranged I'd start in January 1947. That was the beginning of it. There was no tradition of journalism in my family, none whatsoever.

I was born in Edinburgh on the 8th of February 1921, and my earliest recollections are of growing up there. My father was a sheriff officer at the Sheriff Court. In fact he didn't retire until he was 89. He could go back to the days of Oscar Slater and could remember accompanying him between the prison and the court.[2] My grandfather Mackenzie had been a sheriff officer before my father, who, I think, was born in Edinburgh, though there were family connections with Caithness. My father certainly lived in Edinburgh and as a small boy went to school in Edinburgh. He'd wanted to go into the ministry, as his brother did. But when he was at college his health broke down. Whether the strain of study had been too much for him, I'm not sure. He spent some time convalescing from that, then he went and joined my grandfather as a sheriff officer instead. He was self-employed as a sheriff officer, working from the Sheriff Court. When my grandfather became unable to work, dad carried on for both of them, and I think he found it quite a hard job to begin with. So my father was actually maintaining the two households on what he earned. I know it was only after grandfather died that we were able to first of all have a car, and then move house a few years later. I think that was largely because dad wasn't, by that time, responsible for keeping up the two households. He only gave up work at the age of 89 because his car packed in a year or two before. I think he wanted to keep working because my mother had died a few years earlier, and he was missing her dreadfully. They'd just celebrated their golden wedding and a week later mother took a stroke and died a few days later. I think dad felt work was the only thing that kept him going. He was still driving at 87 when his car packed up and he thought it wasn't worthwhile buying a new one. So he carried on just travelling by bus for a while, but he was too frail by that time to be standing in the cold waiting for buses. It didn't do his health any good. So at 89 he decided he would just pack in. He survived another three years and was a fortnight short of his 93rd birthday when he died.

Until she was married my mother had worked as a clerk/typist in her uncle's office. Her uncle was a leather merchant. She was born in Edinburgh, though her family had come from the Borders.

Grandfather Mackenzie had been born, I think, in Caithness. I don't know when he came down to Edinburgh. I remember him very, very vaguely. He died when I was about five, and I just remember him as a sort of whiskered face in bed, because he had a heart condition and spent all his time in bed. I don't know how long he'd been incapacitated before he had to hand over to my father as a sheriff officer.

I went to George Watson's Ladies' College in George Square, primary and secondary, right through from 1926 till 1938. I enjoyed school. I always liked English, and languages and history. Maths and science I was never very good at. Latin I wasn't particularly good at and gave that up early on.

As a teenager I never had any clear ambition. This was the trouble. I kept changing my mind about what I'd like to do. I remember thinking at one time I'd like to do domestic science, but by that time I'd given up science at school, and it would have required that to go to the Edinburgh College of Domestic Science in Atholl Crescent. So that was ruled out. So I left school at 17 at the end of my sixth year, and took French and German at Edinburgh University. Earlier, Latin had been an essential subject, but luckily by then it wasn't necessary. I really set off to do an Honours degree in German but I found I wasn't good enough. I'd had about two and a half or three years of German before going to the university and it wasn't sufficient background for Honours. So I switched to an Ordinary degree, with French and German as my two principal subjects.

By that time a cousin of my father, in age between him and me, had got a job as a secretary, but using languages, with a firm that did a lot of export work. And I was more or less thinking this'd be the sort of thing

I'd want to do. She in fact was a lot cleverer than I am or was. She was a very quiet, studious sort of person. She'd an Honours degree in German and taught herself Spanish, Italian, Dutch, and all sorts of things as well: she'd a gift for languages. So whether I'd have made the grade in that line, I don't know. Anyhow the war came along. It was pretty clear that it would come. I'd completed one year at the university when the war broke out. My parents recommended I should complete my degree before doing anything else, which I did. Women weren't called up anyway till later on.[3] But I wasn't conscripted, I volunteered. It'd be 1941 I graduated, and I applied right away to join the Women's Royal Naval Service. My brother, younger than me, was just called up into the navy towards the end of the war.

I'd made enquiries about the various services. I preferred the WRNS. Then I found that, knowing German, I could use that. There was no family tradition of the navy, I just preferred the navy to the other services. I had all the medical and various interviews and things, and was about to be called up in the spring of 1942, when Greenwich College, their training college, was hit by a bomb and they had to delay intake. So I wasn't actually called up until July 1942, and then went, not to Greenwich, which was still damaged and being repaired, but to Mill Hill College in London. I think we were the first intake to go to Mill Hill.

After a fortnight's basic training at Mill Hill we went for about six weeks to a Wimbledon training college for the specialised training for the job I was doing. Then I was posted to a station up at Sheringham on the Norfolk coast. And I spent the rest of the war at various of these coastal stations, mostly in Norfolk, sometimes down in the south, and a while at Scarborough. It was listening to the naval traffic of German ships at sea, mostly the smaller ones, the E-boats that were attacking the convoys, and trying to pinpoint them by DF – direction finding.[4] We got various fixes on the DF towers all round the coast and got a cross fix and could determine the position of the ships. The Germans had an air–sea rescue service, too, and we'd to listen to any reference, particularly to British servicemen being picked up: that's what we were particularly listening for. A lot of the German boats were based in the Dutch coastal areas. It was very interesting work and I thoroughly enjoyed that. Of course that was top secret work at the time. I think the fact there was such a service is fairly general knowledge now. I think what we're not supposed to tell now or never, are the details – the call signs and codes and whatnot that we had to use.

I was never actually involved in any close action, never served at sea. The nearest I came to any bomb damage was at Sheringham when I was in bed after being on night watch. My bed was right under the window, looking out to sea. And a plane came over and dropped its bomb which luckily fell on the beach in front of us, not on the cliff level with us. I dived under the bed and bruised my leg in the process. But that was the only damage I suffered, apart from a lot of dust and sand being blown into the room. Later in the war these German V1s and V2s were going over, but they were never very close to me.[5] They were horrid. You never knew when they were going to come. I don't know which was worse. You'd hear the V1s coming and then the motor would shut off and you knew it was falling, but you didn't know where it was going to fall! Whereas the V2s, there was just an explosion. You had no pre-warning at all. But I wasn't in London, I never suffered any severe blitz at all. That one bomb at Sheringham was the nearest I came to anything. I was lucky in that respect.

I was put up for a commission and went to officers' training college down in Buckinghamshire. We were called third officers, second officers, and first officers then. We had our own ranking and our own different colour of stripes. We had the blue stripes, not the gold stripes of the navy. The WRNS were unique in that, to begin with, you had to volunteer to join. They were conscripted later on in the war. But the big difference with the other women's services was that we didn't come under the Naval Discipline Act, whereas the WAAFs and ATS came under their respective Discipline Acts. They could be treated just like the men. But we were different. Any misdemeanour that we had, we weren't court-martialled or punished in any way, not the same way as the men were. And the WRNS were a much smaller service than the ATS and WAAF.[6]

After Victory in Europe day in 1945 there wasn't the same need for us on the coast, and I was working at the Admiralty in London, then spent my last year in Germany in the Occupation services. I was at a naval base called Plön near Kiel. It had been built specially as a relaxation and training centre for the German submariners. So it was a very well-equipped and pleasant place to be, rather like a country estate with barrack blocks here and there. I was there from about September, early October, 1945. I was personal assistant to the British naval commander who was in charge of minesweeping in the Baltic. It was all navy because we were dealing with the German navy. Because of my knowledge of German I acted as interpreter, because all the actual sweeping was done by German ships and German sailors. But the officers reported to our commander. He had to plan it all and work in conjunction with them. Most of them spoke reasonably good English, but I'd to be there in case any interpreting was required, and to take notes and that sort of thing. I never went out on the Baltic myself, not operationally. It was too dangerous. The odd ship hit a mine and was blown up. So I didn't take part in any operational minesweeping. It was a tremendous task to sweep the Baltic of mines, because a lot had been laid. All they could do to begin with was simply clear lines through your various channels from port to port and they gradually widened these. It must have taken several years. I was there for a year and they certainly hadn't finished it by then.

We had very little contact with German civilians. Fraternisation was not encouraged, it was virtually against the rules. We had German staff as stewards in the quarters, a German hairdresser who would come and visit us, and we'd contact with people like German dressmakers. But it was only on that very controlled basis, it wasn't on a social basis at all. I didn't find it frustrating that I wasn't able to use my German, I didn't really think as seriously as that about it. I was only in my mid-twenties by then. It sounds rather callous, but it was a very enjoyable life we led out there, because we were very much the winning, the dominating race. The Germans were very much subservient to us. What you did see of the civilians' conditions were appalling. Going into Hamburg was an eye-opener when we drove in there. The first time I saw it I really was appalled. The city was absolutely flattened by the bombing. You were driving along a sort of single-lane track with just piles of rubble and twisted pipes sticking up in the air. The people were mostly living in cellars or just in the ground floors of houses that were crumbled on top of them, like living in a cave. But you got used to it. I think the feeling was more that, well, they asked for it; sorry for the women and the children, but as Germans they really had asked for it. I was certainly thankful it hadn't happened to us the other way round.[7]

Because I was enjoying myself in Germany I'd actually signed on in the WRNS for an extra eight or nine months. But I was demobbed from there and came back home about August/September 1946. I had really enjoyed my service in the WRNS. It had done me a lot of good. Because I'd been very shy when I was younger, and having only been at an all-girls school, I'd had very little chance of mixing in mixed society. My brother was younger than me and therefore his friends were just young boys to me. Even at university the classes I went to were predominantly female. I rowed, but of course that was an all-women's crew. I played a bit of tennis but not a lot. Most of my friends were women at that time. And I hadn't been away from home at all. I'd been very much a sort of home-orientated person, very shy and very unsophisticated, and I think it did me a lot of good getting into the WRNS and being away from home, mixing with other people and giving me confidence. If it hadn't been for that I wouldn't have been able to do the job of a journalist. I'd have been far too shy. Even as it was, I found I was still rather shy about asking questions in, say, a press conference. It took me an awful long time before I'd the courage to speak up and ask something unless I'd been primed beforehand. So service in the WRNS helped a lot.

I don't think I had any feeling that the war was an interference with my life or the prospects of a professional career. I hadn't had any clear line I really wanted to follow. I was not exactly drifting, but rather waiting for an opportunity than heading for anything definite. The war did delay everything by those few years when I was away. On the other hand, it also, I think, prepared me for a working life better than I would have been if it hadn't come, or at least if I hadn't joined the WRNS. I know a lot of people loathed every moment they were away. But I can't say I did. I made a lot of good friends, had some very interesting experiences, and gained a lot of self-confidence.

After four years away I wasn't inclined to leave Edinburgh and go somewhere else. As I've said, I was a very home sort of person. My parents weren't exactly possessive, but they were very protective, and it wasn't so much the custom at that time for girls particularly to break out and go and live in a flat when they had a home they could live in, unless their work took them away. So I was quite glad to get back home and begin to pick up the threads again of friends I'd known beforehand. A lot of them certainly were scattered. School friends I'd had had largely moved away because of the war. Some were married, some were working elsewhere. So it took a while to pick up again and establish myself in Edinburgh. I did to some extent have a difficulty in settling down. But I had to find a job. That was my main concern.

So I went up first of all to the university graduates' employment office and put in some queries there. It was they who put me on to this training down in Newcastle – I think it was Procter & Gamble, but I'm not sure now – where you could train either for the secretarial–management sort of side, or market research. I was offered a job there, although I hadn't actually accepted it, when Bill Coghill, the assistant editor, came up with this idea of joining the Edinburgh *Evening News*. Before then I hadn't had any notion of entering journalism, not at all. In fact, even to begin with, it wasn't journalism I was going to the *Evening News* for. I was going in there as the editor's secretary.

Between seeing Jimmy Seager, the editor, in November 1946 and then, I'd spent the interval brushing up my shorthand, which I hadn't used while I'd been away in the WRNS. Typing I'd used a bit, but shorthand I hadn't. So I took a crash course at McAdam's secretarial college in North Castle Street.

So that's how I began on the *News* in January 1947. Well, I did a year of that, mostly the editor's secretarial work, but I did a bit of book reviewing and I also wrote a few articles while I was there. My first holiday abroad came up that year, and a friend and I went to Corsica, which was virtually unknown at that time, and I wrote an article for the *News* about that. I think Bill Coghill had suggested I should write something about it. So I remember sitting in the garden at home, trying to keep my suntan going, typing away at this article about Corsica. And it made the leader page, it was the main leader page article one day.

I didn't use German very much after the war. It was French that I maintained, we went to France three times, to Spain a few times, to Austria once, and I did learn a bit of Italian, too, because we began going to Italy for holidays. All this travelling on holiday helped me develop an interest in journalism. I'd usually find something to write about every time I came home. To begin with, just after the war, it was more hints on travelling, things to take with you that you might not think about. Things like an air cushion for making it easier on trains if you were travelling overnight – it's useful as a pillow. People wouldn't think of things like that now, but then, when you were spending two or three days travelling to wherever you were going, it could be quite an uncomfortable journey.

My first assignment, so to speak, was another biggish article Bill Coghill suggested. It was about an old castle, one of the old fortified towers of Scotland. I played golf at Turnhouse golf course and I could see this old tower through the trees from there. It belonged to Sir James Maitland Tennant, I think he was, Maitland something anyway. I had no idea what to do, but Sir James took me round and pointed out the house and what he was doing there. And it turned out quite a good article, possibly a bit naïvely written, looking back on it later on. But it was quite an experience for me. And it was published as a main feature in the *News*. James Seager, the editor, was quite pleased with it.[8]

And then, when they realised I could write, I think, I was suddenly asked if I'd like to take on the 'Eve's Circle' women's feature. That was only half a column twice a week at that time, because newspapers were so small. During the war I think a Mrs Dand had been doing Eve's Circle. But she wasn't a trained journalist, I think she was the wife of one of the journalists and had just been brought in. She didn't do much writing as far as I know, it was more or less just a matter of taking in submitted articles and the Ministry of Food recipes and things like that, and preparing them for publication. But they wanted to make it more definitely a journalistic column for women. So I was asked if I would take this on, writing as much as I could myself and of course doing general reporting for the rest of the time. So at that point I became a full-time journalist, and that would be about the beginning of 1948.

In the year I'd worked by then for Mr Seager, the editor, as his secretary, I quite liked him. Relations were quite friendly, we got on very well, he was a man you could respect and work for. I did some special typing for him sometimes, like laying out football teams. Unfortunately, I forgot to reverse them: when you're doing the goalkeeper up there and the other goalkeeper down here, I forgot to reverse the second team, and he pointed that out to me rather scathingly. But otherwise he seemed to approve what I was doing. And I did quite a lot of book reviewing in that time, too, not necessarily just reviews of the books themselves, but taking material out from a book to make an article from it.

When I began on the *Evening News* there were no other women reporters or columnists there, except a girl junior, Margo McGill, who'd been in the WRNS, too. She must have started before me, I think, before going to the WRNS. She was there before me, but I don't quite know in what capacity. I think she was just more a general reporter, not doing the women's page as such. Margo must have been about the same age as me, I think. So I don't quite know why I was asked to take on this Eve's Circle when she had been there and had much more actual reporting experience than I had. I never quite fathomed that one. But later on, as paper became more available and Eve's Circle became bigger, became a page every day, then Margo also became an Eve's Circle staff. We worked together on it, the two of us wrote Eve's Circle, which was a whole page, five days a week, by that time. We didn't have it on Saturday. It was a lot of work for the two of us, but we could use a certain amount of contributed stuff, and of course pictures helped fill it up.[9] So I carried on doing general reporting along with working on Eve's Circle.

Once I became a full-time journalist I worked very irregular hours really. Our regular hours were 8.30am till 4.30pm. But of course any evening work or interviews that could only be done in the evenings had to be done then too. On the other hand, if there was nothing doing in the afternoon, if we'd cleared our desks, and everything was in hand for the next day or two, we could get off at, say, 4pm.

The general reporting I did was, well, if there were certain things that seemed to require a woman's attendance. For a while, when Eve's Circle was still smaller, I was doing the church notes as well every Friday. So I did quite a lot of general reporting on, say, Women's Guild meetings at the General Assembly of the Church of Scotland every May, or some of the special or small meetings during the Assembly. I'd been brought up in a churchgoing family. Our church was the Congregational Church in George IV Bridge. My father was clerk to the deacons there, and he and my mother were both in the choir. She was also the relief organist when necessary. I never considered trying to become church or religious affairs correspondent for the *Evening News*. That didn't appeal to me at all. I can't say I enjoyed that side of reporting particularly.

When I began working in the *News* the chief reporter was Dave Donald. His deputy was John Junor. Lewis Simpson and Vincent Halton, who'd been with the *News* before the war, had just come back from their war service and were the two senior reporters. Then there was Dick Campbell, Logan Robertson, and Donald Esson, and they'd just come back from war service, too. Then there was Margo McGill. And Bill Rae must have just come back from National Service when I became reporting staff. There were some other reporters, too, then but I can't place them, and most of the other ones I can think of came later. And then of course James Seager was the editor, Bill Coghill was there but died quite soon after that, then Bill Barnetson came in as leader writer and later on took over as editor. I found all the journalist staff of the *News* very friendly and extremely helpful, Dick Campbell particularly. He more or less took me under his wing to start with. They were all experienced journalists, and I was completely inexperienced. But they helped a tremendous amount, even in how to write a story, once I got the information how to put it on paper, the sort of questions to ask, the things to look for. Even in interviewing, Dick Campbell helped me with lines to work on before I went out to interview someone, because I'd had no formal training, none whatsoever.

In those days there was no training scheme. And I think I probably made a lot of mistakes, particularly on the practical side, not realising how quickly the material had to be in to give the copy people upstairs time to get it set. I didn't have a telephone at that time at home. When I was doing some musical reviews at concerts on a Friday night – Saturday at that time was usually my day off as I wasn't required to do much sport – they kept saying, 'You must phone your copy in early.' So on Saturday mornings I had to get up, have breakfast, then get out and find a public telephone that was free and phone my copy in. The nearest public phone was about seven or eight minutes' walk from home. So by the time I got to the phone it was probably getting on for 10am and they were screaming at me for not getting it in earlier. I didn't realise at that time just how vital it was to get that stuff in quickly. The first edition was about 12 noon, and 11am was the deadline for getting copy in. And of course they wanted all the non-news items in first, leaving the typesetting machines clear for anything urgent that came in at the last minute. It was only after some weeks or months when I got more into it, watched how the paper was being put together, that I realised how vital speed was. After that we got a phone put in at home and it meant I didn't need to trail out to find a public phone. And of course in those days you had to have a supply of coppers ready. It was only 2d for a phone call, but you didn't know how long it was going to take to get your call through and the copy taken off, so you'd to have a lot of coppers ready and, if necessary, keep feeding them in.

On an evening paper there's no time to think. If it was a morning job you were out on, you simply had to get what you could, rush back to the office, and type it up and get it in as quickly as possible. Quite often I think I missed bits out that I should have put in, simply through sheer desire to get the stuff ready quickly. You learned the hard way. But when I was interviewing someone I was always very reluctant to make too many notes. I think if you're being interviewed it's very off-putting to see the interviewer scribbling down every word said. So I tended just to make a very surreptitious quick note as a reminder, and then rely on memory for fleshing it out. I don't think my memory was as good as it should have been for that method of working. But as soon as I got out of the room where I'd been interviewing anyone, I'd begin jotting down bits I wanted to remember, and then make sense of it when I got into the office. My shorthand was fairly good, but it was never very fast and I could never have taken verbatim reports of a long speech. I honestly don't know what speed I could do, I hadn't been long enough on the crash course to take any certificates in shorthand or typing. I never learned the abbreviations that would have helped me in speed, I never got to that stage of shorthand. And some of my own manufactured abbreviations weren't always intelligible afterwards! But I managed. I was never picked up on having misquoted anyone, so my shorthand must have been reasonably good.

At that time then, from 1948, Margo McGill and I were the only women reporters on the *News*. Then there was a young girl, Joyce Stewart, came in for a while as a trainee reporter. She was very good, but she wasn't with us very long when she got married and went down to London. At that time there were usually one or two women journalists per paper. *The Scotsman* had Elsie Adam. She was the doyenne of the women journalists in Edinburgh. Elsie would be at least 20 or 25 years older than me or Margo McGill. She'd been at *The Scotsman* before the war, and I think she'd stayed there all through the war.[10] And then Dinah Dawson came to the *Evening Dispatch*. Well, Lorna Rhind was with the *Dispatch*, and Dinah may have been there with Lorna or may have followed Lorna, I'm not quite sure. But Dinah was like me, out of the Services and unqualified as a journalist.[11] She, too, was just finding her way, and we got on very well together. Quite often we'd fix up an interview, not stand in for each other but we'd do it together and then compare notes, make sure we got things right. We were, I know, supposed to be from rival papers! One of the funniest interviews I remember was of some African woman chieftain. I can't think what tribe she was the chieftain of, but she was fairly senior. We must have heard about her from the Scottish Office, I suppose. We'd to arrange an interview through them, and it was agreed that as long as we had questions prepared in advance she would see us. She didn't speak English, it had to be done through an interpreter, and we had to go in the evening to her hotel room in, I think, the Caledonian or North British Hotel in Princes Street. She'd only see Dinah and me together, not separately. So Dinah and I got together, prepared our questions, and were shown into this room, rather unsure of the etiquette we had to adopt with this apparently very august personage, rather like interviewing the Queen. She came along with her maid, who never left her, almost like a bodyguard, and who sat on the floor across the doorway, I presume to prevent anyone else coming in. Her interpreter sat beside her. The chieftain herself sat on the bed knitting, a great shapeless mass of pale blue wool round her. So Dinah and I asked the questions we'd prepared about the condition of women in her country, what she'd seen here that she would most like to introduce to her own country, and so on. She was looking more and more puzzled and glum. She would rattle off something to her interpreter, who would say something like, 'She would like to see hydroelectric works in her country.' This was about all we were getting out of her, until completely out of the blue I said to her: 'I see you're knitting. What are you knitting?' Her face lit up immediately, and she began displaying what she was knitting. From then on it became a homely chat about her daughters, her family, how they worked, where they lived – completely at variance with the august personage we'd been led to expect. She was just a very ordinary village-dwelling African woman. But we'd an awful job writing it up because we didn't want to offend anyone by making fun of her. We were rather making fun of ourselves, as our very presumptuous or pompous questions we'd dreamed up to begin with were completely out of keeping with what she really was. So we had to try to sort of fudge the articles to cover all this. Dinah and I kept phoning each other that night as we were writing it up, saying, 'Listen to this: d'you think we should put this bit in?' Dinah and I got on extremely well, we were friends, though our papers were supposed to be hot rivals. But there was a lot of collaboration between individuals on the staffs of the papers.

We met women journalists outside Edinburgh occasionally on some of the big public relations jobs, big fashion shows, we went through to Glasgow for. I remember Dior had a fashion show in Glasgow.[12] It was one of these big charity shows. Princess Margaret was to be at it. So Dinah and I were sent through by our respective papers and we'd to go in evening dress. It was a really big posh affair in one of the big hotels. That must have been very early in the 1950s, because Dinah and I drove through together and the car I got from the *News* was an old Ford that had the old windscreen wipers you switched on by turning the knob in front of you. It was a wretched night of rain and wind. I didn't know Glasgow at all well, and coming home somewhere between 11pm and midnight, I missed the Edinburgh road. We found ourselves heading away down the coast. There was no one to ask, so we'd an awful job finding our way. We finally got on to the Edinburgh road – and that was when the windscreen wipers packed in. By this time Dinah was asleep, so I was driving, trying to keep the car straight with one hand against the buffeting wind, and with the other hand keeping the windscreen wipers going. I was never so glad to get home as I was that night.

But I met other women journalists in Glasgow on that and other occasions. There was Sheila someone I met, and once or twice Mamie Baird – later Mrs Magnus Magnusson.[13] They're the only ones I remember. I did meet others from other parts of Scotland, but not really frequently enough to know them. And of course on an evening paper I was not journeying around Scotland as much as I might have done on a morning or Sunday paper. We did travel around to the Highland Show every year wherever it was, when it was peripatetic.

And I was sent down to cover, or at least to get a woman's angle on, the Knockshinnoch Castle colliery disaster in Ayrshire in 1950. I was sent down a day or two later, I think it was on the Saturday. It was a terrible thing. I don't really remember an awful lot about it now. Most of the miners trapped were rescued but a number were lost. I was never quite sure exactly why I was sent down a day or two later, because it was very difficult finding people who were prepared to speak about it by that time. Those who were closely involved weren't at the minehead any longer, they were away. And it was more or less a matter of going around and trying to find someone prepared to speak. I didn't make a very good job of that. I didn't feel I was really getting my teeth into it at all, and felt what I produced wasn't really worthy of the occasion. I think that's why I tended not to remember very much about it. I wasn't happy either with the doing of it or what came out of it.

There was never any grouping, formal or informal, of women journalists in Edinburgh. I joined the Institute of Journalists as soon as I became a journalist or very soon after. I was more or less talked into it. Lewis Simpson, of course, one of the senior reporters on the *Evening News*, was a very keen Institute man. He became its president eventually. Well, the whole *News* staff really were Institute members at that time. Some of those who came in later and who were trained elsewhere were National Union of Journalists. I never felt any desire to leave the Institute and join the NUJ, anything but. In fact, I was very sorry the Institute wasn't stronger because I felt more in keeping with its aims and way of working than I ever did with the NUJ. I was never a trade unionist at heart. I was never in favour of the closed shop or anything like that. There was no trade union tradition or activity in my family. I was glad that the *News* was an open shop. Even up in the print shop it was open and that, I think, was very exceptional.

But that changed when in 1963 *The Scotsman* took over the *Evening News*. Those of us who had been members of the Institute were allowed to remain members. But those who up to that point had not had any allegiance had to become National Union of Journalists. We were encouraged to leave the Institute and join the NUJ, but we weren't actually banned from the paper because we preferred to remain in the Institute.

The Scotsman takeover was one of the hardest things. It was the same week in November 1963 that President Kennedy was assassinated. It was the Monday. We walked into the *News* on Monday morning that week and found the *Evening Dispatch* staff in command. It was as sudden as that. There had been no warning, none whatsoever, no rumour even, nothing at all. Even Bob Cairns, the then editor, didn't know. He walked into his office to find Max McAuslane, the editor of the *Dispatch*, sitting there. It was just like that. We were absolutely shattered. Oh, I still remember how we felt. It was extremely upsetting. The *News* and the *Dispatch* were different papers with a different way of working, a different style of people. The great majority of the *Dispatch* people were *Daily Record* trained, and that was a complete anathema to the style of the *News*. I couldn't adjust to it. I couldn't adjust to the people either that I was working with. I hated it when the *News* packed in – well, not packed in, when we were taken over by *The Scotsman* and, although the *News*'s name continued, it became the *Dispatch* in practice. I hated the atmosphere. I gave it a trial, but gave up after about six months. I then began looking around for other jobs in journalism or at least journalism-related. I knew there wasn't much chance in Edinburgh itself as far as newspapers were concerned, because they were declining. And as far as I knew there were no vacancies. But I did apply for a few public relations jobs. One was with the Design Council in Glasgow, another was with the BBC, and the other was the Scottish

Office. But I didn't at that time want to leave Edinburgh, because my parents were getting elderly and I didn't want to leave them. Glasgow would have been all right, I could have commuted at least weekends if not daily. I was on the short leet for the Design Council job, which was the only one of the three I really would have liked to get, but didn't get it.

Anyhow that was rather less than a year I spent going after these jobs. Then I went on holiday to one of the remote islands off Sicily, had a thoroughly good fortnight of complete freedom and relaxation, came back home on the Sunday and felt this awful atmosphere at the *Evening News* closing in on me again. So on the Monday morning I decided I just could not stand it any longer, phoned Moray House College of Education that morning and asked if they could take me on their next course, starting in early October – with a degree, yes. So I put in my notice there and then to the *News* as from the end of September 1965, and went then to Moray House. That was a huge change, but I've never regretted it.

I was a year at Moray House and trained as a primary teacher. My degree would have qualified me for junior secondary work, but I didn't fancy teaching the 13–15 year olds. My first job was at James Gillespie's Boys School, then after five years I went to James Gillespie's Girls. Again it took me a while to get into the way of it, because I hadn't had anything to do with young children at all till then. I had asked if I could teach boys. I started at Gillespie's Boys with seven-year-olds and worked up as far as the 10-year-olds. At Gillespie's Girls I was doing Primary 5 to 7, 10 to 12-year-olds, then moving back again. I was there for the remaining 10 years of my teaching career, which I enjoyed thoroughly.

Well, looking back, I enjoyed the first few years of the journalism, when everything was new and fresh and interesting. I found latterly, even before the takeover of the *News*, a lot of it was becoming repetitious. Year by year the same things cropped up, and it was getting more difficult to find a new angle to attack it from – particularly things like the Home Exhibition at the Waverley Market. Every time that came round it was sheer agony, because it was pure commercial advertising, yet it was done as editorial. Margo McGill and I took it in turns to go down there every night to find something to write about, because that was part of the contract. There had to be something in the paper every night about what was going on down there. And we loathed it. That was three weeks of misery.

And the Edinburgh International Festival got more demanding, too. I thoroughly enjoyed the Festival when it first started. I was hardly ever at home. We had these rover passes we could use. If we weren't covering anything we could borrow the rover pass and go and see something we wanted to see. We'd the films, the music, the opera, the ballet. I learnt more about music, opera and ballet in those early years than ever before or since. But then again, as the years passed and the novelty wore off, some of the things I had to cover were not to my taste. Some of the modern music, which I don't understand and don't like, and some of the fringe shows, were pretty grim. Some of the venues you'd to find were very out of the way, and you'd turn up and there'd be about three people in the audience. You'd to try and write a fairly kind sort of notice for someone who was struggling. So that in a way became more a struggle than an enjoyment.

I think journalism is more a young person's job. You can enjoy a fresher outlook on things if you're younger. I never quite understood how Elsie Adam of *The Scotsman* kept going for so long, because she was absolutely as fresh and enthusiastic when I last knew her before she retired as she must have been when she was younger. It was then, when Elsie retired at 60, 65 or 67, that Dinah Dawson moved up from the *Dispatch* and took over on *The Scotsman*. So I didn't see so much of Dinah then because we were working different hours. Dinah was my closest colleague, closer even than Margo McGill. Dinah and I were friends more than Margo and I were. I think Margo possibly resented slightly me coming in at the *Evening News*, because I was in charge of Eve's Circle yet, I think, she felt, she had been there longer. We were never quite on the same wavelength. We got on well enough together but were never close friends.

I don't think I ever had the feeling that the men at the *News* dumped jobs on the women: 'Och, we cannae be bothered with this. The women'll do it.' I didn't have that feeling. The jobs I got were ones obviously more related to women's interests. I did more general work too, though I didn't do much court work. Dave Donald, the chief reporter when I started, I think had a feeling that the courts, for example, weren't a suitable place for ladies. I didn't mind that, I wasn't keen to go to the courts. I think you'd have to be very careful, very accurate, so I didn't do any court work. And I didn't do the City Chambers work, because Lewis Simpson and Vincent Halton, the senior reporters, did that, then Arthur Goodey took it over. I did interview usually the new Lady Provost whenever she took over. But I never had the feeling that the women journalists on the *Evening News*, Margo McGill, the young girl Joyce Stewart, and myself, were being treated as second-class citizens. We mixed freely with the men reporters, went out for coffee and drinks together. We were treated very equally, I felt, and not at all discriminated against. The men were very good colleagues and treated us as equals. So I very much enjoyed my early years of journalism.

I enjoyed the teaching, too. I think I probably enjoyed it more when I was older than I would have done if I'd gone in straight away after the war, because for one thing by that time I'd more variety of experience to draw on. I had a lot of background knowledge of things which came in useful in teaching, which I wouldn't have had if I'd gone straight in, and that was a distinct advantage. What I learnt as a journalist, the history of Edinburgh or people I'd met, provided interest for teaching. If when you become a teacher you've done something else first it's a very good thing, because otherwise if you'd simply school, university, college, and back to school again, it's a very limited outlook and limited experience. So I had roughly 15 years with the *Evening News* and 15 years in teaching.

If I had my time over again I honestly don't know if I'd go into journalism or into teaching. I wouldn't like to do either under present circumstances. I don't think very much of the standard of modern journalism. Even *The Scotsman* is a pretty poor effort sometimes. And as for the tabloid press, I think it's an absolute disgrace. So I don't think I'd necessarily want to be a journalist now. Teaching is also getting more and more difficult. From what I hear of friends who are still teaching, they're only longing for the day when they'll be out. So I don't know which of the two I'd want, if either, now. What I'd do in place of either, I've just no idea. But I enjoyed both journalism and teaching when I was doing them, and that's all I can say.

Gordon Dean

How I became set on becoming a journalist was through a neighbour, Jim Henderson, who was a reporter at the *Daily Record* branch office in Edinburgh.[1] I had spent a year at Nelson's College in Charlotte Square studying shorthand and typing, bookkeeping and English, and looking for a job, when Jim mentioned that one might be coming up in his office and that he would let me know. So I went for an interview with the chief reporter, Tom Nicholson, who said he would be back in touch with me. The next week I met Jim Henderson and he asked if I had heard anything. When I said, 'No,' he said, 'Well, you're starting on Monday.' Apparently Mr Nicholson had forgotten to write me!

I was born in Edinburgh on the 21st of August 1932, and my formative years were spent mostly in the Carrick Knowe, Corstorphine area. My father was born in Elgin about 1900 and was a railwayman all his life, with 51 years of service on the LNER [London & North Eastern Railway] and later British Railways. He came to Edinburgh to find work and started as a ticket boy at Leith station at the beginning of the First World War, became a shunter, then a guard, a foreman and latterly an inspector. During the Second World War he was the guard on trains taking supplies down to England, and recalled how German planes would try to spot a train by following the railway lines which could be seen in the moonlight. Although these goods trains were completely blacked out, the fire box, into which coal had to be shovelled to keep up the steam pressure, could be a dead giveaway. My father died in the early 1970s.

My mother on leaving school became a machinist. She made pram hoods and pram linings for a well-known firm, Scott Brothers, pram makers, who had a display shop in Cockburn Street in Edinburgh. When she got married she ceased to work: my father, who always worked shifts, held that when you married you didn't marry to send your wife out to work – a change from nowadays when mothers have children and then go back to work as soon as possible.

I remember my grandparents on my mother's side. Grandfather worked in the whisky industry, and after several moves ended up at the Distillers Company Ltd in South Queensferry. I vaguely remember him. He died about 1935 or 1936. My grandmother also followed the tradition then of staying at home and looking after the family. She had four sons and three daughters. Two of the sons died in the First World War while serving with the Royal Scots at Gallipoli and in France. She herself died during the Second World War.

In my early years my parents and I lived in Leith, and I started school at Leith Walk Primary, just off Leith Walk and opposite McDonald Road public library. But I was only a couple of years there when, during the early years of the 1939–45 War, we moved from Leith to live at Carrick Knowe, and I transferred to Corstorphine School. Lots of us pupils walked to school from Carrick Knowe, went home at lunchtime and back again, though some boys and girls ate school dinners – usually a plate of soup, half a roll and an apple, all for 1½d [less than 1p]! We didn't get much in the way of PT as the gymnasium was taken over by the ARP (Air Raid Precautions) and was full of blankets, stretchers, stirrup pumps, helmets, and other wartime gear. One of the outstations of the school was across the road in St Margaret's Park, where we spent every Wednesday having classes in the Dower House, now the headquarters of the Corstorphine Trust. It was a very happy school, a great environment, and I liked doing sums, mental arithmetic, and art – painting.

My hopes had always been set on going on to Boroughmuir Senior Secondary in the city centre at Viewforth, but it was not to be. In the Qualifying exam if you got an A you went from Corstorphine School to Boroughmuir, if a B or a C you went to Saughton Junior Secondary, later renamed Carrickvale, in Stenhouse. I got a B!

At the Junior Secondary, boys had the choice of either technical or commercial subjects and usually very few chose commercial, which concentrated on shorthand and typing. These classes were mainly full of girls and it was thought 'cissy' for boys to take commercial. Anyway, I took technical, where we had woodwork, metalwork, technical drawing and mechanics, as well as maths and English. I enjoyed mechanics, geometry and technical drawing, but I was hopeless at algebra. However, I got my Lower Leaving Certificate and was ready to face the wide world. I really wanted an office job. And I had this feeling that Jim Henderson, who lived next door to us at Carrick Knowe, had a good job as a newspaper reporter, and then seeing films like *Call Northside 777*, I was impressed.[2] My father was a great *Daily Record* reader, and I think most working people were, because the *Record* was a working man's paper. My dad always bought the *Daily Record*, though he wouldnae buy it now. All that was why I decided on taking a full-time commercial course at Nelson's College in Charlotte Square. Then, however, my form teacher pointed out I was too young to leave school: as I was still only 14, I would have to stay on until Christmas. But when I told him I had already enrolled for Nelson's College to begin studying shorthand, typing, bookkeeping and English there after the summer, I was allowed to leave school because I was continuing my education full-time.

I had an extra-long summer holiday that year because Nelson's College started later than the schools. And after I'd been to the Boys' Brigade camp at West Kilbride, I worked for the remainder of the holiday in a one-man butcher shop in St John's Road, Corstorphine. That wasn't the first paid job I'd had: as a pupil at Saughton I'd delivered papers morning and evening for a shop next to St Margaret's Park. I was up at six o'clock and had to deliver all over the place. It was a terrible run, covering all of Carrick Knowe and a bit beyond. So the day I left school I was glad to give up the newspapers. My final wages were four shillings [20p] each per week for the morning and evening rounds.

I enjoyed working in the butcher shop, where I'd seen a notice in the window for a message boy and I'd started immediately. The pay was 25 shillings [£1.25] a week, plus tips and wee extras which helped out at home during meat rationing. Those were the days when as a 14-year-old I was able to cycle the message bike, loaded with butcher meat, up Clermiston Hill until I reached the junction with Hillview Road. Then I just had to get off and push. I used to cycle home on the bike in my butcher's overall for my dinner, and my pals and our neighbours thought I was going to become a butcher. But I had other ideas!

The man who ran the shop for the owner, Miss Rankin, liked the whisky, and there was always a tumblerful kept hidden in the back shop. He would disappear now and again for a mouthful. When he reappeared he would breathe into my face and ask, 'Tell me, son, can you smell anything?' Ugh ! Sometimes during that summer's heat wave he never managed to come back to the shop in the afternoon, probably because of the drink, and I was left to run the shop and tidy up at the end of the day. Miss Rankin came in every afternoon to 'cash up', and finding me in charge would say, 'Old Dick has let me down again.' I think she knew he was drinking, but I always made sure the tumbler remained hidden in case she rummaged around. I liked old Dick and didn't want to see him lose his job. Miss Rankin once said to me, 'I've been checking the till and the meat coupons, and everything's in order. You are a very honest boy.' I told her I wouldn't dare be anything else, and that was the way I had been brought up. When I told her I would be going full-time to

Nelson's College, she asked me to change my mind, go to night school, take a City and Guild course and become a butcher, and she would sell me the shop after I returned from National Service in a few years' time. But I turned her down, much to her disappointment.

I started at Nelson's College in September. In typing we had these big manual machines with a tin shield over the keyboard. It was good fun typing to music like 'Run, Rabbit'. Every day we had two hours' shorthand in the morning, and an hour of English; in the afternoon an hour of typing and two hours of bookkeeping. And we got shorthand homework every night. By December we were doing about 60 words a minute in short-hand; and by the time we left in April most of us were doing about 100. Some people who had a particular aptitude were maybe doing about 150.

My parents had paid the fees at Nelson's, £4.50 roughly a term, it was very small really. The Nelson family ran the College. There was an old man Nelson, he was past it, but his two sons carried it on. One was Tom Nelson, we used to call him Mr Tom. He taught us shorthand, his shorthand was tremendous, and bookkeeping. A girl taught us English, another girl typing. Mr Tom's brother ran the general office, and there were a few teachers. The College, which had about 150 or 200 students, had a very good reputation. There were girls there from Dunbar, Port Seton, Falkirk. It was all girls and boys aged about 15, 16, very few older students. But there was an older one who'd worked on marine harvester whaling ships and had a very severe injury. He'd got caught wi' a steel hawser and that was him confined to land. I don't know if he'd lost a leg but he walked with a stick and a limp. We also had half a dozen Polish ex-soldiers who weren't going back to Poland. They'd been demobbed, lived in Edinburgh, and I believe they got their fees paid. They all lived round about the New Town and they were clever. They used to supple-ment their money by makin' things: they'd get a couple of big buttons off an overcoat, solder them together and make a cigarette lighter. Oh, they were clever, nice chaps.

Jim Henderson, our next-door neighbour at Carrick Knowe, had been in the Fleet Air Arm during the war, had come out, and was a reporter with the *Daily Record*. But, as I've said, Jim told me he'd let me know if there was an opening for me in the Edinburgh office of the paper. So about a week later he came to our door and said, 'Would you like to go into the office next week, Monday morning, ten o'clock? There's a man would like to see you – Tom Nicholson, the chief reporter. The office boy has been called up, he's leaving to do his National Service and we're needing an office boy.' So I went to the *Record* office in Bank Street, at the top of the Mound, to see Tommy Nicholson. He was a very nice chap and a journalist of exceptional talent. I mean, the guy could write football on a Saturday afternoon, do a big disaster story on Sunday, cover the Empire or King's Theatre on Monday. You don't get them like that now really. Well, he offered me the job and said he'd get in touch with me. And, typical journalist, he never did! Jim Henderson said to me on the Friday, 'Have you heard from Tommy Nicholson?' 'I haven't heard a thing,' I said. 'Well, you're starting on Monday.' So when Jim went in on Friday afternoon he said to Tommy Nicholson, 'I was speaking to Gordon Dean.' 'Oh, yes,' said Tommy Nicholson, 'we're looking forward to having Gordon on Monday.' 'Well,' said Jim, 'you haven't told him.' 'Oh, hell's bells,' Tommy Nicholson said, 'I forgot to write.' So I was told: 'In on Monday morning.'

So I began as the office boy at the *Daily Record* in Bank Street, a smashin' wee place, on, I think it was, the 5th of May 1948, three months before I became 16. And then George Hodge, the office boy, having shown me the ropes and who was going away to do his National Service, didn't go. George had actually volunteered for the Scots Guards. But he had a medical problem. Anyway, he didn't go. Tommy Nicholson called me in and said, 'You might be wondering what's happening, Gordon, because you've heard George has been turned down for National Service. Well,' he said, 'George is going to be our junior reporter, and you'll just carry on as office boy. So there's no question of you . . .' I said, 'That's very nice.' George, another exceptional Edinburgh journalist, was a great character and also a man of great talent, and I got on well with him. I got on well with everybody in the *Record* office.[3]

At that time the reporters there were Tommy Nicholson as chief reporter, Hammy Neil, Marshall Pugh, Jim Henderson, Ian Smart, and George Hodge as junior. Ross Hall was the sports man. Harold Turner was the *Sunday Mail* man, he didn't work for the *Daily Record* or the Glasgow *Evening News*, just the *Sunday Mail*. Later on other reporters came in, like Hugh Young, Willie Raitt, Dougie Coupar, John Lister, Euan Robertson. Then not long after I began, the office moved from Bank Street to Frederick Street, between Princes Street and George Street.[4]

The work I did as office boy included going to collect copy. The only wee reporting jobs I did was the odd football match, like Edinburgh City and Leith Athletic, and the speedway at Meadowbank on a Saturday night. But as far as news stories was concerned it wasn't till I came back from National Service at the end of 1952 that I started doing the Burgh Court and little odd meetings.

Another job I had to do while office boy was on a Saturday afternoon phoning Tom Nicholson's reports to the Glasgow *Evening News* from

Tynecastle for Heart of Midlothian home games, and at Easter Road for the Hibernians'. That meant I had more or less to give up playing football myself on Saturday afternoons. Then even in the summer you had to go in to cover athletic meetings. There were the Edinburgh City Police sports at Meadowbank, and Edinburgh Corporation Parks Department had great sports events every year.

I'd had a very happy, satisfying boyhood at Carrick Knowe. I was never in the Scouts because most of the guys wanted to be in the Boys' Brigade. The Boys' Brigade had football teams, the Scouts didn't. There was a league, an organised Boys' Brigade football league. So I was in the Boys' Brigade, the 13th Company, attached to the parish church. I was a very keen footballer and played right half every Saturday. We played all over the place. I always remember playin' at the Meadows in Edinburgh. At the start of the game there you went to the parkie's hut and asked for a set of goalposts. You got a set of goalposts but the bar was a tape – it hung, and if you pushed the posts a wee bit it lowered! After the game you put the two stanchions together, wrapped the tape round them, and took them back to the parkie. In my dreams I'd have loved to become a professional footballer, but I was never good enough. There were some other clubs, like Corstorphine Swifts, I played trials for and it looked promising. But when the season started I had to opt out because I had my duties on Saturday afternoons for the paper at Tynecastle and Easter Road.

Carrick Knowe was great when I was a boy. I was a member of the Sunday school, then I joined the Youth Fellowship. And there were great levels at Carrick Knowe: hardly anybody went to fee-paying schools. I can only think of one guy who went to Daniel Stewart's College, one who went to Melville College, and two who went to the Royal High School. Everybody else went to local schools or to Boroughmuir, Moray House, a couple to Leith Academy. I went, as I've said, to Saughton Junior Secondary, which later became Carrickvale Junior Secondary.

     *   *   *

Well, I worked for a couple of years with those lads in the *Daily Record* office, and then I went away on the 27th November 1950 to the RAF to do my National Service. I did my square-bashing at Melksham, Wiltshire. The following year, about April, I flew to Hong Kong and was there for 18 months. I was allocated into the admin headquarters as a clerk and I had to do all these mundane clerical things. But I always kept my shorthand – just practised away on my own. One day somebody wanted something typed, one of the guys who usually typed, with two fingers, was busy so I took it over and rattled the thing off. The Flight Sergeant said, 'Where did you learn to type?' Two or three days later he came to me and said, 'You're a good typist. I've been speaking to the Group Captain. You don't do shorthand do you?' I says, 'Yes.' 'Oh, come with me,' he says. So I followed him into the Group Captain's office just along the corridor. 'Oh, Dean,' the Group Captain said, 'I understand you do shorthand and typing. Tell me about it.' So I told him, and he said, 'Well, I've got a bit of a problem. I'm without a secretary for three months. Do you think you could fill in?' So I moved into the adjutant's room next door to the Group Captain and started doing all his letters, quite a lot top secret. After the three months his secretary came back and I went back to clerical duties. But next day the adjutant said to me, 'We're needing a secretary up at the Flying Wing.' So I went up to the other end of the camp and worked for 80 Squadron and station flight in a small reconnaissance section. It kept my hand in with both typing and shorthand.

During my time there a thing came up about holidays in Japan. Ships came from Bombay to Hong Kong to Japan and there were few passengers. It was decided to let 12 servicemen at a time go on holiday to Japan. So I went on a three-week holiday to Japan. Japan was marvellous. We went first to a wee harbour called Moji, then round to Yokohama near Tokyo, which is like Leith to Edinburgh, then on to Kobe. My impression of Japan was it was becoming very Americanised. We didn't have contact at all really with Japanese civilians, except going into shops or the post office. We ate in restaurants. We slept on the boat. But for the brief time we were ashore we went to these American PX clubs. They were fantastic, they had everything.[5]

I had a great time in the RAF. I played hooker at rugby for the station, and for RAF Hong Kong. There was a pentagonal tournament – the RAF, the navy, the army, the Hong Kong club and the Hong Kong police, and we played each other twice. We also played teams from visiting ships that came in. I also played seven-a-side football for 80 Squadron; and though I could hardly swim I had two or three games of water polo – in goals; and I took up hockey as well. I'd gone to piano lessons when I was young and could play the piano and the organ, so I played the piano in the camp Methodist Church, and once I played the organ in the English church there. The commanding officer came in with his wife and some of the officers, and I'm sittin' there playing the organ. He couldnae believe it. Then at the end of the service I nipped along to the Methodist Church and I'm sittin' there at the piano when in walks the CO and his wife and the same officers; again he couldnae believe it!

There was no RAF station newspaper there so I didn't get a chance to work on anything like that. But I didn't feel I'd marked time as a reporter while doing my National Service. I was asked if I wanted to stay on in Hong Kong for another year. I said, 'No, no. I'd like to get back to my job at home.' If I'd stayed on I wouldn't have been taken back by the *Daily Record*. So I flew back home from Hong Kong on a Friday and started back in the *Record* on the Monday.

And that was me back in November 1952 as a junior reporter. I came into the office about nine o'clock and Tommy Nicholson said to me, 'Gordon, just you go up and have a look at the Burgh Court.' So then I started doing the Burgh Court, and that's where I met reporters like Bill Rae. And, as I've said, I started doing little odd meetings, because the more senior reporters in the office were all doing the main stuff. I just maybe did the odd Sheriff Court and that. I remember going to one AGM. I came back from it and Tommy Nicholson said, 'Well, is there a story?' And I says, 'No. Nobody turned up.' He said, 'Well, that's a story.' And we did a story. As I've said, I found Tommy Nicholson great as a chief reporter, very helpful and very encouraging, a very talented man, who had a presence. He could grace any occasion. You never heard a bad word about Tommy. The reporters like him and John Lister and all the others would turn in their graves about what's appearin' in the *Record* now. People are no longer interested in what a guy's doin', they're more interested in who he's sleeping with and sleaze – terrible. And they were good reporters then, too, in the *Daily Express* and the Edinburgh *Evening News*, like Logan Robertson and Donald Esson of the *News*. Your old *Evening News* was a paper of record of what was going on in Edinburgh, whereas now it's about somebody whose wee laddie's been kept in a hospital waitin' room for four hours because he's skint his knee. It's absolute rubbish. When I was a young reporter you had to do the calls – go up to the Royal Infirmary and check for accidents, go down to the meetings of the Leith Chamber of Commerce and the Leith Dock Commission, and you built up a rapport with all the various people. Now there's nothing like that. So I felt I definitely had a good training on the *Record* and Glasgow *Evening News*. There was no need when I came back from National Service for me to attend shorthand classes. I was probably doing about 140 words a minute, and that was it.

The first major story I was involved in was oddly enough after I met this girl at the dancin'. We started going out, and one night we went to the Palace cinema, in Princes Street and just along from the General Post Office. After the cinema, we crossed the road to get the bus – the girl, a wee smasher, lived in Stockbridge and I was seeing her home. The bus was just driving off when this postman ran up the stairs. One of his mates was on the bus and he says to him, 'Oh, hello, Willie. You've just made it.' 'Aye,' I heard Willie say, 'they've just blown up the pillar box.' His mate says, 'Whereabouts?' 'The one up at . . .' wherever it was in Edinburgh. 'The EIIR – it's been shattered.' His mate says, 'When did that happen?' 'Five minutes ago.' So this bus was going along Princes Street and then up Frederick Street, where the *Record* office was. This girl and I were talking about the postman's story, and she said, 'Oh, that's a great story.' I said to her, 'Look, if you'll excuse me I'm goin' to have to jump off the bus. I'll see you tomorrow.' She says, 'OK.' She wasn't offended. So as the bus got up Frederick Street and slowed down at the junction with George Street, I jumped off and into the *Record* office. I said to the reporters on duty, 'Lads, an EIIR pillar box has been blown up.' And they said, 'How do you know that?' I said, 'I've just heard it on the bus.' So they said to me, 'Would you mind watching the office till we get back?' They ran downstairs to get a photographer, then raced up and got a picture of the pillar box, came back and started sending the story over to Glasgow on the teleprinter. The next morning the *Daily Record* had the best story. When Tommy Nicholson came in he said to me, 'I hear it was you, Gordonio' – he used to call me that. 'Great stuff.' That was what I liked to hear. I didn't write the story but I'd made a contribution. It was just a bit of luck. Some guys might have said, 'Och, I'm seein' my girlfriend home,' and not bothered.[6]

Well, I remained with the *Daily Record* and Glasgow *Evening News* until 1957. I remember being up in the Court of Session when the lad from the *Evening Times* or *Evening Citizen* said to me, 'Have you sent your copy yet to the *Evening News* ?' 'No,' I said, 'I'm about to send it.' 'Well,' he said, 'I wouldnae waste my time. Your paper's closing today.' I said, 'What?!' But I carried on and sent the story over. Later the news came that the Glasgow *News* was closing. It wasn't being taken over by anybody, it was just closing: there were too many evening papers in Glasgow. But what I was told at the time was that the Glasgow *News* circulation had made tremendous progress in the previous six months. It shouldn't have been the paper to go, they reckon that should have been the *Citizen*. But anyway it went. Tommy Nicholson didn't know what was happening. We just got a letter in the post from Glasgow. It just said, 'We regret that due to the closure of the Glasgow *Evening News* your services are no longer required.' There was five of us reporters in the Edinburgh office, including Willie Raitt, Jack Brown, and myself, discovered we'd been employed by the Glasgow *Evening News*, not the *Daily Record*.[7] And by the end of that week I was out of a job. They paid me my week's wages and something like a further month's wages, and that was me out. By then I'd worked for two years as office boy and five years, first as junior reporter then more or less a junior–senior.

Well, Willie Raitt, much older than the rest of us, and Jack Brown, for instance, were both married. I was engaged then and soon to be married. Actually, Jack didn't get his letter from Glasgow, because he'd moved house and thought he was all right. But on Monday morning when he came into the office somebody had readdressed his letter, and he got it then. He didn't get another job for a long time afterwards. I was out of a job for about four weeks. I remember one job I tried for was as a salesman for car batteries. At the very end of the interview, the chap said to me: 'What would happen if you'd been working for us for a short period and a job came up in newspapers and you're offered it?' I said, 'Oh, I'd take it!' That was me scuppered! I also applied for a job in *The Scotsman* and got an interview. I had a cuttings book with me and I showed them my stories. The old guy who interviewed me said, 'I'd like you to take a shorthand and a typing test.' It was ridiculous. But I took a test just to satisfy him, but I never got the job. Anyway I looked in some magazine, there was a job going in Burnley, another in Sheffield, and another in North Shields. So I opted for the one in North Shields – the nearest of the three to Edinburgh, got the job, and went down there to work on the *North Shields News*, an evening paper.[8]

The paper didn't have a big circulation, something like 27,000. But I quite enjoyed it. I got digs and used to come up the A68 to Edinburgh every second weekend and leave the house on my return at six o'clock on a Monday morning when the roads were as quiet as anything. I had a wee 1939 Standard Eight. I worked at the *North Shields News* for three months then I got a telegram one day: 'Phone Tom Nicholson'. When I phoned Tom said, 'George Hodge is leaving the *Record* to take up a position with the *Daily Herald*. Would you like to come back here, or are you happy where you are?' I said, 'I'll come back.' So I gave in my notice and returned to the *Record* in Edinburgh.

But I was there only about three years. Tommy Nicholson, brilliant journalist, wasn't the Glasgow favourite, he was too intelligent by far. Nicholson got the elbow, definitely. He went on to do sport, and Jimmy Allison became the news editor in Edinburgh. Jimmy Allison had worked on the Glasgow *News*, and used to come through to Edinburgh on Saturdays and take charge of the *Sunday Mail* shift. Jimmy was well in. It was all a palsy-walsy act. So Jimmy Allison took over in the Edinburgh office and he wasn't in the same class as Tommy Nicholson. He was a bit of a hard guy to work with. He was awkward, he wasn't a nice fellow. I think he had stomach trouble. He died about the early 1990s. But anyway a lot of people, like Norrie Bryce and wee George Hunter, left the *Record* in Edinburgh. So did I. In all, seven reporters left.[9]

I went to the Edinburgh *Evening Dispatch* in 1960. Max McAuslane, who'd been with the *Record* in Glasgow for years, was by this time at the *Dispatch* and had a job going. 'How much a week?' I asked him. He says, 'What are you gettin' at the *Record*?' I said, '£18.' He says, 'I'll give you £18 10s [£18.50].' So I got a ten shillings rise. But the attraction for me was I was going to an evening paper. At the *Daily Record*, as it had turned out, when there was no longer a Glasgow *Evening News*, you got only one early shift a week. You had one reporter on at 10 in the morning, and the rest were all on from 1pm, 2pm, 3pm, and night shift. It was all night shifts and back shifts. It was dreadful. You couldn't do a thing in your time off. Then if you took your turn at doing a *Sunday Mail* shift on a Saturday, that was your Saturday scuppered.

It was good working at the *Evening Dispatch*. Then one day I was walkin' down the road and met George Millar, who'd moved from the *Dispatch* to the *News*. 'Dick Campbell's looking for you,' he said. 'There's a job at the *News*.' Dick Campbell was the chief reporter of the Edinburgh *Evening News*. I'd always wanted to go to the *News*. They were a great crowd there, Logan Robertson, Bill Rae, George Millar, Bruce Cannon, Hamish Coghill, a super crowd.[10] So I saw Dick Campbell and he said, 'The editor wants to see you.' So I went up to see Barnetson, the editor, and the interview went just as a formality. Barnetson said to me, 'Walk in here, Mr Dean, and you walk into the Bank of England – a safe job.' And, oh, it was a great, a super atmosphere in the *News*. With guys who'd come from Hamilton, Derby, Carlisle, there wasn't the same camaraderie at the *Dispatch* as at the *News*. The *News* was all Edinburgh guys – the Royal High, Portobello, Boroughmuir, we were all the same. And you knew what Edinburgh readers wanted. And of course the whole essence there was competition. We were tryin' to beat the *Dispatch*. Nowadays, with the *Dispatch* long gone, the *Evening News* doesn't have to try to do anything: 'If the story doesn't go in today we'll use it tomorrow.' Oh, there was definitely a strong sense of competition then between the *News* and the *Dispatch*. The *Evening News* were always tryin' to pull one over the *Dispatch* and get things from the High Court and the City Chambers in an edition.

But about two and a half years after I got the job there, the very same Barnetson, editor of the *News*, was telling me, 'Bye-bye.' The *Evening News* had been taken over by Thomson Newspapers, i.e., the *Dispatch* and *The Scotsman*. We were all up in the Court of Session when the blow came. George Millar, who'd been up at the Castle at some military press conference, came back about lunchtime and said to Lewis Simpson, the assistant deputy editor, 'What the bloody hell's goin' on, Lewis? Everybody's talkin' about the *News*.' And it transpired that that afternoon in November 1963, we'd been taken over. We carried on work while talks went on for the rest of the week. The *Dispatch* ceased publication. They hung around, doin' nothin'. Durin' that week they were tryin' to list who would stay and who would go. They had lists of the two staffs, and the decision was on the basis of last in, first out. I was just under where the line was drawn. We didn't hear about this for some days. There was to be a meeting in the *Dispatch* office where they would reveal the names of those who were going and those who were staying. We were sitting at the meeting waiting, when Dunnett, *The Scotsman* editor, came in with Max McAuslane and said, 'I'm sorry lads. We'll have to scrap this meeting. President Kennedy's been shot.' You know how people ask, 'What were you doing on the day President Kennedy was shot?' Well, I always know where I was that day, 22 November 1963. So we didn't know about our jobs until the following day. We went into work at the *News* on the Saturday – the afternoon was mostly sport, and we were told: 'If you're staying the editor will call you in and have a chat with you. If you don't get called, you've had it.' So we're hanging around. No one wanted to leave the office to go out on a reporting job. You were waiting on the editor saying, 'Right, Gordon, come in.' But there was no 'Come in.' Well, on Saturday night I had some copies of the Pink *News*, sports edition, in my car and on the front it had, 'The New Team of Sports Writers for the *Evening News*'. One of them was Jimmy Wardhaugh, the ex-Heart of Midlothian player. So I turned the corner into Lampacre Road and I saw Jimmy himself gettin' out of his car. 'Hello,' I said, 'you're a lucky one. You're staying.' 'Oh,' he says, 'I'm not so sure about that. I was hanging around the office all day and I wasn't called in.' And I said, 'Well, I was hanging around, too, and I wasn't called in either. So I reckon I've had it. But here you are, Jimmy,' and I handed him a copy of the Pink *News*. 'Oh,' he said, 'that's great. But I'm sorry about you, Gordon.' Monday morning Jimmy was called in by the editor: 'I'm sorry. There was a mistake in the paper on Saturday night.' Jimmy Wardhaugh was out, too. But imagine putting his picture in the paper – 'Our New Sports Team'.[11]

So nobody saw me at all. Well, eventually we got a letter saying, 'Your services are no longer required.' And the weekend I got the letter my wife discovered that she was expectin' our second child. Well, I got some money. The *Evening News* had a pension scheme, and what they called a Provincial scheme, where you could put into it what you liked up to a certain limit. I used to put away 12 shillings [60p] a week and they put eight shillings [40p]. If you left it in for over 20 years you got all the interest. But if you left the firm before 10 years or whatever it was, you only got your 12 bob back plus the interest. But, oh, it was a great scheme, a goldmine, if you left it in and you'd been there for over 20 years. Guys like Dick Campbell, Logan Robertson and Lewis Simpson, they'd been in it since they were laddies. So on top of their pension they were goin' tae get this Provincial. At the end of your working career it gave you a big lump sum.

Well, four of us, Bill Rae, Gordon Smith, George Millar and myself, decided hurriedly to start a freelance news service called United News Service. We got an ex-bookie's office in the West End at Prince Albert Buildings. One of the first contracts we got was to handle all the BBC radio work in Edinburgh. They didnae pay us very well, I must admit. They were getting four guys for the price of one, seven days a week. They should have paid us more. Then David Scrimgeour of the *Daily Telegraph* got us some work and that helped us.[12] We worked for a lot of people. But after a couple of years I gave it up because the United News Service just wasn't making money I wanted, and I heard there was a job going in Edinburgh in the *Daily Express.*

So I went then to the *Daily Express.* They'd moved from Bank Street to opposite St Giles' Cathedral in the High Street, and from there to Jeffrey Street. I joined them in Jeffrey Street. Gilbert Cole, another excellent chap, was the chief reporter, and they had guys there like Hugh Welsh, George Crockett, John Vass, and photographers like Stan Hunter and Peter McVean. Bill Harrold was the *Sunday Express* man.[13] Oh, that was a good office. I was there for about six years. But there were so many disputes. There was the journalists now and again, then the machine room were havin' this dispute. I remember one time Gilbert Cole put the phone down and said, 'Right, lads, stop workin'. We're in dispute.' He said to me, 'Do you know, Gordon, they'll never be satisfied in Glasgow till they close the *Daily Express.*' I said, 'Nonsense – with a circulation of 650,000 copies?' Well, things got bad. There was an awful lot of disputes. Beaverbrook Newspapers just got fed up with it and they said, 'Right', and ceased publication of the *Scottish Daily Express* in Glasgow. Now I had had a sense this was goin' tae happen. They were looking for redundancies and I volunteered. The *Express* in Glasgow said, 'No, we don't want you to go. We're coming through to Edinburgh tomorrow and we're goin' tae meet some people who've asked for redundancy.' So I went to the North British Hotel in Princes Street about two o'clock and was summoned into this room where there was one or two bigwigs. They said, 'Gordon, what's the reason for this?' 'Well,' I said, 'there's so much uncertainty.' They said, 'Oh, well, we want you to hang on.' 'Well, gentlemen,' I said, 'you might have invited me to lunch.' The table was all finished, you know, the crumbs and that. I said, 'Supposin' I was to change my mind and stay, what would I be doing?' The guy said, 'You'll be coming to Glasgow to work.' I remember I said, 'Gentlemen, look out that window. There's the most beautiful street in the world and I walk it every night on the way home. I don't want to come to Glasgow.' But they said, 'Go home and talk it over with your wife, and let us know tomorrow morning.' Meantime I got a message from the National Union of Journalists saying, 'You're OK. If you want to go, they asked for it and they got the names.' So next day I phoned Glasgow and said, 'No, I'm no' comin' to Glasgow.' Because I knew what they could do – muck me around all night: a six o'clock finish then, 'Oh, away up to Lochgilphead. There's been a break-in at a bank,' then gettin' home on the last train at the back o' nine o'clock. So I left the *Express*. In the meantime, there was a job going on *The Scotsman*, I went for it and they offered me the job. I had to drop money, from £3,100 on the *Express* to £2,800 on *The Scotsman*. But I got a year's salary in my hand when I left the *Express*.

I was 19 years on *The Scotsman*, from 1972 to 1991. I stayed far too long. I always say the difference between the *Daily Express* and *The Scotsman* was the *Express* was a paper about people doin' things. *The Scotsman*'s a paper about folk talkin': 'Go to this meetin' – 'Gavin Strang, Michael Forsyth, Lord Macfarlane . . .', and others.[14] You know, they're not *doing* anything. With the *Express* you got out more: 'Right, there's two rowing boats missing off Eyemouth. Get down there.' Or 'A canoe's missin' on the River Tweed.' And we're away down to the River Tweed and we're up to here in mud. Oh, the messes Stan Hunter, the *Express* photographer, and I got into! But you were *doing* something. Whereas *The Scotsman* . . .

I did a lot of court work and was the sort of No. 2 when George Saunders, *The Scotsman* court reporter, was off or needed help.[15] I must admit I liked doing the High Court and the civil court. I did a lot of local authority work, well, Lothian Region came in in 1974, and there was that year's build-up to the changes in local government. Then I did a lot of chasin' ambulances and general news. And I did the General Assembly of the Church of Scotland nearly every year. But, as I say, it was all about people talkin'. If you hadn't shorthand you were no use as a reporter in *The Scotsman*. You could get by on the *Express* quite often. But being on shifts on *The Scotsman* I was always at the beck and call of everything Most of the time it was just a bit boring. So I didn't find the work on *The Scotsman* as satisfying as I had work on the *Express* or, in my earlier days, on the *Daily Record*.

Speaking of shorthand, oh, in my career I found a number of reporters who didn't have shorthand, and many who had brilliant shorthand. The finest shorthand writer I ever came across was Ian Smart, who joined the *Daily Record* not long after I started there in 1948 as office boy, then he went to the *Daily Express*. Ian used a fountain pen. He'd just flick over a page and he left it, not rubbing up against the other one, so that it would dry. Ian was a brilliant shorthand writer. So was Bill Rae, and George Millar and Arthur Goodey. Of course, having good shorthand doesn't in itself necessarily make a good reporter. And, mind you, some reporters found difficulty reading their shorthand back. But you also have to have news sense. There's a lot of things go into making a good reporter. You've got to be diplomatic. I'm not being snobbish, but if you knock at somebody's door in, say, Inverleith Terrace in Edinburgh, your attitude's got to be different to somebody you approach up in Craigmillar. I used to shudder at knockin' at the door of somebody killed in a road accident earlier, when you're there to get background and some pictures. Latterly what you learned to do was to go to a neighbour and say, 'Do you know Mrs So-and-so?' She says, 'No. But Mrs So-and-so across the road, she's very friendly with her.' So you went across to the friendly person and said, 'Look, we're from such-and-such a paper. We've heard about the tragic circumstances surrounding Mr So-and-so's death. We don't want to disturb the family if possible. Could you help us?' And she'd say, 'Oh, well, come in. They'd been married . . .', and so on. 'Now is there any likelihood we could get a picture of the dead man?' And quite often the friendly neighbour would go across and ask the widow. So she was doing the dirty work for you. On the other hand, I remember a case of a chap being killed at Monktonhall coal pit near Dalkeith. They were boring the shaft, and this chap was working at the bottom of the shaft when someone up above dropped a spanner. It fell hundreds of feet and, though the chap at the bottom of the shaft was wearing a protective helmet, he was killed. Dougie McCaskill, the *Daily Record* photographer, and I were sent up to St Mary Street in Edinburgh where this chap lived.[16] We knocked at the door and this old woman came to the door. 'We're dreadfully sorry,' we said. 'We're from the *Daily Record*. We came to find out . . . Is it possible?' The old lady said, 'Oh, come in, boys, come in,' and she took us into the kitchen. The young widow was sittin' there with a baby on her knee, and the old lady said to her, 'Maisie, I told you the men from the *Record* would be here.' And she reached up and handed me a packet of photographs, and she says, 'Is there anything you'd like to know?' We got the brief details and left. When we got downstairs Dougie McCaskill said, 'It's unbelievable that, Gordon. All she needed to do was tie a pink ribbon round the packet of photos.' The old lady was waitin' on us, you know. So sometimes the job was made easy by people. Other times they slammed the door in your face. And then of course if you didn't get a picture and the *Daily Express* did, there would be all hell to pay.

The competition was very fierce between the *Scottish Daily Mail*, the *Scottish Daily Express*, and the *Daily Record*. One time when I was working for, I think, *The Scotsman*, though it might have been the *Express*, there was an accident at Harthill, halfway between Edinburgh and Glasgow. A wee girl was knocked down by a delivery van and killed. I went up to her house and saw this car and this guy sittin' in it. There's two things in life I can smell: a detective and a journalist. I presumed he was a journalist and I walked up to the car. 'Hello, who are you from?' He looked at me and says, 'I'm from the *Daily Mail* in Glasgow.' I said, 'What's happened here?' He said, 'Why should I tell you?' 'Because,' I says, 'I'm bloody well asking you.' 'I'm not telling you anything,' he replied. 'Well,' I says, 'that's not the way we work in Edinburgh. We all help each other.' 'Oh?' he says, 'that's not the way we work in Glasgow.' So I jumped in my car and went away. Now my cousin Maisie was the district midwife in Harthill. I knocked at her door and said, 'I'm here about an accident,' and I told her what had happened. 'Oh, no,' she said. 'I delivered that wee girl.' So I told Maisie what I wanted, a picture and background. Maisie gave me all the background then asked me to run her up in my car to the wee girl's house. As we walked up the path this guy from the *Mail* got out his car and followed. 'Excuse me,' I says, 'where are you going?' He says, 'I'm going wi' you.' 'No, you're not,' I said. 'Piss off.' So Maisie knocks at the door, the door opened and she just said, 'Maisie Sneddon' and walked in. I got into the door, the husband was there but I didnae see the wife. Maisie explained, 'Look, I'm awfully sorry about this happening. This is my cousin. He works with *The Scotsman*. Could you give him a picture? And,' Maisie said, 'you don't have to answer the door to anybody else.' So the husband brought some photos and I just took one. I came out the door, walked down the path, and I'm getting in my car when this *Daily Mail* man says, 'What did ye get?' I says, 'Look, son, you do it the Glasgow way. I was willing to do it the Edinburgh way. But too bad for you my cousin is a district midwife.' If the guy had been nice and said, 'Look, we're not goin' tae get in tae the house,' I would have shared the picture. That was the difference between Edinburgh and Glasgow. There was a bit more cut-throat in Glasgow. In Edinburgh the attitude was, well, if he's late on a job – a fire or something like that – you fill him in with all that's happened, because next time it could be you who's late. It was just the general attitude.

Of course, if you went to a job, nobody else was there from another paper and you got clean away, you didn't phone up the others and say, 'This is Gordon Dean of the *Record* (or the *Express*). Who was doing the job for you?' You didn't do that. If you got away you had an exclusive. Sometimes you got people from other papers tryin' to put you off. I remember George Hodge went down to a fire and a policeman said to him, 'You can't go any further. You'll have to park your car there.' So George parked the car, walked along this road to turn the corner into where this inferno was. And Mo Philips of the *Daily Mail* is comin' along the road toward George. Mo says, 'Aw, forget it. There's nothing in it.' George thought, 'Aha.' He went along and of course there was plenty in it.[17]

Then I remember another time when there was a court case, something to do with Glasgow. The *Daily Express* snatched this couple and we couldn't get a picture for the *Daily Record*. The *Express* men sped away in their car, we followed them along Princes Street, but it was hopeless. So once we got to Corstorphine, and the *Express* were still haring on ahead of us, we just phoned the police and told them the car the *Express* men were in had been stolen, and gave a description and number. We drove along the Glasgow road to somewhere about Ingliston and found the police had stopped the *Express* car. All the folk were out on the road, and our photographer just took a picture! These are the things that happened then.

*   *   *

By the time I joined *The Scotsman* in 1972 the old journalists who'd been there for years, like George Philip, who'd covered the Court of Session and the High Court, Pip Stalker, who did the General Assembly of the Church of Scotland, and R.W. Munro, had all disappeared in the 1960s. I think the relationship between the management and the journalists wasn't too bad then, but *The Scotsman* were never great payers. The *Glasgow Herald* men got more in expenses than *The Scotsman*'s. Before I left the paper in 1991 a neighbour of mine, an anaesthetist, and I were talkin' about salaries and he says, 'What is your rate now?' I says, 'I'm on £20,000.' He says, 'Well, I'm on £36,000. If you'd kept up with me you should have been on £24,000.' People who replaced me when I retired, the reporters comin' in then, were not getting that rate: the girl who replaced me got £9,000. She was promised a rise of £500 in six months, but they delayed it. She told me she got it after 10 months. You know, some of the kids in *The Scotsman* and the *Evening News*, they'd be better off working in Marks & Spencer's.

On the *Express* there'd been a very good system where we used to work, say, Sunday to Thursday, then you were off Friday and Saturday. In *The Scotsman* there was a while when we used to work a four-day week from, say, Sunday to Wednesday, and be off the rest of the week. It was great, fantastic.

There were merit awards for people who did their work properly. I remember Malcolm Wilson left *The Scotsman* and went to the BBC. He phoned me up one night when I'd been with *The Scotsman* about 10 years, we were on night shift and we were havin' a wee blether. Malcolm said to me, 'How did you get on in the merit awards this year?' 'Malcolm,' I said, 'I have never had a merit reward in my life. It seems to be an old boys' network. Did you get . . .?' 'Oh, aye,' he says, 'I got a merit award: 12s 6d [62½p] a week.' It was just a case that the news editor and chief sub were told. No, they weren't great payers. But there was a spell in the late 1970s when there was a wee managing director, John Long, and he was pretty determined to close the gap in salaries between the *Glasgow Herald* and *The Scotsman*. We were beginnin' to go in the right direction, but then John Long left. And Ridley-Thomas took over power.[18] He was determined that the journalists were never goin' tae take over the role of the machine men, because they ruled the roost. When we journalists were on £18,000 and £20,000 a year the machine men were on £34,000 and £36,000. And of course management got rid of them, and they got wee lassies up from out of Stevenson or Napier College or University, doing a wee keyboard. They're the type of management who, say, make £6 million and the next year they'll say, 'We're goin' tae make £12 million,' which is ridiculous. So they make £9 million. And you go for a wage award and you say, 'You did quite well last year.' 'Oh, no, we lost £3 million last year.' You say, 'No, you made £9 million.' 'No, no. Our projected sum was £12 million and we only made £9 million. So things are tough.' My God, you could never win wi' them.

The union – the National Union of Journalists – was quite strong, well, it was up until 1987 when they had that dispute and stopped everything in its tracks.[19] After that, the management started to grind in. One of the best union leaders we ever had in *The Scotsman* was Colin Bell. Colin Bell was great and he led us in, I think, two disputes.[20] But the union was just crushed. Of course, there was Thatcherism, too. Before I left *The Scotsman* the union was just discussing things like should we have the canteen vending machines in the right places in the corridor, or how about a smoking room? They did not talk about wages or conditions. At one time they'd gone in and said, 'We want seven', and the management said, 'You'll get two.' Then after negotiation we ended up with four. There was a time in *The Scotsman* when everybody sent their kids to George

Watson's and Daniel Stewart's. That wasn't the case by the time I left the paper. The salaries were poor and got worse.

Well, in 1991 I was called in by the management as one of nine journalists over the age of 50 and we were all told, 'You are too old.' About two weeks later I got a letter from the management saying they agreed to my application for early retirement. I hadn't made an application! I was told, 'We want rid of you.' Magnus Linklater, the editor, was very good and never called me in for about another month. He offered me £16,000. Now the machine room men were getting £30,000-odd. So I held out and Magnus got me another £3,000. So I got £19,000 and a pension of £3,000. He said, 'Now all I want from you, Gordon, is a date. It doesn't have to be tomorrow.' 'Well,' I said, this is March. What about the end of May?', because my car was being paid off in May, and there were one or two other things. Magnus says, 'Fine. I'll just tell the managing director that's your date.' So I left on the 30th May 1991. I had a big do in the Helsinki Room at the Scandic Crown Hotel in the High Street. The local MPs were invited, people from the Church of Scotland, Roman Catholic Church, St Andrew's House, the National Trust for Scotland, Lothian Region and Edinburgh District Council, universities, football folk – all my contacts. To let *The Scotsman* subs come across, we ran it till 11 o'clock. 'Come and have a drink.' Folk thought I was mad. The bill was £800. But it was a great night. I just thought to myself, 'I'm goin' tae go out with a bang.' Frankly, I was glad to be turfed out, even if I'm not making as much money now – though in 1995, for instance, I made £10,000 freelancing. But I didn't want to be the oldest reporter in *The Scotsman*. I didn't want to end up like a constable after 40 years in the police force. I mean, it was my own fault. I had been offered once or twice, in 1977 for instance, the news desk job at night, but I didn't want to go on the news desk and just sit. I liked to be out and meet people. The night desk job might have progressed to the day desk, but I didn't know how long that might take. My kids were up, and I wanted to be able to say to my wife, 'Oh, let's go out and do something,' not to be saying, 'I'm on permanent nights.'

Well, looking back over my 43 or so years in journalism, to me the 1950s and 1960s were the fun times for journalists in Edinburgh. I think the fun has gone out of journalism now. I remember guys going around then with a long face because they'd a couple days off and, if anything, would come into the office: they loved their work. Nowadays they're dyin' to get away and stay out on any excuse. In some respects I think journalists were held then in higher esteem. But I've enjoyed my life as a journalist. There's no doubt about it, you meet people from different walks of life. I have never regretted having gone into journalism. I think what I do regret is staying too long in *The Scotsman*. I enjoyed court work to such an extent that I think, if I'd any intelligence at all and had the chance again, I'd like to have gone into law and been an advocate or a QC. But journalism is definitely changed. The fun days have gone, there's no doubt about it.

James Gunn Henderson

The only journalist in my family that I've ever come across was a great-uncle called James Gunn, who was a printer to trade and moved to Liverpool, where he took up missionary work as well. He published several very strong religious tracts. But my aunt's recollection is that he certainly became a reporter, a full-blown journalist, and worked on, I think, the *Liverpool Echo*. Otherwise there was absolutely no tradition of journalism in my family, and I remember my grandmother asking me when I got my Highers at school what I was going to do. She was extremely keen that I should become a minister, I think to bring in a touch of respectability to the family. But when I told her I was planning to become a journalist, I remember vividly her picking up the poker beside the fire, drawing a circle on the mantelpiece, and saying, 'That's how you'll turn out – a big round 0!'

I was born in Wick on July 10, 1931, at 30 Coach Road, my maternal grandmother's house. My mother wasn't married at the time. I was illegitimate, but was legitimised when four years later she fell pregnant for a second time by my father and they married. So I had the name James Gunn for the first four years of my life and James Henderson after that.

My father was a baker. He belonged to the Pulteneytown side of Wick, which is the fishertown. But not long after he married my mother, and the day after my sister Ella was born, he died of pneumonia at the age of 29, when I was four years old. I barely remember him, just a vague memory when I was being carried shoulder-high with new shoes on. So my mother had the awful experience of being in a nursing home then, after the birth of my sister, and seeing my father's funeral go past.

The Henderson side of the family were mainly fishers. The Gunn side of the family, my mother's side, were principally agricultural workers, carters, horse men, and so on. But both sides were all connected with the herring-fishing trade because Wick, at the turn of the nineteenth/twentieth century, was a huge fishing port. My paternal grandfather was a fisherman, and I know that my great-great-grandfather on the Henderson side was drowned off Stornoway as a fisherman. I remember grandfather Gunn, my mother's father – George Gunn. He was a carter to trade. His job was driving a horse and cart, taking barrels of fish from the harbour, and transporting cargoes all round the town. He died about 1935–6.

My mother was 21 when I was born. She belonged Wick and was in domestic service there. Well, she was wonderful after my father died, in that she carried on working once she was able to, to look after my sister Ella and me. She did cleaning work – she went out cleaning houses and stairs and things like that. She had a very hard life bringing up two kids. In her own family my mother was one of 14 – seven sisters and seven brothers. Her younger sister Joey was only 14 or 15 when I was born. So Joey had the job of babysitter and so on while my mother went out to work. Aunt Joey and I have a tremendous affinity even now. Then when I was about 10 my mother married again – to another baker, Alex Paterson. He came from Fortrose in the Black Isle. And he was a wonderful step-father. He had a daughter, Catherine, from his previous marriage. Then my mother and he subsequently had a son, my brother Alex. So there were four of us children in the family, and we grew up as a very happy family. That was to be repeated in my own life, strangely enough. I was to do almost exactly the same thing, take over a ready-made family, and it worked out very well for us as well.

My earliest years, until I was eight, were spent in my grandmother's house in Coach Road. When I was about eight, I was diagnosed with a spot on my lung and I spent an entire year in the Seaforth Sanatorium at Conon Bridge in Ross-shire. It was the reception point for children from all over the Highlands. There was some 50 of us from Shetlands, Barra, Uist, and so on, who were all looked after under this regimen of fresh air, good food, walks, exercise, and rest. That year is very, very vivid in my memory, because to begin with I came back to Wick with a strange accent. I was now talking Hieland, as they say in Wick. They regarded me there as a teuchter,[1] because Caithness is very much a flat country and it's never regarded as part of the Highlands really. When I came back to Wick with this strange, lilting Highland accent, that was on the very outbreak of war in September 1939, because the Seaforth Sanatorium was closed down and became a military hospital, just as it had in the First World War. They discharged all the children. By then I was well on the way to recovery, and in fact my tuberculosis never developed and I've had no problems ever since.

At the time I came back from the sanatorium my mother had already moved with my little sister Ella from my grandmother's house in Coach Road into a tiny little house at 6 Upper Dunbar Street in Wick. Now at

Coach Road before the war, and into the war as well, my granny ran a little shop in what would have been the parlour, I suppose – the downstairs left-hand-side room, where she sold sweets and groceries and all the rest. Granny Gunn was a great exponent of confectionery known as Gundy. It was a sugar-based rock type thing in a twist. It was a well-known confectionery, and granny made a good job of it in fact. And then at Coach Road downstairs on the right-hand side was the main sitting room, and through the back was the kitchen. Upstairs was the flush toilet, two big bedrooms and a little bedroom. So it was a fairly substantial, fair-sized house. Mind you, it must have been dreadfully crowded in the days when there were 14 of them in granny's family there, though of course they were all staged: my mother was one of the older ones. I can remember Tilley lamps, paraffin lamps and paraffin heaters there, so I don't think we got electricity until the war. We didn't have hot and cold water at Coach Road, or a bath: we had a big zinc bath in front of the fire, where you had to get privacy. Granny did the cooking, mainly on the big old kitchen range, with an oven to the right-hand side, and a wee hot-water tank with a tap at the other side – standard accessories. I don't recall any gas. There was quite a substantial garden, and they grew vegetables there and were quite self-sufficient from that point of view. Coach Road was a very good house to grow up in, a very comfortable, happy house.

On the other hand, 6 Upper Dunbar Street, where my mother moved to with my sister Ella from Coach Road while I was away in the sanatorium, was a very small, cramped house, substantially just one big room and a small one. The little bedroom my mother had herself. My sister slept with my mother. I had the bed in the main room. There was no garden. The lighting was electricity. I can't recall the toilet arrangement at all, but it wasn't a dry toilet: my first experience of that was later on in Benbecula. The cooking arrangement at Upper Dunbar Street wasn't a range as in Coach Road, it probably was a gas cooker.

Once my stepfather Alex Paterson appeared on the scene, that regularised our family life. He was foreman baker with a fairly substantial firm called Nicholson's, grocers, in High Street in Wick. As foreman baker one of the perks of his job was a flat above the shop. I remember moving over from Upper Dunbar Street when I was about 10 or 11, carrying a roll of linoleum or a carpet with my stepfather, to Alexandra Court, Nicholson's Buildings, on the High Street at the junction with Bridge Street. At Alexandra Court there was a flush toilet, but again it was a zinc bath in front of the fire. But I used to go to my uncle's house further up the High Street to have a bath on a Friday night. Uncle Bobby Gunn was the chauffeur to the local doctor and had a tied house, plus bathroom and all mod cons. So when I was 12 years old or so I was able to have a regular weekly bath there. The lighting at Alexandra Court was gas initially, I can remember the mantles. I once burst the gas pipe when I was putting a nail up for a kitchen cabinet or something, and I remember standing there with my finger on the hole while we sent away for somebody to come and turn off the gas. For cooking there was a gas cooker. The house at Alexandra Court became too small once our brother Alex came along – that put a strain on the bedroom space. So in my late teenage years I moved back into the little bedroom in my granny's house in Coach Road, and Aunt Joey and I had a very good kinship again. It's no mistake to say she pretty well mothered me in many ways over the years.

＊   ＊   ＊

I started school at five, at Pulteneytown Academy. I always enjoyed school. I can recall my teachers were quite pleased with me, and my mother used to tell me I got good reports. One of my most influential teachers was Bessie Leith, who took Primary Four. She ended up later as Provost of Wick, the first woman provost in Scotland. She was a very outstanding character, almost Maggie Thatcher-ish except that Bessie was a socialist, very much a Labour councillor. She was very influential in my life because she taught me that learning and education was the most important thing of your life, and that it was a continuing process: when you left school your education still continued day by day. She always imbued in all her children a love of books and reading. Her first election to the council was, I think, in 1945 immediately after the war. She went very quickly up through the ranks and became Provost. The first woman town clerk in Scotland was in Wick as well. So we had a local authority with a Provost and a town clerk, both ladies.[2]

My schooling at Pulteneytown Academy was broken, of course, when I went away to Seaforth Sanatorium in Dingwall when I was about eight. But there was an integral school at the Sanatorium, a composite class with one teacher, and we got an excellent education there. I can remember in my year at school there Hitler's Munich speech on the radio, when he was screaming out, several months before the war was declared. Even in the class we built up a picture of an ogre.

What happened in Wick during the war was that all the schools, except the High School, were evacuated and given over to the military. The churches were used as schools. I always boasted that I had the advantage of a church education, because you moved from vestry one in the parish church to vestry two in the Bridge Street church. Primary Three, I think, were in the Baptist church, Primary Four was in the right-hand vestry of the parish church, and the Qualifying class was in the High School. The headmaster had the job of travelling round all these churches. So from the age of eight upwards, I didn't attend an educational institution as such once the war started. So we'd a very broken education. But it was quite exciting because each class was on its own, or you would have a Primary Four along with a Primary Two. Then we really had a foretaste of secondary education when we were only 11 years old but moved into the Qualifying class which met in the High School.

Wick airport was the main RAF base for the fighters defending Scapa Flow naval base in Orkney, about 15 miles due north. So whenever there was a German air attack on Scapa Flow, the Wick RAF base was attacked. I remember a vivid Saturday afternoon in July 1940 when as children we were playing in Argyll Square in Wick. There was a most incredible explosion and a great sheet of flame and fire and black. These were two German bombs that had been dropped on Bank Row, just two streets down from us. Sixteen people were killed, including one of my own schoolmates, a girl called Amy Miller, who just the previous day had received a Bible for perfect attendance at school. About 23 to 25 other people were very seriously injured. That's my most vivid memory of living at 6 Upper Dunbar Street, when a small town like Wick was under a blitzkrieg as it were.[3]

Then the day we were moving over from Upper Dunbar Street in Pulteneytown to this flat in Alexandra Court at Nicholson's Buildings, when I was carrying a roll of linoleum or a carpet with my stepfather, again there was a German bombing raid. And I remember us sheltering in a doorway in Sinclair Terrace and, as the Germans came in in Heinkel aircraft and strafed the aerodrome, watching all the bombs explode. I was absolutely petrified. We spent a great deal of time in air raid shelters below Nicholson's Buildings, reinforced cellars, with sandbags and special brick walls for anti-blast. The system for the school was that if the All Clear siren went before one o'clock in the morning, we had to go to school that day. But if the All Clear went after 1am, we had the day off. So we used to sit in the air raid shelter and hope the Germans would stay overhead until after 1am to allow us to get a day off school.

But the worst experience my sister Ella and I ever had during the war was when we were dressed up for guising on the night of Hallowe'en in 1941. She would be six and I'd be 10. We were just dressed up in rags, heading from our house up Moat Lane towards my grandmother's house at Coach Road, when three Heinkels came over just at dark. And, oh, tremendous explosions and machine-gun fire quite out of the blue. The two of us were grabbed by servicemen who were coming down from the aerodrome and heading towards the town. They threw themselves on top of us to protect us from shrapnel and machine-gun fire. We regarded this as wonderful that grown men should protect us with their bodies. Then there were incidents during the war when you'd be lying in Argyll Square on a beautiful sunny day and watching in the blue sky the vapour trails of Spitfires chasing Heinkels above us, and shoot-downs and all that. Oh, there were a tremendous amount of raids on Wick. And then it was a protected area. You had to have identification papers to go in and out from Inverness, and there was a tremendous press censorship during the war that I learned about subsequently as well.

When I was growing up I had a lot of interests and activities. I was very keen on football. Well, I was in the Life Boys, graduated into the Boys' Brigade, eventually landed up as a corporal, but was drummed out of the BBs for the extreme treachery of playing football for the Boy Scouts. All this came about because the juvenile league in Wick about 1946–7 was a very keenly fought league, but the Boys' Brigade didn't put in a team. The Scouts had a very good team, and two of my cousins, Peter and Alex Henderson, were the right and left halves. They persuaded me to come and join the Scout team. I did this without demur because there was no BB team anyway. Then as a late entry the BBs decided to put up a team and called me back. But I knew I was on a winning streak with the Boy Scouts because my cousins were very good players and were giving me great support up front as centre forward. So I chose to stay with the Scouts, we tanked the BB team every occasion we met them, and we won the league. And the awful infamy of scoring goals against the BBs! At the same time I was reporting all this for the local paper, you know: 'Henderson scored a brilliant goal'! So the Boys' Brigade decided to dispense with my services.

I had already been playing then for Wick Louisburgh. Louisburgh is a street really, part of the old town of Wick. The reason I was a good centre forward was not through footballing skills at all. I didn't have great ball control. It was purely speed. Given the ball I could get away up the park ahead of everybody. A friend of mine was recalling to another friend my old football days, and he says of me: 'This is the only centre forward I ever knew who could shoot a ball over the bar while standing on the goal line'! So, as I say, my footballing skills weren't great. Then also I was keen on tennis, liked running – sprinting – and was a keen reader. I used to read classics and enjoyed Dickens, Walter Scott, when I'd be 11, 12. I was a member of the public library. I actually became a member of staff of the public library while still at school. There was a job offered by the

Education Authority to a schoolboy or schoolgirl to work at night for an hour, between eight o'clock when the library closed to the public, and nine o'clock when it shut completely. This was the hour in which all the returned books had to be re-catalogued back into their shelves, and all the returns for the day mounted up and entered. That was my job, a paid job – 30 shillings [£1.50] a month, for five nights a week, and I knew all about the Dewey system and all that sort of stuff.[4] I started there at the age of 15, 16, and of course it also meant I could continue my reading and studies. It also meant we could do a lot of cribbing: my pals used to come in to the reading room in that hour and we'd do our homework as a joint effort! Latin was a particularly easy one to do because in the library you had all the reference books you needed. Oh, I loved Latin and I liked French as well. I had a huge interest in Roman history as a result of that and I've been back and forward to Rome, oh, I don't know how many times since then because of that early interest. Then as a laddie I was a regular reader of comics: we had the *Beano* and the *Rover* and the *Adventure*.[5] Oh, we exchanged them around. One of my great heroes was Wilson in the *Wizard*, this athlete, 200 years old, who ran about in his woollen suit and achieved the impossible. Then we also played a lot of games. We would enact, even in young teenage, Bonnie Prince Charlie's rising and so on, and we'd have pitched battles out in the field behind Coach Road. Walter Scott was a great inspiration for that sort of thing.

As well as the library job I delivered papers earlier on at the age of 10 or 11. It was an afternoon and evening job, and I didn't work Saturdays: I played football then. The thing was, in Wick the papers didn't arrive until late: daily papers didn't come up until the midday train. So it'd be after school I'd do the rounds, my memory is from 4 to 6pm. I was paid pennies for that. And I remember we did tattie-picking. We had, I think, something like 10 days' holiday from the school for that. I gave my pay for the papers and tattie-picking to my mother. Well, we'd get a few pennies back to buy sweets and so on. But it was all money for the house, never for yourself. My mother needed the money. I didn't get regular pocket money, it was only on demand – if you needed something.

As I've said, I really did enjoy school very much, it was a pleasure all the way through. I passed the Qualifying exam and went to Wick High School when I was 12. I was good at writing, quite enjoyed art, science was not my favourite subject, but I was hopeless at mathematics. Maths dogged me all through my life really. I was even bad at making up my expenses as a journalist! Both the science master and the maths master didn't appeal to me, and I didn't appeal to them. The maths teacher dismissed me from the start: 'Oh, you've got no head for maths at all.'

I was a dunderhead and I had to admit I was! But the secondary was transcended by another teacher of colossal excellence. A lot of the young male teachers were taken away to the Services in the war, but as a result of war action one came back: John Ross, the teacher of English. He was a first lieutenant on the *Ark Royal*, which was torpedoed and sunk off Gibraltar, and he was slightly wounded and discharged from the navy. Now his return to teaching completely changed my whole idea of life and career, because John Ross fastened on to me as a kid interested in literature, in reading, and gave me colossal encouragement. His background was not unlike my own: he'd begun from lowly beginnings, but had managed to go to university. He was a Lybster man, from just outside Wick. Long after I'd left school he subsequently became rector. He's 86 now and still going strong. He and I still meet and have a very warm affection for each other. He encouraged me to do my best in his class. John Ross was my inspiration for journalism, there's no doubt about that.[6]

I was keen on writing. I've got diaries going back to 1940. I started a regular diary when I was about 16 or 17. I've kept it going since then. It was of daily events in my own life and of public events as well. But it was mainly all football scores when I was younger, little bits and pieces of what happened in the library on a certain night, things like that. Tiny entries to begin with and then they became much more fulsome as I got older.

When I was, oh, 13, 14, I was writing for the *John o' Groat Journal*, established in Wick in 1836, and the *Caithness Courier*, a Thurso paper founded in 1866.[7] I was sending in letters to the editor, ghost stories, and things like that, rather than reporting. My actual reporting began with football reports, because I was playing in matches anyway for Wick Louisburgh and the Boy Scouts. Another game very much in vogue in those days was table tennis, there were great table tennis leagues going. I used to report all these. My name got known by the club secretaries and eventually they used to feed me information.

Another great influence on me at that time was a visit to the 1947 Edinburgh Festival, including a visit to *The Scotsman* office. A very go-ahead youth organiser in Caithness decided that two busloads of Caithness children should have the opportunity of seeing the first Edinburgh Festival. Volunteers to go were drawn out of the hat. It came to about £7 for each of us, and it was subsidised by the Education Authority. The visit to *The Scotsman* was conducted by Sinclair Dunnett, a Caithness man, who was the chief sub-editor in those days. Sinclair Dunnett, a very imposing figure, marched through *The Scotsman* office, lecturing us on how the paper was produced. It was fascinating. I'd never seen an atmosphere like this before, all those linotype machines clicking away, reporters running around, shouts of 'Boy!' and 'Copy!', and the smell of printers' ink was wonderful. As soon as I got back to Wick I wrote Sinclair Dunnett saying: 'How can I become a journalist?' And Sinclair Dunnett wrote me from his house in Morningside this letter, which I still have, saying the first precept should be: get yourself a job on a local paper, learn shorthand, learn typing, take an interest in local affairs, attend council meetings, go to courts, see how things go on. When young journalists write me now I send them a copy of Sinclair's letter, because nothing has changed since 1947. New technology's come in, but the precepts of journalism have not altered in half a century or a whole century. So that then inspired me to continue to write. I used to go into the *Groat* office every Wednesday night with my copy and I'd get the same smells as I got from *The Scotsman*. There's an ambience about the old newspaper office: the heat coming off the melting pot behind the linotype machines, the bubbling metal, the black lead, and all the rest. It gets under your skin. Years later, when the *Daily Express* ceased publication in Glasgow, I more or less cried when the machines stopped, because it's an end of an era. So that's really how I began in journalism. And I was keen to make a start.

Well, at the High School I did the full run until the end of my fifth year. And 1948, the year I sat my Highers, was a watershed in Scottish education, because up to then if you failed a subject you had to resit the whole lot; but after '48 you could pass individual subjects to build up your group. In the Highers I did Higher Latin, French and English, and Lower maths and history. My maths I failed but I got them in the university prelim exam. You had to have three Highers and two Lowers for university entrance. So I applied for admission to St Andrews University and I was accepted. But I always felt I owed it to my mother really that I should get a job and work. And then on top of that there was National Service coming up, and although you went to university you still had to do your National Service at the end of the course.

I didn't go to St Andrews University. What happened was that I was approached by the editor of the *John o' Groat Journal*, who said, 'You've been writing stuff for us now for two or three years. Do you fancy a job as a reporter?' And I leapt at it. The only time I had a regret about not going then to university was later on when I went to Stirling and Newcastle universities on summer courses and thought, 'Now I must have missed something. Maybe I should have gone.' I also reckon that many of the people who came into journalism after me as graduates succeeded in getting very rapid promotion. But it was mainly in features, where I was a news desk executive and was in at the sharp end of the stuff. They generally got soft jobs. I'm talking about men like Magnus Magnusson, who was a contemporary of mine and we worked together, and several others who've done very, very well now on television and so on. But because of their university training and their extra experience, they were able to have a much better picture of the world than I had. They didn't have my experience of starting at the ground level. But I ended up as a leg man to a lot of them, because they said, 'Oh, well, you can rely on him. He knows the background.' So I had to keep them right.

So I left school in July 1948 and started in August on the *John o' Groat Journal* as a cub reporter. I was never a tea boy, I was lucky in that respect. My job was on the office bike and along to do the calls at the harbour, talking to fish salesmen, speaking to the harbour secretary, talking to coastguards, calling at the police station and finding out what was going there, picking up bits and pieces here and there of local news, gossip. The fire brigade was a part-time set-up, and the hospital you tended not to go to unless there was an accident. My main recollection of activity was at the harbour, because it was an important place in those days in Wick. I also went to the courts and the council meetings, always as an understudy at the time: I was never the front man, there was always a senior reporter with me who acted as a sort of tutor. He would introduce me to people, explain to me why such and such a thing was done, and why such and such a sentence came about in court.

There were no shifts as such, except on publication day. It was a 10am to 6pm job, but on a Thursday night you did a double day. You started at ten on Thursday morning and continued up to four o'clock on Friday morning. And then you got the rest of Friday off. When I began on the paper there were three of us on the editorial staff: the editor, the reporter, and myself. Renwick G.G. Millar had been editor for something like 50 years, he retired in 1947, but he was still contributing as a retired editor. His successor by the time I got there was David Oag, who'd been his chief reporter. He had been reporter for something like 30 years, took over the editorship, subsequently became editor–manager, and retired in the late 1960s.[8] David Oag was really one of the exemplary-type journalists, a faultless shorthand writer, very fluent, knew all the ropes, but had never been outside Wick. His whole experience was in Wick. The reporter was Tom Sutherland. Tommy had been a printer pre-war, had been called up as a Territorial into the Seaforths, fought the war, came back, then because there was a surplus of printers and everybody had to get their job back they put him into journalism because he'd a bent for it. He had an enquiring mind. He'd be 30 when I came. Oh, he was a very good, excellent chap, he knew the ropes. And David Oag was a very good editor as well, very strong.

There was quite a substantial number of printers on the paper. Norman Glass was the foreman printer and was author of a book called *Caithness and the War.* So he was an all-round man.[9] Duncan Maclean was the deputy, George Harrold was the senior linotype operator, Acka Doull – that's Alex Doull: Acka was short for Alexander – and Charlie Nicolson, Sandy Cormack, the apprentice, all linotype operators, and an old chap, George Sutherland, who was the printer, and there was another deputy printer, a younger man, whose name eludes me. But there was a considerable team. They were jobbing printers as well. All the printing in Caithness more or less was done in the *Groat* office. And then they'd a very substantial commercial office staff. Renwick Millar's daughter Georgina – Pottie, we called her – was the commercial manager, and she'd a staff of maybe five or six girls in advertising, accounts, and so on. So all in all the *Groat* office had 20.

I think it was selling in those days something close to 10,000 copies a week in a population of 27,000. Then it had a massive worldwide circulation as well: Wick people, Caithness people abroad – in Canada, Australia, New Zealand, America, South Africa – used to get it through postage, I think maybe 500 copies out of the 10,000.

Politically, the *Groat* was independent, but slightly verging to the right, I think, in the days of Renwick Millar. David Oag was very Tory-orientated, I used to think. He was a great friend of the then successful MP for Caithness and Sutherland, Sir David Robertson, and the *Groat* was very much, I would say, pretty close to David Robertson's pocket.[10] The *Caithness Courier* was independently owned and it was more Liberal, following the old Sir Archie Sinclair, who had been the MP for twenty-odd years before 1945.[11] There wasn't much rivalry between the *Groat* and the *Caithness Courier*, because the *Courier* was always regarded as the Thurso paper and the *Groat* more or less Wick and the east of the county. But they both crossed over their boundaries for county council business and the Sheriff Court, because the court, always based in Wick, covered Thurso as well as Wick; so any accused in Thurso were brought down to Wick for appearances. There was no other paper published in Wick in my day, but there was a little paper, the *Sports Favourite*, which came out before the war, and much earlier on there was the *Northern Ensign*, and a couple of other papers that had lived for a very short period.[12]

But there was an incredible rivalry that existed, not between the *Groat* and the *Caithness Courier*, but between the two principal newspapermen in Caithness. David Oag, editor of the *Groat*, represented the local paper. But there was also a freelance journalist in Wick called John Donaldson. The name Donaldson, Wick, was known throughout journalistic circles right down to Fleet Street for a long period after the war, because he came up with some incredible stories. John's father had been a fish curer, so he came from a, well, fairly rich family and he was indulged to an extent. John had taken an MA at Aberdeen University and a BA at Oxford.[13] But he was without a job about 1933–4 when a Danish fishing boat, the *Metha*, was wrecked at Wick harbour with the loss of its entire crew. David Oag and Jimmy More, his sidekick in those days, were down at the harbour picking up the details on the sinking of the vessel. The other newspapers were desperate to get news of what was going on. So Hardy Stewart, news editor in Glasgow of the *Daily Express*, which was only then establishing its reputation in Scotland and trying to build up its circulation, instructed his reporters to phone everybody in Wick connected with the fishing industry and get the answers to 12 questions to form a story. By sheer chance they landed at the house of James Donaldson, fish curer, West Park, and of young John Donaldson, who by then was, as he said, almost suicidal because he'd written a novel and couldn't get it published and had no job in prospect though he'd these university degrees. The *Express's* questions John immediately took on, and he came back to them with the most incredible story that ended up as the page-one lead in the *Daily Express*. It was all about how the Danish skipper of the *Metha* had risked his crew to get ashore in the teeth of a gale and an almost certain death so he could have an assignation with his girlfriend, who lived in Saltoun Street, Wick. Donaldson had all this detail and of course scooped David Oag and Tober More – Jimmy More.[14] So an animosity grew from 1933–4 between Oag and Donaldson. It worsened when Donaldson was called up during the war, became an officer in the Seaforths, while David Oag remained as editor of the *Groat* because he was in a reserved occupation. So David Oag picked up all the freelance journalism going in Wick during the war, although it was censored. When Donaldson came back after the war and tried to re-establish his freelance agency he claimed that David Oag did everything he could to put obstacles in his way. So this rivalry between the two men became very, very bitter. And I got caught up in it, because I was very friendly with John Donaldson. I got on very well with him, had a great admiration for him and his style, liked the quality of his education, and enjoyed his conversation. But this was anathema to my boss, David Oag, who thought John Donaldson was a very bad influence on me. He was worried in case I was leaking secrets from the *Groat* to Donaldson. So an animus blew up which, when I came back from National Service in 1952, made me think, 'The quicker I get out of this the better. I'll have to go.'

As for shorthand and typing when I started on the *Groat* in 1948, I'd learned typing when I was working in the public library as a kid and I was always a good typist. And I had typed the High School magazine. This is also what got me into journalism in a way. At the age of 15, 16, in company with two other guys, I used to do a school scandal sheet full of gossip about teachers and pupils. It came out every week and was called the *Blue, Black and Gold*, the old colours of the school. This was a bit of a rebellion, because after the war a new rector had imposed black and white as the colours and we wanted to revert to the pre-war blue, black and gold. But the sheet was proscribed by the rector because it was too avant-garde for his liking, being critical of teachers and of this and that. But that was the start. Then I'd gone to night school for shorthand and on the *Groat* I was doing maybe about 100 words a minute. But I have to confess I was never a good shorthand writer, it was very sporadic and very chancy, not fast enough for the job. You had to be 140 words a minute or even greater than that. I mean, if you get a guy like Donald Dewar speaking at about 240 . . .! That was one of my really Achilles heels, that my shorthand was never good. This I why I tended later on, when I did get into national newspapers, to move more on to the news desk and into a role where I was dreaming up stories and sending reporters out to do things. To my dying shame, I was chosen to report the Manuel trial and had to turn it down because my shorthand wasn't good enough.[15] That was one example of, when I think of it now, if only I'd studied shorthand harder. But I linked shorthand for some reason with geometry and algebra. I couldn't get my mind round the business of transposing sound into outlines. Shorthand's a brilliant system, I'm full of admiration for it. But much later on, in my last 25 years or so in journalism, I did nothing but tape-record. Were it not for tape recorders, with my very poor shorthand I'd never have been able to do those later jobs. But on the *Groat* my shorthand was adequate for the Sheriff Court or council meetings. And in a small town like Wick you can go back and ask somebody, 'What was it you said actually?' They were very helpful. Well, I go back to Sinclair Dunnett's letter from *The Scotsman* in 1947. Dunnett said to me I had to learn shorthand and that the interesting thing about shorthand to a journalist is it's like a gun in the hand of an African explorer: 'You don't need it often, but when you need it you need it damn badly.' That's absolutely true, and I've been in situations where I've thought, 'Now will I try and get round what this seems to be saying, what it's saying, or should I phone the man and ask him, "Look, was this exactly what you meant to say?" Or did I get it right?' This slows you up, of course, when you're really under pressure. Sometimes taking a chance would land you into a lot of troubles. I tended to pull back rather than take a chance.

Oh, but I remember at the age of 17 being sent back to the Sheriff Court because David Oag, my editor, wasn't at all satisfied with my account of a very complicated legal judgment that Sheriff Reginald Levitt had delivered. David Oag said, 'Go and see the sheriff clerk or somebody and try and sort this out, because I can't understand it.' When I went back the sheriff clerk had gone. So I went up to a door marked Sheriff's Chamber, knocked, and a heavy voice said, 'Come in.' And I went into the august presence of Reginald Levitt, who was about six foot six. I explained my predicament to him and he said, 'Are you old enough to smoke, boy?' I said, 'Well . . .' And he gave me a cigar. 'Are you old enough to drink?' And he gave me a brandy. Then he sat down and wrote my report for me. I went back to the office, typed it up, and David Oag says, 'Ah, that's better'![16]

*   *   *

I'd been 18 months a reporter on the *Groat* when I was called up for National Service in January 1950. I was interested in the Intelligence Corps but I thought, 'Och, well, maybe I won't get in because I haven't got a university education. But I'll have a go at the Education Corps because I've got a good enough Highers group to be accepted.' So I did my six weeks' training at the Brecon Beacons in South Wales, because Brecon and the Welsh Brigade was the training unit for the Royal Army Education Corps. Then I was transferred to Bodmin in Cornwall, then the Army School of Education but in the process of being transferred from Bodmin to Beaconsfield in Buckinghamshire. That's where I graduated from, with the immediate rank of sergeant instructor. I wanted to go to the Far East because I was keen. Well, if you're in the Services, you might as well see the world. And there was a lad from Elgin who wanted a home posting because he was the sole support of a widowed mother and he felt he'd be better quite close to home. So he was sent to Singapore and I was sent to Inverness. I did my 18 months, the rest of my National Service, as an army education instructor teaching illiterate soldiers to read and write, in Cameron Barracks, Inverness.

It was a fascinating experience. In fact, it kept me going: I've been doing adult basic education right up to the last couple of years, because I found you get the satisfaction of teaching and you get such good results from adults. In the army I found that within three months you could teach an 18-year-old lad, who had never been able to put words together, to send a letter home to his mother. It was the huge satisfaction you got as the tutor. These guys were good at calculation. I mean, they could run rings round me running up a darts score or putting a bet on horses, because they'd grown up with that type of mathematics. But when you started teaching them to read from the newspapers the army was way ahead of schools in the use of visual aids: we'd 16mm film we could project to them.

Those lads were all National Servicemen. I got the Regulars later on when the army laid down that every NCO had to have an army first-class certificate of education, because they'd found that the men they'd promoted during the war were illiterates. So I became in huge demand in Highland region, teaching regimental sergeant majors basic English! You had army veterans, guys who'd been through El Alamein and so on. Of course it meant that I could have nights free in the sergeants' mess and as much drink as I wanted – well, provided you got them through their army certificate. I enjoyed that thoroughly, because at 19 and 20 it gave you a power you never imagined you'd have. When I collapsed in front of them one day with pneumonia I was whipped away to hospital in Invergordon, and everybody there wondered why I was so important, with high-ranking army guys coming to see me. It was to find out how quickly I'd recover and get back to teaching them, because their careers were in jeopardy if they hadn't got their first-class certificate. So I was in the army at Inverness until January 1952 and then went back to the *Groat* in Wick.

I've explained the situation at the *Groat*, where things were very uncomfortable before I went to do my National Service. After my return I joined the National Union of Journalists in 1952. John Donaldson, the Wick freelance, proposed me, and Jimmy Angus, editor of the *Caithness Courier*, seconded me.[17] Now for me to join the NUJ was a heinous offence. Tom Sutherland, my senior reporter on the *Groat*, as a former printer, although he'd become a journalist, had retained his membership of the Scottish Typographical Association. David Oag, the editor, was a member of the Institute of Journalists. And I thought the Institute was a bosses' union. Really I also wanted to get myself a decent wage. I'd only been on 28 shillings a week in the army and then I'd suddenly gone up as a sergeant to about £5 a week or something like that, and then I came back to the *Groat* on £3. Well, by joining the NUJ that brought me back up to the fiver again. So David Oag regarded this as a behind-his-back move to get a salary increase. So, as I've said, I thought, 'Well, I'll really have to get out of this.' So John Donaldson and other friends were extremely helpful in trying to get me placed with one of the national papers. But in the end it was Norman Glass, chief printer in the *Groat*, who won me a job on the *Daily Express* in Glasgow.

What happened was that Norman Glass knew Alexander H. Bruce, the *Daily Express*'s managing director, because he came from Wick. Bruce had been a circulation rep in the 1930s, and under Beaverbrook's influence had soared ahead and eventually before he died was managing director of the entire Beaverbrook newspapers in London.[18] Bruce was a brilliant banker, accountant, and so on, one of the new school of newspapermen. Norman Glass wrote him and said, 'Look, I've got a promising young fellow here in Wick who wants to join the national papers. Any chance of getting him an interview?' Within a week I was summoned to meet Jack Campbell, managing editor of the *Express* in Albion Street, Glasgow.[19] I took my cuttings with me and was interviewed. By this stage I had had articles published on a freelance basis in the *Weekly Scotsman* and the *Herald*: 'By a Special Correspondent. TV does reach the north' stuff. This quite impressed Jack Campbell. Once my interview was finished he said, 'Oh, by the way, Mr Bruce wants to see you.' So I was sent off to the management suite and ushered into the presence of this very big man sitting behind a desk. And he says, 'Losh, Jimmy. You're the dead spit of your faither.' He and my long-dead father had been contemporaries at school and Mr Bruce remembered him as a wonderful billiards player. He took me to lunch in the Conservative Club in Glasgow, then for a game of billiards, which I'd never played in my life before. I made an absolute hash of it. But Mr Bruce was good: he'd obviously had a misspent youth just as my father had.[20] And the next I knew I got a job on the *Express*, to start the following week in Dundee. But then I got a further letter from Jack Campbell saying that because of a vacancy created in Inverness, with a reporter being sent to Edinburgh, I would now take over the post of junior reporter in Inverness. So that's where I actually started with the *Express* in March 1953.

I preferred going to Inverness rather than Dundee. I knew Inverness very well because I'd been there in the army and had been reporting there as a soldier. I'd kept my journalism going, working for the *Football Times* and the *Highland News*. Jimmy McEwan, editor of the *Football Times*, had given me regular Saturday employment doing a football match in the Highland League.[21] As a result I had all these contacts. So Inverness suited me ideally. The *Express* office there was in Bridge Street, right next to Gellions Hotel. George Paterson was the senior reporter, there were just the two of us – to begin with, though there was a retained photographer who wasn't a member of staff.[22] But, oh, it's amazing how the *Express* began to burgeon over the years. I was the third junior that George had. The first one was Walter Gunn, who came from Thurso. Walter went from Inverness to Edinburgh, and was succeeded by John

Vass, who also went from Inverness to Edinburgh. Years later I ended up as boss to both John and Walter in Edinburgh, though only for a very short time in John's case, as he moved then to London.[23] Well, I was in Inverness from 1953 to 1955. I was on £8 a week in Inverness, and out of that I'd to pay three guineas a week for my digs. I lived in Gellions Hotel, all found, for three guineas – breakfast, lunch, dinner, tea, and bed. Mind you, three guineas was just under half my pay.

In that time I was in Inverness I'd done a lot of travelling. I used to do stories in the Highlands and Islands – the Uists and Barra, Orkney, Shetland. I used to fly with Captain Fresson on his trips. They had charters, wonderful trips to Stornoway and so on, in a tiny single-engined aircraft, just him and me – marvellous. And of course the *Express* had first call on Captain Fresson's services. They used to pay him a retainer, so that if any story arose they had his plane. We used to fly off the Longman aerodrome, which is now no longer there: it's an industrial site. His wife used to drive their van out to get rid of the sheep and cattle so he could have a straight take-off.[24]

So I was in Inverness until I got married in 1955. And as soon as I announced I was getting married, the *Express* decided to shift me to Glasgow. So I came straight off honeymoon and straight to Glasgow. This was their technique, deliberate policy. They didn't want you to settle in a place. If you were a young man and you had any chance of promotion and so on, if you married a local girl and set up house there they would have the whole problem of transporting you and compensating you – although that wasn't the cachet in those days, because I was subsequently moved from Glasgow to Edinburgh and again got no assistance from the *Express* and had to do it all off my own bat. But anyway this was it: 'If you get married, we'll move you.' So my married home was in Glasgow, I'd to set up home there.

My wife Cath was an Inverness girl. She was a telephone operator. It was all through the most incredible newspaper thingy that we got together. She operated on the trunk exchange in the days when it was all voice-controlled. You'd pick up the phone and ask, 'Can I have Glasgow Bell 3550?' – the *Express* office there. I thought this young lady was rather stroppy and I said, 'You've kept me hanging on for a very long time.' And she said, 'Oh, you reporters are always the same, moaning about this or that.' So we started an argument on the phone. I said, 'Look, I wouldn't mind sorting you out.' She said, 'Well, better still, I'll come round and sort you out.' So she did, and she was bigger than me! And we began going out together and got married. We went on honeymoon to Portobello, came back, and straight to Glasgow, where I began work in September 1955 as a fully-fledged senior reporter. My wife was quite happy to move with me from Inverness, and she got a transfer from the trunk exchange in Inverness to the trunk exchange in Glasgow.

I was lucky in this respect, that on two years previously the *Express* had taken me down to their office in Albion Street, Glasgow, on holiday relief for a month. So I was acclimatised to the set-up, I'd had an indoctrination. I'd stayed in the Ivanhoe Hotel, the lap of luxury, and got jobs to do, among them the McZephyr murder. This was a character in the *McFlannel* radio series, who'd been murdered in Harmony Row in Govan. I think it was a homosexual set-up. And I had the dubious privilege of being ordered off the doorstep by Rev. Dr George MacLeod, who subsequently became Lord MacLeod of Fuinary. He was the minister of Govan High Church and the murderer was one of his Iona community. So George wasn't at all pleased that the *Express* were linking him with a murder, and a rather seedy murder at that. I met him subsequently on other occasions. He was sometimes amusing and very entertaining, and other times he was an absolute ————. Oh, a wonderful preacher, till you started writing him up, because he spoke in images, and never fully-formulated sentences. There was very rarely a verb in there, it was all pictures. I remember a celebrated debate in Springburn Burgh Halls where Rev. Alan Hasson, then the leader of the Loyal Orange Lodge, and George MacLeod were debating the motion 'That Iona is leading us to Rome'. Hasson had it all beautifully organised: as George came on the stage, Mendelssohn's *Hebridean Overture* was being played. But that night when you tried to get George's stuff down on paper, it didn't make much sense, it was all imagery.[25]

In Glasgow it was general reporting I did, right at the blunt end. They threw you at everything: 'Hatchet man goes amok in Gorbals', that type of story, and all sorts. I enjoyed that work. We worked different shifts: 9am to 5pm, 10am to 6pm, 2pm to 10pm, 3pm to 11pm, 4pm to midnight, and 8pm to 4am. There were often occasions when I only met my wife in the lobby of the house we lived in at Langside: she'd be going out to work as I'd be coming in, or vice versa; a strange life. It was a difficult and strenuous life for young couples. Then my wife fell pregnant in 1956 and our first daughter was born in December that year, so she had to give up work, of course. Well, I was in Glasgow five years. It took in the Manuel serial murders: he was charged at one stage with 11 deaths. I was involved in covering every one of these. I landed up in Blackpool doing background on Manuel. I did long, long shifts, far longer than eight hours – sometimes round the clock, and travelling all over Scotland in pursuit of stories. Then we used to have circulation drives as well: a special drive in Kirkcaldy to build up circulation there, a drive in Dumfries, the Borders, Inverness. There was a sort of blitz of the area with local stories. So you were living in these places for a few days at a time, maybe for three weeks sometimes. It was very concentrated work: you lived hard and worked hard. Social life in those days was non-existent, apart from Saturday night with friends, or something like that. Oh, it was completely committed work. And it wasn't hell of a well-paid either. I mean, the *Express* worked a system where you were on merit, and you never knew what your neighbour was earning. We'd no grades or anything, so some were away ahead of others in payment. Recently I came across a letter I wrote to Ian McColl, who was then the editor, making the point that I was earning substantially less than some of the men I was directing.[26] At that time I was looking for an increase in salary from £30 to £35. I think all that led generally to a certain amount of envy, jealousy, backbiting. There were also cliques. I always refused to join groups but always ploughed my own furrow and did my own thing. But I remember vividly there used to be guys who were news editors' and features editors' favourites, and they got the best jobs. There was a lot of that going on. And, I mean, there was a lot of people fiddling expenses and so on.

So I was in Albion Street in Glasgow for five years and then in 1960 I was ordered to go through to Edinburgh as deputy to Gilbert Cole, the chief reporter there. Roger Wood was the editor then and he said the Edinburgh office needed a bit of gingering up.[27] They were slow on their deadlines, their copy was not coming through when it was required. I'd worked on the night desk in Glasgow with Walter Gunn, who'd been brought through from Edinburgh on a couple of occasions, and had experience of running the news desk. And Roger Wood decided to send me through, and I knew the deadlines, and the system in Glasgow and the people, including the chief sub-editor and so on. Gilbert Cole himself had started off in Glasgow but he was sent through to Edinburgh in the late 1930s to set up the Edinburgh bureau and had been there ever since. By 1960 he'd been divorced from the Glasgow set-up for many years, with only occasional visitations to Glasgow or visits from the Glasgow staff to him. But his lines of communication weren't as direct. So they sent me through to Edinburgh as a link man really. Roger Wood said: 'You're through there as the ginger man. You ginger them up.'

Well, I was in the Edinburgh office five years, from 1960 to 1965. The reason I was pulled out of Edinburgh to go back to Glasgow was because there had been a major reshuffle there, and they wanted somebody as deputy news editor in Albion Street who had no knowledge of what had gone on before. In Ian McColl's words, I was 'untainted'. A racket had been running over expenses off the news desk and it was decided to shift certain people or resign or whatever, and they needed somebody to come in from the outside. So I kept that job as deputy news editor, a complete change of role, for four years to 1969. I'd been deputy chief reporter in Edinburgh, now there was major promotion for me as deputy news editor for the whole edition of the *Express* in Scotland. I was under Ian Brown, an Ayrshire man and a considerable character in newspapers in those days. He was a major figure on the *Express* over the years.[28]

But then in 1969 there was again a reshuffle and I was moved to features. The features editor had gone and they wanted to change it around. So I landed up with the very strange title of Features News Editor. It was really deputy features editor, but because the features editor was a technocrat and I was supposed to be the ideas man, they gave me a title as well. My job was to think up ploys for the *Express*'s incredible features staff: Jack Webster, Neville Garden, Mamie Crichton, Molly Kelly, Iris McGill. Bill Allsopp, who became a lecturer in journalism at Napier University in Edinburgh, was on the staff then. All this was in the days of Clive Sandground as editor. So I held that job until 1975.[29]

But I'm qualifying that slightly, because in 1974 all changed: that was when the *Express* stopped publishing in Scotland, and from a staff of 2,000 we were down to 70. Of the 70 of us left I then landed up because of the contraction doing five separate jobs: features news editor, deputy news editor, news desk assistant . . . There was no change in salary. And of course it was a much rockier boat because we were now being printed in Manchester. Our lines of communication, amongst other things, were strained. Some of our staff were working in Manchester. I often went down there as the link man to replace Bruce McLeod, an Edinburgh lad who'd worked with me during my term in Edinburgh and who died suddenly when still a young man. Bruce was the news desk link in Manchester.[30] But I quite enjoyed the Manchester end, because I was back amongst the printing presses again. You could hear the paper being trundled out and see it coming out at night, you got the smell of the ink again, and all the rest. I really loved that. And I daresay if I'd been offered a job in Manchester I might have taken it, but I wasn't. I stood that for a year and then had enough of it. I never had applied for another job until then. I applied for one with the BBC as a news assistant. I didn't get it, and I remember David Scott telling me years later that was because I was too mature.[31]

By 1975 I'd lost my wife Cath. We'd had a very sad marriage actu-ally. What had happened was that our second child, another daughter, was born in 1961, the year after the *Express* had ordered me through to Edinburgh. Then Cath began to show signs of paralysis. It was diagnosed as a sort of deterioration of the motor nerves. It's now called motor neurone disease, but we didn't know it in those days. Cath landed up in an iron lung in the Northern General Hospital in Edinburgh in 1963. She was completely encased in a box apparatus where the pressure allowed her lungs to operate. She was sealed at the neck and was facing upwards to the ceiling, and she had a mirror at the side to correspond to people sitting beside her. Willie Merrilees, then Chief Constable in the Lothians, used to do a great deal of charity work, including visits to hospitals, and on one occasion he brought with him Bill Simpson, who played the part of Dr Finlay in the TV series *Dr Finlay's Casebook*, to visit Cath. Because we'd prior warning I arranged for a photographer to get a picture of Bill Simpson talking to Cath in her iron lung – not for publication in the paper, just for family use. But the matron got to hear about the visit and was furious with Merrilees that he should bring such important people to her hospital without first informing her. So she insisted that if he ever brought any VIPs to the Northern General she ought to be alerted in advance. It was typical of Willie Merrilees's style that he arranged a phone call to the matron to say that indeed he was bringing a VIP to visit Mrs Henderson again. So the matron turned up there with her medals, and the medical superintendent, the assistant matron, and deputy this and that, were all in a line as the police car came in. The chauffeur got out, opened the door for Willie, and Willie stepped out carrying Greyfriars Bobby, the wee dog that played the part in the Walt Disney film. That went down a bomb with the family! And there were other occasions when people were extremely kind to Cath in hospital.[32]

She was transferred to Glasgow as well at the time I was transferred back there by the *Express* in 1965. By this stage she was in a cuirass respirator, no longer a box, and she had had a tracheostomy, and this was straight into her throat and things operated by bellows and so on. The National Health Service wasn't geared to transporting somebody in that parlous state between hospitals. One of the problems was how to work the bellows at the exact interval and over a period where one person would start to get tired and somebody else would have to take over. So it was worked out that a team of five of us could work three minutes at a time, and every one and a half seconds we would depress the plunger. How would you gauge this? Ben Allison, a great old *Express* reporter, came up with the brilliant idea that McLeod Bain, a public relations man at Ferranti's, the engineers, was bound to be able to get a boffin to invent a machine that would do this. Within a week or so arrived a shoebox at the *Express* office in Edinburgh in Jeffrey Street, to which by this time we'd moved down from the High Street where we had been. In this shoebox was a device with a red lamp that flashed every three minutes, and a beeper that went every second and a half. So in this British Road Services van we had Cath in bed with this great big bellows machine, and we'd a doctor, a sister and a nurse, a porter and me. And we were all taking turns under police escort with flashing headlamps and all the rest, travelling at 30 miles an hour between Edinburgh and Ruchill Hospital in Glasgow. What co-operation, but mainly amateurish stuff. Nowadays it'd be a helicopter.

The *Express* were tremendously good to me at that time. They used to provide me with transport. I used to get an *Evening Citizen* van at my disposal any time I asked for it, so I could take Cath to things. Although she was in this strange apparatus, she also had a portable chair with a battery arrangement down below that breathed for her. I took her to the Edinburgh Tattoo with our two kids, Susan, then 10, and Judy would be six. I took Cath to visit Susan when she had an operation for tonsils in Glasgow Royal Infirmary, by just transporting her in this little van and tying her down with ropes to hold the thing. So the *Express* made allowances and were very, very kind to me, provided I did my job to their satisfaction. I never asked for time off for anything special. Well, Cath lapsed into a coma towards the end, remained in a coma for six months and died in June 1971. My children's memory of their mother is just of her in the hospital bed all the time. And of course there was no provision under the social services then for home helps. I'd to provide my own home helps out of my salary. Nowadays you'd get social workers to come and help you out, you'd get assistance, you'd get grants. I had to buy everything, even things like commodes. Then because I lived in Hamilton at that time I negotiated with Dr John McEwan, the Director of Education for Lanarkshire, to try and get Judy into school below her acceptance age. 'Under no circumstances,' he said. 'We can make no exceptions.' I said, 'But look, my circumstances are such that she's a tiny little girl. It's very difficult to get people to look after her and it'd be very helpful if she was in nursery education.' 'No.' Her birthday was March 2nd, and she didn't qualify for entry to school until the following year. Oh, without a doubt the world's improved in some ways, thank goodness.[33]

*   *   *

So, after 22 years, I left the *Express* in 1975. I was not happy under the new set-up because we were working all sorts of hours and it was very, very awkward. And Ian Brown and I weren't hitting it off too well either. He was very domineering and doctrinaire in his way, and I'd my own ideas. I applied for a job with the BBC but, as I've said, didn't get it. Again friends of mine got in touch. Out of the blue I got a phone call: 'You fancy running the *Northern Times*, a local weekly paper in Golspie in Sutherland?'[34] And I said, 'Why? What's happened to Bruce Weir?' 'Oh, well, he's retiring.' I'd known Bruce Weir for years. Bruce had been our correspondent for the *Express* as well. He was a former *Glasgow Herald* man who'd gone up to Golspie in 1949, saved the paper, built up its reputation, and was a very highly regarded member of the community. And I said, 'I'd love the chance.' So he said, 'Well, all you have to do is phone Bruce Weir and show your interest.' I did this, and Bruce then sent me a letter inviting me up for an interview with his board of directors. So I arrived up in Golspie on a Saturday in May 1975 with Judy, my younger daughter, who was 13 and still at school. Susan, my elder daughter, was by then away at nursing college, and in fact at the Western General Hospital in Glasgow. Whether I took the job was all contingent on whether Judy liked Golspie. There was no point in me thinking about my career if my kid was unhappy. So when I was being interviewed, I left Judy to wander around Golspie. And the number of people who spoke to her, asked her who she was, what she was doing there, and they were all saying, 'Oh, it's a great place to live', and so on. So Judy was delighted. She'd made up her mind before I did. I was interviewed on a Saturday morning round the table in the Duke Street office of the Sutherland estates, by the Countess of Sutherland, who was the proprietor of the *Northern Times*, her husband Charles Janson, Michael Scott, the factor and also a director, Bruce Weir, a director and editor, and William Urquhart, the company secretary. They asked me why I fancied the job, and I said, 'Well, because we're in the middle of a Moray Firth/North Sea oil boom.'[35] It looked as if it was going to be an area of great prosperity. There was a huge challenge in the area and it satisfied me. I was 44 years old at the time, and I thought, 'Well, getting back to a local paper is really getting back to the roots.' I'd enjoyed my time on the *Groat*, I'd also enjoyed my 22 years on the *Express*. But I felt that running my own show now I would enjoy much better. I was more or less preaching as sole nominee: they didn't have any other applicants. Well, Bruce Weir, the editor, had been trying for years to find a replacement. He was 67, past his retirement age, and he'd had no luck attracting any attention. So he'd got in touch with Alex Main, the former *Express* man in Inverness. Alex Main had got in touch with Jimmy Buchan on the *Express* news desk and asked him if he knew of anybody. Jimmy Buchan says, 'I've got a man sitting beside me who might be interested.' So that was how it all came about, it was just the network. So I was accepted within a week and was asked how soon could I get to Golspie.

It shows you the animosity that then existed between me and Ian Brown, editor of the *Express*, when I said to him, 'I've got this job up north and they want me as soon as possible. When can I go?' Ian Brown says, 'Your terms are three months' notice. So you'll do your three months.' Then there had been tremendous redundancy packages being offered by the *Express* previous to our closure. Some people were going away with £30,000 in their pockets. I was going to leave with nothing for my 22 years' service – until the union took it up, although not at my behest. Stuart McCartney, father of the chapel, said to me, 'Oh, you ought to get some bucket money, you know.' So he was going down to London on union business and talked to Jocelyn Stevens, managing director there. Stevens gave me an award of £5,000, which set me up.[36] Selling my house in Hamilton and moving into a tied house in Golspie gave me a working capital of £10,000 in 1975 – good from my point of view.

Then the other wonderful thing that happened to me was at Bruce Weir's retiral party. Although he finished as editor in August 1975, they didn't organise his retiral party until March 1976, because that coincided with a whole variety of other people retiring from Sutherland estate management as well. A magnificent function was laid on at Dunrobin Castle, Bruce was given a presentation, and I had to give a speech in honour of him, because by then I'd been six months in the post as editor of the *Northern Times*.[37] Then came the last dance. I was sitting, and there was a lady sitting opposite me, not dancing either. So I went across to her and said, 'Would you like this dance?' 'Sure.' So we began to dance and to talk. I became very intrigued by this young woman. It turned out she was in the middle of a divorce and she'd three sons aged seven, four and three. So we hit it off, decided to get married, and were married in March 1977. I became adoptive father to these three boys, we had another son ourselves through our own marriage, and we've had a very happy family all these years.

When I got the job as editor of the *Northern Times* in 1975 there was no junior reporter, there was just the editor doing the job with the help of a secretary, because it was a tiny paper. It had a circulation of only 6,000, but in a population of 13,000. So, I mean, it's huge, a tremendous sale – for the number of people who lived there. During my editorship I had always a junior reporter. But then that junior would eventually become a senior, and some stayed with me longer than others. My first junior was Donald Maclean, who came from Tiree originally but had West Sutherland connections. Then after about a year he went to Stirling University. Then I had Alison Cameron, a girl of about 20 with a couple of years' experience on the *West Hampstead Express* and who came from Wimbledon, and whose parents moved up to live at Dornoch. She remained 20 years with me and became the deputy editor and advertising manager. Then I had a girl in advertising, Judith Napier, who was doing book reviews for me and had a very nice style of writing. She'd previously been secretary to the advertising manager of the Aberdeen *Press & Journal*. So I had the clever idea of promoting Alison Cameron, my reporter, to advertising manager because she was good on advertising features and very good commercially, and taking Judith out of advertising and making her a journalist at the age of 25. Well, Judith burgeoned, became a wonderful writer, one of the best reporters I've ever come across – and she was snapped up by the *Press & Journal*, tchung! So Judith came in as opposition to us then as the *P&J*'s Caithness, Sutherland and Ross-shire correspondent. Then much later on, when I fell ill, Alison Cameron moved in as editor for a time.[38]

My contract with the *Northern Times*, and Bruce Weir's before me, allowed us to freelance. Because they paid us such a small salary they said, 'You can freelance as much as you like, so long as your first loyalties are with the *Northern Times*.' So Bruce Weir was a BBC correspondent and contributed to all the papers after he'd got his story in the *Northern Times*. When I took over I did exactly the same thing. Apart from that perk, I also got a house and a car. The house, an estate house, was easily provided because the Sutherland estate owned so many houses. I'd lived up on Dunrobin Mains farm in a lovely new house, but then as I remarried and got this new family I needed a bigger house. The estate said, 'Well, where do you want to live?' And I picked a house at Littleferry, near where my wife was born. Her people were the ferrymen there. Alastair Hetherington, former editor of the *Guardian* and BBC Controller Scotland, stayed with us a couple of times at Littleferry. In his funeral service was a little passage he wrote in *The Listener* about our house and our view, which he said was probably the best view that any editor in the world would have.[39]

Well, I settled into a job I loved, enjoyed the *Northern Times*, but didn't increase its circulation massively – just by a few hundred copies maybe over the 1975 figure, because you were at saturation point. And it's a depleting population in Sutherland, now less by some hundreds than when I arrived. Since then the *Northern Times* has had two new proprietors. The Countess of Sutherland gave up control of it in 1988, well, by a nominal sale to our sister organisation called Method Publishing, which published military magazines. Its managing director had been our managing director and a member of the board. It was for a nominal pound or something the company changed hands. The Countess just wanted out, she'd had enough. Well, the Duke of Sutherland, her uncle, took over the paper in 1943, so they'd had all those years. She succeeded her uncle in the earldom. There's another Duke of Sutherland who lives in the Borders but who's got no connection with Sutherland, and he took over the English part of the estate.[40] Then in 1993 Ian Carmichael of Method Publishing sold the *Northern Times* on to Scottish Provincial Press, a big company which publishes almost every title in the north of Scotland.

The *Northern Times* was politically quite independent. There were always allegations that it was the voice piece of the landowner, the laird. The editors before me made the point that they were quite independent and that they got no interference whatever from the House of Sutherland. This was best exemplified within a very short time of me taking over as editor, when in 1977 the National Mod moved to East Sutherland. The Countess of Sutherland was the convener of the local organising committee when Brian Wilson of the *West Highland Free Press* made a vicious attack on her and said there was no way that the National Mod should be associated with the descendant of the man who had cleared that part of the Highlands. There was a lot of recrimination and huge correspondence in *The Scotsman* and the *Herald* and so on over that. At no stage did the Countess, or her husband, ever suggest how I should handle the story. I ended up doing a page one: 'The Countess and her Critic', gave her space to make her point, and Brian Wilson full rein to do his, and published it just like that. But she resigned as convener of the Mod. This was against my advice. Brian Wilson obviously was keen to get her out. I said she ought to stay on and still show the flag, because, I mean, she'd no reason to feel bad about what her ancestors had done years before. The family in recent years had gone the other way and given masses of land to people to develop on their own. However, she decided to resign because she didn't want the local Mod to be spoiled because of a row over the Clearances. Of course Brian Wilson regarded her resignation as a great victory and made great capital in the *West Highland Free Press*. But that's an example of where the Countess and her husband, Charles Janson, a journalist who worked for the *Financial Times* and was an expert on Russia, never said to me, 'Now we don't like what you're doing,' or 'Why don't you give more publicity to so-and-so?'[41]

In all my years on the *Northern Times* the Clearances were always emerging and re-emerging as a continuing topic in the paper, and it's still going on. For example, the SNP had a concerted campaign in the mid-1990s to go for planning approval to demolish the statue of the Duke of Sutherland off the hill overlooking Golspie. Of course, you can't demolish anything unless you own it. The SNP knew that but what they wanted was to arouse the controversy again, because things had gone quiet on the Nationalist scene and this was a good whipping boy. So we'd great publicity over this, a planning enquiry and all the rest. I could fill pages with letters from people from all over the world, because everybody gets involved in this. It's the one major story in Sutherland and it's all of 200 years old but it's still very much a live issue.

Belonging as I did myself to Wick I was of course well aware of the Clearances long before I went to the *Northern Times*. My overall impression is that locally they wished the thing would die down and be forgotten about. It's part of history. They want the Duke's statue to remain there because it's there, it's a landmark. But also, if it were demolished it would then take away the memento of the Clearances, because as long as it stands it's always a reminder that the Clearances did happen. It reminds you of passages in history. But if you knock it down nobody's going to go past Golspie and say, 'What's that cairn of stones up there?' As soon as they see the statue: 'Who's that to?' And then the whole story comes out again. So local people don't want to lose their statue. But equally they don't want to fan the flame of the Clearances. But as soon as you go a generation away and into another country – Canada, Australia, New Zealand, the United States – oh, you find the strong emotion coming back: they come back on holiday and go over it all over again. And they want to stir it all up: 'Oh, my ancestors would have been here but we landed up in Australia.' Then you say to them, 'But would you have preferred to have been here?' 'Oh, well, we've had experience of the way that you live. But no, I think we'll go back to Australia. We don't want to come and stay with you.' I can think of five, I think, who have been known to come back and live again in Sutherland.

I had lots of discussions with the Countess of Sutherland. Her own feeling is that she's not responsible for what her ancestors did. She feels it's most unfair that all this should be visited on her, because succeeding Dukes have bent over backwards to spend masses of money on the county to try and expiate the sins of the factors. The original first Duke – Marquis of Stafford he was then, the guy who is vilified – was an improver. Apart from increasing the influence and wealth of the Sutherland property his idea was to help benefit the local people. The trouble was he went about it in an improving way that the local people didn't like, and of course because his sidekicks implemented it in a most shocking, appallingly cavalier fashion. This will always be remembered as the memento of the Sutherlands. But when you consider that in today's terms the Sutherlands expended millions and millions of pounds on new roads, bridges, inns, afforestation, land improvement, and infrastructure in Sutherland, nobody has really written that story – well, I tell a lie: an Australian Professor Richards, who wrote *The Leviathans of Wealth*, did in fact touch on the major improvements.[42] But the concept of moving people living in impoverished conditions in the strath down to the sea, where the sea was teeming with fish, and making them fish on it – och, a brilliant idea, except that in fact you can't do it. You can't make a landlubber a fisherman. Neil M. Gunn brought that out so much in his *Silver Darlings* and other books.[43] It's all very well to have an idea of how you're going to change the economy of an area and build all these villages – Golspie, Brora, Helmsdale, and up Bettyhill – all built along the coast to bring the people from the straths into the fishing set-up. Then they imported fishermen from Buchan – the Inneses, Cowies, Jappys. All these Buchan names proliferate now along the east Sutherland coast, because they were brought in to teach the Mackays and the Gunns how to fish. But they were seasick, they couldn't stomach the sea. So it was a wrong concept. It was ethnic cleansing in a particular way. But the Countess of Sutherland is aware of all that, and she says that surely by now it ought to be a memory rather than a continuing controversy.

The other thing I would readily agree to would be a memorial to the people of the Clearances as big as or more imposing than the Duke of Sutherland's statue if necessary, on another appropriate hill. Dennis MacLeod, the millionaire from Helmsdale, has already promised £50,000 towards just exactly that. What he envisaged was a beautifully sculptured adult couple and two children clinging to the wife's apron or dress, and the husband looking out to sea, to the lands beyond, where they're going, and the wife looking back on the country they're leaving. That would be a wonderfully symbolic group to show the awful business of how these people were extirpated. We ought to have something to remember them by. Dennis MacLeod saw the spin-off to that would be a museum or genealogical centre where people from abroad could come and look up their ancestry and find where their folk had been cleared from. Instead of keeping on fanning a controversy, from which nothing will ever emerge of any good, it'd be a sensible way of bringing something else constructive and helpful. I have advocated it in the *Northern Times* time after time.[44]

Well, I finished as editor of the *Northern Times* in 1996 after 21 years, almost as long as I'd been with the *Express*. I'd had a couple of heart attacks in October the previous year and had been off work five months, having a bypass. I came back to duty in March 1996 and finished in July, as I deliberately wanted to complete my 21 years. It's been a happy story really.

In my time on the *Northern Times* I have interviewed Prince Charles, Margaret Thatcher, James Callaghan, a huge number of politicians. I'd never have had the guts maybe to go for them if I hadn't had my *Express* experience. Harold Wilson was the only prime minister I ever spoke to when I was on the *Express*. The opportunities you get in a remote area of meeting people you'd never have a chance to see in a city are great. Looking back, I think of all the jobs I've had in journalism the one I enjoyed most was undoubtedly the *Northern Times*. You run the paper on your own, and it gives you lots of worries. I've always intended writing a book, whether a novel or a factual autobiography. I was going to call it *The Hated Mistress*. A mistress is somebody you're passionately fond of, but she makes so many demands on you it's impossible and takes up your time and leads you into all sorts of difficulties. So you hate her one day and love her the next. And that's a local weekly paper. The huge satisfaction you get on a Thursday afternoon from seeing your finished effort. You look at it and say, 'Well, maybe I could have done that a wee bit better. But that's a great story and nobody else has that angle.' You feel wonderful about it. Then maybe next day you've got to face a whole new week and there's very little news. For days you're worrying, 'God, how the hell am I going to fill next week's paper?' Your reporter's on holiday, three or four people are off sick, you're on your own, there are two council meetings in conflict or one council meeting in conflict with another meeting – which one do you go to? And there's a court on you've got to cover. How do you do it?' That's when you hate it. Well, my wife said I was heading for a heart attack because I was under huge strain: you give more than 100 per cent effort to the job. I wasn't aware of it until I began to get short of breath. The next I knew I was in intensive care in Inverness. It all came about very suddenly.

But I've enjoyed the years of retirement, too, because I'm still free-lancing. I do television interviewing and newspapers. I'm still correspondent for *The Scotsman*, the *Herald*, and the *Press & Journal* and I get great satisfaction. I get my byline still. More than half a century on now and I'm still getting a kick out of it. Deadlines seem to get me going. I've promised to write a book about Littleferry, as it's steeped in history. If I'd a publisher who said, 'I have to have it by next month,' then I'd be down to it.

Ron Thompson

From the time I was 9, 10, 11 years old I had to take to my bed for about six weeks each year for at least three years in succession, through an illness which in those days was called old-fashioned growing pains. It was an illness caused by my body stretching too quickly. So in bed I did a lot of reading, and I read boys' stories about reporters, read them and re-read them, and I really became interested both in this business of writing stories and also in the wonderful adventures that these people had. That was what really sowed the seed in my mind at an early age to become a reporter.

I was born at West Ferry, Dundee, on 5 September 1929. And Broughty Ferry is where I was brought up and lived and, apart from five years in Glasgow, I worked nearby in Dundee all my life. I'm an Anglo-Scot. My father belonged to Dover in Kent and was born in 1901. One of a large, poor family, he left home when he was just over 15 and joined the Royal Artillery as a boy soldier. He remained in the army for 12 years until 1928. About 1923–4 he'd been posted to Broughty Ferry Castle, and there he met my mother, a native of Broughty Ferry. After that he went abroad to serve in India and Mesopotamia, then came back, married my mother in Broughty Ferry, stayed there for the rest of his days and never went back to live in England. When he left the army, he got a job with Dundee Corporation as storekeeper in the electricity department. He remained there until 1948–9, and then became an assistant council officer with Dundee town council – a big change of job. A few years after that he became council officer and served as that until he retired when he was 65, about 1966. He was a very smart-looking man who never lost his military gait or bearing. And he had lots of military habits which brushed off on the way that my brother Alan, four years younger than me, and I were brought up. My father was just a bit old for serving in the Second World War, but he was a Home Guard officer then. My father died in 1990, and my mother followed him six months later in 1991.

My mother, a native of Broughty Ferry, became a professional cook and went into domestic service until she got married. Her father was a professional gardener, her mother a professional cook, and they both worked together in service, latterly at Guthrie Castle in Angus. I'm pretty vague about my grandparents on my father's side. My grandfather Thompson died before the war. I never knew him, never met him. My father was away, as I've said, from his family in Kent as a young boy and he never went back there. Och, he may have gone back once or twice, but then the war intervened in 1939, and of course travelling down south became very difficult. My grandmother, who remained in Dover, was a remarkable woman. Many of the people in Dover, who came under German shell fire from the French coast, spent many, many days in caves in the cliffs of Dover. She did that, too, until eventually she said she wasn't going to move again. And she just stayed on in her house in Dover, survived the war, and came up to us once or twice.

My earliest memories are of growing up in Broughty Ferry. We lived in a council house on a council estate at Forthill, built on a hill just to the north of Broughty Ferry. Now that was considered pretty posh council-wise: maisonettes, upstairs and downstairs houses in blocks of four, set in what was then, and still is really, a sort of semi-rural country environment. When my father and mother got married in 1928 they got one of those new council houses. In 1946 we moved to another council house in the same estate, and my father and mother lived there for the rest of their lives. By contrast, my wife was brought up in a tenement in the industrial east end of Dundee, with outside toilet and all the rest of it. She and I even spoke a different language. Now I write a newspaper column every week and whenever I want to revert to the vernacular, it's my wife I consult. She was brought up with Dundonese, the Dundee dialect, whereas a couple of miles away we down in Broughty Ferry and Forthill were slightly posher and spoke rather more correctly and were regarded by people like my wife as a bit posh.

At the age of five in 1934 I went to the local primary school in Broughty Ferry called Eastern Primary School. It's still there, still the original building, still under the local authority. I left in 1939 and was due to go to Grove Academy, a territorial secondary school for Broughty Ferry. It was a comprehensive school long before comprehensive education was introduced. It was the only school in the area where pupils leaving primary could go to, unless you were a Roman Catholic, and then of course you would go to one of the RC secondaries in Dundee. Now I was all set to go to Grove Academy, when the war broke out. Grove Academy was then closed down for about two years, teachers were dispersed, some went away to the Forces, and we had part-time education, perhaps two, three afternoons a week, by going to different people's houses. Sometimes they would come to our house, sometimes we would go to another house. We had an itinerant teacher, retired, who lived in Forthill, went from one house to another, and taught us what she could. That was pretty unsatisfactory, but of course the whole country was upside down. Well, we did that for quite a spell. Then they opened a very old, huge, empty, beautiful, rambling country house called Adderley House in Monifeith, three miles down the road to Carnoustie. They set up a temporary school there, and we were bussed up and down for a period of perhaps 15 months. Then Grove Academy re-opened in 1942 and they got together as many retired teachers as they could. I left school in the summer of 1943, when I was not quite 14, without any certificates and, as I've said, when I was very anxious, and had been for a year or two, to become a reporter.

I didn't like school. I was pretty timid, I was frightened of most of the teachers, and there was a bit of bullying on the part of the teachers and the pupils. I never really took to school. In fact, it wasn't a happy time of my life at all. It certainly wasn't because I spoke with any slightly English accent that I was bullied, because though my father never lost his Kent accent I never in any way adopted any part of his accent.

At primary school I certainly never enjoyed English. I think I quite enjoyed writing – penmanship, because I used to like the handwriting styles: hard up and soft down, and shading. Well, I enjoyed that but not much else, not even at that stage the writing of stories. At secondary school my experience was precisely the same. The two subjects I really enjoyed at secondary were history and geography. But when it came to maths I was totally out of my depth: I could never understand maths and have never understood those subjects to this day, although I've often thought it might be nice to understand algebra, for example. English I didn't enjoy because there was great emphasis placed upon grammar and parsing of sentences, and I certainly didn't get to grips with that either. We had one or two good teachers, but one or two who were really pretty awful, almost, well, not cruel, but I didn't like it at all. Of course many of the teachers had been pulled in from retirement or were actually working beyond their retirement age, and a lot of the younger teachers still hadn't come back from the war. So my whole experience at school really wasn't all that happy a one at all.

When I enrolled at Grove Academy there were different streams: A, B, C and D. A and B were the academic streams. C was more of a commercial stream, which I was interested in because there you were taught to type, do shorthand and book-keeping, and I still had it in my mind I wanted to be a reporter. But unfortunately they didn't have enough pupils to fill that course. I didn't have the brain power to get into the A or B stream, so they put me into D, a technical course: woodwork, metalwork, technical drawing, mechanics. Now these were subjects which have not served me one single purpose throughout my life. I took two years to make an ashtray, which wasn't even fit, even at the end of that time, for a fag end; and I made a poker – with a great bend in the middle of it. I fell behind in the subjects I've mentioned, and was never able to catch up. So I was lost. I didn't know what the teacher was saying half the time. My marks were dreadful. I can still remember how the exam papers were handed out and each person's name was shouted out along with the mark. My marks were very, very rarely above 50: they were away down in the 30s. So I was really glad to get away from school. I found it oppressive.

As a boy I did a lot of reading – nothing classical: detective stories, and I used to be particularly fond of reading books – there seemed to be a lot of them at the time – with stories about English public schools of all things: fags and prefects, the Billy Bunter type of stuff. I was about 10 or 11 when I joined the public library in Broughty Ferry. And then comics: I remember getting the *Dandy* and the *Beano*.[1] My father or my mother used to bring them home regularly, and of course the great D.C. Thomson's boys' papers, the *Hotspur, Adventure, Wizard*, and *Rover*. I was a great fan of *Radio Fun*. We did exchange comics with a pal, because of course we didn't have all that much money, so the comics were handed round.

Then cricket was my consuming passion. The reason for that really was very simple: I was born in a house which overlooked the Forfarshire county cricket ground. They had a wonderful team. So I gravitated to cricket, just as I would have done if I'd been living beside a golf course, I suppose. My father, of course, being English, was a great cricket person, a lifelong supporter of Kent. So obviously I got encouragement from within the house to take up cricket, and there it was on my doorstep. So I started playing cricket up at the Forfarshire county ground during the war, from the year I left school in 1943 into 1945. During the war there was no county championship, but they played every Saturday with a team composed of servicemen stationed in the area: Dundee had a lot of RAF, navy and army installations. So you had a wonderful collection of players at Forthill, some of them very good, from English counties. I played for the County Select Team, as it was called. At the end of the war the good players started coming back from the Forces. I couldn't get a place in the county side and began to play for the seconds as both batsman and bowler. Cricket has remained the consuming passion of my life, but I stopped playing it unfortunately when I became a reporter, because I was working on Saturdays.

As a boy I was in both the Cubs and the Boys' Brigade. My father being English, I was brought up in the Scottish Episcopal Church. I became a server, which meant I helped the minister serve communion in the morning by handing out or helping him hand out the wine and the bread; and I sang in the choir. I also joined Broughty Ferry YMCA in 1946 when I was about 17, and it was there I went to learn to play table tennis.[2] There was a man in Forthill who had been a champion table tennis player before the war, and he came back to Forthill, took about half a dozen of us down to the YMCA, and we all finished up playing in the first division. Table tennis was a wonderful game and I played until I went into newspapers.

Well, what I tried to do when I left school in 1943 was obviously to get a job in the Dundee *Courier*. I made an approach to the *Courier*, but I got a letter back saying that because of my lack of qualifications the *Courier* couldn't really entertain me. It was frustrating. But I had to do something, and I answered an advert for an office boy in a jute merchant's office and I got that job. It was a company called William Wait Sons & Atkinson, a Leeds firm, and it was a very small office in the middle of Dundee. Walter Robertson was the man who ran it, and he had a junior partner called Arthur Miller. They bought and sold jute. They had a clerk, a typist, and I was the office boy. I think I was paid 7s 6d [37½p] a week. The hours were nine till six, and 12 o'clock on Saturdays. Well, I was delivering letters all the time. There were then a tremendous network of jute factories and jute firms in Dundee, and I was despatched at regular intervals during the day to deliver letters to the various factory offices throughout the town. So I did a lot of foot slogging. I was also given very menial tasks to do in the office – putting stamps on the letters, taking a note of where the letters were going to, checking the addresses on the envelopes to make sure the typist had them right, and that sort of thing. So I stayed there for, oh, a couple of years.

From there I went on then to serve a three-year apprenticeship as a jute clerk with another jute merchant, Thomas Bonar; a big Dundee name the Bonars, part of the Low & Bonar conglomerate. Thomas Bonar was quite a big office, employing perhaps 30 or 40 people. The work I did was more interesting than at Wait Sons & Atkinson. I was making out invoices and decoding cables from Calcutta, from the jute growers. You would get by cable and wireless, as I remember it, a page or two or three pages just with codes, which were three or four letters slung together. You had a big book and would simply decode them. I also made out labels for the despatch of goods from Dundee railway station, because we were handling jute goods between factories and customers, and I had to make out railway invoices and that sort of thing. It was quite a rigorous apprenticeship. It was a friendly office, with more people to communicate with and make friends with. I honestly can't remember how much I was being paid at Bonar's, but the annual increments were very small. The hours were the same standard working hours. These were my hours throughout my seven years in a jute office, they never varied.

After I left school I had begun on my own initiative going to evening classes four nights a week at Grove Academy. I went for about three years. I studied English, arithmetic, history, and there may have been one or two other subjects. I didn't do typing or shorthand. I felt a sense of inadequacy and even resentment at the way I'd been treated at school. I had an appetite for learning and found the more relaxed atmosphere at evening classes suited my temperament much, much better. We sat exams and I did get certificates. In those days of course there was no day release to pursue studies as part of my apprenticeship: whatever study you did had to be done in the evening after a day's work. Class fees and other expenses came out of my own pocket. But I didn't have to take certain courses anyway as part of my apprenticeship. At the end of my three years' apprenticeship at Bonar's there was no formal statement that I was now an articled clerk, nothing of that sort, just the three years' training.

I then got a job as a clerk with this other company, David Pirie & Co. That again was a very small merchant office, like the first one I'd gone to. It was right in the middle of Dundee, just next door to the first one. All these jute offices were within a radius of about 250 yards of each other. I was about 19 by then and found myself working under this man, one of the junior directors, who was really very, very unpleasant. He kept picking holes in the work I was doing, and just making life absolute hell for me. He was a very cynical, unpleasant person and he wasn't popular in the office. I don't know why he picked on me, but he seemed to take a dislike to me from the moment I started there, and it just went on like that. So I hated that job.

But it was the best thing that could have happened to me, because it then reactivated my whole desire to become a reporter. I had actually by then given up a bit on that ambition. I had accepted the fact that here I was in jute and I wasn't going to get into newspapers. But when this junior director made me terribly unhappy I decided I must get out of this place, and I began to think, well, let's try again to do what I tried when I left school.

I hadn't done anything at all to prepare myself to work in newspapers, hadn't taken any shorthand or typing courses. Of course, I had led a pretty busy life, because not only was I working in the jute offices but also I was spending every available hour I could playing games – football, cricket, table tennis, swimming, a bit of golf. After office hours that was my life. I played outside right for a couple of seasons for a prominent amateur team in Dundee, YM Anchorage, and for another team as well called Midmill. I was never a competitive swimmer, but we went to the baths two or three times a week.

Well, my parents were obviously conscious of my unhappiness in this office. My father was by then an assistant council officer with Dundee town council and was friendly with several of the Dundee *Courier* reporters who called regularly at the Town House to pick up bits and pieces of news. So he spoke to them about me, and through that channel the *Courier* invited me up for an interview. I got either a phone call or a letter, 'Will you please come for an interview in Meadowside at two o'clock in the afternoon.' Well, how was I going to get off my work to go? I didn't want to tell them at Pirie's I was going away for an interview. So I decided I would go for the interview, go into my work late, and make some excuse about having felt unwell at lunchtime. Well, I went in at two o'clock to Meadowside – and the interview finished at five o'clock. It lasted three hours, during which I was passed from one editor to another and finished up in Bank Street. D.C. Thomson's had two offices in central Dundee, one in Meadowside and one in Bank Street, very close to each other. There were all sorts of questions put to me, to test my general knowledge. I'd seen the personnel officer to begin with and he had just passed me on, and he saw me again after the final interview at five o'clock. He said to me, 'Well, we've decided to take you on our reporting staff for a probationery period of six months, provided you pass the medical examination.' So I staggered out of Bank Street at five o'clock. It was a winter's night. I went home. When I went into Pirie's office next day I simply said to them, very untruthfully, that I'd been rather unwell the previous afternoon and couldn't get into my work although I'd tried once or twice. Well, I did pass the medical examination, had the great pleasure of handing in my resignation at Pirie's, and duly started about a month later in D.C. Thomson's in 1950 at the age of 21.

Medical examinations remind me that I wasn't called up for National Service because I failed my medical then. They discovered something that I had shown no sign of before then nor, thankfully, since: that my heart had a disorganised action. Although it appeared to function perfectly normally, they weren't prepared to take the risk. 'So we'll just stamp you Class 4. Thanks very much. But you're not going into uniform.' This didn't break my heart at all.

So I was late in starting in a newspaper, and to get into the *Courier* then you had to have your Highers – at least Higher English and perhaps one other Higher, which of course I never had and still don't have, not that I'm particularly proud of that. So I was about the oldest tea boy they'd ever had. I don't remember clearly what it was I was paid when I started in the *Courier*, but it was less – maybe £2 a week less – than the salary I was getting in the jute office. I started at the bottom of the ladder and they didn't make any concession at all to me. But of course I was living at home, and my father and mother were quite happy to subsidise me for that period until I caught up again. I suppose it reflected my keenness to become a reporter that I was willing to sacrifice even maybe £2 a week. I do remember that when, aged 24, I got married in 1953, three years after I began in the *Courier*, I was getting five guineas [£5.25] a week. My wife, a secretary in a transport company in Dundee, was then earning £7 a week. So she was earning a couple of quid more than me when we got married.

The work I was doing in the *Courier* to begin with was, well, road accidents in the police court. And I was allocated to whatever reporter was covering stories like that. For the first few months I was always accompanied by a more senior member of the staff, who introduced me to things. They were extremely helpful, very patient, and I remained friends with a lot of them for a long, long time, and am still in touch with some of them, long since retired. There was also a delightful thing called stations, harbour, and hotels. This was a round that you made twice a day. You went to the two railway stations in Dundee, spoke to the porters and any of the officials you could find, and found out if anything untoward had happened in the station that day. You would go round the harbour, a network of docks, where they had little offices where the dock gate men worked from, and ask them, well, 'What are the shipping movements?', and anything untoward again. And you would go to the police station, the fire station, and the ambulance office – all the calls. So I spent possibly the first year just doing things like that. I was very nervous to start with, I can certainly remember that. I must have taken hours to type up a small story. But everybody was very helpful, and they were patient. And no one harassed me. At the end of six months they said I could stay on. There was no question at all. They said, 'Well, that's it. Just settle down.'

The two things I had to learn over and above all of that of course were shorthand and typing. The *Courier* had a marvellous man, Mr Adamson, who was a retired commercial teacher of shorthand. He came into the *Courier* office one afternoon every week and those who were learning shorthand went to him. He put us through it – a crash course in shorthand. And I spent hours and hours at home listening to the radio, taking things down in shorthand until I was reasonably proficient, because I was very conscious that I was late in starting and had to catch up. There were one or two people younger than me on the staff who were, however, quite experienced by then. So I really felt I had to work that extra bit and I did do. I worked very, very hard indeed. It was at least a year before I got up to 150 or 160 words a minute in shorthand, because I was doing court and council work. So, I mean, you couldn't stop and ask people to say it again! You had to get it right. And of course I taught myself to type. I didn't go to typing classes, but taught myself in the office during the day. I was also taught to drive: the *Courier* put me through driving school at their expense. So I had all these things to do on top of learning the actual craft.

I was more mature than the youngsters in the office, so I probably found things less difficult than they did. People often say to me that my seven years in the jute merchants' offices were seven wasted years. Well, they weren't wasted years at all. First of all, I was taught an office discipline, which I've always found very, very useful, particularly later on when I went into television and was running an office in Dundee. Then I was taught to be punctual and tidy and all that sort of thing, and to handle people properly. I learned through those years, unhappy though many of them were. So they weren't wasted years.

There was roughly a score of reporters on the staff at D.C. Thomson's in Dundee. There were actually three women on the staff, and the rest were men. Jessie Milne, who was about 20 years older than me, and Helen Mary Mungo were two of the women reporters. They did general reporting, they were in there, in the trenches with the men, but one of them did the church notes, and there were various features that they did as well that were more suitable for a woman to do. Jessie Milne was there a long time before me. Jessie was marvellous. Apart from all the other things that she had to do Jessie did 'Pulpit and Pew' in the *Evening Telegraph* every Saturday afternoon. She would come in in the morning on the Friday, phone all the ministers in Dundee, and ask them for their news![3] But I cannot remember a single woman sub-editor on the *Courier*, *Evening Telegraph* or the *Sunday Post* staffs.

Everybody started work in the morning. If you were going to the police court you started at nine o'clock. If you weren't, then you would start work just very shortly after that. And we all worked during the day and then, as I remember it, we all had to work two nights a week. So we were working during the day basically for the *Evening Telegraph*, but rewriting our stories for the *Courier* the next day, and then going back two nights a week purely to cover stories for the *Courier* the next morning. We also had to contribute gossip paragraphs for the *People's Journal*.[4] They had a page called 'Bellman's Budget', of just little off-beat stories, and we were expected to supply perhaps one or two of these every week – without any additional payment. And of course you had also a *Sunday Post* rota to work one Saturday evening maybe every four or six weeks – which again was unpaid. On the Saturday night only two of us were on. Of course, we were working on Saturdays as well for the *Evening Telegraph* in the morning. I would then have to perhaps cover a football or cricket match in the afternoon. It was a heavy, demanding job. On the three evenings a week you didn't have to stay on for the *Courier* you would finish at five o'clock. On the two evenings you stayed on you would finish basically after your evening work, your job, was over – any time from 10pm onwards. We did have a late shift which came along perhaps once every six or seven weeks for the *Courier*, and that was starting at 5pm and finishing at two in the morning. The *Sunday Post*, which was largely a feature newspaper, had their own staff, absolutely separate from the *Courier* and *Evening Telegraph*. They came in and occupied the sub-editors' room on a Saturday afternoon. They would come in with their own set of sub-editors between 4 and 5pm as the *Evening Telegraph* subs were packing up to go home. And they would handle the running stories in that way, handle all the stuff coming over the wires, with us two reporters from the *Courier* and *Telegraph* to cover anything local that broke on Saturday evening. The *Sunday Post* staff would have a day off maybe on a Monday or Tuesday, but they were certainly working away all through the rest of the week. I just don't know how many staff the *Sunday Post* had. It wasn't an open editorial floor as they now have. They had their own set of rooms and it was a place that I never really went into. I had no need to have contact with them, only on a Saturday evening when I was working for them did I bump into them.

As I've said, when after six months I'd finished my probationary period successfully and could stay on, it was an immense feeling of relief to me. But I had had sacrifices to make, and one of those was that I really had basically to give up my sport: I was working Saturday afternoons. And I didn't want to start asking for time off, especially during those first six months. I really didn't think about it too much at the time, it wasn't a huge sacrifice at the time at all. But years later, and even yet when I look back, I think it was a pity I had to stop playing at the time I did because I lost a lot of good years in sport. However, I'd had a good fill of sport by the time I went into journalism. The overpowering urge to be a reporter overcame all that, submerged it all.

When I went into the D.C. Thomson press it was strictly non-union.

Nobody said anything to me. But I signed the paper. I can't remember much about it, except that it was just a simple slip of paper in which I had to promise that while I was in the employment of D.C. Thomson I would not join a trade union organisation. And I very quickly signed it. I didn't think twice about it, because I was not brought up in a trade union household, and the jute offices I'd worked in didn't have trade unions. I never heard anybody speak about a trade union in the jute offices. You must remember I wasn't working then in the jute factories but in the merchant offices. There was never any mention of joining a trade union there. So trade unionism just didn't touch me at all. I don't remember any discussion among the reporters in the *Courier* office in the first year or two I was there about trade unionism, or any ill feelings or divisions or anything of that sort. I was never conscious at all of any feeling of that sort under the surface in the office. It was never a talking point, as I remember it, and never a source of dispute or disaffection or anything. Of course, what would happen occasionally was that reporters left the *Courier* and went to national newspapers and they would speak about the better salaries they were going to. It wasn't that D.C. Thomson paid a higher salary in order to dissuade or deter reporters from joining the union. All I know is that when I left in 1954 to go to *The Bulletin* in Glasgow, I think my salary jumped up about £2 a week, which was quite a bit in those days. In 1953, during the time I was with the *Courier*, in fact one of those disputes did flare up between Thomson's and the unions. And the rail people refused to carry our papers. We would very often get phone calls from the railway stations saying would we come down and pick up our papers. They were still lying on the platform. I think one of Thomson's reactions at that time was that when they discovered the railway staffs were not going to carry their newspapers, they went out and bought a fleet of vans and delivered all the papers by road. I don't know to what extent they'd had vans before then, but they certainly increased their fleet of vehicles and got the papers through. But all that didn't affect my work as a reporter in any way at all.[5]

Reporters on the other papers in Dundee, who were in the union, mixed with Thomson's reporters. They found themselves on the same assignments day in and day out, they knew each other and they were civil to each other. There was never any animosity between them at all. And Thomson's supplied copy on a linage basis to many trade union papers. I forget what these papers were, but they must have been something like *The Scotsman*, the *Guardian*, and *The Times*. We did all *The Scotsman* stuff, and they were all trade union there. Then people who sent a big lot of copy to us were the Press Association. That was standard. So they had a linage pool and we all got a cut out of it. That would increase our emoluments a bit. But there was certainly no unpleasantness at all between the staff men of the nationals and the *Courier* people.

So I was at D.C. Thomson's in Dundee for just under four years. Then I went to *The Bulletin* in Glasgow. The *Glasgow Herald* had an office and a staff man, George Mackintosh, a well-known newspaperman, in Dundee.[6] One afternoon I was in the *Courier*'s reporters' room and a phone call came through for me. This was George Mackintosh phoning me from just outside the office, saying, 'Would you be interested in the job in Glasgow in *The Bulletin*?' And I said, yes, I thought I might be. I'd been married then for a year. George Mackintosh came back to me a couple of days later and said, 'They're expecting you through in Glasgow.' I had to report to Buchanan Street at 5pm to see Tom Chalmers, joint news editor of the *Glasgow Herald* and *The Bulletin* and who wore a patch over one eye. I said, 'I don't finish my work in Dundee until 5pm. But I've to go to my shorthand class that day at 3pm. So instead of going to the class I'll go down and catch the train to Glasgow.' So I went through to Glasgow, had an interview, was offered the job, and got the train back. When I went into the office next day, the chief reporter said to me: 'And where were you yesterday afternoon? We were trying to get you. We sent across to the shorthand class and you weren't there.' So I was caught with my pants down and I had to make some sort of feeble excuse! Then a few days later I handed in my notice! I had no hesitation about taking *The Bulletin* job. I had been very, very keen to get into the *Courier*. I realised I had to get in there to get the basic training. But I'd never really made up my mind I would stay in the *Courier* all my life. There was a paper in Broughty Ferry, the *Broughty Ferry Guide*, but I never considered any of those.[7] I knew that the training you got in D.C. Thomson was extremely good and I had wanted to avail myself of that, but never with the long-term intention – oh, I could easily have . . . I mean, I hadn't consciously made up my mind to leave D.C. Thomson. The phone call from George Mackintosh came from out the blue, offering a better salary and an interest-free loan to buy a house. I was then with my wife in a rented property in Dundee in a tenement with an outside toilet. So we were anxious to improve that situation. Going to Glasgow was going to do that. It was going to widen my scope and my horizon as a journalist, and perhaps even at that stage – my wife and I were looking into the future – that would present perhaps a launch platform for going to London. My sights were rising. So for all those reasons we went to Glasgow.

My salary went up quite considerably then. As I've said, I think I was getting about an extra £2 a week. Then at D.C. Thomson's expenses were very basic, you had to justify things. *The Bulletin* of course was a bit better. I think you got paid for lunches and an evening meal there if you were out then on a story and this sort of thing. But of course you didn't get that with Thomson's, a strict organisation; but, I mean, I hadn't taken badly with that, because I had come from working in a jute office which itself had a very tight code of discipline. But *The Bulletin* was a more relaxed atmosphere.

Though *The Bulletin* was sub-titled '*and Scots Pictorial*', I was never conscious in all my newspaper life of having to think in terms of images. The photographer did his job and I did mine. My working relationship with the photographer even on *The Bulletin* was no closer than it was on any other newspaper, although of course it was a pictorial paper.

The Bulletin had a smaller staff than the Dundee *Courier* – perhaps about nine or ten. I also found there I was meeting a different set of people, and again they were all very pleasant. We had an interesting situation, because the *Glasgow Herald*, *The Bulletin*, and the *Evening Times* reporters were all in the same big open space. So you were rubbing shoulders with them all. A reporter with me on *The Bulletin* was Harry Diamond. He was a character. Harry was Jewish and he took me to a synagogue. We had to go to a service one evening in Glasgow, and the two of us were sent there to cover it. I always remember saying to Harry after we got into the synagogue, 'Why are they all wearing hats in your church?' And he says, 'Why do they all take them off in your church?'! Harry went on to become the public relations officer in Glasgow for, I think, the Gas Board, then later on for Glasgow District Council.[8] But there were a lot of interesting people on *The Bulletin*. A real character there called George Harvey finished up as news editor of the BBC in Scotland. George, who stayed in Garrowhill beside me, had been in Bomber Command during the war and had done a tremendous number of missions over Germany. Two or three of us, including Bob Brown, were all grouped together in Garrowhill.

The chief reporter was James Paton, a man of gentle disposition, unmarried, a very, very fine man. I was very lucky having him as chief reporter, because he was really considerate, though a stickler for detail and accuracy that drove me up the wall very often, but a fine man. Tom Chalmers was news editor – actually of *The Bulletin*, the *Glasgow Herald*, and the *Evening Times*: he did all three. Tom was an ex-D.C. Thomson man. There were one or two ex-D.C. Thomson there in *The Bulletin*. That was the thing, you kept on bumping into them, they were all over the place. There were hundreds and hundreds of journalists started off with D.C. Thomson. George Thomson, later Lord Thomson of Monifeith, for instance, he was on the comics – the *Dandy*. In later years that was held against him quite a lot in his CV, you know, sub-editor on the *Dandy*. George stayed in Monifeith, outside Dundee, and I was friendly with him. But he started off on the Dundee *Courier*.[9] Dundee was the city of jam, jute, and journalism – and it was recognised that D.C. Thomson's gave a terrific training in journalism. Then when I went to *The Bulletin* in 1954 there was just one woman reporter out of the nine or ten, but I can't remember her name now. There were a couple of women then on the *Glasgow Herald*, but I don't think there was a woman reporter on the *Evening Times*. Again I can't remember any women sub-editors. But unlike D.C. Thomson's, the staffs at Outrams were absolutely separate – separate for the *Herald*, *The Bulletin*, and *Evening Times*. Another thing was there was really very little transferring from one staff to another. I can't remember any transferring at all from one staff to another by any individual during the three or four years I was there.

When you were on *The Bulletin*, very often you would take a black, or carbon copy, of your story and give it to the *Herald*. So you got a sort of double exposure for your work. That was rewarding, because the *Glasgow Herald* was a very prestigious paper, though you didn't get paid any extra when you did that. The only way we could make extra money was by contributing diary items at 7s 6d [37½p] a head, which was a lot then, for the *Evening Times*. I used to get perhaps two or three a week in, so that was quite valuable.

Then the stories in *The Bulletin* were bigger and more exciting: I was very conscious of the fact that I was working for a Scottish national newspaper. I certainly enjoyed the atmosphere very much indeed. I felt that I was sort of in the big time, I was in a bigger city than Dundee, and the whole thing had just stepped up. The adrenalin was going and I enjoyed it.

When I went to *The Bulletin* I joined the union right away. I think it was more or less a closed shop at that time, and I just joined the union. I had no objection in principle, none whatsoever.

When I was on *The Bulletin* I can't remember any talk about the paper closing. Obviously the circulation wasn't all that healthy. I can't remember what it was, but it wasn't a mass circulation paper at any time. There was occasional talk about the paper's circulation problem. But I never felt that my job there was under threat. There was no crisis of that sort. It was a couple of years after I left that *The Bulletin* went out of publication.

I was with *The Bulletin* about the same number of years I'd passed with D.C. Thomson – about four years. I moved from *The Bulletin* in 1958 to the *Daily Herald*. Now in the last year or 18 months I was with *The Bulletin*

I decided that if I wanted to get on, perhaps one of the ways to do it would be to specialise. So I began to specialise in industrial stories and to exercise a preference for doing industrial stories. The chief reporter was quite happy about that. After I'd been doing that for a few months they decided they would give me a byline. So I became *The Bulletin's* first and only industrial correspondent, and I was bylined as such – a great thrill, and a big step forward in those days, because bylines were very rare. Of course I began to go to the conferences: the mineworkers', the Trades Union Congress, the Labour Party – all the Scottish conferences. So I was in the industrial group of correspondents. Among them was Ian Coulter, the *Daily Herald* man. Ian then was promoted to be northern industrial and political correspondent for the *Daily Herald*, and went down to Manchester. My good friend Bob Brown put in a word for me, I went down to Manchester, was interviewed by Norman Wilson, the northern editor, and he said, 'Right, the job's yours.' So I became the *Daily Herald* man in Scotland for industry and politics.

I was very pleased indeed about that. Of course my salary went up, though again I can't remember just how much. I could then afford to buy a car, and I got mileage. Expenses were good because you were covering the whole of Scotland. Well, the *Daily Herald* had an office in Bothwell Street, Glasgow. They had a small staff: a general or two general reporters, and I of course was there as specialist in industrial and political affairs. The *Daily Herald* of course was, or had been, very much regarded as a Labour paper with a capital 'L'. That didn't present any difficulties to me as a journalist. I was brought up in a house which was totally free from prejudice. It was a house where party politics weren't really discussed, nor differences in religion, and there was absolutely no feeling of prejudice at all in the house against this or that. So when I left home and went out into the world I didn't have any fixed, strongly held opinions on any of these things. Thus I signed the non-trade union paper easily at D.C. Thomson's, and I signed the trade union thing easily at *The Bulletin*. Now I was with a paper that was in total sympathy with the Labour movement, both politically and industrially, and again that didn't pose any problems to me at all. It did pose a problem to me of a different sort after I had been in the job for quite a while, and that was that I felt that with many of the stories that I was working on I had an unfair advantage over many of the other reporters, because the stories were Labour-sourced. I had very quick and easy entry into trade union circles, so I could get those stories much more easily. I just needed to mention I was from the *Daily Herald* and doors would open. Reporters from the *Daily Express, Daily Mail*, etc., wouldn't have that sort of access.

So an exclusive for me didn't give me the same thrill at all as it had done on *The Bulletin*. So later on that became a problem. In fact, I then began to feel that I was working for a sort of propaganda machine. In tandem with that was the feeling that it was perhaps a rather restricted circle of journalism that I was working in. Although I'd wanted to specialise I then decided that perhaps it wasn't a great idea after all, because I was being prevented from covering all sorts of other stories that interested me. So I decided for those two reasons to break out from specialisation – and to break away from the *Daily Herald*.

I intimated to the *Daily Herald* that I was going to leave, my wife and I had decided we'd come back to Dundee, not go to London, because we both missed Dundee and both felt a bit homesick, I suppose. We'd decided to come back to Dundee, or Broughty Ferry, put down our roots and bring up a family. The *Daily Herald* then offered me a job down south and said, 'Well, look, we'll bring you down to Manchester or to London.' And I said, 'Well, that's very kind of you, but I can't really accept that. I really have made up my mind to go back to Dundee.' Geoffrey Goodman, the industrial correspondent of the *Daily Herald* in London, a very nice bloke, wrote me a nice letter. He said, 'I accept the fact that you want to get back to Dundee. But it's very difficult for me working down here in London to understand how someone like yourself doesn't want to come down here and do the same thing.' Geoffrey was obviously puzzled that somebody would want to come back to Dundee rather than go down to London. He'd never lived in Dundee! So we made our mind up.[10]

So after two years with the *Daily Herald* I came back to Dundee at the beginning of 1960. When I was in Glasgow I'd got to hear that the *Sunday Mail* wanted to set up a local man in Dundee to cover this area of Scotland, and another man in Aberdeen. So I approached the *Sunday Mail* and said I was interested. The editor, Jack Robertson, appointed me to the job in Dundee. Before I took the job up a month later Jack Robertson had left the editor's chair and it was taken over by Sandy Webster, a very prominent newspaperman in Scotland.

So I was a one-man band then in the *Sunday Mail* in Dundee for three years. But my work on the *Daily Herald* had to some extent prepared me for that, because as the industrial correspondent I'd been a one-man band there, too. I worked in the same office under the same roof as the *Daily Record* staff – two reporters and a photographer, though I was in a separate room. The photographer worked for me as well. My job was basically to fill a page of local news. I did that under my own name, because by then I had started appearing regularly on television and radio in Glasgow, and Sandy Webster was keen to cash in on that. On the *Daily Herald* I had found myself being invited on to panel programmes for Scottish TV and the BBC, quizzing trade union leaders and politicians. Because I had represented a left-wing paper my presence was desirable.

I found television and radio a bit nerve-racking to begin with. The first programme I ever appeared on was particularly so. It was the first televised election programme broadcast in Scotland, and it was the Kelvingrove by-election in 1958, caused by the death of Walter Elliot.[11] The BBC and STV decided to combine to do two programmes jointly in which the candidates would be questioned by two journalists, with a chairman. I got the job because I represented a left-wing newspaper. Alastair Burnet, its leader writer, represented the *Glasgow Herald* as the right-wing newspaper. I got to know him quite well after I'd left *The Bulletin*, because he and I began to appear on different programmes. The *Daily Herald* had been very good about it. They said to me, 'You can appear on television and do your radio work, provided we always get a credit.' So I would go up to STV at news times and do a report on a political conference or on an industrial story. They would simply hand over to me and I would just give a piece to camera. And then I did the panel programmes. So I did a lot of that. I enjoyed that. Well, it was a wonderful combination of newspaper work and television work, and that is the best combination of all. Although later on I spent 26 years exclusively doing television work I never really enjoyed it as much as when I was on the *Daily Herald* doing a bit of both. I got into radio just the same way. I found myself on radio programmes basically again because I was on a left-wing newspaper, the *Daily Herald*, giving a different point of view, and the radio people were getting the balance they needed. So, as I say, when I came back to Dundee in 1960 to work on the *Sunday Mail* Sandy Webster says, 'Well, we'll keep your name because your name is quite well known.' So I wrote this local page of news in the *Sunday Mail* for just over three years, and was very happy indeed.

Sandy Webster was a good editor, and he never bothered me. The news editor was Charles Smith, who had been the chief reporter of the *Daily Record*. I had worked with him on different stories in Glasgow when he was a reporter. I was no sooner back in Dundee on the *Sunday Mail* when Charles Smith became its deputy editor. I was directly answerable to him, we knew each other, and we got on well together. He was the man who eventually took me into television.[12]

I continued to work in Dundee for the *Sunday Mail* until 1963. That year I got a particularly good exclusive story which the *Sunday Express* liked very much indeed. On the strength of that, they suggested that I work for them in Dundee. So I then started work for the *Sunday Express* and did so for two years. I was on my own, but in the same room as the reporters for the *Daily Express*. I didn't contribute stories to the *Daily Express* at all.

While I was on the *Sunday Mail* in Dundee, Charlie Smith, who by then had left that paper and gone up to Aberdeen to set up news and current affairs with Grampian TV in 1961, had contacted me and said, 'Look, if we send a film unit down to Dundee, in view of the television experience you had in Glasgow will you be able to do a number of stories for us in Dundee, because we have a nightly programme and it eats up an awful lot of material? We can't afford to start an office in Dundee. But we'll send a unit down one day a week.' So I got permission from Sandy Webster as editor of the *Sunday Mail*, to do the work for Grampian TV, again because the *Sunday Mail* got a credit and Sandy felt it was spreading my name around and they would read it in the *Sunday Mail*. But the *Sunday Express* didn't allow me to appear on television. So between 1963 and 1965 I worked exclusively for the *Sunday Express*. That job was a bit less satisfying than the *Sunday Mail* and the *Daily Herald*, because I didn't get that balance between newspapers and television and radio, which was absolutely wonderful. The *Sunday Express*, however, was a good experience. I did get the feeling I was working for a big, big newspaper. They were a very efficient lot, no expense spared at all, and you got the stories, that was it. I definitely got the feeling I was working for a big, powerful organisation.

But when Grampian TV approached me in 1965 and said, 'We're setting an office up in Dundee,' and would I run it for them and cover the news in an area roughly from Montrose down to Edinburgh, I decided this was an opportunity I should take. I thought, 'Well, I'm going to give this a run for a while and see how I enjoy it,' because I had enjoyed doing television before. So for that reason and also because it was something which I would be able to mould to a certain extent to my own shape as I was the first person in the job, I really had no hesitation at all in taking that job. And I did really think that that would perhaps last for a number of years and then I might come back to newspapers. But of course I never did. I remained with Grampian TV for 26 years until I retired in 1991.

Grampian was exciting, particularly in the early years – och, well, I enjoyed it all the time really. The BBC had started television in Scotland at the time of the Coronation in 1953, and STV in 1957. But commercial television in the north-east of Scotland was comparatively new, and at Grampian we were doing stories in interesting ways. I did a lot of feature work, and you did offbeat stories, which I loved doing. So it was really good.

In those early days Grampian struggled. I mean, they made very little at the end of the year, but they held together and got stronger and stronger. My position stayed the same all the time: my title was the Dundee manager, but I was really a senior reporter. But what administrative work had to be done, I had to do it. For the first 15 or so years our office had been in the middle of Dundee, right underneath the Angus Hotel in a row of shops, two of which Grampian converted into a studio and a couple of offices. We operated there from 1965 to 1980. Then I had 10 years down here in Broughty Ferry, just across the road from my house.

There was a lot of travelling involved in the job, and I spent quite a bit of time going up and down to Aberdeen. I travelled about 26,000 miles a year with Grampian. I always remember one day doing stories in each of the four cities – Aberdeen, Edinburgh, Glasgow, and Dundee! We worked enormously long hours, with our overtime. Well, I was starting before nine o'clock in the morning and sometimes not getting home until after seven o'clock at night. I had quite a big catchment area to cover, although most of the stuff obviously came out of Dundee. But we went across to Fife a lot. Then they opened a studio in Calton Road, Edinburgh, basically to produce closed-circuit educational programmes for Edinburgh University. That studio operated for six or seven years, I think, so we very often went through to Edinburgh and I would do interviews in the studio there. It was a very hectic life, but never, never boring. And again I had a lot of freedom.

You were, you know, in a sense pioneering commercial television in the north-east of Scotland. It was great, and a huge area. Our programmes went to the top of Shetland and down to the edge of Edinburgh. I could pick and choose the stories, with nobody breathing down my neck, because I had a good working relationship with Charlie Smith. He could trust me and I was left very largely to my own devices. Charlie, however, sadly died in 1977 from a heart attack. He was only in his mid-50s then.

I worked with a film unit: a sound man and a cameraman, and we had a secretary who manned the office when we were out, which was most of the time. So these were very fulfilling years, though quite stressful. I found the studio work, appearing live in front of cameras, very stressful. So many things could go wrong and frequently did. One often wondered how you even survived it, because there's a lot of rushing around, meeting dead-lines, and sitting in front of a camera. And very often the live programmes you were doing were at the end of the day, when you were at your lowest ebb. I was writing a piece today for my column in the Dundee *Courier*, just reminding readers of the time when Selina Scott arrived in Aberdeen. She and I presented the nightly news programme for about 18 months. Selina went on to big things, to become a millionairess, and I stayed put at Grampian and retired in poverty![13] But the point was the two of us were presenting that programme at six o'clock at night, and we'd been working from nine o'clock in the morning. And then of course at the end of that I'd get into my car and drive home to Dundee. As I've said, I'd found the stress of television was much easier to cope with when I was also doing newspapers. It was a great balance. When I got into Grampian and was doing nothing else but television, I found the strain considerably more.

Many reporters progressed into sub-editing. I never felt attracted to that, never wanted to be a sub-editor. Of the two reasons I'd wanted to become a reporter one was obviously because I wanted to write. The second, equally important, was that there was a big wide busy world out there and all sorts of interesting things were happening in it. I really had a great appetite to know what was happening and why and how it was happening, and to tell people about those things. That was my basic instinct. I never lost it. So I never wanted to be a sub-editor. Similarly in television I didn't want to progress to become a programme director or a head of news or anything like that. I simply wanted to be a reporter, and that's the way I remained all my life.

I was fortunate in the sense that most of the jobs I got were offered to me. And then when I was working in television I contributed articles for three years to the *Scots Magazine*. Ironically, I was stopped by the union from doing those because they then clamped down on union members contributing stuff to D.C. Thomson publications. I was sorry about that because I enjoyed working for the *Scots Magazine*.[14]

Well, I took early retirement from Grampian TV in 1991 when I was just over 60. They were then starting to get rid of people who were a bit older. They offered me a very good package and I decided it was a good time to get out. By then what was happening was there were young lads coming into the newsroom who hadn't even been born when I went to Grampian, and who were coming on the phone to me in the morning saying, 'Go out and do that and do this.' They had me running around like . . . you know. By then I was beginning to feel I was just getting a wee bit past it. And I wanted to do a bit of writing.

I'm back now to where I started, because I'm working for D.C. Thomson, writing a column every Wednesday for the Dundee *Courier*, and I've been doing that since the week I left Grampian in 1991. The other thing that happened was that Dundee was into its octocentenary year in 1991. A local publishing company asked me if I would write a book about Dundee the way it once was, in conjunction with a local man, Douglas Phillips, a very well-known artist. There's no city in Scotland has changed so much as Dundee since the end of the Second World War. So

Douglas did all the illustrations, I did the text, they got the book out in September 1991, it did very well, and we did another three after that. I'm working now on the biography of James McIntosh Patrick, the painter, who died in 1998.[15] He was one of the men I met through television and remained friendly with until the day he died. That was one of the great things about television, particularly in the early days when people were unaccustomed to appearing on it. They depended very much upon the interviewer helping them through this strange experience. As a result you were apt to make friendships, and McIntosh Patrick's was one of that type. So in my retirement I've kept myself reasonably busy! And of course I have a disabled son. Alistair has got muscular dystrophy and my wife and I look after him. One of the other reasons for my taking early retirement was so I could give my wife more of a hand, and that has worked out fine as well.

Well, looking back over my career in newspaper, radio, and television journalism – I worked about 16 years on newspapers and 26 years on TV. Television was entirely different from newspapers. Television's largely showbiz. And I only worked with the one TV company, so I can't compare it with any other. That was a wonderful experience and I don't regret that at all. On the newspaper side, working for the *Dundee Courier* was great. But I was really very conscious of the fact that I was almost a student. I was working like hell to try and catch up. So that wasn't really a very relaxing time. I think the happiest time I had in newspapers was possibly working for the *Sunday Mail*, because then I still had that combination of working and filling a page of my own. Sandy Webster, the editor, said, 'That's your page, the Dundee page. You can treat it as your own newspaper. Do with it as you like. And if you want to do television work as well, as long as you don't neglect your own job, you do that as well.' So I had that wonderful experience for just over three years.

I have no regrets whatsoever about leaving the jute trade. It wasn't a wasted experience. But if that director at David Pirie & Co. had been nice to me I could have finished up being a jute clerk all my days.

John Cairns

Well, you could maybe say my latent talent was there waiting to be tapped and that it came through my father. He seems to have had that flair for writing, and though he would still be working then in the pits full-time, he was into newspapers, did BBC broadcasts, short stories, and all that sort of thing. He was always doing that from when I was a teenager. And I think my grandfather Cairns, a foundry worker, had an ability or a flair for writing as well.

I was born in Shotts, Lanarkshire, on 5 September 1928. There were only three of us in the family: my sister Margaret became Bob Brown's secretary in the *Glasgow Herald*; my brother Raymond, who died some years ago, was a mechanical engineer. I was the oldest, then came Margaret and then Raymond. My mother, before she got married, would be, I think, in domestic service, which was, I would say, the norm for girls at that time in a mining village or town like Shotts. You maybe got a doctor's housekeeper job or something like that for a girl.

My mother's father was a colliery fireman – a deputy or safety man. But he, like my other grandfather and grandmother, had died before I knew him. The only one I can remember is my grandmother on my mother's side.

My father had one of the more hazardous occupations in coal mining: he was a coal-cutting machineman. I think he would probably be working in the pits straight from school, but I'm not absolutely certain. I can't immediately recall the year he was born or the year he died, but it'd be after the Second World War, the late 1950s or '60s, he died. He'd been retired a few years. He was also a training officer with the National Coal Board, so clearly he was still working after nationalisation of the pits in 1947. In his early days he was always involved in the miners' union – it would be the Lanarkshire Miners' Union then. He was also what they called at that time a checkweighman and union representative, I think, at the pit.[1] I certainly never heard of my father working full-time at anything else other than the mining, which was par for the course for male members of families in and around Shotts.

They say there were 20 coal pits within and around Shotts at one time. I can't recall 20, but I can recall certainly several working collieries. Among them there was Southfield, Northfield, Baton, Hillhouserigg, Kepplehill Nos 1 and 2, which was also known as Stane colliery, and there was also a Stane mine where, you know, you walked into. Away back in the seventeenth century, around Shotts and the village of Salsburgh was, it seems, a Covenanter territory. And the story goes that 40 Covenanters were supposed to have sat on a large stone – hence the place name Fortissat, and Fortissat colliery. Then of the pits I couldn't recall and that are long gone there was Belmont, and, going in from Shotts to Fauldhouse, Knowton. I'm excluding the Coltness Iron Company pits at the village of Allanton, a suburb of Shotts, going towards Newmains and Wishaw. There was the Kingshill No.1, and Kingshill No. 3 at Allanton. I think Kingshill No. 2 (also known as Queenshill) was at Forth. So for males in that area in and around Shotts I would say mining would be in those days the principal source of employment. I can't recall seeing girls or women working around the pits in and about Shotts. But women have been pointed out to me who worked on the picking tables on the surface, you know, taking the stone away from the coal, and things like that.

Well, as I say, my father had that flair for writing. He began journalistic work after he was married. From when I was a teenager he was doing paragraphs for the *Daily Record*, other national press, and even a much lamented paper of the past, the *News Chronicle* – he used to do a football column there. As well as things like that he was doing general news reporting, features articles, and short stories, fictional stuff – a theme dreamed up and developed, and that sort of thing, which he got placed in newspapers, not magazines. He wasn't BBC staff but he did scripts, talks, and things like that, and eventually he contributed general news reports also to the BBC. It was quite remarkable for a working man, and that's what encouraged me to do likewise.

Then, too, my grandfather Cairns, who was either a brass or iron foundry worker, but who had died before I knew him, had an ability for writing as well. So I think there was some connection, you know, down the generations. In my grandfather's day the Shotts Iron Company had a brass foundry, iron foundry, blast furnaces, pattern shops, for making the cores for the foundries, and electrical and mechanical engineering, wagon building. It's all gone now: a health centre's built on most of that site now. I think my grandfather was also a brass band man. In Shotts, incidentally, I can recall three brass bands – St Patrick's, Dykehead, and the Foundry Brass Band, in addition to a flute band and the famous Shotts and Dykehead Caledonian Pipe Band. Two or three of these still survive. The basis of all those bands' income would be miners' voluntary contributions, maybe a penny or tuppence taken off their pay on a Friday. And in principle that sustained those bands. When I was a lad there were two cinemas, and a building locally known as The Pav, for Pavilion, that was a theatre and I think became a cinema, or vice versa. Miners were not supposed to be culturally minded, but that was wrong. In more recent times there's been an operetta society, and Gilbert and Sullivan and various other musicals. There was a literary, debating society and public library. The Miners' Welfare Building in Dyfey Street, Shotts, had an international swimming pool: I've attended international swimming galas there where all the great swimmers of the day, Eleanor Gordon, Nancy Riach, Christiansens from Denmark, took part. But that building is now demolished.[2] They also had a large hall for local concerts and public dancing.

At Shotts when I was growing up I always lived in a council house, never in a miner's row, though my father may have in his youthful days. The council house was in the Springhill area of Shotts. I think my parents had had that house since they got married. It had one or two bedrooms, a bath, a garden back and front.

I started school at the usual age of five. My family was Catholic, so I went to St Patrick's School in Shotts. I mentioned there was a flute band in Shotts, but that didn't mean some sort of sectarianism. In the nature of the Shotts men's calling, working beside each other in the pits, dicing with death every day, maybe meant they may have had their arguments and religious difference and things like that. But probably the person you'd been arguing with just a few minutes ago would be running to you to take a stone off you, or something like this. I'm not saying there weren't battles, but I can't myself recall any. You'd maybe get name-calling and things like that, but I can't say I ever saw a street battle. And I don't remember anybody in Shotts purposely going out in gangs looking for trouble. If you went back to much earlier times, the hewers of wood and drawers of water were Irish immigrants – but not exclusively, I mean, you'd Poles and Lithuanians and all that around the Shotts area and, I think, in most mining areas.[3] I would say in West Lothian, too, the likes of Stoneyburn and round about that way, mining was the main source of employment for the men.

Anyway, I got on all right at the primary school. I was never a plugger – a truant: around Shotts they said plugging the school. I can't honestly say one subject at school got more attention than others. I sat the Qualifying exam when I was 11 or 12, passed that for secondary school, and then attended Our Lady's High School in Motherwell.

That was the nearest Catholic secondary school for boys. It was quite a long way off from Shotts. We went there by bus, which took at least half an hour. You'd Shotts, then passed through Allanton, Newmains, Cambusnethan, Wishaw. There were sufficient pupils from Shotts for the bus to run direct without having to pick up pupils from those places. The non-Catholic pupils went to Wishaw High School, which was the nearest. At that time in Shotts the girls from St Patrick's Primary would go even further away to Elmwood Convent at Bothwell, where the nuns ran a secondary school. Our Lady's High at Motherwell was co-educational. But the Shotts girls would go to Bothwell for secondary schooling because I think they were phasing out the girls at Motherwell at that time.

I got on OK at Our Lady's High School. I just took the normal course. I took French and in my first year, I think, Latin. Well, Latin was tagged a dead language: only pharmacists, medical practitioners and priests were the Latin scholars, though it was a good basis, too, for English or for learning other foreign languages. But in a way you'd no option, I mean, you had to take the subjects and that was it, whether you were good at them or not. I managed to cope, but I was not a high flyer.

As a boy I didn't have any formal hobby like stamp collecting, and I wasn't an avid reader or a keen footballer, although there were plenty of football clubs around. There was an organisation called the Boys' Guild. It was a sort of teenage group where you would graduate to the CYMS – the Catholic Young Men's Society. I was in the Boys' Guild and the CYMS. You could enter the Boys' Guild from the age of maybe 14 or 15.

Then I was in – an old word describes it – a kinderspiel, a children's play. It was a stage production, a sort of musical but not as we know a musical society today. It was based in Shotts and was known as the Don Bosco Players. I think it must have been maybe in my late primary or early secondary stage. Two teachers wrote the plays and scripts themselves and conducted the rehearsals. There was a sort of musical ensemble at times for any song-singing and piano and things like that. The rehearsals were sometimes in the teachers' houses or a hall called the Works Corner in Shotts. They would stage it in the Miners' Welfare and it maybe ran for three nights or something like that. I took part as a performer, not a musical performer.

Though, as I've said, I wasn't an avid reader, I can't say I wouldn't sit down and read a novel or any other type of book from cover to cover. The public library I can recall in Shotts was the Miners' Welfare, and you could borrow books there as a sort of junior or juvenile member. I don't think it was confined to miners. The Welfare had a reading room, a dominoes room, snooker and billiards.

As for my ambitions as a boy, my first thought was electrical engineering, because my mother's brother had been an electrical engineer – and then he became a policeman in the Metropolitan Police in London. From Our Lady's High School, where I didn't do the full five-year course, I went to Coatbridge Technical College. There was no pressure on me from my parents to stay on at school, or to leave school and get a paid job. I travelled daily by train from Shotts to Holytown junction, then to Coatbridge. The journey took about half an hour, because the connecting train was always in the station at Holytown when you arrived in the morning, and the same at night when you came back. I took the course in electrical engineering at the Technical College, but I didn't do the full course. I gave it up after a couple of years before I'd completed it. Well, it was all a business of exam passing, that was what it was all about. Maybe I wasn't the studious type or swotter. Whether it was through a pal who was in the foundry or something like that, I don't know, but I went and enquired at the foundry and that's where I ended up. The initial process was core-making with sand, and ramming sand. It started off that way. But after a year or more I left that as well. I think the wages were, oh, maybe 30 bob or £2 a week or something like that. The war was still on at that time, it was maybe 1942, '43, '44. It was maybe just a sickener I got at the foundry, but from there I went to Fortissat colliery, between Shotts and Salsburgh. My parents allowed me to make up my own mind what I wanted to do. They would advise. It wasn't as though they didn't take an interest in what you intended to do.

Well, at Fortissat colliery I worked at the picking tables and what they called drawing off. As the hutches came up the shank or shaft, you'd to draw them off the cage. I also did other jobs on the pithead: maybe if there was spillage from the wagons going under the picking tables you'd to shovel the spillage into the wagons, that sort of thing, odd jobs like that. I don't think there was a Saturday shift, or if there was it'd be optional, I think; and I can't really remember what the wages were there. Then after about two years at Fortissat colliery I went to Organon Laboratories at Newhouse Industrial Estate.

It was a Dutch company, I think. Chemicals – toluene and various other liquids and solids were used in their processes. I was a plant operator there, watching batches being prepared and things like that. Again I think it was just an employment change for me. I don't think the wage issue was paramount. And again I couldn't tell you how long I worked there, not very long anyway, maybe a couple of years.

Well, as I've said, maybe my latent talent for journalism was there waiting to be tapped, and that came through my father's work for newspapers, the BBC, and things like that. Of course, I'd been in the midst of all that since my formative years. I can remember going with press telegrams – my father's copy – to the main post office in Shotts, and they transmitted them just like a telegram: there weren't many telephones at that time. His copy was sent to the likes of the *News Chronicle*, which was Manchester-based, though it had a small Scottish office. So doing that encouraged me to think on similar lines to what my father was doing. And he encouraged me to think in those terms as well. And the market was there at that time, in the late 1940s, early 1950s. I mean, there were three evening papers then in Glasgow and two in Edinburgh, besides the dailies and Sundays. And there were probably more editions then, more editionising for counties and regions. The evening papers used to have maybe five or six different editions, and I can remember the *Evening Citizen*, for instance, used to have a Lanarkshire edition. But those days are long gone now. Nowadays there doesn't seem to be a change from the first edition in the papers: they'll run a story all night rather than replace it with a local story, that sort of thing. So I gave up my job at Organon Laboratories and became a full-time journalist – freelance.

When I began as a freelance, about 1950, '51, I was contributing news and sport to most of the papers, particularly the *Evening Citizen*, *Evening Times*, and I did the Edinburgh *Evening Dispatch*, but not so much for the Edinburgh *Evening News*. I didn't do anything for the *Daily Record* or the Glasgow *Evening News*. But I covered the *Glasgow Herald* and *The Bulletin*, the *Scottish Daily Express*, the *Scottish Sunday Express*, and the *Scottish Daily Mail*. Whether it was news or sport depended on what broke, that was the thing. In sport it was football. There was no cricket in Shotts, though a few miles away at Fauldhouse in West Lothian there was a long tradition of cricket, with a club that had been there for over 100 years. A cricket match can go on to eight o'clock at night, and you were there the whole day waiting on the result. In Shotts, as I've said, there were international swimming galas, and you had the Junior football club, Shotts Bon Accord. Then of course for news you had, for instance, all the coal pits.

So my hours were a bit elastic-sided. If a cricket match maybe started at one o'clock you did a running report on it at one time for, say, the *Evening Dispatch* – the *Green Dispatch* as it was, on a Saturday. But years later they no longer required all that, just the score, and the best of the batting and bowling – but again you'd to wait to eight o'clock at night for that. Whereas a football match took less time – an hour and a half, with maybe a wee bit of extra time with a penalty shoot-out, but you'd know when it was going to finish. There were stories about misprints sometimes in the papers, or misunderstood words taken down over the phone. The famous one was 'So-and-so won the toss and kicked up hell', instead of 'kicked uphill'.

I was still living at home when I began as a freelance. So my father provided me with an oblique sort of supervision in those early days. And if I was stuck I could turn to him for advice. With more experience you acquire a news sense. You know what's likely to be a story or whether there's nothing in it. It just developed like that. Of course at the end of the day the sub-editor determines what's rubbish and what's newsworthy! And I was paid linage for whatever I got published, it was always linage. In the halcyon days, if you can call them that, I can't recall vicious sub-editing. Most papers had a sort of *In Brief* heading for short stuff. Maybe you would keep things down, and then they'd ask, 'Can we have more on this?' Then of course there was the newsprint rationing at that time.

Then, although I can't recall exactly when it was, I had a wee spell as a staff reporter in a local paper up in Alloa in Clackmannanshire. That was after I'd been freelancing for a time. So I was working then on the *Alloa Journal*. There was a pal of mine who worked in, I think, the *Daily Express*. He was going up there and asked me to go too. We used to come home on the Friday train from Stirling to Glasgow, and then Glasgow out to Shotts, and then back that way the next morning to report football and that.

Everything was there for you on the *Journal* staff at Alloa. They had the diary there, you knew what was coming off. And then as a staff reporter I had a steady income there. I went to digs there and just came home, as I say, on Fridays. I wasn't married at that time. I got married in 1954. So it was certainly before then that I was working on the *Alloa Journal*, and I was there for maybe a couple of years.[4]

Even before then, I'd joined the National Union of Journalists as a freelance. It was the Lanarkshire branch and they held their meetings in Hamilton in, I think, the *Hamilton Advertiser* office. How many members attended the meetings depended when they were held and what commitments you had. I went to the meetings as often as I could, but it was quite a long road to Hamilton and the meetings were mostly on Saturday mornings, because too many journalists would be busy with sport in the afternoon. I certainly had football to do on Saturdays.

Making a living in my first years of journalism when I was freelancing was – well, you couldn't sit back on your laurels, because you were only paid for what actually appeared in the papers. That was the thing. But you had your regular stand-bys, the likes of your sport would be a regular commission. As I've said, there was a Junior football team, Bon Accord, in Shotts from about 1949–50. And you'd council meetings, the likes of

Lanarkshire Seventh District Council. You had three tiers of local government then: your county council, your town councils, and your district councils. The district councils covered landward areas, you know, outwith the burghs, and you covered those. One of them was based in Shotts. Shotts included Salsburgh, Harthill, Newmains, Bunkle, Overtown. Of course Wishaw was a burgh, and they held meetings once a month. And there were sort of area education sub-meetings, and things like that. But there were no courts. The Sheriff Court was in Hamilton, and of course there'd be a reporter there all the time. Airdrie would have a Sheriff Court, too. And then you'd have your magistrates' or Justice of the Peace courts. You'd have that in the burgh of Motherwell and Wishaw. But I never did any. Of course, when I was up at Alloa working for the *Alloa Journal* I did courts. There was a Sheriff Court and a Burgh Court there; and Alloa and, I think, Clackmannan, Tillicoultry, Alva, and Tullibody, too, had a town or district council. So working at Alloa wasn't a dramatic change from working as a freelance at Shotts: you could say news was all there waiting on us. You had your courts and your regular council meetings. Well, maybe the court work was a change, because there were no courts in Shotts.

Well, I think it was when I was at Alloa that I was invited by the Glasgow *Evening Citizen* to take a staff reporter's job with them. It wasn't because it was Glasgow that I wasn't attracted by the invitation. It was probably because when you're on your own as a freelance, you're your own person. Whereas if you were on the staff in a newspaper office there'd be somebody breathing down your neck all the time. So I valued my independence. To me that was an important part of the job. But I suppose you could also say in a staff job it would be a complete contrast. In offices you were doing diary things. They were there, you didn't need to go out and search for news as you did as a freelance.

I mean, as a freelance you've plenty of people coming with tip-offs and things like that. Of course you may think – no chance. But you don't want to say to your informants, 'Don't bother me with these things,' because you'd maybe get one good tip-off out of half a dozen! If you said that, they wouldn't come back to you. And of course contacts, which are so important in journalism, take a year or two to build up for a freelance journalist like me. I mean, you could be walking down the street and somebody would come and offer you this piece of information, maybe not knowing they were telling you about a story! At that time it was national stuff I was doing, and unless the tip-off or the story was something out of the ordinary there was no chance of getting it in the evenings or dailies, unless it was something tragic or something like that that had happened.

In those years what happened at the pits in and around Shotts was an important part of my work. What happened in the coal industry was of concern not only to that locality but to other mining localities, and even non-mining areas, because stories would arise or could be developed that were not exclusively of interest to those in mining areas. And Shotts was a particularly militant area as far as the miners were concerned – or at least they had that reputation, and it was justified. They would sacrifice for a principle. It wasn't like later on at your big modern pits. At Shotts it was about the height of the workings, and water, and all this sort of thing. And there was that bond, probably resulting from the large number of pits within the small area, where they'd all be not only unionised, but would meet at their work, meet on the street, meet socially, and talk about their work – that they thought they were getting a raw deal, and all this. At a rough guess, in my early years as a freelance journalist there must have been 1,500 or 2,000 miners in and about Shotts. The National Coal Board started Kingshill No. 3 pit about 1951 at Allanton Moor, between Shotts and Newmains. Now I think there were almost 1,000 men there. That was a relatively big pit, with one of the largest workforces in the Shotts area. I can't recall a mining disaster, nothing like that, in the area. But there were quite often fatalities, maybe single or double, in the pits. I can't recall any railway accidents in the area either. But in an instance like that they would send out staff reporters from Glasgow or Edinburgh, and you as a freelance would just be used by them for your local knowledge. I do remember being at an aircraft crash many years ago at Breich, 10 miles east of Shotts, but apart from it being, I think, an RAF plane, I can't recall any details about it.[5]

Informants, as I say, were very important for a freelance. But I can't honestly say that anyone who came to inform me of something solicited financial reward. And I didn't myself employ anyone who would pass me information in return for payment. No, there were never any hands being crossed with silver. It was all voluntary, people told me because they knew me, that was it – what you call a tip-off. There was nothing asked in return, say, that I should help publicise maybe their group or club activities or something like that. They were just genuine people. What they told me might make a story – though many times it wouldn't have made a story. But you were supposed to have the news sense to judge whether it really was newsworthy. Even then of course you had to deal with the copy tasters or sub-editors on the papers after that.

I always had a phone at home. My father hadn't had a phone in the early days, because there was the messing about I mentioned with press telegrams. But once I became a freelance I always had a phone. It was essential. But I never had a car. You might laugh at this and say it's an excuse, but I never even had any dreams to graduate to a car. If you were just driving along in your car all the time how and where are you going to meet people who would tell you about this, that, and the next thing? So I found it essential to be on foot. People could then come to me. They might not have any news insight or sense, but they would hold some tip-off for your consideration. To make sure the flow was there it was important to get people coming. I can't say that I had maybe half a dozen people coming to me with wee snippets. Many times it would be just a chance meeting with them. And, as I say, most of the time you would realise there wasn't much in the tip-off. But you wouldn't say, 'Oh, rubbish.' You'd be cutting yourself off from the flow. Of course, too, you'd maybe think it was a good story, spend time on it, but when it reached the Taj Mahal – spiked. I can't, however, recall any major disappointments of that kind.

As for taking holidays, well, if I went on holiday that was everything dead then. There was no deputy or stand-by or anything like that for me. I had no arrangement with any other local freelance. Any regular holiday had to be in the period of the Edinburgh or Glasgow annual Fair or Trades week or fortnight, and in the football close season. Anyway the likes of the Glasgow Fair or the Edinburgh Trades holidays, they didn't really bother me. I didn't say, 'Right, I'm off.' In a way you developed a sense of responsibility: if you knew something had to be covered you'd didn't walk away from it. But when things maybe tapered off, my wife and I went away for a week or something like this.

There was one other freelance in Shotts, Jim Rodger, who mainly did Kemsley papers – the *Daily Record*, Glasgow *Evening News*, and *Sunday Mail*. Jim and I would inform each other what was likely to transpire. Oh, there was a friendly, close relationship between us. We didn't see each other as deadly rivals, but co-operated together. But there were times when you got a commission, say, from the office, with that famed word 'Exclusive' on it. And that was understood and respected by Jim and me. And his superiors were quite happy until they said: 'How did you miss that?' You couldn't be expected to know everything that was going on, and again, you were reliant in the main, apart from your regular things, on people tipping you off. There's no other freelance that I'm aware of who's come to work in this area in recent times: so our numbers have fallen by 50 per cent.

There had at one time for a short period been a Shotts newspaper. But Shotts as far as I can recall was always covered by the *Hamilton Advertiser* and the *Wishaw Press*. But in more recent years I covered Shotts and

Fauldhouse for the *West Lothian Courier*. They include a column, though it's not big, because you could write till the kye come home, and there's nothing worse when you've maybe done a dozen paragraphs and you see only about four in the paper.[6]

Well, looking back to what I've called the halcyon days of my early years in the 1950s and '60s in freelance journalism in and around Shotts, the number of outlets you had then for sport and news is there no longer. During the half-century or more years I was freelancing there've been changes in fashion in news as in everything else. But in those earlier years you were getting more space in the papers. The market for commissioned copy, shall we say, was greater then. But I've never had any great urge to become a staff reporter. You could say you've more freedom freelancing in a way, although you're tied more. You're not working a shift and then you know all the time's yours. Of course, it's a less secure job, because you haven't got a regular salary cheque at the end of the month. As for whether I have no regrets about taking up journalism as a freelance, well, there's an old saying that when you've made your bed you've got to lie on it. So, to paraphrase that famous song, I've no regrets.

Christopher Reekie

In my early teens I think my mother encouraged me to aim towards journalism. I don't think I really had a burning ambition but I'd a kind of vague idea I'd like to go into journalism. There was no tradition of journalism in my family, except that in her later years my mother wrote a number of articles which were published in Selkirk in the *Southern Annual*, recalling her youth and old times and so on. So I'm the first journalist in the family.[1]

I was born in Selkirk on 20 July 1931. I was an only child. My earliest memories are of growing up in Selkirk. Before the First World War my father had been a stonemason. He was in the war in the Royal Scots Fusiliers,[2] but he was invalided out about 1917; and when he came back from the war he got a job as a postman at Selkirk Post Office, and he did that until he retired. He was a bit older than my mother and he retired from the Post Office at the beginning of the 1939–45 war. It was necessary to find another job. So my parents bought a small general merchant's shop, mainly groceries with some elements of things like knitting wool, at Eskbank, at the edge of Dalkeith, and my mother ran the shop with my father's assistance. So about April 1940, shortly before Dunkirk, we came from Selkirk to Bonnyrigg Road, Eskbank.

My mother was the daughter of a shepherd and was born at Ashkirk, between Selkirk and Hawick. Before her marriage she had a variety of jobs: she was in service, she worked as a maid, and in hotels as a cashier.

My grandfather on my father's side, Christopher Reekie, died before I was born. But he came from Falkland in Fife and settled in Selkirk and they'd rather a large family who grew up there. I don't know if he worked in the mill at Selkirk, or what he did. But he was a bailie of the burgh of Selkirk and the bandmaster of Selkirk Silver Band.

At Selkirk we lived in a bungalow, but it wasn't an expensive bungalow. It was a place called The Huts, in Viewfield Park. They were huts or long bungalows that had been specially built, I think, after the First World War. There was a scheme of these wooden huts, possibly for ex-servicemen, with a number of families living there. The houses were reasonably spacious. There was a big kind of lounge in the middle and maybe two rooms at each end. The house was big enough for my mother to cater for boarders, a couple – couples came and went, and we also had visitors who could stay. We ourselves could easily be accommodated at one end of the house, and that's why there were boarders at the other end. But that did not indicate wealth or anything like that at that time. We had a flush toilet there, a bath, and I think it was for quite a long time gas lighting. I don't remember clearly what my mother did for cooking, maybe she had a gas cooker or possibly a cast-iron range. As I say, we left Selkirk when I was eight years old.

I started school in Selkirk at Knowepark Primary School. I remember my mother taking me to school when I was five years old, and I remember being in a big class on the first day there. Then when we moved to Eskbank in 1940 I moved from Knowepark School to the primary department of Dalkeith High School at King's Park. The primary department was housed in the main building. Oh, it was indeed quite a daunting experience to change schools. I'd lost all my old friends in Selkirk of course. At Dalkeith there was a big class of boys and girls. Some of the boys were inquisitive about where I'd come from and all that sort of thing. I suppose my accent was different from theirs. Well, I came up through the primary department and the Qualifying class, taken by Mr Cattenach, an old, slim, stern sort of man. Then I came across the playground into the secondary department, and stayed there till I was 18 in 1949. I repeated my third year. I didnae do well at the secondary school at all.

I remember very little about Knowepark School in Selkirk. But throughout my school life I think I was always good at English and art, and I liked history. But I was terrible at maths, and didn't like Latin much either, which with French I did in secondary. I used to write good essays in English. I was a keen reader from an early age, and joined the public library in Dalkeith. Of course, I was very keen from 1940 onward on the boys' comics and got the *Wizard*, *Adventure*, *Rover*, and *Hotspur*. There was a school library but we also got books in the English class. And I remember reading books in the Qualifying class in the primary department, too, because Mr Cattenach had a wee library in the classroom and you were allowed to take a book. There was what you'd call adventure stories and things like that. So I remember reading these. When I was in Miss Dalgleish's class in the secondary department, oh, I was then about 12 or 13, I read an awful lot of Sir Walter Scott. I deliberately set myself to read the *Waverley* novels. It was quite an ambitious read at that age. Scott's a bit heavy. So I read a lot of Walter Scott at school. I havenae read much of it since.

I think, as I've said, my mother encouraged me in my early teens to aim towards journalism. I was fairly clear by the time I came to leave school that I wanted to be a journalist. I did sit the Highers but I didnae get them. At that time I think you needed two Highers and two Lowers, or something like that. But I didnae actually complete what was needed, because in my teens I was ill. I had a kind of virus for quite a number of years from about 1945, when I was about 14. So that really blighted my teenage years, and though I sat them I didn't get my Highers. But I was quite pleased to leave school in 1949.

At that time you felt you would get a job somewhere, but that even so the whole of life was kind of uncertain. There were jobs, but it was entirely different from nowadays, and it was a big daunting world. As you get older, you just forget how young, inexperienced, and lacking in know-ledge of the world you were. Well, after I left school my mother sent me to Skerry's College in Edinburgh to study shorthand and typing, and there was some English there, too.[3] But the main thing was shorthand, which I hadn't had at school because I hadn't taken the commercial course there. I was at Skerry's for quite a long time because the illness I had went on for quite a while even after I left school. I got a course of injections at the Edinburgh Royal Infirmary in 1950–1. I took a bloodshot eye, a sign of illness; so I was in the Infirmary for a short time in 1950, and then in the Astley Ainslie Hospital – about six months altogether. Then I went back to Skerry's College. Eventually by 1953 I got 110 words a minute in shorthand and in typing about 40 a minute.

Well, my first job was junior reporter on the *Southern Reporter*, a weekly paper published in Selkirk. I joined the *Southern* on October 28, 1953. I think the vacancy was advertised. But my mother, having been in Selkirk previously, actually knew the editor, David Mackie. He was an old friend of hers and, not that she was pulling strings, she put in a good word for me.[4] So I was returning to Selkirk 13 years after we'd left it in 1940. And a lot of people there knew me.

At that time the staff of the *Southern Reporter* was the editor, David Mackie, maybe just one or two reporters, a compositor that maybe did a bit of sport for them, me as junior reporter, and a photographer, Gordon Rule.[5] And they got local correspondents, on whom they were very dependent, to send stuff in. There were quite a lot of local correspondents; and the *Southern* would get even amateur sort of people – secretaries of organisations and so on, to send in stuff.

After these years when I'd been ill and hoping for a job and so on, I never really looked back when I got that job. I worked very hard and went round all kinds of organisations in Selkirk collecting local news.

There was a Selkirk column in the paper so I got a lot of the products of my work – paragraphs or longer stories – in that. It gave me a great deal of satisfaction. Oh, I was very encouraged and felt I'd arrived in a job I really wanted to do.

I just did about everything. Well, I went round the ministers, for instance, to get church news. I called on all the ministers at their manses, a fairly regular tour every week. I went round all kinds of local organisations to get stuff. It was a journey of discovery really, because David Mackie, the editor, would say, 'You haven't done this. You'd better go to the Sheriff Court.' Or, 'There's a meeting in the county council. You haven't been there. Go and see what this is like.' Or 'There's a bird show . . .': an enormous range and variety of stories. I did that from the beginning almost.

The population of Selkirk at that time was about just a few thousand. It's not one of the bigger Border towns. Gala and Hawick were the two largest towns in the Borders and kind of industrialised in a way. Selkirk had mills, but it was more a place from which people travelled to other places to work. It was a busy enough town in its own way, but compared with some other places that I was later to experience it wasn't as busy. Sometimes I did go down to the mills in Selkirk in search of news stories, but I would say that kind of industrial news was a bit beyond me at that stage. David Mackie, the editor, covered that himself. He also covered all kinds of other things. He wrote about the Common Riding, the big event of the year in Selkirk, and he always wrote a very colourful account. Actually David was a published poet, and used to write poems in the *Weekly Scotsman*. As junior reporter I didn't at that time cover the Selkirk Common Riding, apart from subsidiary events that took place.

The only other newspaper in Selkirk was a small Saturday morning paper, just a folded four-page sheet, the *Selkirk Saturday Advertiser*, which I think was published free at one time but later on it was 1d [½p] or something. The *Saturday Advertiser* carried a lot of advertising but there was a fair bit of local news in it as well. It was a family firm with a printing business and the main man was Walter Thomson. His family had founded the *Advertiser* about 1897. Walter was printer, compositor, reporter, a Johnny a'thing. In addition he covered rugby for some Scottish papers and, I was delighted to discover, was 'Fly-Half' of the *Sunday Post*, a talented writer whose reports of international, district, and club matches over many years were always a joy to read.[6] The *Advertiser* wasn't a serious rival to the *Southern*. The *Southern*'s main rival, I would say, was the *Border Telegraph* at Galashiels, another weekly paper.[7] But the *Southern Reporter* was one of the leading papers in the Borders. It would have a good circulation as it went in these days, though I couldn't tell you exactly what its circulation was then.

My working hours at the *Southern* were from about nine in the morning till about 5.30 in the evening. I probably went home to the digs to get something to eat. But I worked all day long because I wanted to. I didnae think about hours. We were working morning, afternoon, and then I'd be out most evenings, sometimes attending meetings, looking for news. I really got stuck into it. I was very keen. Even if I hadn't been keen, the hours would have been very long anyway, and I'd have had to go out and work in the evenings. Sometimes you had to go out of the office to finish stuff, and so on, and it'd be quite late before you got home to the digs. But I didn't mind that at all. Of course I didn't have much time myself to take part in any organisations or activities. Then on Saturday afternoons I did some rugby matches for the *Southern*. I'd played some rugby myself towards the end of my schooling at Dalkeith that gave me some knowledge of the game. Selkirk was in a rugby stronghold and it was the Selkirk home matches that I normally covered. I enjoyed that and it was good experience. And I did the series of five Borders Sevens tournaments for the *Southern* in the spring of 1954. Occasionally on Saturday evenings there were dinners and meetings to be covered. Then on Sundays there were church services and events, and I was reporting sermons and things. So working for the *Southern Reporter* was very much a seven-day-a-week job and from time to time quite demanding. To work on a weekly like that was an excellent apprenticeship in journalism. Then it gave you a chance, too, to see the compositors at work. You took stuff through to them because they were in an adjoining room. I didn't get any experience of sub-editing there, because the editor, David Mackie, would just sub the copy.

I started at the *Southern* in 1953 on £4 5s [£4.25] a week. But I really can't tell you what the wage was after that. We didn't have conversations at the office about the union or trade unionism in a general way. At that time I didn't even know about the union. That was one of the things David Mackie encouraged me to do – to get under the umbrella of the National Union of Journalists because of the protection it was going to give. But it was after I left the *Southern* that I actually applied to join the Union.

I got on extremely well with David Mackie. And he always encouraged me to get on. And he encouraged me also not to stay with the *Southern* but to move on. Well, by that time the paper had been taken over by Colonel Smail of the Tweeddale Press. Colonel Smail was a New Zealander who had come over to this country and he took over the Tweeddale Press about 1948. His headquarters were at Berwick-on-Tweed. Tweeddale Press took over the *Southern Reporter*, and I don't think relations were very good between Colonel Smail and David Mackie. David had been editor of the *Southern* for a long, long time. I think Colonel Smail was wanting to make changes. They were pushing advertising for one thing, and that meant that some news was kept out to make room for advertising. David Mackie was not too keen on that. And then I don't think the Tweeddale Press were too sympathetic to unions! Well, obviously Colonel Smail didn't want people coming along and saying, 'This man should have a wage rise.' That was the attitude.

The Tweeddale Press had also taken over other papers. So in August 1954, after 10 months with the *Southern*, I was transferred to the *Kelso Chronicle*. It was part of the Tweeddale Press group. I had been living in digs in Selkirk, though my home was still at Dalkeith where my mother lived, and then in 1954 I moved to digs in Kelso. It was after I'd gone to Kelso that I applied to join the National Union of Journalists. I suppose it took a wee while for the paperwork to go through, because officially I was admitted as a member in February 1955. It was the Edinburgh branch of the NUJ actually, but it covered the Borders, or part of the Borders, as well. I went to meetings of the Edinburgh branch occasionally from Kelso. They met on a Sunday in the Press Club in Rutland Street. My father died in 1951 and my mother was a widow, so some weekends I went home to Eskbank, and it was easy enough to go into the union meeting in Edinburgh on the Sunday. But for a number of years I didn't take much interest in the union, I was a member but not active, I paid my subscription and that was it.

My new paper in 1954 was, to give its full title, the *Kelso Chronicle & Mail*, an amalgamation of the *Kelso Chronicle*, founded in 1783, and the *Kelso Mail*, 1797. Both of these original papers were older than the *Southern Reporter*, which was founded in 1855. When I went to Kelso the office was at the far end of the Horsemarket. It was up a stair in a building kind of standing on its own or jutting out. The circulation of the *Chronicle & Mail*, well, I couldn't tell you what that was then, but it was maybe not as much as the *Southern Reporter*.

On the staff there was the editor, James Faill, I think one other reporter, me as the junior reporter, and there was always at least one photographer. Jimmy Faill was a very good, very keen, shorthand writer, and he attended the council, even the Sheriff Court, and things like that. I think he had come from Berwick.[8] But anyway I did a whole range of things again. I went sometimes to the town council, and, oh, maybe once or twice to Jedburgh Sheriff Court, and I did some Kelso rugby matches, just about the same as I'd done in Selkirk, and one or two football matches. It was earlier in that same year that I was transferred to Kelso that the James Goldsmith–Patino runaway marriage took place there. Goldsmith married Isabel Patino in the registry office at Kelso. The big stories about it would be done by Jimmy Faill, and I remember him talking about it.

When I first went to Kelso I didn't know anybody there. But there was a newsagent, Charles Wilson, there in the Square, well, I suppose he was a kind of tip-off man. But I became very friendly with him, and I was invited to his house, so that gave me someone to visit. And then there was John Rennie, a reporter for the *Daily Mail*, who was covering the Borders and used to come about Kelso.[9] He became friendly with Charles Wilson. So that was two people I was friendly with while I was there. But in a way it was a kind of more lonely life for me in Kelso than it had been in Selkirk.

Kelso was a different town from Selkirk. Kelso was very much a county town and there were more, well, sort of county people conspicuous – the landed gentry and all that, and Floors Castle, where the Duke of Roxburghe was, was just visible down the road. And more of the shops catered for the landed gentry than most of the shops at Selkirk did. But I got into the life of Kelso, though it was more difficult than at Selkirk.

Well, I didn't enjoy working on the *Kelso Chronicle & Mail* as much I had the *Southern Reporter*. Partly it was because of a difference between David Mackie as editor of the *Southern* and Jimmy Faill as editor of the *Chronicle & Mail*. I certainly felt closer to David Mackie. He gave me more encouragement. I didn't know Jimmy Faill so well. And of course David Mackie was well aware I didn't have experience when I first began on the *Southern*, whereas Jimmy Faill would see me as a junior reporter who'd already been working on the *Southern*. I was working hard at Kelso. But I found it, as I say, more difficult to get into the town. Of course, I'd been born at Selkirk, whereas Kelso was unfamiliar to me.

And all this time I was very keen to get on. There was the temptation or attraction, you see, of the daily papers. You wanted to get on, either to evening papers or to move up. Och, I think that was an ambition I had really from an early stage in my career as a journalist. I didn't think I'd be on the *Southern Reporter* for several years. I realise now it was a very good apprenticeship. I knew it was a start. But while you were there you realised that this was just a low rung on the ladder and you wanted to get on. You heard about people working on national or evening papers in Edinburgh. Of course I don't think I was proficient enough really then to write for, say, the Edinburgh *Evening News* or *The Scotsman* while I was working in Selkirk or Kelso. Well, I applied for jobs in the likes of the *Evening Dispatch* in Edinburgh, but I didnae get them. So, I mean, if one moved up to a weekly paper with a larger circulation than the *Kelso Chronicle & Mail* that would have been a good step.

Oh, I was looking round for jobs. And I applied and got a job in May 1955 in the *Fife Herald*, a weekly paper in Cupar, Fife, which was a tremendous geographical jump really from working in the Borders.[10] So I'd worked in Kelso for a short time till then, from August 1954. But in a way I was glad to get away from there, I had no regrets at all about leaving Kelso. I didn't know Fife at all, but, och, I was keen to get away. What attracted me to the *Fife Herald* was that it was just another opening.

The staff at the *Fife Herald* was, well, William Taylor, the editor, and I think about three reporters, including me.[11] There was a woman reporter who was senior, but she moved on shortly after I arrived. And J. & G. Innes, owners of the *Herald*, were a printing business, too, so there was a big composing room. They had a huge, very unsightly building, at Burnside, Cupar. I don't know if the *Fife Herald* had a bigger circulation then than the *Southern Reporter*. But it was certainly in a different area of the country and for me was another band of experience.

The *Fife Herald* was entirely different because Fife then was a much more industrial, more active area than Selkirk and Kelso, which were sort of rural. Fife was an industrial and varied county because in the west you had the coal-mining area, and in the north-east, where Cupar itself was, that was agricultural. Cupar was the county town, so you had the county council there, a very active body. I was sent there from a very early stage to cover its meetings.

It was my first experience of a really energetic local authority. I was immediately sent to cover its committee meetings. The county council met about once a month and they had a cycle of a whole shoal of committee meetings. And the *Fife Herald* demanded verbatim reports, which were also new to me. The two previous papers I'd been on allowed you to do a digest. But the *Fife Herald* published verbatim reports of meetings, long columns, and that was very demanding. So I had to improve my shorthand. I'd got 110 words a minute at Skerry's College in Edinburgh. When I was in Kelso I'd gone for private tuition to a woman, sat a private examination and I got 120 – the most speed officially I got. It was all put to the test when I was in Cupar at these committee meetings. So to begin with I had some stumbles, sometimes quite a bad time really for a year or two. But I just got my head down and got stuck in, just practised my shorthand speed and thought about how you would tackle this and that. I didn't take any more classes or tuition, because of the hours I worked.

Well, once again in Cupar, where I was in digs all the time, I was working very, very hard – round the clock really. It was in the nature of weekly journalism. I think it may still be. Because, you see, the paper only comes out once a week but you're really working the whole week for that day. And that day is very intense when the paper comes out – and the day before, when you're getting everything together. You've still got to gather news even on the slack days. So I would encourage anybody interested in becoming a journalist to get a training on weekly papers. It's very hard just to jump straight into an evening or morning paper.

Anyway, at those Fife county council meetings at Cupar there was undoubtedly a much higher, more intense political atmosphere than at Kelso or Selkirk. At that time, in 1955, Labour had won the elections for the county council for the first time. The majority of councillors were from the industrial areas in west and central Fife and many were miners. They outnumbered the opposition, who were Independents from the better-off parts of the county to the east and north. That made a very marked division. Labour seized all the main positions in the council. John Sneddon, a veteran miner, was elected Convener. Two members who were prominent then and later became well known nationally were George Sharp, a powerful personality and strong speaker, and John McWilliam, a businessman at Crossgates, who was finance convener. Both later received knighthoods. And as well as these there was a number of other very vigorous Labour councillors, like Norman Graham and Frank Gibb. Then there were also maybe one or two Communists. Rab Smith was one of them. He came from Lochgelly or Lumphinnans.[12] Oh, there was nothing like it in either Kelso or Selkirk, where the councillors had been mainly Independents, Conservatives, Liberals, or whatever they called themselves.

And in the Borders also it's mainly a rugby place. Rugby of course is a working-class game in the Borders. It's not to do with schools, it's to do with the ordinary people. Association football was a very poor relation. Though in Fife it was the opposite, Cupar actually had a very good rugby club – Howe of Fife, and I used to report their matches all the time I was there.

I also did the Sheriff Court at Cupar most days or maybe twice a week. It was a busy court, very much busier than at Selkirk. Oh, Fife was absolutely different, and Cupar, too, was much more lively and stimulating than Kelso had been. I worked mostly in Cupar. Just occasionally I was sent out of Cupar to do things. To begin with, I didn't have a car, but bought one in 1959 for the first time. Until then I got around on foot, and I had a push bike. If I went outside Cupar I'd just take the bus or get a lift from someone. The J. & G. Innes group of course published a similar weekly paper, *The Citizen*, at St Andrews, and a similar paper, the *Fife News*, for the outlying parts. Fife has always been a journalistic place. There were papers in Leven, Kirkcaldy, Dunfermline. There were a lot of local correspondents in Fife, too.[13]

I didn't become active in the National Union of Journalists in Fife. I just paid my subscription and I heard about meetings that I couldnae go to. There was a Fife branch and they used to meet about Kirkcaldy, I think, on a Sunday. I attended the meetings spasmodically or periodically. It was difficult to get there and, as I've said, I didn't have a car until 1959.

So my journalistic experience was very much broadened and deepened on the *Fife Herald* at Cupar. I'd been only 10 months in Selkirk and about the same in Kelso. But I was in Cupar more than four years in 1955–9. I was thinking about moving from there but I had just got kind of settled down. I was enjoying the work and finding it satisfying. But then I got a job with Kemsley Newspapers, who published the *Newcastle Journal*, a daily paper, and I moved to the north of England in June 1959.

I didnae go to Newcastle itself, I went to Jarrow. Kemsley had a number of branch offices on Tyneside, going down the river from Newcastle. They had a vacancy in their branch office at Jarrow, so that's where I went to the *Newcastle Journal*. I had to run the office single-handed. But what you'd to do at that time was to work for three papers all from the same stable: the *Newcastle Journal*, the *Evening Chronicle*, and the *Sunday Sun*. You were expected to produce stories for all of them. And it was very, very difficult. But the job was a big step forward for me. It was going closer to what I really wanted to do. It was a kind of convenient step over the Border, because at that time the natural place to go from Scotland, if you wanted to broaden your experience and especially if you wanted to get on to a daily paper, was into the north of England, either to Newcastle or Manchester. Possibly I had considered the *Daily Record*, *Daily Mail*, *The Scotsman*, the *Glasgow Herald*, but nothing occurred – no vacancies.

Being on my own in the office in Jarrow gave me a very busy life. And I can't say that I handled it all that well, because it was far too demanding. I tried to do too much, you see. They had a number of branch offices in various towns like Morpeth and Blyth. One bloke there once told me: 'Concentrate on doing one good story a day.' I tended to be dutiful, so I went to the magistrates' court and I'd get fastened down there waiting for some story to come up or for a trial to finish, whereas you could maybe have been doing something else that would get in the paper more. This was my first experience of working for a daily, an evening, and a Sunday paper, and they were very different from a weekly. So it was very diffi-cult. I was too loyal and dutiful in just pursuing the news of the day that was available, rather than trying to concentrate on something that would be really good and make a splash. In Selkirk, Kelso and Cupar I'd been accustomed to the more routine stuff, community news, and non-sensational reporting. Well, the demands of serving three papers was really excessive, and that would have been objected to by the National Union of Journalists and may well have been amended later. And then I might have got a bit cleverer and saved something up for the Sunday paper, instead of doing it during the week. But these are just things you learn how to handle. It was particularly difficult on Thursday, Friday and Saturday, because you had deadlines on the Saturday evening for the Sunday paper, and you had the evening and the daily paper still on the Saturday. But all the days were very busy, and it was a worry. You couldn't possibly meet these demands every week. You just tried to space it out so that you gave all of them something some of the time. The *Newcastle Journal* was the main one, I would say. You were doing a story for the next day and if you had to break off and send something to the evening paper it was a kind of rushed story. Or they might want you to do an overnight, as they call it: a wee special that can be held over. But all that was difficult to produce. And I didn't feel I was on top of the job; I think that from time to time it got on top of me.

They had, as I say, a series of branch offices in the area. I was supposed to be covering Hebburn, another small community a mile or two along the Tyne, as well as Jarrow. Down at the mouth of the Tyne was South Shields, where there was an office with about two or three staff. So I kind of kept in touch with the South Shields office, and they were supposed to give me some help. Sometimes I was down there actually, doing a bit for them.

My salary was increased considerably compared with my earlier jobs, though I cannot tell you what it was. I was certainly working for it, and I was on my own, which I found a bit difficult. I found the job really a bit lonely. And again I was in digs. The only colleagues I had at Jarrow in that office, where I had a room upstairs, were two guys downstairs who handled circulation.

Jarrow itself was a depressing place altogether. There was a great deal of deprivation and poverty. It was awful. They still had the memory of the 1936 Hunger March to London, and there were actually veterans of that March still living in the town, some of them on the council. Alderman Rennie, Paddy Scullion and George Rose were, I think, still there and were councillors.[14]

I didn't join any organisations myself there or find it easy to make social contacts, and I'd no friends or relations there. So, as I say, it was quite a lonely life.

Well, I stayed at Jarrow on the *Newcastle Journal* and its stablemates for about 18 months, then I was quite glad to move on in February 1961 to Wearside, still in the north-east of England, to the *Sunderland Echo*, an evening paper, as a general reporter. I think I made a conscious decision then not to go back onto weeklies. I was wanting to move up or to something on the same level as the *Newcastle Journal* and the *Evening Chronicle*. The *Sunderland Echo* looked a more attractive and congenial prospect.[15]

Again Sunderland was for me unknown territory. But the job there was really easier for me to manage because it was just the one paper, and also they'd quite a big staff there – it might have been about six or seven. So I was quite glad to go there. And Sunderland itself was quite a bright place. There were a lot of local organisations active in the community, though I wasn't quite so interested in that aspect now as I had been earlier on. Then, of course, there was Sunderland football team: everybody was interested in that. Len Shackleton had retired from football by that time and was, I think, a sports writer. I actually saw him in person.[16]

Working to the deadlines of the *Sunderland Echo* as an evening paper was to begin with in a way a challenge, but you had time. One of the things I did was I went to the magistrates' courts an awful lot. They had to cover that every day. You had to go to the police CID department every morning and an inspector would tell you what was coming up, because they did the prosecutions. Then you went upstairs into the court. And there were coroners' inquests and things like that. I enjoyed court work. It's an awful trap to get into but it's a staple really. A lot of the main stuff every day is what's in the courts. So some poor unfortunate reporter has to cover it! But, oh, I did a lot of general news, too. The news editor and the chief reporter went to the council meetings, and I sometimes went to help them. It was one of the main sources of news. And then I did a lengthy public enquiry there into a major development in the town centre, and provided a story each day for the paper. By that time I'd learned to fasten on to something someone, such as a QC, had said and which would form a headline. So I think they were quite pleased with the way I did the story. Oh, I learned quite a bit while I was with the *Echo*.

So I enjoyed working for the *Sunderland Echo*, and I enjoyed Sunderland. It was much more friendly, and you formed friendships with people you were working with. Your working hours were more limited than they'd been at Jarrow, because you'd free evenings. We worked from nine o'clock or half past eight through to five o'clock in the evening, then most evenings you were free. That was a big change, the first time in my life as a reporter I found it so. So I was able to develop my personal interests. Oh, I read a lot and went to the pictures. Then at the weekends, maybe about once in three weeks, I used to visit my mother at home in Eskbank and drive back to Sunderland on Sunday night.

I stayed almost four years with the *Sunderland Echo* until December 1964. By then I'd been away from home in Eskbank since 1953, and away from Scotland for over five years. From Sunderland I could have maybe gone to Manchester or even applied for a job in Fleet Street. But I didnae want to do that. I really felt my roots were in Scotland. So while I was in Sunderland I always wanted to come back to Scotland, though Sunderland provided me with a lot of useful experience in general reporting and allowing me to work for the first time specifically for an evening paper and no other paper.

So by that time I was applying for jobs in Scotland, and in November 1964 I was invited to go to Glasgow for an interview with the *Glasgow Herald*. I was interviewed by George Fraser, the deputy editor. He later became well known as George MacDonald Fraser, author of *Flashman*.[17] There was a vacancy in the *Herald*'s Edinburgh office, and I got the job. It was ideal from my point of view. I was able to live at home at Eskbank with my mother again, who was also very pleased about it. So I came then into the office of the *Glasgow Herald* in South St Andrew Street, Edinburgh, which later moved about 1976 or '77 to 37 York Place. I remained 32 years as a general reporter with the *Herald* in Edinburgh until I retired in 1996. I suppose working for the *Herald* satisfied my ambition to get on to a daily paper in Scotland. Well, it obviously took a few years to achieve that.

During those 32 years I covered a whole range of general news. The first job I got was to go over to the North British Hotel for a meeting of the electricity consultative committee, one of these watchdog bodies. Then I covered Edinburgh town council meetings and its committees from 1965 until 1974–5, when local government was reorganised, and did the same after that for the new bodies Edinburgh District Council and Lothian Regional Council. Then in the early 1980s the *Herald* appointed Frances Horsburgh as its local government correspondent and my coverage kind of fell away and I made maybe only periodic or occasional visits to the councils.[18] But the whole range of things I covered included political speeches, and there was the Scottish Office, too. In later years we used to go up to the information office in the Scottish Office at St Andrew's House to see what was happening and to collect the news releases. Then I reported the General Assembly of the Church of Scotland for a long, long time, too. Throughout my time I did what could be called the heavy stuff, you see – council meetings and all these formal occasions, one of them the General Assembly, which is seen as a very formidable assignment and something a lot of journalists would avoid: it's far too difficult and obscure – and you're there for a week or more. The *Herald* usually sent a team up, so I became one of the team of two reporters who reported the Assembly right through. My first General Assembly was in 1966 and I reported every one of them since then up to 1996. David Douglas used to go up and write a kind of sketch of the day. Anyway I learned a great deal at the Assembly and enjoyed it. It was really a hard job but I felt it was good for me. You were working away at taking down speeches and then you had to go and write them up. Having good shorthand I didn't find it difficult to get everything down – well, you learn what to take and what not to take. And you got a lot of contacts there with clergymen, elders, commissioners. But latterly I was in the office doing stories that just came up.

Later on, from about 1987, when electronic means came in, we worked on screens. The news from the Scottish Office was simply sent out on the wire, and you could see the press releases on your screen. The news editor would say, 'There's a speech by Lord James Douglas-Hamilton. Can you write that up and do any follow-up or reaction that's necessary?' So that was quite a change, when in those later years work came into the office that you could do at your desk and use your phone, from the tradition of a reporter like me going out to meetings and using shorthand. I can't say I welcomed the change. It just made things maybe a bit easier for you. You weren't having to scrabble around to get a handout or a copy of somebody's speech. But I've always thought you should spend about half the day out the office, because it's not good to be sitting all day long in the office doing things by phone calls. All through I've always relied on my shorthand. You learn to take people. This is the main thing. It's not just the speed.

There was a time in my early years when I was very vague about what the story was. But I taught myself to understand what people were saying, to listen to every word they say, and to know what the important bits were. It can be difficult for reporters when you go into meetings you haven't been to before, and there's a kind of atmosphere of understanding around those on the committee. They know, and can make allusions the reporter doesn't understand, and especially if the reporter doesn't get the chance to ask questions of anybody at the end of the meeting. Well, I think things have improved in recent years, in that organisations have become more aware of the need to spread information and allow people to understand what they're talking about. Some of these councils you went to were sitting mumbling away about local allusions. You'd no idea what on earth they're talking about, and you were supposed to report this.

There's also been a growth in public relations departments being set up and press officers appointed to put out news to newspapers. For instance, Lorna Rhind was appointed by Edinburgh town council in 1960 as its first publicity officer and she became the District Council's public relations officer in 1974–5. That is a contrast to my early days in Selkirk and Kelso. At one time it was very difficult to find out what was going on and people were very unwilling to tell you. In that sense, the reporter's job, in my view, has become easier than it used to be. And, as I've said, all my time I've relied on shorthand and it's been invaluable to me, because you get down exactly what people say. That helps to make up the body of your story. But all through my life, too, there's been a lot of reporters with deficient shorthand, and they have to resort to other means – maybe to question people afterwards, though nowadays reporters'll just get out their tape recorders to record the spoken word. Oh, I think reporting is very difficult if you don't have shorthand. Well, I don't know how reporters without it survive. Of course, for a reporter to have shorthand is not in itself enough. You've also got to have news sense, curiosity, the ability to write, and so on.

I never myself felt inclined to enter public relations work. I've stuck to reporting all the time because I think it's a much more varied activity. You get a variety of things to do, instead of just working with one aim in mind: to promote your employers. There was a time in the late 1960s or early 1970s when the clever, fashionable thing to do was to go into public relations from journalism. I think public relations officers were well paid – better paid at that time, when journalists' wages were low compared with those of other people. In fact, in 1969 Barbara Castle, Employment Minister in the Labour government, published a white paper, *Journalists' Pay*, which showed that even, I think, in Fleet Street journalists were being low-paid.[19] And as I remember that led to an explosion of journalists' wages throughout Britain and benefited everybody in the profession. Wages went up for quite a long time from about 1969–70. It may have had the effect later of restraining journalists from going into public relations.

When I started in the *Glasgow Herald* Edinburgh office in December 1964 there was quite a big staff of about ten or a dozen. The chief reporter was Bob Yeats, who I think had been chief sub-editor in Glasgow and was also a former editor of the *Weekly Scotsman*. Jimmy Tosh was the deputy to Bob Yeats. David Douglas, former chief reporter, I think, of *The Bulletin*, was the senior reporter and had the responsibility of going every day to St Andrew's House to cover the government stuff. The other five or six reporters were all experienced fellows like myself. There was one woman reporter, Jean Smith, and later there was Dorothy-Grace Elder. I hadn't run across all that many women reporters in my previous offices, though there'd been at least one on the *Sunderland Echo*. In those days women still weren't very common among reporters. I think it was about 1965–6, for instance, that Lorna Rhind made some kind of protest in the Edinburgh Press Club about the Club being a male preserve. But there are certainly many more women reporters now: that's one of the changes I've seen in my time. Then the *Herald* Edinburgh office had two photographers, Jimmy Thomson and Duncan Dingsdale, who were there for a long time.[20]

Bob Yeats as chief reporter obviously had to report to Glasgow every day and give them a schedule, tell them what was happening in Edinburgh. And he used to mark a big desk diary with the engagements for the day. You looked at that first thing in the morning or the night before, to see your initials and what you were to be doing. The diary was marked maybe about six o'clock in the evening for the next day, though Bob might revise it the next morning. If you were on a day off you would phone in to ask the person on duty, 'What am I doing tomorrow?'

At that time they sent the news from the Edinburgh office to Glasgow by wire – teleprinters. Our newsroom was on the first floor in South St Andrew Street and there were two wire men who worked in an upstairs room there. There was a kind of dumb-waiter system. Yeats would sub-edit the reporters' copy, fold it up, put it into this dumb-waiter, pull a string, and it went up to the wire room, where the two wire men put it through to Glasgow. I didn't have much contact with the Glasgow office or the senior men there. All my time in the *Herald* I was very seldom through in the Glasgow office. As reporters we received our orders from the chief reporter in the Edinburgh office. And even if a Glasgow person came through to our office there was a certain strangeness about it – looking into the office, you know. Of course, we were always subject to direction from the news editor and chief reporter in Glasgow.

I spent quite a lot of my time as a reporter reporting council meetings and election meetings. But I've never been politically active or in a political party myself. I never felt any sort of tension or conflict about politics with the papers I worked on, because I've never paid much attention to what newspaper leaders say. Well, journalists should be neutral and I've always tried to be neutral and balanced and give a fair report. You have to report both sides, no bias. It's very difficult: you want to be friends with councillors and so on, but you've just got to report them objectively. Political views really are comment. There's a section of the paper for that such as the leader column or some article somebody writes. I would support the traditional view that factual reporting should be distinguished from comment. But I think there's much less objective reporting now, because so many journalists now want to be writers, go along to something and express their own view about it. I think at one time you could say a lot of journalists were shy about putting forward their own views: they were backward about being articulate. But now there's ever so many articles and features expressing views. And something I've noticed, too, is that there's a much higher standard of education. If it's a good thing or a bad thing, I don't know, but there are more people with university degrees now, with some kind of learning behind them.

Well, I've just learned the job as I've gone on from my own experience. I didn't even have any formal training in journalism, because when I started as a junior reporter on the *Southern Reporter* in 1953–4 I think the formal training was just coming in – and I missed it. So the nature and the terminology of local government, the law courts, and so on, I had to learn myself as I went along. I would regard the training that has come in since those days for young journalists as in theory a good thing. I have heard criticisms of it though that it's all theory and doesn't really teach you very much. The job itself is different. It's not like that at all when you get out on the job. But I would in principle support training.

As I said, I had joined the National Union of Journalists in 1955 when I was with the *Kelso Chronicle & Mail*, and I'd attended branch meetings periodically in Edinburgh and later in Fife. The NUJ had a branch in Sunderland which I attended but took very little part in. Then when I came to the *Glasgow Herald* in Edinburgh I didn't really pay much attention to the branch until about the end of 1968, when I started going to branch meetings because there were things going on then about wages and staffing and so on.

At that time, when the *Scottish Daily Mail* was about to cease publishing in Edinburgh, the branch membership was possibly about 400. That was a kind of medium-sized branch. Glasgow branch would have about 700 members then to Edinburgh's 350 or 400. The Edinburgh branch meetings were very poorly attended. All through my time they've been poorly attended – not even a dozen members present. I think the NUJ activities have always been carried on just by a small number of enthusiasts. This goes back beyond my time and even Ernie McIntyre and before him. There were actually just about half a dozen people attending meetings in the late 1960s. The branch was very fortunate to even get a quorum. It's very difficult to tell why there was so much apathy. Of course, the NUJ has got a chapel in the individual paper offices, and the branch itself covers the town or district, a wider area. So many members just feel their contact with the union is in the chapel, rather than in the branch. If they have to discuss a wage claim or something like that, they'll do it in the chapel. It's an effort to go to the branch meeting and discuss wider issues. It isn't easy for them to go because, well, a lot of journalists work in the evenings, so they cannae go to an evening meeting of the branch. The Edinburgh branch has met Saturday night, Sunday afternoon and evening, and on all kinds of days during the week, in an attempt to draw in more people. But none of these has succeeded.

In the *Glasgow Herald* Edinburgh office we had our own chapel and there were chapel meetings. The chapel didn't meet regularly but from time to time when there was maybe an issue came up or there was something else to talk about. You'd get most of the members at the chapel meetings, nearly everybody. I think everybody in the office was in the National Union of Journalists, even after the employment legislation changes in the early 1980s which gave people the right not to belong to a union.[21] I think that in the middle of all that legislation against trade unions, NUJ membership stood up particularly well. The *Herald* really was one of the best places in Scotland for the survival of trade unionism. All through my working life with the *Herald* the management had an agreement with the NUJ. That's not been the case in some other newspaper offices. In my own latter years with the *Herald*, *The Scotsman*, for instance, didn't officially *not* recognise the NUJ, but they didn't pay any attention to it. So we had NUJ members in *The Scotsman* and its stablemate, the Edinburgh *Evening News*, but they really had a very, very hard task. The management wouldn't talk to them – not officially anyway.

In the 1960s and particularly in the 1970s there was legislation much more friendly toward trade unions, although some employment law specialists deny that.[22] So journalists' conditions advanced considerably from the late 1960s into the 1970s. They got higher wages, better holiday entitlements, even sabbatical leave, and things like that. There were a whole lot of gains. And then things changed of course from 1979 into the 1980s, and some of those improvements in pay and conditions were lost. But I think in all that time conditions for journalists on the *Herald* remained largely unscathed. Incidentally, I never myself took sabbatical leave. That was a kind of extravagance really. You had to attach a project to it. If you went to, say, Austria for a month you had to write something about it when you came back. So sabbatical leave wasnae just a holiday.

Ownership of the *Herald* changed several times during my 32 years on the paper: Outram's, then Lonrho, Caledonian, Scottish Media.[23] But throughout those years the management has appeared to want a relationship with the NUJ, so their journalists have benefited, and there was a house agreement. On the other hand, journalists at *The Scotsman* had a much bleaker time, as anyone on the editorial staff there would tell you. So by the time I retired in 1996 the NUJ was in a weaker position than it had been earlier on. But it was remarkable that it managed to survive. There's always been a lot of active people in the NUJ in Scotland and Ireland. But by the end of the twentieth century in parts of England the union had been wiped out entirely.

The National Union of Journalists defines itself as a trade union. On the other hand, the Institute of Journalists, which is still going, has a royal charter. The Institute might claim to be a union but it's really a chartered institution. At one time, in the late 1960s and into the 1970s, there was a trial marriage between the two organisations. There was a conference in 1971 about a merger between them, with a proposed new constitution. But it all fell through. After that, the National Union of Journalists proscribed membership of the Institute of Journalists. The Institute is still there, but it's had a very small membership, particularly in Scotland. Well, the Edinburgh branch of the NUJ, as I've said, probably had its largest membership in the days from 1946 to 1968 when the *Scottish Daily Mail* was being published in Edinburgh. A lot of members left when the *Mail* ceased publication then. But at the end of the twentieth century the Edinburgh branch of the union still had about 350 members, which was remarkably good. Young journalists were still joining then. Probably they realised they still need to be able to talk among themselves, have some means of discussing their common interests, and having some protection and help, rather than being isolated and having to depend on a personal contract.

It was in the late 1960s, as I've said, that I became more active in the NUJ. At that time there were very few members carrying on the work of the Edinburgh branch. The leading lights mainly were Stewart Boyd, Allan McLean, Ernie McIntyre, and the treasurer, George Strathie.[24] Anyway I was kind of roped in to help them at that time. So I became membership secretary in 1970, then secretary in January 1971, and secretary and treasurer from about 1990. At the annual conference of the union in 1994 I was made a Member of Honour of the NUJ, which is awarded in recognition of long and distinguished service to the Union. There were at that point only about 130 people who had been given this in the history of the union since it was formed in 1907. Then when I retired from the *Herald* in 1996, John Foster, the General Secretary of the union, came up to Edinburgh and I was presented with life membership.[25] A life member's really a retired member, and life membership enables me as well to hold office in the union. So even though I retired from the *Herald* in 1996, as a life member I continued as secretary of Edinburgh branch of the union until 2003, and completed 32 years in the post.

Well, looking back over my years of journalism with the *Southern Reporter*, the *Kelso Chronicle & Mail*, the *Fife Herald*, the three Newcastle papers at Jarrow, the *Sunderland Echo*, and the *Glasgow Herald*, I don't know which I enjoyed working on most. But I think they've all made a contribution.

Liz Taylor

Even as a girl of 14 I wanted to be a journalist. I saw that film *The Front Page*. I think I read Ben Hecht's book first, and I was completely knocked out by the idea of being a newspaper reporter. I'd never had any idea that men could do things and women couldn't, I think because my father never treated women as if they were a different sex. I mean, he was totally egalitarian about men and women. So I never felt there was a job that I couldn't do. And I read this book *The Front Page*, and then I saw the film, and I just thought, 'That's what I want to be.'[1]

I was born in Newport, on the opposite side of the Firth of Tay from Dundee, in April 1931. My father's family on his mother's side, the Mudies, were a very old established Dundee family. My father, Archie Pennie, was a master butcher and had a shop, bought for him by his mother, in Newport, where we lived till I was three. He hated being a butcher, he hated it. He wasn't really suited to it. He was more or less dragooned into it by my grandmother, who had several butcher's shops in Dundee. She was getting older and she did the 'I've sacrificed my life for you' stuff on him, as she did on my Aunt Ivy, his sister, and prevented her ever getting married. She'd sent my aunt to St Andrews University, from which she was a very early graduate, about 1910, and of course they were paying for it in those days. When my grandmother died in 1939 my father took over the shops in Dundee and sold the Newport one. Yet he stuck the job until three years after my grandmother died, then he gave up the butcher's business, sold it off about 1942, and bought a pub in Galashiels.

My grandmother was a very matriarchal lady. Her husband, my grandfather Pennie, a master butcher with a shop in Dundee, had died when he was only 30. So grandmother took over the running of his shop, added two more in Dundee, always in fairly working-class districts up near the jute mills. I think she must have had managers. But her aim in life was to get her will published in the paper. The Dundee *Courier & Advertiser* only printed your will if you left over a certain amount of money. So my grandmother was determined to get her will in the paper. And she did! She made it! She wasn't there of course to read it, but it was just a matter of, you know, keeping your end up. They were very money-conscious people. I think people who owned their own shops were like that. It was a funny society: very property-conscious, very conscious of clothes, dressed terribly well, went to Draffens, a very big department store in Dundee – Dundee's equivalent of Harrods, bought very fancy clothes, went there every Wednesday afternoon for tea, just to show off really. I was taken along, dragged along by my grandmother because I was her first grandchild. My father was nearly 40 when he got married. Grandmother was a tremendous influence on me. She was not interested at all in my brother, three years younger than me. He wouldn't go to my grandmother's, he used to cry. Then she announced she didn't want him in the house because he was such a cry-baby; and when she made her will she deliberately said she was leaving nothing to my brother because, she said, he was such a moaner. I think she was only interested in training up this other female, me, in her own image! And she had a tremendous influence on my life because when I wanted to leave school and wanted to be a journalist I pleaded with my father to let me just try and find a job. But he insisted that I go to university, because, he said, his mother was left widowed at the age of 28, and he said, 'You've got to have something to fall back on. Look what happened to my mother.'

I don't remember anything really about living in Newport, which I left when I was only three. But I can remember as a small child crossing the Tay there on the paddle steamer ferry *The Fifie*, and loving it. *The Fifie* was all shiny brass. I've got a thing about the sea, I just love it. But I remember growing up in Dundee, where I had no contact at all really with working-class children. But my father, because he had a butcher's shop, had a round, and when I was very small he had a pony and trap and he used to take me round farms in Letham in Fife, and before the war he used to deliver from Newport also to the Air Force base at Leuchars, and he delivered in Angus. We used to go off for the afternoon and he loved it. My father was terribly sociable. He went into all the farms and had a crack and a cup of tea, and this went on for the whole afternoon. Then sometimes he'd go round the housing estates in Dundee, and I can remember being absolutely horrified, not snobbishly horrified, but moved, by the sight of children with only little vests on and no shoes. I can remember my father pointing them out to me and I thought, 'Oh, my God, it must be so cold.' Some of them had no shoes. They had poor little bare feet, and they were blue with the cold. This was just before the 1939–45 war. There was a big housing estate that had been built, I think in the 1930s, as one of those projects to give men work, and these children were in there. I can remember it was on the Forfar side of Dundee, on the road to Blairgowrie.

My father, by the way, was in the Canadian army in the First World War. He had an Uncle George, my grandmother's brother, who had TB, was advised to try a different climate and decided to go to Canada. My father, who was born about 1894, was 15 by then and giving a lot of trouble: he was a very rebellious child and never did anything he was told. Uncle George volunteered to take him to Canada to see if they could find anything there for him to do. But Uncle George was homesick in Canada, and came back. My father refused to come back with him, and at 15 took off across Canada, working as a bookkeeper at the building of the Canadian Pacific Railway. He worked in a bogey that was pulled along at the back of the train, paying out the wages. He was about 16 when he was held up by two bandits. They came into the bogey where he had the safe and said, 'Well, just open the safe for us or we'll shoot you.' So he opened the safe, and one of them patted him on the head and said, 'You'll go a long way, son.' But when father got to Vancouver the First World War broke out. He and his friend were desperate to fight, so they trekked to the other side of Canada to join up in the Canadian Scottish. I think he was 19 when he joined up. They landed in this country, were put up for the night in Buckingham Palace stables, and shipped straight out to France to the trenches. His friend was dead within six weeks. My father had a horrible war. He was badly wounded on the Somme and was shipped home. And that's the only reason he lived, because he missed the rest of the fighting and didn't get back to the front till, I think, 1917. By that time everybody in his regiment, except the colonel, had been killed. He and Colonel Peck were the only two that survived the war. He said, 'Every morning I thought, "This is going to be my last day. I'm going to be dead before tonight."' When it got to 1918 and he wasn't dead he couldn't believe it. And he had a terrible guilt complex because every-body else was killed. He used to say, 'I should have died like the rest of them.' But what he did was – I reckon it saved his life – he decided he was going to be a despatch rider. He wasn't just going to get thrown over the side. The only ones that were doing it were Red Indians in the Canadian Scottish. They gave them bikes and they rode between the lines on these bikes. Father said he was with the Red Indians, and the Red Indians didn't mind because they thought they were going to go to the Happy Hunting Ground if they got killed. He said as soon as the shooting started he just threw his bike into a shell-hole and lay there till the shooting finished. It was the only way he survived. He was terribly lucky. Later on, when we lived in Earlston, people used to joke and say,

'If ye threw Archie Pennie intae the Tweed he'd come up wi' his pockets fu' o' troots!' But my father had horrible, horrible memories of that war. He never talked about it, except on New Year's Eve. He wasn't a heavy drinker, only on New Year's Eve would he have too much to drink. So every New Year's eve we went through the Somme, and he got more and more maudlin, the lice, the mud, the screaming. He was really freaked out by it. I said to him once when he was in his seventies, 'Look, dad, if you like, I'll drive you to France, so you can see these places.' He said, 'No way. I never want to go back there. I still dream about it.' In his seventies he was still dreaming about it. So when he was demobbed at the end of the First War he came home to Dundee: his mother wouldn't let him go back to Canada, and forced him to become a butcher. He was very sentimental, had very strong family feeling, and was absolutely devoted to his mother though, as I've said, he hated being a butcher.

*   *   *

I started school when I was five in 1936 at Morgan Academy primary in Dundee. I was there until I came down to the Borders at the age of 11. My whole primary education was in Morgan Academy. I was very impressed by it. It was a beautiful building, with pinnacles, and a huge lawn in front of it. Of course, when the war broke out they covered the lawn with air raid shelters, and I can remember being put down into the shelters. I was very happy at the Academy. But I was only an intermittent student, because when I was six I got double pneumonia and was ill for a year. Then as soon as I was getting better, I broke my arm, so I was off for another six months. So I missed about a year and a half of schooling, and when I went back they put me back a year. So throughout my entire school career I was always a year older than the people I was in class with, because I had missed so much schooling. But I loved school and never had any problems.

Morgan Academy was fee-paying. I went there because we lived in the Forfar road, just beside the Academy. My father and my aunt went to Harris Academy, because they lived out at that Perth end of Dundee. Harris Academy was also fee-paying, and both Academies were co-educational. Then there was Dundee High School, which was also fee-paying. The High School was reckoned to be where the top society went in Dundee. Then the next layer, the shopkeepers, their children went to Morgan or Harris Academy: they were on a level, simply at different ends of the town. The sort of people I went to school at Morgan with, their fathers were mill managers or lawyers or doctors on their way up.

But the really top lawyers and doctors, their kids went to the High. I can remember it was very closely marked in those days.

I always enjoyed English. Fortunately, I was able to read before I was taken ill when I was six, and I spent my entire life reading books. I was reading stuff at age five and six I shouldn't have been reading till I was about 10 or 11. I remember reading *The Saint* by Leslie Charteris when I was six. I loved it. I got through the fairy stuff, and that was boring. I would read anything. My parents used to bring me in the *Weekly News* and the *People's Journal* and I just devoured them. I don't think I belonged to the public library in Dundee, but there was a lending library at the end of our street, and I can remember reading all the *Scarlet Pimpernel* books out of that library. And Mazo De La Roche – I read all these things.[2] I read anything I could get my hands on, except comics, which I didn't read very much. We used to get the *Dandy* and the *Beano*, but I wasn't ever terribly interested in comics. They didn't have enough words for me. I didn't mind the pictures, but I liked words, I just wanted words. I wanted stories, and I loved things that excited my imagination. Then I loved writing essays, and I loved what they called comprehension. I'd fallen in love with words and reading at a very early age, and I reckon it was because I was ill. I had patches on my lungs, and the cure was just to be kept in bed and entertained, so they just gave me books, and it was wonderful.

I sat the Qualifying exam at Morgan Academy and passed everything with flying colours. When my father sold his butcher's shops in Dundee and bought a pub in Galashiels in 1942 and we went to live there, my mother took me up to Galashiels Academy and the headmaster said, 'Well, we never start anybody in the top class. We'll put her in the B class.' But Morgan Academy had given me a letter to give the headmaster at Gala, and when my mother handed over the letter and he read it, he said, 'We'll put her in the top class.' I didn't find the transition from Dundee and Morgan Academy to Galashiels and its Academy difficult. I loved Galashiels Academy and was very happy at school. I loved English and was very, very good at history: I remember I got 99 per cent for the history paper one year. And I was very good at art and used to get the art prize every year. And I edited the school magazine. In the Highers I passed English, history, French, physics, chemistry, and art, all Highers, and I had Lower Latin and maths. It was easy, I never had any problem. Because I was a year older, I was 19 when I left Galashiels Academy in 1950.

My father had always wanted a pub. He was very convivial, never happy unless he was with a crowd of people. So, as I said, we came to Galashiels, to the Railway Inn there, about 1942. We lived in a flat above the Inn. When the war finished in 1945 I can remember the bonfires, and fighting in the streets in Galashiels between the Canadians and the Poles. There were a lot of Poles there, and there must have been Canadians stationed there, too. But there was a lot of fighting on the night of the end of the war, I can remember that. But then my father bought a hotel in Earlston and we lived in Earlston till I went to the university in 1950. Galashiels was in Selkirkshire, Earlston in Berwickshire – a different education authority, so I ought to have been transferred then to the secondary school at Duns. But my father said he didn't want me to move, and he paid the bus fares from Earlston for me to continue to go to Galashiels Academy.

The hotel he bought at Earlston about autumn 1945 was the Red Lion. My father did everything on impulse. He used to go jaunting off in his car, and one day he saw this hotel on the square in Earlston that was up for sale. It was a wreck. I remember when you went into it, it smelt of urine. It was dreadful. Father just went in and said, 'How much do you want for this place?' There was a woman there – her husband had left her or something – and she said what she wanted for the hotel. So he just phoned his cousin John, a lawyer in Kelso, and said, 'I've bought a hotel.' John was nearly driven to a nervous breakdown by the things my father did, because to a lawyer's way of thinking they were totally wrong. Eventually John refused to be father's lawyer any more because it was getting too difficult.

And my mother freaked, she just about went mad over this. Poor thing, she started off being terribly house-proud and it just degenerated. There was no point. She didn't know whether she was going to be in that house next week. It was dreadful. Oh, father was impossible, utterly impossible. I don't think anybody could have lived with him. My mother had been a nurse in Perth Infirmary, and as a young woman she was very pretty. She was just like the Queen Mother – dark hair and a very pretty profile. My father saw her standing at a bus stop! He had a car in those days, and she said this car drew up at the bus stop. He was wearing a straw boater, and he invited her out to dinner. She reeled in horror. She wasn't going to have anything to do with this. But he just got his eye on her and he was a collector, my father. He'd more or less stalked her. He kept hanging about outside the hospital. Like his mother, he would collect things, and he collected my mother: eventually he prevailed on her to marry him. He was nearly 40, she was more than 10 years younger. They really had very little in common, absolutely nothing in actual fact. In the early years of my childhood there was terrible arguing, constant battling, terrible fighting between them. That went on until we got the hotel in

Galashiels then in Earlston, and then I think they felt they couldn't fight in public. So things quietened down, and it was much easier after that for my brother and me anyway.

My mother came from a labouring family in Perthshire. My grandmother Pennie didn't like her: I don't suppose she'd have liked anybody my father married. My mother's father was a quarry contractor. He rented a quarry, worked it, used up the stone, and then moved to another quarry and rented it. My mother had three brothers and one very much younger sister, but none of the three brothers would go into the quarry business with my grandfather. So when he got old, there was nothing for him. He'd only rented his quarries. I remember him quite clearly. He was a very nice, gentle, but quite a sad little old man. He used to smoke one of those pipes with a wee metal hood on it with holes in it, and he always wore a cloth cap. But my grandmother, my mother's mother, was a termagant. She threw her weight about a bit. They lived in Muthill and they called her the Duchess of Muthill. I think they were illegitimately connected with the Bowes-Lyon family, because my mother actually was the spitting image of the Queen Mother! When I used to see the Queen Mother I had a double take: she was just like my mother, the same teeth and hands, just everything. But my grandmother on that side was a menace, she really was, and she and my father had a running war. She didn't get on with my father because she looked on him as an infinite source of money, and he resented this very badly. So really the not getting on was more from his side than from hers.

Well, at the Red Lion in Earlston we lived in a flat upstairs in the hotel. There were only about three letting rooms in the hotel, we occupied the rest! It was mainly a drinking place. It had a very good restaurant, did very good food. But the reason my father had bought the Red Lion was because of its stable. At one stage we had 24 horses standing in behind that hotel. And he was buying and selling horses, running race horses. It was a maelstrom of activity. It was great, oh, it was great fun. You never knew what was going to happen next. And he bought me a horse called Comet that I loved devotedly. Two horses were with us all the time: a grey pony called Denote he'd bought me in Galashiels, and Comet. We prevailed on him never to sell these two. Father sold everything else that came in and out. You never got fond of anything, you knew not to, because it would be away next week. But Comet and Denote stuck with us right till the end.

Father had bought me a pony first in Dundee. He went to an auction sale one day – he couldn't resist auction sales – and bought this little Shetland pony that was pregnant. So we got two ponies for the price of one. And I was taught to ride by this lady friend of father's – he had a lot of lady friends as well. She was a really nice woman and took me out every Sunday morning. I just loved that pony, but we left it with her when we left Dundee, because we had no field and she had a big house with a field. Well, when we came down to Galashiels I just got mad on horses and was mad on them until I left home to go to university. I thought of nothing else but horses. I used to hunt every winter with the Buccleuch Hunt. My father had all these contacts, and bribed people with bottles of whisky. He got anything he wanted. The Hunt was fairly upper-class. I don't know how the hell we got into it! But my brother and I used to hunt, and we had a groom and everything. I mean, father spent money that he didn't have.

At Earlston my father had Hughie Fairbairn as groom. My brother and I both say we were brought up by a groom. Hughie was like a governess to us. Our sense of what was right and wrong, and so many things – everything was given us by Hughie. He was not a perfect role model at all, but he had very strict Victorian ideas about things. Hughie had a very chequered career. He had been married and had left his wife, and she kept coming back, trying to ask him to come back. I once said to my father, 'Why will Hughie not go back to his wife?' My father said, 'Hughie's wife is a high-stepper.' Hughie, a Galashiels man, was an alcoholic all his life and used to go on binges. My brother and I used to hide that from my father and do Hughie's work for him. Then my father would find out Hughie hadn't been out for about three days. He'd shout through the window, 'You're fired, Fairbairn.' Hughie was only Fairbairn when he was getting fired. 'You're fired, Fairbairn. A week's notice.' Then my brother and I would have a week of sheer hell, knowing our lives without Hughie would have been absolutely devastated. But we'd always prevail on one or other of them to make it up, and of course they were just waiting for the opportunity to do that: my father couldn't have done his horses without Hughie, and Hughie was happy enough really. It was maybe odd that my father put his daughter and son under the control of Hughie. He had more control over us than our parents did. My mother wasn't interested in me at all. But she was interested in my brother, absolutely doted on him.

Another thing I remember about that summer in Earlston at the Red Lion when I left school. When I was born I had a big mole about the size of a ten pence piece on my forehead. I felt more conscious of it in Dundee than I ever did in Galashiels. And my mother wouldn't have it removed. Before the war my grandmother Pennie had kept sending doctors and making appointments at hospitals for this mole to be removed.

But my mother used to throw wobblers and wouldn't allow it to be done. As a former nurse she had medical knowledge, but in fact she should have allowed it to be removed, because it was a terrible thing to grow up with. It was very obvious, very dark and very big. That summer my father kept on at me to go to university, but I was afraid to go there. I really just wanted to stay where I was safe and everybody knew me and nobody used to stare and say things. Well, I was serving the tables in the Red Lion that summer, when two very nice women came in for lunch. One of them said to me, 'Are you the daughter of this house?', and she said, 'I wonder if you'd mind asking one of your parents to come and speak to me?' I thought, 'God, I wonder what I've done.' So my father went up, with me behind him, and this woman said to my father, 'I'm a doctor and you should do something about that girl's face.' I was in the pantry and heard her. She didn't think I was there. My father came out, I was standing with my hands in the sink, just weeping, and he said to me, 'Get your coat.' And he drove me up to Edinburgh right away to a plastic surgeon and I had the mole off next morning. My father never asked my mother, he just took me. Well, I'm glad he did. It should have been done years before when I was small, because it was a very simple operation. I'm not at all self-conscious now. I mean, I felt invisible for a long time. I think my mother was so resistant to the removal of the mole because my grandmother Pennie was so insistent, and I think also it was that my grandmother seemed to put it on my mother that I'd had this mole. I remember once going with my father to one of those farms he visited as a butcher, and a woman leaned over and said to him, 'Erchie, was her mother frichted by a moose?' I think they put it on my mother and so she was determined that she wasn't going to do anything about it. I was the pig in the middle.

So when I left Galashiels Academy aged 19 in 1950 I knew what I wanted to be. I wanted to write things, I loved writing things. I wanted to write books. And I went round all the local newspapers asking for a job. I even went to the *Daily Express* in Glasgow, and they said: 'It's not a job for a woman.'[3] That was the most embarrassing experience. Nobody would give me a job. Oh, my father approved of what I was wanting, oh, he was all for it. But he wanted me to go to university first. His sister, my Aunt Ivy, had a degree, and he wanted me to get one, too. I was persuaded then by my father to go to university, plus the fact I hadn't been able to get a job on a newspaper. I was very depressed, really low that summer – and then of course that was the summer I had the operation to remove the mole on my forehead. Once that was off, I thought, 'Oh, great. I'll go out and I can take the world on. I'll try this.' And I went to Aberdeen University, of which the headmaster of Galashiels Academy was a graduate.

My father wanted me to do medicine, and I do regret not having done medicine, because I like people and would have loved to have been a GP. But I didn't do medicine. I wanted to do a double degree in English and history. In fact, English was a bit of a bore because the first year, well, you did a lot of essays and they did Anglo-Saxon and I found that boring. But I got so interested in the history course, really loved it, liked the lecturers, and decided to do Honours history. And I was very happy at Aberdeen, had a marvellous time there. I lived in digs, there were no residences. We moved around in gangs from digs to digs. I was on the Student Union Management Committee and the charities committee, and I edited the charities magazine in my third year – again, journalistic. And I was assistant woman editor of *Gaudie*, the student newspaper:[4] I still wanted journalism. I was at Aberdeen University in 1950–4 and I got a good second-class degree. They thought I would get a first, but I really didn't do any academic work, though I did a lot of other things. I didn't really want to leave!

The summer of 1954, when I had to come home and I didn't know what to do, was miserable. I still wanted to be a journalist. I hadn't tried to get into the *Press & Journal* in Aberdeen. I really wanted to go to Fleet Street: I wanted to start at the top. But it was my father who got me my first job. He said to me, 'I'll give you six weeks and if you haven't found a job in six weeks, you've got to enrol for Moray House Teacher Training College in Edinburgh. You've got to be a teacher.' I had no interest in teaching at all, I wasn't the type. I thought, 'I cannot face this. What am I going to do?' By this time my father had two bars and the Berkeley restaurant in Lothian Road, Edinburgh. A lot of people came in, and Jack Miller, who had just taken over the editorship of the *Evening Dispatch*, was one of his customers. And of course they got on like a house on fire, they were exactly the same kind. Jack Miller said to him, 'Well, send her up and I'll have a look at her. I'm not promising her.' So I went up to the *Dispatch* office, and that day a young girl, Evelyn somebody, a nice girl, had been fired and she was sitting at her desk crying. She'd gone out and said to somebody, 'If you don't give me this story my editor'll fire me.' So when he heard the story Jack Miller fired her. Jack Miller was a rough man to work for.

But he looked at me and said, 'Oh, yeah. I know who you are. You're Archie Pennie's daughter. Right,' he said, 'you can have her [Evelyn's] job, she's going. But you're only getting a fortnight's trial.' And I knew he reckoned I wasn't going to survive a fortnight! Well, they never gave me anything to do. I trailed along behind established *Dispatch* people like Tom Campbell, Bob Stewart, Ronnie Robson.[5] I didn't know what the hell they were doing. And I didn't know any shorthand: I was teaching myself shorthand out of a book. That summer I'd gone for two weeks to Skerry's College to learn shorthand and typing, but I wasn't interested in it. At my interview with Jack Miller he said, 'Do you do shorthand?' And I said, 'Oh, yes, yes. I've been at Skerry's.' So at the end of my trial fortnight at the *Dispatch* the last day was a Friday and I'd done nothing, I'd not put a hand to paper. I knew Jack Miller was always looking at me and I could see him thinking, 'Well, that one's out. She's going.' And on the Friday morning I thought, 'The only thing I can do is be first in the office.' So I was in the office about half past seven in the morning. Robert Leishman was the chief reporter. The phone rang, he lifted the phone and said, 'I've got nobody here, just her.' Then he looked over to me and said, 'You'll have to go down to Leith. There's a fire in Leith.' So I got on the tram, went right down to the bottom of Junction Street, and there was a fire. A man had been killed. It was so unlucky for him, but lucky for me! There was only one other reporter there, Alan or Algie Brown from the *Evening News*.[6] Algie took pity on me because he could see I didn't know what on earth to do. He said, 'I've got the man's name, his age, and two wedding photographs of him. I'll give you one of the photos.' Oh, Algie was an angel to me, he really was. I went back up to the office with all this information and this photograph. Jack Miller looked at me and said, 'I was going to fire you. But you're bloody lucky. I'm going to keep you because you're lucky.' And he kept me on.

After that he used to send me on all the murders, all the really rough incidents, because he reckoned that I was so naïve that policemen would speak to me – and they did! I used to go up and say to them, 'What's happened here?' And they would tell me! They wouldn't tell anybody else. I looked like a wee lassie, younger than I was, I looked about 17. I was coming back to the office with the most amazing stories because I could get people to speak to me, they always spoke to me. I became one of Jack Miller's star reporters.

My shorthand was never good but it was adequate. I never timed myself for speed, but I could do a court case, though nobody else could read my shorthand. It was my shorthand, it wasn't Skerry's. And I taught myself to type. I had no typewriter at home and never thought to buy one. I never had any money when I was younger, my father never gave us any pocket money. We used in those days to get our money by going for Hughie Fairbairn's cigarettes, and then I had enough for a bus fare to get back to Galashiels! If somebody gave me half a crown I would save it up and buy a book. I had a terrific collection of books – but no typewriter.

When I got my job on the *Dispatch* there were four women in the office. Muriel Poole wrote the women's page, Marjory Edwards was the artist. Dorothy Young was a reporter at the same time as me, and there was a sort of floating other girl – different girls came and went.[7] The rest were all men. And in most papers the women reporters only got women's jobs. It was awful: you got the Women's Rural Institute annual general meeting, and flower shows, and that sort of stuff to cover. But Jack Miller gave us anything. He sent Dorothy Young and me on all sorts of stuff.

I really liked Jack Miller. He was more like my father, and I was used to that kind of person. I had a great regard for Jack Miller, a very interesting man. He had a demonic reputation. He used to drink gin in the office in the morning, and he had the bottle of gin on his desk. Sometimes if he was really angry he used to lift his typewriter – we had those little typewriters – and hold it up so that everybody could wait for the crash, and then drop it on the floor. There was a clanging of keys and bits of typewriter went flying everywhere. And the language was horrific. I'd never heard some of the words in my life until Jack used them. He wouldn't let you swear in anything except four-letter Anglo-Saxon words! He said, 'Use your own language, use your own f—— language!' He was great, an absolutely brilliant journalist. He could teach you, I mean, he'd say, 'Get everything in the first paragraph. If you can't get it in the first par, don't bother writing the story.' And you daren't go out and come back and say, 'They won't speak to me, Jack.' You had to get the story. I reckon I would never have made it in journalism if it hadn't been for Jack Miller. He was brilliant.

We were very well paid on the *Dispatch*. I got £7 a week when I started in 1954, and that was a married man's wage. My father couldn't believe it when I came home and said I was earning £7 a week. They paid us the same wage as the men reporters. But if we women reporters got married we were fired from the Thomson organisation. It was *The Scotsman*'s rules: no married women. You got fired. Then I remember my first expense account at the *Dispatch*. I put in something like: bus fares, 2s 4½d [12p]. Jack Miller looked at it, then looked at me and said, 'You're mad! You're mad!' I thought, 'God, what have I done?' And I said, 'But I really did spend 2s 4½d.' He said, 'Christ, you can't put in that! None of us'll get our decent expenses.' So he put down £4 something for me – £4 2s 4½d!

I joined the National Union of Journalists when I was in the *Dispatch* in 1954. Somebody came round and said, 'We're collecting for the union,' and I just joined. We were always NUJ in the *Dispatch*. Many years later when I came back to Scotland, I hadn't paid my sub for the NUJ all the years I was married, but we came to some arrangement. I paid something and I got back into the NUJ. I was never an active member. I was always too busy to have time to sit on committees.

Well, I was on the *Dispatch* for two and a half years and Jack Miller got fired in my second year there. After that it got terribly boring. Alec Bowman, I think he was a sub-editor on *The Scotsman*, took over from Jack as editor, and he was just put in by Roy Thomson to sort of run things.[8] I had been writing a column from the Burgh Court in the style of Damon Runyon, all about people getting drunk and falling off their bikes and everything.[9] And they stopped it because it was all about drinking and swearing. When they did that I thought, 'I can't stick this.' So I started writing off for jobs. I wanted to go to Fleet Street. Jack Miller gave me the name of an editor in Fleet Street – *The Sphere*.[10] But at that time I met my husband-to-be, and six weeks later we got married.

Well, after Jack Miller got fired I went and saw him in London. And in later years I used to go and see Jack and we had drinks in various underground clubs. But he was rejected. He couldn't work in Fleet Street again because he had run the story of the verdict on one of the murderers, I think it was Christie. Jack was working as night editor on the *Daily Mirror*, and he knew the man was going to be found guilty in the morning. So he put out a headline: 'Guilty'. The paper was on the street before the verdict was announced and, although the verdict was guilty, the editor was sent to jail and served six weeks or something for pre-empting the verdict. Jack was blackballed in Fleet Street and could never work there again. That was when he came up to Edinburgh to the *Dispatch*.[11] Well, he went back to London after being fired from the *Dispatch*. He was unemployable at anything except journalism, so he ghosted. He ghosted footballers' memories, film stars' revelations, and all that sort of stuff. He never got back into newspapers, and he died very young in his 40s. That was terribly sad. He was a very talented man. I liked him. You either liked him or you hated him. I mean, there was nothing in between.

Though women on the *Dispatch* got fired when they got married, I didn't get fired. I got married on my afternoon off, because my father didn't like my husband Addie and he wouldn't come to the wedding. So I didn't have a wedding. I went into the office next day and said to Alec Bowman, the editor, 'I'm leaving. I'm giving a fortnight's notice.' He said, 'Don't leave. I'll raise your money.' I said, 'It really wouldn't make much difference, Mr Bowman, because I'm going to India.' Muriel Poole, the woman's editor, was sitting typing with red fingernails, hammering away on the typewriter, and she looked up and said, 'People in this office do the maddest things' – and went back to typing!

My husband Adam, I called him Addie, wasn't a journalist, he was a mechanical engineer – piping. He came from Musselburgh and he'd gone out to work with an Indian engineering company. He built factories and chemical plants, and that sort of stuff. He was home on leave from India. The day after we got married I got a letter from *The Sphere* in London saying they wanted me to come for an interview. Oh, God! Well, two weeks after we were married I went to India, to a bungalow where Addie lived outside Bombay. I'd been abroad before – to Italy twice on holiday, and with my father we used to go to Ireland every year to the Dublin horse show. I wasn't afraid of travelling, but I'd never been in an aeroplane before.

I was very unhappy for the first year I was in Bombay. I missed my friends, missed working, and was stuck 15 miles outside Bombay with no phone, no European neighbours. We had Indian film stars as our neighbours. They were great, and one of them in particular I was very fond of. But I was very, very lonely and used to write letters home to my friends on the *Dispatch*. I remember getting one letter back from Drew Townley, a *Dispatch* reporter, and Drew said, 'God, you sound so unhappy. Why don't you just come back?' I was isolated. Addie went into his office every morning about seven o'clock and never came back till seven at night, and I was left with all these servants who didn't know a word I was saying and I didn't know a word they were saying. I had nothing to read except piles of the sort of books, adventures, mysteries and things I'd never have bothered reading before. It was awful. Anyway eventually I sort of got myself in hand and I got a job. I went to work three days a week for *Onlooker*, a magazine in Bombay. It was run by a European family who'd had it for generations. The editor, a girl called Norma, and I got on great. She had done her training on *Lilliput*.[12] I used to write the political articles for *Onlooker*, and I remember writing an article about why Harold Macmillan would make an excellent prime minister, better than Anthony Eden.[13] I knew nothing about the subject, it was all culled from newspapers. Then the man in Norma's life was a gun-runner, and he was killed in a plane crash while running guns to the Pathans. Norma then went off to Switzerland, married a Swiss, and *Onlooker* more or less folded up or was bought by Indians. I had worked for the magazine for about a year.

I'd only had two years' experience under Jack Miller at the *Evening Dispatch* and I was really sort of green. I sent a piece to *Woman's Hour*, which you couldn't receive in India on the radio, but I got it back.[14] I thought they just read the pieces in *Woman's Hour*, I didn't realise you actually had to read them yourself. But then, after three and a half years in India, Addie and I came home on six months' leave, we met a chap who knew somebody in the *Daily Herald* and he said to me, 'Just go along to the office, tell the foreign editor you're going back to Bombay, and if he ever wants anything from Bombay you'll send it.' So I went along and there was this guy with one of those dark blue suits with white stripes and miles between them, like a bookie. He said to me, 'Oh, yeah, you can be our stringer in Bombay. We'll get you a press card and credentials, but we won't pay you unless we use the stuff. And,' he said, 'remember, if there are three million Indians killed in a flood, I don't want to hear about it. I only want to hear about it if there's one European among them.' And again I was lucky, because the week I went back all of Bombay closed down because the astrologers had predicted a tidal wave, and everybody left the city. The stock exchange closed, the city was deserted and in the grip of paranoia. This was in 1961. I sent the *Daily Herald* man a story on this and he cabled back: 'Great stuff. Keep it up.' So after that I interviewed Krishna Menon, followed the Pope, reported air crashes and gold smugglers, and did a lot of stuff for the *Herald*.[15] We used to get cables in the middle of the night: 'Gold smuggler arrested Bombay. Send story at once.' Of course the time in India was different from in Britain. The *amah* used to come downstairs in the middle of the night and whisper outside our bedroom door, 'Madam, madam, cable, cable.' And you'd say, 'Oh, for Christ's sake, just leave it till the morning.' But it was great, I loved it. I was beginning to settle down in India and, oh, I knew a lot of people – the police, and all that sort of stuff. I then began to feel as if I had begun to know a little bit about journalism, though I didn't really. I didn't know how to sub-edit a story properly, for instance. I think journalism has to be learned on the street. I don't think you can really teach people it. I think you've either got it or you don't, it's like dancing. Well, I saved all the money from the *Herald* and just blew it when I came home. And I only did the occasional thing because by that time I had three children, two girls first then a boy.

Then in 1966 Addie got offered a very good job as managing director of an engineering company in Manchester, and we came home. Well, we'd been in India, with home leaves in the middle, for a period of 10 years. I wasn't happy being back home, I really hated it. I missed India, missed not having anything to do, because the *Herald* – well, it was *The Sun* by that time – wasn't interested in anything from Manchester. Then I had another daughter in 1969. Addie had changed his company and we'd moved to London.

Then Addie had a heart attack in Singapore in 1971 and died. I was left with four kids, no money, and an enormous house in Blackheath, which we'd over-extended ourselves buying and which we were doing up. Addie'd cashed in his insurance policy to buy the house, it had a huge mortgage, and I was stuck with this. And Addie died intestate, that was another thing, and so we had a terrible job. It took five years to get the will, and all the children of course had to have their share of it when I sold the house, so I didn't even get the money from the house entirely to myself. It was all very complicated. But I was again lucky. Addie had worked for a marvellous man called Oliver Poole, the head of Pearsons, though Addie wasn't working for Pearsons when he died.[16] Oliver Poole phoned me up when he heard about Addie dying and said, 'Are you all right?' I said, 'No, quite frankly, I'm not.' Oliver Poole sent me John Webster, his company lawyer, and that man worked for me for five years and never sent me a bill. It would have cost me thousands. It was such a kind thing to do. Oh, John Webster was a marvellous person. I said to him, 'Where did you go to school ?' And he said, 'Actually, I went to Eton.' He was ashamed to admit it!

When Addie died, Pennie was 12, Sarah was 10, Adam was eight, and Ellie two. I couldn't take a job. That was the only time in my life I thought my father had been right: I should have been a teacher. But that feeling only lasted a wee while. Again I was lucky. Algie Brown, the Edinburgh *Evening News* reporter who'd given me my first story when I was on trial with the *Evening Dispatch*, was in London.

Algie had been in Bombay for a bit, running a very odd news agency called Near and Far East News. I could never quite work out the reason for its existence, because it never seemed to do anything. Algie had an office down in the Fort, and I'd met him there and then lost touch with him. But I met him at a party in London given by Lorna Blackie, who had a flat in London at that time.[17] Algie knew Addie, and I told him what had happened to Addie and he said, 'Oh, God, that's awful.' Algie said, 'I'm running this news agency called Forum World Features in Lincoln's Inn. If you ever do a feature we can sell, send it to me and I'll try and sell it for you.' So I went straight home and did a feature on buying second-hand clothes in London. I sent it to Algie and he sent me an American dollar cheque with the equivalent of £20, a lot of money in 1971. After that I was doing maybe three and four stories a month for him. I was just churning out these features and I could never understand who was buying them! I'd friends in Cyprus and they'd phoned and said, 'We saw your piece in a Cyprus newspaper.' I thought, 'Blimey!' And I'd get cuttings from Malta. Then Philip Agee, a CIA renegade, spilled the beans on the CIA.[18] My eldest daughter Pennie had started her training as a journalist with D.C. Thomson in Dundee, and one night she phoned me in a terrible panic and said: 'Mum, you've got to stop selling these stories to Algie Brown. I've just been to a talk given by Philip Agee in Dundee's Caird Hall, and he says that one of the chief agents for disseminating CIA propaganda in the West is Forum World Features!' So Algie Brown was a CIA agent. I knew there was something going on, especially in Bombay. I went along and said to Algie, 'You're in the CIA, Algie.' He said, 'Yes. But I was just going to ring you and tell you – no more features, because I'm splitting.' Algie bolted to Spain. But before he left he said to me, 'Can I leave my papers in your house?' I said, 'No, Algie. I don't want your papers. I've got my kids to think about. I don't want anybody coming and turning up my house looking for papers. I'll take your clothes for you, but I'm not taking your papers.' I don't know what papers they were, but I didn't want them. So he said, 'OK.' He left his clothes with me for about nine months and then he came and collected them. He was living in Chelsea and had an office in Northumberland Avenue, which he shared with an ex-major. I had lunch with them once or twice. There was nothing on their desk except this microfilm-reading thing. Then Algie disappeared. I was leaving London then in 1976 and coming back to live in the Borders. I phoned this ex-major in Northumberland Avenue and said, 'If you see Algie, will you tell him I've gone back to Scotland?' The ex-major said, 'Algie who?' I said, 'Alan Brown, who shared your office.' 'I've never heard of him,' the ex-major said. So I've never seen or heard of Algie since that day. Algie disappeared literally off the face of the earth. I don't know what happened to Algie. But I reckon he was rubbed out. He used to hang out in the Geographical Society, and I tried to leave a message for him there, but nothing happened, I never got a reply. Well, Algie was certainly recruited to the CIA before he went to Bombay, because there was something very funny going on in Bombay. He'd been in Australia and in New Zealand since he'd worked with us on the *News* and the *Dispatch* in Edinburgh. He was an Edinburgh man. But Algie was a romantic who'd got bitten by the same bug as I had, because when we were young reporters, Algie used to wear a snap-brimmed hat with a press card stuck in it, and one of those raincoats with epaulettes – and so did I! Oh, he wasn't a political animal, not even when he was in the CIA. He was in for the fun. Oh, no, Algie wasn't ideological about anything. If he was, he kept it well hidden. I'd love to know what happened to Algie. I asked people in Edinburgh, but nobody had heard anything about him, he'd just disappeared off the face of the earth. And there was no point in arguing with that ex-major guy who swore blind he'd never heard of him: I just didn't want to draw attention to myself. The best thing is to keep out of that sort of stuff.

What made me decide to come back to the Borders in 1976 was that, though I was doing all right freelancing in London, because I had all Algie Brown's stuff, and I sold regular pieces to *Woman's Hour*, I was working very hard and didn't realise how stressed I was. I was reacting to Addie's death really. I had just got a message from two policemen that he'd died, and he'd been perfectly well when he'd left for Singapore. I mean, he just literally dropped dead. It was awful. The only thing I could do was work, and I really almost worked myself into a nervous breakdown and was not at all well. I was getting heart problems, went to a most unsympathetic doctor who just said, 'Take these pills.' 'For how long?' He said, 'For the rest of your life.' And then my son Adam, aged 10, got mugged at a bus stop and got his head split open. I thought, 'I cannot go on like this. I've got to get out.' A month before Addie died we'd seen this cottage in Newstead in the Borders and bought it for £1,000, and we used it for holidays. Then another bigger cottage in Newstead came up for sale and I bought it in 1972, again for £1,000. We used to have our holidays in it because we couldn't afford to go abroad. But once I sold my dining-room table and we went to Russia, and I did a *Woman's Hour* piece saying, 'I've just sailed to Russia on my dining-room table.' But I knew I couldn't live in the Newstead cottage with four children, though by this time Pennie was 18 and working in Dundee with D.C. Thomson's, and I wanted to be nearer her as well. Eventually I found a buyer for my house in London, after all sorts of people, including the Bishop of Woolwich, looked at it. The kids and I used to sit at the kitchen table with maps and say, 'Will we go to Canada or to Australia? Where will we go?' I would never have gone back to Dundee or to Edinburgh. I was very fond of my Aunt Ivy, who was still living in my grandmother's house in Dundee, and I went to see her there until she died when she was 84, so that was a continuity. I did have that link with Dundee but would never have gone back there to live. But all the time I knew I was coming back to the Borders, because I had memories of Hughie Fairbairn and the horses and really the happiest time of my single life was in the Borders. I felt safe when I was in the Borders, and I just wanted to be going back to where I was safe. And by that time I had made enough contacts with, and was selling stuff to, magazines and newspapers to think I could live as a freelance. Well, I was at my lowest ebb, getting heart flutters and my lips were turning blue, when I saw in the *Sunday Times* a house advertised for sale in the Scottish Borders, at the side of the A68, just north of the village of Ancrum. I went up, bought it, and we moved there.

I remember the first Christmas there. I had no work. I'd sold most of my furniture in London so that we didn't have to pay for a flitting. I sat on the floor. The sitting room didn't have a carpet, and I had a single cyclamen in a pot in the middle of the floor, and I thought, 'Have I gone completely mad? Is this going to be a disaster?' But we had wonderful neighbours. They said, 'Come up for Hogmanay and see the New Year in with us.' So I got myself all dressed up in my London gear, went up with the kids, and found the neighbours all drunk. They were a farmer and three sons and a housekeeper. They were all drinking and singing *The Flower o' Scotland*, but they didnae know anything except the first verse, so they just sang it over and over again. They gave me a tumbler of whisky and every time I took a sip they filled it up again. I didn't know what I was drinking and I just kept drinking this whisky. I got absolutely legless and the kids had to take me home about three o'clock in the morning. It was a frosty night, the path from their house to our house was downhill. I had on high-heeled shoes which I never wore again, and my feet went from underneath me. I was wearing a mink coat and lay on my back in this mink coat, looking up at the stars. I said to the kids, 'We're gonna be all right.' And we were! It was amazing.

The kids were great, marvellous. I wrote a lot for *The Scotsman*. That was my main source of income. I still did *Woman's Hour*, but then it was difficult doing *Woman's Hour* in Scotland, because you had to go down to London and record it. I did it occasionally from the BBC Edinburgh studio, but they only did an Edinburgh thing about once every three months and that wasn't enough for me, I needed more. I did a lot for women's magazines, and a lot for *Country Life*,[19] and occasionally for foreign magazines like *Golf International* in America. If you got a story that fitted, by that time I knew where to put it. It was tremendously hard work, but it was great fun. And by the time I was there near Ancrum for six months I knew so many people in the Borders. I had all those children and I couldn't leave them, that's why I freelanced. I didn't want to go into an office. I was probably unemployable really, because I like working my own time, and being my own boss.

In those days I was banging the stuff out on a typewriter and posting it. Though the kids and I had this old Volvo car, if the car was broken down I've seen me going up to Edinburgh on the bus to deliver a piece because it had to be there at a certain time. But the kids were great. It was great, I had a wonderful time. I just went anywhere and I did anything. I was a genuine freelance. I just sold to whoever would buy my stuff. I never got a retainer from anybody. I'd make a trip to London about every three months, go round the magazines and say, 'I've got a good idea for this . . .', and sell stuff in advance. I never wrote or sold a story without knowing I had a market for it.

In my early days a woman journalist was a great rarity. What they said to me at the *Daily Express* when I was 19, 'It's not a job for a woman,' was the general thing. Lorna Blackie had exactly the same experience. Lorna and I met at that time, when we were both working. Lorna's wonderful. She's the godparent to my youngest daughter, and Lorna helped me tremendously when Addie died. She's been a very close friend over the years. I think it's great what's happened during my working life in journalism. And the idea of a woman being an editor is great. That was unheard of in my early days. So there have been tremendous changes. Well, I've seen the rise of women. My daughter, for instance, became health correspondent for Scotland on TV. She'd never have got that job even in the 1970s. It's wonderful that women are being treated as equals in newspapers. I don't like complaining about newspapers, because they're still good reading, I couldn't live without them. But we were taught not to be biased, that you had to try and present both sides to the story. They don't do that now. I mean, they take up attitudes, which I don't really think is a newspaper's job. You should if possible entertain and inform. But to try and shape opinion I don't think is a newspaper's job. The leader writer, yes. But I'm talking about reporters: they shouldn't be grinding their own axes. And of course the critic is entitled to an attitude. If you're a critic you've got to take up an attitude, but not a reporter.

Lorna Blackie was a better news reporter than I was. I could write a news story but my heart wasn't in it. I love writing features, love trying to describe a place and people, what people are doing, and the individuality of people. I love trying to put that on paper. An awakening of the imagination and trying to summon something up on paper is a great skill, and I love doing it. Nowadays I write novels mostly, and I'm a member of the Society of Authors. I've done nine novels and five non-fiction books. Then two partners and I opened and ran The Talisman bookshop in Melrose. I always wanted a bookshop. But after Addie died I never had any capital, and you need it. The Melrose shop was really more of a dilettante occupation because it didn't yield much money. But I was fascinated by the shop. I went there every day.

Well, looking back, I liked living on a knife-edge. I was just so lucky that when I look back I can see sort of fairy godmothers popping up just when they were needed. I always felt that when I got to a stage of total desperation, something solved it and it was great. I've enjoyed every minute of it.

Lorna Blackie

'You were a funny little girl,' my aunt, who lived in Edinburgh, said. 'I remember once you came through from Glasgow, you were about six or seven, and you just sat there on the couch reading the newspaper.' So maybe that was an early sign! I think just from an early age I enjoyed looking at newspapers, and I was the first in my family to become a journalist.

I was born in Edinburgh in 1928, but actually my family comes from Glasgow and my parents moved back to Glasgow when I was about a year or two years old, and I was brought up really in Glasgow.

My father, an only child, was born in 1898 and he'd been in the First World War. He joined up under age. He was in the Highland Light Infantry, the Glasgow regiment, rose through the ranks and won the Military Cross. He was quite badly wounded, and ended up in the Royal Flying Corps.[1] He volunteered into the army in the Second World War, fought through the desert and latterly in Europe, and ended up as a colonel. He had his own business, called Tubular Scaffolding, which I believe was the first scaffolding business in Scotland.

My grandfather Blackie, a Glasgow man, was a ship's engineer. I think my grandmother Blackie's family originally had come from Ireland. I've got the family Bible which shows they came from round about Cork.

My maternal grandfather Dobson was a self-made man. He'd come up from the Borders, started work as an office boy in a Glasgow warehouse, ended up owning it, and made money. That would be round about the 1860–70s, I suppose, maybe a bit later. Then, much further back, there's supposed to be some relation whose descendant was the Empress Eugénie, wife of Napoleon III.[2] I suppose, too, there was a strain of writing running through my mother's side of the family, though they weren't professional writers. One of grandfather Dobson's uncles, for instance, wrote a book about Innerleithen. But, as I've said, none of them were journalists.[3]

My mother never worked before her marriage. And I don't think she'd got much schooling at all really. Well, she went to a young ladies' seminary. I mean, in a sense she was the end of the Victorian era, and she was older than my father. She was 38 when I was born and over 40 when my sister was born. I had just the one sister, no brothers.

My earliest recollections are of growing up in Glasgow, where we lived on the west side, in Jordanhill. It was quite a smart, big house, on three floors and probably about eight or nine rooms. It had just been newly built when my parents moved into it. So my background was very different from that of many other people in Glasgow. Well, I think it was probably due to grandfather Dobson, who made money.

I don't know why, but I didn't start school till I was six and I went to Miss Bishop's Kindergarten in the Kirklee area of Glasgow, near where we were living. From there I went to Westbourne School for Girls, a fee-paying private school. That was at the top of Cleveden Road, still in the West End in Glasgow. Westbourne School later on merged with Glasgow Academy.

But when the war came in 1939 children were all evacuated from the big cities. So I went then for a year to Balfron Primary School in Stirlingshire. I was about 11 or 12 then. I really enjoyed Balfron school very much. My mother came with us. I was there as an individual evacuee with my mother and sister. We weren't part of a school evacuation. I think my father knew somebody in Balfron and we shared this cottage there and I loved it. The class of course was a mixture of the local kids and evacuees from Maryhill in Glasgow and people like me, I suppose.

Westbourne School had actually gone to Symington near Biggar in Lanarkshire. After a year, I think, we left Balfron – we seemed to move around all the time – and went to Largs. But my father decided we should go back to Westbourne School. So I stayed at Biggar with Westbourne School till 1944. By this time of course the school numbers had dropped, and it was a limited education because, for instance, they didn't have any science labs. It must have happened in lots of these schools: no science, they didn't get proper games or anything, people started drifting back to the town, and numbers fell.

At Symington the school was in a big mansion house which they must have just taken over. The pupils lived in the mansion house as well as pursuing their classes there. I remember a lot about it. It was very, very cold, and I remember also being hungry, because of course this school was dumped down there. They'd no connections with the locals, and I suppose they were having to manage on their rations. It was a very restricted existence. It was a very long half-mile drive, and even if you went down the drive where would you go? Symington was quite a small village, nothing much there. Eventually, when we got a bit older we'd bicycles, and I think they allowed us out in groups to cycle around, because the traffic would be minimal. There was an Italian prisoner of war camp there, and you would see the Italians working in the fields or the officers walking around amazingly smart in sky-blue uniforms. Latterly we went to church in Biggar, so we cycled to that. And we played tennis: there were quite a lot of big houses round about there and we'd go and play on their tennis courts, because there wasn't a court at Symington. So really the only games we got were netball, which we could play at Symington, or tennis. Well, there was some fun, but most of it was pretty boring at school. In the school holidays we went to Largs, where my mother was still at that point. In fact, our house in Glasgow had been damaged. I don't know if it was the Clydebank raid or it might have been a bit later, because we were in a kind of direct line with Clydebank, but a landmine had been dropped so all our windows were blown out and the ceilings came down. Nobody was there at the time.

At school, English certainly interested me. The headmistress of Westbourne, Rose Rebecca Harris, was a very good English teacher, and she was quite young, I think only in her mid-thirties. It must have been pretty hard for these women, too, dumped in the middle of nowhere with all these unruly schoolchildren to look after. We were always getting rows for talking at night in the bedrooms, the usual thing. There were maybe about 10 teachers, all women, there at Symington. When Westbourne was in Glasgow it'd be all women teachers, I think. I don't recollect any men teachers. Although in Balfron I had had a male teacher and I always used to argue afterwards he was the best teacher I ever had.

I didn't really have much difficulty with my lessons. But I don't remember there being many books at Symington. And if there was a public library you wouldn't have been able to get to it. The school itself had limited resources, and the owners of the mansion house would have taken all their things away. I remember we had to provide our own beds and bedding there, because again they wouldn't have had them as it was just an ordinary mansion house turned into a boarding school. My mother didn't know where to find a bed and I ended up with something like a big hospital bed. All the beds there were different sizes. It wasn't a very big mansion house and we had to sleep in the attics and in every possible space there was. And there wasn't much heating in a place like that.

So, though I enjoyed reading, my reading was a bit restricted in the war years. During our holidays in Largs I discovered Boot's lending library there, so I used to use that a lot. I don't know whether I or my mother didn't know about public libraries. I suppose I must have got comics but

I don't particularly remember that. Again, where would we get them? – unless somebody had some. We did go into Symington occasionally but spent our money on sweets rather than comics. We'd be limited, too, in the pocket money we'd be given. I don't remember any newspapers being delivered at the school in Symington. Certainly we had newspapers at home before the war: *The Bulletin* and, though I remember my mother saying they shouldn't be buying it, my parents got the *News of the World* on Sundays.[4] Then my father would take us over to my grandmother Blackie – my mother had fallen out with her early on and would have nothing to do with her – on Sundays, and she used to get the *Express*. So I remember these.

My ambition, well, I think that as a girl I might have gone into medicine – if I'd had science. But in those days, particularly in these girls' schools, I don't think people thought of you having careers. I don't remember anybody discussing the question 'what career are you going to follow'. Nobody gave me any advice. You were just brought up to be a nice young lady who'd be a wife and mother, and that seemed to be about it really. Well, certainly we had a good education. We did French, German, and Latin.

I left Westbourne in 1944 when I was 16. I don't think I had sat any exam before I left. I would have been doing my Highers the following year. I seemed to make my own decisions about my education. It was all kind of a mystery to my mother, because, as I've said, I don't think she'd got much schooling herself at all really. So she didn't try to influence my decisions in any way. My father was away in the army at that point. I think Westbourne School was then going back to Glasgow because the numbers of pupils had fallen to about 40-something, and the danger of being bombed had been lifted. I liked the thought of going off to a proper boarding school. I think somebody else was going to this school down in North Wales, so I said to my mother I wanted to go there. So I went then to this even more ludicrous girls' school called Lowther College near Abergele, not very far from Rhyl.

At Lowther College I suppose there were about 200-something girls, mainly from Lancashire, Manchester, round about there, quite a few Scots girls – some of them from Westbourne – but not many Welsh girls. It was certainly much bigger than the number at Westbourne. The headteacher, Miss Sayers, a remote figure, was a relation of Dorothy L. Sayers.[5] I had in a sense to go back a year then so that I could get my Lower School Certificate, which I did. It was too late by then to be taking science, and the only additional thing I did, which the teacher thought I should do, was trigonometry! I don't know why; anyway I passed it. I did eight or nine subjects and passed most of them at the highest level. Anyway what I'd got in my Lower School Certificate was enough to get me into university. I was at Lowther College two years and left at 18.

I remember Miss Sayers calling me into her study and saying, 'Now I think you should go to university. You've got the qualifications and you should apply.' So at least I got that advice. I had a cousin, daughter of my mother's brother, who was the first member of our family to go to university before I did. She went to St Andrews University and I'd like to have gone there. But it was definitely too expensive: in those days there weren't grants unless, well, the kind of Highland local authorities gave grants or you won bursaries. Of course I wasn't in for any bursaries, and my mother – by this time we were back in Glasgow – couldn't then afford to send me away to St Andrews. So I went to Glasgow University, where I could live at home and it would be much cheaper.

I did Honours English, which included literature and language – we had to do Anglo-Saxon and Tudor sound shift. I did English, Latin, and history in the first year, failed the Latin, resat it, and still failed it. When I first went to university the only person I knew there was my next-door neighbour's daughter, but she was doing medicine so you didn't see her in the arts classes. I walked around for about six weeks not speaking to anybody. I thought, 'This is ridiculous. This cannot go on.' I looked around in the history class and I thought, 'I'm going to speak to somebody today.' So I picked out this girl and she said, 'But I know you.' She'd come from Craigholm School on the south side of Glasgow and everybody would play netball against them at some point. Anyway I then became a very firm friend of hers, and still am. After that I got much more involved. University could be a very lonely experience, particularly at Glasgow, because the students there were mostly non-residential. They would come up from Renfrewshire, Ayrshire, go to their classes, and then just disappear home again. Another problem with Glasgow University at that time was of course the vast number of ex-servicemen, who were mostly interested in either drinking and having a good time or getting their qualifications as quickly as they could. So we had enormous classes, hundreds in the first year classes, and over 40 in the Honours English class. Alistair Maclean, the author, was in my year. You said afterwards, 'Oh, yes, Alistair Mac . . .' But really I did not know him.[6] So obviously, even in the smaller groups you weren't really getting to know many people.

After my second year, this woman adviser said, 'Well, I don't think you've done well enough to go on to Honours English.' And I said, 'But that's what I want to do.' 'Well, you'll have to go and speak to the professor.' So I went to see the professor of English, a very nice chap, who said, 'Well, if you want to do Honours English, you can.' Anyway, I enjoyed my course and at the end got quite a good second-class degree.

As for a career, I'd thought early on that I wanted to do journalism. I'd given up completely the idea of entry into medicine. This friend I'd picked out to speak to in the history class, she'd wanted to do medicine, and was interviewed by the University medical people. They said to her, 'Oh, you're very pretty, Miss Duncan. Do you think it's worthwhile doing medicine?' I mean, that was the attitude. And they wouldn't let her into medicine. So she did history. So I probably wouldn't have got in even if I'd done science.

I'd worked on the University newspaper *Gilmorehill Guardian*.[7] I was looking for practical experience. I don't think I was much use to them but I did try, and that encouraged me to proceed further by the time I graduated in 1950. But the first setback was when I wrote to one of those big newspaper groups – I think it was Kemsley – for an application form for a trainee post. They wrote back and said there was no point because they never took women trainees. Really, that's what it was like in those days. So I then thought, 'Well, what do I do now?' And my mother very sensibly said, 'Oh, well, if you do shorthand and typing you'll always have something to fall back on and also you'll have shorthand for newspapers.' At that stage I had no shorthand or typing at all, so I went off to some kind of private place in Glasgow for shorthand and typing. I didn't mind the typing so much, but I found the shorthand quite difficult. I'm not a neat writer – illegible. But this place went bust in the middle of my course! I'd mastered the typing by then but I hadn't really mastered the shorthand. So my shorthand was always a little bit dodgy. After that I kept practising and did eventually get up to 120 words per minute, which wasn't too bad.

Meantime I was still applying for jobs – and not getting anywhere. I seem to remember at one point going out as a kind of typist to this administrator in the Royal Beatson cancer hospital in Glasgow. It was my first paid job and kind of temporary. It was very weird. The job was obviously too much for this administrator, who kept phoning up his wife called Pearl. I sat in the same room as him and I think he was very odd really. Then there was great drama when two lots of people were trying to claim a dead body. I was glad to get away from that job! Then my friend Strona Duncan had been working for a university lecturer who was writing a book, but she was going on to a job in the Scottish Conservative and Unionist or Tory Party, helping to write speeches and things for people. So would I be interested in this job with the university lecturer? He worked in the department of physiology, and was writing a history of that department and the biochemistry one. So I had to go out and interview people, come back, and write it up. I sat in this lab where they were dissecting animals behind me! He was doing this history privately, so he was employing me privately. The job was very good because it was in a field of medicine I was interested in, and at the same time it was writing. I did that for nearly two years. It was just a waste of the poor man's money, because he never got his work published. He went off later to work in America, and died quite young.

By this time I think I'd kind of slightly abandoned the thought of journalism – or at least I couldn't see how to get into it. For women it was almost impossible then, actually. I remember getting an interview with the *Peeblesshire Advertiser*, because people said you should start on a small paper.[8] I got an interview but I didn't get the job. I don't think it was because I was a girl. It was because I don't think my shorthand was good enough. The job involved a lot of council meetings and that kind of thing, and I had to admit I didn't think my shorthand was all that great. He was a nice chap who interviewed me. So at that point I thought, well, a bit of travelling would be quite nice. And by this time my father had come back from the army.

My father got me into the Foreign Office, so I went down to London as a secretary. The only foreign posting they offered me – and, looking back now, I wish I'd taken it – was to Saigon. But that was just after Dien Bien Phu, and the girl who'd been in Saigon before me had died of polio. There was no Salk vaccine at that point, and I was a bit apprehensive at the thought of polio. I did go briefly to Holland with the Foreign Office job, just for a case at the International Court of Justice.[9] But I couldn't see where I was ever going to escape from being a Foreign Office secretary. They did offer me a job in personnel but I turned that down. Incidentally, once when I was on holiday in Paris, I did work for one of the English-language papers there – a very small Left Bank thing. Just one article I did, although I started off trying to sell advertising for them in French, which I wasn't very good at. So I saw a job advertised in a London publishing firm and thought, 'Well, this is maybe a step towards . . .' And I went to work for the Burke Publishing Co., a very small firm, in Britain Street, near Smithfield Market.

They published a lot of coffee-table stuff, but also they had Patrick Moore as one of their authors, and they did children's books.[10] I had the grand title of Personal Assistant, which just meant secretary. Well, the man I was working for there really was mad, paranoiac. He could be absolutely charming, then he would accuse me of listening to his telephone conversations and going through his files. Fortunately I had very good friends from university who were in London at that time, and if they hadn't been there maybe I would have thought it was not him but me, that I really was going mad. Anyway, six months at Burke's was enough. I thought, 'Before I go, I must tell him why.' You'd to screw up your courage to do that: when you're young you don't have much confidence. But he took it amazingly calmly: he probably knew himself he was a bit unbalanced.

I had to have money to survive and went to one of these temping agencies. Then I saw a job advertised for a sub-editor-cum-librarian in the Institute of Ophthalmology at London University. I was still hoping that this was all going to lead me to journalism. I hadn't given up hope. The Institute was very prestigious, they had all these different journals they published, and there was a woman editor. You had people writing from all over the world in kind of fractured English and you had to turn it into . . . and you had to help run the library there. But mainly it was sub-editing, that suited me and gave me excellent experience. I can't remember now the name of the woman editor, but she was in her forties and very nice. She'd had rheumatoid arthritis and was terribly badly crippled. The head of the Institute was Duke Elder, a Scot, who had written a classic textbook on ophthalmology. He used to come in and say to the woman editor, 'Get all your teeth and your tonsils out.' He was very fond of her and he was trying to help her. Anyway I did that job for about a year.[11]

Before then, my parents had split up. My father went off with another woman. My sister was still at home but then she decided to go abroad and work. She'd done a teacher training course at Jordanhill College, so she went off to teach in Rhodesia, as it was then. I thought my mother might not cope on her own, and also I was finding I wasn't getting anywhere much in London. Well, I had these other friends – again from university – in London, and the husband of one of them was an accountant with one of the big newspaper groups. They had a lot of provincial papers, and he arranged an interview for me with the editor, who also was Scottish, of the Derby *Evening Telegraph*. And just after I got back to Scotland he offered me a job. But my father also knew I wanted to get into journalism, and he'd become very friendly with Sandy Trotter, editor of the *Scottish Daily Express*. So my father put a bit of pressure on Sandy, and I got an offer from the *Express* at the same time as from the Derby *Evening Telegraph*. So I took the *Express* offer.[12] It meant I stayed in Scotland. After all these years, it all happened. It was 1956 and I was 28. I'd tried very hard and until then had got nowhere but, well, I should have tried harder. I should really have gone and knocked on doors, but I don't think I had the courage to do that. So knowing this accountant chap proved that's how, well, for women anyway, you got into newspapers. I mean, I'd been so knocked back by this thing saying, 'Well, we never take women.' And by then it was getting difficult because I was getting older, and most of the men started straight from school as copy boys. And a degree was no help at all.

So I started that summer in the Edinburgh office of the *Scottish Daily Express*. One who did have a degree and who was working on the *Express* with me when I first joined the paper in Edinburgh was Magnus Magnusson. He'd been at Oxford. Then Gilbert Cole, a charming man, who'd started with the *Express* when it started up in Scotland about 1932, was the Edinburgh news editor.[13] Poor Gilbert was given the task of having to train these sons and daughters of Sandy Trotter's friends. Well, there weren't very many, but certainly there was another woman reporter, Patsy Budge, there when I started, and she was there because her father, like mine, knew Sandy Trotter. Patsy, from Wick, was a young graduate and was very bright, very clever. Later on she married Stan Hunter, an *Express* photographer, whose brother George was a reporter on the Edinburgh *Evening News*, and another brother, Archie, worked on the circulation side in London, I think, for the *Observer*. There were very few of us women reporters in Edinburgh in those days. April Angus of the *Scottish Daily Mail* at Tanfield was one.[14] And, as well as Patsy Budge, two other women I remember and stayed friendly with were Dorothy Young and Liz Taylor. We were all young journalists together. There were a few others who were women's page editors: Nancy Mackenzie, Muriel Poole, Dinah Dawson, with the *Evening News*, *Dispatch*, or *The Scotsman*. I absolutely took my hat off to Dorothy Young, because she did it the hard way, without getting in through influence. She started as a copy taker – but not a copy girl: they wouldn't take copy girls in those days – on the Edinburgh *Evening News* or *Dispatch*, I can't remember which, and then she graduated to being a journalist. I think she was down in London working on magazines when I first joined the *Express*, but she came back later and joined the *Express*.

Since I'd thought I was never going to get a start in newspapers it was exciting to begin in the *Express*. Its Edinburgh office then was on the Mound. In physical terms it was a small office, but there were a lot of us in it, maybe a dozen, only two of us, Patsy Budge and I, as I say, women. I can't remember how long Patsy had been there when I arrived, but the predecessor to Patsy had been a girl who was really a debby type. They sent her out on a story and she never came back. She would go off and look at the shops. So I felt personally that I really had to work hard. I didn't want to be tarred with the same brush, just a kind of debby type filling in my time. So I decided I definitely would work very hard at whatever I was given to do. And, I mean, you go on thinking, 'Well, I can write. I'm a writer. I can write anything.' But of course that's not what journalism is about at all. I think it really took about two years before I knew what it was all about. And I think Gilbert Cole was marvellous at training people. It must have been pretty hard on him. In those days there was no formal training, and I don't think there were courses. I remember earlier writing to the National Union of Journalists and saying, 'Could I join?' They wrote back, 'No, not until you're on newspapers.' But they didn't say to me, 'A way to get on is to go on a course.'

In the office I didn't feel any prejudice among the male reporters against women reporters. Once they realised you were really serious, unlike this earlier debby girl, it was all right. I felt very lucky actually because the men worked shifts but I didn't. I kept saying, 'I don't mind doing shifts.' But I just did the 10am to 6pm shift. I think this was because Mamie Baird – Mamie Magnusson as she became – who worked in Glasgow had gone out at night (she did shifts) to interview somebody there and got attacked.[15] After that they said, 'No women on shifts.' So I always felt rather guilty, because the men were doing all these different shifts and I was just sailing in 10 till 6. But I never detected any resentment by the men about it.

I used to get slightly irritated when, if there was a really big story, they used to send teams of reporters out. Then, if they failed, they would turn to me and say, 'Well, let's have the woman's touch', as though I would get in there where they'd failed! But anyway I never seemed actually to succeed where they failed. I remember being sent out when there'd been an awful murder on the Lanark Road, it'd be in the late 1960s. It was two of them stopped this man in his car and were alleged to have murdered him for no very good reason that anybody could see. One turned Queen's Evidence. The other one lived in Armadale, West Lothian, and he got off on a not proven verdict.[16] The men were at the court, I was sent out to Armadale, it was pouring with rain, everybody was there of course, and I was to get into the house but they weren't letting anybody in. I did get as far as the door and I did get the mother to say something to me. Anyway he later was involved in two hold-ups and ended up in prison. But I remember having to take the other one who'd turned Queen's Evidence out in a car with one of the photographers. We were being chased by other people, and I felt slightly apprehensive. I remember saying to Gilbert Cole, 'There are only two things you shouldn't send me out on.' One was to interview Catholic priests. Occasionally I did interview them, but I always felt that they saw this as a diminution of their status if a woman rather than a man was sent to interview them. In those days they didn't take women very seriously in the Catholic church. The other place I asked Gilbert not to send me was into a male lavatory, because in those days quite often there were murders in lavatories. So I said, 'I can do anything else!' Though I didn't do very much court work, for which I was truly grateful. Probably they thought my shorthand wasn't good enough, but also they had dedicated court reporters, like Hugh Welsh, who sat in the court day after day.

I didn't really have any difficulty with my shorthand, though I remember getting into trouble once. I was sent down to a Women's Guild meeting in the Church of Scotland. It was at the time they were introducing women elders. I was sent to this meeting and told to get 50 or so people and ask them what they thought of women elders. They were all streaming out of the meeting and it was all quite difficult. I stopped this woman and said, 'What do you think?', and I wrote it down. She turned out to be the Duchess of Hamilton.[17] When it appeared in the *Express* she said, 'That's not what I said at all.' Actually it hinged on the way that what she had said was interpreted, rather than any failure of my shorthand. But that's the only time I remember somebody saying, 'That's not what I said.' It was only what you put in quotes that had to be accurate. And there were always other reporters there you could chat with afterwards. Of course, it depended on the story, how big the story was. I don't think you did that with big stories, especially if you had an exclusive.

In those days, certainly in the 1960s, competition between papers was quite intense. The *Express* was the top paper, closely followed by the *Daily Mail*. The *Express*'s key rival was the *Mail*, rather than the *Daily Record*. The *Daily Mail* had some very good reporters. You'd be fighting to get the story before them. I tended to get these kind of stories like miracle babies to do. I remember once I'd got to know the mother of this miracle baby and I was in the hospital with her. And the *Daily Record* chap Gordon Airs came in and said to me, 'I'm going to report you to the hospital authorities.' And I said, 'But I'm here with the mother. You're the one who shouldn't be here.' So you got a little bit of that, but it wasn't very common that you'd fall out with a reporter, except, you know, you didn't want to lose out on anything.[18]

One reporter who I always remember was great at sharing things was George Millar of the *Dispatch* and later the *Evening News*, and then later on the agency United News. George was great, super, you could always rely on George to fill you in. The *Express* also had the Glasgow *Evening Citizen*. If you were out on a story and you were told you had to give the story to the *Citizen* – though they supposedly had one *Citizen* reporter – you had to go out of the meeting or whatever it was and phone it over to the *Citizen*, and then go back in, having missed whatever had happened in between. Well, I objected to this and actually took the issue up with the union. But if you were on these big stories, you know, chasing people, trying to track people down, you were then a bit more ruthless, I suppose.

Again maybe if a child had died, or if it was a woman, a mother, they would maybe send me rather than a man reporter. But I used to find that it was a kind of release for people. It was almost better that a stranger was talking to them about it rather than a member of their family, because you weren't so emotionally involved. I think the worst story I ever had to do, and that came out of a court story, was once when I was actually sent in by the other reporters because they said, 'Well, it's got to be a woman that does this.' It involved a woman who was heavily pregnant and whose husband, whom she'd separated from, had raped their 14-month-old child – absolutely incredible. He'd been sentenced. So we were all sent down to see the mother of the child. But she wasn't seeing anybody. And then they asked me to try. The woman's mother was there and they did let me in. They absolutely opened up and told me everything. By the end of it the woman was posing for photographs. I think that was my worst experience really.

Of course the intense circulation war tended to have the effect of depressing standards. I remember one case in the days when Ian Brown was the news editor in Glasgow. It was when they did the first lung transplant at the Royal Infirmary. It was a boy from Lewis, about 15, I think, who'd drunk paraquat. They took the lungs from a girl who'd committed suicide. I'd been down seeing the father of the Lewis boy, a very nice man, and I think I'd had dealings with the parents of the girl as well at that time. Anyway I came back with a story from the father of the boy and did it up.[19] Then, I think, the same day we'd heard the *Daily Record* had scooped us by bringing the father of the boy and the mother of the girl together. Ian Brown was incandescent with rage, frothing at the mouth, at the *Record*'s scoop. I had then to go to the boy's father and the girl's mother and say, 'Would you again go through this, for the *Express?*' I said, 'I hope . . .' 'No, no,' the father said, 'I understand why you're doing this.' So I actually did get the story but a bit later than the *Record*. And Ian Brown was still furious. I said, 'We've got it. What's all this fuss about?' And I walked out of the office.

Although I'd remained at school longer than most of the men reporters, who'd left school at 14 or 15 and plunged into papers at the deep end, and also I was a university graduate, I didn't find that created any tensions in my work with the *Express*. I never felt I was better than the men were. I always felt they were much more skilled at their job than I was. I didn't feel that they were intellectually beneath me at all. And I didn't feel that the *Express* was asking me to do things that went against the grain.

I thought some of the things were stupid maybe, you know, sending me after stories that were not worth doing, were trivial. We were constantly out in West Lothian, for instance, following up ridiculous stories. But I still found journalism really exciting. I didn't find that it wasn't challenging my intellectual abilities, because by the time I got into journalism I had realised that a degree was of little worth really in those days in the employment market. I was just so glad to be in newspapers, and I just felt most of the men were much better qualified than I was, and that some day somebody was going to find out that I really wasn't very good at my job anyway! I think that's what I felt. I always felt I might just make some dreadful error that would catch up with me or I would be exposed. It was so easy to make errors, well, that's why I was glad not doing court work, because I always felt the weight of the law might come down on me. And reporters were working under great pressure, meeting deadlines for editions. Fortunately, I never had any great disasters. But you did feel that it could happen at any moment. On the other hand, I didn't feel that what I was doing was beneath my abilities. Maybe I felt, as I say, it was a stupid story to send me out on. But then, poor Gilbert Cole, he had a big staff in the Edinburgh office and he had to try and find something for everybody to do.

Gilbert was a very good boss, on the whole sympathetic and encouraging. A lot of my old colleagues turned up for his funeral when he died in his eighties. He'd worked all these years for the *Express* and he retired just before it disappeared. I don't know what kind of pension scheme they'd had on the *Express*. When I myself got to 60 I got this letter from the *Express* saying I'd worked for them for 13 years, so, 'You are due a pension from us of £30 a year.' Anyway inflation took off in the 1970s, and I think Gilbert Cole retired on a pension which cannot have increased at all. John Vass, a former *Express* reporter, came back from London to work in Edinburgh for the *Evening News*, and John went to stay with Gilbert and Vivien Cole in a great big house they had down at Trinity. They were living absolutely on the breadline, Gilbert's pension must have been very poor. John said, 'Sell the house and go into a flat.'

Well, I was with the *Express* in Edinburgh from 1956 till 1969. I was always doing general reporting and never specialised in women's work or sport. I felt I was very privileged to be able to do that, and doing what I wanted to do. I did the odd feature, but I didn't feel particularly happy in features. Anyway I enjoyed my 13 years with the *Express*. Well, in 1961 my father had died and left me about £4,000.

But latterly, before I left it in 1969, I had slightly fallen out with the *Express*. I was their lobby correspondent in Edinburgh, which sounds great. The Scottish Office had decided they were going to be more open, so they asked all the newspapers to appoint a lobby correspondent. Every day somebody from the *Daily Record*, *The Scotsman*, the *Glasgow Herald*, and I would tramp up to the Scottish Office in Regent Road and be briefed. Of course, the briefings were all from the press officers. You weren't actually meeting the civil servants. It was all a bit ridiculous. I said to Gilbert Cole, my news editor, 'I need to get *Hansard*,' because often you could get a good story out of it.[20] I was interested in politics because a great friend of mine from university days was Winnie Ewing, and when she got into Parliament in 1967, quite often I would go down into the House of Commons and listen to her. Of course the word came back from Glasgow: 'Can't have you sitting around reading *Hansard* all day.' Of course I was doing other stories anyway. So I said, 'Well, that's it. I've had enough,' and I sent in my resignation to Ian McColl, the editor. Ian Brown, news editor, invited me through for lunch in Glasgow to talk me out of it. And I said, 'No.' By this time I'd started in 1966 with a friend a clothes shop called Campus in the Grassmarket in Edinburgh. It was one of the first boutiques in Edinburgh and really was very successful, though there wasn't enough money for both of us to make a living out of it, so I had carried on doing journalism. Then in 1967 we opened a shop in Glasgow, and in 1969 a third in Oxford. So there was enough to keep me busy with these shops.

But after I'd resigned from the *Express* I got a call from the *Daily Record* asking me to work for them in Glasgow as their women's editor. So I went through and worked there. But the editor of the time was away when I arrived and nobody quite knew what I was supposed to be doing. So after six weeks or two months I gave that up, though they offered me a job with a lot more money. That was a very strenuous time for me: three shops and a newspaper job, and I travelled daily between Edinburgh and Glasgow while I was with the *Record*.

When I first came to work in Edinburgh with the *Express* and its office was at the foot of Lady Stair's Close at the top of the Mound, I always thought that the old town was a super place and decided this was where I wanted to live. I had a series of bedsits around the town, and then bought my first little flat, across the courtyard from the office, for £200 in 1960. And coming back again to the way women were perceived in those days, I had just enough money to buy the tiny, tiny flat, but I didn't have enough to do it up: it had no hot water, and needed rewiring and everything. So I went to the bank, where my salary was being paid in every week, and said could I have a loan, and they said, 'Oh, no. We never lend money on houses.' I said, 'Why not?' 'Oh, well, we might have to put you into the street.' And I thought they wouldn't have said that to a man. I was furious. Then I went to the building societies and they said, 'What age is the property?' I said it was about 150 to 170 years old. 'Oh, we never lend money on property of that age.' The building societies wouldn't lend on it if it was older than 1919. I said, 'But the government has just brought in a thing that says they'll provide back-up money for older houses.' 'Oh, well, we don't understand that yet.' So the building societies wouldn't lend, the bank wouldn't lend. The old Edinburgh Corporation at the end were the only people who would. So that's where I started, in Lady Stair's Close. Though the *Express* office by then had moved to the High Street and finally to Jeffrey Street, the flat was still very handy. And then in 1970, by which time I had more money because I was at last getting money out of Campus, I bought my present flat in nearby Blackie House, Lawnmarket, where Dorothy Young had lived as the tenant for years but had moved out when she remarried. Winnie Ewing had had a case in the Court of Session and came up afterwards to see me, bringing with her her junior QC, James Douglas-Hamilton, whose father and family trust owned the whole building.[21] I wasn't interested in renting the flat, James said he'd speak to the lawyers about it, and so I bought the flat without it ever being on the market. Of course, in those days people didn't think the old town was the place to live: it was seen as quite dangerous actually. It'd started going down years before, but there's been a big change, it's perfectly safe, and like living in an urban village.

Well, at Campus we ended up with another branch in Nottingham, making four shops. I don't think I was earning all that much from journalism really – about £30 a week when I started Campus in 1966, which was not bad but didn't allow you to live in any great style. Campus was a gamble, I could have lost it all. But all went well, and it was the right time to do it. In the 1960s people had more money to spend on clothes and things.

So apart from that two months as women's editor with the *Daily Record*, I was always with the *Express*. And of course if you didn't move you didn't earn so much. In those days you increased your salary by moving. I had applied once about 1964 or so for the women's editor job with *The Scotsman*, but got no reply at all, not even an acknowledgement. Looking back now of course I should have phoned up and said, 'Did you get my application?' So I suppose I was getting restless then at the *Express*. And then I thought I might go and work on newspapers in America. A chap who had worked with me in Edinburgh was over there working for *Time* or *Newsweek*,[22] and I went over on holiday. But after about three days in New York I realised the American newspapers weren't very good, I mean, they were light years behind the British newspapers. And the only comparable things to our newspaper standards were those like *Time* and *Newsweek*. So I decided pretty quickly that for me that wasn't the answer either. But I must then have been quite restless at the *Express*. I must have been thinking I could be doing better.

I had moved around a lot – Glasgow, Symington, Largs, North Wales, Glasgow University, London, Holland, and thinking of going to Saigon and of working in America. It wasn't as if I'd grown up in Edinburgh and stayed there all my life and never worked anywhere else. But I don't think settling down for any length of time more than two or three years was difficult for me. I'd certainly always at the back of my mind that I must be able to support myself. I mean, I'd seen the situation my mother was in, having to keep us and keep us going after my father went off. In those days you were supposed either to be a career woman or you married. It didn't always seem possible to do both. I never felt being a university graduate was any great asset really.

So I'd had 13 pretty intensive years' experience in the *Express*. We used to have to do three or four news stories in a day, depending what was happening of course. But as a reporter you weren't expected to sit around doing nothing. Then some people got merit payments on the *Express*. I don't know how you qualified for these! I never got one, so I never found out. I never liked to ask for more money in case they said, 'Well, you're not really worth what we're paying you anyway.' And also I was in this fortunate position of only doing day shifts, which made me feel, well, I don't deserve to get more because I'm not really subjecting myself to the full intensity of doing night shifts or early morning shifts or whatever. Merit payments could be divisive. Some reporters in the Edinburgh office received them, others probably not. It was never clear who was getting what.

I don't think I joined the union straight away when I came to the *Express* in 1956. Hugh Welsh was the father of the National Union of Journalists' chapel in our branch office. I think eventually I said to Hugh I should join the union, but by then a year or two had passed. I don't think anybody asked me to join. I made up my own mind to join. Then later on I thought this business of doing work also for the *Evening Citizen* was ridiculous, because the other papers had their evening staff, and here was the *Express* kind of getting double out of us. And actually more than anything else, it was the way Hugh Welsh, a hard, hard-working chap, was being treated, because Hugh was having to do work for both papers. I thought that was very unfair. And I think he was hauled up because the *Citizen* hadn't got something or other. It was ridiculous what they were expecting of him. It started to get a bit nasty towards the end of the 1960s. But it wasn't any particular incident that made me join the union. At first I didn't become active in the union, later I did. After I came out of journalism in 1969 I kept on my NUJ membership because I thought, well, I never know what's going to happen.

From 1969 until 1981 I worked full-time with Campus. It was great fun at the beginning, and a complete change from journalism. I handled the financial affairs and all the nitty-gritty stuff of administration, pretty boring actually, and when VAT came in, it got worse. Then my business partner and I disagreed about the way the business should go. In the late 1970s, early 1980s, the first recession, things were starting to get difficult, and I felt we weren't doing the right thing for the hard times that were coming. So she carried on in Campus but I came out in 1981.

Even after I'd left the *Express* in 1969 I hadn't entirely given up journalism, because in 1970, when the Commonwealth Games were in Edinburgh, I was asked to go and work in the press office for four or five weeks. I certainly worked very hard at it, and afterwards I had the reputation of having been the only press officer there that knew what he or she was doing. So that was quite nice. When the Commonwealth Games came back to Edinburgh in 1986 I got involved again in that. It was a public relations firm that were really running things, and then of course Robert Maxwell came in. But that was the disastrous affair when it all fell apart. Then sometimes I was asked to be a broadcaster by BBC Radio Scotland, usually about fashion. I didn't terribly enjoy broadcasting. I remember once being on an *Any Questions*-type panel, but that's not my mode. I don't feel particularly articulate, you see. And I was asked both by the SNP and the Tories – why both should think I could do it, I don't know – to be a candidate for election. But that would not be my sphere, I'm not good on public platforms. Being a writer and being a speaker are very different. Some people can combine both but I never felt I could. As for public relations, I don't think I ever applied for a full-time permanent appointment in that. It didn't attract me. Various PR companies employed me to do bits of work for them. For instance, I was the PR for Scotland's Gardens Scheme, which was very pleasant, though I never felt they quite understood what the publicity was they were looking for. They'd no money and you couldn't charge them very much. What was also very nice was working at the National Trust for Scotland, when they had big campaigns on and I went in and worked in the office for two or three days a week, whatever was necessary.[23]

After I left Campus in 1981 I started freelancing. I had tried to get other kinds of jobs, too. One job I applied for was in the Scottish Office.

I got an interview but didn't get the job, and I began to realise I was a bit old by then as I was about 53. It was just when the age thing was coming into focus. So then I was very lucky. There were a lot of people still in jobs in journalism whom I knew, and so I started using my contacts. That was when the *Sunday Standard* was started up, and I applied for a job there. Charlie Wilson, the editor, wrote he was sorry there was no job, but the women's page editor would be interested to meet me. So I did stuff then for the *Standard*. The old *Express* had gone years earlier, and there was only a very small *Express* office in Edinburgh. But I also knew people in the *Daily Record*, so I did stuff for them and for *The Scotsman*. Sheila MacNamara, whom I'd worked with in the *Express*, was then women's editor of the Edinburgh *Evening News* and I did fashion things for them.[24] So I was very fortunate that I had enough contacts to make a living freelancing from 1981 until 1995, actually a longer period than I'd been with the *Express*.

But freelancing got more and more difficult. Various people that had commissioned me fairly regularly either retired or were made redundant. Latterly also I was doing work for the National Trust for Scotland in their press office for three summers running, and then that came to an end. So it all just seemed to happen at the one time that my normal sources dried up. I thought, 'Am I going to start all over again with people I don't know and who've never heard of me?' So I just thought, well, I'll stop. If anybody wants me, they can phone me. But nobody did.

As I've said, after I came out of journalism with the *Express* in 1969 I kept on my National Union of Journalists' membership. At that time there were very few of us who were freelances in Edinburgh, about eight or nine of us, including photographers like Tug Wilson. We met in a pub, Sandy Sutherland, who did sports journalism and had an agency, was the secretary. I just kept going to the meetings, and because there were only a few of us, I suppose, I ended up as the vice-chairman of the freelance branch. Then at one meeting about 1985 – there were more women had come in by then – Frank Walker, who'd been in the *Daily Mail* and did motoring and property, was the chairman and he was being asked questions. Frank said, 'I'm fed up with all these questions from these women' – and he resigned. So, though I didn't go out seeking it, I became the first woman chairman of the Edinburgh freelance branch of the NUJ. The secretary was Joyce McMillan.[25] I was the chairman for ten years. Many more people had become freelances. I think when I became chairman we had about 40 members. It increased to over 120 by the time I retired from the chair in 1995. The freelance branch was quite separate from the Edinburgh NUJ branch, which is the kind of district branch and which also takes in people like those in public relations. I got fed up with staff journalists saying, 'Oh, well, all these freelances, they're just making pin money, they're just playing at it.' So I kind of set up a system in which we interviewed all applicants for membership of the freelance branch, and if we didn't think they were serious journalists we didn't let them in or, if we weren't sure, we said that after a year they had to come back and show what work they'd done. Later that all went, because the Union just took anybody that applied. When I stopped working in 1995 the NUJ made me a life member of the union. Joyce McMillan arranged a lunch for me, and said that I'd done a lot to encourage and make it easier for other women, and I thought that was one of the nicest things.

I should maybe add that I nearly resigned from the union at one point when I think they went terribly wrong. The NUJ always seemed to me to be more allied with the print unions than anybody else. At the time of Wapping, the journalists from *The Times* certainly went happily to Wapping – well, maybe some of them didn't – but they went to Wapping because they were offered £2,000 more or whatever. There was a young girl, just starting out and with no other income at that point, in our union who'd seen that she could maybe make a bit of a living doing freelance theatre criticisms for *The Times* and whoever else. But the NUJ decreed that anybody who was supplying News International was to stop immediately. There was no question that freelances were going to be recompensed by the union. And I thought, 'There's something absolutely ridiculous here. There are the staff people there earning even more, and they're telling us freelances that we're to stop working for News International!' The union were going to haul this little girl up in front of them on a kind of charge. I said, 'Well, if you do this I'm resigning.' I think they've never recovered from that ridiculous stand they took. I mean, we all knew the printers had been getting away with murder and holding up everything. Maybe they were losing their jobs and it was a great pity. But the National Union of Journalists should have been looking after our interests rather than the printers'.[26] I remember when the general secretary of the union was at an Edinburgh NUJ branch meeting in the mid-1990s, the members were saying to him: 'We have had no negotiations with *The Scotsman* for four years. We're still being paid what we were paid four years ago. Don't you think it's time something was done about this?' 'Oh, well, yes.'[27] Well, I mean, that's it, you see. At that time all negotiations seemed to be falling apart, nothing was being done to improve things. Again, when I was chairman of the freelance branch it maybe got to the point where one-sixth of the members of the union were freelances, then by about 1996 we were pretty near one-third or more. It was a huge change. But again did the NUJ take this on board? Not really, I don't think. They should have been helping freelances, for instance to be trained as sub-editors, because there was plenty of work as a sub-editor. They should also have been changing the rules a bit, because if as a freelance you were unemployed you got no unemployment help from them. It was all geared to the staff members – and the staff members were often no longer in chapels. So it was by then a very different world. There was talk of the NUJ going in with the broadcasting unions, and I think that's what they should have been doing. But I do believe if you work in an industry you should be in a union. Well, I never aspired to any kind of the top offices. But I should have done if I felt as strongly as I did.

I suppose I've had an eventful and interesting life. I think I've got a reputation as a journalist I don't necessarily deserve. It was in two separate periods mainly I worked, of 13 years and 14 years, separated by the dozen years I was full-time in the Campus clothes shop business, during which from time to time I was still doing a bit of reporting or writing. Looking back from a woman's point of view on my life in journalism, it was very difficult, when I started, for women to get into journalism and to be taken seriously. I think the amazing change that's taken place is that women now are seen as absolutely equal to men, if not almost more equal than men. I mean, when I was a young journalist they used to say, 'Oh, of course, you couldn't have a woman sub-editor, because she wouldn't understand all the *double entendres*.' You were almost seen as too innocent to be able to – which probably we were actually. And now you've had women editors of the *News of the World* and all sorts of papers.[28] I think that's an amazing change, the result of a general social change in the position of women rather than something specific to journalism. I come back to the business of my flat in Edinburgh. Nobody would lend me money because, I'm sure, I was a single woman, and because women were not seen as actually going to make all the payments. You were not seen as a serious worker, I suppose. My friend Winnie Ewing, for instance, when she married she was a lecturer in law. She had a child and after the child was about a year old she applied for a job in legal research, where there was a Carnegie Scholarship. She went along to be interviewed and I think it was the old Lord Cameron said, 'Now tell me this, Mrs Ewing, you, I believe, have a child?' 'Yes,' she said, 'and do you ask men that question?' Of course they didn't ask the men. The implication was that as she had a child she wasn't going to be a serious worker. And I think that's the amazing change for women: even if they've more than one child they're seen as being able to have both a career and a job. It's a major change in my lifetime. Certainly, when I was starting out, there were women in teaching and in banks, but if they married they had to give up their jobs. I think in my day women were seen as being in the marriage market, and if you didn't marry then there was something peculiar, and then you were a bluestocking or an unattractive spinster, whatever. That's all gone. Well, I think the best years in journalism were in the 1960s. Certainly if you were working on the *Express* it was a good time. Now, with the upsurge of public relations, as far as I can make out reporters sit in their offices and just rehash the PR. In a sense it's all to do with cheap labour – get rid of all the senior people. It is depressing, it's not confined to journalism, everywhere's the same. Why they can't understand that what people want is some good journalism, I don't know. I mean, that is why people buy papers. But of course they all want the young readers. Now the young readers are not what they should be going for. This pursuit of youth is so ridiculous. Young people are not going to buy papers to read them, but to see what's on in the cinema or whatever. It's as you get older you can afford to buy newspapers and you want to buy newspapers.

George Hume

Then came the day, toward the end of my ultimate school year, my parents said to me, 'Well, we're perfectly happy to keep you there if you think you can make anything of it.' I thought, 'Forget it.' It was best that I go. Then I thought, 'What skills do I have?' And these were few. But I thought: newspaper trade. So I'm the first journalist in my family.

I was born in Edinburgh on July 19th, 1939, just before the war broke out. The family home was in Craigentinny, but by the time I was a few weeks old they'd moved to a brand new bungalow in Corstorphine in Tyler's Acre Road, built on what had been farm fields. The only thing built in 1939 was this street and then nothing was built until the 1950s. When we went there we had vacant blocks of ground between the bungalows. They had put up the metal palings, but a year or two later they came with an oxyacetylene torch and cut them all down for making munitions. The bulk of them were never used, but rotted over at Inverkeithing in Fife. But my earliest recollections are of growing up in Corstorphine, and I can remember back to the age of four very clearly. I lived there in Tyler's Acre Road until I left home to go to work when I was 17.

I can genuinely say I had a Victorian father, born in Edinburgh in 1900. He was a mercantile clerk with the Distillers Company Ltd. He joined it when he was 16 and he nearly made it to 65 and retirement, but died a few months before at 64. His father, my grandfather Hume, came from the Borders, but I don't know from which town or village there, and he was a portrait artist: I have a portrait he did of my father when he was 13. But I never knew grandfather Hume: he died in 1916, when my father was 16. Perhaps typical of that time, my grandmother went into widow's weeds in 1916 and never came out of them. She died in 1947 when I was eight. I only remember her vaguely, an elderly lady dressed totally in black, à la Queen Victoria. She came from Dunblane originally, but I don't think she did anything before marriage. She came from a background which had been modestly comfortable, and the girls were just not trained to do anything.

My mother's family came from Dundee originally. My grandfather George Doig was a Royal Marine and had fought at Omdurman and in the Boxer Rising in China.[1] I was called after him – and my middle name is Doig – to please him, because he'd had five daughters but never a son: his fifth daughter he called Georgina, the closest he got. But I've no recollection of him: he died just after I was born. When I started school at five I went for some reason to the Royal High School primary department at Piershill. So my father put me aged five on the tram in the morning at Corstorphine and I travelled alone right through the city all the way to Piershill to the school. It would have been about 50 minutes' journey. And the same back home in the afternoon. Until he died when he was about 60 I had a brother Guy, two years older than me, and he went to James Gillespie's School for Boys in Marchmont Road, near the Meadows. I wasn't at the Royal High primary very long, maybe a term, because my brother wasn't very happy at Gillespie's. So my parents sent him then to the Edinburgh Rudolf Steiner School, which in those days was in Colinton Road. Within weeks my brother was ten times the happy chap, so I too was then sent to the Steiner School and was there for the rest of my school life – and very happy.

There were two ways to go from Corstorphine to the Rudolf Steiner School. You could take a tram, or later on a bus, into the West End, cross from Shandwick Place to Lothian Road, then catch a No. 9 or a No.10 and get off at, or very near, Colinton Road. That way my brother and I were accompanied by my father, who was something of a champion walker and who would walk us through the traffic, a mere fraction of what it is now, between Shandwick Place and the No. 9 or 10, then he just walked back to Torphichen Street nearby, where the DCL office was. When we got older, however, we tended to walk to the end of Tyler's Acre Road and pick up the No.1 bus, which wound its way past the Heart of Midlothian FC ground in Gorgie Road. But we got off at the bottom of Robertson Avenue, walked past McVitie's biscuit factory there (although we never got any biscuits it was always great to go past: Tuesdays they made ginger snaps and the air was full of spice, Friday was chocolate robing day!), and up Shandon – 15 minutes' walk. Everybody walked in these days.

The Rudolf Steiner School was very different to any form of school education in Britain at that time.[2] In the Steiner system there's the Lower and Upper School. The Lower School goes beyond the state sector primary school, where they change at about age 12; the Steiner changes at 14. Then you do four years in the Upper School. In the Lower School you have a class teacher who is your friend and mentor for the first eight years of your school life. That teacher takes the first two hours of every day. They teach a system of what they call main lessons, and each main lesson lasts four weeks. So you start doing languages in the Lower School. Obviously, you're not studying the grammar, but you learn to sing songs in German and French. One of the favourite main lessons is the building lesson, where you learn about bonding brick and you have to put a foundation down; so practical work is done. Then the rest of the day you have your other lessons, where you have teachers who teach specific lessons. When you move into the Upper School at 14, the system changes. You have much more in the way of specialist teachers preparing you for the exam work. In those days the School only did the Oxford O and A Level exams.

The School aims to have very rounded pupils, so there is no streaming into, say, chemistry where you'd never do art. Nobody goes through the Upper School only doing their exam subjects. Somebody who is maybe going for the sciences and maths will also still be doing art, language, etc., lessons, and vice versa. And it's very friendly, very informal. The children are referred to by their first names. I remember thinking how nice this was when I went there: instead of being Hume I was George. Then in my day you shook hands with every teacher you encountered, and before you all sat down in main lesson in the morning your class teacher went along the rows and shook hands with every one of you. Now there's a lot in this, because if you've been planning to blow the door off the school safe or something of that sort, it's quite hard to look somebody in the eye and say, 'Good morning, Docky.' My teacher was Dr Pelham Swinton Moffat, from the Moffat family of photographers in Princes Street and one of the founders of the Edinburgh School in 1937–8, and he was known to everybody – children, staff, parents – as Docky, and this was to his face. You didn't say 'Docky' behind his back and Dr Moffat to his face.[3] The school was based on the principles of this Austrian philosopher Rudolf Steiner, and when my little school opened in Edinburgh ours was the first in Scotland and, I think, the sixth in Britain.

When I joined in 1944 we only had a Lower School up to 14-year-olds, they hadn't then grown into an Upper School. The numbers were of the order of 60; by the time I left in 1956 it was 180. So I saw quite a period of growth. When I got there they were already into No. 38 Colinton Road, then they got 14 Spylaw Road, which was acquired for the growing Upper School. There'd be eight teachers in the Lower School, one for every class. But you'd also have various teachers doing French, music, handwork, PT, German – so probably another 10, making maybe 18, 20 altogether. And then of course as they needed more specialist teachers as the pupils got higher, in came people teaching chemistry, biology, whatever. My own class was the biggest – 32, 24 boys and eight girls: Steiner's was co-educational. On the other hand, my brother's class – he was two years older than me – was small: eight.

So the Steiner School was proving more attractive each year to parents in Edinburgh. For many decades from its earliest days the school sought – before there was an assisted places scheme – to have as broad a social range of pupils as possible. If parents were not able to afford the fees there was a concession panel. Many years after I left the school I became chairman of the trustees, so I'm well aware of the internal workings of the school. The budget was so drawn that there was always a little bit scope to reduce the fees for parent applicants who couldn't look at the full fees. I haven't a clue what the fees would be when I was a pupil there. It would be wrong to say the school was utterly integrated and that 50 per cent of the pupils came from poorer working-class backgrounds and the others didn't. Generally speaking they came from lower-middle-class to middle-class, white-collar workers mainly, rather than blue-collar. The school has always attracted in large numbers the children of academics. When you're reading the parent list it sometimes reads like a staff roll of Edinburgh University. I think the Steiner philosophy would attract this element. On the other hand, if somebody living in working-class areas like Niddrie or Craigmillar did hear of Steiner and really took an interest, it was perfectly possible for them to come to the school.

When I was a youngster there, and even as a young fellow, there was a prejudice against the school, with the bizarre idea going the rounds that if you went to the Steiner you were either educationally subnormal, not quite up to speed, or that it was a school where you did exactly what you wanted. But that was not the case, I mean, you turned up at nine o'clock and started lessons on time. You assembled outside the front door after break time and you were taken in by the handbell. It was rung in each class and a class was ignored if it wasn't silent and in order. They took them in, little ones first; but if, say, Class 4 were still pushing and shoving they would just be given a serious look and Class 5 would be pulled in. Class 4 would be left there to realise that their behaviour was not acceptable. So it was perfectly formal in that way.

One of the other things, of course, other children couldn't believe was that there was no corporal punishment there. There were lines to write, and there was gardening. How could any teacher possibly keep order unless there was the ability to hang two or three unruly pupils every morning? I think we were very lucky. There were none of the teachers, male or female, that I could say we could take a loan of. And some of them were absolutely magnificent in their ability to hold and control a class. The method of punishment was quite good, because it involved your parents knowing in almost every case. In other schools if you were belted and your parents said, 'Did you have a nice day?' 'Oh, yes' – great, you'd been a good boy: thus children'd cleverly introduce a wedge between school and home. But if at Steiner we misbehaved we had to go in on a Saturday morning to do gardening in the grounds. So then you had to go home and say so: 'Oh? What have you done ?' 'Well, there was a bit of riot, and three of us have got to go in for an hour and a half.' And your teacher came in and supervised it. So there wasn't a feeling of oppression, you did your work properly and it was seen to be done properly. For other things, when you were older, you would get lines to write. I had a great chum in my class, Ian Wight, who lived down at Trinity. He came up from there to school every day by tram, and every other day he was late. He simply could not eject himself from bed in time. Our teacher used to make up his own lines. One little couplet he made up for Ian to write 100 times was: 'Early to bed and early to tram would obviate a hasty scram.' And of course Ian's parents would know. But the discipline at Steiner School was maintained, I would say, through this close contact and affection. Really there was great warmth between the teachers and the pupils, and there were clever items to keep this maintained, such as shaking hands in the morning. All right, there was a them and us feeling in that we were the kids and you knew which teachers you could endeavour to wind up and how far you could wind them up, as all children do. But that said, there wasn't a 'I hate school and all teachers' atmosphere. I mean, nobody ever wired a teacher's bicycle to explode or anything of that nature. And mainly this was mutual respect, and mainly it went beyond respect: it was affection. I always felt my teachers there cared for me as a person. So you really didn't have to have draconian punishment, because you were more embarrassed to be caught doing something really silly, particularly when you got into your teens. Then in the Upper School the teacher was called the class guardian, and was much more a friend and mentor. If any other teacher had trouble with you he or she would tell your class guardian, and then: 'Oh, by the way, a word. I hear there's difficulty in the class. Now what is the matter here?' And it would be sorted out that way. So there was a very high expectation of good behavior, and by and large it was met.

As a boy I was a keen reader and read anything I could get my hands on. I just consumed books. In my day 13, 14 year olds went to bed even in the summer by 8.30pm, and of course you were by no means ready to sleep. So I used to read under my blanket with a torch, and many's the time my parents, just passing on their way to bed at 11 or 11.30pm, would open the door to see that my brother Guy and I were still alive, and very gently the bedding would be lifted off while I was absolutely into a book. Well, by the time I was 10 the reminiscences of men who'd fought in the Second War were beginning to come out in large numbers, so there were any number of stories about fighting their way up through Italy, or escaping, or doing this or that. The escape genre was very strong – *The Wooden Horse*, and so on.[4] There was also a great writer, Richard Gordon, who wrote the *Doctor in the House* series. A female cousin, eight years older than me, was very good at choosing books for my birthday and my Christmas, and she gave me the *Doctor* books, which of course weren't written for children. Some time later my parents read one of them, *Doctor at Sea* – quite advanced, quite racy. But I thought, 'Ooh, ooh,' this was living.[5] And I just devoured tons of Robert Louis Stevenson, though I found Walter Scott then, and I still do, not terribly accessible, awfully chewy. I joined Corstorphine public library at an early age. It was a super little library with a polished beech floor, you could have eaten your dinner off it. And from when I was about 13 I used – well off my way home from school! – to wander round the old town near the University, where there were lots of little second-hand bookshops, and I remember getting my first copy, translated, of *Les Misérables* in two volumes for 3s 6d [17½p].[6] I mean, I haunted these places and did so until very recently. And then of course I was also into the Central Public Library in George IV Bridge. Across the street they'd started to build the National Library of Scotland just before the war broke out. The steel frame for the building was there all through the war until they finished building it in 1956. But starlings by the million used to roost in the steel frame. If you went past in the evening and there was a loud noise, clouds of starlings went up. Anyway as soon as the National Library was going, I was 17 or 18, got a reader's ticket and got in there. I remember the best line I got out of a book in those early days at the National was when a university economics tutor had said to Alec Douglas-Home: 'When a man says that his word is as good as his bond, always remember to take his bond.'[7] I slipped it into an article this morning for the Edinburgh *Evening News*.

As for reading comics, there was what you can only call a class prejudice in those days. I hadn't seen comics until when I was 10 I had a bad accident at school which damaged my legs, and I was in hospital for almost three years at the Princess Margaret Rose Hospital in Edinburgh. The Hospital was absolutely stiff with Fife miners' boys suffering from a wasting disease of the bone. These Fife boys always had stacks of comics. There was the *Dandy* and the *Beano*, and then there were the several reading comics, which weren't pictures but were mainly text: the *Hotspur*,

Rover, Wizard . . . I think they all came from D.C. Thomson in Dundee. But certainly I never saw a comic at my school nor in the possession of any of my friends, and my parents wouldn't have let me buy one, as they were just disapproved of as being pulp and trash. And I have to say that, at the age of 11, having looked at them in hospital over a period of many months, I was very much of the same impression about the *Beano* and the *Dandy*. I mean, I really couldn't see that Desperate Dan with his stubbly chin eating cow pie . . . It's all right if you're intellectually challenged, but to see boys of 14 and 15 reading this . . .[8]

Then as a boy I was interested in writing as well, and I used to write stories at the table. Remember also that people then didn't have television. It had come, but not all that many people had it. We didn't get TV into my house until the mid-1950s, when I was about 16. We rented one from the shop at the top of the road. We took it back after three months and I remember my father saying to the shop man, 'Mr So-and-so, we would like actually now to cease renting the TV.' The man said, 'Is there something wrong with it?' 'No,' my father said, 'we just think it's appalling rubbish.' We didn't have a television set after that until after my parents died in 1964–5. When many years later I was working for BBC TV it came out that I didn't have a television set myself. One of my bosses said, 'But how can you work on TV and you don't have one?' I said, 'Well, I get by.' 'Oh,' he said, 'I think you better get a TV.' So I rented one then.

Well, as I've said, I had a bad accident at school when I was 10. I was larking around in the playground with a great chum, Julian Rowe, and I had a bad fall. We were both big heavy lads, but if I was big, Julian was 50 per cent bigger. It was one of those games where, boy-like, you jump on each other's backs. Anyhow Julian jumped on my back and I went down very awkwardly and got a great pain in my left hip. After a day or two my parents took me to the doctor, who said, 'Ah, you've a pulled muscle. You've got to exercise furiously.' So for the next few weeks I exercised furiously and it didn't get any better, and my parents noticed that I walked with a roll like an old sea dog. So the doctor sent me to a specialist, who said the ball had moved out of its socket. It's called a slipped epiphysis. So in the Princess Margaret Rose Hospital at Fairmilehead they put it back and pinned it with a metal pin. I was in the PMR for 10 months, out for 10 months, back for 10 months and then back in again briefly – over two years altogether. I went in just before my 11th birthday and I wasn't back at the Rudolf Steiner till I was 13. PMR did a very good job of glueing me back together.

Being in hospital was an amazingly educational and enriching experience. Of course, at that age you were saying, 'I'd love to be home.' It was like being a prisoner of war: you dreamt about getting under the wire! But that said, it was fascinating to find another side of life in there in the PMR, because, as I say, the place was absolutely stiff with Fife miners' boys: 50 or 60 per cent of the ward came from Fife. These boys were fluent in two languages: fluent in proper English, but fluent also in ethnic or patois. To our teacher, it was 'Miss Tilley, could I shut the window?' But if Miss Tilley, the sister or the doctor weren't involved, it was 'widnae, didnae, cannae'. I was amazed, I'd never encountered this before. Where I lived in Corstorphine we just spoke one form of English and that was it.

At the PMR a teacher came in from 10 o'clock till 12. But the ward size was 25, the age range eight to 16: so it was really a holding operation and, in my view, very poor-quality teaching. Schools' radio, a thing I'd never encountered before, was heavily relied on, and it was pretty crass. One series I remember – it was to teach you Scottish geography – was a man who drove a lorry and he had his nephew Wullie with him. The sound effects of this lorry, well, they must have recorded them when lorries were first invented. And the lorry driver had one of those ethnic voices you could grate cheese on. If he had been my uncle I would have refused to get into his lorry, because wherever you went it was: 'Now, this is the River Tay, Wullie. See, the Tay runs from so-and-so to . . .' Our teacher, Miss Tilley (as in lamp) used to make a dirty dive for this radio, the ward radio of course was turned on, and then you did whatever else you wanted – carried on reading, or . . . So the hospital schooling wasn't even a holding operation. It didn't amount to a row of beans.

So if you miss two and a bit years at the Rudolf Steiner you're really toiling to catch up. I mean, for example, they'd started chemistry, Latin, logarithms, algebra, all these things, while I was tucked up between the sheets in Fairmilehead. Well, I caught up in the things that were easy to me, I suppose. So I managed to get my O Level in English language and literature. I had a stab at French: it won, I didn't. These were the only three exams I tried. And so I left in 1956 when I was 17, because there was really no point in going on another year, I was never going to make it in any other subjects in Oxford Os or As. So I went into the newspaper industry.

When I'd got into my mid-to-late teens I began to have ideas of what I wanted to do. One which caused my father great amusement and about which he used to tease me, was that because my reading had given me this wonderful picture of the world to be explored, I was terribly keen to become a trader in Hudson Bay. I'd be 16 when I wrote off and asked what were the criteria for joining the Hudson's Bay Company. I got back a letter which said, you know, 'No way, José.'[9] The other thing I wanted to be was a deck officer in the merchant service, and that was much more serious. In those days, in the 1950s, the merchant service in Scotland was still very big, with quite a number of shipping companies to be found down in Leith.[10] But what precluded that ambition of course was my complete lack of maths. It was after that I thought, 'Now what skills do I have?' And these were few, but I thought: newspaper trade.

So I left school and immediately went off on a one-month walking holiday through Brittany with three of my school mates. When I came back that was it, now the die had to be cast. So on my own initiative I went into the *Glasgow Herald* branch office in [South] St Andrew Street and met a very nice gentleman, David Douglas, then the Edinburgh editor of the Outram papers. This charming man with appallingly bad teeth said to me, 'It's far better if we change places at this table. You can interview me.' Great psychology, and at the end of all that he said, 'Well, no, you can't really join a big daily paper at 17. You must get yourself trained on a weekly. And,' he said, 'don't go to Dalkeith. Avoid Colonel Frew!'[11] Anyway David Douglas tried to push me along that line. Then, however, I went to see Frank Walker, a very tall chap, lean, and a little trim moustache, down at the *Scottish Daily Mail* at Tanfield. Of course the *Mail* was the real McCoy, the paper was printed there: here were wires, boys running about, folk saying, 'Boy! Copy!' And the smell of the ink – I was getting high on the ink! But Frank Walker was very kind, gave me 10 or 15 minutes, said, 'Now, no, no,' and gave me exactly the same advice as David Douglas had. I also managed to get an interview with Mr Barnetson, boss of the Edinburgh *Evening News*, a rotund gent with a fierce moustache, and I got the impression he had a considerable opinion of himself. At the *News* they had pulleys flying over the roof and I saw men putting copy into clips and it went round and round corners, and I thought, 'This is something.' At any rate I got that far at the *News*. I was beginning to get the message loud and clear: 'Get yourself fixed.' Then a day or so later my mother said, 'There was a Mr Douglas phoned.' David Douglas had phoned a chum of his, Donald Mackintosh, editor of the *Fifeshire Advertiser* in Kirkcaldy, a weekly paper of slender sale but great age, and had very kindly said about me (this is what I found in my early days in the newspaper industry, that these people were wonderful): 'This boy is dead mustard keen.' And he must have added, 'He can at least spell his name and will not eat peas off his knife in the company's time. You can trust him.' So I phoned Mr Mackintosh in Kirkcaldy and he said, 'Yes, yes, come and see me.'[12]

My whole relationship with Donald Mackintosh was quite quaint: he seemed to think you knew what he was thinking. So I arrived at his office and I was polished: I'd even ironed the seams of my underpants. I'd never been in Kirkcaldy before and waded my way through the smell of the linoleum down to the High Street and had my interview. It became obvious that Mr Mackintosh seemed to imagine I was already working at the *Fifeshire Advertiser*. I had expected things'd be along the lines, 'Well, I'll consider it and let you know.' But as our conversation wore on he was saying, 'So Monday would be all right to start then would it, George?' I could not believe it. I said, 'Oh, Monday would be very all right for starting.' He said, 'Well, this is what we would offer' – it was £3 3s 3d [£3.17].

And I was formally indentured. My father had to sign forms that I would be hard-working in the interests of the Fifeshire Advertiser Co. Ltd, would do as I was told, and would present myself sober, neat, smart, and ready for work as and when required. Mr Thallon Wood, chairman of the company and I think its major shareholder, and who was a solicitor and burgh prosecutor, and Donald Mackintosh signed for their part that the Company Ltd would teach me my trade, not expose me to moral turpitude, and . . . I wish I still had the document today because even in 1956 it was something! It was a long tradition, they were keen on their youngsters.

And they were very good. As soon as I got there they got me into the recently established training course. I was in fact the 16th person in Scotland to get my ticket, and that was four years later. So when I got in the course was obviously just under way. And because at that stage I had no shorthand at all I used to have to go out in the evening once a week to No. 9 Douglas Street to my shorthand teacher, Mrs Gourdie, an amazing shorthand guru, whose husband was the great calligrapher Tom Gourdie.[13] I went to night school in Kirkcaldy High for my typing and sat with about 30 girls at these enormous Underwood machines, with a shield over your fingers and a metronome that went *pitong-pitong*. If you'd mounted a four-inch gun on the typewriters you could have sent them to sea: they were like battleships. And of course I had to study for my Joint Councils exams. You didn't get day release.

Donald Mackintosh's cogs were, I think, slightly worn. The first three months I worked for the *Fifeshire Advertiser* he insisted on calling me David. Donald smoked a pipe and he was all *cough, cough*, and his front was covered in blazing flecks of boggy roll. Albert Crichton, the very able, very witty deputy editor, an awfully nice man, who had fought in the war, used to have great fun with Donald. Basically Bertie ran the

517

show. Then there was Jimmy McGregor, the chief reporter, Christine Shepherd, and Betty Carr, reporters,[14] and then they would always have two youngsters, of whom I was one and the other was just ahead of me; ultimately I became one ahead of somebody else. It was quite a sizeable staff for a local weekly paper. Well, we did cover a lot, we covered the Sheriff Court and we did the councils, and we'd two journals: along in Leven we had the *Leven Mail,* no editorial, just advertising with a few bits of Scottish Women's Rural Institute notes and 'Round the District' kind of crap.[15] The real reporting was in the *Fifeshire Advertiser.*

The very first job I did on day one was to go along to a hotel in Kirkcaldy High Street. They'd said, 'Go along to the Conservative person there. They're having a baby show.' When you're 17 and you've just come from school you don't have a lot of brass neck. I hadn't even been in many hotels. But I found this person in her room, asked all about this baby show, came back, wrote it up, and it went into the paper. I couldn't believe it: my very first published piece.

And then I used to get sent out to do things like, 'Go up to the Beveridge Park. We want 800 words on the rose garden.' And I remember taking down all these rose names, roses called Ena Harkness.[16] And they put that on the front page of the *Advertiser* and it had my name on it – a byline! That was very unusual in those days. Oh, they did it plainly to tickle me. But it must have been at least competent. I just thought, 'This is it.' Well, they were just very good with young people.

But at first, my overwhelming job during the week was to read proofs. I read proofs till they were coming out my ears and I got quite fast at it. We had four councils under our auspices, and I had three: Burntisland, Kinghorn, and Leslie. At Kinghorn the Provosts were always pork butchers all the years I was there. At Leslie, away up in the hinterland where they made paper, the family that owned the paper mill had two members, a husband and wife, who were both on the council. Even at that tender age I thought, 'This cannae be right.' But Jimmy McGregor, the chief reporter, he did the Kirkcaldy council, because that was real.

I wasn't allowed to do Kirkcaldy Sheriff Court for a bit, but I started on the juvenile court – no names, you see. Everything was read by Bertie Crichton, and so that you couldn't get it wrong you'd already been told, 'No way do you identify the person. So if the boy's father is a deep sea diver you can't say, "A Leslie boy whose father is a deep sea diver", because there's only going to be one boy in Leslie whose father is a deep sea diver.' You could say, 'A Kirkcaldy boy whose father is a miner,' because that covered 2,000 men in the local pits and probably 4,000 local boys. And the juvenile court was another ethnic experience, similar to the one in the Princess Margaret Rose Hospital, because I discovered at the court that boys from a very Scottish working-class background can use the word 'sir' to denote an enormous range of reactions, all done on inflection. The Sheriff might say, 'Well, John, this is very serious.' 'Sir.' 'Is it going to happen again?' 'Sir.' 'What did your mother think about it? Was she a bit upset?' 'Sir.' There were about eight or nine inflections to 'Sir', and there was a shake of the head up or down, there was denial and even askance. 'So am I right in thinking that you're an absolute rascal then, John?' 'Sir.' You couldnae translate it into newspaper copy. But this was the way the interrogations went.

Ultimately I got to different stories. I used to go along and keep an eye on the boats in Kirkcaldy harbour. They used to still ply across from the Baltic, though very seldom, and if there was anything with a mast and sails . . . And of course I was always doing up stories on linoleum companies. Oh, Kirkcaldy was bustling and busy. It had two major companies manufacturing linoleum. It was my first experience of religious prejudice. I quickly discovered that if you worked for Nairn's, the big successful company, you were a Protestant. I mean, that was it. Barry, Ostlere & Shepherd, the other company, which wasn't quite so successful, although it had a mix, basically the bulk of them were Catholics. And then a local music whiz, Drake Rimmer, was the musical director of the Barry, Ostlere & Shepherd's brass band. Nairn's may have made the profit, but Barry's band run by Drake Rimmer was the *crème de la crème* and just whacked the pants off everybody all over Britain.[17] So Kirkcaldy was a great place to grow up in, away from the temptations and pitfalls you might run into in a city where you might not get people who were so kind.

So I had great colleagues on the *Fifeshire Advertiser* and great fun. They were good at showing you your trade. But they weren't in any way avuncular, in the sense of your social life. In the four years I was there I was never invited to anybody's home, although they knew I was in digs. So here was a 17-year-old lad in Kirkcaldy, and when my work was finished in the evening what was I doing? Nobody ever said, 'Would you like to come home to supper tonight, George?' I think today I would do that, if I was in a wee office and we had a laddie from, say, Perthshire and he was living in digs. So that was very striking. But they had a very warm interest in your professional welfare and they really did help you along, instruct you, and so on. And of course the place was full of good fun. The editor, Donald Mackintosh, wrote a leader which was just incredibly turgid. Its heading was 'Something I want to say', by D.R.P.M. (I don't know what the R.P. was). One day when I hadn't been there very long and was learning to read proofs, Donald, who never took his bloody pipe out of his mouth, stuck his head round the editorial door and said, 'David', which was what he called me and I would always say, 'George.' 'Yes, George. Now, David.' It took about six months for him to get this right. Anyway this day he said, 'David.' 'Yes?' And he said, 'Something I want to say.' So I said, 'Yes, Mr Mackintosh?' 'Something I want to say.' And I thought, 'Come on, you're over 21 – say it.' I became aware that a silence had fallen in the room and that several people were convulsed. And of course it was the silly old bugger's editorial, which he always insisted on reading himself. On the one or two occasions I got it there was a syntax error once, and I remember thinking 'I'll correct that.' And he came back with more sparks flying out of his pipe and said, 'What was wrong with that?' 'Well, you know, it's the wrong thing to say.' He didn't mind if I'd picked up a literal, but otherwise it was holy writ. And when he went on holiday I discovered that, like a minister with sermons, he could buy editorials in a book. And Donald subscribed to this service that sent him ten at a time. Some he did write himself, but they were unusual. Normally he just took one of the subscription ones and he adapted it for Fife. So all this was an education and good fun.

The *Advertiser*'s main rivals were the *Fife Free Press*, whose office was in Kirk Wynd.[18] Ours was in about the middle of the High Street in Kirkcaldy. We'd a great big coal fire there in the winter, and in my early days there one of my duties was to go and get the coal and light the fire first thing in the morning. The cleaner had set the fire, so when I came in last night's ashes had disappeared and there were crumpled up papers, sticks and some coal. But I'd to go down to a cellar one floor below and fill up two buckets and yank them upstairs. Of course, as you rose in rank you no longer had to light the fire. One of my other duties which wasn't strictly editorial was to go to the end of the High Street, which is a long one, to a butcher's shop near the harbour to get thin-cut corned beef for Bert Crichton's lunch. This was the keenest price: Bert, a true Fifer, watched the ha'pennies.

I lived in digs at No. 108 Nicol Street. Nicol Street was in two distinct parts. The top end, the higher numbers, up by Beveridge Park, was posh, the bottom end was a festering slum. It was a very long street. So if you said to anybody local, 'I live in Nicol Street', their eyebrows would immediately go up and you had to add, 'Up beside Beveridge Park.' The digs were run by Kate Wilson, from the west coast of Scotland, whose late husband had been a shipwright. For £2 10s [£2.50p] a week you got your room, your breakfast, and your dinner. To supplement my pay from the *Advertiser* I got ten shillings [50p] a week from my father – provided I didn't drink. We used to buy our lunches out. There were two or three middle-aged ladies who ran a refectory near one or two small engineering works, at the west end of Kirkcaldy High Street. There for a shilling [5p] you could get soup, a main course, and pudding. It was good home-made soup, and the main course was mince and potatoes and a green or it was stew and something, and the puddings were all of the steamed sponges, spotted dick and custard variety. You took your plate to a trestle table with benches, so you had to climb over. As young men at the *Advertiser* we had to wear suits, or at least pressed flannels and a proper jacket. The social mix in the refectory was amazing: you were sitting maybe beside a boy in blue overalls that were absolutely saturated in grease and oil. Opposite you was maybe a bank clerk who was so young he still had acne all over his face. And here was I, the *'Tiser*'s young man, travelling the world as far even as Burntisland and Leslie to find out what was going on. These refectory middle-aged women were obviously able to turn a profit off this and provide a very good service. But the interesting thing wasn't so much that, it was the fact that so many young people used the place. There would be no one there under about 15 or 16 and probably no one over 20. We were essentially kids and we wanted lots of hearty food. I suppose we were never more than 16 or 20 sitting down at a time. So they maybe did 30, 40 covers at lunch. To stride out there from the office took me about five minutes. I didn't go there every day, but most days: I couldn't afford anything else.

In giving me a 10 shillings [50p] supplement, subject to not drinking it, my father himself wasn't at all TT. Though he worked for the Distillers Company Ltd he didn't drink. If we were on holiday he would maybe have a small glass of lager, which I think he thought was quite daring. But our house was awash with drink, whiskies particularly. At Christmas time the DCL directors used to send him, because by this time he was in a more elevated position, bottles of Johnnie Walker, Vat 69, King George IV, all these things. A very smart three-ton platform lorry used to draw up outside our house and a man in overalls would bring in a case with six bottles of KG IV or of . . . Some cases brought gin. My father used to give it away, because he didn't drink spirits. But, I mean, there were always six, seven, eight unopened bottles of whisky in the house.

I couldn't live on my *Advertiser* pay of £3 3s 3d [£3.17] a week, because my digs cost me £2 10s [£2.50] a week, but also my return rail fare home at the weekend was 4s 8d [23½p]. I came home late on a Friday virtually every weekend. In the summer I didn't get home every weekend, because we covered agricultural and Highland shows. In those days, Fife heaved with agricultural shows and these little awful Highland shows. In the latter you had basically thousands of tiny girls with insanely ambitious mothers who used to strip clothes off them right on the edge of the platform. There were three dances – the Highland, the hornpipe, where they had to dress up as little sailors, and an Irish jig with shillelaghs. I used to watch this absolutely dumbstruck. You had these shows all over the place, oh, we did them endlessly for the *Advertiser*. You had endless lists of stuff to type out for the cattle and things shows, so there had to be two of you, as we printed a whole page of results. And woe betide you if you got the bullock's name wrong. Of course, the names of the farms were unbelievable. Lothendie of Buchholt Backfart would be the name of the bloody place. You couldn't use any core of knowledge to get to it, you just had slavishly to follow this off the programme. Oh, a marvellous training in accuracy. The only way we could get this down was for one of us to read it and one of us to type it. We used to rush out to the judges, get a handful of results, and rush back. We had a portable typewriter, one banged away at that while the others spelled it out almost letter by letter. And of course also there were also the different categories. I remember them yet: a pen of store stotch of not more than two broad teeth. Pale fed calves was another one. I mean, it was hell. The Highland shows were a bit more fun, they had running, cycle races, and sports. I'd never seen cycle races and the bookies that came for them. I didn't realise this whole sub-milieu existed in Scotland. People came even from the north of England. There were bicycle sprints, and they were a right rough, tykey-looking lot, I wouldn't have tangled with any of them! They were professionals who moved round all the shows: oh, there was money, cash prizes, heavy betting. It was just amazing.

Then also I was introduced to the four local cinema managers. That meant you could go to the cinema free of charge. But what films you saw you didn't review. They used to send you handout material which we just used to top and tail and bang it in the paper: 'Wonderful film! Better go and see it!' In the winter you might want to go to a cinema. Three were respectable and one was a fleapit, though it had perfectly good films. That one was along at the foot of Nicol Street, as I say, a rough district. And we had the Regal, where I met Sean Connery. The manager phoned up one day and said to Bertie Crichton, the deputy editor, 'Could you send a reporter? We've got a young actor along here and we're showing a film called *Darby O'Gill and the Little People*. He's the star. He's an Edinburgh fellow called Sean Connery, and he's on holiday in Fife playing golf.' So I was told, 'Go along and see this Pat.' When I got there, sitting in the manager's office was this fellow Sean Connery. He wore golfing trousers and a startling canary yellow sweater, very à la golf course. He was perfectly pleasant and told me how he'd been a milk boy in Edinburgh and so on. I never saw him again until a good few years ago he was receiving an honorary degree at St Andrews University and I was working for television. By this time of course he was mega. I went up to him, we chatted away, and I got an interview with him. 'We've actually met before,' I said to him. 'You were playing golf in Fife and you'd just opened at the Regal in Kirkcaldy in *Darby O'Gill and the Little People*.' And his face – froze! Had I said the wrong thing? That film was obviously a lemon, and he didn't want anybody to know. It would be the very first film probably he'd ever made with anything other than a walk-on part.[19]

I didn't feel lonely or homesick in Kirkcaldy. I mean, it really was an experience. Well, you were working probably one night in the week, then you had the two publication nights. So that was three nights in a week. And then Friday night, as soon as I finished I went home to Edinburgh. And I had my regular routines – went out for lunch, worked hard in the office, had to go to night school in the evenings in winter. Like my father I was a very keen walker, and in the summer months I walked every night. There were a lot of little paths all round. I would walk from Kirkcaldy to Aberdour and back along the front. My legs only fell off a few years ago (till then they'd been very successful in dealing with them all those years earlier at Princess Margaret Rose Hospital), so in those days I was a great walker. I was at the *Advertiser* four years but the time did not hang heavy, not at all. So it was a marvellous training for me in Kirkcaldy. You learned proofreading, and my shorthand built up to a speed of 140 words a minute. But it was also such a wonderful life experience, discovering things you never thought existed.

I did pit accidents. We used to do Fatal Accident Inquiries. You picked up a mining vocabulary: trepanners, shears, sylvesters, lipes, horizons.[20] I'd never been underground before in a coal pit and that was an experience going down in the cage. They kick the brake off and just drop the cage. I became weightless, felt I was six inches off the floor, just floated down in this cage. Coming up was equally very odd. The speed of the wind-up was such that you actually felt as if your shoulders and your hips were being pressed down. The Frances colliery, known as The Dubbie, was always very wet because it ran out under the Firth of Forth, as did Seafield colliery of course at the west end of Kirkcaldy.[21] And further east along the shore of the Forth was Methil which in those days they used to work coal boats out of. There was a brothel in Methil High Street (I never went into it) which was always the subject of great hilarity, because you'd get right rough-looking dames involved in offences coming up in court in Kirkcaldy. And when they were asked for their address they would say Number such-and-such High Street, Methil. It was absolutely notorious. Methil docks was a busy, busy coal port. Some of the collier crews must have been right hard guys, and they came in and had a wild night in Methil – which is almost beyond conception, having a wild night in Methil. But I think it included a visit to No. such-and-such in the High Street.

And then, as I say, there were stories from the linoleum works. The workers there were very poorly paid. It was almost essentially labouring work, there was very little skilled element then. In those days you would see men with bogies under enormous loads of God knows what, staggering up and down the public streets with these things. Nairn's was reckoned to be the better employer and payer. But, as I say, there was a very caste system. Barry, Ostlere & Shepherd's, I think, was a jollier place in some respects. And it wasn't a factory each, I mean, both companies had factories, it wasn't a question of one here, one there: around every corner you went was a lino factory. Barry's were behind the railway station mainly, and they had three or four factories. Nairn's were spread more toward the little harbour and up the hill at the Dysart end of Kirkcaldy. And then the town also had in those days McIntosh's Furniture, famous for their inlay, beautiful work. So there was a tremendous amount going on in Kirkcaldy to report and also for me to become personally interested in. It was just an eye opener, particularly when you're that age. One wasn't blasé about it. Then the High School was very much part of the place, we had a very good rep theatre company which played in the Adam Smith Hall, and the library, museum and art gallery were absolutely excellent. I used to spend hours in there in the winter. And they'd just built the new Town House when I got there.

The *Fifeshire Advertiser* was a union paper. Well, I was introduced to the union and there wasn't the feeling that you absolutely had to join it. But I joined the National Union of Journalists because everybody else there was in it. Albert Crichton or Jimmy McGregor – I forget which one – was the father of the chapel. So one paid one's pennies. I'd be 17 when I joined, so I joined more or less from starting work there. In those days there was also the Institute of Journalists, and Donald Mackintosh, the editor, was in the Institute. This was somewhat derided because the Institute was not a trade union but a sort of gentleman's association. Anyway, I wasn't active in the union. I was a member but it didn't mean anything to me, and we never had any hassle with the company. I mean, it wasn't that kind of place, although again the attitudes to young people could be quite funny. We had a jobbing printing shop in the back and we printed the Kirkcaldy Town Diary. We got them bound at Oliver & Boyd's in the High Street in Edinburgh.[22] The cheap way to get the diaries over to Edinburgh for binding was for me to carry this whopping parcel to Kirkcaldy station, get a ticket to Edinburgh, stagger up – no taxis – from the Waverley station to Oliver & Boyd's in Tweeddale Court, and hand it in. Then a week or so later, go back, get two even bigger parcels of the diary with the bound covers on them, and stagger down with them to the train. One day I was doing this and Thallon Wood, chairman of the Fifeshire Advertiser Co. Ltd, this enormous puffed-up lawyer, had seen me in Edinburgh probably at three in the afternoon or something. He was in the *Advertiser* office one day about a week later and said to me, 'I'd like a word with you. You know when you come here,' he said, 'you're here to work for the company, not to take afternoons off and jolly about in Edinburgh.' 'Well, sorry,' I said, 'I haven't taken an afternoon off and jollied about in Edinburgh. What's the problem?' 'I saw you in Edinburgh last Wednesday and you were looking in the shop windows in the High Street.' 'Well,' I said, 'I was on my way to pick up a parcel of Kirkcaldy Town Diaries from Oliver & Boyd's.' 'Oh,' he said, and just walked away. But it tells you the attitude in those days: 'I'm keeping an eye on you,' because you were still of school age.

*   *   *

Well, I came to the time when my four-year indenture, my apprenticeship, at the *Fifeshire Advertiser* was completed. You had to do the National Joint Training Council's exams at about three and a half to four years into the course and, as I say, I think I was the 16th in Scotland to pass them. The *Fifeshire Advertiser* and the *Leven Mail* had put through eight of them. The company reckoned to lose you after the four years' training, that was virtually the understanding. I could have stayed on of course, but, oh, I wanted to see a wider world. I was waiting for the day I'd passed my exams, stayed a month or so afterward, and then – typical of the arrogance of youth – left the *Advertiser* without another job to go to. There was no way I was ever going to be a Kirkcaldy-ite, a member of the Lang Toon fraternity.[23] Edinburgh, my home city, had two evening papers that beckoned, and there were other papers there, too.

I had a great scheme to go round Europe on a motorbike with a chum. I didn't have much in the way of savings; my £3 3s 3d [£3.17] at the *Advertiser* had risen to perhaps just over £4. Anyway my chum had this old motorbike, and we put our pennies together. We slept under a wee tent all over Europe, climbed the high mountain passes over Switzerland into Italy, would eat just boiled rice with a can of sardines on our pressure stove. It was great fun. But we had a bad accident in France: a loony drove over the top of us, which didn't improve our condition. But we got ourselves home in one piece, well, in several bits. My parents were very accommodating, weren't barking at me to get a job. Though I was swathed in bandages I realised I would have to find one. Meantime the *Daily Mail* man in Paris had picked up that two Scots had been mown off their motorbike just outside Paris. His paragraph lay about somewhere in the *Daily Mail* office for about a week, then they printed it as if the accident had just happened. The Edinburgh *Evening News* reproduced the *Mail*'s story. Then Fergus Taylor, a young *Evening Dispatch* reporter, turned up at our door. There am I standing, a bandaged apparition. Fergus said, 'Is this the home of George Hume?' 'Yes,' I said, 'he is I.' So Fergus came in, had a coffee, and said, 'Where are you a journalist?' I said, 'Well, I've left my job in Fife and I was having a holiday.' He said, 'There's a vacancy in the *Dispatch*.' That afternoon I went in, saw the editor, and got the job: general reporting.

On the first day the boss on the *Dispatch* news desk called me over and said, 'You can drive, can you?' 'Yes.' He said, 'Set of car keys. There's a Hillman Minx parked up in the back of Cockburn Street, registration . . . There's your job.' And he handed me a chit of paper about an uncovered drain up the back of the city. It should have been culverted but wasn't. Some kiddie had fallen in and just been rescued from a terrible fate. And there were women chanting, 'Down with the council.' And that was the first job I did for the *Dispatch*.

The second job was when I came back from that, typed it up rapidly, and then they said, 'Go along to the Caley Hotel. Wolf Mankowitz, the writer, is holding a press conference there.' With a photographer I went along to Wolf Mankowitz, who was sipping a gin and tonic at the Caley. And I thought, 'Wow! All in one day. You wouldn't get that in Kirkcaldy.'[24]

It was 1960 and I was 21 when I started in the *Dispatch*. My pay was £575 a year, more than double what I'd had when I left the *Fifeshire Advertiser*. I was 18 months on the *Dispatch*, for a year of which I was their High Court man and did the Court of Session as well. I did a lot of murder trials for them, and they used to send me through also to trials in Glasgow. I did the Walter Scott Ellis murder trial, which became something of a *cause célèbre*.[25] Intellectually, the Court of Session was extremely engaging, and the murder trials were very good experience, just slapping the stuff down to excellent copy takers, of whom the fastest was an amazing woman, Ann Coomb, a real character, and could she type!

It was a big contrast between working for an evening paper in a big city like Edinburgh and working for the *Fifeshire Advertiser*. It brought you right up to speed. I had the basic skills and felt I was probably no longer easily shockable. But I didn't have the speed. Then suddenly I'm driving off with an A to Z street map in one hand, coming back with the copy quotes, and being asked very hard questions: 'Have you checked with the council? Have you phoned up so-and-so department?' I'm thinking, so-and-so department: what's that? And having to hammer in the copy, then on to your next job, 'And get back here,' this kind of thing. Then when I was doing the High Court I had to serve every edition of the *Dispatch*. It was a big contrast with the *Fifeshire Advertiser*, but it was great fun.

We did three shifts on the *Dispatch:* 6am to 2pm, 8am to 4pm, 4pm to midnight. If you were on general reporting, you got your murders at night. You'd phone the police – hourly checks, and they'd say, 'We've got a body in a dunny down at so-and-so.' You'd get into your car and away down, and true enough there'd be a corpse stretched out. You got to know the CID guys and they'd say, 'Ah, it's just a natural.' But sometimes they'd say, 'Ooh . . .' So I saw quite a few bodies down in back courts and things. But after a short time the *Dispatch* moved me on totally to the Court of Session and High Court. I enjoyed that.

While I was working there one day, George Watt, one of the *Glasgow Herald*'s two High Court men, came up to me and said, 'Would you like to work for the *Evening Times* as their Edinburgh man? Angus Shaw has been reading your stuff in the *Dispatch* and he'd like to have a word with you.' So I phoned Angus, news editor of the *Evening Times*, and went through to Glasgow, where I was interviewed by him on board that ship that used to be tied up near the High Court there. Angus himself was ex-navy and he'd definitely got a quarterdeck bearing, a very distinguished-looking man.[26] Well, Angus asked me a few questions and so I joined the *Evening Times*. That job came in at £12 a week. They wanted me as their Edinburgh man. I became a king with my own little fiefdom, which ran into Fife and down to the Borders.

I was based in the South St Andrew Street branch office. I sat with all the others, had my own wee desk, and used to go in about quarter to eight in the morning. I was purely *Evening Times*. That was a super job and they were a great staff. David Douglas, who'd given me my start in newspapers, was still there though by this time he'd been moved sideways and the news editor was Bob Yeats. Because he never smiled, Bob was nicknamed Stoneface among the staff, but not to his face. Charlie McCorry, a great chap, a card, one day said of Bob: 'You see that bugger there. Even when he smiles it's like the screeching of a coffin lid.'

A dozen or 14 of us reporters went down in those days to press conferences at the Miners' Union office in Hillside Crescent. They had this tiny wee room at the back with highly polished brown lino. It was like getting an audience at the Kremlin. Michael McGahey, and the two presidents Abe and Alex Moffat before him, used to call in two shorthand typists to take down every word that was said.[27] I mean, you just were not trusted. The relationship was quite unnecessarily abrasive. Anyway we were waiting to go into a meeting there to interview them and out of the blue it was announced that the Edinburgh *Evening News* had been bought by Roy Thomson, who wanted it shut. I remember Charlie McCorry getting this information as we sat there, and he said, 'Oh, aye, *Evening News*. Well, as the saying goes, when one door closes another one shuts.'

My *Evening Times* job coincided with the building of the Forth Road Bridge. I had three years of going up and down these towers and elevators and walking over the cables before they were finished off. I've walked from bank to bank of the Firth of Forth over the towers. Of course there was always a good story during the building of the bridge. I covered the Queen's opening of it in September 1964. Then apart from keeping an eye on the two solemn procedure days at the Sheriff Court, which in Edinburgh were Tuesdays and Fridays, I always had to keep an eye on them daily at 10am, just in case we got a cracker. But also at that time of course we had the Argyll divorce case, and I was involved in covering that and all the skirmishes beforehand. So I reckon I got a front-page splash in the *Evening Times* once a week. It was just tremendous for the ego, and I never had a nicer boss than Angus Shaw. And I was still then only in my earlier twenties, just a kiddie.

So I was three years with the *Evening Times*, very happily. But the need did come to earn a bit more crust. I heard from somebody on the *Daily Express* that if I applied for a job there I had a chance. So I applied and I got it, and went from what was probably only about £17 a week to £1,500 a year or £30 a week. I was 24. But I'd just started working for the *Express* a few weeks before my mother died on Christmas Day 1964, and my father died just a few weeks later.

So I joined the Edinburgh office of the *Express*, and I was three years with them, great fun. That was a total cracking up of the pace, because now you were working for a big boys' paper and suddenly you found it wasn't enough to cover the news that emerged. You had to get exclusives and collect pictures that nobody else got, and you had to make sure nobody else got them. The tricks and techniques one learned!

The Edinburgh office covered from Bathgate down to the Borders, on to the Lanark Moor and up into Fife – a huge area. We had huge resources. We had 18 reporters based in Edinburgh, six photographers, three chauffeurs, one dedicated PBX operator in the room, just doing the editorial telephone calls. We had two boys on shift – pit ponies in the darkroom – who did nothing but develop and print pictures. The office itself had moved down to Jeffrey Street when I got there.

Gilbert Cole was then still the chief reporter or Edinburgh news editor. One of the company cars would pick him up and bring him in in the morning. Once the day was well under way he would call for his tea. Then he would take out of his drawer a Club biscuit, slide the wrapper off, reverse the biscuit, open it up almost in a surgical way, take a knife, and cut it into exactly six equal parts, then drink his tea and eat the six biscuit parts. Gilbert was a great boss, a gentleman, very witty and very able. Many funny stories surrounded Gilbert. We had a bit of a Jack the Lad called Len Shearer, who later died in New York in a taxi, which I thought very appropriate. Len was besotted with working for the *Express* in a romantic movie type of way. He lived in Portobello, took a bus from there to the cab rank at the east end of Princes Street, there boarded a taxi and had it drive him to the front door of the *Express* in Jeffrey Street. He could have walked through Waverley station to the office, but you had to have style. Len couldn't afford the taxi all the way from Portobello so he did it that way. Len was an absolute scamp and a charmer. One day he was very late arriving. Gilbert looked up and said, 'Leonard Shearer!' – you always knew if you got your full name you were getting a ticking off, always very elegantly done – 'Leonard Shearer! I'm used to you coming in 10 or 15 minutes late. But, Leonard – one bloody hour?!' With the whole office listening and watching, Len walked across to Gilbert, bent over his desk, beamed at him in a seraphic manner, and said, 'Yes, Gilbert, but so well worth waiting for.' Gilbert for, I think, the first time in his career did not know what to say. He just grinned and said, 'Leonard, go away!' We always admired Gilbert because he cut off completely from work. As soon as the working day finished, that was it. One of the chauffeur cars took him back home. The drivers used to tell us that as soon as he stepped into the car he was witty, urbane, charming, and he was always going out to dinner with his wife. He was a great music lover, a great member of the Gramophone Society.

We had an *Express* driver called Teddy. I don't think he had a driving licence, and it was terrifying: he used to go through red lights. And we had two huge Fords in those days. There was a wonderful story that Teddy'd been driving Gilbert home and for some reason he couldn't go directly but had to go via Danube Street. That's where the famous Dora Noyce's brothel was. Apparently they'd been driving along Danube Street and Teddy, coarse as always, said, 'Dora Noyce's?' And Gilbert had said, 'Dora Noyce's?' 'The brothel,' said Teddy. 'Oh,' said Gilbert, 'oh, that's

Dora Noyce's?' Gilbert had a delicate edge to himself and always tried to pretend not to know about these things. But he knew fine, because we were always writing stories about it.[28]

When the *Express* in Glasgow were short of staff, they always pulled people in from the branch offices. So I spent quite a bit of three summers working shifts in Glasgow. That was interesting and entertaining. Joe Megin sat at the news desk there in the evenings. Risen to his full height he'd be about four feet something. He had his hair plastered down with, I think it must have been, sausage grease. But there was always a stray bit that came up at the top, like a caricature out of one of the comics. And he had a voice that you could have cropped steel with. Once he'd read the copy and wanted it sent down, it was almost like he was going to be sick the way his voice sounded: 'Boy! Copy!' It was just such an eye-opener. And you worked away at the reporters' desk, to which the typewriters were chained in case they were stolen. They had bits of chain from a shipyard shackling the typewriters to the desk. So – rough! You've no idea! There were lots of queer things. I mean, there were no knives in the *Express* canteen in Glasgow, because the *Citizen* van boys used to fight with them. So the knives were withdrawn.

Joe Megin used to read the schedule at 4.30 in the afternoon. It was 4pm in Edinburgh. Joe used to pick up the phone, dial a number, a split second later one of the two very able secretaries sitting opposite him three or four feet away would pick up her phone. She'd say, 'Right,' put on her headphones, and start to tinkle away on her typewriter. This was Joe dictating the schedule to her. What was to prevent him saying across his desk, 'Ann, here's the schedule,' and she'd have heard him. He used to sink lower and lower in his swivel chair till only his eyes and this amazing patent leather hairdo were visible above the desk. And he swivelled, he spent the entire day swivelling. Anyway I couldn't believe it because when, after three years with the *Express*, I started working on *The Scotsman*, I was in the sub-editors' room one night and it was absolutely silent.

I had realised after about three years I needed to move on from the *Express*, because it wasn't quite what I'd want to do for the rest of my life. A chum working on *The Scotsman* said if I applied there was a job there for me. So: 'Yes, there certainly is. Come this way.' And I was the first *Express* man they'd ever employed. There was almost an aura of prejudice, particularly among the sub-editors. You know, a hooligan! I mean, here was a fully-fledged *Daily Express* thug that somehow had got into their building. In those days some of the sub-editors, these old boys, used to go round with carpet slippers on. I was in one evening from the news room and heard a beautifully modulated voice saying in Morningside tones, 'Down, please, down, please.' I thought there was a wee doggy jumping up on somebody. But this was their equivalent of: 'Boy! Copy!' And it was wonderful, the voice was never raised above a library type whisper: 'Down, please.' A young man would go forward, get the copy, put it in a pneumatic tube, and *pphhaatt*, down it went. Oh, I think the slippers were worn to ensure silence and the comfort of their feet.[29]

In those days, when I joined *The Scotsman* in 1967, its approach to work was that if you didn't have your name in the diary for a set job, you could actually disappear. For example, if the Lord Provost had been machine-gunned in Princes Street and some citizen phoned in to *The Scotsman*, there'd have been no question of sending a reporter and a photographer. They would get the official statement later off the police book. The headline wouldn't have been *Lord Provost Slaughtered in Machine-Gun Attack*, it would have been probably *Untoward Event in Capital*. *The Scotsman* was that kind of place. They lived only off the diary. They never did jobs about people. They only did stories about organisations and associations. The National Trust, the council, the Royal Society, the Society for the Prevention of Cruelty to Birds: these were the jobs they did. It was run as a sort of news-sheet for people who lived in the Grange. So much so that some people who lived in the Grange actually thought it was one of the emergency services. They would phone up and say, 'Oh, we're having a small sherry do for the Binkie, who's retiring as lecturer. And we thought it'd be nice if you'd send a man.' I mean, you were literally summoned.

So between the *Daily Express* and *The Scotsman* there could be no greater contrast. You can understand why the carpet-slipper brigade looked at me. I was the very first person they'd ever employed from the *Express* – the *Express*, my God! But basically your parents had to live in the Grange. I mean, if you actually put them all through a riddle you found that was the case. The features editor when I joined was Bill Watson. Bill had been there for years and, I mean, he came from a well-to-do background. He was a clever lad, and when he left *The Scotsman* he started writing books and plays which never sold. Anyway I wasn't long with *The Scotsman* and I would pass Bill in the corridor and I'd say, 'Hi, Bill,' and Bill would say something like: 'When the cranes fly at night they fly not alone. But man stands ready.' And I'm thinking, 'That has to be some very, very deep literary reference.' A few days later I'd pass him again and I'd say, 'Morning, Bill. Lovely day.' He'd say, 'The sun shines. But what is to be done when the crop's grown and the leaf is yellow or seared?' I couldn't keep up with this.

Well, when I joined *The Scotsman* they had news on the front page.

Some years later *The Scotsman* got a new editor – Eric Mackay, and Arnold Kemp was the deputy. And that worked well for me, because they both wanted to sell more papers and realised that this kind of crap was nonsense. So there was a core grew up within the building which was really more involved in getting stuff in the paper. Well, I wasn't long there when I uncovered a scandal of enormous Edinburgh proportions. It involved the man who was due to be the next Lord Provost, Bailie Craig Richards, and the Corstorphine mansion – a fascinating story.[30] That kept me going, and at the end of that they just said, 'Well, do investigative work all the time.' So I had the most amazing *carte blanche*. But also this period coincided with the development of North Sea oil.[31] And of course if you took a car out to the airport and sat, the crooks were coming down on the planes. It was a wonderful time and all the funny money banks moved in. So I just had a great few years, it was just fabulous.

Again I was just three years at *The Scotsman* until 1970. Then I got an invitation to go to BBC Television in Glasgow and I was there two years. But unfortunately because of a personal affair between two people there the department fell apart, virtually everybody left. I went back to *The Scotsman* and did six years there this time, exclusively investigative journalism – just great fun.

Then in 1978, when I was down at the BBC in Queen Street, Edinburgh, doing a wee freelance piece for radio, I bumped into Ross Anderson, who said, 'Had you ever thought to work for radio?' I said, 'Is there a job?' He said, 'There certainly is.'[32] So I just chipped in my notice there and then to *The Scotsman*, and joined the BBC Radio Scotland news service a few weeks after they'd started and was one of their radio reporters very happily for again three years.

I was having breakfast one morning in 1981 when Charlie Wilson phoned to say he was setting up the *Sunday Standard*, and wanted me as the number two to David Scott in a small investigative team. David Scott (not the David Scott who became *The Scotsman* local government correspondent)[33] came from the Borders and worked for many years for the *Express*, the BBC, and later STV. Though the *Sunday Standard* lasted two years, I only stayed a year because I couldn't stand the pace: it was far too slow. We worked only a four-day week and I couldn't gear down to this club-like atmosphere. But David Scott was great and we got some super stories in the paper.

I went back then to BBC Radio Scotland, where I'd made sure they knew that I'd be perfectly happy to leave the *Titanic*, as we called the *Sunday Standard*. I had another three very happy years with radio. I'd worked there before on the basis that I couldn't freelance. But I made sure when I went back the second time that I could freelance, because I'd seen the market was huge. So, based in Edinburgh, I did a lot of freelancing within the BBC. As well as my core duties, I did stuff for Radio 4, for features, current affairs.

Then Donald Munro, in charge of the television side, which was very small, in Edinburgh at that time, said George Sinclair, the boss in Glasgow, had asked him to sound me out.[34] So then it was back to telly, and I did telly news for about three years. Then, though I was still based in Edinburgh, I worked in Glasgow doing current affairs for many years till the early 1990s.

By then I'd gone totally freelance though actually all my work was for the BBC. Well, I was beavering away and one day in August 1993, sitting at my desk in my house, I had a stroke. When I got back on my feet after that, I just started doing what I'm doing now, which is newspapers, radio, some television. I do scripts for a film company in Scotland, I do magazine work for Germany and America, I have a column in the *Herald* and the Edinburgh *Evening News*, and I just stay very gainfully employed. I am also getting more and more agency teaching work, teaching fatheads who are in charge of huge corporations. So for very fat fees one goes and does a day with somebody wearing a suit. And there's more and more of that. So it's a varied life still, which is terrific.

Surely the charm of journalism is the richness of it? You meet mass murderers, High Court judges, comic singers, fading actresses, (and) the wonderful rich pattern of loonies that keeps the country going, I mean, wonderful. So I don't understand anybody that goes into the press and says, 'Now I just want to do local government, or be the water or the air correspondent.' I mean, if you're going to do that why not do it properly and get a job in, say, local government? Well, we're all different, but that narrow specialism wouldn't interest me. Then, though I never applied for a job abroad, I'm disappointed with myself for not having used my trade to go abroad. If I had my life again I wouldn't just change from Edinburgh to Glasgow to Perth, I would go Britain–Morocco. I'm chilled nowadays when I speak to young men and women in their late teens or early twenties, and find they have a master plan: 'My career,' they say. And in almost every case they're not talking about a career to do something they like doing, it's a career to rise in a corporate structure: 'I want to be a corporate cog, and by the time I'm 30 I should be an under-manager in charge of 10 people.' Now that certainly worries me when I meet these people. In my day we were happy with little and we got great fun from our work.

Well, until a very few years ago if somebody had come to me and had the right attitude for the job of journalism, I would have said, 'Go for it. It's given me great fun.' In my youth and until very recently any newsroom I worked in was just a laugh a line. The one-liners people used to come out with, the wit, the humour, the erudition! Even when I was older, we used to go into BBC Radio in Edinburgh and laugh until our ribs ached. We got through a hell of a lot of work, but the camaraderie was terrific. I don't know now if I would encourage someone to go into the trade, because it seems to me to have changed so radically and to have lost a lot of its fun element. I think the reason for this is that when I and my colleagues went to work we all just went to get a job. Nobody used the word career. But when I speak to young journalists nowadays, just going into the industry, they all want to be Jeremy Paxman.[35] They're looking for stardom and a quarter of a million quid a year. The thought that they would work on a weekly or an evening paper, well, you have to be joking. They tell me this quite unabashed, and 'How many years do you reckon before I could get a top telly job presenting?' A young woman came to see me the other day and she wanted to go from being a student journalist to writing her own light entertainment programme and producing it – she was going to do the two together, without getting any practice writing. She wanted to know how she could copyright it so that no one could pinch it, and then she was going to take this to the BBC in Glasgow and sell it to them. I thought, 'I've heard of vaulting ambition, but this is unreal!'

Notes

An attempt has been made, where relevant and, it is hoped, helpful to the general and young reader, to provide in these notes some basic or further information at least about events, institutions, newspapers, etc., but particularly persons, and especially journalists, mentioned *en passant* in the 22 veterans' recollections. Some journalists, like old soldiers, seem to have faded away without leaving much trace of themselves.

Abbreviations and contractions, other than everyday ones, used in these notes are: Bn – battalion; capd – captured; C-in-C – Commander-in-Chief; Cons. – Conservative; dept – department; *ED – Evening Dispatch*, Edinburgh; *EN – Evening News*, Edinburgh; educ. – educated; *GH – Glasgow Herald*; grad – graduated; I(i)nfm. – I(i)nformation; IoJ – Institute of Journalists; Lab. – Labour; Lib. – Liberal; m. – married; NEC – National Executive Committee; NUJ – National Union of Journalists; Parl. – Parliament or Parliamentary; PPS – Parliamentary Private Secretary; PS – Parliamentary Secretary; *P&J – The Press & Journal*, Aberdeen; regt – regiment; sqn ldr – squadron leader; STUC – Scottish Trades Union Congress; *TH – The Herald*; *TJ – The Journalist*; *TS – The Scotsman*; WW – *Who's Who*; *WWiS – Who's Who in Scotland*; WWW – *Who Was Who*; WWI – World War I; WWII – World War II.

Max McAuslane, pp. 17–41

1. *Glasgow Herald*, est. 1783 as the Glasgow *Advertiser* (retitled *GH*, 1804, then, Apr. 1992, *The Herald*), oldest surviving national newspaper in Britain. (The even older *Aberdeen Journal*, est. 1747, merged 1922 with the *Aberdeen Free Press* to form *The Press & Journal*, a regional, not a national, paper.) Alastair Phillips, *Glasgow's Herald* (Glasgow, 1983), 11, 14, 46; Joe Fisher, *The Glasgow Encyclopedia* (Edinburgh, 1994), 247–9.
2. The Scottish Rifles, or Cameronians, 26th Foot, formed 1689, disbanded 1968. The Boys' Brigade, founded 1883 in Glasgow by William Smith (1854–1914), businessman, for 'the advancement of Christ's Kingdom' among boys. Based on Christian principles, the BBs, a uniformed organisation, inculcated discipline and provided camps and other recreational activities for members, and had spread throughout the world by the end of the nineteenth century.
3. Robert M. Ballantyne (1825–1894), Scots prolific author of boys' books, including *The Coral Island* (1857) and *Martin Rattler* (1858).
4. Glasgow *Evening Citizen*, 1864–1974, from 1940 a sister paper of the *Scottish Daily Express*. Jack Campbell, *A Word for Scotland* (Edinburgh, 1998), 67.
5. General election, Nov. 1922, Glasgow Camlachie: Rev. Campbell Stephen (Lab.):

535

15,181, Sir H. Mackinder (Cons.): 11,459; W. (Walter) C. Smith (Lib.): 1,896. Smith forfeited his deposit. *GH*, 15 Nov. 1922.

6. The *Daily Record*, begun in 1847 in Glasgow as the *North British Daily Mail*, bought by Lord Northcliffe (1865–1922) in 1901, then retitled *Daily Record & Mail*, acquired 1926 by the Berry brothers (Lord Kemsley), '*& Mail*' dropped from its title 1954, acquired 1955 by the *Daily Mirror* Group. Fisher, *Glasgow Encyclopedia*, op. cit., 244–5. *Sunday Mail*, 1919 to date, a sister paper of the *Daily Record*.

7. *Willings Press Guide*, 1874 to date (with several changes of title, 1874–99).

8. *Govan Press*, 1878–2008 (from 1885 it included the earlier *Partick & Maryhill Press* of 1881–5, though there was a later *Partick & Maryhill Press*, 1892–1917); *Southern Press*, 1892–1943; *Clydebank & Renfrew Press*, 1891–1921, cont. as *Clydebank Press*, 1921–83, then to date as *Clydebank Post*; *Renfrew Press*, 1921–83, then with two changes of title, 1983–6, cont. 1987–9 as *Renfrewshire Post*. The Pollokshaws paper seems to have been the *Pollokshaws News & East Renfrewshire Advertiser*, 1885–1940. Fisher, *Glasgow Encyclopedia*, op. cit., 247; Alice Mackenzie, *NEWSPLAN: Report of the NEWSPLAN Project in Scotland* (London, 1994), 100, 101, 220, 320, 339, 347, 348, 349.

9. *Manchester Evening Chronicle*, 1897–1963, merged into *Manchester Evening News*. Dennis Griffiths, *Encyclopedia of the British Press* (London, 1992), 192, 399. The Singer Manufacturing Co. Ltd, est. 1867 in Glasgow, moved 1885 to Clydebank, where it developed into the largest sewing-machine factory in the world before closing in 1980. Catriona M.M. Macdonald, *Whaur Extremes Meet* (Edinburgh, 2009), 71–2.

10. Linage: payment for the number of lines published.

11. *Daily Express*, 1900 to date (acquired, 1917, by Lord Beaverbrook). The *Scottish Daily Express*, its Scottish edition, began publication in Glasgow in Nov. 1928. Campbell, *A Word for Scotland*, op. cit., 11.

12. *The Scotsman*, 1817 to date.

13. *Evening News*, Glasgow, 1915–57.

14. *The Bulletin*, 1915–60. (The *Scots Pictorial* merged into it in 1923.)

15. For the work of a sub-editor, see e.g. pp. 115, 116, 275, 276.

16. John Allan, editor, *Daily Record*, for several years until 1937; no other infm. about him has been found. Alastair Dunnett, *Among Friends* (London, 1984), 26, 100.

17. For *The Press & Journal*, see above, Note 1. Between the late 1930s and late 1940s, Kemsleys became the largest newspaper empire in Britain, with morning, evening and Sunday papers that included in Glasgow the *Daily Record*, *Evening News*, and *Sunday Mail*; in Aberdeen the *Evening Express*; and in England the *Sunday Times*, *Sunday Graphic*, several other national Sundays, and papers in half a dozen cities other than London.

18. David Russell Anderson (1883–1976), managing director, Associated Scottish Newspapers Ltd, Glasgow; educ. Allan Glen's School, Glasgow, Glasgow University, Glasgow Technical College, the Sorbonne and École des Beaux Arts, Paris. *Scottish Biographies 1938* (London and Glasgow, 1938), 20.

19. *Sunday Chronicle*, 1885–1955, acquired 1937 by Lord Kemsley, and became one of the first Sunday papers to be published in three cities: London, Manchester and Glasgow. Griffiths, *Encyclopedia*, op. cit., 544. *Sunday Express*, 1918 to date (though retitled, 1996, *Express on Sunday*); *Scottish Sunday Express* ceased publication in Glasgow, 1974, as did the *Scottish Daily Express* and the Glasgow *Evening Citizen*, but the two former were then published from Manchester. *Catalogue, Newspaper Library* (British Library, Colindale, 1975), Vol. I – London; Griffiths, *Encyclopedia*, op. cit., 205, 346.

20. Barbara Hutton (1912–1979), daughter and heiress of Frank Hutton, founder of Woolworth. Carol II (1893–1953), king of Romania, 1930–40.

21. The *Scottish Daily Mail* began publication in Edinburgh on 4–5 Dec. 1946. At its launch then, its proprietor, Lord Rothermere, said plans to publish the paper there had almost

been completed in 1939, but the outbreak of the war had forced postponement. *The Scotsman*, 5 Dec. 1946.

22. Clement B. Livingstone, editor (from age 27), 1937–46, *Daily Record*, then successively managing editor, 1946–?, managing director, and, from 1958, chairman, Daily Record & Sunday Mail Ltd. Dunnett, *Among Friends*, op. cit., 100, 111; *GH*, 21 Aug. 1958.

23. On those two successive nights in Mar. 1941, the bombing of Glasgow and Clydeside by the German air force killed 528 people (including 14 from one family, and including six of six years of age or less) in the burgh of Clydebank (including Dalmuir), and seriously injured 617 others. Of the 12,000 houses in the burgh, 4,300 were either completely destroyed or damaged beyond repair, and only eight were undamaged. Of Clydebank's population of more than 50,000, over 40,000 had been evacuated by 15 March. In Glasgow and elsewhere on Clydeside more than 700 people were killed then, and more than 500 others seriously injured. I.M.M. MacPhail, *The Clydebank Blitz* (Clydebank, 1995), 56, 68, 89, 90.

24. Max McAuslane's account of the parachuted landing by Rudolf Hess, Hitler's deputy leader of the Nazi Party, from a stolen twin-engined, long-range Messerschmitt Me. 110 fighter plane that crashed near Eaglesham, Renfrewshire, eight miles south of Glasgow, illustrates, among many other aspects, how a good newspaper reporter has to be inquisitive, observant, resourceful, energetic and persistent. Hess's flight, unknown to and unauthorised by Hitler, and threatening to affect his secret plans to invade the Soviet Union the following month, was doubtless not as great a shock to the Führer as was the Nazi invasion itself to Stalin. Nonetheless, Albert Speer, Hitler's architect, testified how from a room adjoining the Führer's office, he heard him emit in horror 'an inarticulate, almost animal outcry' when the news of Hess's flight was brought to him. Yet Max McAuslane's claim to have secured an exclusive story in the *Daily Record* may in fact have been a little exaggerated – an exclusive, but published perhaps only a few minutes before the story appeared also in its rival papers. All the morning newspapers, including the *Record*, first published the story on the same day: Tuesday, 13 May 1941. Nor, perhaps, may Max McAuslane have secured the exclusive story even before publication, since the *Glasgow Herald* claimed it knew before any other paper who the parachutist was, as the Renfrewshire police had asked for and been given biographical details of Hess from the *Herald*'s files. Moreover, an article by John Shaw in *The Scotsman* in 1996, concerning the sale next day in London of a nine-page contemporary typed report by Daniel McBride, a young Scots soldier in the Royal Signals, stationed in May 1941 at Eaglesham and said to have detained Hess (though McBride did not at that point know he was Hess) when he landed near there by parachute, showed that, as well as informing his Signal unit's headquarters by phone about the parachutist, McBride had also contacted 'a friend who was news editor of a national paper'. The paper was not identified. But if it was not the *Daily Record* itself or the *Sunday Mail*, a colleague on which had left a note on 11 May 1941 for the *Record* staff about the newly crashed Messerschmitt, then it must have been a rival paper. The controversy about Hess's landing continues, with press reports of a document said to have been written in 1948 by Hess's adjutant, and evidently found in 2011 in an archive in Moscow, that is said to show Hitler knew in advance of, and indeed ordered, Hess's flight. *Daily Record*, 13 May 1941; *GH*, 13 May 1941; *TS*, 13 May 1941, 27 May 1996, 30 May 2011; Campbell, *A Word for Scotland*, op. cit., 69; Albert Speer, *Inside the Third Reich* (London, 1971 edn), 174; Adolf Hitler, *Mein Kampf* (London, 1939), 128. See also, e.g., Winston Churchill, *The Second World War* (London, 1950), Vol. III, 43–9; William L. Shirer, *The Rise and Fall of the Third Reich* (London, 1970), 834–8; A. Bullock, *Hitler: A Study in Tyranny* (London, 1952), 591–3; Ian Kershaw, *Hitler: 1936–45: Nemesis* (London, 2000), 369–81; Martin Gilbert, *Second World War* (London, 2000), 181; James Douglas-Hamilton, *The Truth about Rudolf Hess* (Edinburgh, 1993).

25. The battle of El Alamein, 23 Oct.–4 Nov. 1942, a turning point in the North African campaign. Tripoli, capital of Libya, was capd by the Eighth Army, 23 Jan. 1943. Allied forces had landed on the French Riviera near Toulon on 15 Aug. 1944 and rapidly joined up with the forces advancing eastward from the earlier landings in Normandy.

26. The first to elect a majority Lab. government, the 1945 general election returned 393 Lab. MPs, 213 Cons., 12 Lib., three Indep. Lab., two Communist, one Commonwealth, and 16 others. Of 25,085,978 votes cast (a 72.7% turnout), Lab. won 11,995,152 (47.8%), Cons 9,988,306 (39.8%), Libs 2,248,226 (9%). Alan Sked and Chris Cook, *Post-War Britain: A Political History* (London, 1993 edn), 15; David Butler and Jennie Freeman, *British Political Facts 1900–1960* (London, 1964), 106, 124.

27. Racial segregation was legal and widely practised in South Africa, as Max McAuslane indicates, even before the election to power in 1948 of the National Party, whose government then extended and systematised racial segregation and discrimination by, e.g., the Population Registration Act, 1950, which classified the people of South Africa as white, 'coloured' (mixed race) or Bantu (i.e., all black Africans; Asians were added later as a fourth group). This racist system of 'apartness' (in Afrikaans, Apartheid) was systematically and brutally applied by the National Party government for more than 40 years.

28. Alastair M. Dunnett (1908–1998); educ. Hillhead High School, Glasgow, worked in a bank, 1923–35, then successively for the Glasgow *Weekly Herald*, *The Bulletin*, and, 1937–40, the *Daily Record*; chief press officer, Secretary of State for Scotland, 1940–6; editor, 1946–55, *Daily Record*, 1955–72, *The Scotsman*; successively, 1962–78, managing director and chairman, Scotsman Publications Ltd; member, 1974–8, executive board, Thomson Organisation Ltd; director, 1975–9, Scottish TV Ltd; author of several books, including his autobiography *Among Friends* (London, 1984); knighted, 1995. *Who Was Who, Vol. X, 1996–2000*, 166.

29. *Daily Mirror*, 1903 to date.

30. Hugh Cudlipp (1913–1998), born Cardiff, youngest of three brothers who all became editors of national newspapers; left school at 14 and began as junior reporter, *Penarth News*; aged 19, features editor, *Sunday Chronicle*, then of *Daily Mirror*; aged 24, editor, *Sunday Pictorial*; in army, 1940–6, editor from 1943 of Forces newspaper *Union Jack*, demobbed as Lieut. Col., OBE; dismissed, 1949, as editor, *Sunday Pictorial*, he became managing editor, *Sunday Express*, then editorial director, Mirror Group; knighted 1973; life peer 1974.

31. Tom Nicholson (1908–1969), educ. Boroughmuir Senior Secondary School, Edinburgh; began aged 15, 1923–4, as junior reporter, *Evening Dispatch*; from 1930, reporter, later chief reporter, Edinburgh office, *Daily Record*; a major in WWII; from c. 1959 a *Record* full-time football correspondent. *Daily Record*, 9 Jan. 1969. Marshal Nikolai Bulganin (1895–1972), chairman, 1955–8, Council of Ministers, USSR. Nikita Khrushchev (1894–1971), First Secretary, Soviet Communist Party, 1953–64; at 20th Party Congress, 1956, he denounced Stalin's crimes. As part of their ten-day visit to Britain, Bulganin and Khrushchev came to Edinburgh, 26 Apr. 1956, visited Holyrood Palace, the Forth Bridge, and City Chambers, and watched the beating of retreat on the esplanade before attending a banquet in the Castle, where they both expressed a wish for peace and co-operation. *TS*, 27 Apr. 1956.

32. Roy Thomson (1894–1976), born Toronto, began, 1928, as a radio salesman in Ottawa; by 1944 he owned eight radio stations and several newspapers. He bought *The Scotsman* for £393,750 from the Findlay family, its owners since it began publication in 1817. He bought in 1959 Kemsley newspapers, including the *Sunday Times*, two other national and one provincial Sunday newspapers, 13 provincial dailies and several weeklies. He acquired in 1966 *The Times*, enlarged his Thomson Regional Newspaper group, became involved in North Sea oil and in Thomson Travel, and described his acquisition in the 1950s of the franchise for Scottish TV as 'a licence to print money'. Lord

Thomson of Fleet from 1964. His autobiography (1975): *After I was Sixty*. Dennis Griffiths, *500 Years of the Press* (London, 2006), 317–18. On his first day as proprietor of *The Scotsman*, Thomson had gone round the office introducing himself: 'My name's Thomson, call me Roy.' But in his first week as proprietor, 41 people were sacked. *The Glorious Privilege: The History of The Scotsman* (Edinburgh, 1967), 160, 161.

33. James Vassie, born Bathgate, grad MA (Hons), Economics and Economic History, Edinburgh University; on editorial staff, Wm Collins Ltd, publishers; Lab. Parl. candidate, Moray and Nairn, 1935; 1945–75, sub-editor then leader writer, *TS;* an active member, NUJ; on Economic Affairs Committee, STUC; continued to write occasionally for *TS* and edit its daily crossword until shortly before his death in 1989, aged 81. *TS*, 23 Sep. 1989. Arthur J. Arthur (1928–), reporter, then sub-editor, in Stirling, 1952–5; leader writer, *TS*, 1955–64; Central Office of Information, 1964–78; freelance writer from 1978. Infm.: Andrew Hood.

34. Calderhall opened in 1956.

35. *Izvestia*, 1917 to date.

36. George Philip began, 1906, aged 16, on the Edinburgh *Evening Dispatch*, but soon moved to *The Scotsman*, where he reported the trial in 1909 of Oscar Slater and his appeal in 1926. George Philip was full-time Court of Session and High Court reporter for *TS*, 1911–57, when a presentation was made him by the Lord Justice General, Lord Clyde, who said: 'We must rely on the reporters to give fair and objective reports of what goes on and not to sacrifice truth on the altar of sensationalism . . . We owe a great deal . . . to the wisdom and discretion of the reporters, among whom, for at least 50 years, George Philip has been such an outstanding figure.' He died 1975, aged 85. *TS*, 30 May and 13 Jul. 1957, 18 Feb. 1975. Philip ('Pip') Stalker, born Dundee, son of professor of medicine, St Andrews University; educ. Dundee High School; apprentice marine engineer, 1917–18; joined RAF, 1918; reporter, Dundee *Advertiser*, 1922–4, then *TS*, 1924–67, becoming features writer then, 1950–67, churches correspondent: reported Church of Scotland General Assembly for 40 years, and on his retirement tribute was paid him by the Moderator; life member, NUJ; MBE, 1968; author of two books and co-author of *The Glorious Privilege*, history of *The Scotsman*; his brother Kenneth was killed in action with the International Brigades in the Spanish Civil War. Philip Stalker died 1971, aged 71. *Journalist*, Dec. 1969; Dec. 1971; *TS*, 28 Oct. 1971.

37. Stuart Brown (1920–), began, 1937, on *Berwick Advertiser;* joined Territorial Army (7th Bn, Northumberland Fusiliers), Apr. 1939; capd Jun. 1940, Saint Valéry-en-Caux, PoW till 1945, then returned to *Berwick Advertiser;* later news editor and managing editor, *TS*; author of *Forbidden Paths* (Edinburgh, 1978), about his war experiences. Allen Wright (1932–1997), educ. George Watson's College, Edinburgh; copy or tube boy, *TS*, 1949–50; National Service, 1950–2; reporter then deputy news editor, *TS*, 1952–65, highly respected arts editor, 1965–93, when ill health forced his retirement; noted for his constant encouragement to young journalists, 'his death marked a major loss to journalism in Scotland.' *TS*, 18 Nov. 1997; *TJ*, Mar. 1998.

38. Albert David Mackie (1904–1985), born Edinburgh, educ. Broughton Senior Secondary School, MA (Hons) English, Edinburgh University, where he was editor, *The Student* and lightweight boxing champion. A teacher before entering journalism in Glasgow, then news editor, *Daily Gleaner*, Jamaica, 1928–32; assistant leader writer, *TS*, 1932–5; leader writer, Glasgow *Evening News*, 1935–?; sub-editor, *TS*, ?–1945; editor, Edinburgh *Evening Dispatch*, 1945–54; afterwards a regular contributor of his 'MacNib' verses to *Evening Dispatch* and Edinburgh *Evening News*, and of a column in the *News* and articles in other publications; author of several books (including a history of Heart of Midlothian FC) and a play. *Scottish Biographies*, op. cit., 489–90; *TS*, 15 May 1985. Jack Miller, trained on a north-east England evening paper, then by age 23 had become, on a sports paper, Fleet Street's youngest editor; volunteered into army, Sep. 1939,

invalided out, 1942; then successively chief sub-editor, *Daily Sketch*, and senior jobs on *Daily Express, Daily Mirror, Daily Mail* in Paris and London, and *Sunday Express*. He was night editor, *Daily Mirror*, when it reached four million copies, the biggest daily circulation in the world. 'Miller was a man of enthusiasm and brought with him a species of spectacular tabloid journalism such as Edinburgh had never been exposed to before.' But the sensational coverage he gave in the *Evening Dispatch* to aspects of the Tron Square murder, 1954, in the city led to 'the swift and explicit' rejection of Miller's zeal: the *Dispatch*'s circulation fell by 6,000 in a fortnight. *The Glorious Privilege*, op. cit., 160; *ED*, 1 Feb. 1954. The *Dispatch* editor after Miller (1954–5) was Alex Bowman (d. 1971), a sub-editor from *TS. TS*, 27 Dec. 1971.

39. The *Evening News* since 1925 had been part of United Newspapers Ltd and its subsidiary Provincial Newspapers Ltd, the owner of which from 1946 was Harley Drayton (d. 1966), a Yorkshire big businessman who controlled many companies, including British Electric Traction, which owned thousands of buses and tramcars. It appears to have been William Barnetson, editor, *Evening News*, a board member of Provincial Newspapers Ltd and from 1962 managing director of United Newspapers Ltd, who suggested ownership of the *News* be exchanged for Roy Thomson's two Sheffield newspapers, the *Telegraph* and the *Evening Star*, accompanied by a balancing payment to Thomson of £564,700. Guy Schofield, *The Men That Carry the News: A History of United Newspapers Ltd* (London, 1975), 2, 29–30, 36, 37, 41, 44–5.

40. The Press Association, est. 1868, the only national news agency for Britain and Ireland, employs staff journalists and also correspondents throughout the world, and is owned by the regional press. Griffiths, *Encyclopedia*, op. cit., 672–3.

41. George Byron Millar (1925–1991), began aged 14 as copy boy, *ED;* 1943–6, in RN as gunner on merchant ships; successively, reporter, *ED*, then briefly with a London news agency, then until 1964 *EN*; 1964–c. late 1980s, United News Service. Obit. by Bert Morris, *TS*, 14 Aug. 1991. *Sunday Times*, 1821 to date; *Sunday Graphic*, 1915–60 (1915–27 titled *Illustrated Sunday Herald*). Griffiths, *Encyclopedia*, op. cit., 544–5. Max McAuslane is therefore mistaken in recalling the paper was still being published in 1963–4. For Bill Rae, see above, pp. 322–49.

42. William D. Barnetson (1917–1981), born Edinburgh; educ. Royal High School and Edinburgh University, MA (during his studies there he went aged 19 to Spain as a freelance correspondent to report the Civil War); major, Royal Artillery, 1940–c.1948; after WWII he took part in reorganising publishing in West Germany; 1948–62, successively leader writer, editor, general manager, *EN*; during 1962–79, a director, then chairman, United Newspapers Ltd, and a director of 24 other companies, chairman, Reuters, and of *The Observer*, a member of the Press Council, and from 1979, chairman, Thames TV; knighted 1972, life peer 1975. Griffiths, *Encyclopedia*, op. cit., 90–1; *TJ*, Jan. 1974.

43. Full front-page news was introduced in the *Evening News* on Monday, 6 Apr. 1964.

44. 'haudin' doon' – afflicted, oppressed. The National Union of Journalists, 1907 to date, the first journalists' trade union in the world.

45. Oliver Brown, a lifelong Scottish Nationalist, several times an SNP Parl. candidate, and the first of them to save his deposit; a teacher of modern languages, author of many pamphlets, a regular columnist in *Scots Independent*; died 1976, aged 73. *TS*, 31 May 1976.

46. Other than that he was the son of William Regan, Catholic Socialist Society and Independent Lab. Party, no more infm. about Liam Regan has been found.

David M. Smith, pp. 42–62

1. *Perthshire Constitutional*, 1835–1951, then merged into *Perthshire Advertiser*.
2. *Rover*, 1922–73. *Wizard*, 1922–63, cont. 1963–9 as *Rover/Wizard*, 1970–3 as *Wizard (Picture*

Stories), and 1973–6 as *Wizard and Rover*. Infm.: D.C. Thomson & Co. Ltd, publishers.

3. Dundee *Courier*, 1861–1926, amalgamated with Dundee *Advertiser* to become Dundee *Courier & Advertiser*, to date. *People's Friend*, weekly, 1869 to date.

4. *Perthshire Advertiser*, 1829 to date (amalgamated 1929 with *Perthshire Courier*, and 1951 incorporated *Perthshire Constitutional*). J.P.S. Ferguson, *Directory of Scottish Newspapers* (National Library of Scotland, Edinburgh, 1984), 97.

5. Sir Thomas Hunter (1872–1953), educ. Perth Academy; Fellow, Institute of Journalists; Perth town councillor from 1919, Lord Provost, 1932–5; Cons. MP, Perth & Kinross, 1935–45; head of several Masonic Orders; author of two books about Perth; knighted 1944. Lieut. Col. T. Harris Hunter, TD, JP (1898–1970). *Scottish Biographies 1938*, op. cit., 366. During the fall of France in 1940, most of the 51st Highland Division was cut off and surrounded at St Valéry-en-Caux on the Channel coast south of Dieppe, and forced to surrender on 12 Jun. Only about 1,350 men escaped; some 8,000 of the Division became prisoners of war. Winston Churchill, *The Second World War, Vol. II: Their Finest Hour* (London, 1949), 134–5.

6. The Munro Press, est. in Perth, 1915, by Henry Munro Ltd, publishers, Glasgow and Aberdeen, to print the *Perthshire Advertiser*, was later taken over by Geo. Outram & Co. Ltd, Glasgow. (Infm.: Scottish Print Archive, provided by Business @ The Mitchell (Library)). The partnership that published the *Glasgow Herald* became titled Geo. Outram & Co. when in 1836 George Outram, an Edinburgh advocate, was appointed the paper's editor. Outram & Co. was superseded in 1969 when ownership of the *Glasgow Herald* and *Evening Times* passed to SUITS (Scottish and Universal Investments), owned by Hugh Fraser, later Lord Fraser of Allander. Fisher, *Glasgow Encyclopedia*, op. cit., 247–9. *Evening Times*, 1876 to date.

7. Led by Sir John Simon (1873–1954), 25 Lib. MPs separated in 1931 from their party and formed the Liberal Nationals (retitled 1948 National Liberals) The number of seats they won fell from 35 in the 1931 Parl. election to 13 in 1945. Butler and Freeman, op. cit., 107; C.L. Mowat, *Britain Between the Wars, 1918–1940* (London, 1962), 407, 411, 554. The historian A.J.P. Taylor's view was that the National Liberals became Conservatives in all but name. *English History, 1914–1945* (Oxford, 1965), 334. Sir Francis Norie-Miller (1859–1947) had stood unsuccessfully as Lib. candidate for Perth in 1929 and 1931, but won the by-election there in Apr. 1935 as Liberal National, when no Cons. candidate stood. Sir Thomas Hunter succeeded him as Cons. MP in the Nov. 1935 general election. F.W.S. Craig, *British Parliamentary Election Results 1918–1949* (Glasgow, 1969), 643.

8. Eddie Balfour began, 1926, on the *Perthshire Constitutional*; 1930–3, *Mearns Leader*, Stonehaven; from 1933 (apart from service in WWII) until his retirement, *Perthshire Advertiser*, as chief reporter from 1942; for many years secretary and treasurer, Perth & District branch, NUJ, and life member of the union; died 1987, aged 76. *TJ*, Jan. 1988.

9. Founded as a memorial to soldiers killed in the Boer War, the Queen Victoria School, Dunblane, was open to sons, especially orphans, of soldiers from any Scottish regt, and there are also reserved RN and RAF places; it became co-educational in 1996. D.B. Taylor (ed.), *The Counties of Perth & Kinross: The Third Statistical Account of Scotland* (Scottish Council of Social Services, Dundee, 1979), 623–4.

10 LNER – London & North Eastern Railway (1923–48); LMS – London, Midland & Scottish Railway (1923–48): nationalised in 1948, along with other railways in Britain, they became part of British Railways. National Union of Railwaymen est. 1913 as an industrial union, from a merger of the Amalgamated Society of Railway Servants (1872–1913), the General Railway Workers' Union (1889–1913), and the United Pointsmen and Signalmen's Society (1880–1913). In 1990 the National Union of Railwaymen amalgamated with the National Union of Seamen to form the National Union of Rail, Maritime, and Transport Workers (RMT).

11. As David M. Smith says above, p. 49, the NUJ members in Perth were actually

members of the Stirling branch in 1935–7 (when Stirling branch itself was formed awaits verification). Eddie Balfour (above, Note 8), re-elected Perth branch treasurer in 1970, was said then to have 'held the post since 1935'. *TJ*, Nov. 1970.

12. *Stirling Observer*, 1873 to date.

13. At the end of the 1926 General Strike, D.C. Thomson, newspaper and magazine publishers, Dundee, had become and (unlike most other newspaper publishers) remained for many years non-union and, as David M. Smith says, even anti-union, by requiring their employees to sign a document renouncing trade union membership. (See also below, p. 553, Colin Dakers, Note 5, and, above, Ron Thompson, pp. 424, 425). In 1952 matters came to a head when the firm dismissed several employees found to be members of printing or paper workers' unions. Workers in some paper mills refused to handle, and some Transport & General Workers' Union lorry drivers to deliver, paper supplies for D.C. Thomson, and some workers in Glasgow came out on strike against the firm. A Ministry of Labour Court of Inquiry investigated the dispute, and one of its recommendations was that D.C. Thomson reconsider their insistence on their employees signing the no-union document. A judge simultaneously ruled against granting D.C. Thomson injunctions against union leaders for any further action to prevent supplies of newsprint, etc., reaching the firm. The outcome of the dispute was that D.C. Thomson ceased to insist on employees signing the no-union document, although the firm continued to refuse to recognise trade unions, nor did it reinstate the dismissed employees. Mr L. Moncrieff, Scottish Secretary, National Society of Operative Printers & Assistants, told the STUC annual congress in Apr. 1953 that, though as a result of the struggle D.C. Thomson might no longer be insisting on employees signing the no-union document, when printers had applied recently for vacancies at the firm, 'they were presented with the usual questionnaire asking if they were trade unionists or union officials, or if they knew any trade union officials. Being honest, the printers answered truthfully, and did not get the jobs.' STUC *Annual Report*, 1953, 61–3, 175–9; James Moran, *Seventy-Five Years: The National Society of Operative Printers & Assistants, 1889–1964* (Oxford, 1964), 123–30; C.J. Bundock, *The Story of the National Union of Printing, Bookbinding & Paper Workers* (Oxford, 1959), 518–24.

14. John Keir Cross, *nom de plume* of Stephen MacFarlane (1911–1967), novelist, author or editor of almost a score of books.

15. The Scottish Typographical Association, formed, 1853, from earlier local typographical or compositors' societies such as Glasgow (est. 1817) and Edinburgh (c.1836), changed its title, 1973, to Scottish Graphical Association, then became in 1975 Scottish Graphical Division of the Society of Graphical & Allied Trades (SOGAT 75), which in 1982, on amalgamation with the National Society of Operative Printers, Graphical and Media Personnel, became SOGAT 82. The amalgamation of SOGAT 82 with the National Graphical Association in 1991 formed the Graphical, Paper & Media Union (GPMU), which merged in 2004 into the union Unite.

16. Tweeddale Press, so titled from 1951, was earlier known as the Tweeddale Trio: *Berwick Advertiser*, *Berwickshire Advertiser*, *Kelso Chronicle*. Infm.: Tony Langmark, Berwick-upon-Tweed. *Berwick Advertiser*, 1808 to date. Major Henry R. Smail, TD (1889–1948), mentioned in dispatches, 1915, served, 1908–25, with 7th Bn, Royal Northumberland Fusiliers; president, Scottish Newspaper Proprietors' Association. *Scottish Biographies 1938*, op. cit., 691; *TS*, 31 Aug. 1948.

17. *Berwickshire Advertiser*, 1893–1957, merged into *Berwickshire News*. *Kelso Chronicle*, 1832–1949, then with the inclusion of the *Kelso Border Mail & Gazette*, 1934–45 (which, 1797–1934, had been the *Kelso Mail*) became, 1949–57, *Border Counties & Kelso Chronicle & Mail*, retitled, 1957–64, *Border Counties Chronicle & Mail*, then merged with the *Jedburgh Gazette* (1870–1964) to form the *Kelso Chronicle & Jedburgh Gazette*, 1964–83, when it merged into the *Southern Reporter*. Ferguson, *Scottish Newspapers*,

op. cit., 70, 72; infm.: Hawick Heritage Hub. *Berwick Journal*, 1855–1957, merged into *Berwick Advertiser*. *Berwickshire News*, 1869–1957, then retitled *Berwickshire News & Berwickshire Advertiser*; in 1983–4 it was incorporated into the *Berwick Advertiser*, but from Sep. 1984 was reissued as *Berwickshire News & East Lothian Herald*, to date. David Parry, *NEWSPLAN: Report of the NEWSPLAN Project in the Northern Region, Oct. 1987–Sep.1988* (London, 1989), 81, 82, 84; infm.: Hawick Heritage Hub.

18. *Newcastle Journal*, 1832 to date (a weekly to 1860, then a daily). Griffiths, *Encyclopedia*, op. cit., 344.

19. *Scottish Farmer*, 1893 to date.

20. Mary Gray (1887–1968), born Berwick-upon-Tweed, daughter of a solicitor; in WWI, a Voluntary Aid Detachment nurse and dept head in a war hospital; joined *Berwick Advertiser*, 1918, its editor, 1937–48, one of the first woman newspaper editors in Britain; active in Red Cross and other voluntary organisations in and after WWII. *Berwick Advertiser*, 28 Mar. 1968.

21. The 'Phoney War', 1939–40, in the west ended with the German invasion of France and the Low Countries on 10 May 1940. The German blitzkrieg then rapidly drove the British Expeditionary Force and many French troops back to the Channel ports, especially Dunkirk. From there, during the nine days from 27 May to 4 Jun., through the determination and skills of the Royal Navy, supported by French warships and many small civilian boats from Britain, 338,000 troops were evacuated, almost two-thirds of them British and about 120,000 French. As Winston Churchill said, 'the miracle of Dunkirk' was a deliverance, not a victory: 'Wars are not won by evacuations.' The Black Watch infantry regt, so called because of its dark-coloured tartan uniform, originated in independent Highland companies raised in Perthshire in 1725, est., 1739, as a regt, became, 1751, the 42nd of Foot. Recruitment to the regt was long associated with Perthshire, Angus, and Fife. In 2006 the regt became 3rd Bn, Royal Regt of Scotland.

22. Colonel James I.M. Smail, born New Zealand; grad University of Canterbury, NZ, and Heriot Watt University, Edinburgh; in NZ army in WWII in North Africa and Italy: MC, Cassino, 1944; president, Scottish Newspaper Proprietors' Association; a founder-director, Border Television; Norham and Islandshire District, Berwick Town, and Northumberland County councillor for altogether 50 years, mayor, 1971–2, and sheriff, 1964–5 and 1975–6, of Berwick, deputy lord lieutenant, Northumberland, 1971; OBE, 1963, for long service in the Territorial Army; died 1995, aged 73. *Berwick Advertiser*, 29 Jun. 1995; *TS*, 28 Jun. 1995.

23. Denis Straughan (b.1935), began 1951, aged 15, on *Berwick Advertiser*, joined David M. Smith, 1951/2–5; National Service, 1955–7; then with *TS*, 1957–99. Infm.: Denis Straughan.

24. *Evening Chronicle*, 1885 to date; *Sunday Sun*, 1919 to date.

25. *Sunday Post* (D.C. Thomson Ltd, Dundee), 1914 to date.

26. Joan Crawford (1904–1977), actress and star of many films.

27. *Mearns Leader*, Stonehaven, 1913 to date.

28. *People's Journal* (D.C. Thomson, Ltd, Dundee), 1858–1990.

29. *Daily Herald*, 1912–64, then retitled *The Sun. News Chronicle* (an amalgamation of the *Daily News*, 1845–1930, and *Daily Chronicle*, 1856–1930), 1930–1960, then incorporated in *Daily Mail*. Griffiths, *500 Years of the Press*, op. cit.,183–4.

30. Andrew Neil (b.1949), born Paisley, educ. Paisley Grammar School, Glasgow University, MA (Hons); 1971–2, Cons. Research Dept; 1973–82, journalist, *The Economist*, 1983–94, editor, *Sunday Times*, 1996–2006, editor-in-chief and, 1999–2006, publisher, *TS*, *Scotland on Sunday*, and *EN*; chairman, 1988–90, Sky TV; 1999–2002, Lord Rector, St Andrews University; broadcaster; his autobiography is *Full Disclosure* (London, 1996).

31. Border TV, 1965–2009, merged with ITV Tyne and Tees to form Tyne and Tees and Border TV. BBC Radio Tweed, 1983 to date.

32. *Southern Reporter*, Selkirk, 1855 to date.

Ernie McIntyre, pp. 63–87

1. Unemployment in Scotland, never from 1923 onwards less than 10 per cent of insured workers, averaged 14 per cent in 1923–30, but 22 per cent between 1931 and 1938. A peak of 27.7 per cent was reached, not in 1931 but in 1932, when about 400,000 were unemployed. Averages meant there were cities, towns and regions that suffered even higher rates of unemployment – and particular industries, too, such as coal-mining and shipbuilding, in which respectively 34 per cent and 62 per cent were unemployed at the height of the Depression in 1931–2. *Stirling Journal*, 1833–1970.

2. The Wallace Monument, 200 ft high, built 1861–9 on Abbey Craig overlooking the scene of the battle of Stirling Bridge, 1297, includes a statue of William Wallace.

3. Pontoon – a card game (French, *Vingt-et-un*) in which the object is to have a score of – or as near as possible to, but not exceeding – 21.

4. Wendy Wood (1892–1981), an Englishwoman brought up in South Africa, studied art under Walter Sickert (1860–1942); came to live in Scotland on her marriage; a founder, 1928, of the National Party of Scotland, but left the Party in 1949 to found the Scottish Patriots. At a Bannockburn Day rally on 25 Jun. 1932, as one of the speakers she called on and led a group of young men to remove the Union Jack flying from the ramparts of Stirling Castle as it was 'a slight on Scotland'. As they entered the Castle, one of its guides, believing they were sightseers, stopped Miss Wood and told her: 'You have got to pay.' Several of the young men scaled the wall, pulled down the Union Jack, and replaced it with the Lion Rampant on the Saltire – flag of the National Party. Soldiers promptly replaced it with the Union Jack. Lewis Spence, vice-chairman of the National Party, afterwards repudiated the action of Wendy Wood and her supporters in substituting the flags: '. . . all right-thinking Scotsmen and Scotswomen have no desire to antagonise the English nation . . . our cause . . . is a pacific and constitutional one, and not in any sense a revolutionary or violent one.' *TS*, 27 Jun. 1932. Wallace's sword (transferred there in 1888 from Dumbarton Castle, where it had lain since his capture by the English in 1305) was stolen from a glass case at his Monument on Sunday evening, 8 Nov. 1936, by four masked men, 'suspected to be Scottish Nationalists'. The sword was recovered by police at Bothwell, Lanarkshire on 7 Oct. 1939, when children playing at the river Clyde there discovered it lying in mud when the water was very low. *TS*, 9 and 10 Nov. 1936, 12 Oct. 1939. Robert Bontine Cunninghame Graham of Ardoch (1852–1936), educ. Harrow; socialist, Scottish Nationalist; a rancher in Argentina, 1869–83; Radical MP, North-West Lanarkshire, 1886–92; jailed for six weeks after 'Bloody Sunday' unemployed demonstration, London, 1887; president, 1888, Scottish Lab. Party, 1928, National Party of Scotland, and, 1934, Scottish National Party; author of many books. Bannockburn Day is normally held on the Saturday nearest the date of the battle in 1314, Sun. and Mon., 23 and 24 Jun.

5. *Stirling Sentinel*, 1888–1961. J.P.S. Ferguson, *Scottish Newspapers*, op. cit., 120.

6. Thomas Johnston (1881–1965), born Kirkintilloch, grad Glasgow University; journalist; founder, 1906, and editor, 1906–31, *Forward*; Lab. MP, Clackmannanshire and West Stirlingshire, 1922–4, 1929–31, and 1935–45, and Dundee, 1924–9; Under-Secretary of State for Scotland, 1929–31, Lord Privy Seal, 1931, Secretary of State for Scotland, 1941–5; founder, 1943, of North of Scotland Hydro-Electric Board and, 1945–59, its chairman; Chancellor, 1951–65, Aberdeen University; author of several books, including *History of the Working Classes in Scotland* (Glasgow, 1920). Capt. Guy D. Fanshawe, joined RN, 1898; served in Boxer Rising, China, 1899–1900, and in WWI and WWII; Unionist MP, Clackmannanshire and West Stirlingshire, 1924–9, PPS, Secretary of State for Dominions and Colonies, 1928–9; died 1962.

7. *Falkirk Herald*, 1845 to date; *Falkirk Mail*, 1886–1962; *Grangemouth Advertiser*, 1900 to date. Ferguson, *Scottish Newspapers*, op. cit., 46, 60.

8. James MacIntosh, reporter from 1931, *Stirling Journal*; before and after WWII (in

which he served five years in army) worked for Outram Press, Glasgow, till 1950s, then for 20 years a sub-editor successively on *ED* and *EN*; life member, NUJ, after 47 years' membership from 1931; died 1992. *TJ*, Dec. 1992–Jan. 1993.

9. At Hampden Park, Glasgow, in season 1934–5, a second-round third replay was won 2–1 by King's Park against Ayr United; but King's Park were beaten in the third round 6–2 by Airdrie. John Byrne, *Scottish Cup 1873–1986* (Basildon, 1986), 149.

10. Voluntary Aid Detachments, formed 1910 as part of the Territorial Army and consisting of men and women from the Red Cross and St John's Ambulance Assn, were trained in first aid and nursing. By 1914, 46,000 mainly upper- and middle-class women were in the VADs. Only 'mobile' VADs were in the Forces (in the army till 1944, the RAF till 1945, and the RN till 1960); the 'immobiles' were in civilian hospitals. Anne Powell, *Women in the War Zone: Hospital Service in the First World War* (Stroud, 2009), 18, 19; Arthur Marwick, *Women in War 1914–1918* (London, 1977), 21.

11. George Younger (1931–2003), Cons. MP, Ayr, 1964–92, Secretary of State for Scotland, 1979–86, for Defence, 1986–9; life peer, 1992, Viscount Younger of Leckie from 1997.

12. Sheriff John Dean-Leslie (1860–1946), born Glasgow, educ. Glasgow Academy, grad Glasgow, Leipzig and Berlin Universities; advocate, 1886; sheriff-substitute of Stirling, Dumbarton and Clackmannan, 1901–40; member, Cons. Club, Glasgow. *Scottish Biographies 1938*, op. cit., 184; *WWW Vol. IV, 1941–1950*, op. cit., 300.

13. Stirling Castle was the depot of the Argyll and Sutherland Highlanders from 1881. Raised in 1794, the regt became, 2006, 5th Bn, Royal Regt of Scotland.

14. Major General His Highness Maharajah Pratapsinka Gaekwar of Baroda (1908–1968). Said at one time to be the second-richest man in the world, in his earlier years he ruled with more or less absolute power over three million people; his state merged with Mumbai in 1949, and he himself was deposed in 1951. *TS*, 20 Jul. 1968; *WWW, Vol. VI, 1961–1970*, 61.

15. *Birkenhead News*, 1877 to date.

16. *Liverpool Daily Post*, 1855 to date. Griffiths, *Encyclopedia*, op. cit., 186.

17. *Birkenhead Advertiser*, 1860–1956.

18. The Cunard Line's second *Mauretania*, 35,750 tons, for many years the largest merchant ship ever built in England, was launched at Birkenhead on 28 Jul. 1938. After her last voyage in 1965 she was broken up at Inverkeithing. W.R.P. Bonsor, *North Atlantic Seaway* (Newton Abbot, 1975), 118, 122–3, 126–7, 130.

19. HMS *Prince of Wales*, 35,000 tons, launched in May 1939, was sunk, along with the WWI battle cruiser HMS *Repulse*, 26,500 tons, by Japanese bombers on 10 Dec. 1941 off the east coast of Malaya. Neither ship had had air cover. Of the 3,000 crew, more than 2,000 were rescued. The C-in-C, Admiral Phillips, and his flag-captain were among the hundreds who lost their lives. The loss of these two major warships three days after the destruction wrought by the Japanese on the American fleet at Pearl Harbor crippled British and American sea power in the western Pacific, badly affected the morale of British and Allied forces in Malaya and at Singapore, and gave the Japanese freedom to attack where they chose in that huge area. The loss of the two British warships also showed the vulnerability of capital ships to air attack. Churchill afterward wrote: 'In all the war, I never received a more direct shock.' Capt. S.W. Roskill, RN, *The Navy at War 1939–1945* (London, 1960), 175–81; Winston Churchill, *The Second World War*, Vol. III, op. cit., 548–51; J.J. Colledge, *Ships of the Royal Navy* (London and Mechanicsburg, PA, 2003 edn), 258.

20. HMS *Thetis*, launched 29 Jun. 1938, foundered 1 Jun. 1939 in, as Ernie McIntyre says, Liverpool Bay, with the loss of 99 lives and only four survivors – the worst submarine disaster in the world until then. *Thetis* was raised and renamed in Apr. 1940 HMS *Thunderbolt*, but was sunk by an Italian warship north of Sicily, 13 Mar. 1943. Colledge, *Ships of the Royal Navy*, op. cit., 324; Paul J. Kemp, *The T-Class Submarine* (London, 1990), 107–11.

21. The construction in 1888 of Port Sunlight on Merseyside, three miles south of Birkenhead, was funded by the brothers William (from 1917, Lord Leverhulme) and James Lever, makers of Sunlight soap. Workers at Port Sunlight were provided with medical care, free insurance, compensation when unemployed, pensions, and profit-sharing.
22. *Liverpool Echo*, 1879 to date.
23. *Liverpool Evening Express*, 1870–1958, merged into *Liverpool Echo*.
24. The *Empress of Britain*, built by John Brown & Co. Ltd, Clydebank, for Canadian Pacific Railways, to voyage between Britain and the St Lawrence river, and carrying in peacetime up to 1,200 passengers, had made its maiden voyage in May 1931. Norman L. Middlemiss, *British Shipbuilding Yards, Vol. 2: Clydebank* (North Shields, 1994), 128.
25. The Russo-Finnish 'Winter War', Nov. 1939–Mar. 1940, launched by Stalin mainly to strengthen Soviet defences around Leningrad (St Petersburg) by pushing back 30 or 40 miles the existing frontier near there with Finland (an attempt to achieve which by agreement the Finnish govt had rejected), proved far from being the easy victory expected for the Soviet forces. Their heavy losses to the determined and skilful Finnish resistance showed how the Red Army had been weakened by Stalin's extensive and ruthless purges in 1937–8 of so many of its leading generals and other senior officers. Britain and France, although already at war since Sep. 1939 with Nazi Germany, came close to intervening in the Winter War by sending, as Ernie McIntyre indicates, a large expeditionary force. The Finns were, however, forced to make peace and accept the loss of the frontier areas concerned (which in fact pushed the frontier back about 100 miles from Leningrad). The war strengthened Hitler's belief that his own forces could and would in due course defeat the Soviet armies. See, e.g., Alexander Werth, *Russia at War, 1941–1945* (London, 1965), 84–96; John Erickson, *The Road to Stalingrad* (London, 1993), 13–14; Peter Calvocoressi, Guy Wint and John Pritchard, *The Causes and Courses of the Second World War* (London, 1989 edn), 115–18; Richard Overy, *Russia's War* (London, 1998), 54–7; Taylor, *English History*, op. cit., 468–9.
26. Nazi Germany had invaded Denmark and Norway on 8–9 Apr. 1940. British and French troops were landed at several places on the west coast of Norway a week or so later and, supported by Norwegian forces, fought the Germans until 8 Jun. when, because both of the crisis in France resulting from its invasion by Germany and of the much greater German air power in Norway, all remaining Allied troops were evacuated from Narvik in the north. HMS *Victoria* has not been identified: Ernie McIntyre may have meant HMS *Victorious*, a recently launched aircraft carrier. Roskill, *Navy at War*, op. cit., 62–71; Colledge, *Ships of the Royal Navy*, op. cit., 345, 346; Richard Holmes, *The Oxford Companion to Military History* (Oxford, 2001), 663–4.
27. Of the 1,561 crew of the aircraft carrier (not cruiser) HMS *Glorious* and the two escorting destroyers sunk with her on 8 Jun., all but 46 lost their lives. Roskill, *Navy at War*, op. cit., 69–70.
28. Field Marshal Viscount Montgomery of Alamein (1887–1976), joined the army, 1908; fought in WWI; from major general to field marshal, 1938–44; commanded Eighth Army in North Africa from Jul. 1942, and 21st Army Group, 1944–5; Deputy Supreme Allied Commander in Europe, 1951–8.
29. Patrick J. Dollan (1885–1963), rope worker, grocery apprentice, miner, journalist; as a conscientious objector in WWI, jailed in 1917; a leader, Independent Lab. Party, in Scotland, then, 1933–6, of the Scottish Socialist Party; Glasgow town councillor from 1913, Lord Provost of Glasgow, 1938–41; knighted, 1941. *Scottish Biographies 1938*, op. cit., 195. William Knox (ed.), *Scottish Labour Leaders, 1918–1939* (Edinburgh, 1984), 92–9.
30. The *Daily Herald* in Jun. 1933 was the first newspaper in Britain to achieve a daily circulation of two million copies – though that was soon surpassed by the *Daily Express*. Julius Elias (1873–1946), Lord Southwood from 1937, rose from office boy to managing

director, Odhams Press Ltd, printers and publishers, which in 1929 acquired a 51 per cent share in the *Daily Herald*. R.J. Minney, *Viscount Southwood* (London, 1954), 17, 20, 162–3, 229–30, 242–3, 292–3.

31. Arthur Woodburn (1890–1978), educ. Boroughmuir School and Heriot Watt Coll., Edinburgh; engineering and foundry office worker; jailed as a conscientious objector in WWI; office-bearer in Labour College movement, 1920s–30s: Scottish Secretary, Lab. Party, 1932–9; Lab. MP, Clackmannan and East Stirling, 1939–70; PPS to Secretary of State for Scotland, 1941–5, PS, Ministry of Supply, 1945–7, Secretary of State for Scotland, 1948–50.

32. There is no reason to doubt the accuracy of Ernie McIntyre's recollection but, curiously, David Moir has not been found among lists of Edinburgh town councillors between 1944 and 1953.

33. James Dollan (1913–1991); in RAF in WWII; succeeded his father as Scottish editor, *Daily Herald*; later a freelance journalist; West of Scotland member, NUJ NEC, 1955–63 and 1969–71; president, 1974–5, STUC; honorary member, NUJ, and OBE for his services to journalism. *TJ*, Jun. 1975, Sep. 1991; *TS*, 24 Jul. 1991.

34. Douglas Henderson, deputy leader, Scottish National Party, 1970–2 and 1979–81; SNP MP, East Aberdeenshire, 1974–9; died 2006, aged 71.

35. Magnus Williamson, a sports journalist for over 50 years, founded his own sports news agency in Edinburgh; played a leading part in bringing the Commonwealth Games, 1970, to Edinburgh; NUJ NEC member for Central and North Scotland, 1955–65; president, NUJ, 1960–1; Lab. councillor, Edinburgh, 1952–77; narrowly defeated as Lab. Parl. candidate, Edinburgh Pentlands, 1964; OBE, 1970; died 1978, aged 69. *TJ*, Jul. 1970, Mar. 1978; *TS*, 13 Feb. 1978. *The Clarion*, Official Organ of the East of Scotland Labour Movement (Edinburgh, Feb. 1948–Dec. 1960). Earlier issues were titled *Edinburgh Clarion*, published by Edinburgh West Constituency Lab. Party, Mar. 1939–May 1947. Harold Wilson (1916–1995), Lab. MP, Ormskirk, 1945–50, Huyton, 1950–83; Leader, Lab. Party, 1963–83; Prime Minister, 1964–70, 1974–6; life peer from 1983.

36. Joseph Westwood (1884–1948), industrial organiser from 1916, Fife miners' union; political organiser, 1918–29, Scottish mine workers; Lab. MP, 1922–31, Peebles and South Midlothian; Parl. Under-Secretary of State for Scotland, 1931; Lab. MP, 1935–48, Stirling and Falkirk Burghs; Secretary of State for Scotland, 1945–8; killed in a road accident.

37. William Maxwell Aitken (1879–1964; from 1917, Lord Beaverbrook), born Canada; Unionist MP, Ashton-under-Lyne, 1910–16; Chancellor, Duchy of Lancaster and Minister of Information, 1918; newspaper proprietor from 1919: *Daily Express, Sunday Express* (1921), and London *Evening Standard* (1929); minister successively of three govt depts, 1940–5; author of several books, including *Politicians and the Press* (London, 1925).

38. The Edinburgh International Festival of Music and Drama, begun in 1947, has long since become one of the world's largest and most successful annual festivals of all the arts. It now includes film, television, book, and Fringe festivals.

39. Percy Cudlipp (1905–1962), born Cardiff, began work on *South Wales Echo*, then reporter, *Evening Chronicle*, Manchester, film critic, *Evening Standard*, London, successively assistant editor, editor, editorial manager, 1931–53, *Daily Herald*; columnist, 1954–6, *News Chronicle*; editor, 1956–62, *New Scientist*.

40. Hannen Swaffer (1879–1962), on *Daily Mail* from 1902, then editor, *Weekly Dispatch*, a decade with *Daily Mirror*, then on *Daily Graphic*; dramatic critic, *Daily Express*, 1926; on *Daily Herald* from 1931. Harry Lauder (1870–1950), born Portobello; began work in an Arbroath flax-spinning mill, then a miner; became an internationally known Scots comic song composer and singer; knighted, 1919.

41. *Time*, New York, 1923 to date.

42. Maurice Linden as a young Glasgow journalist had joined the Scottish Ambulance Unit which went to Spain during the Civil War, 1936–9, there. Edinburgh *Evening Dispatch*, 14 Jan. 1937, reported Linden was also to 'write for the press and the various aid, etc.,

organisations about the Unit's work there'. For references to Linden and other members of the Ambulance Unit who later resigned from it and joined the International Brigades to fight General Franco's forces, see the recollections of Roderick MacFarquhar in I. MacDougall, *Voices from the Spanish Civil War* (Edinburgh, 1986), 81–3.

43. Cheque-book journalism: news or feature articles based on information *bought*, sometimes at a substantial price. 'Cheque-book journalism is degrading to the profession and to all those who trade in grisly or prurient information for personal gain. The practice has been condemned repeatedly by the Union in the past and it is still our policy to outlaw it. There can be no excuse for any journalist to entertain doubts about this.' Jake Eccleston, deputy general secretary, NUJ, in a formal statement, 6 May 1981 (published in that month's *Journalist*), arising from the Peter Sutcliffe 'Yorkshire Ripper' case. *The Sun*, 1966 to date. In 1959 Odhams Press Ltd and the *Daily Herald* had been acquired by the International Publishing Corporation, owners of the *Daily Mirror*, who in 1966 re-titled and relaunched the *Daily Herald* as *The Sun*, then acquired, 1969, by Rupert Murdoch of News International.

44. St Andrew's House, headquarters, Scottish Office, built on the site of the former Calton Jail, Edinburgh, was completed and opened 1939. William Ballantyne began work on *Weekly Record*, later assistant editor, *Sunday Mail*; 1934–8, successively on *Weekly Herald*, Glasgow, and editor, *Bon Accord*, Aberdeen (and, n.d., but before 1938, editor, *Scottish Field*); 1938–70, successively press officer then from 1946 director, Scottish Information Office; author or editor of four books on Scottish subjects; MVO, 1954, CBE, 1962; died 1974, aged 66. *EN*, 30 Apr. 1969; *GH* and *TS*, 28 Sep. 1974.

45. There were 21 US servicemen, out of all those taken prisoner during it, who refused repatriation to the USA at the end of the Korean War. Virginia Pasley, *22 Stayed* (London, 1955), 7.

46. John Blackwood, editor, 1962–8, *Scottish Daily Mail*; died 1978.

47. Hugh Farmer was later editor, *Scottish Catholic Observer*. *TJ*, Nov. 1999. *The People*, 1881 to date.

48. Andrew Condron, a Regular ex-Royal Marine, the only British serviceman taken prisoner in the Korean War to refuse repatriation after it, returned from China to Britain at Southend, 11 Oct. 1962, accompanied by his Chinese–French wife Jacqueline and their son aged two. *TS*, 12 Oct. 1962.

49. George Strathie began, 1961, on *Falkirk Herald*, then moved to *Scottish Daily Mail*; assistant chief press officer, Commonwealth Games, Edinburgh, 1970; columnist, *EN*, 1970–83; treasurer, Edinburgh branch, NUJ, 1968–83; died 1983, aged 44. *TJ*, Feb. 1983; *TS*, 11 Feb. 1983.

50. Bay City Rollers, Scots pop group, formed 1966, originally as The Saxons, broke up in 1986. See, e.g., Les McKeown with Lynne Elliot, *Shang-a-Lang: Life as an international pop idol* (Edinburgh, 2003).

51. Hugh Fraser (1903–1966; from 1961, Lord Fraser of Allander), educ. Glasgow Academy; chairman and managing director from 1941, House of Fraser Ltd, and from 1948 of Scottish & Universal Investments Ltd; deputy chairman then chairman from 1959, Geo. Outram & Co Ltd, publishers, *GH* and *Evening Times*; acquired Harrods, 1959; treasurer, Scottish Cons. and Unionist Party. *WWW, Vol. VI, 1961–1970*, op. cit., 398, 399; Griffiths, *Encyclopedia*, op. cit., 253–4.

52. The Printing & Kindred Trades Federation, 1891–1973, existed to further the common interests of trade unions and their members in printing, bookbinding, paper-making and kindred trades. The NUJ affiliated to it in 1919. The P&KTF was replaced in 1973 by the Printing Trade Unions Co-ordinating Bureau. Sarah C. Gillespie, *A Hundred Years of Progress: The Record of the Scottish Typographical Association 1853 to 1952* (Glasgow, 1953), 127–9; Clement J. Bundock, *The National Union of Journalists: A Jubilee History 1907–1957* (Oxford, 1957), 70–1; *TJ*, Jun. 1973.

53. The Federated Society of Electrotypers and Stereotypers, formed 1893, changed its

title, 1917, to the National Society; merged, 1967, into National Graphical Association.

54. Jim Bradley (1904–1991), began work on *Craven Chronicle*, Yorkshire, moved to *Evening Chronicle*, Manchester; joined NUJ 1923, member from 1945 of its NEC, general secretary, 1951–69, during which NUJ membership doubled to 24,000; president, and Member of Honour, NUJ, 1970; president, 1964–70, International Federation of Journalists; OBE, 1969. *TJ*, Oct.–Nov. 1991.

55. The *Scottish Daily News*, May–Nov. 1975 (plus some emergency editions to Jul. 1976), was published at first by a workers' co-operative formed after the cessation of publication in Glasgow in Mar. 1974 of three Beaverbrook newspapers (and the transfer of publication to Manchester of the first two), the *Scottish Daily Express*, *Scottish Sunday Express*, and the *Evening Citizen*, and described by the general secretary, NUJ, as 'the worst blow ever in Scotland' to newspapers and newspapermen. Of 1,942 workers employed at the Beaverbrook plant in Albion St, Glasgow, more than 300 were NUJ members. At its launch there, with funding raised from the government, Beaverbrook Press, the newspaper magnate Robert Maxwell, trade unions, and not least from the workforce itself, the new paper employed some 500, about 100 of them journalists. Circulation at first was encouraging, but difficulties soon arose, particularly over costs, circulation, funding, and the divisive influence from the outset of Maxwell. *TJ*, Apr. 1974, May, Jun. 1975; STUC *Annual Report, 1976*, 106, 107. For a detailed account, see Ron McKay & Brian Barr, *The Story of the Scottish Daily News* (Edinburgh, 1976).

56. Robert Maxwell (1923–1991), born Jan Hoch in Slovakia; most of his family died in Auschwitz; served in WWII in Czech then British army: MC, 1945; founded, 1949, Pergamon Press; 1964–70, Lab. MP, Buckingham; from 1984, chairman, Mirror Group Newspapers Ltd; author of several books. *WWW, Vol. IX, 1991–1995*, 374–5.

57. Sir James Miller (1905–1977), architect; educ. George Heriot's School, Edinburgh; managing director, Jas Miller & Partners Ltd, building and civil engineering contractors; Edinburgh Progressive town councillor, 1936–54, Lord Provost, 1951–4, Lord Mayor of London, 1964–5.

58. Jack Moffat (1894–1961), Edinburgh branch secretary, National Society of Brushmakers; chairman, Edinburgh Lab. Party; 1937–61, a director, and 1950–61, president, St Cuthbert's Co-operative Association; 1944–61, a director, Co-operative Press. The first supermarket in Scotland was opened by St Cuthbert's Co-op. at Leven St in 1959. George Davidson, *Scotmid – Past, Present & Future* (Newbridge, 2009), unnumbered pps.

59. Abe Moffat (1896–1975), a Fife miner; from 1920s a leading member of the Communist Party in Scotland; general secretary, 1931–6, United Mineworkers of Scotland, president, 1942–5, National Union of Scottish Mine Workers, and, 1945–61, of National Union of Mineworkers (Scottish Area). His autobiography is *My Life with the Miners* (London, 1965). The Knockshinnoch Castle colliery disaster near New Cumnock, Ayrshire, on 7 Sep. 1950 was caused, after heavy rain, by a huge mass of liquid peat or moss rushing from the surface into the underground workings. Thirteen miners were missing, a further 116 were trapped. Through the skill and courage of the rescue teams all 116 trapped men were brought out of the pit safely by 9 Sep. The 13 men missing lost their lives. A public inquiry in Nov., with Abe Moffat representing the miners and a KC the National Coal Board, established there had been a major breach of the regulations governing the dangers of moss to coal-mining under it. There followed a lengthy but eventually successful struggle by the union, led by Abe Moffat, to secure from the Coal Board unprecedentedly substantial compensation for the families of the 13 miners killed in the disaster. Four NCB officials, including the colliery manager, charged with breaches of the safety regulations were found not guilty, and an appeal against the verdict was dismissed in the Scottish Court of Criminal Appeal. The miners' union then pressed for a new Coal Mines Act, duly passed in 1954, that made clear the legal obligation on the NCB and its managers to ensure the safety of miners at their work. R. Page Arnot, *A History of the Scottish Miners* (London, 1955), 369–98.

Hector McSporran, pp. 88–104

1. Vivien Leigh (1913–1967), stage and film actress, Academy Award winner; wife, 1940–60, of Laurence Olivier. *WWW, Vol. VI, 1961–1970*, 665.
2. Tranent beat Petershill 6–1 in the final, 1935, of the Scottish Junior Cup. David McGlone and Bill McLure, *The Juniors – 100 Years: A Centenary History of Scottish Junior Football* (Edinburgh, 1987), 76, 98.
3. Jimmy Caskie was signed, 1933, from Ashfield FC by St Johnstone, played 110 times for the latter and scored 16 goals. Transferred, Mar. 1939, to Everton FC, he seems to have made only four wartime appearances for them, and played for Glasgow Rangers FC, 1939–49, as well as in eight internationals, 1939–44, for Scotland against England. Ian Ross and Gordon Smailes, *Everton: A Complete Record* (Derby, 1993), 405; infm.: St Johnstone FC and Sandy Jardine, Rangers FC.
4. *Campbeltown Courier*, 1873 to date.
5. *Argyllshire Leader & Western Isles Gazette*, Campbeltown, 1929–34. Ferguson, *Scottish Newspapers*, op. cit., 6.
6. Monotype: a composing machine where each letter was individually cast in metal (unlike the linotype, which produced slugs, or lines of type). Hand-set: manual composition from previously cast metal sorts in a fount-case.
7. About Alex Ramsay no more infm. has so far been found.
8. Angus MacVicar (1908–2001), born Duror, Argyll; son of a minister; educ. Campbeltown Grammar School; MA, Glasgow University; assistant editor, 1932–4, *Campbeltown Courier*; teacher in Argyll of journalism, 1934–8; author from 1933 of more than 70 books, several plays, and hundreds of radio and TV scripts; capt., Highland Light Infantry in WWII in Madagascar, India, Middle East, Italy; hon. doctorate, Stirling University, 1985. *Scottish Biographies 1938*, op. cit., 523; *TH*, 3 Nov. 2001.
9. *Kirriemuir Free Press*, 1884–1975.
10. Anna Neagle (1904–1986); stage and film actress; m., 1943, Herbert Wilcox (1890–1977). He began as a journalist, then became a film producer, director, and author; in WWI in infantry, RFC and RAF. J.M. Barrie (1860–1937), born Kirriemuir; son of a weaver; educ. Glasgow, Dumfries and Edinburgh Academies, and Edinburgh University; leader writer, 1883–4, *Nottingham Journal*, and contributed to other newspapers, including *ED*; from 1888 novelist and playwright; *Peter Pan* first staged, 1904; knighted, 1913; Chancellor, Edinburgh University, 1933.
11. Charles Mactaggart (1898–1984); solicitor; enlisted aged 17 in WWI in 8th Bn, Argyll and Sutherland Highlanders, and became capt.; MC for conspicuous bravery, Cambrai, Nov. 1917; cont. working in his family legal firm C. & D. Mactaggart until he was 85. Infm.: Angus Martin, Kintyre Antiquarian & Natural History Society.
12. Tom Chalmers, born Kirkcaldy; began there in journalism, then worked in Dundee and Edinburgh; 1934, joined Outram Press, Glasgow, and became news editor of its three papers: *GH*, *Evening Times*, and *The Bulletin*; in Machine Gun Corps in WWI, lost an eye in Flanders; later became editor, Earl Haig Fund Scottish magazine for disabled ex-servicemen; died 1959, aged 63. *Evening Times*, 30 Dec. 1959. James Ross, born Stranraer; began, 1912, on *Wigtownshire Free Press*, then on *Northern Whig* and *Belfast Newsletter*; 1930–62, successively reporter, chief reporter, deputy news editor, *Glasgow Herald*. *GH*, 11 Jan. 1962. James MacArthur Reid (1900–1970); MA, Glasgow, BA, Oxford (and won, 1922, Newdigate Poetry Prize); began, 1922–3, as features writer, *The Bulletin*, successively from 1936, *Glasgow Herald*, assistant editor, editor, *The Bulletin*; author of a dozen books. Sir William Robieson (1890–1977), born Fossaway, Kinross-shire; educ. Dollar Academy and Glasgow University; assistant, 1913–14, to professor of history, Glasgow University; in WWI in Cameron Highlanders and Gold Coast Regt; successively, 1914–37, sub-editor, leader writer, assistant editor, *Glasgow Herald*, editor, 1937–55; knighted 1948. *Scottish Biographies 1938*, op. cit., 650; *WWW,*

Vol. VII, 1971–1980, op. cit., 676.

13. Donald Dewar (1937–2000), educ. Glasgow Academy, Glasgow University; solicitor; Lab. MP, South Aberdeen, 1966–70, Glasgow Garscadden, 1978–97, Glasgow Anniesland, 1997–2000; PPS to President, Board of Trade, 1967; Opposition: spokesman, 1981–92, on Scottish Affairs, 1992–5, on Social Security, 1995–7, Chief Whip; Secretary of State for Scotland, 1997–9; First Minister, Scottish Executive, 1997–2000. Winston Churchill (1874–1965), son of Lord Randolph Churchill; educ. Harrow and Sandhurst; an army officer, 1895–9, fought in battle of Omdurman, 1898; journalist, orator; a leading politician in Lib. and Cons. Parties alternately: among successive Parl. seats he held he was as Lib. MP, Dundee, 1908–22; a govt minister, 1906–16, 1917–22, 1924–9; 1939–40, anti-Appeaser in 1930s; Prime Minister, 1940–5, 1951–5; author of 15 histories and biographies.

14. British Association for the Advancement of Science, founded 1831, holds annual meetings and seeks to stimulate scientific inquiry. Ben Allison (1912–1978), born Edinburgh; reporter, 1930–73, *Scottish Daily Express* (apart from war service, 1939–45). When police refused him an interview with Benny Lynch, world boxing champion in 1930s who was arrested on a driving charge, Ben Allison threw a brick through the police station window and, put in the same cell as Lynch, got his interview. Infm.: Hector McSporran; *TJ*, Mar. 1978; Patricia Allison, *Rare Ben Allison* (Edinburgh, 1979).

15. Joe Louis (1914–1981), American world heavyweight boxing champion, 1937–49.

16. Hector McNeil (1907–1955); educ. Woodside School, Glasgow, and Glasgow University; journalist; Glasgow Lab. town councillor, 1932–8; Lab. MP, Greenock, 1941–55; PPS to PS, Ministry of War Transport, 1942–5, Parl. Under-Secretary of State, 1945–6, and Minister of State, 1946–50, Foreign Office, Secretary of State for Scotland, 1950–1. *WWW, Vol. V, 1951–1960*, 719.

17. All but one of the 30 passengers, and all the crew of 10, were killed in the crash on 21 Oct. 1948 – 'Scotland's worst civil aviation tragedy' – of the KLM (Royal Dutch Airlines) plane a mile from Tarbolton, while it was attempting to land at nearby Prestwick airport. The sole survivor of the crash died two days later. *TS*, 21–4 Oct. 1948.

18. *Dumfries & Galloway Standard*, 1843 to date.

19. The Institute of Journalists, formed 1884 and granted a royal charter in 1890, is, in the words of its published literature, the 'world's longest established professional association for journalists', with 'an independently certificated trade union arm, the IoJ (TU)', and a code of conduct 'to ensure that members adhere to the highest professional standards'. It 'has always been willing to work with media owners, and is respected by employers' organisations as a responsible trade union which prefers negotiation rather than confrontation'. Nothing in its Charter, Rules, etc., 'prevents its members from going on strike'. But by 1907 many journalists, concluding that the Institute, whose members included some newspaper employers, had failed to secure reasonable wages and working conditions, formed then the National Union of Journalists, which specifically excluded from membership newspaper proprietors, directors and managers. In 1919 the NUJ affiliated to the Printing & Kindred Trades Federation, and in 1920–1 to the Trades Union Congress, to which it re-affiliated from 1940. During the twentieth century several attempts to achieve a merger of the IoJ and the NUJ failed, e.g., in Oct. 1971, over 'fundamental and irreconcilable differences' between the two bodies. The nature of some of these differences was illustrated when, in 1991, the IoJ was briefly enrolled into the Confederation of Professional Associations organised by the Electrical, Electronic, Telecommunication & Plumbing Trades Union, and the NUJ pointed out that the electricians' union, expelled by the TUC in 1989, had 'collaborated with Rupert Murdoch to smash the print unions and to seriously weaken the NUJ at News International' [newspapers owned by Murdoch]. Infm.: IoJ; *TJ*, Dec. 1971, Oct./Nov. 1992; Bundock, *National Union of Journalists*, op. cit., 1, 5–7, 8, 70–1, 85–6, 150.

20. Alexander G. Williamson (1914–1993), assistant editor, 1952–4, managing editor, 1954–7, *Dumfries & Galloway Standard*.
21. Niall Macpherson (1908–1987), born Newtonmore; educ. Edinburgh Academy, Fettes College, and Oxford University; National Liberal & Cons. MP, 1945–63, Dumfriesshire; Joint Under Secretary of State for Scotland, 1955–60, PS, Board of Trade, 1960–3; Lord Drumalbyn from 1963. *TS*, 12 Oct. 1987.
22. James Dewar, an Aberdeen town councillor and managing director and superintendent of the crematorium, and Alick Forbes, an Aberdeen undertaker, were unanimously convicted by a jury at the High Court, Edinburgh (where the trial, to ensure it was fair, had been transferred from Aberdeen): Dewar, between Jul. 1939 and Apr. 1944, of the theft of two coffins and 1,044 coffin lids, and Forbes, of resetting 100 lids. Dewar was sentenced to three years' penal servitude, Forbes to six months' imprisonment, though Dewar was liberated on bail pending an appeal. Productions in the well of the court during the trial included eight coffins (six of them for children), 120 coffin lids, and 90 wooden name plates. A witness testified that coffins had been saved by putting two bodies in one casket for cremation. A gardener at the crematorium gave evidence of having made blackout shutters and seed boxes from coffin lids. Public interest in the trial was so great that admission to the court was by special ticket; and it was the first criminal trial in Scotland in which women formed a majority of the jury. *EN*, 10 and 14 Oct. 1944. Peter Craighead, born Aberdeen, began 1921 as office boy, Aberdeen Journals Ltd; 1941–4, deputy chief reporter, 1944–52, chief reporter, 1952–70, news editor, *Press & Journal* and *Evening Express*; died 1973, aged 67. *P&J*, 17 Apr. 1973. *Evening Express*, 1879 to date. *Weekly Journal*, 1876–1957. George Ley Smith began aged 15 on the *P&J* in 1915; 1918, wounded in France, serving with the Gordon Highlanders; then successively reporter, chief reporter, and, 1950–6, editor *P&J*; ill health ended his editorship, but he contributed to the paper until his retirement, 1960; died 1968, aged 68. *P&J*, 20 Mar. 1968.
23. James C. Grant, born Elgin; began as office boy, *Northern Scot*, Elgin; joined, 1936, Aberdeen Journals Ltd, and represented them in Edinburgh and Glasgow; in Royal Artillery, 1939–45; post-war, successively sub-editor, assistant editor, deputy editor, 1953–60, editor, 1960–75, associate editor, 1975–6, *P&J*; chairman, NUJ, Aberdeen branch; CBE, 1975, for services to journalism (1936–75, circulation of *P&J* increased from 25,000 to over 110,000); died 1998. *P&J*, 6 Sep. 1998.
24. Kenneth Peters (1923–2000), educ. Aberdeen Grammar School, Aberdeen University; capt., KOSB, in WWII; on editorial staff, *Daily Record*, 1947–51; assistant editor, *Evening Express*, Aberdeen, 1951–2, and, 1952–3, Manchester *Evening Chronicle*, editor, *Evening Express*, 1953–6, *P&J*, 1956–60; director, 1960–90, managing director, 1960–80, chairman, 1980–1, Aberdeen Journals Ltd; director, Thomson Regional Newspapers, 1974–80, and Thomson North Sea, 1981–8; president, Scottish Daily Newspaper Society, 1964–6 and 1974–6; member, Press Council, 1974–7; author or editor of three books; CBE, DL. *WWW, Vol. X, 1996–2000*, op. cit., 453.
25. Thomson's sold Aberdeen Journals Ltd to Northcliffe/*Daily Mail* at the beginning of 1996. The big strike had begun in 1989 when 100 of the 180 journalists at Aberdeen Journals Ltd stopped work over union recognition and an attempt by the Thomson Organisation to introduce personal contracts. An agreement was reached after three weeks. But a bitter strike, lasting almost a year, began on 3 Oct. when 116 journalists were sacked. The sacked journalists produced their own newspaper; those others who remained at work were regarded as blacklegs. Aberdeen Journals Ltd expected the strike to collapse on 3 Jan. 1990, when they became legally entitled to re-employ strikers selectively: but only one striker returned then to work. Sales of the *P&J* and *Evening Express* slumped badly as many local bodies boycotted the two papers. The dispute cost the NUJ £1 million, and Thomson's probably more. The strike was called off on 14 Sep. 1990 after lengthy negotiations (a delegation of the strikers

had gatecrashed Thomson's annual shareholders' meeting in Toronto in May and secured assurances the dispute would be resolved). Neither side could claim outright victory, but the strikers succeeded in forcing Thomson's to negotiate despite their declaration that they never would, and also that none of the strikers would ever be re-employed. In fact, the agreement allowed more than 20 jobs to be available to the strikers (though only 14 journalists remained interested in returning to work there), and strikers not returning were paid compensation of between £2,500 and £12,500. But most of the sacked journalists did not secure their reinstatement, and Thomson's ceased to recognise the NUJ. *TJ*, Oct. 1990; W. Hamish Fraser and Clive H. Lee (eds), *Aberdeen 1800–2000: A New History* (East Linton, 2000), 464; Norman Harker, *First Daily: A 250-year Celebration of the Press & Journal* (Aberdeen, 1997), 175.

26. Grampian Television, est. 1961 in Aberdeen, was acquired by Scottish Media Group in 1997, and was renamed in 2006, along with Scottish Television, as STV.

27. The trial of his wife, Mrs Sheila Garvie, her lover, Aberdeen barman Brian Tevendale, and Alan Peters, for the sensational murder in May 1968 of Maxwell Garvie, a wealthy Kincardineshire farmer, took place at the High Court in Aberdeen between 19 Nov. and 2 Dec. that year. Mrs Garvie was found guilty by a majority, Tevendale unanimously, and both were sentenced to life imprisonment. The case against Peters was found not proven. *P&J*, 20 Nov.–3 Dec. 1968.

28. Sandy Mutch (1924–2000), Aberdeen businessman; Cons. town councillor, 1961–74, Grampian Regional councillor, 1974–90, convener, 1974–82; president, 1972–3, Scottish Cons. and Unionist Association; a leading figure in the creation of Aberdeen as 'the oil capital of Europe'. *P&J* and *Evening Express*, 8 May 2000.

29. John Cameron (1900–1996), educ. Edinburgh Academy and Edinburgh University; in RNVR in WWI, 1918–19, and WWII (mentioned in dispatches, DSC); advocate, 1924, Advocate Depute, 1929–36, KC, 1936, sheriff, 1945–8, Dean of Faculty of Advocates, 1948–55; Senator of the College of Justice, 1955–85; knighted, 1954, Knight of the Thistle, 1978; awarded several hon. degrees. *WWW, Vol. X, 1996–2000*, op. cit., 85.

30. John Reith (1889–1971), born Glasgow, son of a minister; educ. Glasgow Academy, Gresham's School, Norfolk and Glasgow College of Technology; began work as an engineer in London; badly wounded in WWI; administrator, munitions work; general manager, 1920–2, Beardmore & Co. Ltd, Coatbridge; BBC managing director, 1922–7, director general; 1927–38; 1938–40, chairman, Imperial Airways and of British Overseas Airways Corporation; National MP, Southampton, 1940; minister successively of three government depts, 1940–2; in RNVR and Admiralty, 1942–5; two autobiographies, *Into the Wind* (London, 1949), *Wearing Spurs* (London, 1966); knighted, 1927; from 1940 Lord Reith of Stonehaven. *WWW, Vol. VII, 1971–1980*, op. cit., 661.

Colin Dakers, pp. 105–19

1. *Arbroath Herald*, 1885 to date.
2. *Weekly News*, 1855 to date.
3. James Gair Henderson (1913–1970) worked all his life for Geo. Outram & Co., successively as copy boy, telephonist, sports reporter until 1954 in its Edinburgh office, where he was chief football correspondent for *GH*, *Evening Times*, and *The Bulletin*; moved, 1954, to Outram's Glasgow office and was chief football writer, *Evening Times*; a major in Cameron Highlanders and Parachute Regt in WWII. *GH*, 4 May 1970.
4. *Evening Telegraph*, 1877–1905, merged then with *Evening Post*, 1900–5, to become *Evening Telegraph & Post*, Dundee, to date. Mackenzie, *NEWSPLAN Scotland*, op. cit., 172–3.
5. See also above, p. 542, David M. Smith, Note 13. Even as late as 1977 the NUJ had only one member out of some 330 journalists at D.C. Thomson's, Dundee; in the firm's Glasgow office 13 of the staff of 37 were then in the union; in both offices the numbers increased in 1978; and in 1982, the Dundee office had 65 NUJ members.

TJ, Mar. 1977, Apr. 1978, Nov. 1982. In 1985 there was said still to be no equal pay at D.C. Thomson's, no right for pregnant women to have the same job on their return to work, no part-time work for mothers, and management retained the right to transfer staff around the different editorial offices, to prevent each office becoming fully unionised. *TJ*, Jul.–Aug. 1985. Harry was Harry Boyne (1910–1997); son of a journalist; educ. Inverness High School and Inverness Royal Academy; reporter, *Inverness Courier*, 1927; Dundee *Courier & Advertiser*, 1929; major, Black Watch, in WWII; staff correspondent for *GH*, 1945–9, in Dundee, and from 1949 in Edinburgh; political correspondent, *GH*, 1950–6, *Daily Telegraph*; 1956–76; chairman, 1958–9, secretary, 1968–71, Parl. Lobby Journalists; Political Writer of the Year, 1972; knighted 1976; director of communications, 1980–2, Cons. Party Central Office; author of two books. *WWW, Vol. X, 1996–2000*, op. cit., 61; infm.: George MacDougall.

6. Professor Jim Tomlinson, Dundee University, who has carried out detailed research on Dundee jute workers in the 1930s, says there was no big strike by them at that time, though there was a vote for a strike. There was, however, he says, at that time serious unrest in Dundee over the Means Test and new scales of benefit for the unemployed.

7. See above, p. 545, Ernie McIntyre, Note 19.

8. Quintin Hogg (1907–2001); educ. Eton College and Oxford University; barrister; Cons. MP, 1938–50, Oxford City, 1963–70, St Marylebone; officer, Rifle Brigade, in WWII; succeeded, 1950, as 2nd Viscount Hailsham, renounced his peerage, 1963, life peer, 1970; held ministerial office, 1945, 1956–64, Lord Chancellor 1970–4, 1979–87; author of several books, including *The Case for Conservatism* (London, 1947). *WWW, Vol. XI, 2001–2005*, 220–1.

9. Sir Oswald Mosley, Bart. (1896–1980); educ. Winchester Coll. and Sandhurst; badly wounded in WWI; Cons. and Unionist MP, Harrow, 1918–22, Independent, 1922–4, Lab., 1924, for Smethwick, 1926–31; Chancellor, Duchy of Lancaster, 1929–30; founded, 1932, British Union of Fascists; interned during WWII. By 1934 the BUF, whose members wore black shirts, was estimated to have about 20,000 members and some 400 branches. The *Sunday Dispatch* awarded prizes to readers who sent in postcards saying, 'Why I like the Blackshirts'. But because of the brutal handling of hecklers at the BUF mass meeting at Olympia, London, in Jun. that year, and that same month the bloody 'Night of the Long Knives' purge by Hitler of some of his fellow Nazis in Germany, support for the BUF began to decline. Mowat, *Britain between the Wars*, op. cit., 473–5; Noreen Branson and Margot Heinemann, *Britain in the Nineteen Thirties* (London, 1971), 307; *WWW, Vol. VII, 1971–1980*, op. cit., 563.

10. Stukas were Junkers (JU 87) two-seat dive-bombers, 1937–45, which, tested by the Nazis against Republican forces in the Spanish Civil War, contributed to the success of the German blitzkrieg against Poland and France in 1939–40 but suffered disastrous losses in the Battle of Britain, 1940. A distinctive feature of the plane, intended to terrify its victims before dropping its bombs, was a piercing whistle emitted as it dived.

11. Donald McKay Elliot, born Edinburgh, 1902; educ. George Heriot's School; began, 1921, as junior reporter, *Evening Dispatch*; joined NUJ, 1922, president, 1942, life member, Edinburgh branch, 1975; in WWII, PRO, Air Training Corps in Scotland; left journalism on appointment as director, 1947–68, Scottish Film Council and Film Library; secretary, Educational Films of Scotland, and of Scottish branch, Great Britain–USSR Assoc., president, Edinburgh Cine and Video Society, and a member of the Franco-Scottish Relations Committee; OBE, 1962; died aged 89. Infm.: Janet McBain, Scottish Screen Archive, National Library of Scotland; *TJ*, Feb. 1975, Oct. 1983.

12. Colin Dakers overlooks the publication in Glasgow from Nov. 1928 of the *Scottish Daily Express*.

13. Reuters, named after its founder Julius Reuter (1816–1899), a German journalist, was est. 1851 in London as a speedier agency for providing news by means of telegraph and carrier pigeons. Reuters soon developed into what it has since remained – a

leading agency for providing an accurate and speedy foreign news service.

14. Frank Walker, began in Edinburgh office, *Daily Record*, before WWII, returned there post-war, then, 1946–68, was with *Scottish Daily Mail*, and after 1968 was a freelance motoring correspondent; died 1987, aged 70. Charlie McCorry (1918–1993), son of a miner; began, 1936, on Edinburgh *Evening News*; after service in WWII, moved to *Glasgow Herald*, then in 1960s to *Scottish Daily Mail*; 1968–81, PRO, Scottish Transport Group, and editor, *Scotland's Magazine*; 'a distinguished figure in Scottish journalism'. *TJ*, May–Jun., 1993. For Ernie McIntyre, see above, pp. 63–87.

15. Nothing more has been found about Frank Stefani. For John Blackwood, see above, p. 548, Ernie McIntyre, Note 46.

16. *The Independent*, a national daily, 1986 to date. Rupert Murdoch (b.1931), newspaper and other media proprietor; among companies he is, or has until recently been, chief executive and/or chairman of, are News Corporation, USA, News International plc UK, Fox Entertainment Group Inc., and British Sky Broadcasting. *WW 2010*, op. cit., 1639.

R.W. (Billy) Munro, pp. 120–41

1. George Waters (1880–1967), born in Thurso; educ. Thurso Academy, George Watson's Coll., Edinburgh University (MA (Hons) and Vans Dunlop Scholar in English Poetry, 1903), Berlin University, and Sorbonne, 1903–4; teacher, 1904–5, Hillhead High School, Glasgow; 1905, joined The Scotsman, successively sub-editor, leader writer and reviewer, chief assistant editor then, 1922–44, editor; hon. DL, St Andrews University, 1938, knighted, 1944, Chevalier de la Légion d'Honneur, 1946. Scottish Biographies 1938, op. cit., 771–2; WWW, Vol. VI, 1961–1970, op. cit., 1173–4.

2. Ronald C. Munro-Ferguson (1860–1934), Lib. MP, Ross and Cromarty, 1884–5, Leith Burghs, 1886–1914, private secretary, Secretary of State for Foreign Affairs, 1886 and 1892–4; Provost, Kirkcaldy, 1906–14; Governor-General and C-in-C of Australia, 1914–20; Viscount Novar from 1920; Secretary for Scotland, 1922–4.

3. The report on truck in the Shetlands is in *Reports from Commissioners, Inspectors and Others on Employment of Children (Departmental Committee); Factories and Workshops, Session 15 February 1910–23 November 1910, Vol. XXVIII, Annual Report for 1909, Appendix*, pp. 166–8, by Miss Isabel Meiklejohn, who had visited the Shetlands in Jun. 1909 to enquire into truck in the hosiery trades.

4. Cranley School (est. 1917) merged, 1979, with St Denis School (est. 1855); the merged school then itself merged, 1998, into St Margaret's School (est. 1890), which closed in 2010. (Press cuttings, Edinburgh Room, Edinburgh Public Library.) Edinburgh Academy, 1824 to date.

5. James Taylor, maths teacher, was on the Academy staff 1886–1926; Robert 'Boab' McEwan from 1904 to 1939, when he retired as senior master. Magnus Magnusson, *The Clacken and the Slate: The Story of the Edinburgh Academy 1824–1974* (London, 1974), 246, 278, 413, 415.

6. William, 8th Earl of Douglas, after receiving a safe-conduct from King James II, was murdered by him at Stirling Castle in Feb. 1452.

7. Lady Harriet Findlay had m., 1901, Sir J.E.R. Findlay, proprietor, *The Scotsman*; she was president, 1927–8, Scottish Unionist Association; died 1954. *WWW, Vol. V, 1951–1960*, op. cit., 374.

8. James W. Herries (1875–?), born Maxwelltown; began as a law apprentice; then journalist, 1895–1900, *Dumfries & Galloway Standard*, 1900–4, reporter, Glasgow office, *The Scotsman*, 1904–5, assistant editor and leader writer, *Carlisle Journal*, 1905–12, reporter, *The Scotsman*, Edinburgh; 1912–16, civil servant, National Health Insurance Commission; 1916–46, chief reporter, *The Scotsman*; author of several books; hon. vice-president, IoJ, 1946. *TS*, 26 Oct. 1946; *Scottish Biographies 1938*, op. cit., 347.

9. For Nelson's College, see above, Gordon Dean, p. 369.

10. James Mollison (1905–1959), educ. Glasgow Academy and Edinburgh Academy; RAF officer, 1923–8, then air mail pilot in Australia; in 1930s made several record-breaking intercontinental flights, some with Amy Johnson, his wife, 1932–8. *WWW, Vol. V, 1951–1960*, op. cit., 776. Amy Johnson (1903–1941), CBE; educ. Sheffield University; first woman to fly solo from London to Australia, 1930; died 1941, when her plane crashed (or possibly was shot down) in the Thames Estuary. *WWW, Vol. IV, 1941–1950*, 606–7.

11. Barrie (see also above, Hector McSporran, p. 550, Note 10) was inducted as Chancellor of Edinburgh University on 25 Oct. 1933. Alexander Pope (1688–1744). No report of the speech or broadcast in the Assembly Hall that day by George Bernard Shaw (1856–1950) has been found in the press.

12. Compton Mackenzie (1883–1972), born West Hartlepool; educ. St Paul's School and Oxford University; as capt., Royal Marines, 1915–16, at Dardanelles; Military Control Officer, Athens, 1916, director, Aegean Intelligence Service, 1917; OBE, 1919, hon. LL D, Glasgow, 1932, Rector, Glasgow University, 1931–4; literary editor, 1931–5, *Daily Mail*; editor, *Gramophone*; author of numerous books, including *Whisky Galore* (London, 1947); knighted, 1952. *Scottish Biographies 1938*, op. cit., 484.

13. Stanley Baldwin (1867–1947), Cons. MP, 1908–37, Prime Minister, 1923–4, 1924–9, 1935–7, Lord President of the Council, 1931–5; Rector, Edinburgh University, 1923–6, Glasgow University, 1928–31, Chancellor, St Andrews University, 1930–47; Earl Baldwin, 1937. *WWW, Vol. IV, 1941–1950*, op. cit., 52. Neville Chamberlain (1869–1940); Cons. MP, 1918–40, government minister intermittently, 1922–37, Prime Minister, 1937–40; author of *The Struggle for Peace* (London, 1939). *WWW, Vol. III, 1929–1940*, 235. Anthony Eden (1897–1977); with King's Royal Rifle Corps in WWI, MC; Cons. MP, 1923–57, in government office intermittently, 1926–57, including Secretary of State for Foreign Affairs, 1935–8, 1940–5; Prime Minister, 1955–7; author of several books, including his memoirs (London, 1960–5, 3 vols); Earl of Avon from 1961. *WWW, Vol. VII, 1971–1980*, op. cit., 32.

14. Jan Christian Smuts (1870–1950), commanded Cape Colony Boer forces in the South African War, 1899–1902; South African representative, Imperial War Cabinet, 1917–18; Prime Minister, 1919–24, 1939–48; Field Marshal, 1941. *WWW, Vol. IV, 1941–1950*, op. cit., 1075–6.

15. Robert Urquhart (1910–1990), born Banff; educ. Banff Academy; began aged 17 on *Banffshire Journal*, 1933–47, *Press & Journal*; gained his pilot's licence, 1939, and joined RAF Volunteer Reserve; in WWII, pilot, sqn ldr, Bomber and Coastal Command, shot down or crashed thrice; infm. officer with bomber group that attacked Gestapo HQ and broke the walls of Amiens prison, Feb. 1944, to allow Resistance and Allied PoWs to escape; 1947–75, agricultural correspondent, *The Scotsman*; winner, Fison Award, 1963 and 1966, for best contribution to informing general public about farming; author of two books, including *Farming in Scotland* (1967). *TS*, 21 Jul. 1990.

16. The sketch appeared in *The Scotsman*, then a large broadsheet, 24 Jul. 1930, p. 12, and covered a third of the page.

17. *Dundee Advertiser* (originally, 1803–61, titled *Dundee, Perth and Cupar Advertiser*), 1861–1926, when it merged with the Dundee *Courier*, 1816–1926, to form the *Courier & Advertiser*. R.M.W. Cowan, *The Newspaper in Scotland* (Glasgow, 1946), 15–16.

18. Patrick Geddes (1854–1932), born Aberdeenshire; a pioneer of town planning; professor of botany, Dundee, 1888, of civics and sociology, Bombay, 1919; founder of the Scots College, Montpellier; as a polymath, his best-known achievement may have been the Outlook Tower, Castlehill, Edinburgh, which he acquired in 1892 (from 1846 it had been an observatory, in which was placed first in 1855 a camera obscura that gave a panoramic view of the city) and which was said to have been the world's first sociological laboratory; knighted 1932. David Daiches (ed.), *The New Companion to Scottish Culture* (Edinburgh, 1993), 127–8; J.F. Birrell, *An Edinburgh Alphabet* (Edinburgh, 1980), 168.

19. Frank Moran (1885–1975), began, 1904, as a junior on *The Scotsman* in its then Cockburn Street offices, and sometimes reported football matches for its sister paper, the *Evening Dispatch*, sending half-time scores back to the office by carrier pigeon; golf correspondent, *The Scotsman*, 1913–65; president, 1948, Association of Golf Writers; author of *Golfers' Gallery* (1946); Frank Moran Trophy est. by *TS*, 1963, for annual award to a Scot giving notable service to golf; MBE, 1965. *TS*, 24 Dec. 1975; *The Glorious Privilege*, op. cit., 55–6.

20. Charles Graves, born Warwickshire, began there in journalism before WWI, in which he served as an army officer and then led a Chinese labour bn back to China from France; worked, c.1919–21, on Glasgow *Evening Citizen*, then successively reporter and dramatic critic, 1921–61, *The Scotsman*; member, until 1963, Scottish Committee, Arts Council of Britain; author of several volumes of poetry (e.g., *The Bamboo Grove* (London, 1928)), and a close friend of many contemporary poets; 'a man of exquisite manners and exceptional erudition'; died 1976, aged 84. *TS*, 29 Apr. 1961, 20 Dec. 1976.

21. General Sir Ian Hamilton (1853–1947), in army from 1873, in numerous wars or campaigns from the Afghan War, 1878–80, to WWI at Gallipoli; Lord Rector, Edinburgh University, 1932–5. *WWW, Vol. IV, 1941–1950*, op. cit., 492. Field Marshal Earl Roberts of Kandahar (1832–1914), in army from 1851, won VC in Indian Mutiny, relieved siege of Kandahar in Afghan War, 1878–80, C-in-C in India, 1885–93, and, 1901–2, in Boer War. *WWW, Vol. I, 1897–1915*, 441–2. Earl Kitchener of Khartoum (1850–1916), in army from 1871, won battle of Omdurman, 1898, chief of staff and C-in-C, Boer War, C-in-C, India, 1902–9, consul-general, Egypt, 1911, Secretary for War, 1914–16, died in explosion on HMS *Hampshire* off Orkney, 1916. *WWW, Vol. II, 1916–1928*, op. cit., 456.

22. Sir Ernest Shackleton (1874–1922), made four expeditions to the Antarctic, 1901–22, and died in South Georgia on the last. Magnus Magnussson (ed.), *Chambers Biographical Dictionary* (Edinburgh, 1990), 1332.

23. Wilfred Taylor (1909–1987), born Dundee; grad St Andrews University; sub-editor, 1936–7, Glasgow *Evening News*; book reviewer, columnist, etc., *The Scotsman*, 1937–86; author of *Scot Free* (1953). Infm.: Andrew Hood. *The Glorious Privilege*, op. cit., 122, says that *The Scotsman*'s 'Log' began in late 1939, and was originally suggested by Taylor.

24. Elsie Adam, 'the second woman to join the reporting staff' of *The Scotsman*, was asked in 1925 by Sir George Waters 'to introduce a Woman's Page . . . headed "Woman to date", [it] took a whole page, and appeared each Friday'. *The Glorious Privilege*, op. cit., 122. Miss Adam retired in 1954. Infm.: Mrs Dinah Stevenson.

25. Neil Fraser was succeeded as news editor of *The Scotsman* by Max McAuslane in 1957. Infm.: David Scrimgeour.

26. James Murray Watson (1888–1955), born Kirkcudbright; educ. George Watson's College and Edinburgh University; editorial assistant, Thos Nelson & Sons, Ltd (publishers), 1911; *Weekly Scotsman*, 1912; assistant editor, *Evening Dispatch*, 1912–16, chief assistant editor, *The Scotsman*, 1924–44, editor, 1944–55. *WWW, Vol. V, 1951–1960*, op. cit., 1141.

27. Sir J. Edmund R. Findlay (1902–1962), born Edinburgh; educ. Harrow and Oxford University; Cons. MP, Banffshire, 1935–45. *Scottish Biographies 1938*, op. cit., 239; *WWW, Vol. VI, 1961–1970*, op. cit., 375.

28. David John Colville, Lord Clydesmuir (1894–1954), born Lanarkshire; educ. Charterhouse School and Cambridge University; in Cameronians in WWI; director, David Colville & Sons Ltd; and of other steel and engineering companies; Unionist MP, North Midlothian, 1929–43, a government minister, 1931–40, Secretary of State for Scotland, 1938–40; army staff officer, 1940–2; Governor of Bombay, 1943–8. *Scottish Biographies 1938*, op. cit., 144; *WWW, Vol. V, 1951–1960*, op. cit., 219.

29. Hon. James Stuart (1897–1971), born Edinburgh, third son of Earl of Moray; educ. Eton Coll.; in Royal Scots, 1914–19, MC and bar; Unionist MP, Moray & Nairn, 1923–59; Joint PS to Treasury and government Chief Whip, 1941–5, Secretary of State for Scotland, 1951–7; Viscount Stuart of Findhorn from 1959. *Scottish Biographies 1938*, op. cit., 726; *WWW, Vol. VII, 1971–1980*, op. cit., 767.

30. Resulting from a police raid by more than 30 plain clothes detectives on the Kosmo dance club, Swinton Row, off Elder St, Edinburgh, the trial took place within closed doors at the Sheriff Court between 27 Nov. and 7 Dec. 1933 of the club's owner, Asher Barnard, and two of its managers, James Black and Edwin Jones, on charges of contravening the Immoral Traffic Act and the Criminal Law Amendment Act. Women employed at the club as dance instructresses were paid 50p per week plus one-third of their dance earnings. A system of 'booking out', which meant for 'immoral purposes', enabled men to take instructresses away from the club in cars or taxis, sometimes to where the women lived. The 'booking out' fee of £1.50 was shared between Barnard (who got £1) and the instructress (50p); the wages of Black and Jones were paid out of Barnard's £1 fee. The charges against the three accused were of living wholly or partly on the immoral earnings of the instructresses. The jury unanimously found Barnard guilty, and also Black and Jones of aiding and abetting in prostitution, but with a strong recommendation to mercy for the two latter. Black and Jones were each sentenced to three months' imprisonment, but appealed successfully; Barnard's appeal against an 18-month sentence failed. A detailed account of the police action in the case is given by William Merrilees, who took part in it, in his autobiography, *The Short Arm of the Law* (London, 1966), 83–106; *TS*, 2 Aug. 1933; *EN*, 1 Aug, 27 Nov.–7 Dec. 1933.

31. Frederick M. Johnston (1903–1973); educ. Daniel Stewart's College, Edinburgh; journalist, 1922, *Dumfries & Galloway Courier*; editor, 1927, *Evesham Standard*; with *The Scotsman*, 1931–5; from 1935, chairman, Johnston & Co. Ltd, Falkirk, group of weekly newspapers; president, 1950–2, Scottish Newspaper Proprietors' Association. *WWW, Vol. VII, 1971–1980*, op. cit., 417.

32. Arthur H.C. Hope (1896–1986), born Edinburgh; Lieut. Col., TA, WS, NP; educ. Edinburgh Academy, Rugby School, Edinburgh University; served 1914–19, Seaforth Highlanders, RFC and RAF, mentioned twice in dispatches, OC, 4/5 Bn, Royal Scots, from 1936; law agent to Edinburgh Royal Infirmary from 1926. *Scottish Biographies 1938*, op. cit., 355; infm.: Signet Library. J.A.D. Hope, Rt Hon. Lord Hope of Craighead (b.1938), advocate from 1965, Advocate Depute, 1978–82, Dean of the Faculty of Advocates, 1986–9, Senator of the College of Justice; Lord Justice General of Scotland and Lord President of the Court of Session, 1989–96; a life peer from 1995; a Lord of Appeal in Ordinary, 1996–2009, from 2009 Deputy President, Supreme Court of the UK. *WW, 2011*, 1109.

33. The Seaforth Highlanders, 1881–1961, originated in 1778–93 as the 72nd and 78th Highland regts. The Seaforths merged with the Cameron Highlanders in 1961 to form the Queen's Own Highlanders, which merged, 1994, with the Gordon Highlanders to form The Highlanders; in 2006 The Highlanders became 4th Bn, Royal Regt of Scotland. Trevor Royle, *Queen's Own Highlanders: A Concise History* (Edinburgh, 2007), 211–12.

34. The British and Allied (Australian and Indian) forces at Singapore, estimated at 85,000 – twice as many as their Japanese attackers – surrendered to the Japanese on Sunday 15 Feb. 1942. The capture of Singapore, regarded as the chief bastion of the British Empire in the Far East, was a massive victory for the Japanese and a disaster for Britain and its forces. See also above, p. 545, Ernie McIntyre, Note 19.

35. Field Marshal Earl Wavell (1883–1950), commissioned in Black Watch, 1901, served in Boer War, WWI, and Palestine and Trans-Jordan, 1937–8; C-in-C, Middle East, 1939–41, C-in-C, India, 1941–3, Supreme Commander, South-West Pacific, Jan.–Mar. 1942; Viceroy and Governor-General of India, 1943–7; author of several books. *WWW, Vol. IV, 1941–1950*, op. cit., 1213. Field Marshal Sir Claude Auchinleck (1884–1981); in army in India from 1903, in Middle East in WWI, in India, 1930s, in Norway, 1940; C-in-C, Middle East, 1941–2; C-in-C, India, 1941 and 1943–7; Field Marshal, 1946. *WWW, Vol. VIII, 1981–1990*, 28. VE (Victory in Europe) Day was 8 May 1945, VJ (Victory in Japan) Day was 15 Aug. 1945.

36. Earl Mountbatten of Burma (1900–1979), Supreme Allied Commander, South-East Asia, 1943–5; last Viceroy of India, 1947; First Sea Lord, 1955–9; assassinated, 1979, by an IRA bomb. *WWW, Vol. VII, 1971–1980,* op. cit., 565. On the establishment in Aug. 1947 (ten months earlier than previously envisaged) of India and Pakistan as independent states, a disastrous accompaniment was the murderous communal religious violence in the Punjab and Bengal among Hindus, Muslims and Sikhs, in which tens of thousands lost their lives.

37. Mohammed Ali Jinnah (1876–1948), Indian Muslim leader who from 1940 led their demand for a separate Muslim state, which at the partition of India in 1947 became Pakistan, and of which he was head of state until his death a year later. *WWW, Vol. IV, 1941–1950,* op. cit., 606.

38. David Terris, joined *The Scotsman,* 1912, from the *Evening Dispatch* as a junior reporter; became successively its political, industrial, and education correspondent, and was also for some years rugby correspondent; succeeded, 1946, J.W. Herries as chief reporter; chairman, Edinburgh & East of Scotland District, IoJ, and a Fellow of the IoJ. *TS,* 26 Oct. 1946.

39. *Highland News,* 1883–1963, cont. as *Highland News & Football Times* to 1969, then merged with *Forres News, North Star* and *Northern Chronicle* to form *Highland News & Northern Chronicle* until 1976, when it cont. as *Inverness & Highland News* to date. J.P.S. Ferguson, *Scottish Newspapers,* op. cit., 68; Mackenzie, *NEWSPLAN Scotland,* op. cit., 238. *Inverness Courier,* 1817 to date. The Battle of the Braes, eight miles south of Portree, Skye, took place on 19 Apr. 1882, between police sent from Glasgow to arrest several Braes crofters who, with the support of others and their womenfolk, had prevented their eviction by a sheriff officer on 7 Apr. The issue concerned disputed grazing rights on the adjoining Ben Lee, which, once a common pasture, had been taken from the crofters in 1865 and let to a sheep farmer by the factor of the landowner, Lord Macdonald, but with the promise the rights would be restored to them on the expiry of the farmer's lease in 1882. The crofters' refusal to pay their rents until the grazing rights were returned to them had led to the eviction order against several of them. The crofters arrested by the police were found guilty on 11 May at Inverness Sheriff Court, but given relatively light sentences. The Battle of the Braes proved one of the first encounters in the Crofters' War that decade, arising from the acute agrarian depression in the Highlands, reduced incomes from fishing, the example of Irish peasant land agitation, and the Irish Land Act, 1881. Among results of the Battle of the Braes were other cases of resistance by crofters, the formation in 1883 of the Highland Land Law Reform Association and of the Napier Royal Commission of inquiry into the condition of the crofters and cottars. In 1887 the Commission reduced the rents paid by the Braes crofters by almost half, cancelled almost all their arrears of payment, and decided the issue of Ben Lee in their favour. I.M.M. MacPhail, *The Crofters' War* (Stornoway, 1989), 36–52; James Hunter, *The Making of the Crofting Community* (Edinburgh, 1995 edn), 133–7, 143–5; Derick S. Thomson (ed.), *The Companion to Gaelic Scotland* (Glasgow, 1987), 237.

40. Evan Macleod Barron (1879–1965), born Inverness; educ. Inverness Royal Academy and Edinburgh University (editor, 1902–3, *The Student*); a solicitor in Inverness, 1903–11; succeeded, 1919, his father as proprietor and editor, *Inverness Courier;* Chief, Inverness Gaelic Society, 1935; author of several books, e.g. *The Scottish War of Independence* (London, 1914; 2nd edn Inverness, 1934) *Scottish Biographies 1938,* op. cit., 45; WWW, Vol. VI, 1961–1970, op. cit., 61.

41. See also Note 39 above. The Dingwall paper was the *North Star* (1893–1969), the *Forres News & Advertiser* dated from 1905, the *Caithness Courier* (Thurso), 1866 to date. These three papers were acquired by Scotsman Publications Ltd in 1957, and the *Northern Chronicle* (Inverness) and *John o' Groat Journal* (Wick) were added to its Highlands News Group soon afterward. Mackenzie, *NEWSPLAN Scotland,* op. cit., 86, 187, 303; *The Glorious Privilege,* op. cit., 173.

42. Sandy MacRae, BEM, CBE, proprietor, *North Star*, managing director, Highland News Group; Provost of Dingwall, 1947–64 and 1970–4; died 1988, aged 84. *Ross-shire Journal*, 19 Aug. 1988.

43. In addition to those Billy Munro names, William Watson is said on the page facing the title page of the book to have been one of the members of staff who contributed to it. Magnus Magnusson (1929–2007), son of the Icelandic consul for Scotland; educ. Edinburgh Academy and Oxford University; journalist, broadcaster, scholar, author; assistant editor, *Scottish Daily Express* and *The Scotsman*; Rector, 1975–8, Edinburgh University; awarded several hon. degrees. *WW, 2005*, 1455–6. Robert Warren as Robert Conisborough also compiled crosswords for *The Scotsman*. Matthew J. Moulton (1911–1991), a leader writer, feature writer and reviewer for the paper for many years, retired 1978; died as a result of a walking or climbing accident in Lochaber. Infm.: Christopher Reekie. William Watson was features editor, *TS*, for several years.

44. W. & A.K. Johnston Ltd, est. 1825, became, 1953–4, Johnston & G.W. Bacon, taken over, 1968–9, by Morrison & Gibb, which dissolved, 1982. Books by R.W. (Billy) Munro are: *Kinsmen and Clansmen* (Edinburgh, 1971), *Johnston's Gazetteer of Scotland* (Edinburgh, 1973 edn), *Highland Clans and Tartans* (London, 1977), *Scottish Lighthouses* (Stornoway, 1979). His books jointly with his wife Dr Jean Dunlop are: *Tain through the Centuries* (Tain, 1966), *The Scrimgeours* (Edinburgh, 1980), and (eds) *The Acts of the Lords of the Isles, 1336–1493* (Edinburgh, 1986). Dr Jean Dunlop's books are: *The Clan Chisholm* (Edinburgh, 1953), *The Clan Gordon* (Edinburgh, 1955), *The Scotts* (Edinburgh, 1957), *The Clan Mackintosh* (Edinburgh, 1960), *The Clan Mackenzie* (Edinburgh, 1963), *The British Fisheries Society* (Edinburgh, 1978).

Tom McGowran, pp. 142–63.

1. Tom McGowran, *Newhaven-on-Forth: Port of Grace* (Edinburgh, 1994 edn).

2. Bruce Peebles & Co. Ltd, 1866–1999, manufacturers of electrical (and, from 1960s, electronic) equipment, merged 1969 with Peyrolle-Parsons, later retitled Parsons Peebles Ltd, then NEI (Northern Engineering Industries) Peebles.

3. *The Water Babies* (1863), a story for children, by Charles Kingsley (1819–1875), novelist and historian. *Don Quixote de la Mancha* (1605), by Miguel de Cervantes Saavendra (1547–1616), Spanish novelist, poet and playwright. Nathaniel Hawthorne (1804–1864), American novelist, author of many works, including *Tanglewood Tales for Boys and Girls* (1853).

4. Robert H. Leishman, born Edinburgh; educ. Boroughmuir Senior Secondary School and Heriot Watt Coll.; joined *Evening Dispatch* as a reporter, 1911, successively to 1963 chief reporter, news editor, deputy editor; responsible for organising training of young journalists on the paper; in WWI served with Lothian & Border Horse and Cameron Highlanders, commissioned in Royal Scots; life member, Edinburgh branch, NUJ; died 1977, aged 81. *ED*, 30 Jan. 1963; *EN*, 27 May 1977; *TJ*, Jul. 1977.

5. The Creed was a form of teleprinter.

6. Lorna Rhind (1914–2006); educ. James Gillespie's High School for Girls, Edinburgh; worked successively for *Evening Dispatch* from 1930s, then, 1950–2, as infm. officer, St Andrews House, 1952–60, as reporter then deputy chief reporter, Edinburgh office, *Glasgow Herald*, 1960–74, as publicity/press officer, Edinburgh Corporation, and, 1974–6, as PRO, Edinburgh District Council; first woman chair, 1945, and first woman life member, Edinburgh branch, NUJ, which she joined in 1938. Infm.: Bill Rae; *TJ*, Apr. 1968; Jan. 1977; *GH*, 1 May 1970. Neville Garden (1936–2002), born Edinburgh; educ. George Watson's College; 1953–63, successively reporter, sub-editor, feature writer, *Evening Dispatch*; 1963–4, columnist and music critic, *Evening News*; 1964–78, *Scottish Daily Express*; 1978–93, broadcaster, BBC Scotland Radio and TV, then returned to journalism; author of *Good Music Guide* (London, 1989); killed in a car accident. *TS*, 25 Sep. 2002.

Pat Garrow later became a PRO for RAF, Leuchars, Fife. Infm.: Walter Gunn.

7. Thomas B. MacLachlan (1865–1952), educ. George Watson's College and Edinburgh University; successively reporter, sub-editor, then, 1909–43, editor, *Evening Dispatch* (editor, dates uncertain, *Weekly Scotsman*); author of several novels and biographies. *Scottish Biographies 1938*, op. cit., 495; *WWW, Vol. V, 1951–1960*, op. cit., 711. Some 18 letters were published in the *Evening Dispatch*, 13–20 Feb. 1936, from readers about blue tits (some other feathered birds were mentioned, too). Of the 18, two written by 'Bird Lover' and one each by four other readers, seem fairly obvious leg-pulls, full of double entendres.

8. Edinburgh Trades Council (est. c.1853) consisted of delegates from affiliated local branches of trade unions, from whom its Executive Committee and office-bearers were elected. The Council was affiliated to the STUC, whose General Council always included one elected representative from its affiliated trades councils. In Dec. 1936, the Trades Council carried by a large majority a recommendation from its Executive that 'the Press . . . criticised for some of its reports of Trades Council meetings', should continue to be allowed to attend them. *ED*, 30 Dec. 1936.

9. See above, p. 558, R.W. (Billy) Munro, Note 31.

10. William C. Murray was editor, 1935–40; his father, George Murray, had been editor, 1890–1910. Infm.: *Falkirk Herald*.

11. In the mistaken belief the battleship HMS *Hood* was at Rosyth in the Firth of Forth (in fact it was HMS *Repulse*), German Junkers JU 88 bombers made their first attack in WWII on the British mainland there on 16 Oct. 1939. Their bombs hit the cruisers HMS *Edinburgh* and *Southampton*, causing some damage to the latter and wounding a dozen seamen, and killed 16 on the destroyer HMS *Mohawk* nearby. Two of the German planes were shot down by Spitfires. Les Taylor, *Luftwaffe over Scotland* (Dunbeath, Caithness, 2010), 7–9. H.G. Wells (1866–1946), prolific author, including of *The Shape of Things to Come* (London, 1933). The title of the 1936 Alexander Korda (1893–1956) science fiction film based on Wells's novel was shortened to *Things to Come*.

12. George Drever's account of his experiences before, during and after his service with the International Brigades in Spain is in I. MacDougall, *Voices from the Spanish Civil War* (Edinburgh, 1986), 277–87. News items about George Drever appeared in the *Evening Dispatch*, 1 and 8 Apr. and 1 Jul. 1938.

13. *Daily Worker*, newspaper, 1930–66, of the Communist Party of Great Britain, then changed its title to *Morning Star*, to date. Within three weeks of the outbreak of the military and right-wing rebellion in Spain in Jul. 1936, the formation of special military units to support the Republic was considered by the Spanish Communist Party. The idea was taken up by the Executive of the Communist (or Third) International (1919–43) and approved by Stalin. Formation of the International Brigades was formally authorised by the Spanish Republican government in Oct. By then the earliest foreign volunteers to arrive in Spain had already formed units such as those named after Tom Mann (1856–1941), the veteran British trade union and Communist Party leader, and Ernst Thaelmann (1886–1944), German Communist Party leader, later murdered by the Nazis. During the Spanish Civil War six or seven International Brigades, about 50,000 men altogether, were formed on the basis of language spoken. The British Bn was part of the XVth Brigade.

14. The admiral was Rear-Admiral William Beveridge Mackenzie of Caldarvan, Dunbartonshire, his son David, aged 20, educ. Marlborough College (he had joined the Young Communist League then or soon afterward) and University of Oxford, before becoming an Edinburgh University medical student, was one of the first Scottish volunteers to arrive in Spain, in Sep. 1936, in support of the Republic. He had been reported killed on 25 Nov. in the fighting at Madrid, a memorial service was held for him at Alexandria, Dunbartonshire, and a group of Edinburgh University medical students formed themselves into an ambulance unit for Spain titled the David

Mackenzie Memorial Ambulance. Early in Dec., however, it was reported that David Mackenzie was alive and well, and he spoke at a meeting at Coatbridge on 6 Jan. 1937. Nine reports about, and one photograph of, David Mackenzie appeared in the *Evening Dispatch*, 1 Dec. 1936–9 Jan. 1937.

15. *Mit Hitler Nieder* – Down With Hitler. There is no reason to doubt the reliability of Tom McGowran's memory of this, but a search of the *Evening Dispatch* for 1934–8 has not so far found a report of the German cruise ship at Leith. Between 27 Jul. and 1 Aug. 1938 the *Dispatch* carried three reports and five photographs (one of them of an anti-Fascist speaker from the Communist Party) of a visit to Leith by the German sailing training ship *Horst Wessel*, which attracted 50,000 visitors there; but it seems unlikely this was the vessel he refers to.

16. J.C. Park, Communist Party secretary in Edinburgh. MacDougall, *Voices from the Spanish Civil War*, op. cit., 34.

17. The Japanese attacked Pearl Harbor, Hawaii, 7 Dec. 1941, and made their first landings on the east coast of Malaya, some 400 to 550 miles north of Singapore, on 8 Dec.

18. Buffaloes, obsolete or obsolescent American planes disposed of by the US navy, were designed to fly from aircraft carriers. Early in Feb. 1941 some 266 RAF Hurricane fighters were ordered to the Far East, but only 99 of them arrived, and not all of them went into action, before the fall of Singapore. Brian P. Farrell, *The Defence and Fall of Singapore 1940–1942* (Stroud, 2003), 330–1.

19. See above, Ernie McIntyre, p. 545, Note 19.

20. Johore: the southern part of the Malayan (now Malaysian) Peninsula, immediately north of Singapore island.

21. *Straits Times*, Singapore daily paper, 1845 to date. Since 1931, when its troops had seized all of Manchuria, Japan had been increasingly encroaching on north-east China. In Jul. 1937 a major Sino-Japanese war began that by 1941 resulted in the Japanese overrunning still more of north-east China, including Pekin (Beijing), Shanghai and Nanking, and parts also of China's south-east coast. But the vast area of China, its huge population, and the resistance by both the Chinese Nationalist government forces and, in two provinces, the Communist guerrilla army, made it seem unlikely that, as Tom McGowran and others believed, the Japanese could win outright victory in China, still less decide to widen the war by attacking in Dec. 1941 the USA at Pearl Harbor and then the south-east Asian colonies of the West European states Britain, France, and the Netherlands. In fact, events in China, 1931–7, had arguably marked the beginning of WWII.

22. Raffles Hotel was named after Sir Stamford Raffles (1781–1826), British East India administrator, and founder, 1819, of Singapore. Magnusson, *Chambers Biographical Dictionary*, op. cit., 1210. Sir Shenton Thomas (1879–1962), was Governor of the Straits Settlements and High Commissioner for the Malay States from 1934; interned by the Japanese, Feb. 1942–Aug. 1945, *WWW, Vol. VI, 1961–1970*, op. cit., 1113.

23. Richard Gough, *The Escape from Singapore* (London, 1987), Appx I, 194–239, lists more than 150 mainly small vessels that left Singapore with civilians and servicemen during its fall, and the known fate of these vessels.

24. Lieut.-General Arthur Percival (1887–1966), GOC, Malaya; 1941–2; a PoW, 1942–5; author of *The War in Malaya* (1949). *WWW, Vol. VI, 1961–1970*, op. cit., 886.

25. Farrell, *Defence and Fall of Singapore*, op. cit., 418, puts the number of British, Australian, Indian, and other British Empire forces taken prisoner or missing at Singapore at more than 120,000.

26. Greta Garbo (1905–1990), born Stockholm, a leading Hollywood film actress, 1925–41.

27. *The Bridge on the River Kwai* (1957), a British film based on the novel by Pierre Boulle and directed by David Lean, with Alec Guinness, William Holden, and Jack Hawkins.

28. Korea, though with its own dynasty, had long been a tributary state of China. But Japan, after its successful war of 1894–5 against China and of 1904–5 against Russia, had annexed Korea in 1910.

29. Camp Kanchanaburi, about 60 miles slightly north-west of Bangkok, was near the bridge over the river Kwai. Huntley & Palmer – a firm of biscuit makers. The Kempetai, or Kempei Tai, were no less fiendish and murderous than the Gestapo. Eric Lomax (b.1919), born Edinburgh; developed as a boy a profound interest in railways, worked as a Post Office clerk and telegraphist, volunteered into the Royal Signals in 1939, arrived as an officer in Singapore in Oct. 1941, and at the surrender to the Japanese in Feb. 1942 was stationed like Tom McGowran in Fort Canning. In Oct. 1942, like so many thousands of other prisoners from Singapore, Eric Lomax was sent to work on building the Siam–Burma railway, and became actively involved in the prisoners' secret radio work. His account of his captivity is given in his book *The Railway Man* (London, 1995).
30. Kanburi was a shortened form of Kanchanaburi.
31. The original diary kept by Alex Young is now preserved in the Imperial War Museum, London. But copies and a microfilm of the diary, which covers the period from 25 Jul. 1941 to 12 Nov. 1945, are preserved in the Mitchell Library, Glasgow.
32. Of the 2,500, 2,000 were Australians, 500 British. Martin Gilbert, *Second World War* (London, 2000 edn), 635.
33. The first atomic bomb was dropped on Hiroshima, the second on Nagasaki. Emperor Hirohito did not inform (by radio) the Japanese people of the unconditional surrender of Japan until the day after the 14th, which became Victory in Japan Day and the end of WWII.
34. The total number of prisoners of war from several nationalities who died building the Siam–Burma railway has been estimated at 15,000. Gilbert, *Second World War*, op. cit., 345.
35. Tom McGowran was secretary, Scottish Far East Prisoners of War Association. *TS*, 3 Jul. 1995.
36. *Hamilton Advertiser*, 1837 to date.
37. Carron Iron Works, 1759–1982.

R.J. (Bob) Brown, pp. 164–215

1. William Arrol & Co., engineers; built the Tay Bridge and Forth Bridge; Sir William Arrol (1839–1913) was Liberal Unionist MP, South Ayrshire, 1895–1906.
2. The submarine (in fact K13, not K37), built by Fairfield, Glasgow, and launched 11 Nov. 1916, sank during its trials in the Gare Loch on 29 Jan. 1917, with its crew of 53 officers and men, plus 14 directors and employees of Fairfield, 15 other civilians, and two RN officers as observers. All the men in the flooded stern section of the sub died, and one RN officer was killed while attempting to escape. But after almost two and a half days of rescue attempts, 47 men, including the sub's commander, were saved. Raised to the surface on 15 Mar. 1917, K13 was refitted and returned to service as K22. Submarine Association, Barrow-in-Furness branch, www.rnsubs.co.uk; Colledge, *Ships of the Royal Navy*, op. cit., 176.
3. Stewart & Lloyds, leading tube manufacturers in Scotland, founded, 1860, in Glasgow by Andrew Stewart, amalgamated, 1903, with Lloyd & Lloyd, Birmingham, to form Stewart & Lloyds. J. Cunnison and J.B.S. Gilfillan (eds), *The Third Statistical Account of Scotland: Glasgow* (Glasgow, 1958), 166–7.
4. John Brown & Co. Ltd, Clydebank, 1899–1968, built some 400 merchant ships, liners, and warships, including the *Queen Mary* (1934), *Queen Elizabeth* (1940), and *Queen Elizabeth II* (1969). Brown became part of Upper Clyde Shipbuilders, 1968–71, then was taken over first by a US then a French company. Fisher, *Glasgow Encyclopedia*, op. cit., 345–6.
5. *Cork Examiner*, founded 1841, retitled, 1996, *The Examiner*, then, 2006, *Irish Examiner*, to date. *Forward* (published to 1956 in Glasgow, then London), 1906–60.

6. James H. Aitken (1890–1955); born Dundee; educ. Harris Academy, Dundee; Glasgow correspondent, *The Times*, from 1914; in Cameronians in WWI; president, NUJ, 1933–4, and of Glasgow Press Club, 1928–35. *Scottish Biographies 1938*, op. cit., 10; *WWW, Vol. V, 1951–1960*, op. cit., 11.
7. Libby – an American tinned food company est. 1869, acquired by Nestlé, 1971, and since then by Seneca Foods Corp.
8. Neil Carmichael (1921–2001), born Glasgow; educ. Eastbank School and Glasgow Royal College of Science and Technology; a gas engineer; conscientious objector; Lab. MP, Glasgow Woodside, 1962–74, Glasgow Kelvingrove, 1974–83; PPS, Under-Secretary, and PS, several govt depts, 1966–76; life peer, 1983. Obit. by Janey Buchan, *TS*, 25 Jul. 2001. James Carmichael (1894–1966), Glasgow ILP town councillor, 1929–47; ILP MP, Glasgow Bridgeton, 1946–7, Lab, 1947–61. *WWW, Vol. VI, 1961–1970*, 181. James Maxton (1885–1946); conscientious objector in WWI; ILP MP, Glasgow Bridgeton, 1922–46; chairman, ILP, 1926–31, 1934–9. Clifford Hanley (1922–1999), born Glasgow; journalist, novelist, songwriter, broadcaster, speaker; began as court and crime reporter in a Glasgow news agency, then worked for Kemsley Newspapers, Glasgow, and briefly for Scottish *TV Guide*; his first book, *Dancing in the Streets* (London, 1958), enabled him to become a full-time writer; writer in residence, 1979–80, York University, Toronto. *TH*, 10 May 1999; *TS*, 11 May 1999.
9. *Eastern Standard*, 1923–61; *Airdrie and Coatbridge Advertiser*, 1868 to date; *Motherwell Times*, 1883 to date; *Rutherglen Reformer*, 1875 to date.
10. *Ayr Advertiser*, 1803 to date. George Goodfellow began, 1903, as office boy *Ayr Advertiser*, editor, 1938–53; director, T.M. Gemmell & Son Ltd, the proprietors. Rob Close, 'Two Hundred Years of the *Ayr Advertiser*', *Ayrshire Notes*, Winter 2003, 22–3.
11. *Poems, Chiefly in the Scottish Dialect*, by Robert Burns (1759–1796), were first printed and published in Jul. 1786 at Kilmarnock, and immediately established his reputation as a great poet.
12. Col. Sir Charles Dunlop (1878–1960), proprietor, *Ayr Advertiser*, 1900–38, when it became a limited company; officer, Ayrshire Yeomanry, at Gallipoli, Palestine and France in WWI, commanded the regt, 1928–31, and the Ayrshire Home Guard in WWII; treasurer, 1934–60, Western Meeting Club, Steward at Ayr, Bogside and Perth race-courses; knighted, 1955. *Ayr Advertiser*, 18 Aug. 1960.
13. *Ayr Observer*, 1832–1930, merged into *Ayr Advertiser*.
14. *Ayrshire Post*, 1880 to date.
15. Green Howards, a Yorkshire infantry regt formed 1688, and so called because it wore in its early years the green livery of the local Howard landowning family; from 1782, the 19th of Foot.
16. The lookalike was M.E. Clifton Jones, an actor, who had served in the army in WWI, volunteered in 1939, was commissioned in the Pay Corps, and became author of *I Was Monty's Double* (London, 1954).
17. *Cumnock Chronicle*, 1901 to date.
18. *The Times*, London, 1785 to date. *Daily Telegraph*, London, 1855 to date.
19. James Boswell Talbot, 6th Lord Talbot de Malahide (1874–1948), great-great grandson of James Boswell (1740–1795), biographer of Samuel Johnson, had inherited a large number of Boswell's papers that were rediscovered at Malahide Castle, County Dublin, in the 1920s and sold to an American collector. Their publication in 18 vols. led to a revival of interest in Boswell and his writings, and to the discovery of further Boswell papers and to further publication. Alexander Boswell (1707–1782), father of James, was laird of Auchinleck, Ayrshire; an advocate, 1729, a judge as Lord Auchinleck from 1754. Robert MacQueen, Lord Braxfield (1722–1799), an advocate, a Lord of Session from 1776, Lord Justice Clerk from 1788, sentenced to transportation Thomas Muir and other 'political martyrs' in 1793–4, and was the model for Robert Louis Stevenson's Lord Hermiston in his novel *Weir of Hermiston* (1896). *ED*, 6 Apr. 1937;

The Times, 25 Aug. 1948; Trevor Royle, *The Mainstream Companion to Scottish Literature* (Edinburgh, 1993), 36–8, 212.

20. John Ferguson Macnair began as a junior reporter, *Clydebank & Renfrew Press*, moved to *Aberdeen Free Press*; seriously wounded in WWI; reported from Press Gallery, House of Commons till 1920; reporter, 1920–5, *Glasgow Herald*; editor, 1925–58, and director, 1950–8, *Ayrshire Post. Ayrshire Post*, 1 Aug. 1958.

21. James Brown (1862–1939), began work aged 12 in Ayrshire pits; president, 1895, Ayrshire Miners' Federal Union, a full-time official from 1904, secretary, 1908–18; secretary, 1917–36, National Union of Scottish Mine Workers; originally a Lib., he joined the ILP c.1899, Lab. MP, South Ayrshire, 1918–31, 1935–39; Lord High Commissioner, Church of Scotland, 1924 and 1929–31. James Ramsay MacDonald (1866–1937), born Lossiemouth; Lab. Prime Minister, 1924 and 1929–31, and Prime Minister, 'National' govt, 1931–5. Alexander Sloan (1879–1945), began work aged 12 in an Ayrshire ironstone mine; secretary, Ayrshire Miners' Union, and, 1936–40, National Union of Scottish Mine Workers; an Ayrshire county councillor from 1919; Lab. MP, South Ayrshire, 1939–45. W. Knox, *Scottish Labour Leaders 1918–1939* (Edinburgh, 1984), 252–3. Emrys Hughes (1894–1969); educ. Abercynon Council School, Mountain Ash Secondary, and City of Leeds Training College; teacher, journalist; editor, *Forward*, 1931–46; author of many books and pamphlets; pacifist; Lab. MP, South Ayrshire, 1946–69. *WWW, Vol. VI, 1961–1970*, op. cit., 562. James Keir Hardie (1856–1915); from age 10 to 23 a Lanarkshire and Ayrshire miner; journalist; secretary, 1879–81, Hamilton Miners' Union, 1886–91, Ayrshire Miners' Union, 1886–7, Scottish Miners' National Federation; a founder and leader, 1888, Scottish Lab. Party, 1893, ILP, 1900, Lab. Party; Lab. MP, West Ham, 1892–5, Merthyr Tydfil, 1900–15. Nan Hardie m. Emrys Hughes, 1924; Cumnock town councillor, 1933, Provost, 1935–8. Lieut. Col. Sir Thomas Moore (1886–1971), knighted 1937, bart., 1956; in army, 1908–25, in Ireland, 1916–18 and 1920–3, in Russia, 1918–20; Unionist MP, Ayr Burghs, 1925–50, Ayr, 1950–64. *WWW, Vol. VII, 1971–1980*, op. cit., 555.

22. George S. Lindgren (1900–1971); railway clerk and trade unionist; Hertfordshire county councillor, 1931–49; Lab. MP, Wellingborough, 1945–59; PS, Ministry of Civil Aviation, 1946–50, and PS of five other govt depts, 1945–51, 1964–70; a life peer from 1961. *WWW, Vol. VII, 1971–1980*, op. cit., 470.

23. *The Observer*, 1791 to date.

24. An imperfect series of *Prompter*, 1943–57, is preserved in the Mitchell Library, Glasgow, and another run, 1943–53, in the National Library of Scotland.

25. John MacCormick (1904–1961); first chairman, 1928, and Hon. National Secretary, Scottish National Party, 1928–42; founder and chairman, Scottish Convention, 1942; chairman, Scottish Covenant Association, 1949–61; Glasgow University: Rector, 1950–3, hon. LL D, 1951; unsuccessful Parl. candidate six times, 1931–59; author of two books, including *The Flag in the Wind* (1955). *WWW, Vol. VI, 1961–1970*, op. cit., 708.

26. Bilbao, largest city in the Basque country and a major Spanish port and centre of industry, fell, 19 Jun. 1937, to General Franco's forces and their Italian Fascist allies.

27. The Amalgamated Society of Engineers, est. 1851, retitled, 1920, Amalgamated Engineering Union, then, after amalgamations in 1968 with foundry unions, to Amalgamated Union of Engineering Workers. After further amalgamations the union is now titled Unite. John Wheatley (1869–1930); born in Ireland; from age 13 worked for more than a decade as a miner; est. 1906 Hoxton & Walsh, printers and publishers; active in United Irish League, then joined ILP and est., 1906, the Catholic Socialist Society (the 'riot' Bob Brown mentions was in 1912); Lanarkshire Lab. county councillor, 1910–12, Glasgow town councillor, 1912–22; opposed WWI; Lab. MP, Glasgow Shettleston, 1922–30; Minister of Health, 1924; author of many pamphlets on labour and socialism. Knox, *Scottish Labour Leaders*, op. cit., 274–82. Willie Regan, born1884; secretary, and a founder member with John Wheatley of the Catholic Socialist Society,

1906; as a conscientious objector in WWI dismissed from his job as a Post Office telegraphist; Rutherglen town councillor, 1910–20; organiser, Glasgow ILP, 1919–20; secretary, Hoxton & Walsh Ltd, 1930; managing editor, Glasgow *Eastern Standard* (1923–60*)* and *Western Leader* (1930–40). Harry McShane and Joan Smith, *No Mean Fighter* (London, 1978), 17, 28, 80; *Scottish Biographies 1938*, op. cit., 631; Iain Mclean, *The Legend of Red Clydeside* (Edinburgh, 1983), 156. About Liam Regan no further information has so far been found.

28. *Socialism in Our Time* was the title of the policy statement adopted by the ILP annual conference, Apr. 1921. Ian S. Wood, *John Wheatley* (Manchester, 1990), 161.

29. Allan Hewitson (1910–1974); reporter, 1927–36, *Ayrshire Post*, 1936–8, *Bolton Evening News*, 1938–61, Ayr office, *Daily Record* and Glasgow *Evening News*; 1941–6, in RN; Lab. town councillor, Ayr, 1946–61; chief reporter, briefly of *North West Evening Mail*, Barrow-in-Furness, then, until his death, of *Ayrshire Post*; a founder, Ayr branch, NUJ. *Ayrshire Post*, 27 Sep. and 8 Nov. 1946, 11 Aug. 1961; *TJ*, Apr. 1974.

30. H. Lester Hutchinson, a left-wing journalist; one of the 32 'conspirators', mainly trade union and labour leaders, arrested and tried at Meerut, 1929–33, for conspiracy to overthrow British rule in India, and sentenced to savage punishments, including transportation, that aroused memories of the Tolpuddle Martyrs, 1834, and widespread protests. Hutchinson was sentenced to four years' 'rigorous imprisonment', but on appeal was soon afterward acquitted and released. Lab. MP, 1945–50, Manchester Rusholme; joined the Labour Independent Group, 1949; bottom of the poll at Walthamstow West, 1950. *Report, 29th Annual Conference, Labour Party, 1929*, 190–4, and *Report, 33rd Annual Conference, 1934*, 19; Craig, *British Parliamentary Election Results, 1918–49*, op. cit., 193; F.W.S. Craig, *British Parliamentary Election Results, 1950–70* (Chichester, 1971), 300. Clement R. Attlee (1883–1967), Earl, 1955; educ. Haileybury College and Oxford University; barrister, lecturer; major in WWI; first Lab. mayor, Stepney, 1919–20, Lab. MP, Limehurst, 1922–50, Walthamstow West, 1950–55; PPS to Ramsay MacDonald, 1922–4, held junior and senior govt office, 1924, 1930–1; Leader, Lab. Party, 1935–55; minister, 1940–3, Deputy Prime Minister, 1942–5, Prime Minister, 1945–51; author of several books: his autobiography, *As It Happened* (London, 1954). *WWW, Vol. VI, 1961–1970*, op. cit., 39.

31. *Guardian*, 1821 to date (est. as *Manchester Guardian*, dropped '*Manchester*' 1959). The 13 'wasted years' was Lab.'s description for the period of Cons. govt, 1951–64. Lab's majority in the Oct. 1964 Parl. Election was only four over the combined Conservatives (304) and Liberals (9). Lab. was returned in the Mar. 1966 election with an overall majority of 98.

32. David Scrimgeour (see below, p. 591, Note 12) recalls that for some time from 1958, when he also became a *Daily Telegraph* correspondent in Scotland, he worked jointly with Frank Gillespie, who was based in Glasgow.

33. William Ernie Cockburn (1903–1957) had begun as a reporter, 1943, with the *Manchester Guardian*. Infm.: *Guardian* Archives. Robert M. Dobson (1914–1961), began as a junior reporter on a Torquay local paper, then sub-editor, to 1937, *Morning Post*; leader writer, *Daily Herald;* in WWII, news section, Air Ministry; *The Times*: 1943–7, Parl. reporter and lobby correspondent, 1947–53, assistant Home News editor, 1953–61, Home News editor. *The Times*, 5 Jan. 1961.

34. Sir William Haley (1901–1987), began, 1922, on Manchester *Evening News*, chief sub-editor, 1925, managing editor, 1930; director, 1930, Manchester Guardian & Evening News Ltd, joint managing director, 1939–43; director, Press Association and Reuters, 1939–43; BBC: editor-in-chief, 1943–4, Director General, 1944–52; editor, *The Times*, 1952–66, Director and Chief Executive, *The Times* Publishing Co. Ltd, 1965–6, chairman, *Times* Newspapers Ltd, 1967. *WWW, Vol. VIII, 1981–1990*, op. cit., 319.

35. Iverach McDonald (1908–2006), born Caithness; educ. Leeds Grammar School; began work on Yorkshire local weekly papers; assistant editor, *Yorkshire Post*, *The Times*,

1935–73, successively a sub-editor, diplomatic correspondent, Assistant Editor, 1948–52, Foreign Editor, 1952–65, Managing Editor, 1965–7, Associate Editor; 1967–73; author of *A Man of The Times* (1976), and *The History of the Times*, Vol. V (1984). *The Times*, 18 Dec. 2006. Sir Edwin Landseer (1802–1873), painter and sculptor, especially of animals, e.g. his painting of a Highland stag, *The Monarch of the Glen*.

36. John Hennessy (1918–2009), born London; began work with a firm of stockbrokers; in army in WWII; 1948, sports sub-editor, *The Times*, 1954–79, sports editor, then golf correspondent; author of a book (1983) about the ice-skaters Torvill and Dean. *The Times*, 7 Oct. 2009. Roy Hodson moved, 1968, from *The Times* to the *Financial Times*. News International Newspapers Ltd, Infm. Services. Frank Roberts (1909–1979), began as a reporter, 1928 (with diploma in journalism from London University) on Wolverhampton *Express & Star*; 1935–40, *Birmingham Post*; in RAF in WWII; 1947–72, with *The Times*, successively Parl. staff then, 1948–68, Home News room, for many years as Deputy News Editor, then 1965–8, News Editor, 1968–72, local govt correspondent; later worked in obituary dept. *The Times*, 21 Nov. 1979.

37. Jeffrey Preece (1927–1994), began aged 18 on *Tamworth Herald*, moved to *Birmingham Post*, then to *Birmingham Evening Mail*, then became *The Times* Midlands correspondent; 1960–70, was BBC Midlands industrial and political correspondent; 1970–92, was in public relations, latterly as Director, Information Services, British Nuclear Fuels. *TJ*, Sep. 1969; *The Times*, 1 Aug 1994. Francis Mathew (1907–1965), worked in printing for years, joined *The Times*, 1948, manager, 1949–65. *The Times*, 30 Mar. 1965.

38. James Holburn (1900–1988); grad Glasgow University MA (Hons); sub-editor, leader writer, *Glasgow Herald*, 1921–34; *The Times*, 1934–55: foreign or diplomatic correspondent successively in Berlin, Moscow, Ankara, New Delhi, United Nations, Middle East; war correspondent, Middle East, 1941–2; editor, *Glasgow Herald*, 1955–65. *WWW*, *Vol. VIII, 1981–1990*, op. cit., 359; *The Times*, 17 Sep. 1954.

39. The doo man has not been further identified. The Gangrel, Harold Stewart, 'a brilliant man . . . of scholarly wit and spirit. He invented fictional characters ranged in their adventures over the whole scene of satire and political ineffectuality.' William 'Elky' Clark (1898–1956), born Glasgow; in the 1920s, Scottish, British, and European flyweight champion, and unsuccessful contender for the world flyweight title, when permanent blinding in one eye forced his retirement from boxing; boxing correspondent of the *Daily Record* for many years. Dunnett, *Among Friends*, op. cit., 115–16.

40. Bob Brown's report in *The Times*, 22 Sep. 1955, on the annexation of Rockall, 250 miles west of the Hebrides, by a landing party from HMS *Vidal* ran to three-quarters of a column on page 8. An Admiralty statement said the annexation was necessary as it was within the sector of the sea likely to come within the orbit of the projected guided missiles range on the Hebrides; and a Ministry of Defence statement said that Rockall (on which from 1810 several previous brief landings had been made) belonged to no nation and had been formally annexed by the Crown 'to eliminate the possibility of embarrassing counter-claims' once the guided missile project had begun. It seems 'the embarrassing claims' to Rockall, said to be potentially rich in oil and gas resources as well as in fishing, might have come from Iceland, Ireland and Denmark. *TS*, 22 Sep. 1955. Basil Gingell worked on several newspapers in England before joining the Exchange Telegraph News Agency in 1941 as a war correspondent and, post-war, was the Agency's chief correspondent for southern Europe; with *The Times*, 1957–72, as general reporter and naval correspondent and later also religious affairs correspondent; one of two British correspondents drawn by lot to witness the execution of 10 leading Nazi war criminals convicted at Nuremberg; died 1979, aged 70. *The Times*, 17 Feb. 1979.

41. The Suez Crisis, Jul.–Dec. 1956, begun by the nationalisation by Egypt of the Suez Canal, was a turning point in twentieth-century history, aroused enormous controversy in Britain, was marked by secret agreements by the British, French and Israeli govts

to invade Egypt, the deliberate failure to inform the US govt, the insistence of the latter and the Soviet govt that Anglo-French troops landed in Egypt cease action, the resignation of the British prime minister Eden, and also was generally regarded as a factor that facilitated the Soviet decision to intervene on 4 Nov. in Hungary to suppress the uprising there.

42. Jeannie Robertson (1908–1975), daughter of a travelling pedlar and hawker, was regarded as the finest traditional singer discovered by the Scottish folk song revival of the 1950s. E. Ewan, S. Innes, S. Reynolds, R. Pipes (eds), *The Biographical Dictionary of Scottish Women* (Edinburgh, 2006), 305, 306.

43. John Cole (b.1927), successively 1956–75, reporter, labour correspondent, news editor, deputy editor, the *Guardian*; 1975–81, successively assistant editor then deputy editor, *The Observer*; 1981–92, political editor, BBC; author of several books, including *As It Seemed To Me: Political Memoirs* (London, 1995). *WW, 2010*, op. cit., 464. *Belfast Telegraph*, 1870 to date. Alastair Hetherington (1919–2000); educ. Gresham's School and Oxford University; in army, 1940–6; editorial staff, *Glasgow Herald*, 1946–50; 1950–75, *Manchester Guardian*: assistant and foreign editor, 1953–6, director, 1956–75, *Guardian* and Manchester *Evening News* Ltd, and, 1967–75, of Guardian Newspapers Ltd; Controller, BBC Scotland, 1975–8; winner of several journalist and press awards, and author of several books. *WWW, Vol. X, 1996–2000*, op. cit., 266. Sir Hector Hetherington (1888–1965), born Cowdenbeath; professor of moral philosophy, Glasgow University, 1924–7; Vice Chancellor, Liverpool University, 1927–36; Principal and Vice Chancellor, Glasgow University, 1936–61; author of several books. *Scottish Biographies 1938*, op. cit., 348; *WWW, Vol. VI, 1961–1970*, op. cit., 196. Hugh Cochrane (1932–1995), copy boy, Glasgow *Evening Times*, junior reporter, *Kilmarnock Standard*, then with *Noon Record*, Glasgow; briefly with *The Scotsman*; Scottish correspondent, *The Times*, 1960–8; BBC Scotland, 1968–c.1974; features and leader writer, columnist, *Glasgow Herald*; c.1974–94; author of two books on Glasgow. *TS*, 3 and 4 Mar. 1995; *TH*, 3 Mar. 1995.

44. John Hossack (1917–2004); son of a Kelso baker, began as junior reporter, *Kelso Chronicle*, then successively worked in Newcastle and on *Daily Herald*, Glasgow; was six years in Eighth Army in WWII; post-war, industrial correspondent, *Scottish Daily Express*; BBC Scotland, 1959–mid 1960s, then to Scottish TV; a socialist. *TH*, 2 and 8 Sep. 2004. Phil Stein (1922–1996), born in Gorbals, son of Lithuanian immigrants; educ. Allan Glen's School; in Highland Light Infantry in WWII; a teacher, then, 1954–c.1968, Scottish correspondent, *Daily Worker*; Scottish TV news, then freelance and public relations in London, mainly in motor trade; active in Communist Party, NUJ, other bodies, and later in Lab. Party; a Burns scholar, and friend of Hugh MacDiarmid. Obit. by R.J. (Bob) Brown, *TH*, 30 Nov. 1996; *TJ*, Sep. 1991, Jun./Jul. 1992, Mar./Apr. 1997; infm.: Professor John Foster.

45. Charles P. Scott (1840–1932); educ. privately and at Oxford University; Governing Director, *Manchester Guardian*, editor, 1872–1929; Lib. MP, Leigh, 1895–1906. *WWW, Vol. III, 1929–1940*, op. cit., 1206, 1207.

46. Harry Whewell (b.1923), worked, 1950–87, for the *Guardian*. Infm.: Archivist, *Guardian*. Peter Jenkins (1934–1992); educ. Culford School and Cambridge University; journalist, *Financial Times*, 1958–60, *Guardian*, 1960–85, successively as journalist, labour correspondent, 1963–7, Washington correspondent, 1972–4, political commentator and policy editor, 1974–85; theatre critic, *The Spectator*, 1978–81; political columnist, *Sunday Times*, 1985–7; winner of several journalism awards; author of, e.g., *The Battle of Downing Street* (1970).

47. Scottish Trades Union Congress, est. 1897: for a scholarly history of it, see Keith Aitken, *The Bairns o' Adam* (Edinburgh, 1997).

48. Tam Dalyell (b.1932), Lab. MP, West Lothian, 1962–83, Linlithgow, 1983–2005. *The Observer*, 26 May 1968, published a detailed account of a report of a visit to Porton Down, Wiltshire, the govt germ warfare centre, by the House of Commons Select

Committee on Science and Technology. A copy of the unpublished report, which he had believed was in the public domain, had been given an *Observer* journalist by Tam Dalyell, a member of the Select Committee. A large majority of MPs voted to reprimand Tam Dalyell for 'a breach of privilege and a gross contempt of the House'. See, e.g., Greg Rosen (ed.), *Dictionary of Labour Biography* (London, 2001), 155–6.

49. Bernard Ingham (b.1932), reporter, 1948–65, on several Yorkshire papers, reporter and later labour staff, *Guardian*, 1965–7; in public relations, 1967–8; information officer, then director of information, two govt depts, 1968–77; Chief Press Secretary to Prime Minister, 1979–90; head of govt infm. service, 1989–90; columnist, 1991–8, *Daily Express* and *Yorkshire Post*; author of several books. *WW, 2010*, op. cit., 1162.

50. The Scottish Council (Development and Industry), est. 1946, an independent organisation with wide-ranging membership that sought to influence the development of, and strengthen, the Scottish economy.

51. Nine miners were killed in the Michael Colliery fire on 9–10 Sep. 1967, and some 3,000 jobs there lost with the consequent closure of the pit, then the largest producer of coal in Scotland. *TS*, 11 Sep. and 22 Nov. 1967.

52. Fourteen men, including a Free Church minister, were charged with breach of the peace after they had formed a human barrier across the only road exit from the Kyle of Lochalsh–Kyleakin ferry on Sunday, 6 Jun. 1965. That day 350 passengers used the ferry to and from Skye, 72 cars had crossed to Skye, and 85 from Skye. The Caledonian Steam Packet Co. said it had already run ferries on 18 of the 22 Sundays so far that year, to provide emergency medical, police, and veterinary services. Ten of the Company's 16 ferrymen had refused to work on Sundays; the Company said it would not force any men to do so who had strong Sabbatarian convictions. *TS*, 7 Jun. 1965. Allan Campbell McLean (1922–1989), motor mechanic, junior accountant; in RAF in WWII; post-war, became a full-time writer, including of children's novels, and lived on Skye; unsuccessful Lab. Parl. candidate, 1964 and 1966, Inverness-shire; chairman, 1974, Scottish Council, Lab. Party. *TS*, 28 Oct. 1989.

53. James Cagney (1899–1986), American actor who starred in many films, particularly about gangsters, for half a century from 1931. In *Johnny Come Lately* (1943) and *Come Fill the Cup* (1951) he played the role of a journalist. *Radio Times Guide to Films* (London, 2000), 288, 743.

54. Robert Kemp (1908–1967), born on Hoy, Orkney; educ. Aberdeen University; began as a journalist on *Manchester Guardian*; 1937–48, a BBC producer; Scots language scholar; playwright (and adapted *The Thrie Estaits* for the Edinburgh Festival, 1948); est. Gateway Theatre, Edinburgh, 1953–65; novelist and prolific journalist. Royle, *The Mainstream Companion to Scottish Literature*, op. cit., 168–9.

55. A stringer – a non-staff local correspondent. Bert (Albert) Morris (b.1927), left school at 14, studied shorthand and typing, Skerry's College, Edinburgh; worked in courts for a year; copy and phone room boy, 1944–5, Edinburgh *Evening Dispatch*; in army, 1945–8; *Dispatch* reporter, 1949–54; *Scotsman* reporter then columnist, 1954–92. Infm.: Bert Morris. Hugh Davidson, born Berwickshire, educ. Gretna Green School; editor, *Campbeltown Courier* and *Port Glasgow Guardian*, then full-time freelance in Glasgow as a correspondent for the *Guardian*, *The Times*, *Daily Telegraph*, and other papers, as well as for Reuters, Agence France Presse, and UPI; died 1981, aged 65. *TJ*, Oct. 1981.

56. In the worst Scottish pit disaster for 70 years, 47 miners at Auchengeich colliery, Chryston, Lanarkshire, lost their lives in the fire on 18 Sep. 1959. *TS*, 19, 21, 22, 23 Sep. 1959.

57. Toward the middle of his second term in office as President of the USA, allegations from early in 1998 into 1999 of a sex scandal said to involve Bill Clinton and Monica Lewinsky led to court action, in which Clinton admitted to an 'inappropriate relationship' with Ms Lewinsky, and to his impeachment by the House of Representatives but his acquittal by the Senate.

58. Dick Sharpe, began from school in advertising dept, *Glasgow Herald*; National Service with Scots Guards in Malaya; worked in early 1950s on *Bon Accord*, an Aberdeen weekly owned by Outram; reporter then industrial correspondent, *Glasgow Herald*; 1968–70, Scottish correspondent, *The Times*; 1970s–84, associate news editor, Edinburgh office, *Glasgow Herald*; died 1984, aged 54. *TJ*, Feb. 1984.

59. Margaret Cairns was the sister of John Cairns, above, pp. 436–46.

60. The *Daily Worker*, 1930–66, changed its title to *Morning Star*, 25 Apr. 1966.

61. Contrary to Bob Brown's belief, the *Daily Worker*, 21 Jan. 1936, devoted to the death of George V its front page lead story, headlined over all six columns, 'The King is Dead', and also the back page (page 8), with a bold headline, 'The Story of the Dead King' over all six columns, a sub-heading, 'Royal Power in the Last Stage of Capitalism', and a sub-sub-heading, 'George V and the National Government', with three and a half full-length columns of a survey of the king's reign, which concluded: 'As the reign ended supporters of capitalism and the Monarchy could not refrain from reflecting on the immensity of the services rendered to the ruling class by the Monarchy during the reign of King George V.'

62. The Bonus Joe strike began at the Rolls-Royce factory, Blantyre, on 26 Oct. 1955, when all 600 workers downed tools because a polisher there, Joe McLernon, was earning more than his fair share of bonus. His General Ironfitters' Union card was withdrawn and he was expelled from the union. The management rejected the workers' demand that McLernon be dismissed as a non-unionist. The strike extended to include 10,500 other workers at Rolls-Royce factories at East Kilbride and Hillington. The dispute arose from a shortage of work that had resulted in men being transferred 18 months previously from Blantyre to other Rolls-Royce factories in Scotland. But the transferred men were not given their own kind of work – only labouring jobs were offered them, and if the men refused they were given seven days' notice. The workers had then appealed to Rolls-Royce management to send more work to Blantyre, and had introduced a bonus limitation scheme to ensure the work available was fairly shared. Joe McLernon had not observed the limit. The strikers resolved on 14 Dec. 1955 at meetings at Hamilton and in Govan Town Hall to return to work next day on the basis of no victimisation, and that all Rolls-Royce workers would be urged to join their appropriate trade union. Joe McLernon had continued working throughout the strike. *Hamilton Advertiser*, 29 Oct., 19 and 26 Nov., 3, 10, and 17 Dec. 1955.

63. R. Page Arnot, *A History of the Scottish Miners* (London, 1955).

64. Joe Minogue (1923–1996), worked for the *Guardian*, 1958–c.1980s: Infm.: Archivist, *Guardian*.

65. David Murison (1913–1997), born Fraserburgh; leading philologist of Scots, and editor, *Scottish National Dictionary* in 10 vols.; author of over 60 other publications on Scots and its history, including *The Guid Scots Tongue* (Edinburgh, 1977). *TS*, 17 Feb. 1997.

66. *The Economist*, weekly, 1843 to date.

67. Sir Kenneth Alexander (1922–2001), professor of economics, Strathclyde University, 1963–80; economic consultant to Secretary of State for Scotland, 1968–91; Chairman, Highlands and Islands Development Board, 1976–80; Principal and Vice Chancellor, Stirling University, 1981–6; prolific author on economics and industrial relations. *WWW*, *Vol. XI, 2001–2005*, op. cit., 8. Sir Samuel Curran (1912–1998), Principal and Vice Chancellor, Strathclyde University, 1964–80. *WWW*, *Vol. X, 1996–2000*, op. cit., 136–7.

68. Alastair Burnet (1928–2012), journalist and broadcaster; sub-editor and leader writer, *Glasgow Herald*, 1951–8; leader writer, *The Economist*, 1958–62; political editor, Independent Television News, 1963–4, and broadcaster, ITN, 1976–91; editor, *The Economist*, 1963–74; editor, *Daily Express*, 1974–6; knighted, 1984; hon. vice-president, IoJ, 1990. *WW, 2011*, op. cit., 330.

69. Chris Baur (b.1942), copy boy, 1960, then industrial reporter, 1963–73, *The Scotsman*; Scottish correspondent, *Financial Times*, 1973–6; Scottish political correspondent, BBC,

1976–8; assistant editor, 1978–83, deputy editor, 1983–5, editor, 1985–7, *The Scotsman.* Infm.: Andrew Hood. The only seats the SNP had ever won in Parl. elections before 1970 were one each in by-elections in 1945 (very briefly) and 1967 (lost in 1970). From one seat won in 1970, the SNP's total rose to seven in Feb. 1974 and 11 in Oct. 1974.

70. Hamish MacKinven (1921–2010), born Campbeltown; educ. Campbeltown Grammar School; reporter, *Campbeltown Courier*, 1938–40; in RAF, 1940–6; with Forestry Commission, 1946–8, while also active as freelance journalist; assistant editor, *Forward*, 1948; press officer, Lab. Party headquarters, 1948–52; assistant information officer, Scottish Hydro-Electric Board, 1952–84. MacDougall, *Voices from Work and Home*, op. cit., 465–504.

71. Jim Sillars (b.1937), born Ayr; an official, Fire Brigades Union; 1963, full-time Lab. Party agent, Ayr; Ayr town and county councillor; 1968–70, dept head, STUC; MP, South Ayrshire, Lab., 1970–6, and Scottish Lab., 1976–9; a founder, 1975–6, Scottish Lab. Party; SNP MP, Glasgow Govan, 1988–92; author of *Scotland: The Case for Optimism* (1986). Rosen (ed.). *Dictionary of Labour Biography*, op. cit., 524–5. Alex Neil (b.1951), Scottish Research Officer, Lab. Party, 1975–6; general secretary, Scottish Lab. Party, 1976; SNP MSP, Central Scotland, from 1999; Minister for Housing and Communities, 2009–11. *Who's Who in Scotland* (Irvine, 2009), 407. The Scottish Lab. Party was est. in Dec. 1975. *TS*, 23 and 31 Dec. 1975.

72. Lewis Grassic Gibbon, *nom de plume* of James Leslie Mitchell (1901–1935), born Aberdeenshire, journalist, soldier, RAF clerk, socialist, above all author of the trilogy *A Scots Quair: Sunset Song* (1932), *Cloud Howe* (1933), *Grey Granite* (1934), and of a dozen other books.

73. Hugh MacDiarmid, *nom de plume* of Christopher Grieve (1892–1978), born Langholm; educ. Langholm Academy; pupil teacher, journalist, prolific poet, editor, polemicist, pioneer of the Scottish literary renaissance; reporter, Edinburgh *Evening Dispatch*, 1911; in Medical Corps in WWI; reporter and editor, *Montrose Review*, 1920–9; Montrose town councillor, 1920s; a founder and member, National Party of Scotland, 1928–33; member, Communist Party of Great Britain, 1934–9 and from 1956; hon. LL D, Edinburgh University, 1957. He came third as SNP candidate in the Glasgow Kelvingrove Parl. election, Jul. 1945, and lost his deposit. Alan Bold, *MacDiarmid* (London, 1990), *passim*.

74. John S. Maclay (1905–1992), Viscount Muirshiel from 1964; shipowner; National Lib. and Cons. MP, Montrose Burghs, 1940–50, Renfrewshire West, 1950–64; successively PS or minister of three govt depts, 1945, 1951–2, 1956–7, then, 1957–62, Secretary of State for Scotland. *WWW, Vol. IX, 1991–1995*, 394.

75. Steven Bilsland, Lord Bilsland (1892–1970), born Glasgow; educ. Cambridge University; MC in WWI; a leading Scottish industrialist; chairman, Bilsland Bros Ltd, Glasgow (bakers), and a director of many other companies; chairman, Scottish Economic Committee, 1936, and of the Scottish Council (Development and Industry) to 1955, president, 1955–66. *TS*, 11 Dec. 1970; *Scottish Biographies 1938*, op. cit., 58.

76. *Scots Independent*, 1926 to date. Bob Brown's story, on page 8 (back page) of the paper, Nov. 1942, and signed 'R.J.B.', is headlined: 'Comic Opera in Edinburgh starring Lauder and Churchill', and begins: '"The national comedians of England and Scotland on the same bill" was how one Scot described Mr Churchill's admission to the freedom of Edinburgh last month. His speech was an ill-assorted mixture of soft-soap and stale-ginger, ludicrously out of touch with the spirit of the New Scotland.'

77. The Scottish Convention, est. 1942 by John MacCormick (see above, p. 565, Note 25), till then secretary of the Scottish National Party, and some other Party members, was a breakaway from the Party and sought to make itself a broad front, supported by members from other political parties, trades unions, local councils, churches, and other bodies that favoured self-govt for Scotland. The Lab. Party leadership was, however, antagonised from MacCormick and the Convention by what it regarded as his over-close association with the Conservatives, particularly at the Paisley by-election, 1947, when he stood against the

Lab. Candidate. The Convention launched a National Covenant in 1949 that was said to have attracted two million signatures in favour of self-govt or Home Rule for Scotland. Neither the Lab. nor Cons. Party, despite support from some rank and file sections of the former, and by some unions, was willing to press for devolution. See, e.g., Michael Keating and David Bleiman, *Labour and Scottish Nationalism* (London, 1979), 130–49; Andrew Marr, *The Battle for Scotland* (London, 1992), 92–106. William Power (1873–1951); born Glasgow; left school at 14; bank clerk, 1887–1907; journalist and author; on editorial staff, *Glasgow Herald*, mainly as literary editor and leader writer, to 1926; editor, *Scots Observer*, 1926–9; on literary staff, Scottish Associated Newspapers from 1929; president, Scottish PEN Club, 1935–8; SNP Parl. by-election candidate, Argyll, 1940; chairman, 1942, Scottish Convention; and, 1949, Scottish Covenant Association; author of many books inc. his autobiography *Should Auld Acquaintance* (1937), and contributor to many journals. *Scottish Biographies 1938*, op. cit., 622; *GH*, 14 Jun. 1951. Douglas Young (1913–1973), born Tayport; spent some of his childhood in Bengal; educ. Merchiston Castle School, Edinburgh, and St Andrews University; poet and scholar; lecturer in Greek, Aberdeen University, 1938–41; joined Lab. Party, 1935, SNP, 1938: chairman, 1942; imprisoned in WWII as a conscientious objector (on Scottish Nationalist grounds); unsuccessful SNP Parl. by-election candidate, Kirkcaldy, Feb. 1944, left SNP, 1948, when it forbade membership of any other Party; lecturer in Latin, University College, Dundee, 1947–53, in Greek, St Andrews University, 1953–68; professor of classics, McMaster University, Canada, 1968–70; professor of Greek, North Carolina University, 1970–3. Daiches (ed.), *The New Companion to Scottish Culture*, op. cit., 345.

78. Winnie Ewing (b.1929), born Glasgow; educ. Queen's Park School and Glasgow University, qualified, 1952, as a solicitor; lecturer in law, 1954–6; SNP MP, Hamilton, 1967–70, Moray and Nairn, 1974–9; SNP MEP, 1979–99; president, SNP, 1987–2005; MSP, 1999–2003; hon. LL D, Glasgow and Aberdeen Universities. *WW, 2011*, op. cit., 729.

79. Alex Eadie (1920–2012), Fife miner from 1934; Fife county councillor; Lab. MP, Midlothian, 1966–92; Parl. Under-Secretary, Dept of Energy, 1974–9. John Robertson (1913–1987); a senior west of Scotland Engineering Union official; Motherwell and Wishaw town and Lanarkshire county councillor, 1948–52; Lab. MP, Paisley, 1961–78; a founder member, Scottish Lab. Party, 1976–9. *WWW, Vol. VIII, 1981–1990*, op. cit., 646. Harry Ewing (1931–2007), Lab. MP, Stirling and Falkirk, 1971–4, Stirling, Falkirk and Grangemouth, 1974–83, Falkirk East, 1983–92; Parl. Under Secretary, Scottish office, 1974–9; life peer, 1992. *WWW, Vol. XII, 2006–2010*, 162. James Frame (b.1927), from age 16 successively copy boy, copy-taker, junior reporter, *Evening Citizen*, Glasgow, 1943–5; in army, 1945–8; reporter, *Evening Citizen*, in Ayr, 1948–9, in Glasgow office, news and sports, 1949–58; news and sports reporter, and sub-editor, sports, 1958–63, *Evening Dispatch*, Edinburgh; industrial correspondent, *Evening News*, Edinburgh, 1964–90. Infm.: James Frame. Neal Ascherson (b.1932); journalist and author; educ. Eton College and Cambridge University; in Royal Marines, 1950–2; reporter and leader writer, *Manchester Guardian*, 1956–8; Commonwealth correspondent, *The Scotsman*, 1959–60; *The Observer*, 1960–3, correspondent, Central Europe, 1963–8, Eastern Europe, 1968–75; Scottish politics correspondent, *The Scotsman*, 1975–9; columnist, associate editor, *Independent on Sunday*, 1979–89; reporter of the year, 1982, journalist of the year, 1987; author of several books, including *Black Sea* (1993), and *Stone Voices* (2002); has several honorary degrees. *WW, 2010*, op. cit., 68.

80. Edward (Ted) Short (b.1912), Lab. MP, Newcastle, 1951–76; govt minister successively of three depts, 1967–70, 1974–6; deputy leader, Lab. Party, 1972–6; life peer, 1977, as Baron Glenamara.

81. Don Robertson, Lab. Party, St Andrews, had been vice-chairman of the Steering Committee of the Scottish Lab. Party; died 2011. *TS*, 23 Dec.1975; infm.: George MacDougall.

82. George Foulkes (b.1942); educ. Keith Grammar School, Haberdashers', Aske's School, and Edinburgh University; chairman, Lothian Region Education Committee, 1974–9; Lab. and Co-operative MP, Carrick, Cumnock and Doon Valley, 1979–2005; Parl. Under-Secretary, International Development, 1997–2001, Minister of State for Scotland, 2001–2; MSP, Lothians, 2007–11; Lord Foulkes from 2005. *WWiS, 2009*, op. cit., 197–8; *WW, 2011*, op. cit., 794.

83. Jim Sillars, SNP, won the Glasgow Govan by-election, 10 Nov. 1988, with a majority of 3,554 over the Lab. candidate Bob Gillespie, in a 30% swing from Lab. to the SNP. *TH*, 11 Nov. 1988.

84. Judith Hart (1924–1991), Lab. MP, Lanark, 1959–83, Clydesdale, 1983–7; held junior office, 1964–6, then a minister for two govt depts successively, 1968–70, 1974–5, 1977–9; life peer from 1988. *The Biographical Dictionary of Scottish Women*, op. cit., 160–1.

85. S.G. Edgar Lythe (1910–1997); grad Cambridge University; lecturer, Hull University, then Dundee School of Economics, 1935–62; in RAF in WWII; professor, economic history, Strathclyde University, 1962–75; Vice-Principal from 1972.

Bob Scott, pp. 216–34

1. Sean Connery (b.1930), born and grew up in Edinburgh; served in Royal Navy; a world famous actor and film star; Oscar winner; 1987, BAFTA Award, 1988, for Best Actor, BAFTA Lifetime Achievement Award, 1990; hon. D Litt, 1981, Heriot Watt University, 1988, St Andrews University; Freedom of City of Edinburgh, 1991; knighted, 2000; Legion of Honour. *WW, 2010*, op. cit., 480. Bob Scott was in fact almost five years older than Sean Connery.

2. *The Skipper*, 1930–41, *Hotspur*, 1933–59; and *Adventure*, 1933–59, were all D.C. Thomson & Co. Ltd publications; *Champion*, 1922–55 (revived 1966, but ceased publication), and *Triumph*, 1924–40, were Amalgamated Press publications. *The Magnet*, 1908–40 (in which the Billy Bunter stories appeared), and *The Gem*, 1907–39, were Harmsworth, London, publications. *Biggles*, by Capt. W.E. Johns (1893–1968), was a series of almost 100 books published during three decades from 1932 and whose hero was Captain James Bigglesworth, RFC/RAF.

3. Edward G. Robinson (1893–1973) starred in *Five Star Final* (1931) as a principled editor instructed by the paper's proprietor to lower its standards drastically in order to increase its circulation. *Radio Times Guide to Films*, op. cit., 499.

4. There was in fact no air raid on 3 Sep. 1939: it was a false alarm.

5. Smith has not been further identified, except that he was editor, 1943–5.

6. James Robertson (33), a Glasgow policeman, was convicted, 13 Nov. 1950, of the murder of Catherine McClusky (40) in Glasgow, and was executed there, 16 Dec. 1950.

7. In Dec. 1943 Ernest Bevin, Minister of Labour and National Service, introduced a balloting system for young conscripts: one in 10 was directed by ballot to work in the coal mines. By the end of the war 21,000 balloted young conscripts were employed in the mines, plus 16,000 who had volunteered to work there. The last of the Bevin Boys were not released until 1949. Unlike demobbed members of the armed forces, they received no issue of civilian clothing, nor a Defence Medal, nor were they considered eligible to take part in the annual Armistice Day service of remembrance. Warwick Taylor, *The Forgotten Conscripts: A History of the Bevin Boys* (Bishop Auckland, 1995), 4, 5, 89, 96, 98.

8. Gilbert Cole, joined NUJ, 1927, in South Wales; reporter, 1928–c.1931, *Scottish Daily Express*, in Glasgow; c.1931–1934, *Daily Express*, London; 1934–71, chief reporter or bureau chief, Edinburgh office, *Scottish Daily Express*; died 1994, aged 87. *TJ*, Aug–Sep. 1994; *TS*, 2 Jun. 1994; Campbell, *A Word for Scotland*, op. cit., 51. The *Scottish Daily Express* office moved, 1946–7, from India Buildings to No. 10 Bank St; the *Daily Record* office moved, 1948, from No. 8 Bank St to No. 32 Frederick St; the *Sunday Post* and

Weekly News were still at India Buildings in 1948. No address in the city for the *News Chronicle* at that period has been found. *Edinburgh & Leith Post Office Directory, 1947–8* and 1948–9. See also above, Gordon Dean, p. 370.

9.   Helen Elliot (b.1927), born Edinburgh; World Ladies' Doubles champion, 1949 and 1950; Scottish Ladies' Singles champion for 13 consecutive years, and champion of Ireland, Wales, Germany, and Belgium.

10. Hearts made a summer tour of Australia in 1959. Tommy Walker (1915–1993), born Livingston; played for Hearts, 1932–46, then Chelsea; played 20 times for Scotland; in army in India in WWII; assistant manager, 1949–51, manager, 1951–66, of Hearts, later of Raith Rovers and Dunfermline; OBE, 1960. The Association of Football Statistics, *Report No. 79, Feb. 1973*, 28.

11. Tommy Muirhead, born Cowdenbeath; played in Fife junior football, then for Hibs, and, 1917–30, Rangers, and eight times for Scotland; manager, 1930s, St Johnstone and Preston North End; became a sports journalist and chief football writer, *Scottish Daily Express*; died 1979, aged 82. *TJ*, Aug. 1979; Bob Ferrier and Robert McElroy, *Rangers: The Complete Record* (Derby, 1993), 153.

12. Errol Flynn (1909–1959), an Australian actor and star, 1933–58, of several dozen films.

13. *Sunday Standard*, 1981–3.

14. *Dalkeith Advertiser*, 1851 to date. Scottish County Press, est. 1944 as Peebles County Press by Dr David Frew and a partner, changed its title, 1945, when the company bought the *Dalkeith Advertiser* and moved its office to Dalkeith. The Press was taken over by Johnston Press in 2002. Infm.: The *Advertiser* and Johnston Press. See also below, George Hume, Note 11, p. 607. Leith Gazette, 1952–86.

15. Doon Campbell (1920–2003), born Annan; in fact, born with only one hand, his left hand a wooden one, always covered with a glove; began on *Linlithgowshire Gazette* and *West Lothian Courier*; cycled six miles to the Forth Bridge to report German air raid there in Oct. 1939; with Edinburgh *Evening Dispatch* to 1943, then with Reuters to 1973, successively as sub-editor, science correspondent, war correspondent (battle of Cassino, then landed in Normandy on D-Day with the commandos, then Far East), post-war reported assassination, 1948, of Mohandas ('Mahatma') Gandhi, then worked in Middle East and Paris; became an editor and a deputy general manager, Reuters. Infm.: Bert Morris; *TS*, 31 May 2003.

Jack Sutherland, pp. 235–51

1.   The Gordon Highlanders originated from the 75th and 92nd Highlanders, raised respectively in 1787 and 1794: the latter from 1798 were titled the Gordons; the two regts merged, 1891, as the Gordon Highlanders. The regt merged in 1994 with the Seaforth and the Cameron Highlanders in the Queen's Own Highlanders, which in 2006 became 4th Bn, Royal Regt of Scotland.

2.   Highland Clearances: the forced, often brutal removal, particularly during the later eighteenth and earlier nineteenth century, by oppressive and grasping landlords, including numbers of hereditary clan chiefs, of masses of native Highlanders from their traditional lands, to make way for sheep or deer-hunting.

3.   The battle of Arnhem, part of Operation Market Garden, 17–25 Sep. 1944, intended to outflank German defenders by Allied forces advancing northwards through Holland then turning east into Germany, was fought by the British 1st Airborne Division there to secure the bridge over the Lower Rhine, while two U.S. airborne divisions seized bridges over other rivers further south at Eindhoven and Nijmegen. Once these bridges were secured other troops were to advance over them northwards by road. Arnhem, however, proved 'a bridge too far'. Owing to unexpectedly large German forces there, and other factors, the attempt to seize and hold the bridge at Arnhem failed. Of the 10,000 British and Polish airborne troops engaged, 1,000 were killed; 6,000, many

of them wounded, were capd; and only about 2,600 were safely evacuated. Several hundred others escaped capture by remaining in hiding. See, e.g., Chester Wilmot, *The Struggle for Europe* (London, 1954 edn), 555–83.

4. The Royal Northumberland Fusiliers, 5th Regt of Foot, formed 1674, merged 1968 into the Royal Regt of Fusiliers. The 2nd Bn was at Dunkirk; the 9th Bn, part of the 18th Division, landed at Singapore a few days before its capitulation to the Japanese, and 151 of its men died in captivity. Basil Peacock, *The Royal Northumberland Fusiliers* (London, 1970*)*, 95.

5. The Air Training Corps, for boys aged 16–18, was est. by the Air Ministry, Jan. 1941, and within six months had a membership of 200,000, dressed in RAF uniforms. Angus Calder, *The People's War: Britain 1939–45* (London, 1969), 345.

6. The disaster occurred on 26 Oct 1947; four days later the death toll had become 28. *TS*, 27 and 30 Oct. 1947.

7. Capt. George C. Grey (1919–1944) was in fact Lib. MP, Berwick-upon-Tweed, 1941–4. *WWW, Vol. IV, 1941–1950*, op. cit., 470. Sir William Beveridge (1879–1963), a leader writer, 1906–8, *Morning Post*; Director, 1919–37, London School of Economics, Master, 1937–45, University College, Oxford; Lib. MP Berwick-upon-Tweed, 1944–5; chairman of a committee of civil servants appointed to survey all existing social insurance schemes, and whose report – the Beveridge Report, published Dec. 1942 – aroused huge public discussion, and formed much of the basis of the post-war Welfare State. *WWW, Vol. VI, 1961–1970*, op. cit., 91–2.

8. *East Essex Gazette* (with several changes of title), 1913 to date. Selwyn Eagle and Diana Dixon, *NEWSPLAN: London and South-Eastern Library Region* (London, 1996), 64, 65. Arnold Bertram Quick, born 1915, played, 1936–52, for Essex, and once, 1948, for MCC. Robert Brooke, comp. and ed., *The Collins Who's Who of English First Class Cricket, 1945–1984* (London,1985), 231.

9. *Northern Echo*, 1870 to date. The Westminster Press was part of Pearson Longman. The Press was said some years later to be 'the largest publisher of weekly newspapers in Britain'. *TJ*, Jul. 1973.

10. The 1951 Census showed Glasgow's population then to be 1,089,767, Edinburgh's 487,000. Cunnison and Gilfillan (eds), *Third Statistical Account of Scotland: Glasgow*, op. cit., 48.

11. The splash sub-editor dealt with the main story on the front page.

12. The death of Stalin in 1953, the revelatory speech by Khrushchev, secretary of the Soviet Communist Party, to the Party's 20th Congress in Feb. 1956, in which he denounced Stalin's abuses of power, led, along with ongoing de-Stalinisation, economic, nationalist, and other factors, to revolts in Poland and Hungary later that year. In Hungary, a reformist Communist govt led by Imre Nagy announced the withdrawal of Hungary from the Warsaw Pact, 1955 (an equivalent of NATO for the Soviet Union and the East European Communist states). Consequent Soviet military intervention on 3 Nov. and its suppression of the uprising was made easier by the simultaneous Suez Crisis. Large numbers of Hungarians were deported to the Soviet Union; others were executed or sought refuge abroad. Other consequences included the withdrawal of considerable numbers of members from Communist Parties in Western European countries, including Britain.

13. Len Lord joined the *Scottish Daily Mail* in 1957 from Nottingham and became 'one of Scotland's best-known reporters'; died 1968, aged 37. *TJ*, Mar. 1968.

14. Alex Cameron, formerly chief sports writer, *Scottish Daily Mail*, retired in 2000 after 55 years of reporting sport; Scottish Press Lifetime Achievement Award, 2001; NUJ life member. *TJ*, Jul.–Aug. 2001. John Rafferty (1911–1976), born Glasgow; began work as a shipbuilder's cost clerk; took part in training the world flyweight champion boxer Jackie Paterson; after WWII, awarded a teaching diploma by Jordanhill College and for 15 years was a primary teacher in Govan; he became a contributor of sports

reports to several national newspapers, and a sports writer with *The Scotsman*, 1962. Infm.: Mr Brian Rafferty; *TS*, 4 Apr. 1976. At Aberfan, Mid Glamorgan, on 21 Oct. 1966, 144 people, 116 of them children, lost their lives in a horrific colliery spoil-heap disaster.

15. Slip edition – one dealing with a particular subject or place (as Fife) and slipped in between main editions.

16. James Goldsmith (1933–1997), son of a director of the London Savoy hotel and owner of a leading hotel in Paris; educ. Eton College; m. at Kelso registry office, 7 Jan. 1954, his fiancée Isabella Patino, aged 18, daughter of an extremely wealthy Bolivian tin magnate, who sought by interim interdict to prevent or delay the marriage on the grounds she was too young. In Scotland, however, where the young couple had arrived in Edinburgh and stayed from 13 Dec., marriage from age 16, with or without parental consent, was legal, provided 15 days' residential qualification was fulfilled. Isabella Patino Goldsmith died in childbirth in Paris in May 1954. James Goldsmith, knighted 1976, became a leading businessman, founded the Referendum Party, an MEP, 1994–7, and author of several books. *WWW, Vol. X, 1996–2000*, 215; *TS*, 5–8 Jan. and 17 May 1954. George MacDougall says Jack Sutherland is mistaken about his having been chief sub-editor on the night of President Kennedy's assassination: in fact, he was not on duty, but he cannot now recall who was along with Jack Sutherland that night.

17. The back bench in the sub-editors' room consisted of senior journalists: night editor, chief sub-editor, deputy chief sub-editor, and copy taster. Infm.: George MacDougall.

18. In fact, there were two separate appearances by Bill Matthewman at the High Court in Edinburgh. The first was on 7 Nov. 1953, when the Court upheld a petition, on behalf of four men due to appear for trial on 17 Nov., prohibiting Matthewman, as editor, *Scottish Daily Mail*, and its publisher, Associated Newspapers Ltd, publishing any article or comment concerning the indictment against the men that might prejudice their trial, until the proceedings against them had been concluded. The petition referred to an article in the paper on 30 Oct. headed 'Scots linked with terror plot'. Lord Cooper, the Lord Justice-General, said the article had followed one the previous day setting out the indictment and the names of the accused. Lord Cooper said the High Court had already laid down that, once a person had been apprehended and committed for trial, the function of the press in commenting on the guilt of the accused and nature of the offences charged was, at least for the time being, at an end. The second appearance of Matthewman and the paper's publisher at the High Court was on 4 Dec. 1959 before Lord Clyde as Lord Justice-General, when they were called to account for the appearance in the *Scottish Daily Mail* on 25 Nov. of a photograph and an article which, it was claimed, would prejudice a fair trial of the accused man Jack Sutherland refers to. After counsel for Matthewman and the publisher tendered an 'unqualified apology' to the Court, it awarded the accused man 100 guineas costs, and fined Matthewman £500 (not £10,000) and the publisher £5,000 (not £15,000). Lord Clyde, who said the Court had decided with some hesitation not to impose a sentence of imprisonment, declared: 'Conduct of this kind will not be tolerated and it must be punished if justice is to prevail in Scotland, if it constitutes an interference with the due administration of that justice and therefore amounts to contempt of court.' Matthewman ceased to be editor of the *Scottish Daily Mail* two months later. *TS*, 5 Dec. 1959; cutting, n.d., *World's Press News*. Mike Randall (1919–1999), began, 1940, on *Daily Graphic*, moved to *Sunday Chronicle*, then to *Sunday Graphic*, of which he was editor, 1952, then successively to *Daily Mirror, News Chronicle* (assistant editor), and *Daily Mail*, editor, 1963–6, then managing editor (news), *Sunday Times*, 1967–79; Journalist of the Year, 1965. Infm.: *Daily Mail* Reference Librarian. Donald Todhunter (1926–1996), began on *Chester Chronicle*; in armed forces in WWII; reporter, *Sunday Chronicle*, 1948–9, Manchester *Evening Chronicle*, 1949–50, *Daily Mail*, 1950–2, news editor, 1952–3, *Scottish Daily Mail*, night news editor, 1953–4, then news editor,

1954–8, *Daily Mail* in London; Northern editor, 1958–9; assistant editor, 1959–60, editor, 1960, *Scottish Daily Mail*; assistant editor, 1960s, *Daily Sketch*; Director, Public Affairs, Hill Samuel Merchant Bank. Infm.: *Daily Mail* Reference Librarian.

19. For John Blackwood, see above, Ernie McIntyre, Note 46, p. 548. Pat Ford (1930–1992); an antiques dealer after the *Scottish Daily Mail* ceased publication in Edinburgh in 1968; a sub-editor, *The Scotsman*, 1980–91: Infm.: George MacDougall.

20. Larry Lamb (1929–2000), journalist on *Brighouse Echo*, *Shields Gazette*, *Newcastle Journal*, London *Evening Standard*; sub-editor, *Daily Mirror*; Manchester editor, *Daily Mail*, 1968–9; editor, *The Sun*, 1969–72, 1975–81; director, 1970–81, editorial director, 1971–81, News International Ltd; director, News Corpn (Australia), Ltd, 1980–1; deputy chairman and editor-in-chief, Western Mail Ltd, Perth, Australia, 1981–2; editor-in-chief, *The Australian*, 1982–3; author of *Sunrise* (1989); knighted, 1980. *WWW, Vol. X, 1996–2000*, op. cit., 333.

21. The Thistle Foundation, est. 1943 by Lord and Lady Tudsbery in memory of their son killed in the war, to provide care for badly wounded ex-servicemen (and now also for civilians). Infm.: the Foundation.

22. Eric B. Mackay (1922–2006), born Aberdeen; educ. Aberdeen Grammar School and Aberdeen University; in Fife & Forfar Yeomanry in WWII; worked on Aberdeen *Bon Accord*, 1948, moved to *Elgin Courant*, 1949, *The Scotsman*, 1950, *Daily Telegraph*, 1952, *The Scotsman*, 1953, London editor of, 1957, deputy editor, 1961, editor, 1972–85. Of him, James Seaton, editor, *The Scotsman*, 1995–7, wrote: 'He was a very great man . . . the most principled and decent journalist I have ever worked with.' *TS*, 17 May 2006; *WWW, Vol. XII, 2006–2010*, 1385.

23. Ian Nimmo (b.1934), began freelancing as a schoolboy for the Dundee *Courier* in Perthshire; National Service, 1955–7: 2nd Lieut., Royal Scots Fusiliers; reporter and sub-editor, 1957–9, *Sunday Post* and Dundee *Evening Telegraph*; moved to Scotsman Publications Ltd: *TV Guide*, 1959–60, then, 1960–6, successively sub-editor, assistant editor, editor, *Weekly Scotsman*; features editor, 1966–8, Aberdeen *Press & Journal*; assistant editor, 1968–70, then editor, 1970–6, Middlesbrough *Evening Gazette*; editor, 1976–89, Edinburgh *Evening News*; post-1989 worked around the world for many years as a consultant, mainly with the Thomson Foundation; author of 10 books and writer of a musical; still working. Infm.: Ian Nimmo.

24. *Edinburgh Advertiser*, 1978–89, then cont. to date as *Edinburgh Herald & Post*.

25. Apart from some college or correspondence courses, there was no formal or professional training for journalists in Britain until in 1952, following the report, 1949, of the Royal Commission on the Press, the National Advisory Council for the Training and Education of Junior Journalists was established. Its title was changed three years later to the National Council for the Training of Journalists. The Council was composed of representatives of newspaper proprietors and managers, and of the NUJ and the IoJ. Courses in journalism are now available at many colleges and universities. Richard Keeble, *The Newspapers Handbook* (London, 2006 edn), 260–1.

George MacDougall, pp. 252–98

1. The Royal Scots, formed 1633, First of Foot, oldest infantry regt in the British army, became in 2006, along with the King's Own Scottish Borderers, 1st Bn, Royal Regt of Scotland.

2. The Ben Line (William Thomson & Co.), est. 1839, so-called when, in the second half of the nineteenth century, its ships were named after Highland mountains. After WWI the Ben Line concentrated on Far East trade, and its base moved from Leith to London.

3. The Dandy 9th was so called as the only Lowland TA Bn that wore kilts.

4. *Radio Fun*, 1938–61, *Film Fun*, 1920–62, both published by Amalgamated Press.

5. Harry Wharton and Bob Cherry were characters in the Billy Bunter stories in *The Magnet*.
6. The weekly sum paid householders in 1939 who took in, and provided full board and care for, one child evacuee was 10s 6d [52½p], and 8s 6d [42½ p] for each child if they took in more than one. Juliet Gardiner, *Wartime Britain 1939–1945* (London, 2004), 36.
7. Finnan haddie – a smoked haddock: *finnan* derived probably from Findon, Kincardineshire.
8. Queans – girls; loons – boys.
9. There were 16 German air raids on Edinburgh (including Leith), the first on 25 Jun. 1940, the last on 25 Mar. 1943. In raids on Leith on 18 and 22 Jul. 1940, eight people were killed and others injured, and several others were also injured on 23 Jul. in a raid around Granton harbour. On 7 Apr. 1941 two landmines dropped on Leith killed three people, injured 132 others, 37 of them seriously, and 600 people were made homeless. Taylor, *Luftwaffe over Scotland*, op. cit., 119–23; Andrew Jeffrey, *This Present Emergency: Edinburgh, the River Forth, and South-East Scotland and the Second World War* (Edinburgh, 1992), 67–9, 83.
10. The Army Cadets had been est. in 1859. Infm.: Edinburgh Castle Museum.
11. George Reith, CBE, MA, BSc, MEd, PhD, FEIS, a maths teacher before he became during WWII an educational administrator; Director of Education, Edinburgh, 1961–72; chairman, Schools Broadcasting Council for Scotland and of Educational Films for Scotland; Chevalier Dans L'Ordre National du Mérite, 1969, for furthering cultural relations between Edinburgh and France; died 1987, aged 79. *EN*, 27 Oct 1987; *TS*, 28 Oct. 1987.
12. It was the passenger liner *City of Benares*, torpedoed by a U-boat, 17 Sep. 1940. Of the 400 passengers, 90 were evacuee children. More than 300 passengers and 77 of the evacuees lost their lives. G.H. and R. Bennett, *Survivors: British Merchant Seamen in the Second World War* (London, 1999), 162.
13. Mrs Kitty Wintringham came third in the 1945 election and lost her deposit; died 1966. Tom Wintringham (1898–1949, not 1944), who had left the Communist Party in 1938, failed by only 869 votes, out of 22,371 cast, to beat the one other (Cons.) candidate in the Feb. 1943 by-election. Craig, *British Parliamentary Election Results, 1918–1949*, op. cit., 638; Joyce M. Bellamy and John Saville, *Dictionary of Labour Biography, Vol. VII* (London, 1984), 255–64.
14. About the sergeant and the ILP meeting nothing has been found for the period in the Edinburgh *Evening News*, *The Scotsman*, or the local Lab. paper *Edinburgh Clarion*, although there was an advertisement in the *Evening News*, Sat. 5 Dec. 1942, for an ILP open discussion next day at 7pm at 31 Lothian St on the war in North Africa; but there were no reports of that meeting in Monday's papers.
15. A major turning point in WWII, the battle of Stalingrad on the river Volga from Sep. 1942 to Feb. 1943, was a shattering defeat for Hitler's forces.
16. *The Orcadian*, 1854 to date.
17. David Douglas (1906–1995), born Perth; educ. Hutcheson's Grammar School, Glasgow; began, c.1922, as junior reporter, Glasgow, on *Motor World*; worked for two Glasgow weekly papers owned by John Wheatley, MP; then for *Glasgow Herald* in Paisley then Glasgow, as a news reporter, then 1936–8 as a sub-editor; in Edinburgh office, 1938–71 (apart from a brief period post-WWII as an information officer at St Andrew's House), successively as court reporter, chief reporter, feature writer, leader writer; reported for many years the General Assembly of the Church of Scotland, and when he retired was publicly thanked by the then Moderator, Very. Rev. Andrew Herron. Infm.: Mrs Marjorie Crawford, his daughter; *TH*, 8 and 11 Jul., 1995; *Fife Herald*, 31 Jan. 1986.
18. Willie Raitt, born and educ. at Blairgowrie; served in Mesopotamia in WWI; took a course in journalism then began, 1921, on *Dundee Advertiser*; moved briefly to Aberdeen, then, from 1923, to *The Scotsman*; from there for 18 years to Linlithgow; during WWII,

in Edinburgh office, *Glasgow Herald*; c.1948–58, *Daily Record*, Edinburgh office, as daily columnist of 'Raitt's Progress'; with *The Scotsman* and *Evening Dispatch*, 1958–63; died 1976, aged 78. 'One of Edinburgh's best-known journalists', many stories or legends about Willie Raitt included one said to have occurred in his first job in Dundee, when he was sent to check a report that an important local jute merchant had died. Clad in bowler hat and black overcoat, Willie arrived at the merchant's house, where the maid who opened the door assumed Willie was from the undertakers. After confirming with his own eyes that the merchant had indeed passed away, Willie then departed, telling the maid he had forgotten to bring his measuring tape. *TJ*, Jun. 1976; *TS*, 26 Apr. 1976; private infm.

19. William Morren (1890–1972), chief constable, Edinburgh, 1935–55; knighted, 1952.

20. Jack Radcliffe (1900–1966), born Cleland, Lanarkshire; miner; stage performer from 1926, specialising in working men, characters, drunks; performed all over Britain after WWII, including at the London Palladium. Vivien Devlin, *King's, Queen's and People's Palaces: An Oral History of the Scottish Variety Theatre, 1920–1970* (Edinburgh, 1991), *passim*.

21. James Bridie, *nom de plume* of Osborne Henry Mavor (1888–1951), born Drymen; educ. Glasgow High School, Glasgow Academy, Glasgow University; served in Royal Army Medical Corps in WWI and II, mentioned in dispatches; post-1918 a doctor in Glasgow; playwright, whose many plays included *The Anatomist* (1931), *Mr Bolfry* (1943), and *Dr Angelus* (1947). *WWW, Vol. V, 1951–1960*, op. cit., 135. William Burke and William Hare, Irishmen, indicted in 1828 for murdering people in Edinburgh in order to sell their bodies for anatomical research; Hare turned king's evidence, Burke was hanged. Alastair Sim (1900–1976); educ. in Edinburgh; stage actor from 1930, in films from 1934, producer; Rector, Edinburgh University, 1948–51, and hon. LL D, 1951. *WWW, Vol. VII, 1971–1980*, op. cit., 727.

22. Harry Pollitt (1890–1960), a boilermaker; educ. elementary school, Lancashire; secretary, 1919, 'Hands Off Russia' Movement, general secretary, 1924–9, National Minority Movement, general secretary, 1929–56, and chairman, 1956–60, Communist Party of Great Britain; author of several books, including (autobiography) *Serving My Time* (London, 1940). *WWW, Vol. V, 1951–1960*, op. cit., 881; Ian MacDougall, *Militant Miners* (Edinburgh, 1981), 174. John Strachey (1901–1963); educ. Eton College and Oxford University; Lab. MP, 1929–31, Birmingham Aston, 1945–50, Dundee, 1950–63, Dundee West; wing commander, RAFVR in WWII; Parl. Under Secretary, Air Ministry, 1945–6, Minister of Food, 1946–50, Minister of War, 1950–1; author of many books, including *The Theory and Practice of Socialism* (1936). *WWW, Vol. VI, 1961–1970*, op. cit., 1086.

23. NAAFI – Navy, Army & Air Force Institute.

24. Emanuel Shinwell (1884–1986), born London; seamen's union leader; Lab. MP, 1922–4 and 1928–31, Linlithgow, and, 1935–70, successively Seaham and Easington; junior then senior minister in five govt depts successively between 1924 and 1951; life peer from 1970; author of several books, inc. his autobiography *Conflict without Malice* (London, 1955).

25. The Young Communist League, est. Oct. 1921, a year after its parent body, the Communist Party of Great Britain. James Klugmann, *History of the Communist Party of Great Britain, Vol. I* (London, 1969), 223.

26. William Gallacher (1881–1965), born Paisley; a leader of the Clyde shop stewards' movement in WWI, and from 1920 of the Communist Party of Great Britain; Communist MP, West Fife, 1935–50; author of several books, including *Revolt on the Clyde: An Autobiography* (London, 1936). The *Communist Manifesto*, by Karl Marx (1818–1883) and Friedrich Engels (1820–1895), published Feb. 1848, when Europe was at the beginning of 'The Year of Revolutions'. The *Manifesto*, a fundamental text of Marxism, insisted that the struggle between social classes explains historical change, that in a revolutionary struggle with capitalism the victory of the proletariat is

inevitable, and it concluded: 'The proletarians have nothing to lose but their chains. They have a world to win. Working men of all countries, unite!'

27. David Robert Gent (1883–1964), schoolteacher and journalist; played rugby for Gloucester and Cornwall and, 1905–10, five times for England; rugby correspondent, *Sunday Times*, post-WWI to 1955. Infm.: World Rugby Museum, Twickenham.

28. Murdoch Taylor (1917–1992), an active Communist all his life, a national organiser, Young Communist League, then full-time Party worker in Fife, election agent for William Gallacher, MP, West Fife; secretary, Kirkcaldy Trades Council; a founder member, Communist Party of Scotland. *Morning Star*, 5 Sep. 1992; infm.: Kirkcaldy Registrar's office.

29. Harry McShane (1891–1988); a Glasgow engineer; from 1911, member, British Socialist Party; a Clyde shop steward in WWI and a close associate until after the war of John Maclean, the Clydeside revolutionary; in the inter-war years a leader of the National Unemployed Workers' Movement, and a member, 1922–54, of the Communist Party, and politically active almost until his death; member, NUJ, as Scottish correspondent, 1940–54, *Daily Worker* (except when its publication was forbidden by govt, Jan. 1941– Aug. 1942); co-author with Joan Smith of *Harry McShane: No Mean Fighter* (London, 1978). *TJ*, Aug. 1979.

30. Fred Pateman had been a paratrooper in WWII. Walter Holmes had worked, 1920s, on the *Daily Herald*; editor, *Sunday Worker* (1925–9); joined *Daily Worker*, 1930, and from then wrote its 'Worker's Notebook' feature, and was also the paper's correspondent in 1930s in Moscow, the Abyssinian war, 1936 (where he also represented *The Times*), Shanghai, 1937, and at the Nuremberg Trials, 1946. W. Rust, *The Story of the Daily Worker* (London, 1949), 9, 17, 25, 36, 104; Noreen Branson, *History of the Communist Party of Great Britain 1927–1941* (London, 1985), 53.

31. William Rust (1903–1949); secretary, Young Communist League and editor, *Young Worker*; imprisoned for a year, 1925, for incitement to mutiny; editor, 1930–49, *Daily Worker*; correspondent, 1937–8, with International Brigades in Spain; author of *Britons in Spain* (London, 1939). MacDougall, *Militant Miners*, op. cit., 330–1. John Ross Campbell (1894–1969), born Paisley; member from 1912 successively of British Socialist Party and Communist Party; in Naval Division in WWI, wounded and decorated, MM; editor successively of *The Worker*, 1921–4, *Workers' Weekly*, 1924–6, and *Daily Worker*, 1949–59; his arrest but release, 1924, in the 'Campbell case', led then to the fall of the first Lab. govt; member, Executive and Central Committee, Communist Party, for many years, and, 1925–35, of Executive, Communist International; imprisoned for six months, 1925–6, for seditious conspiracy. MacDougall, *Militant Miners*, op. cit., 170, 174; Branson, *History of the Communist Party of Great Britain 1927–1941*, op. cit., *passim*; *TJ*, Oct 1969.

32. G. Allen Hutt (1901–1973); educ. Cambridge University; joined Communist Party early 1920s; began work in journalism on *Daily Herald*, 1923–5; editor, 1925–9, *Trade Union Unity*; 1929–30, chief sub-editor, *Sunday Worker*; 1930–66, chief sub-editor, *Daily Worker* (he was also chief sub-editor, then night editor, *Reynolds News*, 1936–42); joined NUJ, 1925, a member, 1946–72, of its Executive, president, 1967–8, and editor, 1948–72, *Journalist*; author of several books, including *The Condition of the Working Class in Britain* (London, 1933). *TJ*, Aug.–Sep. and Oct. 1973; MacDougall, *Militant Miners*, op. cit., ii, iii, 327, 328, 334.

33. George A. Watt (1921–1997), born Elgin but grew up in Edinburgh. As a result of an accident he suffered as a baby, George Watt developed tuberculosis of the spine, spent his childhood and youth at home in bed, able to attend school for only two or three years, although he read widely. His father (also George Watt) was assistant editor, Edinburgh *Evening Dispatch*. Able to begin work there when he was about 17, George Watt vividly recollected his great difficulty climbing the lengthy flight of steps up from Waverley station to the back door of the then *Dispatch/Scotsman* building. Interviewed

a few months before his death, to record and include in this book his recollections of his years in journalism, for services to which he was awarded the MBE in 1980, very sadly he found as the interview reached the years of his life's work that he had no recollection at all of his work at the *Dispatch* or of his later distinguished career during several decades as Parliament House courts correspondent in Edinburgh for the *Glasgow Herald*. The much later decision not to include George Watt, a highly respected journalist and a most courageous man, in this present volume was taken with the greatest reluctance. A memorial to his life and work is his co-authorship, with Dr Eric Clive, of *Scots Law for Journalists*, first published in 1965, and since then reissued in several new editions. As Lord Emslie, Lord Justice-General of Scotland and Lord President of the Court of Session, 1972–89, said of George Watt, he was a master of his craft. Interview with George Watt, 21 Jan. 1997; *TH*, 5 Apr. 1997.

34. *Reynolds News*, 1850–1967, originally a Chartist newspaper, it became successively Liberal–Radical, Labour, and Co-operative; retitled, 1962–7, *Sunday Citizen*.

35. Associated Press, est. 1848, an American news agency equivalent to the Press Association and Reuters.

36. John Christie, who lived in the same house as Timothy Evans, was convicted and hanged in 1953 for the murder of his own wife and confessed to the murders of six other women, including the wife of Evans. Belief was widespread that Christie had also murdered the Evans's child. Evans was given a free pardon posthumously in 1966.

37. Further references to these and other *Daily Worker* staff mentioned by George MacDougall can be found in Alison Macleod, *The Death of Uncle Joe* (Woodbridge, Suffolk, 1997) – she herself had joined the Communist Party in 1939, was a sub-editor, from 1944, then, from 1953, TV critic, for the *Daily Worker* in the years recalled by George MacDougall – and in Francis Beckett, *Enemy Within: The Rise and Fall of the British Communist Party* (Woodbridge, Suffolk, 1998 edn).

38. Ruth Hingston had begun work, 1947, as a sub-editor at Newnes, publishers. In 1969 she failed to be elected the third woman member of the NUJ Executive, and later that year moved from British Plastics to join the Overseas Press Services Division, Central Office of Information. *TJ*, Feb., Jun., and Jul. 1969.

39. A testimonial was launched in 1970 by London Central branch, NUJ, for George Sinfield, for many years industrial correspondent, *Daily Worker* and *Morning Star*, as he had by then become paralysed and had lost the power of speech. *TJ*, Jun. 1970.

40. Malcolm MacEwen (1911–1996), son of Sir Alexander MacEwen; educ. Edinburgh University; a senior journalist, *Daily Worker*, 1943–56; assistant editor, 1956–60, *Architects' Journal*, head successively, 1960–72, of Information and Publicity Services and Public Affairs, Royal Institute of British Architects, editor, 1964–71, *RIBA Journal*; Hon. Fellow, RIBA, 1974; Leverhulme Research Fellow, 1972–3; Research Fellow, University College, London, 1977–84, Birkbeck College, 1985–8; author of several books, including *The Greening of a Red* (London, 1991). *WWW, Vol. X, 1996–2000*, op. cit., 367.

41. Rosina (Rose) Smith (1891–1985), born Putney; grew up near Chesterfield; an infant teacher, c.1909–19; joined, 1909–10, Social Democratic Federation, then, 1922, the Communist Party; Party Parl. candidate, 1929, Mansfield; Party National Women's Organiser, 1929–33; a leader of women's section, Hunger March to London, 1930; imprisoned for three months, 1931; 1934–55, reporter, special correspondent, editor of women's page, *Daily Worker*; worked in China, 1962–9 and 1971 to early 1980s; given a state funeral in China, and her ashes were buried in Beijing. Keith Geldart, David Howell, and Neville Kirk (eds), *Dictionary of Labour Biography Vol. XI* (Basingstoke, 2003), 262–6.

42. *Workers' Weekly* 1923–7, official organ of the Communist Party of Great Britain.

43. John Gollan (1911–1977), born and grew up in Edinburgh; joined, 1927, the Communist Party; successively editor, Young Communist League paper *Challenge*, general secretary, Young Communist League, secretary, North-East England Committee, then Scottish

Committee, Communist Party, assistant general secretary, 1947–9; assistant editor, *Daily Worker*, 1949–54; Party national organiser, 1954–6, general secretary, 1956–76. MacDougall, *Voices from Work and Home*, op. cit., 531.

44. The Communist or Third International (the Comintern), est. at Moscow, Mar. 1919, as a complete break from the Second or Socialist International, est. 1889, was dissolved in 1943 during WWII. J.R. Campbell was a member, 1925–35, of the Communist International Executive Committee.

45. *Challenge*, est. 1921 as *Young Worker*, retitled later that year *Young Communist*, then again, 1926–7, *Young Worker*, then *Challenge*, 1935–85, then retitled *Young Communist*. Royden Harrison, Gillian B. Woolven, and Robert Duncan, *The Warwick Guide to British Labour Periodicals 1790–1970* (Sussex, 1977), 72, 454; private infm.

46. British–Soviet Friendship Society est. in England, 1946–c. early 1990s. Infm.: Anna Dyer, Scotland–Russia Society.

47. The World Youth Festival, attended by delegates from 103 countries, ran for a week from 5 Aug. 1951 in East Berlin, with 900 British youth delegates sailing to the Festival on a Polish passenger liner; but 300 others travelling by train were stopped by the American authorities for two days in Austria, and there were complaints by those delegates of assault and mistreatment. *Daily Worker*, 6 Aug. 1951.

48. In the 1951 election Lauchlan came third with 4,728 votes, in 1955 again third, with 5,389 votes; in the 1959 and 1964 elections, the last in which he stood in West Fife, his successive percentage vote fell. *TS*, 28 May 1955; Craig, *British Parliamentary Election Results 1950–1970*, op. cit., 649.

49. David Ainley, an expert on the Co-operative movement, had worked out the constitution of the People's Press Printing Society shortly after WWII, and it was approved as a Co-operative by the Registrar of Friendly Societies. The *Daily Worker* then ceased to proclaim itself as the Organ of the Communist Party, and instead described itself as 'The Only Daily Paper Owned by Its Readers'. Thus organised as a Co-operative, the shareholders could, if they so decided, make the paper independent of the Communist Party – and years later, when the Party had become 'liberal', they did so. Macleod, *The Death of Uncle Joe*, op. cit., 240.

50. The World Youth Festival in Bucharest, with delegates from more than 100 countries, took place from 6 to 16 Aug. 1953. *Daily Worker*, 7 and 17 Aug. 1953.

51. At Christmas 1989, the Soviet Union cancelled 6,000 copies of the *Morning Star* (formerly, till 1966, titled the *Daily Worker*). That cancellation reduced the daily circulation of the paper from 12,000 to 6,000. *TJ*, Mar. 1990; Macleod, *The Death of Uncle Joe*, op. cit., 243.

52. The 'Great Terror' trials and purges unleashed by Stalin in the 1930s are generally considered to have begun from the assassination (which Stalin himself may have arranged) of Sergei Kirov, head of the Communist Party in Leningrad (now St Petersburg), in Dec. 1934. By 1939 enormous numbers of those – whether old Bolsheviks, army officers, Trotskyists, or others – whom Stalin regarded as opposed to his policies had been 'liquidated', in many cases along with their family members. Willie Campbell, born 1910 in Paisley as William Carlin, changed his name to Campbell when his mother m. J.R. Campbell in 1922. Willie worked in the Soviet Union from 1932 as an entertainer and eventually for the Soviet State Circus as Villi the Clown, before returning to Britain in 1977. There is no evidence in his book *Villi the Clown* (London, 1981) that he was ever sent to prison or a labour camp in the Soviet Union. But Alison Macleod, *The Death of Uncle Joe*, op. cit., 268, says that shortly before Stalin's death [in 1953] Villi *was* in prison.

53. *Neues Deutschland*. Zentralorgan der Sozialistischen Einheitspartei Deutschlands, 1946–89/90.

54. James Klugmann (1912–1977), born London; his father a City merchant; educ. Gresham's School, Norfolk, and Cambridge University; joined, 1932, Communist Party at Cambridge and, with John Cornford (later killed in the Spanish Civil War), he helped

build there a strong Party branch among the students; research at Cambridge, 1934–5; secretary, 1935–9, in Paris, World Student Association for Peace and Freedom; an army major in WWII in Middle East, Italy, and liaison officer with Yugoslav partisans led by Tito; 1945–6, assistant to head of UNRRA (United Nations Relief and Rehabilitation) in Belgrade; editor, 1947–50, *World News and Views*, Communist Party weekly; head, 1950–60, of the Party education dept; member, 1952–63, Party executive, and later of its Political Committee; a founder and later successively, 1957–77, assistant editor and editor, *Marxism Today*; tutor, lecturer, writer; 'remarkable for his friendliness'. *Morning Star*, 15 Sep. 1977; *Marxism Today*, Nov. 1977. At Easter, 1952, the Communist Party held its first Congress for three years, and publicised the Party's new programme, *The British Road to Socialism*. Macleod, *The Death of Uncle Joe*, op. cit., 29.

55. Peter Kerrigan (1899–1977); a Glasgow engineer; member, 1927–9 and 1931–65, Executive Committee, Communist Party; a leader, 1934 and 1936, of Hunger Marches from Glasgow to London; successively Scottish secretary, national organiser, and industrial organiser, Communist Party; a political commissar in Spanish Civil War. Wilfred Macartney or McCartney, a left-wing journalist and author of *Walls Have Mouths: a Record of Ten Years' Penal Servitude* (London, 1936).

56. In the 1930s Peter Zinkin had been industrial organiser for the London District Committee, Communist Party. Branson, *History of the Communist Party of Great Britain 1927–1941*, op. cit., 179, 282. According to Macleod, *The Death of Uncle Joe*, op. cit., 248, Peter Zinkin was 'the Russians' man in the [*Daily Worker*] office. I know now that he made regular reports to the Soviet Embassy on all of us.'

57. Llew Gardner, born Glasgow; trained on *Northampton Chronicle and Echo*, moved to London as a feature writer, *Daily Worker*, but left the paper and the Communist Party over the invasion of Hungary, 1956; worked briefly for *Tribune*; political correspondent, *Sunday Express*, but resigned in protest against its attacks on the Lab. govt; joined, 1967, Rediffusion TV programme *This Week*, and remained with the programme after Thames TV took over; freelance from late 1970s; died 1990, aged 60. *TJ*, Apr. 1991.

58. Arthur Christiansen (1904–1963); began, 1920–4, on *Wallasey Chronicle*; 1924–5, *Liverpool Courier*, 1925–6, London editor, Liverpool *Evening Express*; 1926–9, news editor, *Sunday Express*; 1928–33, assistant editor, 1933–57, editor, and, 1957–9, editorial director, *Daily Express*; 1941–59, director, Beaverbrook Newspapers Ltd; 1960–2, editorial adviser, Associated TV Ltd; author of *Headlines All My Life* (1961). *WWW, Vol. VI, 1961–1970*, op. cit., 203, 204.

59. Allen Hutt, *Newspaper Design* (Oxford, 1960).

60. *New Statesman*, 1913 to date.

61. Nine doctors, six of them Jewish, were said to have been involved in the 'plot'. Soon after Stalin's death in Mar. 1953 all nine doctors were freed and rehabilitated. Alan Bullock, *Hitler and Stalin: Parallel Lives* (London, 1991), 1048–9.

62. It was in fact in May 1955 that Nikita Khrushchev, Soviet leader for a decade after Stalin's death, visited Marshal Tito (1898–1980) in Yugoslavia to effect a reconciliation between the two govts, bitterly divided as they had been since 1948 by ideological and other factors. Many other opponents, actual or alleged, of Stalinism since the late 1920s (when Leon Trotsky, a leader of the 1917 Bolshevik Revolution had been expelled by Stalin from the Soviet Union) had also been denounced as Trotskyists. The Vienna Talks in May 1955 resulted in the signing, by the four Powers that had jointly occupied Austria since 1945, of the treaty of Austrian independence, and the withdrawal from Austria that autumn of all foreign troops.

63. Khrushchev's speech denouncing the appalling crimes of Stalin (in some of which Khrushchev himself had played some part), at the closed or secret session of the Soviet Party Congress in Feb. 1956, created a huge sensation around the world – not least among many other Communist parties, once its contents became generally known, as they soon afterwards did.

64. Lazlo Rajk, Communist Minister of the Interior in Hungary, had been an early victim of Stalinist post-war purges there when he had been executed in 1949. Destalinisation, divisions in the Communist Parties in Poland and Hungary between Stalinists and reformers, and growing national feelings in both countries made 1956 a fateful year in eastern Europe. In Poland, a steelworkers' pay dispute at Posnan in Jun. led to troops killing or wounding more than 300 peaceful demonstrators. In Hungary, the increasing unrest led to the uprising of Oct.–Nov. that year.

65. Cayton (*nom de plume* of Alf Rubin), began, 1935, on the *Daily Worker* and was its (and later the *Morning Star*'s) racing tipster for 60 years; his *nom de plume* came from Cayton St, home in 1935 of the *Daily Worker*; died 1995, aged 79. *TJ*, Apr.–May 1996.

66. Gabriel (*nom de plume* of Jimmy Friell), born and grew up in Glasgow; cartoonist with *Daily Worker*, 1936–56, when he resigned from it and from the Communist Party because the paper refused to print a cartoon equating Soviet troops in Hungary with the simultaneous Anglo-French invasion of Egypt; with *Evening Standard*, 1956–61, then with TV; a life member, NUJ; died 1997, aged 84. *TJ*, Mar.–Apr., 1997. Mick Bennett, died 1997, had been a member of the Central Committee, Communist Party, in the 1930s. Branson, *History of the Communist Party of Great Britain 1927–1941*, op. cit., 342; Macleod, *The Death of Uncle Joe*, op. cit., 264. In the NUJ (as traditionally in printing unions) the in-house membership is known as the chapel, and its chair or chief officer as the father (or mother) of the chapel (FOC or MOC). Peter Fryer (1927–2006); joined the Young Communist League, 1942, and the Communist Party, 1945; began, 1943, as a reporter, *Yorkshire Post*, but was sacked, 1947, for refusing to leave the Communist Party; 1948–56, parl. and foreign correspondent, *Daily Worker*, and reported the trial, 1949, of Lazlo Rajk; his reports from Hungary about the 1956 uprising were censored or suppressed by the *Daily Worker*, from which he then resigned, and he was expelled from the Communist Party for his criticism of the suppression of the uprising; became a founder member of the Socialist Labour League and editor, *The Newsletter*, a Trotskyist journal; author of several books, including *Hungarian Tragedy* (London, 1956); posthumously awarded the Knight's Cross of the Order of Merit of the Republic of Hungary. Obit., Terry Brotherstone, *Guardian*, 3 Nov. 2006.

67. Rajani Palme Dutt (1896–1974), grad. Oxford University; imprisoned for refusing to serve in armed forces in WWI; founder member, Communist Party of Great Britain; founder, 1921, and first editor, *Labour Monthly*; editor, 1923–4, *Workers' Weekly*, and, 1936–8, *Daily Worker*; member, 1922–65, vice-chairman, 1945–65, Central Committee, Communist Party.

68. After dropping the first atomic bombs on Japan in 1945, the USA had developed by 1952 the much more powerful hydrogen bomb. The Soviet Union had first tested an atomic bomb in 1949, and had developed a hydrogen bomb by 1953. The *Daily Worker*, 6 Apr. 1957, reported the Soviet Union had tested its second hydrogen bomb. Macleod, *The Death of Uncle Joe*, op. cit., 239.

69. *Tribune*, 1937 to date.

70. *World's Press News*, 1929–68, merged into *Campaign*.

71. Granada Television, 1956–2004, then merged with Carlton Television to form ITV plc.

72. Arnold Kemp (1939–2002), son of Robert Kemp, playwright; educ. Edinburgh Academy and Edinburgh University; sub-editor, 1959–62, *The Scotsman*, 1962–5, the *Guardian*; production editor, 1965–70, London editor, 1970–2, deputy editor, 1972–81, *The Scotsman*; editor, 1981–94, *Glasgow Herald* [*The Herald*, from 1992]; consultant editor, 1994–7, Caledonian Publishing; contributor and desk editor, 1996–9, *The Observer*; three hon. degrees from Scottish universities; author, *The Hollow Drum: Scotland Since the War* (Edinburgh, 1993). *WWW, Vol. XI, 2001–2005*, op. cit, 292. Ronald Munro (1930–2007), began from school on *Banffshire Journal*; National Service, RAF, 1949–51; reporter, then sub-editor, 1951–5, *Press & Journal*; 1955–6, *Scottish Daily Mail*; 1956–61, sub-editor, 1961–70, deputy chief sub-editor, 1970–8, chief sub-editor, 1978–86, production editor,

1986–93, successively night editor and associate editor (production), *The Scotsman*. *TS*, 12 Jan. 2007.

73. Magnus Linklater (b.1942), born Orkney; author, broadcaster, journalist; educ. Eton College and Cambridge University; 1965–87, successively, reporter, *Daily Express*, *Evening Standard*, a supplement editor, *Sunday Times*, news, features, managing editor, *Observer*, editor, 1988–94, *The Scotsman*; chairman from 1996, Scottish Arts Council; hon. DA, Napier University.

74. Andrew Hood (b.1940); 1961–4, sub-editor, 1964–72, a leader writer and, from 1972, editor of letters to the editor, 1973–89, assistant editor, *The Scotsman*; 1990–4, sub-editor, and, 1994–2007, involved in letters-editing, *The Herald*. Infm.: Andrew Hood.

75. The Campaign for Nuclear Disarmament (CND), est. 1958 by Bertrand Russell (1872–1970) and Canon John Collins (1905–1982), was said to have 200,000 people affiliated to it by the 1980s. Sked and Cook, *Post-War Britain*, op. cit., 421.

76. Alex Reid stood as Lab. candidate in only the Oct. 1964 North Edinburgh election, when he came second. In the 1966 election the Lab. candidate there was W.S. Dalgleish. *TS*, 16 Oct. 1964, 1 Apr. 1966.

77. George MacDougall as SNP candidate came second in the municipal elections in Edinburgh Broughton ward in 1968 and 1969, and third in 1970. He was fourth in Lothian Regional Council elections for Edinburgh Murrayfield/Dean ward in 1994, and third in the City of Edinburgh Council elections for Dean ward in 1995. *TS*, 8 May 1968, 7 May 1969, 6 May 1970, 7 May 1994, 7 Apr. 1995.

Ethel Simpson, pp. 299–321

1. James M. Chalmers, began as an apprentice reader and compositor, *Banffshire Journal*, then joined *Northern Herald*, Wick, as reporter, proofreader, clerk, accounts collector, and advertisement canvasser; from age 20, reporter, Aberdeen *Free Press*, for Buchan, based at Peterhead; acting capt., Gordon Highlanders, in WWI; 1927–35, deputy chief reporter, 1935–44, news editor, and, 1944–50, editor, *Press & Journal*; with Kemsley Newspapers, in London, 1950–6; died 1963, aged 71, in Paris as a result of a car accident. *P&J*, 13 Aug. 1963.

2. Kitchen deem – kitchen maid.

3. Chaumers (chambers) – sleeping places for farm workers.

4. Caff beds – beds where the mattresses were stuffed with chaff, husks of grain.

5. William Veitch (1885–1968), born Edinburgh; educ. George Watson's College; trained on Edinburgh *Evening Dispatch*, moved, 1910, to a news agency in London; chairman, 1923, Parl. Press Gallery; London editor, 1910–23, Aberdeen *Daily Journal*, and, 1923–7, of *Press & Journal*; editor-in-chief, 1927–57, Aberdeen Journals; and managing director; director, 1937–57, Kemsley Newspapers Ltd; treasurer, NUJ, 1917–23; president, 1942–6, Scottish Daily Newspaper Society; a member, 1953–7, of Press Council; CBE and Chevalier de la Légion d'Honneur. *P&J*, 13 Aug. 1968; *Scottish Biographies 1938*, op. cit., 759.

6. George Inglis, born Methlick; educ. Ellon Senior Secondary School; joined, 1927, *Mearns Leader*; 1938, *P&J* and *Evening Express*, of which latter he became chief reporter; chief sub-editor, 1958–60, deputy editor, 1960–71, *P&J*; died 1971, aged 62. *P&J*, 10 Nov. 1971.

7. Helen Fisher, women's editor, *P&J*; died 1995, aged 79. Infm.: Ethel Simpson.

8. George Fraser (1895–1998), born Newmachar, son of a stationmaster; educ. Inverurie Academy and Aberdeen University; 1917–19, sub-editor, Aberdeen *Daily Journal*; 1919–21, Liverpool *Daily Post*; chief sub-editor, 1921–2, *Daily Journal*, 1922–6, *P&J*, 1926–45 (he and a few others produced a typewritten version of the paper during the 1926 General Strike); 1926–45 also chief sub-editor, *Evening Express*, then its editor, 1945–53; literary editor, *P&J*, 1953–61, and weekly columnist, 1961–98; in 1993 the

Dept of Employment declared George Fraser was the oldest working journalist in Britain. *P&J*, 22 Apr. 1998; *TJ*, Dec. 1995–Jan. 1996.

9. William Alexander (Sandy) Mitchell; educ. Aberdeen Grammar School and Aberdeen and St Andrews Universities; joined, 1931, Aberdeen Journals; an RN officer in WWII; 1950–71, London editor, *P&J*; died in London, 1979. *P&J*, 12 Dec. 1979. George Rowntree Harvey (1891–1951); seriously wounded in RFC/RAF in WWI; post-war, worked at night as a sub-editor on Aberdeen *Free Press* and *P&J*, and attended Aberdeen University by day; for many years literary, dramatic, and music critic, *P&J*; author and playwright, actor, and Community Drama adjudicator. *P&J*, 12 Jun. 1951.

10. The siege of a house in Sydney St, Stepney, on 3 Jan. 1911, by police and Scots Guards, with Winston Churchill, Home Secretary, also present, was of three or four Baltic immigrants, said to be anarchists, who had tried to break into a jeweller's shop and had killed two policemen. The siege ended with another policeman killed and two of the besieged men found dead inside the burned-out house, the other one, or two, having escaped.

11. James Gomer Berry (1888–1968), Lord Kemsley; 1937–59, chairman, Kemsley Newspapers Ltd, and editor-in-chief, *Sunday Times*; his wife was Edith Meraudon du Plessis. In a book review in *TJ*, Dec. 1972, of a history of the *Sunday Times*, Allen Hutt, a past president, NUJ, and editor, *The Journalist*, took a critical view of Lord Kemsley and wrote that he 'appears in these pages, for all their kindly stress on his personal virtues, as the most appalling publisher British newspapers have ever known. Kemsley was not just a snob, he was the Matterhorn of the snob world. And his fingers were ever in the editorial pie of every newspaper he owned, above all in that of the *Sunday Times*.' *WWW, Vol. VI, 1961–1970*, op. cit., 620, 621.

12. There was also published *The Kemsley Manual of Journalism* (London, 1950), 424 pp.

13. The *P&J* and *Evening Express* were both issued during the General Strike, but only as duplicated sheets. Liz Kibblewhite and Andy Kirby, *Aberdeen in the General Strike* (Aberdeen, 1977), 12. See also above here, Note 8.

14. Alex Dempster, fishing correspondent, Aberdeen Journals, died 1984, aged 84. James Forbes (1916–1980); joined, 1933, Aberdeen Journals Ltd as trainee news reporter but transferred to sports; in RAF Coastal Command in WWII; became associate sports editor, *Evening Express*; chairman for many years, North of Scotland District, IoJ; died on his way to work, then the longest serving member of staff. *P&J*, 5 Jan. 1980. Gordon Forbes (b.1926), chief sports editor, *P&J*. Alistair Macdonald (b.1930); chief football writer, *P&J*. Norman MacDonald, joined Aberdeen Journals aged 15; sports editor, 1932–73, *P&J* and *Evening Express*; in KOSB in WWII, later capt., Pioneer Corps; died 1976, aged 68. Infm.: Ethel Simpson; *P&J*, 23 Dec. 1976, 5 Jan. 1980.

15. *Aberdeen Bon Accord and Northern Pictorial*, 1926–59.

16. See above, David M. Smith, Note 15, p. 542.

17. Lady Tweedsmuir (1915–1978), born London, as Priscilla Thomson; educ. in England, Germany and France; m., 1934, Sir Arthur Grant of Monymusk (killed in action, 1944); m., 1948, John Buchan, Lord Tweedsmuir (son of the novelist); 1948–66, Cons. and Unionist MP, Aberdeen South; Parl. Under-Secretary of State for Scotland, 1962–4; life peeress from 1970; successively, 1970–4, Minister of State, Scottish Office, then Foreign Office; 1974, Deputy Speaker, House of Lords. *The Biographical Dictionary of Scottish Women*, op. cit., 51. Hon. Mary Pamela Berry, daughter of 1st Lord Kemsley, was wife of the 12th Marquess of Huntly; she died 1998. *WW, 2011*, op. cit., 1151.

18. From 1928 onwards Communist candidates usually stood in Aberdeen North Parl. elections but usually also lost their deposits. Bob Cooney (1910–1984); began work as a pawnbroker's assistant; political commissar, 1938, British Bn, International Brigades; in Royal Artillery in WWII; Communist Party Parl. candidate, 1945, Glasgow Cathcart; blacklisted by Aberdeen building employers, he lived for many years in Birmingham. Dave Campbell, a farm worker then engineer; vice-president, Aberdeen Trades &

Labour Council; leader, Hunger March from Aberdeen to London, Nov. 1938; post-1945 a full-time trade union official. Jimmy Milne (1921–1986); a patternmaker; secretary, 1947–69, Aberdeen Trades Council; a member, 1954–69, General Council, Scottish TUC, its president, 1959–60, assistant general secretary, 1969–75, general secretary, 1975–86.

19. For Donald Dewar, see above, Hector McSporran, Note 13, p. 551.

20. Robert Boothby (1900–1986), born Edinburgh; educ. Eton College and Oxford University; Cons. MP, 1924–58, East Aberdeenshire; PPS, 1926–9, to Winston Churchill as Chancellor of the Exchequer, and, 1940–1, in Ministry of Food; in RAF in WWII; Lord Boothby from 1958; author of several books, including *I Fight to Live* (1947). *WWW, Vol. VIII, 1981–1990*, op. cit., 77. Boothby's love affair with Lady Dorothy Macmillan, wife of the later prime minister (1957–63) Harold Macmillan, appears to have begun in 1929–30 and evidently lasted until her death in 1966. Robert Rhodes James, *Bob Boothby: A Portrait* (London, 1992), 114, 117, 120, 122–3.

21. Emma Simpson (b.1968).

22. Sandy Meston (1894–1980); became chief sub-editor, *P&J*, shortly before WWII, then assistant editor till he retired, 1968. Infm.: Ethel Simpson; *P&J*, 15 Nov. 1980.

23. Ethel Simpson recalls that she and her colleague Helen Fisher, as friends of Poppy Mitchell, who ran the family-owned but men-only Bond Bar, were allowed into it. The two were sitting in the bar one day when two men arrived with their women partners. Poppy Mitchell told the four, 'Sorry, no ladies here, men only.' One of the men pointed to Ethel and Helen and said, 'What about those ladies there ?' 'Oh,' said Poppy, 'they're nae ladies, they're *P&J* reporters'.

24. For the dispute, see above, Hector McSporran, Note 25, pp. 552, 553.

Bill Rae, pp. 332–49

1. For Bruce Peebles, see above, Tom McGowran, Note 2, p. 560.

2. David Donald, born Liverpool; PoW in WWI; reporter, 1922–9, Edinburgh *Evening Dispatch*, joined *Evening News*, 1929, was for many years its municipal correspondent, then became chief reporter; chairman, Edinburgh branch, NUJ, but later joined IoJ; died 1953, aged 57. *EN*, 24 Dec. 1953.

3. For Smith, Berwick, see above, David M. Smith, pp. 42–62.

4. Alexander (Lex) McLean (1908–1975). The Palladium Theatre, East Fountainbridge, Edinburgh, was originally, 1886–1911, a circus, then, 1911–32, a cinema, and 1935–84, a theatre. Lex McLean often appeared at the Palladium Theatre. J.H. Littlejohn, *The Scottish Music Hall, 1880–1990* (Wigtown, 1990), 44, 59.

5. Lewis Simpson (1907–1993), worked from age 14 with the Edinburgh *Evening News* until he retired, 1973. Infm.: the late Mrs Jean Simpson. Arthur Thomas Goodey (1918–2008); post-WWII, municipal correspondent, *Evening Dispatch*, then of *Evening News* to 1964; public relations officer, 1964–74, Midlothian County Council, 1974–83, Midlothian District Council. Death notice, *TS*, 24 Sep. 2008; private infm.

6. Dick Campbell retired from the *Evening News*, c. 1976. Infm.: Ian Nimmo.

7. James Donaldson Heatly; grad Edinburgh University; 12 years in court work (six of them as a clerk, Parliament House), then, 1948–70, Edinburgh City Prosecutor; died 1977, aged 72. *TS*, 27 Jun. 1977. As early as 1942 (when in that year alone she had had 28 such convictions), Isabella Nicol or Freeman had appeared a total of 127 times at the Burgh Court. *EN*, 15 Dec. 1942.

8. John Logan Robertson; educ. George Heriot's School, Edinburgh; joined from school, 1935, reporting staff, *Evening News*; in RAF in WWII; post-war, covered major news stories throughout Scotland for *EN*, and football (under *nom de plume* Restalrig), as well as for several years the 'Turret Window' and 'People' columns; as chief reporter, covered early stages, 1969–74, of the Troubles in Northern Ireland; chairman,

Edinburgh branch, IoJ; a founder, the William McGonagall Club; died 1974, aged 53. *EN*, 7 and 8 Jan. 1974. Donald Esson (1920–1979); educ. Royal High School, Edinburgh; began, from school, 1936, as a copy boy, *Evening News*; in WWII in Lothians & Border Yeomanry in North Africa, Italy, and Palestine; post-war, general news reporter, *EN*, then its Court of Session correspondent (he secured a world exclusive story on the Goldsmith–Patino marriage, 1953), as well as sports writer (*nom de plume*: Dunedin); from 1960s, news editor, from 1972, a leader writer; member, NUJ, for 15 years. Infm.: Peter Esson; his son; *EN*, 8 Oct. 1979; *TJ*, Nov. 1979. Willie Ross later moved from *EN* to *Scottish Daily Mail*, then to Middlesbrough *Evening Gazette*, from which he retired, but he remained on Teesside until his death. Infm.: Ian Nimmo.

9. James Seager; began, 1904, on *Evening News* as a copy boy aged 14 (one of his first jobs was to collect messages from the legs of carrier pigeons arriving in their loft at the *News* office, Market St); became chief sub-editor; introduced the 'Turret Window' column, 'Eve's Circle', and the Saturday features page; editor from 1941, editor-in-chief and general manager, 1954–6; 'His was the edict, since observed, that what one would not like one's own daughter to read did not go in the paper'; chairman, Edinburgh District, IoJ, and Fellow, IoJ; CBE, 1951; died 1964 aged 73. *EN*, 5 Mar. 1964; *TS*, 6 Mar. 1964.

10. William R. Milligan (1898–1975); educ. Sherborne School, and Oxford and Glasgow Universities; in Highland Light Infantry in WWI; advocate from 1925, QC from 1945; Solicitor General for Scotland, 1951–4, Lord Advocate, 1954–60; Cons. MP, 1955–60, Edinburgh North; as Lord Milligan, Senator of the College of Justice, 1960–73. *Scottish Biographies*, op. cit., 552; *WWW, Vol. VII, 1971–1980*, op. cit., 544.

11. George Robertson was hanged at Edinburgh, 23 Jun. 1954, for murdering his former wife, Elizabeth Greig or Robertson or McGarry, by stabbing her in the house at 57 Tron Square, Edinburgh, and for murdering his son, George Robertson, at 42 Tron Square. *TS*, 24 Jun. 1954.

12. Fifty reporters representing the world's press were present in court when Lord Wheatley (1908–1988) delivered his judgement, 8 May 1963, on the divorce action brought by the 11th Duke of Argyll (1903–1973) against the Duchess. The judgement, of some 40,000 words, granted divorce on the ground of adultery by the Duchess, and was one of the longest judgements ever delivered concerning a Scottish divorce action. The Duke's second wife had divorced him in 1951 because of his adultery with the defender. Lord Wheatley described the Duchess as 'a completely promiscuous woman . . . whose attitude to the sanctity of marriage was wholly immoral'. The *Evening News* report carried a three-deck headline over five columns. *EN*, 8 May 1963; *TS*, 9 May 1963.

13. For Gordon Dean, see above, pp. 366–85.

14. Andrew Fyall (b.1932); began, 1949–56, on *Fifeshire Advertiser*; 1956, *Scottish Daily Express*; 1956–76, *Daily Express*, London, as foreign correspondent, 1961–7, in USA, then in 71 countries, including coverage of the Biafran War; head of public relations, 1976–89, Edinburgh District Council; bureau chief, Scottish Television, 1989–97; consultant, 1997–2000. Infm.: Andrew Fyall.

Nancy Mackenzie, pp. 350–65

1. Bill Coghill worked for the *Evening News* from the 1930s; died 1947.

2. Oscar Slater (c.1870–1948), a German Jewish immigrant, was found guilty by a majority at the High Court, Edinburgh, in May 1909 of the murder in Glasgow in Dec. 1908 of an octogenarian spinster, Marion Gilchrist, in her flat in West Princes Street. He was sentenced to death, but was reprieved and his sentence commuted to penal servitude for life. He remained in prison until 1927. His conviction was quashed by the Scottish Court of Criminal Appeal in Jun. 1928.

3. Conscription of unmarried women and childless widows aged from 20 to 30 was introduced in Dec. 1941. The age was extended early in 1943 to women aged 19. Calder, *The People's War: Britain 1939–45*, op. cit., 268; Gardiner, *Wartime Britain 1939–1945*, op. cit., 433.

4. German E-boats were small and speedy motor torpedo boats, skilled in using smokescreens to hide their movements at close quarters.

5. V1s were flying pilotless bombs, the first of which were directed across the Channel against London and the south of England on 13 Jun. 1944, a week after D-Day. At the beginning of Sep. 1944 the first V2s, long rockets each carrying about a ton of explosives, were likewise launched from Holland. The loss of life and destruction of houses, etc., caused by these two weapons was very severe. Many people living in the areas where they fell considered the V1 and V2 attacks were worse than the Blitz of 1940–1.

6. The ATS (Auxiliary Territorial Service), est. Sep. 1938, had by 1943 more than 200,000 women in its ranks. The WAAFs (Women's Auxiliary Air Force), preceded by the Women's Royal Air Force, 1918–20, and re-formed in 1939, had by mid-1943 over 180,000. The WRNS (Women's Royal Naval Service), also re-formed in 1939, had enrolled more than 100,000 women by 1945. Gardiner, *Wartime Britain 1939–1945*, op. cit., 433, 434, 436; Sqn Ldr Beryl Escortt, *Women in Air Force Blue* (Wellingborough, 1989), 296.

7. Between 27 Jul. and 3 Aug. 1943 four night raids by RAF bombers and two daylight raids by US bombers killed at least 45,000 people in Hamburg, about 900,000 were rendered homeless, and over a million inhabitants left the city. Destruction of and damage to factories, etc., was equivalent to that by an earthquake. During the entire eight-months-long Blitz on Britain in 1940–1, the total number of civilians killed was more than 43,500. See, e.g., Denis Richards, *RAF Bomber Command in the Second World War* (London, 1994), 190–5.

8. The article, headed 'A Baronet Takes Off His Coat to the Job', by A.M.M. [Nancy Mackenzie], appeared in the *Evening News*, 25 Jun. 1947, and concerned the restoration of Gogar House by its owner, Sir James Steel-Maitland. The main part of the house dated back to 1625. It had been used during WWII by the RAF, when Sir James himself had been in the Australian Air Force.

9. Margo McGill is understood to have moved afterward to London, and worked there for the Lab. Party before her death. Infm.: Hamish Coghill.

10. For Elsie Adam, see also above, R.W. (Billy) Munro, Note 24, p. 557. She appears to have worked for *The Scotsman* for several decades until her retirement in 1954, when she had been in charge of the women's page and was also the paper's ballet critic. She is believed to have died c. 1970s.

11. Dinah Dawson (b.1923); served five years in the WAAFs in WWII; worked for a year in Vienna with the Control Commission for Austria; grad. Durham University; women's page editor, 1950–4, *Evening Dispatch*, 1954–5, *The Scotsman*; then left journalism to train as a teacher and to marry. Infm.: Dinah Dawson.

12. Christian Dior (1905–1957); French couturier, opened his own establishment in Paris, 1947; author of several books; a Dior fashion collection was shown in Glasgow on 29 Apr. 1955.

13. Mamie Baird (1925–2012); left Rutherglen Academy aged 17 and worked first on the *Sunday Post* and *Weekly News* as a reporter, then joined the *Scottish Daily Express*, where she became chief feature writer. She retired from the paper, 1954, when she m. Magnus Magnusson, but cont. to write freelance columns and features for the *Express*, *Evening Citizen*, and later *The Scotsman*: Infm.: Sally Magnusson.

Gordon Dean, pp. 366–85

1. Jim Henderson served in the Fleet Air Arm in WWII; post-war, a reporter, *Daily Record*,

Edinburgh office; moved, c.1949, to the *East African Standard*. Infm.: Gordon Dean.

2. The American film *Call Northside 777* (1948) featured James Stewart as an investigative newspaper reporter.

3. George Hodge (1930–1995); born Edinburgh; educ. Broughton Senior Secondary School; learned shorthand and typing at a local commercial college; began, c.1946 as office boy, then reporter, Edinburgh office, *Daily Record* and Glasgow *Evening News*; succeeded, 1957, Ernie McIntyre as *Daily Herald* Edinburgh correspondent; moved, 1963, into public relations and, 1969, formed George Hodge Associates; 'one of Scotland's best known and respected journalists and public relations consultants', he collapsed and died at work. *TJ*, Oct.–Nov. 1995; *TS*, 28 Apr. and 2 May 1995.

4. Hamilton Neil, in RAF Bomber Command aircrew in WWII; post-war, deputy chief reporter, Edinburgh office, *Daily Record*; moved, 1948, to London. Succeeded as deputy chief reporter by Hugh Young, who had begun work on *Kelso Mail* and *Southern Reporter*; after WWII service with Black Watch, had been *Daily Record* reporter in Galashiels; later became chief reporter, Edinburgh office, and was for many years *Daily Record* rugby correspondent; died 1988, aged 66. Marshall Pugh (b.1925), later author of several works of fiction and a biography of Commander Crabb, RN. Ian Smart moved c.1950–1 to *Scottish Daily Express*, Edinburgh office; later a press officer, Lothian Regional Council; died 2009. Douglas Coupar, after WWII service in the army, reporter, *Daily Record*; moved, c.1950, to *East African Standard*, where Euan Robertson recalls meeting him in the 1960s, when Douglas Coupar was about to become editor of a newspaper in Dar es Salaam, Tanzania. John Lister moved, early 1950s, from the *Daily Record* to become a press officer with the Scottish Tourist Board or National Coal Board. Euan Robertson, after WWII service in Bomber Command, became a reporter, for two years with *The Scotsman*, in early 1950s with *Daily Record*, then emigrated to USA, and afterward lived in Europe and London. Infm.: Euan Robertson and Gordon Dean; *TJ*, Jan. 1983, Jul.–Aug. 1988.

5. PX (Post Exchange) clubs were more bountiful equivalents of the British armed forces' NAAFI.

6. The pillar box, 'the only one in Scotland to bear the controversial EIIR cypher', had been installed on 28 Nov. 1952 in the Inch housing estate, at the corner of Walter Scott Avenue and Gilmerton Road. There were in fact six attacks on the box between 30 Nov. and 12 Feb. 1953, and it seems to be that last one to which Gordon Dean refers. On 30 Nov. the numerals had been daubed with tar. On 6 Dec. 'a primitive bomb' was dropped into the box but did not explode. On 22 Dec. the front of the pillar box was smeared with cream paint. On 2 Jan. a postman making a routine collection found in the box an explosive charge of gelignite from which the detonator had become detached. On Saturday afternoon, 7 Feb, a man wielding a 7lb stonemason's hammer wrapped in a sack attacked the pillar box, but was disturbed at his task and ran away, leaving the hammer behind him. The front of the box was damaged. After a postman had made the day's final collection from the box at 8pm on 12 Feb., the box blew up: witnesses had seen a man posting 'a parcel' in it, smoke was soon afterwards observed coming out of the post-box, then there was an explosion that left the box a shattered stump. Fortunately, no one was injured. Police later found a small Lion Rampant flag on a pile of rubble where the box had stood. A temporary postbox with only GPO on it, not EIIR, replaced the box blown up. The Executive of the Inch Community Association, representing 350 families in the area, declared on 16 Feb. that unless the authorities could guarantee absolute safety to the public it did not want another EIIR postbox. The Scottish Covenant Association called on the Secretary of State for Scotland to ensure that, in the interests of public safety, no more EIIR pillar boxes should be erected anywhere in Scotland. The Executive of the Scottish National Party went further, and called on the Secretary of State to prevent the official and public display anywhere in Scotland of the 'incorrect and unacceptable' Royal cypher EIIR. An EIIR

notice board outside the Royal Scots officers' mess in Colinton Road, Edinburgh, was badly damaged on 22 Feb. by someone who had set it alight, and another EIIR sign at nearby Dreghorn Barracks was found daubed on 27 Feb. On 5 Mar. posters appeared in Glasgow, Perth, Dundee, and Stirling, offering a £2,000 reward for information leading to the identification 'dead or alive of Elizabeth the First of Scotland'. The controversy was hardly new: for example, a reader's letter in the Edinburgh *Evening Dispatch*, 27 Jan. 1936, had suggested the re-numbering of monarchs should have begun with the Treaty of Union in 1707, and that the 'wrong precedent' had begun with William IV. *EN*, 2 Jan, 9, 13, 14, 16, 17, 20, 23, 28 Feb. and 5 Mar. 1953.

7. Jack Brown, a recently married young man, remained unemployed and suffered considerable distress until he eventually found work with the *TV Times*. Infm.: Gordon Dean.

8. The (North) *Shields Evening News* had begun, 1864, as the *Shields Daily News*; with amalgamations and changes of title, its final title, 1975–85, was *Shields Weekly News*. Parry, *NEWSPLAN Northern Region*, op. cit., 202, 207.

9. George Hunter moved from the *Daily Record* to *The Scotsman*, then to John Menzies & Co. Ltd, newspaper distributors and booksellers. Infm.: Gordon Dean. Norrie Bryce (b.1935) worked on the *Linlithgowshire Gazette* before and after service, 1952–6, in the RAF; then on Edinburgh *Evening Dispatch*, *Daily Record*, 1958–60, *Scottish Daily Express*, 1960–4, *Scottish Daily Mail*, 1964–6; press officer, 1966–9, for Secretary of State for Scotland; Cruden, builders, 1969–74; in logistics, 1974–82; editor, 1982–90, *Majorca Daily Bulletin*; logistics, 1990–9; author of *My Thoughts* (Kidderminster, 2006). Infm.: Norrie Bryce.

10. Bruce Cannon (b.1932), began, 1949, as a copy boy, Edinburgh *Evening News*; 1951–3, National Service in RAF; 1953–64, successively junior reporter, reporter, sub-editor, and occasional leader-writer, *Evening News*; successively, 1964–96, assistant editor, *British Weekly*, press officer, director of publicity, and director of communication, Church of Scotland. Infm.: Bruce Cannon. Hamish Coghill (b.1936), began, 1953, as a copy boy, Edinburgh *Evening News*, then junior reporter; National Service, 1957–9; successively, 1959–96, reporter, municipal correspondent, deputy news editor, news editor, and assistant editor, *Evening News*; author of several books, including *Lost Edinburgh* (Edinburgh, 2004). Infm.: Hamish Coghill.

11. Jimmy Wardhaugh played, 1946–59, for Hearts, when, during 1954–8, Hearts won the Scottish Cup, the League championship, and twice the League Cup; played 1959–61 for Dunfermline Athletic; emigrated briefly, 1961–2, to Australia; 1962–78, successively a sports writer with Edinburgh *Evening News* then *Scottish Daily Express*; then publicity officer, BBC, in Edinburgh; died 1978, aged 49. *TJ*, Feb. 1978; *TS*, 4 Jan. 1978.

12. David Scrimgeour (b.1931), began, 1947, as a tube boy, Edinburgh *Evening Dispatch*; by 1950 a junior reporter, *The Scotsman*, then reporter until 1958; 1958–75, a Scottish correspondent, *Daily Telegraph*; a publican, 1975–99, in Edinburgh until he retired. Infm.: David Scrimgeour.

13. Hugh Welsh (c.1922–c.1970s), a highly respected reporter, was with Edinburgh *Evening Dispatch* till c.1950; *Scottish Daily Express*, c.1950–74. Infm.: Walter Gunn and Stan Hunter. George Crockett, born Galashiels but spent most of his childhood in Edinburgh; educ. Royal High School, where he won a school writing competition, the prize for which was a job with the *Evening Dispatch*, which he held until 1950; reporter, c. 1950–74, *Scottish Daily Express*; moved for a time to London and a leading news agency; worked last on the *Kilmarnock Standard*; a noted jazz drummer, he played with leading bands in Scotland and abroad, presented a jazz programme on West Sound Radio, and as a member of Equity played small parts in TV programmes such as *Taggart*, *Rab C. Nesbitt*, and *Para Handy*; d. 1996, aged 75. *Kilmarnock Standard*, 12 Jan. 1996; infm.: Walter Gunn and Stan Hunter. John Vass (b.1930); began, 1947, on *Inverness Courier*; National Service in RAF; reporter, *Scottish Daily Express*, in north of Scotland and Edinburgh and later in London; 1970 to late 1970s, press and public

relations officer, Beaverbrook Newspapers; late 1970s, est. Northpress, independent printing press, in Highlands; subsequently feature writer, Edinburgh *Evening News*; 1990–5, *P&J*, in Inverness. *P&J*, 7 Feb. 1995; infm.: Walter Gunn. Stan Hunter (b.1932), photographer, 1947–86, *Scottish Daily Express*; freelance, 1986–8; pictures editor, 1988–90, *Scotland on Sunday*; freelance, 1991–2001. Infm.: Stan Hunter. Peter McVean was chief photographer, Edinburgh office, *Scottish Daily Express*, but died very young. Infm.: Walter Gunn. Bill Harrold, born Caithness; in RN in WWII; had worked in Canada as a journalist before joining *Scottish Daily Express*, Edinburgh office, then, until 1974, *Scottish Sunday Express*; thereafter information officer, RAF, Pitreavie, Fife. Infm.: Walter Gunn and Stan Hunter.

14. Dr Gavin Strang (b.1943); Lab. MP, Edinburgh East, 1970–97, Edinburgh East and Musselburgh, 1997–2010; intermittently, 1972–97, an Opposition front bench spokesman, held junior and senior office in govt depts, and was Minister for Transport, 1997–8. *WW, 2008*, 2226. Michael Forsyth (b.1954); Cons. MP, Stirling, 1983–97; held junior and senior office in five govt depts, culminating, 1995–7, as Secretary of State for Scotland; life peer from 1999. *WW, 2008*, op. cit., 791. Norman Macfarlane (b.1926); a leading Scottish businessman, chairman of many companies; a life peer as Lord Macfarlane of Bearsden. *WW, 2008*, op. cit., 1467.

15. George Saunders (1923–1995); began as a junior reporter, *Stirling Sentinel*, then with *Stirling Journal*, Derby *Evening Telegraph*, Edinburgh *Evening Dispatch*, where he was news editor on its merger, 1963, with *Evening News*; chief law reporter, 1963–88, *The Scotsman*; Scotland's Specialist Journalist of the Year, 1994; MBE, 1988; author of *Casebook of the Bizarre* (Edinburgh, 1991); after retirement, worked for National Council for the Training of Journalists, and was said 'to have represented all that was best in traditional Scottish journalism'. *TS*, 18 May 1995.

16. Douglas McCaskill, apart from National Service in RAF, was all his working life a *Daily Record* photographer; died 2007, aged 76. Infm.: Eric Rutherford.

17. Mo Philips, after his years of work on the *Scottish Daily Mail*, retired to London and is now dead. Infm.: Walter Gunn.

18. John Long, managing director, 1981–4/5, *The Scotsman*. Roger Ridley-Thomas (b.1939); managing director, 1984/5–early 1990s, *The Scotsman*. Infm.: Andrew Hood.

19. See above, pp. 294–5.

20. Colin Bell (b.1938), born London; educ. St Paul's School and Cambridge University; journalist, 1960–2 and 1975–8, *The Scotsman*, and on staff of, or contributed to, other papers, including *Sunday Times, Sunday Telegraph, Daily Record*, etc.; lecturer, 1965–8, Morley College, supervisor, 1968–75, King's College, Cambridge; 1979, SNP Parl. candidate, Edinburgh West, and European Parl., North-East Scotland; vice-chairman, SNP, 1978–84; Rector, 1991–3, Aberdeen University; hon. LL D, Aberdeen; broadcaster, and author of several books, including *Scotland's Century* (Glasgow, 1999). *WWiS, 2010*, op. cit., 66.

James Gunn Henderson, pp. 386–414

1. Teuchter – a disparaging term for a Highlander, especially a Gaelic speaker.

2. Bessie Leith (1896–1976), a Wick town councillor, 1948–58, Provost, 1949–58. The woman town clerk, 1951–5, was Miss Jess Page (Mrs Campbell): Infm.: Highland Council Archives, Caithness Archive Centre; Mr Leslie Gunn, deputy rector, Wick High School.

3. Apart from German bombing raids (on 17 Oct. 1939, 31 Mar., 2, 8, 10, and 24 Apr. 1940) on nearby Scapa Flow in the early months of the war, Wick itself was, as James Gunn Henderson says, attacked several times. A German plane on 1 Jul. 1940 dropped two bombs on Bank Row near the harbour, killing 15 people (seven children, five men, and three women), and injuring 22 others. A much heavier attack, mainly directed

against Wick aerodrome, was made on 26 Oct, when three people were killed in Wick (a girl, a boy, and a woman), and three Heinkel bombers machine-gunned parts of the town. On 17 Mar. 1941 a German bomber sprayed parts of Wick with machine-gun fire, and children playing at the Riverside were fortunate to escape injury. On 4 Jun. 1941 in the early evening a German plane bombed Wick and sprayed the streets with machine-gun bullets. At the children's playing field at Northcote St, children panicked, and soldiers and others rushed to shield them. Norman M. Glass, *Caithness and the War, 1939–1945* (Wick, 1994 edn), 2–3, 6, 13.

4. The Dewey system of classifying and cataloguing books so they may be easily stored and accessed was devised by the distinguished American librarian Melvil Dewey (1851–1931).

5. The *Beano*, 1938 to date, published by D.C. Thomson Ltd.

6. John Ross (1911–2005), a pupil at Wick High School, spent his whole teaching career there. He was principal teacher of English, then, 1964–76, rector. The *Ark Royal* was sunk by a U-boat, 14 Nov. 1941. Infm.: Highland Council Local Studies; Mr Leslie Gunn, deputy rector, Wick High School.

7. *John o' Groat Journal*, 1836 to date. *Caithness Courier*, 1866 to date.

8. Another source says David Oag retired as editor in 1975.

9. See Note 3 above here.

10. David Robertson (1890–1970); officer, Argyll and Sutherland Highlanders, in WWI; an accountant and businessman; MP, Cons., Streatham, 1939–50, Unionist (Independent from 1959), Caithness and Sutherland, 1950–64; knighted, 1945. *WWW, Vol. VI, 1961–1970*, op. cit., 965.

11. Sir Archibald Sinclair (1890–1970); in army, 1910–21; Lib. MP, 1922–45, Caithness and Sutherland; Secretary of State for Scotland, 1931–2; leader, 1935–45, Lib. Party; Secretary of State for Air, 1940–5; Viscount Thurso from 1952.

12. The *Sports Favourite* has not been traced. *Northern Ensign*, 1850–1926. The other short-lived papers were *Northern Herald*, 1844–6(?) and another, 1903–15, with the same title, and *Northern Star*, 1836–9.

13. John Donaldson (1907–1967), born Wick; educ. Aberdeen University, MA (Hons), 1928, Historical Research Fellow, 1928–30, and BA, 1936, Corpus Christi College, Oxford; freelance journalist, Wick, 1934–67; capt., 1939–45, Seaforth Highlanders, then Royal Engineers; author of *Caithness in the 18th Century* (Edinburgh, 1938), *The Mey Letters* (Edinburgh, 1984), and *Tales of Turly Town* (place and date of publication not yet found). Infm.: Noel Donaldson, his son; Leslie Gunn, deputy rector, Wick High School; Walter Gunn.

14. Early on 15 Mar. 1934, huge waves were breaking all over Wick bay and dashed high over the quay wall. Coastguards warned vessels not to try to enter Wick harbour, and several trawlers and drifters that had entered the bay put out to sea again. That evening between 7 and 8pm the lights of a boat sailing up the bay were seen, and the coastguards, seeing the vessel was in dangerous waters, fired maroons to call out the rocket apparatus crew. The oncoming vessel, the Danish seine-net motor boat *Metha* of Frederickshaven, in attempting nonetheless to enter the harbour, was caught broadside on by the heavy seas and toppled over. In a few seconds she was a wreck, floating keel up. Smashed again by the sea, the *Metha* was reduced to matchwood. The skipper, Karl Nielsen, and his crew of three, one a boy of 15, had had no chance to save themselves. A few days after the salvaged wreckage of the *Metha* had been sold by auction for firewood, the first body, that of the boat's engineer, was recovered on 26 Mar. from the sea, that of the cook, Borga Quest, aged 15, on 1 Apr., the skipper's on 2 Apr, and the mate's on 9 Apr. All four bodies were sent to Denmark for burial. *John o' Groat Journal*, 16, 23, 30 Mar., 6 and 13 Apr. 1934.

15. The 16-day trial in May 1958 at the High Court in Glasgow of Peter Manuel was one of the most sensational in Scottish legal history. Manuel, an Uddingston woodworker,

who dismissed his counsel halfway through his trial and skilfully conducted his own defence, was unanimously found guilty, by the jury of nine men and six women, of murdering five women, a man, and a boy aged 10, though not guilty of murdering another woman; and guilty also of several charges of housebreaking, theft, assault, and discharging loaded firearms. The offences with which he was charged (as well as one where he was found not guilty, and one found not proven) had taken place between Jan. 1956 and Jan. 1958. Manuel was sentenced to be hanged. His appeal to the Scottish Court of Criminal Appeal was dismissed, and the Secretary of State for Scotland rejected a petition for Manuel's reprieve. He was hanged at Barlinnie prison, Glasgow, on 11 Jul. 1958. Infm.: the contemporary press.

16. Sheriff Reginald Levitt (1913–1982), sheriff substitute of Caithness, Sutherland, Orkney and Zetland at Wick, 1951–5, of Ayr and Bute at Kilmarnock, 1955–82. Stephen P. Walker, *The Faculty of Advocates 1800–1986* (Edinburgh, 1987), 98.

17. Jimmy Angus, in RAF in WWII, died before he was of age to retire from the editorship of the *Caithness Courier*. Infm.: Walter Gunn.

18. William Maxwell Aitken (1879–1964), Lord Beaverbrook from 1917; born Ontario; Unionist MP, 1910–16, Ashton-under-Lyne; govt minister for several depts successively in WWI and II; a newspaper press magnate from 1919 when he acquired the *Daily Express*; author of several books, including the two-volume *Politicians and the War* (London, 1928 and 1932).

19. Jack Campbell (1913–2004); began, aged 15, as a copy boy on the *Scottish Daily Express* four days after it began publication in Glasgow on 8 Nov. 1928, then successively reporter, sub-editor, deputy chief sub-editor, night editor from 1946, news editor from 1948, and managing editor, 1951–7 and again from 1961–(?); editor, 1957, Glasgow *Evening Citizen*, and, 1974–8, of the *Scottish Sunday Express;* in RN in WWII; author of *A Word for Scotland* (Edinburgh, 1998). *Daily Express*, 13 and 20 Feb. 2004.

20. Campbell, *A Word for Scotland*, op. cit., 118, 146, says Alexander H. Bruce was from 1940 until at least the late 1950s Group general manager, and by 1961 was deputy to the Group circulation manager.

21. *Football Times* (titled, 1904–7, *Inverness Football Times*), 1907–63, the Saturday evening edn of the *Highland News*. Mackenzie, *NEWSPLAN Scotland*, op. cit., 185.

22. George Paterson, in RN in WWII, afterward remained in Inverness with the *Scottish Daily Express* until he retired or it ceased publication in Glasgow in 1974. Infm.: Walter Gunn.

23. Walter Gunn (b.1929), began, 1947, as junior reporter, *Caithness Courier*; National Service, RN, 1948–50; 1950, *Caithness Courier; Scottish Daily Express*, Inverness, 1950–1, Glasgow, 1951–2, Aberdeen, 1952–3, Edinburgh, reporter, 1953–74; unemployed nine months after cessation of publication in Glasgow, 1974, of *Scottish Daily Express*; press officer, British Leyland, Bathgate, 1975–6; Senior Information Officer, Scottish Office, 1976–94. Infm.: Walter Gunn.

24. Capt. Edmund E. Fresson, pioneering airman; in RFC in WWI; worked post-war in China, and flew air trips in England; est., 1933, Highland Airways, the first internal air service in Britain, covering the Highlands, Hebrides, Orkney and Shetland, and later including the first air mail service and an air ambulance service; OBE, 1943; area manager, 1947–8, Scottish Division, British European Airways; then worked for some time in Kenya, before returning to Inverness to run an air charter service; author of *Air Road to the Isles* (1967); died 1963, aged 71. *TS* and *GH*, 26 Sep. 1963.

25. 'McZephyr' was George McNeill, a BBC radio actor, formerly secretary of the Iona Youth Trust and at the time of his murder welfare officer at Fairfield Shipbuilding & Engineering Co., Glasgow. John William Gordon, a freelance journalist with a prison record, was convicted of the murder by a majority verdict of the jury at his trial at the High Court, Glasgow, on 3 Mar. 1955, and was sentenced to death. Rev. Dr George MacLeod of Fuinary, who had known and tried to help Gordon since he was a boy,

was principal defence witness at the trial. A petition to the Secretary of State for Scotland signed by 14,000 people, which drew attention to the recent Timothy Evans case (see above, p. 276) and expressed 'uneasiness at the circumstantial nature of the evidence' and also about 'the way of life' of George McNeill, was followed by the commutation of the sentence to life imprisonment for Gordon. *TS*, 12, 22–5 and 28 Feb. and 1–4 and 24 Mar. 1955. Baron the Very Rev. Dr George MacLeod of Fuinary (1893–1991); MC and Croix de Guerre in WWI; founder and first leader, 1938, Iona Community; Moderator, 1957–8, General Assembly, Church of Scotland; life peer from 1967; author of several books, including *Govan Calling: A Book of Broadcast Sermons and Addresses* (1934). *Scottish Biographies* 1938, op. cit., 504; *WWW, Vol. IX, 1991–1995*, op. cit., 356–7. Rev. Alan Hasson (1926–1991), former Church of Scotland minister, joined the Orange Order in 1953 and was Grand Master, 1958–60, of the Grand Orange Lodge of Scotland. He was found guilty at the High Court in Glasgow on 22 Jun. 1971 of fraud and embezzlement involving a total of £10,330 while acting as Grand Master, and was sentenced to three years' imprisonment. After he claimed in mitigation of sentence that he had been threatened with physical assault on his return to Barlinnie prison to serve his sentence, the judge granted a special court order for his protection. *TS*, 8, 17, and 23 Jun. 1971.

26. Ian McColl (1915–2005), born Glasgow; an active Lib. from his teens, and Parl. candidate, 1945 and 1950; from 1933, reporter, *Scottish Daily Express*; in RAF Coastal Command in WWII; editor, 1961–71, *Scottish Daily Express*, 1971–4, *Daily Express*, London; chairman, 1975–82, Scottish Express Newspapers; CBE, 1983, for services to journalism and the newspaper industry. *Daily Express*, 23 Jun. 2005; *TH*, 24 Jun. 2005; Campbell, *A Word for Scotland*, op. cit., 206.

27. Roger Wood, editor (?)–1959, Manchester edn, *Daily Express*, 1959–61, *Scottish Daily Express*, briefly of *Daily Express*, London, then editor in New York of a Rupert Murdoch newspaper. *TS*, 30 Dec. 1959; infm.: Andrew Fyall.

28. Ian Brown (1926–1996); capt., Cameron Highlanders, in WWII; began as a journalist, 1947, on *Ayrshire Post*, moved, 1950, to *Scottish Daily Mail*; then, 1952, to *Daily Express* in London; news editor, 1963–74, *Scottish Daily Express*, editor, 1974; remained with the *Express* in Glasgow till 1986. *TH*, 27 Sep. 2010.

29. Jack Webster (b.1931), born Maud, Aberdeenshire; educ. Peterhead Academy and Robert Gordon's College; reporter and sub-editor, *Turriff Advertiser* and Aberdeen *P&J* and *Evening Express*; chief sub-editor, *Scottish Sunday Express*; feature writer, *Scottish Daily Express* and *Sunday Standard*, columnist, *The Herald*; Columnist and Speaker of the Year, 1996; author of many books, including a biography of Alistair Maclean, and screenwriter of several TV films. *WWiS*, 2009, op. cit., 544–5. Molly Kelly (1926–2004), began as a copy taker, became a leading *Scottish Daily Express* journalist, *Daily Express*, 13 Feb. 2004. Clive Sandground (1932–1993), born Paisley; worked for many years for *Scottish Daily Express*: editor, 1971–2; editor, 1973–81, *Sunday Mail*; features editor, 1981–3, *Sunday Standard*; executive editor, *Scottish Field*. *The Times*, 6 Sep. 1993.

30. Bruce McLeod died in 1991 aged 51, while working as a freelance journalist. *Daily Express*, 2 Sep. 1991.

31. David Scott had begun work as an office boy in the *Scottish Daily Express* office in Edinburgh. Infm.: Walter Gunn.

32. William Merrilees (1898–1984), born Leith; chief constable, 1950–68, Lothians and Peebles Police; his autobiography, *The Short Arm of the Law* (London 1966). *TS*, 23 Aug. 1984. Bill Simpson, born Dunure, Ayrshire; STV newsreader for two years; first role as an actor in TV series *Z Cars*; he played, 1962–71, Dr Finlay in *Dr Finlay's Casebook*; died 1986, aged 54. *TS*, 22 Dec. 1986. The 1960 film *Greyfriars Bobby*, starring Donald Crisp, concerned the eponymous Skye terrier that for years after the death of John Gray, his master, faithfully visited his grave at Greyfriars Church, Edinburgh.

33. Dr John S. McEwan, MA (Hons), LL B, DL (h.c.), taught in Ayrshire, Lanarkshire,

Glasgow Academy, and Fettes College, Edinburgh; in forces in WWII; depute director of education, Lanarkshire, 1945–50, director, 1950–75; died 1993, aged 79. *Hamilton Advertiser*, 22 Oct. 1960, 28 May 1993.

34. *Northern Times*, 1899 to date.
35. The Countess of Sutherland (b.1921), Lady Strathnaver, chief of Clan Sutherland; in Land Army, 1939–41; hospital laboratory technician, Inverness, 1941–3, London, 1943–5; succeeded, 1963, to her uncle's (5th Duke of Sutherland) earldom of Sutherland; her husband, Charles Janson, died 2006. *WW, 2011*, op. cit., 2230. From the late 1960s oil wells began to be drilled in Scottish areas of the North Sea. The first major finding was the Forties Field, 100 miles north-east of Aberdeen, in 1970. In the Cromarty Firth and Moray Firth, Nigg and Ardersier became important oil platform building sites by the early 1970s. The North Sea oil industry gave employment to huge numbers of people.
36. Stuart McCartney (b.1935); began aged 15 as a copy boy, *Evening Citizen*; c.1956–65, reporter, *Scottish Daily Mail*; 1965–78, *Scottish Daily Express*; 1978–93, *Daily Star*; retired, 1993. *Daily Star*, 1 Jul. 1993; Campbell, *A Word for Scotland*, op. cit., 125–6, 161. Jocelyn Stevens, a grandson of the press magnate Sir Edward Hulton (1906–1988); educ. Eton College and Cambridge University; worked, 1955–6, as a journalist with Hulton Press Ltd; bought, 1957, and was editor of the magazine *Queen*, sold it, 1968; managing director, 1969–72, London *Evening Standard*, 1972–4, of the *Daily Express*, and from 1974 of Beaverbrook Newspapers. Griffiths, *Encyclopedia*, op. cit., 347.
37. Dunrobin Castle, Golspie, residence of the Countess of Sutherland.
38. Judith Napier, circulation worker, 1987–9, then reporter, 1989–92, *Northern Times*; from 1992 with *Press & Journal*; at the time of writing a freelance, but writes a regular recipe column for *Northern Times*. Alison Cameron, began, 1973, as junior reporter, *Weekly Post*, north-west London; 1977–2009, successively reporter, deputy editor, advertising manager, and from 2009, editor, *Northern Times*. Infm.: Alison Cameron.
39. *The Listener*, published by BBC, 1929–59, then cont. as *The Listener and BBC Television Review*, 1960–91.
40. The Countess's uncle, the 5th Duke, was succeeded by the 6th Duke, and he in 2000 by the 7th Duke, his cousin, who lives at Mertoun, Roxburghshire. *WW, 2010*, op. cit., 2229, 2230.
41. The National Mod annual competitive festival of Gaelic music, literature, and speech, organised by the Highland Association (An Comunn Gaidhealach) since 1892. The Sutherland clearances, 1807–20, have generally been regarded as particularly savage. Patrick Sellar (1780–1851), sub-factor of the then Countess and her husband the Marquis of Stafford (from 1833 first Duke of Sutherland), was tried in 1816 for culpable homicide, cruelty, and other offences, but the jury found him not guilty. Brian Wilson (b.1948); educ. Dunoon Grammar School, Dundee University, and University College, Cardiff (Diploma in Journalism Studies); 1972–97, founding editor and publisher, *West Highland Free Press*; Lab. MP, Cunningham North, 1987–2005; govt minister successively of several depts, 1997–2006; a visiting professor, from 2007, Glasgow Caledonian University. *WW, 2011*, op. cit., 2497. *West Highland Free Press*, 1972 to date. *Financial Times*, 1888 to date.
42. Eric Richards, *The Leviathan of Wealth: The Sutherland Fortune in the Industrial Revolution* (London, 1973).
43. Neil M. Gunn (1891–1973), born Dunbeath, Caithness; educ. Highland school, privately; resigned, 1937, from civil service; author from 1926 of many novels, including *The Silver Darlings* (London, 1941), short stories, essays and plays; his autobiography: *The Atom of Delight* (1956).
44. Dennis MacLeod (b.1941), born Sutherland; a gold-mining entrepreneur. A memorial to victims of the Sutherland clearances was erected and unveiled in Jul. 2007 at Couper Park, Helmsdale. Infm.: James Gaukroger and Alison Cameron.

Ron Thompson, pp. 415–35

1. *Dandy* (D.C. Thomson & Co. Ltd), 1937 to date. (From Aug. 2007 to Oct. 2010 it was titled *Dandy Xtreme*.)
2. YMCA – Young Men's Christian Association.
3. No information has been found about Jessie Milne or Helen Mary Mungo, other than that they had left D.C. Thomson & Co. Ltd by 1978.
4. *People's Journal*, 1858–1990.
5. See also above, David M. Smith, Note 13, p. 542.
6. George A.J. Mackintosh; educ. Dundee High School; began work on *Fife Herald*, Cupar, moved to Aberdeen Journals, then to *Scottish Daily Express* in Glasgow; co-founder, 1980, and programme director, 1980–5, Radio Tay; also helped found Kingdom FM in Fife and Radio Discovery in Dundee; died in Dundee, 2000, aged 54. Dundee *Courier*, 12 Aug. 2000.
7. *Broughty Ferry Guide*, 1887 (with many changes of title) to date.
8. Harry Diamond (b.1926), born Glasgow; his father and grandfather Lithuanian Jewish immigrants; left school at 14, had several brief office jobs, one of them with Scottish Newspaper Services news agency, and taught himself shorthand; began, c.1940–1, as office/copy/telephone boy, *Glasgow Herald*; and, 1944, its youngest reporter; in army, 1944/5–8; 1948–50s, reporter and crime reporter, *The Bulletin*, *Glasgow Herald*, and *Evening Times*; briefly in 1950s, reporter, *Scottish Daily Mail* and also worked in London on *Woman's Own*; sub-editor, then chief sub-editor, *The Bulletin*, until 1960; then briefly, 1960, a sub-editor, *Scottish Daily Mail*, in Edinburgh; sub-editor, 1960–2, *Scottish Daily Express*; public relations officer, 1962–9, Scottish Gas Board; 1969–70, in an advertising agency; 1970–4, assistant public relations officer, Glasgow Town Council; head of public relations, 1974–92, Glasgow District Council. After he left school Harry Diamond met one of his old teachers, who asked what he was doing for a living. 'I'm a newspaper reporter.' 'I always knew,' said the teacher, 'you'd come to no good, Diamond.' Infm.: Harry Diamond, and his autobiography, *Can you get my name in the papers?* (Glasgow, 1996), *passim*.
9. George Thomson (1921–2008), Lord Thomson of Monifeith; began from school as a journalist in Dundee with D.C. Thomson & Co. Ltd, and became a chief sub-editor, then an editor; in RAF in WWII; assistant editor, 1946–8, editor, 1948–53, *Forward*; Lab. MP 1952–70, Dundee East; a senior minister, 1964–70, in several govt depts; Commissioner, 1972–7, European Economic Community; a life peer from 1977; head, 1980–8, Independent Broadcasting Authority; joined Lib. Dem. Party, 1988. *TS*, 7 Oct. 2008.
10. Geoffrey Goodman (b.1921), journalist and broadcaster; in RAF in WWII; *Manchester Guardian*, 1946–7, *Daily Mirror*, 1947–8, *News Chronicle*, 1948–59, *Daily Herald*, 1959–64, *The Sun*, 1964–9, industrial editor then assistant editor, *Daily Mirror*, 1969–86; author of several books, including *The Miners' Strike* (London, 1985), and ed., *British Journalism Review* from 1989. *WW, 2011*, op. cit., 887.
11. Walter Elliot (1888–1958); in army in WWI, MC and bar; Unionist MP, 1918–23, Lanark, 1924–45, Glasgow Kelvingrove, 1946–50, Scottish Universities, 1950–8, Kelvingrove; held junior and senior govt ministerial posts in several depts, 1923–9, 1931–42, including Secretary of State for Scotland, 1936–8; and Minister for Health, 1938–40; Rector, 1933–6, Aberdeen University and, 1947–50, Glasgow University; author of two books, including *Toryism and the Twentieth Century* (London, 1927). *WWW, Vol. V, 1951–1960*, op. cit., 343. The Kelvingrove by-election, 13 Mar. 1958, was won by Mrs Mary McAlister, Lab.
12. Charles Smith, born Glasgow; began, 1937, on *Glasgow Herald*; in RAF in WWII; returned, 1947, to *Glasgow Herald*, and later moved to *Daily Record*, Glasgow *Evening News*, and, as news editor, *Sunday Mail*; head, then controller, of news and current

affairs, Grampian TV Ltd, Aberdeen, 1961–77; MBE, 1970, for services to TV journalism; died 1977. *GH*, 18 Apr. 1977.

13. Selina Scott (b.1951), born Scarborough; journalist, TV newsreader, producer and presenter, author.

14. *Scots Magazine*, 1739 to date.

15. Douglas Phillips and Ron Thompson, *Dundee: People and Places to Remember* (Dundee, 1992); Douglas Phillips and Ron Thompson, *Dundee: A City Made of Memories* (Dundee, 1993). Ron Thompson, *Easel in the Field: The Life of McIntosh Patrick* (Coupar Angus, 2000). James McIntosh Patrick (1907–1998), OBE, RSA, grad Glasgow School of Art, painter and etcher; army capt. in WWII; his paintings are preserved in galleries in several countries. *WWW, Vol. X, 1996–2000*, op. cit., 447. Ron Thompson on his retirement was awarded the MBE for his 26 years of service to TV journalism.

John Cairns, pp. 436–46

1. A checkweighman or checkweigher, sometimes also termed a justiceman, was a miners' elected paid representative, and very often a leading member of the union at the colliery, who checked that coal produced by each miner was correctly weighed at the pithead and duly paid for.

2. Eleanor Gordon, Hamilton, was awarded in 1950 the Nancy Riach Memorial Medal, as the swimmer who did most to enhance the reputation of Scottish swimming during the year. Nancy Riach (1927–1947), born Motherwell; outstanding swimmer in the Motherwell Amateur Swimming Club, by age 17 she held 28 Scottish and British swimming records. She died from polio while preparing with the British swimming team for the 1948 Olympic Games.

3. Lithuanians (often wrongly referred to as Poles) began to arrive in considerable numbers in Scotland in the 1890s. As well as in Lanarkshire and West Lothian, some settled and worked in the Ayrshire and Midlothian coalfields. By 1914 they had est. in Lanarkshire their own newspapers and, at Wishaw, their own Provident Society, Sandara, until its winding up in 1905. See, e.g., John Millar, *The Lithuanians in Scotland* (Colonsay, 1998); Murdoch Rodgers, 'The Lanarkshire Lithuanians', in Billy Kay, ed., *Odyssey: Voices from Scotland's Recent Past* (Edinburgh, 1980), 18–25; Ian MacDougall, *Mungo Mackay and the Green Table* (East Linton, 1995), 31, 59–61, 84, 113, 122–3.

4. *Alloa Journal*, 1859–1972, then merged with *Alloa Advertiser* and *Alloa Circular* to form the *Alloa Advertiser-Journal*, 1972–6, retitled, 1976, *Alloa & Hillfoots Advertiser-Journal*, retitled, 1988, *Alloa & Hillfoots Advertiser*, to date. Mackenzie, *NEWSPLAN Scotland*, op. cit., 44–5.

5. The crash at Breich, of a Hawker Hind bomber from 603 City of Edinburgh Sqn, Royal Auxiliary Air Force, in which the pilot, Flying Officer C.A.G. Thomson, Glasgow, and air-gunner R.H. Starrett, Edinburgh, were killed, occurred on 26 Mar. 1938. *ED*, 28 Mar. 1938; *West Lothian Courier*, 1 Apr. 1938.

6. *Wishaw Press*, 1875 to date. *West Lothian Courier*, 1872–1974, when title changed to *Lothian Courier*, to date.

Christopher Reekie, pp. 447–66

1. *Southern Annual*, a magazine published, 1930s–c.1969, by the *Southern Reporter*.

2. The Royal Scots Fusiliers, raised 1769, became the 21st of Foot, merged, 1959, with the Highland Light Infantry to form the Royal Highland Fusiliers, which, 2006, became 2nd Bn, Royal Regt of Scotland.

3. Founded, 1878, by George F. Skerry, Skerry's College, in Edinburgh, Glasgow and Newcastle upon Tyne, offered secretarial courses, including shorthand and typing, and also prepared students for civil service, university entrance, and various professional examinations. The Colleges closed in 1968. *TS*, 22 Oct. 1953 and 23 Feb. 1968.

4. *Southern Reporter*, 1855–1957, when it merged with the *Border Standard* and became *Southern Reporter and Border Standard*, to date. David Mackie (1891–1956); born Tarbolton; educ. Ayr Academy; in Yeomanry in WWI; editor, 1925–55, *Southern Reporter* and *Southern Annual*; author of several books, including *Songs of an Ayrshire Yeoman* (Paisley, (1920)). *Scottish Biographies 1938*, op. cit., 490; infm.: Christopher Reekie, and Edith Scott, *Southern Reporter*.

5. Gordon Rule was later for many years pictures editor, *Glasgow Herald*. Infm.: Christopher Reekie.

6. Walter Thomson (1913–2001), born Selkirk; educ. Selkirk High School and Heriot Watt College, Edinburgh; editor (dates uncertain), *Selkirk Saturday Advertiser*, member, IoJ. *Scottish Biographies 1938*, op. cit., 746; infm.: Christopher Reekie. *Selkirk Advertiser*, 1883–1939, then resumed as *Selkirk Saturday Advertiser*, 1946–86, then 1992–3, when it merged with *Selkirk Week-ender*, and became *Selkirk Week-end Advertiser*, to date. Infm.: Heritage Hub, Hawick.

7. *Border Telegraph* (titled, 1896–1902, *Galashiels Telegraph*), 1896 to date. Mackenzie, *NEWSPLAN Scotland*, op. cit., 74, 190.

8. No further information about Jimmy Faill has been found, except that he is now dead.

9. John Rennie later worked in the 1960s on the Middlesbrough *Evening Gazette*. Infm.: Christopher Reekie.

10. *Fife Herald* (began, 1822, as *Cupar Herald*), 1823–1974, when it merged with the *Fife News* to form the *Fife Herald News*, to date. Mackenzie, *NEWSPLAN Scotland*, op. cit., 112, 180, 181.

11. William Taylor (1892–1963), born Glasgow, grew up in Elgin; began, aged 15, as a reporter on the *Northern Scot*, Elgin; moved, 1912, to the *People's Journal* and Dundee *Advertiser*, in their Dundee, Montrose and Forfar offices, and, from 1920, as chief reporter at Cupar, Fife; from 1925, editor, *Fife News*; from 1935, managing editor, *Fife Herald*, *Fife News*, and *St Andrews Citizen*; from 1938, director, J. & G. Innes, Cupar; retired from journalism, 1957; in his youth, played for Elgin City FC, but declined an offer to play for Swindon Town FC. Dundee *Courier*, 26 Oct. 1957, 12 Oct. 1963.

12. John Sneddon, Kelty, was elected county council convener by 46 votes to 36, John McWilliam, Crossgates, vice-convener by 43 to 39 for Sir John Gilmour, Montrave. *TS*, 25 May 1955. McWilliam (1910–1974), knighted 1970, became county council convener, 1961–70, and lord lieutenant of Fife, 1965–74. *WWW, Vol. VII, 1971–1980*, op. cit., 510. George Sharp (1919–2000), an engine driver, Fife county councillor, 1945–75; president, 1975–8, Convention of Scottish Local Authorities. *WWW, Vol. X, 1996–2000*, op. cit., 525. For Rab Smith's account of his life, see Ian MacDougall, *Voices from the Hunger Marches* (Edinburgh, 1990–1), Vol. I, 83–110.

13. *St Andrews Citizen*, 1870 to date. *Fife News*, 1870–1974, when it merged with the *Fife Herald* to form the *Fife Herald News*. Mackenzie, *NEWSPLAN Scotland*, op. cit., 182–3, 354. Newspapers were, or had been, also published in Fife at Anstruther, Cowdenbeath, Inverkeithing, and Pittenweem.

14. Jarrow, 'the classic town of unemployment in England', had suffered especially severely in the interwar depression, particularly with the closure in 1933 of Palmer's shipyard there. The rate of unemployment was 80 per cent. The Medical Officer of Health estimated that out of the then population (35,000), 6,000 were on the dole and 23,000 were living on relief. The Jarrow Hunger March in Oct. 1936 (unlike virtually all the other national Hunger Marches of the interwar period that were organised by the National Unemployed Workers' Movement and denounced by the national leaders of the Lab. Party and Trades Union Congress as Communist-inspired) was suggested and led by the Lab. councillor David Riley and supported by the Lab. mayor Alfred Rennie, and two other workers' leaders, councillor Paddy Scullion and George Rose, was 'non-political', and was supported by the whole town, the Town

Council, the local Cons. Party, and blessed by the bishop of Jarrow. As a result the Jarrow Marchers were much better funded, clothed, fed, and equipped than the far more numerous NUWM national Hunger Marchers of 1922–36. The Jarrow March is almost always the one that is shown on television or mentioned in the newspaper press. Ellen Wilkinson, *The Town That Was Murdered: The Life-Story of Jarrow* (London, 1939), 191–213; Richard Crouch, *We Refuse to Starve in Silence: A History of the National Unemployed Workers' Movement* (London, 1987), 179–82; Ian MacDougall, *Voices from the Hunger Marches* (Edinburgh, 1990–1), Vol. I, 25, 37, 201–2, Vol. II, 388.

15. *Sunderland Echo*, 1873 to date.
16. Len Shackleton (1922–2000), played successively, 1940–57, for Bradford, Newcastle United, and Sunderland FC. Barry J. Hugman, *The PFA: Premier & Football League Players' Records, 1946–2005* (Harpenden, 1998), 354.
17. George MacDonald Fraser (1925–2007); served in Burma in WWII; post-war, a reporter, *Carlisle Journal;* sub-editor, then assistant editor, *Glasgow Herald*, until 1969; author of the *Flashman* series, and other books, including *Quartered Safe Out Here* (London, 1993), his recollections of his war experiences in Burma, and three works on the Border reivers. *TS*, 4 Jan. 2007.
18. Frances Horsburgh (b.1946); grad. MA (Hons), 1968, Glasgow University; 1968–73, trainee graduate, Thomson Regional Newspapers, with Aberdeen *Press & Journal*, and 1973–7, in London, as feature writer and political correspondent; 1977–80, feature writer, Edinburgh *Evening News*; 1980–2, BBC Radio Scotland; *The (Glasgow) Herald*, 1982–99, local govt correspondent then, 1999–2003, Scottish Parl. correspondent; retired, 2003; 2005 to date, research worker and political adviser to Lord James Douglas-Hamilton (now Lord Selkirk of Douglas). Infm.: Frances Horsburgh.
19. Barbara Castle (1910–2002), Lady Castle from 1974, Baroness Castle of Blackburn in her own right from 1990; Lab. MP, 1945–50, Blackburn, 1950–5, Blackburn East, 1955–79, Blackburn; a Cabinet minister, 1964–70, and 1974–6; MEP, 1979–89; in 1969, she produced as Secretary of State for Employment a highly controversial white paper, *In Place of Strife*, concerning industrial relations but which was abandoned after strong trade union and widespread other opposition; author of several books, including *The Castle Diaries* (London, 2 vols, 1980, 1984). Rosen, *Dictionary of Labour Biography* (2001), op. cit., 108–11.
20. Robert Yeats, began as a journalist in the Borders; from 1924 a reporter, *The Scotsman*; in WWII Scottish press officer, Air Ministry; 1946–56, editor *Weekly Scotsman*; 1956–71, *Glasgow Herald*: successively chief sub-editor then, in Edinburgh office, chief reporter and education correspondent; after he retired he cont. as part-time education correspondent; from 1976, a Fellow of the Educational Institute of Scotland, 'the first working journalist to receive the honour'; died 1979, aged 73. *TS*, 13 Nov. 1979; *TJ*, Jan. 1971. Jimmy Tosh (1903–1970), worked for *The Scotsman*, then for many years *Glasgow Herald* in its Edinburgh office until he retired, 1968. Infm.: Christopher Reekie. Jean Smith, born 1931, grad. Glasgow University; 1953–5, in library, *Glasgow Herald*, then reporter, 1955–65 (1958–65 in Edinburgh office); 1965–92, features writer, *The Scotsman*. Infm.: Jean Smith; died 2011. Dorothy-Grace Elder, journalist; SNP, then Independent, MSP, Glasgow, 1999–2003; on staff of or contributor to D.C. Thomson & Co. Ltd newspapers, *Glasgow Herald*, BBC TV and radio news, *Scottish Daily News*, *Scottish Daily Express*; British Reporter of the Year, 1996–7. *WWiS, 2010*, op. cit., 170. Jimmy Thomson (1921–1998); began on *Sunday Post* as a darkroom boy; in RAF in WWII; post-war with *Scottish Daily Mail*, then *The Bulletin* and, 1951–84, chief photographer, Edinburgh office, *Glasgow Herald*. *TJ*, Aug.–Sep. 1998, Jan.–Feb. 1999; infm.: Christopher Reekie. Duncan Dingsdale (1931–1999); began, 1950s, with *Scotnews*, est. by *The Scotsman*; then freelance and, 1957–94, *Glasgow Herald*, 1984–94 as chief photographer, Edinburgh office. *TJ*, Aug.–Sep. 1999. Infm.: Christopher Reekie.

21. The Cons. govt led by Mrs Thatcher from 1979 undertook by a series of Acts to reduce the power and the rights of trade unions. The Employment Act, 1980, first of these Acts, made secondary strike action unlawful, and picketing lawful only if carried out by workers at their own place of work. The Employment Act, 1982, prohibited pre-entry closed shops, provided there must be 85 per cent approval for post-entry closed shops, and that unions must compensate workers refusing to accept a closed shop, and allowed employers to sue for damages and secure court injunctions to stop industrial action. In the miners' lengthy strike in 1984–5, their union, traditionally regarded as the vanguard of the trade union movement, was heavily defeated by the govt. In 1984 ballots were made obligatory before industrial action could be lawfully taken; and an Act in 1990 terminated the closed shop in any form, and held unions liable for unofficial action taken by their members. Keith Aitken, *The Bairns o' Adam: The Story of the STUC* (Edinburgh, 1997), 265–6; W. Hamish Fraser, *A History of British Trade Unionism, 1700–1998* (London, 1999), 235, 237, 243.

22. The principal Acts passed in the 1960s and 1970s dealing with trade unions' and workers' rights were the Lab. govts' Trades Disputes Act, 1965, which reaffirmed the unions' immunity from legal action when they went on strike to maintain closed shops, the Equal Pay Act, 1970, the Trade Union and Labour Relations Act, and the Health and Safety at Work Act, both 1974, the Employment Protection Act and the Sex Discrimination Act, both 1975. The main relevant Act passed in 1970–4 by the Cons. govt was the Industrial Relations Act, 1971, which had aroused vehement opposition by trade unionists.

23. George Outram & Co. (Outram was editor, 1837–56, *Glasgow Herald*), was the title of the company, 1837–1992. In 1964 the new owners of the company became Scottish & Universal Investments (SUITS), headed by Sir Hugh Fraser (Lord Fraser from Dec. 1964). Lonrho took over the ownership in 1979. In 1992, in a management buy-out, Lonrho were succeeded as owners by Caledonian Newspaper Publishing Co. In 1996 the latter was bought by Scottish Television plc, whose name was soon changed to Scottish Media Group plc. In 2002 Newsquest plc, a subsidiary of the US news company Gannett Co. Inc., succeeded the Scottish Media Group as owners of *The Herald*, Glasgow *Evening Times*, and *Sunday Herald*. Phillips, *Glasgow's Herald*, op. cit., 50, 52, 152, 167; infm. from the papers' Research Library.

24. Stewart Boyd (b.1940), worked for many years for *The Scotsman*, and c.1973–93, when he took early retirement, was pictures editor. Allan McLean (b.1946), journalist, *The Scotsman*; later for many years Public Affairs Manager, Scotland, Virgin Trains. George Strathie (1939–1983), journalist, *Scottish Daily Mail* to 1968; assistant press officer, Commonwealth Games, Edinburgh, 1970; then worked for Edinburgh *Evening News* until his death. Infm.: Stewart Boyd and Christopher Reekie.

25. John Foster was general secretary, NUJ, 1992–2002. *TJ*, Oct.–Nov. 1992, May 2002.

Liz Taylor, pp. 467–86

1. Based on a play by the American novelist and playwright Ben Hecht (1894–1964), himself a newspaperman in the 1920s, and Charles MacArthur, the 1931 film *Front Page* is set mainly in the press-room of a Chicago court.

2. Leslie Charteris (1907–1993), author of *The Saint* crime novels, c.1931–83. *WWW, Vol. IX, 1991–1995*, op. cit., 94. *The Scarlet Pimpernel* (1905), by Baroness Orczy (1865–1947), a novel whose English hero Sir Percy Blakeney eludes and outwits bloodthirsty French Revolutionaries in the 1790s. Mazo De La Roche (1885–1961), Canadian novelist, author of a series of novels from 1927 about the *Whiteoaks* family.

3. In the following decades the prospects for, and numbers of, women journalists improved markedly, e.g., in 1978 the NUJ appointed Linda Rogers its first woman full-time official as a national organiser, and a second, Peta Van den Bergh, was

appointed the following year. By 1981 the union had some 8,000 women members, and in the early 1980s the union held its first national and regional conferences for women members. *TJ*, Nov. 1978, Jun. 1979, Feb. 1981, Feb. 1982, Apr. 1981.

4. *Gaudie* (newspaper of Aberdeen University Student Association), 1934 to date. Infm.: Library and Historic Collections, King's College, Aberdeen.

5. About Tom Campbell no more information has so far been found. Bob (or Bert) Stewart (Robert Banks Stewart, b.1931), born Edinburgh; moved briefly to the *Daily Record* in the mid-1950s, and later established himself as an author, TV script writer (e.g. for *Doctor Who*), and producer (e.g. of *Bergerac*). Ronnie Robson (1920–1995), began in the *Evening Dispatch* before WWII and post-war returned to it till 1954; in WWII, a capt., Royal Signals: at Dunkirk, in North Africa, Italy (including Monte Cassino) and Burma; as a BBC reporter from 1954: at Suez, 1956, the Congo, Cyprus, the Franco-Algerian war, and correspondent, Southern and, 1964–9, Central Africa (expelled by Ian Smith's 'govt' from Rhodesia), East Africa, India/Pakistan, 1969–71 (covered campaign for Bangladeshi independence from Pakistan); Bangkok and Far East, 1971–4, radio reporter, London, 1974, Foreign Duty editor, London, 1974–80, acting New York correspondent, 1978; died at Royal Star and Garter Hospital, London. *TJ*, Nov. 1969; *TS*, 7 Oct. 1995; *Ariel* (BBC in-house magazine), 15 Aug. 1995; infm.: Louise North, Archives Researcher, BBC; Laura Maffioli-Brown, Royal Star and Garter Homes, Richmond, Surrey; Bert Morris; Mrs Dinah Stevenson.

6. Nothing more than Liz Taylor recalls here has so far been found about Algie Brown.

7. Agnes Muriel Poole (1922–2006); with the *Evening Dispatch* from c.1950 until, it seems, its merger, 1963, into the *Evening News*, of which she then became and apparently remained women's editor until she retired c.1978(?). Infm.: Christopher Reekie. Dorothy Young moved from the *Dispatch* to the *Scottish Daily Express*, then to the BBC; her second marriage was to a lecturer in Russian, with whom she briefly ran a Russian restaurant in Edinburgh. She died quite young. Infm.: Mrs Dinah Stevenson. About Marjory Edwards no further infm. has yet been found.

8. Alexander Bowman, born Darlington; began aged 18 as a reporter, *Berwick Advertiser*; on staff of *The Scotsman* for many years, and became its chief sub-editor; editor, *Evening Dispatch*, 1955–c.1960; chief press officer, Livingston Development Corporation, 1964–71; died 1971, aged 61. *TS*, 27 Dec. 1971.

9. Damon Runyon (1884–1946), American journalist and writer whose writing was racy, full of slang, generally in the present tense, and dealt with characters on the seamy side of life.

10. *The Sphere*, 'an illustrated newspaper for the home', 1900–64.

11. The relevant murder trial may have been that not of Christie, but of John George Haigh in 1949. On the latter occasion Sylvester Bolam, editor, *Daily Mirror*, was sent to prison for three months, and the *Mirror* fined £10,000, for contempt of court by prejudicing the course of justice. See, e.g., Roy Greenslade, *Press Gang: How Newspapers Make Profits from Propaganda* (London, 2004 edn), 39–41.

12. *Lilliput*, 1937–60, merged into *Men Only*.

13. Harold Macmillan (1894–1986); in Grenadier Guards in WWI; Cons. MP, 1924–9, 1931–45, Stockton-on-Tees, and, 1945–64, Bromley; Resident Minister, Allied HQ, North Africa, from 1942; 1951–7, successively Housing, Defence, Foreign Minister, and Chancellor of the Exchequer, 1957–63, Prime Minister; author of several books; Earl of Stockton from 1984. *WWW, Vol. VIII, 1981–1990*, op. cit., 726, 727.

14. *Woman's Hour*, broadcast by the BBC since 7 Oct. 1946.

15. Vengalil Krishna Menon (1896–1974), Indian statesman, lawyer, journalist; member, Home Rule League and Indian National Congress; St Pancras borough councillor, London, 1934–47; Lab. Parl. candidate, Dundee, 1938–41; hon. president, World Peace Council; High Commissioner for India, 1947–52; Indian representative, 1952–62, United Nations General Assembly; Indian Minister of Defence, 1957–62. *WWW, Vol.*

VII, 1971–1980, op. cit., 446. Paul VI, Pope 1963–78, visited India in 1964, the first Pope to visit Asia.

16. Pearson's Industries, a conglomerate company, in an engineering section of which Liz Taylor's husband was employed. Pearson's were also publishers, e.g. of the *Financial Times*.

17. For Lorna Blackie, see above, pp. 487–507.

18. Philip Agee (1935–2008) was author of *Inside the Company: CIA Diary*, written with the help of the Cuban govt and published in 1974 in England, outside the reach of the US courts. Agee had served in Latin America in 1969 and had become sympathetic to Marxist ideas. Cuban agents persuaded him to name everyone he knew and was associated with in the Central Intelligence Agency. The book named several hundred CIA officers and identified cover organisations and relationships with govts and companies. Names of agents were also revealed in *Counterspy*, an anti-CIA newspaper published by radical American journalists. In one edition of *Counterspy* the name and address of Richard Welch, CIA station chief in Athens, was published. It was reprinted in the English language *Athens News* on 25 Nov. 1975, and a month later Welch was murdered on his own doorstep. Philip Agee denied that his revelations had anything to do with Welch's murder, that an East German publication in 1967 had identified Welch as a CIA officer, and that his Athens address was well known as that of the CIA station chief. In 1981 the United States Supreme Court deprived Philip Agee of his passport. Agee and Mark Hosenball, who to a lesser extent had also exposed CIA activities, were deported by the then Lab. govt in 1977. Both men were members of the NUJ, and were invited by its NEC to attend the union's Annual Delegate Conference that year. The former US Attorney-General Ramsay Clark, who in Feb. that year had given evidence on behalf of Agee to a tribunal in London that was considering the proposal to deport the two men, declared the tribunal's procedure was 'lawless', as it was based on unnamed informants and unstated information, and that what was at stake was 'the right for the people to know the truth'. Merlyn Rees, Lab. Home Secretary, confirmed on 16 Feb. 1977 the deportation orders against Agee and Hosenball. That same year Agee was also expelled from France; in 1978, when it was reported he was to be deported from Holland, the NUJ invited him to address its annual ADM in Apr. *TJ*, Dec. 1976, Feb. and Mar. 1977, Mar. 1978.

19. *Country Life*, a weekly, 1897 to date.

Lorna Blackie, pp. 487–507

1. The Highland Light Infantry originated from two Highland regts raised in 1777 and 1787, numbered the 71st and 74th, and which merged in 1881 to form the HLI. The HLI merged in 1959 with the Royal Scots Fusiliers to form the Royal Highland Fusiliers, which in 2006 became 2nd Bn, Royal Regt of Scotland. Diana M. Henderson, *The Scottish Regiments* (Glasgow, 1992), 54. The Royal Flying Corps (Naval and Military Wings) had been est. in 1912, but in 1914 the Naval Wing became the Royal Naval Air Service. The RFC remained part of the army until in Apr. 1918 it became separate as the Royal Air Force.

2. Empress Eugénie (1826–1920), daughter of the Duque de Peñaranda and María Manuela Kirkpatrick of Closeburn, Dumfriesshire, m. Napoleon III in 1853.

3. Thomas Dobson, *Reminiscences of Innerleithen and Traquair* (Innerleithen, 1896).

4. *News of the World*, 1843–2011.

5. Dorothy L. Sayers (1893–1957), educ. Oxford University; author of many books (e.g. *The Nine Tailors* (1934)) and essays, and a playwright. *WWW, Vol. V, 1951–1960*, op. cit., 969.

6. Alistair Maclean (1922–1987), educ. Glasgow University; Scots author of many thrillers, e.g. *The Guns of Navarone* (1957), on many of which films were based.

7. There seems a contradiction here in dates. *GH*, 6 Jan. and 14 Mar. 1956, and infm. from Glasgow University Library, say the *Gilmorehill Guardian* was launched in Jan. 1956 by Glasgow University Student Representative Council as a weekly newspaper. It continues to date as *Glasgow University Guardian*. In 1952 the University Senate had stopped publication of an earlier student newspaper, the *Gilmorehill Girn*, as it 'was considered to have overstepped the bounds of propriety'. Copies of the *Girn* have not so far been found, but it may be that Lorna Blackie worked on the *Girn* rather than the *Guardian*.

8. *Peeblesshire Advertiser*, 1853–1954, merged into the *Peeblesshire News*.

9. The protracted major battle (Mar.–May 1954) at Dien Bien Phu in northern Indo-China, in which the Vietnamese Communist and Nationalist forces led by Ho Chi Minh and General Giap decisively defeated the French troops led by General Henri Navarre, ended the war in Indo-China that had begun in 1946. The subsequent Geneva Agreement of Jul. 1954, however, divided Vietnam along the 17th Parallel into North and South Vietnam. A decade later, conflict resumed, this time with the US govt making a massive armed intervention against North Vietnam. The war ended in 1975 with the victory of North Vietnam and the unification of the whole of Vietnam. See, e.g., Holmes (ed.), *The Oxford Companion to Military History*, op. cit., 260, 953–7. Professor Jonas Salk (1914–1995) developed at the University of Pittsburgh in 1954 the first effective vaccine against polio, and it was first used in 1955 in the USA. The International Court of Justice, a United Nations body since 1945, is a continuation of the Permanent Court of International Justice, est. in 1921 by the League of Nations, to settle international disputes submitted to it by the govts involved.

10. Patrick Moore (1923–2012), author, radio and TV broadcaster on astronomy; knighted 2001. *WW, 2010*, op. cit., 1821.

11. Sir William Stewart Duke Elder (1898–1978), author–ed. of the 15 vols of *Textbook of Ophthalmology* (1932–54) and of *System of Ophthalmology* (1958–76).

12. *Derby Evening Telegraph* (with changes of title), 1879 to date. Infm.: Derby Daily Telegraph Ltd. Alexander (Sandy) Trotter (1902–1975); educ. St Mary's Cathedral Choir School, Edinburgh; began as a copy boy in Edinburgh; joined Beaverbrook Newspapers in Fleet Street, editor, 1934–59, *Scottish Daily Express*, chairman, 1959–70, Beaverbrook Newspapers, Scotland. Infm.: *Daily Express* Library; *TS*, 11 Oct. 1975; *WWW, Vol. VII, 1971–1980*, op. cit., 806.

13. It was in fact Nov. 1928 when the *Scottish Daily Express* began publication in Glasgow.

14. Patsy Budge (1933–2005), born Wick; educ. Edinburgh University, MA; reporter, 1954–8, *Scottish Daily Express*; m., 1957, Stan Hunter; later, till 1986, a primary teacher then headteacher, Lismore School, Edinburgh. George Hunter (1930–2002), began aged 15 on Edinburgh *Evening News*; reporter, c.1956–60, *Scottish Daily Express*, 1960–c.1972, *Daily Express*, London; 1972–95, successively *National Examiner* in New York and Florida, and *The Globe*, in Florida. Archie Hunter (1928–2000); began work as a civil servant; in Paratroops, c.1946–9; from 1949, circulation representative, Edinburgh, of *The People*, then of *The Observer*; circulation manager, London, *The Observer*. Infm.: Stan Hunter. April Angus (1930–2005); began as a junior reporter on *Mearns Leader*, Stonehaven, but was paid off after asking for union rates of pay; then briefly with *Brechin & District News*; moved, c.1953, to *Scottish Daily Mail*, Edinburgh, where she was the only woman reporter, became a features writer, and worked also for BBC Scotland TV, and was active in publicising the work of many voluntary bodies. *TH*, 3 Oct. 2005.

15. For Mamie Baird, see above, Nancy Mackenzie, Note 13, p. 589.

16. The murder by shotgun, of John Brown, a Buchlyvie butcher aged 60, on the desolate moorland A706 road between West Calder, Midlothian, and Forth, Lanarkshire, in fact took place in early Jan. 1962. Two young West Lothian miners were initially charged with capital murder, but one was released after the charges against him were

withdrawn; and after a four-day trial in Mar. at the High Court the case against the other accused was found, as Lorna Blackie says, not proven. *Midlothian Advertiser* and *West Lothian Courier*, 12 Jan. 1962; *TS*, 6 Jan., 2, 7, 17, and 27–30 Mar. 1962.

17. Elizabeth Percy, daughter of the Duke of Northumberland and wife of the 14th Duke of Hamilton and Brandon (1903–1973).

18. Gordon Airs (b.1939); a *Daily Record* reporter in Edinburgh, then, 1971–94, its chief reporter in Glasgow. In May 1975, after appearing at the High Court, Edinburgh, as a witness in the trial of seven men (the 'Tartan Army') charged with plotting raids on banks, military establishments, and other key installations in the cause of Scottish independence, Airs was himself charged with contempt of court for refusing, on the grounds that it was against his professional ethics to do so, to name a confidential source of information. One of the seven accused, however, did not dispute he was Airs's source and did not object to being identified. The judge said Airs's refusal could not, however, be overlooked and he was kept in custody overnight, and the following month fined £500 for contempt of court at the High Court, where Lord Emslie, who presided, said the Court was treating the case with 'special leniency' because of the circumstances. Counsel for Airs (who himself later said he had expected to be sent to prison) argued that he had been engaged in investigative journalism, which if it were not to operate, 'many facts which are very much in the interests of the public might not come to light'. In 1979 Gordon Airs won the Scottish Arts Council Munro Award for his services to journalism in Scotland and was joint Reporter of the Year in the Fraser Press Awards for journalists contributing to newspapers and magazines published in Scotland. *TJ*, Jun. and Jul. 1975, Apr. 1980; *Daily Record*, 27 Mar. 1979.

19. The lung transplant at Edinburgh Royal Infirmary on 15 May 1968 was in fact the first such in Europe. Alex Dan Smith, aged 15, a schoolboy from Lewis, had swallowed poisonous liquid weed-killer. After the operation his condition was said to be satisfactory, but he died at the Infirmary on 28 May. *TS*, 17 and 29 May 1968.

20. *Hansard*, the printed official reports of proceedings in Parliament, and named after Luke Hansard (1752–1828), printer.

21. James Douglas-Hamilton (b.1942), now Lord Selkirk of Douglas, second son of the 14th Duke of Hamilton; advocate; Cons. town councillor, 1972–4, Edinburgh; Cons. MP, 1974–97, Edinburgh West; held junior and senior govt appointments in several depts, 1983–7; MSP, 1999–2007; author of several books, including two concerning Rudolf Hess's landing in Scotland in 1941. *WW*, *2011*, op. cit., 2063.

22. *Newsweek*, New York, 1933 to date.

23. Scotland's Gardens Scheme, a registered charity founded 1931, which, by encouraging and arranging opening of gardens not normally open to the public, raises funds for other charities. Founded in 1931, the National Trust for Scotland owns, maintains, and keeps open to the public scores of buildings and sites of historical, architectural and cultural interest.

24. Sheila MacNamara (b.1938), born and grew up in Newcastle upon Tyne; left school at 15 and found it difficult to get a job on a newspaper; began, 1963–4, as junior reporter, *Galloway Gazette*, Newton Stewart; feature writer, *Scottish Daily Express*, 1964–72; returned, 1972–6, to *Galloway Gazette*; at Newcastle upon Tyne, 1976–8, caring for her ill father; women's editor, Edinburgh *Evening News*, 1978–89; feature writer in London: *The Observer*, 1989–92, and *Sunday Times*, 1992–3; leader writer, *Eastern Express*, Hong Kong, 1993–6, then *South China Morning Post*, 1996–2002. Infm.: Sheila MacNamara.

25. Alex 'Tug' Wilson (1929–c.2005), photographer, *Scottish Daily Mail* until its closure in 1968, then a freelance until he retired. Infm.: Christopher Reekie. Sandy Sutherland began as a sub-editor, 1967–8, on *The World*, then 1968–9, on *The Scotsman*, 1969–70, sports sub-editor, Edinburgh *Evening News*; 1970–3, public relations, Church of Scotland; 1973–2011, freelance; 1974–c.1984, secretary, NUJ freelance branch, Edinburgh, c.1984–c.1987, its chair. Infm.: Sandy Sutherland. Joyce McMillan (b.1952),

journalist and arts critic; educ. Paisley Grammar School and St Andrews and Edinburgh Universities, MA (Hons), Dip Ed, D Litt (h.c.); columnist, *The Scotsman*; theatre critic, *The Scotsman*, BBC Radio Scotland, *Sunday Standard*; radio critic, 1983–95, and columnist, 1997–8, *The Herald*, Scottish theatre critic, the *Guardian*, 1984–93; chair, NUJ freelance branch, Edinburgh; member, NEC, NUJ; author, e.g., of *Arts for a New Century* (Scottish Arts Council, Edinburgh, 1992). *WWiS*, 2010, 345.

26. Wapping in east London was the centre of a bitter and protracted struggle in 1986–7 between the several newspaper unions, including the NUJ, and News International, whose new printing and publishing plant there, surrounded by a 12-foot-high fence, was to produce its four newspapers hitherto published in 'Fleet Street' (actually Bouverie Street and Gray's Inn Road): the *Sun*, *News of the World*, *The Times*, and *Sunday Times*. Taking advantage of the anti-trade union and employment legislation passed since 1979, News International sought to reduce the number of workers employed at their new plant and to impose on them a series of demands, including no strikes or other forms of industrial action, no demarcation, no recognition of union chapels, and complete acceptance of management's 'right to manage'. For refusing to accept such anti-union conditions, some 5,000 News International workers were dismissed, though they did succeed in securing some redundancy compensation. Mass protest demonstrations were severely handled by the police, who arrested hundreds of the demonstrators. One union, SOGAT 82, was heavily fined and its funds sequestrated by the courts. Most journalists employed on the four newspapers agreed to work at Wapping under the pressure of threatened dismissal and, on the other hand, offers by News International of substantial wage increases for them. See, e.g., John Gennard and Peter Bain, *SOGAT: A History of the Society of Graphical and Allied Trades* (London, 1995), 601–29; *TJ*, Nov. 2000, which described the struggle at Wapping (where 'Unions were quickly destroyed . . . their strength broken by the combination of the mass sackings, formal de-recognition, generous pay rises, and good conditions') as 'the most traumatic upheaval in British newspapers in the turbulent 1980s . . . a revolution in the production of newspapers and in employment conditions'.

27. The NUJ general secretary in the mid-1990s was John Foster. See above, Christopher Reekie, Note 25, p. 601.

28. The first woman associate editor of a British national newspaper was Felicity Green at the *Sunday Mirror* in 1955, then at the *Sunday Pictorial*, 1959, *Daily Mirror*, 1961, and, 1980, at the *Daily Express*. More or less simultaneously Joyce Hopkirk became assistant editor, *Daily Mirror*, and Anne Robinson likewise there in 1982. In 1996 Rosie Boycott was appointed editor of the *Independent on Sunday*, then in 1999 editor of both the *Daily Express* and the *Express on Sunday* (in a merger in 1996 the *Daily Express* had been retitled *The Express*, and the *Sunday Express* the *Express on Sunday*); and in 2000 Rebekah Wade (Mrs Rebekah Brooks) became editor of the *News of the World*, and, 2009–11, chief executive, News International. Greenslade, *Press Gang*, op., cit., 364–71, 634–6, 653; contemporary press. Women editors, if few, were not unknown on local weekly papers in the mid-twentieth century – for example, Mary Gray, whom David M. Smith mentions above (p. 53) as editor, *Berwick Advertiser*, which sold some copies also over the border in Berwickshire.

George Hume, pp. 508–34

1. At the battle of Omdurman, near Khartoum in the Sudan, on 2 Sep. 1898, General Kitchener's Anglo-Egyptian army defeated the huge Sudanese army of Islamic jihadists, followers of the Mahdi (who had died in 1885) and of his successor Khalifa Abdullah. The battle resulted in the addition of the Sudan to the British empire. The Boxer Rising by peasants in China in 1899–1900, supported by the Empress Dowager and most of her govt, attempted to eject all foreigners from China. But an

international armed force capd Beijing, lifted the Boxers' siege of the foreign lega-
tions, and looted the city. Subsequent negotiations forced the Chinese authorities to
make reparations to the foreign powers.

2. Rudolf Steiner (1861–1925), scientist, philosopher, editor, author. His ideas about
education led to the establishment in the twentieth century of scores of Steiner schools
in Europe and the USA. The Edinburgh school was est. in 1939. George Hume in
TS, 2 Mar. 1995.

3. Dr Pelham Moffat (d.1978), taught at the school, 1939–73. Moffat, Scotland's oldest
firm of photographers, est. 1853 in Nicolson Square, Edinburgh, moved, 1856, to
Princes Street, in 1861 to No. 103 there, in 1922 to No. 126. The firm closed in 1961.
TS, 29 Apr. 1953; *ED*, 31 Mar. 1961; infm.: Edinburgh Steiner School.

4. Eric Williams, *The Wooden Horse* (London, 1949).

5. Richard Gordon (b.1921), *nom de plume* of Dr Gordon Ostlere; an anaesthetist in
London and at Oxford, ship's surgeon, assistant editor, *British Medical Journal*; author
of many books, including *Doctor in the House*.

6. *Les Misérables*, the great novel by Victor Hugo (1802–1885), published in 1862.

7. Alexander Douglas-Home (1903–1995), Earl of Home from 1951; as Lord Dunglass,
Cons. MP, South Lanark, 1931–45, Lanark, 1950–1, and (after renouncing his peerage)
Kinross & West Perthshire, 1963–74; PPS to Neville Chamberlain, Prime Minister,
1937–40; held senior govt office in several depts, 1951–63, including, 1960–3, Foreign
Secretary; Prime Minister, 1963–4. *WWW, Vol. IX, 1991–1995*, op. cit., 262–3.

8. Desperate Dan, a character in the *Dandy* comic since its first publication in 1937.

9. The company had been founded in London in 1670, with a charter granted by Charles
II to trade goods with the Indians in exchange for furs, especially of beavers, over a
vast area of North America centred on Hudson Bay in north Canada.

10. Although the Ben Line Ltd (William Thomson & Co.) had moved its base after
WWI from Leith to London, other shipping companies based at Leith in the 1950s
included the Currie Line, George Gibson & Co., London and Edinburgh Shipping
Co. Ltd, and Henry & MacGregor Ltd.

11. Dr David B. Frew (1919–1997; 'Colonel' Frew is a misnomer), born Glasgow; as a
schoolboy there he began a class newspaper and also one for his Scout troop, and wrote
a column of Scout news for *Govan Press*; began aged 14 as a copy boy on *Evening Citizen*;
successively reporter then, before 1939, sub-editor Glasgow *Evening News*; volunteered
for RAF in WWII, invalided out, 1942; returned as a sub-editor to *Evening News* then
moved to *Evening Citizen*. In 1944, with a partner, he bought the *Peeblesshire Advertiser*
and the *South Midlothian Advertiser*, and titled the firm Peebles County Press; in 1945
the partners bought the *Dalkeith Advertiser*, moved their base there and retitled the firm
Scottish County Press. Frew's partner left in 1950 to take over a group of newspapers
in the west of Scotland. In 1956 Frew decided to study medicine and grad., 1962, as
a doctor, working for many years at Edinburgh Royal Infirmary, while continuing as
chairman, Scottish County Press. The Press took over in the early 1960s the *Musselburgh
News*, the *Leith Gazette*, and the *East Lothian News*, and moved in 1979 to larger premises
at Bonnyrigg. In 1986 the *Lothian Times* and in 1990 the *Peebles Times* were begun as
freesheets. Scottish County Press and its papers were acquired by Johnston Press plc
in 2002. *Dalkeith Advertiser*, 9 Oct. 1997; *TS*, 11 Oct. 1997.

12. Andrew Fyall, a reporter, 1949–56, *Fifeshire Advertiser*, recalls that Donald Mackintosh,
a Borderer, was then quite old. The *Fifeshire Advertiser*, 1838–1965, merged with the
Leven Mail to form the *Fife Mail*, which then cont., 1966 to date, as the *East Fife Mail*.
Mackenzie, *NEWSPLAN Scotland*, op. cit., 183.

13. Tom Gourdie (1913–1995).

14. Albert Crichton later became editor, *Glenrothes Gazette*. He died suddenly after a heart
attack. When the *Fifeshire Advertiser* amalgamated, 1965, with the *Leven Mail* Jimmy
McGregor became Fife and east of Scotland reporter for the *Scottish Daily Express*, but

he died suddenly that year, aged 36. Betty Carr, the first woman journalist in Scotland to gain the NUJ certificate of proficiency, m. Andrew Fyall in 1958 and retired from journalism. Infm.: Andrew Fyall.

15. *Leven Mail* (see also Note 12 above here), 1913–65.

16. Ena Harkness roses, a very well-known species, grown by the Harkness firm of rose breeders.

17. Drake Rimmer (1901–1978), born Southport, but lived most of his life in Kirkcaldy; a brass band conductor and composer with a national reputation, who conducted bands in Fife, Dundee and Arbroath. Many of his compositions were played on radio and chosen as test pieces at brass band competitions, at more than 500 of which he adjudicated; the first Scot to be elected a full member of the Performing Rights Society, and received the National Brass Bands Association Musician of the Year Award, 1967. *Fife Free Press*, 24 Mar. 1978.

18. *Fife Free Press*, 1871 to date.

19. For Sean Connery, see above, Bob Scott, Note 1, p. 573. *Darby O'Gill and the Little People* appeared in 1959.

20. Trepanner – a type of coal-cutting machine like an augur. Shears – cuts of coal. Sylvester (its trade name) – a ratchet type of tool for removing temporary pit props. Lipes – a formation of other minerals in the roof of the workings, or (pugs) when coal on the floor has not been cut. Horizons – undulations in the coal, the rise of the coal when coal does not lie flat and goes uphill until it is end-on. Infm.: Eric Clarke, general secretary (retired), National Union of Mineworkers, Scottish Area.

21. Frances colliery, Dysart, at the eastern edge of Kirkcaldy, produced coal from the mid-nineteenth century until 1985 and closed in 1988. Seafield colliery, a very modern one, had produced coal for only 22 years when it closed in 1988. There was a serious accident at the colliery in 1973 that killed five miners and injured several others. Miles K. Oglethorpe, *Scottish Collieries: An Inventory of the Scottish Coal Industry in the Nationalised Era* (Royal Commission on the Ancient and Historical Monuments of Scotland, and the Scottish Mining Museum, Edinburgh, 2006), 144–5, 158–9.

22. Oliver & Boyd, publishers and printers, 1807/8–1962, taken over by Pearson's.

23. The extension of Kirkcaldy from the eighteenth century, with its inclusion of settlements such as Gallatown, Sinclairtown and Pathhead, led to its becoming known as the Lang Toon.

24. Cyril Wolf Mankowitz (1924–1998); educ. East Ham Grammar School and Cambridge University; in WWII a volunteer coal miner and in army; author, playwright, and film producer. *WWW, Vol. X, 1996–2000*, op. cit., 383.

25. The charge against Walter Scott Ellis of shooting John Walkinshaw, a taxi driver, at Castlemilk, Glasgow, on 23 Jul. 1961, was unanimously found not proven by the jury at the High Court, Glasgow, on 1 Nov. that year. He was also found not guilty, on the direction of the judge, of possessing 11 cartridges. *TS*, 2 Nov. 1961.

26. Angus Shaw (1907–2010), born on the island of Luing, Argyll and Bute; a native Gaelic speaker; came to Glasgow after WWI, and began work there from school on the *Evening News*; he reported, e.g., the release, 1927, of Oscar Slater, the Paisley Glen cinema disaster, 1929, in which 70 children died and where he helped lay out their bodies in the mortuary; and the evacuation, 1930, of St Kilda; in RN (Lieut. Commander) in WWII; news editor (?)–1957, Glasgow *Evening News*, 1957–8, *Sunday Mail*, and, 1958–72, *Evening Times*; his daughter Winnie, died 1992, aged 45, was a leading Scottish tennis player and golfer. Angus Shaw was described as one of the most gentlemanly journalists in Scotland. *Evening Times*, 31 Mar. 1972; *TJ*, May 1972; *TS*, 23 Oct. 2010. The ship tied up near the High Court was the old clipper *Carrick*, formerly the *City of Adelaide*, and later reposed as a hulk at Irvine, Ayrshire.

27. Michael McGahey (1925–1999), born Shotts; went down the pits at age 14 and at the same age joined the Young Communist League, and later became a leading national

member of the Communist Party; chairman, from age 18, Shotts branch, miners' union, and later a full-time official; vice-president, from 1961, president from 1967, National Union of Mineworkers, Scottish Area, and vice-president, NUM, until 1987. Alex Moffat (1904–1967), a Fife miner, younger brother of Abe Moffat; Fife county councillor, 1929–45; president, 1961–7, NUM, Scottish Area; president, 1958–9, STUC.

28. Mrs Dora Noyce (1901–1977), widow of a joiner, had bought a house in Danube St in 1943. By Jun. 1974, when she pleaded guilty in Edinburgh Sheriff Court to keeping, managing or assisting with the management of a brothel at her Danube St property, she admitted to 29 previous such convictions dating back to 1934. She was fined many times and sometimes sent to prison. In its heyday, her establishment was said to employ up to 40 women and girls. Her clients (especially, it was said, when the US fleet was in the Firth of Forth) sometimes formed long queues in the street outside her establishment. On at least one occasion a respectable resident of Danube St, struggling to enter his home through the crowds of waiting men, was sharply told to 'Get in the queue'. A librarian from the nearby Stockbridge public library, sent to Mrs Noyce's to collect unreturned books borrowed by her girls, found himself arrested in a police raid immediately after his arrival, and the City Librarian had to vouch for his *bona fides* before he was released. Mrs Noyce, who was reported to have at least once placed in her house window a Cons. Party election poster, was described as a High Tory as 'she believed in promoting enterprise'. She declared, 'My house is just like the YMCA – apart from one little difference.' In 1972 she had been jailed for four months for living on immoral earnings, and by then had been charged 47 times with that offence. *EN*, 3 Jun. 1974.

29. George MacDougall (above, pp. 252–98), a *Scotsman* sub-editor, 1969–91, says no sub-editors there in those years wore carpet slippers at their work.

30. The jury at Edinburgh Sheriff Court on 26 Oct. 1970 took only 12 minutes to find, by a majority, former senior bailie Craig Richards guilty of forming a fraudulent scheme over the sale of Hillwood House, a 33-room mansion in seven acres of grounds on the slopes of Corstorphine Hill and which the Corporation had decided, as surplus to its needs should be leased or sold. After the jury's verdict the Sheriff said that on the evidence he would not be entitled to send Richards (who had ceased to be a councillor in 1968) to prison, but imposed on him a fine of £500, with one week to pay, or three months' imprisonment. *TS*, 17 Sep., 20, 24 and 27 Oct. 1970.

31. See above, James Gunn Henderson, Note 35, p. 596.

32. Alexander Ross Anderson (b.1928); educ. Hillhead High School, Glasgow, and Glasgow University, MA, 1949; National Service, RASC, 1949–51; reporter, 1951–3, *Perthshire Advertiser*, 1953–7, Edinburgh office, *Glasgow Herald*, sub-editor, 1957–8, Glasgow, *The Bulletin*; 1958–87, BBC Scotland, successively news assistant, senior news assistant, chief news assistant, current affairs producer, TV, assistant news editor, news editor (1968–74), editor – news, editor – radio news and current affairs. Infm.: Ross Anderson.

33. For a scrap of information about David Scott, BBC, see above here, James Gunn Henderson, Note 31, p. 595. David Scott (b.1943), *The Scotsman* local govt correspondent, began, 1958, as junior reporter, *Hawick News*; briefly with *Cumberland News*, Carlisle, in late 1960s, before returning to *Hawick News*; 1968–71, general reporter, *The Scotsman*, 1971–98, its local govt correspondent, 1998–2003, local govt editor. Infm.: David Scott.

34. No more has so far been found about Donald Munro, except that he died some years ago, or about George Sinclair.

35. Jeremy Paxman (b.1950), educ. Malvern College and Cambridge University; journalist, broadcaster, and author of several books, including *The English: a Portrait of a People* (London, 1999). *WW, 2011*, op. cit., 1787.

Index

The Scottish Working People's History Trust

Founded in 1991, the Scottish Working People's History Trust finds and encourages the depositing in libraries and archives of all surviving documentary sources of working people's history north of the border. A key element of its activities is recording and making accessible the oral testimony of the lives of working men and women throughout Scotland. The Trust has been responsible for a number of publications based on the collected oral testimony.

Over the last twenty years the Trust's research worker, Dr Ian MacDougall, has interviewed in depth hundreds of working men and women in many occupational groups – including miners, journalists, Leith dockers, railway workers, Borders farm workers, textile millworkers, librarians, co-operative society workers, blacksmiths, shipyard workers.

As a result of the work of the Trust many important historical records, banners, artefacts and photographs have been deposited in Scottish libraries and archives.

The Trustees come from a wide cross section of occupations and institutions. They are people of experience in a variety of areas who feel it is vital that these priceless written and oral records of the past be preserved and, at the same time, that the scholarship behind their presentation is of the highest quality.

The experiences of so-called 'ordinary working people' in Scotland deserve to be a much better known part of history than has hitherto been the case. The hope is to arouse greater awareness of the important contribution that oral recollections about work, housing, education and recreation can make to the understanding of our heritage. It will encourage people to identify working men and women in their own areas whose spoken recollections can be recorded and preserved for posterity before it is too late. For veteran working men and women to recollect and record their experiences can contribute distinctly both to their recognition that their own lives have been meaningful and to a greater knowledge and better understanding of history by other people.

The Trust is glad to receive names and addresses of veteran working men and women in Scotland who might have their recollections recorded. It is also always keen to learn of any documentary sources of working people's history in Scotland, such as minutes of organisations, photographs, reports, financial records, membership lists. The Trust can give advice on how these might best be preserved in such a way as to make them accessible to as wide an interested audience as possible. If you know of such people or of records please contact the Trust Secretary:

Janet McBain, 86 Marlborough Avenue, Glasgow G11 7BJ
e-mail secretary@swpht.org.uk

Why not become a Friend of the Scottish Working People's History Trust?

The Trust is wholly dependent on voluntary donations to finance its activities. Joining the Friends is an easy way to support the Trust's activities. For just £10 per annum you will be kept informed of the Trust's activities and receive mailings of new publications.

www.swpht.org.uk